PROGRAMMING
FROM
FIRST PRINCIPLES

Prentice-Hall International
Series in Computer Science

C.A.R. Hoare, Series Editor

BACKHOUSE, R.C., *Program Construction and Verification*
BACKHOUSE, R.C., *Syntax of Programming Languages, Theory and Practice*
de BAKKER, J.W., *Mathematical Theory of Program Correctness*
BJØRNER, D., and JONES, C.B., *Formal Specification and Software Development*
BORNAT, R., *Programming from First Principles*
CLARK, K.L., and MCCABE, F.G., *micro-PROLOG: Programming in Logic*
DROMEY, R.G., *How to Solve it by Computer*
DUNCAN, F., *Microprocessor Programming and Software Development*
ELDER, J., *Construction of Data Processing Software*
GOLDSCHLAGER, L., and LISTER, A., *Computer Science: A Modern Introduction*
HAYES, I., (Ed.), *Specification Case Studies*
HEHNER, E.C.R., *The Logic of Programming*
HENDERSON, P., *Functional Programming: Application and Implementation*
HOARE, C.A.R., *Communicating Sequential Processes*
HOARE, C.A.R., and SHEPHERDSON, J.C., (Eds.), *Mathematical Logic and
    Programming Languages*
INMOS LTD., *Occam Programming Manual*
JACKSON, M.A., *System Development*
JOHNSTON, H., *Learning to Program*
JONES, C.B., *Systematic Software Development Using VDM*
JONES, G., *Programming in Occam*
JOSEPH, M., PRASAD, V.R., and NATARAJAN, N., *A Multiprocessor Operating System*
LEW, A., *Computer Science: A Mathematical Introduction*
MacCALLUM, I., *Pascal for the Apple*
MacCALLUM, I., *UCSD Pascal for the IBM PC*
MARTIN, J.J., *Data Types and Data Structures*
POMBERGER, G., *Software Engineering and Modula-2*
REYNOLDS, J.C., *The Craft of Programming*
TENNENT, R.D., *Principles of Programming Languages*
WELSH, J., and ELDER, J., *Introduction to Pascal, 2nd Edition*
WELSH, J., ELDER, J., and BUSTARD, D., *Sequential Program Structures*
WELSH, J., and HAY, A., *A Model Implementation of Standard Pascal*
WELSH, J., and MCKEAG, M., *Structured System Programming*

PROGRAMMING FROM FIRST PRINCIPLES

Richard Bornat
Queen Mary College, University of London

Prentice/Hall International

Englewood Cliffs, NJ   London   Mexico   New Delhi
Rio de Janeiro   Singapore   Sydney   Tokyo   Toronto

sci
QA
76.6
.B66
1987

Library of Congress Cataloging-in-Publication Data

Bornat, Richard, 1944–
  Programming from first principles.

  Includes index.
  1. Electronic digital computers——Programming.
I. Title.
QA76.6.B66   1986   005.1   86–18706
ISBN 0–13–729104–3 (pbk.)

British Library Cataloguing in Publication Data

Bornat, Richard
  Programming from first principles.
  1. Electronic digital computers——Programming
  I. Title
  005.1   QA76.6
  ISBN 0–13–729104–3

Prentice-Hall Inc., Englewood Cliffs, New Jersey
Prentice-Hall International (UK) Ltd, London
Prentice-Hall of Australia Pty Ltd, Sydney
Prentice-Hall Canada Inc., Toronto
Prentice-Hall Hispanoamericana S.A., Mexico
Prentice-Hall of India Private Ltd, New Delhi
Prentice-Hall of Japan Inc., Tokyo
Prentice-Hall of Southeast Asia Pte Ltd, Singapore
Editora Prentice-Hall do Brasil Ltda, Rio de Janeiro

Printed and bound in Great Britain for
Prentice-Hall International (UK) Ltd,
66 Wood Lane End, Hemel Hempstead, Hertfordshire, HP2 4RG
by A, Wheaton & Co. Ltd, Exeter.

1 2 3 4 5 90 89 88 87 86

ISBN 0-13-729104-3

CONTENTS

7 PROOF BY INDUCTION 185

8 CHOICE 205

PREFACE

This book is not the usual sort of introduction to programming. It is unusual in at least three ways: it is very long, it takes a formal approach to the subject based on reasoning about programs, and it is not based on a particular mechanical code or 'programming language'.

From my experience of teaching programming to novices, and from watching other people do it, I have become convinced that it takes quite a while to learn to program. The principles of programming can be very concisely stated, but there is plenty to learn. Programming is sufficiently different from what is taught in other subjects and requires such mental discipline that it takes time to absorb and command the subject. This book is designed to take the novice slowly through the first stages of learning, through those subjects which seem so easy to the skilled practioner but are real obstacles to so many novices. It takes pains to explain the simple things at sufficient length that they can be understood and to make a firm foundation for the development of later ideas. The book is long because there is more to the teaching and the learning of those simple things than might at first appear.

I am equally convinced that reasoning about programs lies at the heart of programming. Skilled programmers can write programs that work - that's why we call them skilled - but that's not all that they can do. When writing a program it is normal and sensible to make several designs, several sketches of a solution before settling on one which appears to be the most promising to develop. Skilled programmers can analyse the properties of a design without developing it into a program; they can discover when a particular development has gone wrong and correct their mistake; they can take a working program which does one thing and convert it into a working program that does something similar but significantly different. All of this requires that they can tell what a program does just by looking at it, without running it on a machine, and tell what the properties of a program would be if they got around to writing it. This book teaches some of those skills to novices.

Mechanical codes - Pascal, BASIC, FORTRAN, Prolog, LOGO or whatever - shouldn't be dignified with the title of 'language'. They are systems of notation which are designed to be mechanically processed and they fall considerably below the standards of flexibility, subtlety and expressiveness required for communication between intelligent beings. The design of any code can only be partly a matter of principle: mostly it has to do with historical accidents and concessions to software and hardware technology. The notation used in this book is based on Landin's ISWIM (*If* you *See* *W*hat *I Me*an). Although ISWIM isn't confined by the straitjacket of a mechanical implementation it is restricted by the need to express only computable programs. I have restricted it further in order to make it fit the requirements of my system of reasoning. But like any other abstract notation it is more flexible, more capable of abstraction, than any mechanical code and I use it for that reason.

Truth doesn't reside in any particular system of description. There is not and never will be a Programmers' Stone. The principles of programming are independent of notation and a skilled programmer can write working programs in *any* mechanical code. The 'damage' caused by early exposure to a particular code (BASIC is often singled out in this regard) is real enough but is not caused by the evil properties of any particular notation: it is the delusion that to learn a code is to learn to program which is truly harmful. I believe that it is possible to isolate the principles of programming and to teach them abstractly, separately giving rules by which abstract programs may be transcribed into a mechanical code so that novices can experiment with working models of their programs. With the arrival of personal microcomputers, novices will often have access to several different codes. It can be very helpful to them that, given the transcription rules, they can really write programs which can be transcribed into several different codes and run that program on several different programming systems. To help make this point, students should be given every encouragement to transcribe their programs into as many codes as possible[†].

Small examples and sound reasoning

I have concentrated in this book on the design and analysis of small example programs. The first examples are based on the printing of asterisk patterns on a screen or a sheet of paper, using a small set of basic instructions. The use of such simple problems facilitates analogies with simple mathematical ideas. In particular it is possible to base some program proofs on nothing more than the counting of asterisks. There is a great deal to be learnt from small programs, as the numerous examples at varying levels of difficulty are designed to demonstrate.

When people begin to learn to program, their reasoning skills are usually either rusty or under-developed. The teacher's task is to develop those skills to a level where they can be used to construct and analyse worthwhile programs. This book attempts to teach those skills directly by concentrating on calculations of the effect of programs and proofs about programs. The technique of reasoning which it introduces isn't necessarily the best technique for proving that programs meet their specification, but it is simple to understand and to teach and it serves

---

[†] In its present form the coding appendices in this book tell only how to transcribe programs into Pascal, though Part Five gives some guidance on how to transcribe into other codes. I have prepared appendices giving details of transcriptions into BBC BASIC, a dialect widely used in Britain. I would be glad to provide assistance to anyone who wishes to prepare transcription rules for other codes.

to illustrate that reasoning about programs is a practical proposition.

Program proving has a desirable side effect in teaching, surprising when you first encounter it but extremely useful. Students who have already learnt to program, but learnt badly and picked up bad habits on the way, typically do not respond to exhortations about 'good programming style'. They *do* respond to the challenge 'can you prove that your program has such-and-such a property?', and they learn quickly to adopt habits which lead to provable programs. Those habits are mostly the ones which we call 'good style'. Program proving is a sure cure for the BASIC addict, and it is one which they will undertake.

Mathematics and programming

The mathematics in this book is simple in principle. Students are assumed to have a background no more advanced than the average English sixteen-year-old. It requires formula manipulation skills which are learnt around the age of fourteen but which are regrettably rather rusty by the beginning of a university course. It explains all its mathematical developments, including proofs by induction, so that even a mathematical drop-out can learn to program.

Programming is a creative activity requiring real mental effort and ingenuity and no conceivable developments in the subject will change its character. All but the most trivial program requires a repetition or a recursion. To develop a repetition or a recursion it is necessary to solve particular cases and to generalise: that is, to use a form of scientific induction. Once a putative solution has been invented it is necessary to justify the design and that must involve a form of mathematical induction, whether formally expressed or not. As part of the justification it is necessary to develop a provable specification of the program. The proofs in this book use mathematical induction and the examples teach the skill of designing provable propositions as specifications of programs.

The creative ability required to make both scientific and mathematical induction, and the mental discipline required to produce convincing reasoning which connect them, make programming the challenging subject that it is. To become a skilled programmer is a worthwhile ambition.

Acknowledgements

This book is the result of a six year experiment in undergraduate teaching in the Department of Computer Science and Statistics at Queen Mary College, University of London (QMC for short). In 1979 we collectively decided to stop teaching our first year students to program in the old way, indirectly via a computer language course, and to try instead to teach them the principles of programming directly. This book represents the course more or less as we taught it in 1986 with some extra embellishments (for example, the treatment of recursive value structures in Part Four). It is similar in structure to the course we designed in 1979, but vastly different in detail. In particular I have learnt as the course developed how valuable it is to give a formal presentation of the meaning of instructions using algebraic substitution rules.

I owe an enormous debt to all my colleagues at QMC, who have by their relentless criticism turned the course and therefore this book in directions which have immeasurably improved it. I owe a particular debt to Peter Landin, who was involved in the earliest design discussions and in the first couple of year's teaching: his contributions include much of the notation, the choice of basic instructions, the environment diagrams and the emphasis on small exercises to drill the student. Many other colleagues were involved in the original design meetings and in the almost continuous discussion groups which accompanied early course development and which haven't yet died down. To every one of you - Samson Abramsky, Don Beal, Cameron Burton, Hilary Buxton, Keith Clark, Keith Clarke, Mike Clarke, Steve Cook, George Coulouris, Allan Davison, Jean Dollimore, Alan Frieze, Peter Hemingway, Paul Howells, Chris Hudson, Peter Johnson, Isaac Khabaza, Heather Liddell, Colin Low, Bob Newman, Ian Page, Steve Reeves, William Roberts, Jon Rowson, Dave Saunders, Mel Slater, Harold Thimbleby, Sylvia Wilbur - thank you for what you did.

The evolution of the course was influenced by developments in computer science teaching and thought during the last couple of decades. Two particularly important borrowings are from Thomas Green, whose work on the understanding of conditional instructions influenced me to teach guarded commands rather than *if-then-else*; and from Tony Hoare, whose transformation rules for Communicating Sequential Processes inspired all of mine and whose rules for assignment are lifted wholesale in chapter 12.

The students who laboured over the exercises in tutorials and laboratory classes deserve a special acknowledgement. As a body they helped me realise just how many conceptual difficulties there can be even in the earliest stages of learning to program. As individuals their criticisms helped correct many mistakes. No doubt it hurt them more than it hurt me. Sorry folks: hope I got it right in the end.

I wouldn't have written this book without the encouragement of Tony Hoare. I am particularly grateful to my reviewers (Jane Hughes, UMIST; Bernard Sufrin, Oxford; Keith Clarke, QMC) who have enormously improved the book by their suggestions. With more than usual fervour I acknowledge that all the mistakes are all my own.

The typographical mistakes are mine, too. This book was typeset using ditroff™ running on a DEC™ VAX™ 11/750 under BSD 4.2 UNIX™ and printed on an Apple™ LaserWriter™. I wouldn't have completed the job without the expert help of William Roberts. I think desktop publishing has a way to go yet.

Chapter 0
HOW TO USE THIS BOOK

This book will teach you how to program - or rather, it will take you the first part of the way down the road to becoming a skilled programmer.

Programming is a special sort of reasoning. To become a programmer requires lots of practice in designing and in analysing programs. So although programming goes on in your head and is mostly thinking, learning to program means spending lots of time doing things, practising to gain fluency and experience. This book is full of exercises which are designed to give you practice in designing, analysing and proving programs. You can skip the text if you like, but you should certainly not skip the exercises.

Programming shouldn't be confused with coding, which is a matter of writing programs down in a form that can be understood by computer programming systems (compilers, interpreters or whatever). Once you can program you can code with ease, but not vice-versa. At the end of most chapters there is an appendix giving details of how to transcribe programs into the well-known mechanical code Pascal, and a set of exercises to help you practise that skill. Your teachers may be able to provide you with instructions for transcribing programs into other mechanical codes. Sometimes you may find that program structures are difficult to transcribe into any of the codes you are familiar with. Don't despair: there are other codes and by the end of the book you will be so expert that you will be able to invent ways round those difficulties.

This book puts great emphasis on reasoning about programs because reasoning is at the heart of programming. It is used every time we locate and correct a mistake in a program. Increasingly it is coming to be used to prove that a program contains no anticipated mistakes. The reasoning we use in programming involves jumps of insight, backwards arguments to justify guesses, false starts and trips down blind alleys. It is the nature of human reasoning to be like that, not nice and smooth like a proof in a textbook. You can learn to do it (and you can learn at the same time how to write down a nice smooth version of your final argument so that others can follow it). To the beginner, skilled programming may seem more like jumping to a conclusion than careful work towards a solution but it is really reasoning.

Reasoning skills can be taught and they are polished by practice and experience. This book uses a particular kind of formal reasoning to establish the properties of programs and teaches you how to use the same kind of reasoning with your own programs. It uses simple algebraic substitution of equals by equals, treating a program as a formula and replacing pieces of one formula by other formulas with identical meaning so as to change a program from one form into another. You don't need to be a mathematician to follow the proofs in this book or to make up your own proofs about programs.

How this book is laid out

In this book I have chosen to explain the fundamental ideas which underly the most common mechanical codes used in programming today. These codes are called 'sequential' or 'imperative' codes. Examples are BASIC, Pascal, Ada, Modula-2, Algol 68, FORTRAN, PL/1, LOGO and COBOL.

The book is divided into five parts. Part One introduces the ideas which the rest of the book develops and at the same time it introduces the mathematics which the proofs later on in the book will use. Chapter 1 introduces the program structures which are discussed in later chapters and in later parts. Chapter 2 discusses sequential execution. Chapter 3 introduces procedures and chapter 4 deals with parameterised procedures. Chapter 5 discusses some of the intricacies of programs which have definitions within definitions and which use a single name for more than one purpose.

Part Two is about structured instructions and is the heart of the book. It introduces lots of different sorts of instructions together with the mathematics and the algebraic rules you need to reason about programs which include those instructions. Chapter 6 is about counting repetition. Chapter 7 is about proof by induction, the main form of reasoning used in this book. Chapter 8 is about choice instructions and chapter 9 is once again about proofs by induction. Chapter 10 is about assignment instructions and chapter 11 about input and interactive programs. Chapter 12 deals with a different form of repetition. Chapter 13 discusses repetitive calculations. Chapter 14 is about premature termination of a program execution.

Part Three deals with some examples of larger programs, going into the design of programs as well as their analysis. Chapters 15 and 16 concentrate on the problem of printing a numeral representation of a number. Chapter 17 designs a calculator program. Chapter 18 discusses how to print a calendar.

Part Four discusses some ways in which information within a program can be organised. Chapter 19 introduces sequences of values and indexed sets. Chapter 20 uses value sequences in an illustration of how to solve the famous eight queens problem. Chapter 21 introduces structured values - trees and lists - and chapter 22 uses graphs in a discussion of searching and mapping mazes. Chapter 23 discusses some more searching problems, ending up with a solution of the knight's tour problem.

Part Five discusses how to transcribe programs into some of the other mechanical codes which you may come across.

How to learn from this book

Each chapter in this book after this one introduces a single topic and explains it in two ways. One explanation is based on an *operational* or *executional* description, explaining what happens when you give a particular program to a computing machine. The other explanation is based on *algebraic substitution rules*, explaining how to calculate the meaning of a program in terms of the meanings of its parts. The exercises in each chapter give you practice in using each of these forms of description: they test your knowledge and ask you to explain particular programs. Other exercises ask you to invent programs, or to invent proofs that your explanations of programs are valid.

To learn to program you must learn how to invent programs and to reason about programs. In particular you must practise writing down proofs which explain why you believe a particular program does what you think it does.

This book takes things slowly. It is designed to be easy to read. But reading a book, or listening to lectures, isn't enough to make you a programmer. I repeat: to learn to program you must *practise*. Reading the text should make the ideas plausible to you. That is the first stage of your learning, and the one which requires the least effort. The second stage of understanding is to be able to follow other people's reasoning. Many of the exercises, especially at the beginning of the chapters, are designed to confirm that you can follow the reasoning in the text and to move you from the first to the second stage of understanding. The third stage is to be able to use what you know: for example, to invent explanations of existing programs, or programs which fit existing explanations. The fourth stage is to be able to use the ideas creatively, inventing new programs and new explanations for them given no hint of a solution. There are exercises in each chapter designed to help you move from the second through the third to the fourth stage.

Programmers must be creative, but I can't teach creativity. Nobody can. You can learn it, but only if you work at it. Practice and yet more practice is what you will need. Practice especially in reasoning, in writing down plausible explanations of the effects of programs. Practice in inventing programs. Practice in proving that your invention is worthwhile. Programming isn't knowing, it's doing. Get out there and do it!

What to do if you think you can already program

If you have already learnt to program in some mechanical code or other then you are both at an advantage and at a disadvantage compared with the complete beginner. Your advantage is that you have an idea about some of the basics of programming. Your disadvantage is that some of what you know may be severely misleading. If your knowledge isn't soundly based then, in a sense, you will have to start all over again.

You will almost certainly know little or nothing about program proving and about the mathematics used in this book. Since that mathematics is introduced and used very early in the book you will have to start reading at the beginning like everybody else. In Part One at least you will be able to skip large chunks of textual explanation but, for your own sake, please don't skip the exercises. Don't miss chapters 5, 7 and 9, whatever else you do.

Some of this book will be familiar to you. Some of it will be quite new. Some of it may directly contradict what you have already learnt. If it does, that is where your greatest danger lies. Please don't fall into the trap of imagining that, because you can write a program to solve a particular problem, you needn't think about alternative solutions or try to understand them when they are shown to you.

But I'm sure that you are far too intelligent to fall into any silly traps. You've started once, you know a lot and you're ready to learn some more. Get in there and do it!

Part One
BASIC CONCEPTS

The hardest step in learning to program is the first one. This part of the book shows you that you took that step years ago. The way you organise your life, the way you use language, perhaps even the way you think - in all these ways you already use ideas and concepts which are fundamental to programming. The basic principles of programming are already a part of you. To become a programmer, all you need do is generalise a little from what you already know.

I don't say that programming is trivial or programmers are brainless. It isn't and they aren't. Conversely, programming isn't impossibly difficult and programmers need not be infinitely intelligent. The difficulties you will face - and overcome - arise from the need for precision and the need for simplicity when writing programs. You will already know how hard it is to be precise and straightforward at the same time.

You must be precise when you write a program because the action of computers is controlled by rules. Computers follow their rules very carefully and with absolute precision: in order that a computer should produce a particular effect it must be instructed by a program which is equally precise. The good news is that because your instructions are always obeyed with such precision it is possible to deduce what will happen when they are followed: that is, you can use reasoning to discover the meaning of a program.

Programs must be simple because you must be able to understand the programs you write, if only to be sure that they have the effect you want them to have. The need for precision makes some programs large, but even the largest programs must be kept simple enough to be understood. The most effective way to keep a program simple is to make it out of a small number of pieces, joined together to form one of the standard program structures. Understanding a program that is *structured* in this way is a matter of understanding its various parts separately and, separately once more, understanding the way they fit together.

Chapter 1 shows how each of the program structures introduced in this book corresponds to one of the ideas you already use when you make a plan of action. Chapter 2 introduces some *basic instructions* from which programs can be built and expands on the description of *sequence*, the most fundamental program structure discussed in this book. Chapters 3 and 4 deal with *procedural abstraction*, the fundamental way of giving large-scale structure to a program. They also introduce the technique of *substitution of equal formulas*, which is the basis of the reasoning system introduced in this book. Chapter 5 deals with the ways that names can stand for things in programs and describes how to deal with the conflicts that can arise when the same name is used for more than one purpose in a single program.

By the end of Part One you should be able to write, read, understand and reason about simple programs - and some not so simple ones!

Chapter 1
PLANNING EQUALS PROGRAMMING

This chapter is based on a single observation. A *program* (of instructions) is nothing more than a *plan* (of future action). You already know a lot about planning because you have been doing it all your life. You know about its advantages and its drawbacks: how a plan made beforehand simplifies decision-making but how tedious it can be to make the plan; how a plan makes it possible to solve problems systematically but how a faulty plan can so easily lead you astray. This chapter explains how your hard-won knowledge of everyday life can be used in the study of programming.

1.1 ARCHITECTS' PLANS, GAME PLANS AND METHOD PLANS

First I must explain my terms. 'Plan' and 'planning' are English words and like all English words they have a variety of meanings. One kind of plan is a blueprint, an architectural design, a picture of how things might be in the future without instructions about how to make them so. A second kind of plan is a plot which you might make in a card game or a game of chess: an overall approach, a flexible plan of attack, a way of doing things which you fully expect to be successful for a little while and then to break down because your opponent finds out what you are doing or does something totally unexpected (and then you expect you will have to make a new plan for those new circumstances). A third kind of plan is made by the robbers in a crime movie when they decide to attack a bank: a fixed and very detailed set of instructions to follow which makes everyone very rich provided everybody follows it exactly. It is this last kind of plan which is closest to a computer program: a *method* of solving a problem or making something happen which is fixed on beforehand, thought about and reasoned over, then followed through carefully, right to the end.

Circumstances in real life are unpredictable. The baddies' plan in a crime movie often fails because of an unforeseen event: somebody treads on the Boss's cat, which must be taken to the vet by one of the gang; it is raining and he puts on his raincoat; the vet notices the bullet hole in the raincoat sleeve .. Method plans can't cater for unforeseen circumstances, but the baddies' Boss is in a dilemma. His gang is made up of idiots who must be given a method plan to follow. If he lets them follow a flexible game plan they will mess it all up and it will be more than the cat who suffers injury. He must hope that everybody will follow the method plan without argument, and that nothing unexpected will turn up. Method plans are for idiots, for armies, for times when you don't trust yourself to think clearly on the spot, for times when you dare not go wrong.

Real life always throws up unforeseen circumstances. Method plans don't provide a sensible basis for human actions and real-life planners - even the baddies' Boss in a crime movie - can never expect their human agents to take a method plan absolutely literally. Even the most authoritarian planners will expect their agents to use their intelligence if some little part of the plan goes wrong because something unexpected turns up.

Computer programming, fortunately or unfortunately, isn't exactly like real life. Computers aren't intelligent agents and they are mechanical in the sense that they follow instructions precisely, without understanding and without argument. The only sort of plan they can follow is a method plan. If anything unexpected turns up then the computer, like the most brainless screen villain, will blunder along trying to follow the original plan as long as any action at all is possible.

Computer programming is method planning. For the rest of this chapter, please suspend your disbelief in the real-life usefulness of method plans. Just suppose that there really are circumstances in which method plans are the best alternative.

1.2 THE SIZE OF PLANS

Consider as a first example something which most of us make an attempt to plan - our career for the year ahead. In life we make decisions on a second-by-second basis, so our plan must cover every second of the year or at least every waking second. Every day you are awake for about sixty thousand seconds. In the year ahead you will live through about twenty million waking seconds. This suggests that a plan of a year's action could be a list of twenty million separate decisions. This isn't a practical sort of plan simply because most decisions would take more than a second to record, so it would seem that it must take you more than a year to write down your plan.

A plan of twenty million actions may seem very large, but in computer programming plans of that size are quite usual. A modern computer will carry out millions of separate actions every second, every one of which must be described in the program which is its plan of action. Indeed a program which described only twenty million actions would be thought to be relatively simple, and we often write programs which describe unlimited sequences of actions. We have developed special techniques of description to cope with the very large plans we must construct, which are intended to make our plans small enough to comprehend. This book is about just those methods of description.

1.3 GOALS, PLANS AND MISTAKES

Suppose that you have time to make a plan of your actions in the year ahead; that you have found a way to write it down economically; that the plan would be useful when you made it. Before you can start to make a plan you need a *goal* - something you want to achieve which is sufficiently important to make the effort of planning worthwhile. For example, your personal goal might be to pass some important examinations next year, or your goal might be to cycle around the world, or it might be to grow the country's biggest outdoor tomato. You might have several goals, which is the same as having a single goal with several parts: you may want to learn to play the guitar *and* to improve your parachute jumping *and* to pass your examinations *and* to grow that monster tomato. You might have a goal with several parts but you don't want to choose between them: you might want to grow that tomato *or* pass your examinations *or* write a bestseller (*or* all three if possible). You might have a goal which is difficult to pin down because it doesn't correspond to any definite achievement. For example, you could just want to enjoy as many as possible of those twenty million seconds - your aim is to be happy but aimless.

Once you have fixed a goal you can make a plan. Once the plan is made you can start carrying it out or, if you are making a plan for somebody else's life, they can start carrying it out instead. Usually this is where the fun starts because whoever is carrying out the plan - the *agent* - often finds that, because there is a mistake in the plan, it doesn't work entirely as it should. Sometimes the agent finds that the mistake is so serious that the plan doesn't work at all. Most plans have mistakes in them and when a plan proves faulty the mistake must be repaired or the plan replaced. The planner must reconsider, rethink, replan. If the tomatoes all die, stop weeding and plant new seed. If you break your leg, stop parachute jumping and concentrate on the guitar or the tomatoes.

You can only know that a plan is failing if you notice that it isn't moving towards its goal. If the agent who is following a plan doesn't know the goal then they can never know whether the plan has gone wrong or not and they must follow it willy-nilly as if they were playing a game of 'follow my leader'. It is essential to know the goal when making a plan, checking a plan for mistakes or re-making a plan so as to avoid the mistakes you have found.

1.4 STRUCTURE AND LEVELS OF DESCRIPTION IN A PLAN

Suppose that you have settled on a goal and are ready to write down your plan of action for your next year of life. How is it possible to reduce the size of the plan so that it can describe an action for each of the twenty million seconds of the year ahead? Or even actions for three hundred thousand minutes, or six thousand hours, or three hundred and sixty-five days?

To overcome the problems of size it is essential to introduce *structure* into a plan. Structure enables us to describe a plan at various different levels and to break it down into separate components. At one level we can describe the structure (shape) of a plan and give brief descriptions of its components; at another we can describe the components. Usually there are many levels of description of a computer program, far more than are normally required in everyday planning.

Hierarchical structure

A house is a structure of rooms; a room is a structure of walls, ceiling and floor; walls are structures of bricks and plaster; floors are structures of wood; ceilings are structures of wood and plaster. Is a house then a structure of bricks, plaster and wood *or* is it a structure of rooms? *Or* is it a structure of levels, each a structure of rooms? Is a housing estate a structure of bricks and wood and plaster *or* is it a structure of houses? The answer is that they are each of those things, and that there are advantages in different forms of description for different purposes. Another answer is that you can often deduce the information which one sort of description would give you from a different sort of description.

The plan of a housing estate[†] can be examined from many different points of view. If you are a brickmaker you need to know how many bricks the whole housing estate will need; if you are a bricklayer you need to know where to put the bricks. The electricity board needs to know the total energy demand; the electrician needs to know where to put the cables. The council planning committee needs to know what the estate will look like; the builder needs to know what it will cost; the building society needs to know how long a single house will last. How can one plan provide all this information, all this detail, unless it is as big as the housing estate? The trick is performed using repetition of elements within a hierarchical structure.

The *hierarchical* structure - found in some schools, every army, most programs and almost every textbook - is one in which every part except one is subordinate to every other part. It is like a diagram of the root system of a tree. For example,

---

[†] House plans and estate plans are mostly description, hardly method plans at all. Nevertheless we can learn something from the way that they exploit structure to simplify a description.

this book is made up of parts, each part of chapters, each chapter of sections, each section of paragraphs and exercises. This organisation is intended to help you find your way around, to make the book easier to read and to understand. An army is made up of divisions, a division of regiments, a regiment of companies, a company of squads. The idea is to make the army easier to control, by splitting it up into units that one person can effectively command.

A hierarchical plan of a housing estate shows where each of the houses should be placed in the estate and it gives a separate plan of each type of house. The plan of a house is another hierarchical structure. Normally it is given as several separate plans covering its features: roof, different floor levels, foundations, wiring, and so on. Usually there are hierarchies giving information about each feature of the house at different levels of detail. A collection of separate plans, each separately understandable, gives all the detail required. It is called a hierarchical structure because each plan shows part of some larger plan, which is part of some larger plan still and so on until you reach the largest plan of all, which covers the whole estate.

A hierarchial plan can be a basis for calculations, just as if it was an unstructured plan. Even though there is no single plan describing every detail of an estate you can calculate the total energy demand: by calculating the energy demand of one type of house from its own plan, finding the number of that type of house by looking at the outline plan and multiplying by that number you find the energy demand of that type of house. If you do the same for the other types of house and add it all up you arrive at the total energy demand. Even though there is no single sheet of paper which gives a picture of the position of every brick on the whole estate you can calculate how many bricks the whole estate needs. Similarly for cabling, timber, plaster, road surfacing, and so on.

A complete plan of a housing estate at the minutest level of detail never exists because it would be ridiculously expensive to prepare, far too large to scrutinise and no more use than the hierarchical plan in any case. If it were split into a number of sheets each small enough to handle, such an unstructured plan would be useless for the purpose of building the estate because a single sheet might not include all of one house or might even include part of one house, part of a road and a garden and a corner of a neighbouring house[†].

[†] Survey maps - like those which make up the Ordnance Survey of Britain - are unstructured in just this way. Separate sheets fit together to form one enormous map of an area. In mapping, planning and programming, purpose defines structure and when surveyors can't predict the purpose their maps will be used for they can't reasonably impose any particular structure. But when purpose is declared - say when you need a map for a walking holiday in a National Park - you will often find a map specially designed to give you the information you require at the scale you prefer.

Parts within parts, wheels within wheels

The advantage of a hierarchically-structured plan is that you can concentrate on parts of the structure separately. For example, when building a house you needn't worry about the estate layout. And when making a roof in a workshop you needn't worry about where it is to go in the estate. Just as the housing estate plan is a structure of smaller descriptions of parts of the whole, so a method plan is usually a structure of *sub-plans*, each with a *sub-goal*. Breaking a plan into parts means splitting the planning problem into sections which you can tackle separately, each of them small enough to understand, plus an outline section which describes how those sections fit together. If you do it properly the outline will be small and simple enough to understand immediately. If you are lucky the other sections will be small and simple as well, but if the problem is too big to allow this then they in turn can be split into sub-sections, with a description of how the sub-sections fit together.

In this way a large plan can be made up of a number of smaller plans, each of them separately understandable. It is possible to understand how the parts fit together without necessarily completely understanding the parts or vice-versa. Understanding can be acquired piecemeal. For example, you can understand why a motor car needs an engine and how an engine fits into a car even if you are hazy about how an engine works. And if your car's engine goes wrong you can read a book about engines, and find out how to fix it without having to know about the steering gear, or the gearbox, or the body, or the controls.

Structure in a plan helps resolve the conflict between detail and clarity. A small plan is easy to read and to understand and easy to change if it goes wrong, but it may be too small to contain essential detail. A large plan can contain all the detail, but it may be so large that you can't remember everything, or you might forget your place while you are carrying it out, or it may be so complicated to understand that you can't change it if it goes wrong.

Unstructured plans

Not every human plan has a discernible structure. Sometimes plans are made that are intentionally intricate and difficult to understand: think of the plans made by spies or by diplomats. To see a notorious example of an unstructured plan, peer into the back of an old-fashioned television set (circa 1970). You will see a jumble of wires and components without any obvious structure. Then look into a modern set and you will see instead a few printed circuit boards which plug in and out for easy maintenance. Or perhaps, in the most modern sets of all, just a few massive integrated circuit chips.

TV sets once used intricate and unstructured circuit plans because clever design can reduce the number of components in a circuit and if a company could save 50p on each of a million sets then it would make an extra half a million pounds profit (the same arithmetic works in dollars, yen, roubles, francs, pesetas, galactic mega-credits, ..). But the cost of components has been constantly falling whilst labour has become ever more expensive. First transistors replaced valves, then chips began to replace transistors: at each stage the total component cost of the set fell but the labour cost of replacing a faulty component on the production line or during the free guarantee period became ever higher. In the end it became profitable to build sets from circuits which can be easily repaired even though their components cost more, and TV set designers learned the value of structure. Programmers, of course, knew it all the time. We shouldn't be too proud of our achievement: perhaps we knew it first because we make more mistakes than other people.

1.5 DIFFERENT KINDS OF STRUCTURE

Programs are method plans and are normally made up of a number of parts, put together to form some grand structure. The parts themselves will normally be structures, whose parts are structures, and so on until the division of parts into ever smaller parts can usefully go no further.

This book describes many of the ways in which we can fit together the parts of a method plan. This applies not only to the 'grand structure' of a program, but to each of the structures it contains and to those which they contain, and so on. The structures I shall describe are:

> Sequence
> Repetition
> Procedures (abstraction)
> Choice
> Memory

It is quite normal to have repetitions of choices of sequences of procedure calls, to take a simple example. Structures within structures are what programmers build, day in and day out.

1.6 SEQUENCE

So far as this book is concerned the simplest form of program structure is the sequence, in which a plan is made up of a number of smaller sub-plans which must be carried out in order. This structure immediately makes it easier to understand a program or a plan. It makes it easier to change it if it goes wrong because only part of the plan will go wrong - the part which covers a particular step in a sequence of steps - and you may be able to alter the faulty part of your plan without affecting any of the other parts.

Consider once again the problem of planning your next year's activity. One obvious way of dividing a year plan is to make it into a sequence of season plans. If you are growing a champion tomato your plan will probably describe what you are going to do in Winter, Spring, Summer and Autumn. Spring and Summer are pretty busy growing times so you might divide them more finely - perhaps into early and late Spring, early, middle and late Summer. Or you might choose a different time interval for each sub-plan, based on your own special knowledge of the life cycle of the monster tomato plant.

Seasons aren't the only way of dividing the year into a sequence of shorter periods: if your goal is to save enough money so that you can buy each of your friends a Christmas present, your plan might be a sequence of month plans, each describing how much money to save from that month's pay packet.

When following a sequence of actions you first do this action *and then* do that action *and then* some other action, .. For example, to travel from home to work you might have sub-plans with sub-goals:

> *get out of the front door*
> *go from front door to bus stop*
> *get on first bus which is going my way*
> *get off bus at work stop*
> *get from bus stop to work place*

If you can achieve each of these sub-goals, in the order I have given them, you can travel from home to work.

Now none of these separate activities is so basic as to be a simple action: each of them requires a complicated activity to ensure that it comes about. (If you think they're basic actions, ask yourself why you don't see robots riding to work on the bus, or cats, or mice!) Each of them requires a large number of separate actions to carry out: for example, the bus stop may be a couple of hundred metres from your house, and therefore will take at least two hundred steps to reach. But although we know that each of these sub-goals is not immediately achievable, we know that each is somehow achievable, either because we have heard about other people who regularly achieve these goals, or because we have achieved similar goals ourselves. So we can go ahead and make an outline plan, leaving until later the detailed planning about how to achieve each sub-goal. Sometimes we may already know how to achieve the sub-goals because of earlier planning: for example, the plan which gets you from front door to bus stop is the same whether you are going to work, on holiday, to the cinema or to meet your best friend the bus driver.

By stringing activities which achieve sub-goals together in sequence, we have planned an activity which achieves the overall goal 'go from home to work place'. Now we must plan the activities which achieve those sub-goals separately: many of us will know more than one route from home to bus stop, perhaps more than one nearby bus stop, and can choose the most effective sub-plan, considering now only the sub-goal and not how it fits into the entire plan.

Typically each sub-plan will require more than a single action and our plan will become multi-layered or multi-level, with plans containing sub-plans containing sub-sub-plans, and so on.

-=-=-=-=-=-=-=-=-=-=-=-=-

Exercise 1.1
Make a plan of one of your own activities with at least three levels of structure (for example, seasons, parts of seasons, actions within parts of seasons; or terms, subjects, parts of subjects; or some other structured organisation).

Exercise 1.2
Choose one of the descriptions at the lowest level of structure (a sub-sub-plan) from your answer to exercise 1.1 and make a plan for it with at least two more levels of structure.

Exercise 1.3
Write a travel plan for your journey to school, to college or to work with at least four levels of description. For example, the following plan has three levels of description:

> *to travel to college*:
> *walk to bus stop*
> *travel on bus*
> *walk from bus stop to college*

> *to walk to bus stop*:
> *leave house*
> *walk 50 metres to left*
> *cross road*
> *walk 20 metres to right*

> *to leave house*:
> *open door with right hand*
> *walk two steps forward*
> *pull door shut with left hand round its edge*
> *– but be sure to move your*
> *hand out of the way before the door slams*

-=-=-=-=-=-=-=-=-=-=-=-=-

Effects in sequence

One very important thing about sequences of actions in a plan is that the order in which you choose to carry out the actions can sometimes determine the effect you produce. This can be for one of two reasons. First, different orderings may give different effects. In particular some orderings may give an unintended effect. For example, you must first dig the ground *and then* plant the seed: if you do it the other way round you may bury the seed so deep that it can't grow. If you want to eat a chocolate you must put the chocolate in your mouth *and then* start chewing: if you do it the other way round you may bite your finger instead of the chocolate. Second, certain orderings of sub-plans may be impossible to carry out. You must take the lid off the box *and then* take a chocolate: if you try it the other way round you can't reach a chocolate at all.

-=-=-=-=-=-=-=-=-=-=-=-

Exercise 1.4
Consider the problem of getting dressed, using four items of clothing: knickers, trousers, socks, shoes. How many possible dressing sequences are there? How many of them lead to a 'normal' or 'average' dressed appearance?

Exercise 1.5
Suppose that your trousers are so tight that you can just pull them over your feet (with or without socks), but you can't pull them over your shoes. How many of the dressing sequences from the previous exercise are 'impossible'? How many are both 'abnormal' and 'impossible'?

-=-=-=-=-=-=-=-=-=-=-=-

The order of actions in a sequence is important when the effect we want is some change in the *state of the world*, *state of things* or *state of affairs* (usually abbreviated simply to *state*). A change in the state of the world can be brought about as the result of a sequence of smaller changes. Each action in a sequence of actions changes the state of the world a little, and the change it produces usually depends on the state in which it takes place.

-=-=-=-=-=-=-=-=-=-=-=-

Exercise 1.6
Consider the action 'walk one step forward'. Define states of the world in which this action will take you

- a metre closer to the supper table
- one metre north
- nowhere
- to the bottom of a cliff
- to the bottom of a cliff with all your bones broken
- to the bottom of a cliff without hurt

-=-=-=-=-=-=-=-=-=-=-=-

Before-after diagrams

In a sequence of actions which describe how you do this *and then* do that *and then* do some other thing, each action takes place in the state of affairs produced by the *previous* action in the sequence and in its turn produces the state in which the *next* action will take place. The first action takes place in an *initial* state of affairs and the last action produces the *final* state.

Take the example again of a travel program. Program 1.1 describes a possible route from my home to my place of work. If I follow that program when the state of the world happens to include 'me at home' it will produce a final state which includes 'me at work'. I can draw a *before-after* diagram to show this, as illustrated in figure 1.1.

> *go to bus stop*
> *wait for bus and get on it*
> *wait until bus reaches Mile End*
> *get off bus and go into work*

program 1.1

Before   *program* 1.1   **After**
me at home   ——————————▶   me at work

figure 1.1

The diagram as it stands isn't very convincing. It is no more than an assertion that the whole program, the entire sequence of actions, will produce a particular effect. It is made more convincing if I expand the diagram to include all the in-between states of the world. The result is shown in figure 1.2 overleaf: I have had to turn the diagram on its side to fit in all the states on the page, but the content is unchanged.

-=-=-=-=-=-=-=-=-=-=-=-

Exercise 1.7
Suppose that the actions 'go to bus stop', 'wait for bus and get on it', 'get off bus and go into work' can themselves be expanded into sequences as follows:

> *go to bus stop*:
>   *go through door*
>   *cross street*
>   *walk 50 metres east*
>
> *wait for bus and get on it*:
>   *wait until a bus arrives*
>   *get on bus*
>
> *get off bus and go into work*:
>   *get off bus*
>   *walk 50 metres west*
>   *cross street*
>   *go through door*

Draw plausible before-after diagrams showing the detail of the state changes between the states of figure 1.2.

Before
me at home

go to bus stop

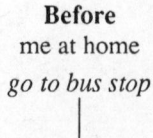

In-between 1
me at bus stop near home

wait for bus and get on it

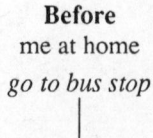

In-between 2
me on bus going to Mile End

wait until bus reaches Mile End

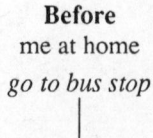

In-between 3
me on bus at Mile End

get off bus and go into work

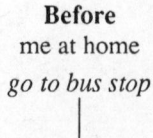

After
me at work

figure 1.2

Exercise 1.8
If you replace each of the actions of program 1.1 by their definitions in exercise 1.7 you should get a program which is a sequence of ten actions. Construct that program.

Exercise 1.9
In the program you constructed as the answer to exercise 1.8, the sixth action should be 'wait until bus reaches Mile End', the seventh 'get off bus'. If these two actions are transposed, draw before-after diagrams which show the effect of the altered program. [Hint: the seventh and subsequent actions in the altered program *are* sensible and *can* be carried out.]

-=-=-=-=-=-=-=-=-=-=-=-=-

1.7 REPETITION

A plan can be shortened and simplified if it contains repeated elements: you describe just once the action that is repeated and separately describe when and how often it is repeated. For example, a school or college timetable needs only to describe how teaching takes place in a sample week of a term and when terms start and end. The timetable for a term is a *repetition* of the sample timetable. Such a plan is remarkably short considering the amount of teaching which it describes, but it describes the term in just as much detail as if a separate timetable were given for each week. If the teaching timetable is the same for each term, then the plan of a whole year can be given with little more description than that for a single term.

In programming we identify two kinds of repetition. One kind is *counting*, *bounded* or *definite* repetition, in which you do something a fixed number of times. 'Press the left-hand button three times' describes bounded repetition; so does 'add two eggs'; and so does a school timetable. The other kind is *unbounded* or *indefinite* repetition. 'Press the button until the light comes on' and 'stir as long as you can see white flecks in the sauce' each describe indefinite repetition; so do 'stay in the classroom until you get your sums right' and 'keep taking the tablets'.

-=-=-=-=-=-=-=-=-=-=-=-

Exercise 1.10
Identify three activities which can be planned using repetition. Classify the plans as either definite or indefinite repetition.

Exercise 1.11
Similarly classify the two sentences of exercise 1.10.

Exercise 1.12
Similarly classify the activities implied by:

> Stay young and beautiful if you want to be loved
> Knock three times and ask for Charlie
> Keep right on to the end of the road
> It's the third house on the left
> Play it, Sam
> I close my eyes and count to ten
> Close the door after we've gone

-=-=-=-=-=-=-=-=-=-=-=-

Converting between repetitions and sequences

In principle any repetition describes a sequence: first you do this *and then* you do it again *and then* you do it again *and then* .. and so on until the repetition finishes. So it is a fact about repetitions that you can always *unroll* them into sequences.

If you unroll a definite repetition you get a finite sequence. Unrolling indefinite repetitions is more difficult because the number of repetitions depends on circumstances: for example, when you are making a sauce, the time you have to stir depends on the quality of the ingredients and the temperature of your cooker. So you can't be sure how long an unrolled indefinite repetition will be. But given a description of a particular initial state, and knowledge of how each individual action will change a state, you can unroll an indefinite repetition into a particular sequence.

-=-=-=-=-=-=-=-=-=-=-=-

Exercise 1.13
Take each of the repetitions which you classified as definite in previous exercises and unroll them to give the corresponding sequence.

Exercise 1.14
'Knit until the garment measures five and three quarter inches' is indefinite repetition. But suppose that the tension is thirteen rows to the inch: roughly how many repetitions are required?

Exercise 1.15
For each of the repetitions which you classified as indefinite in previous exercises, say what kind of information about particular circumstances and the effect of actions would be required to enable you to unroll them into particular sequences.

Exercise 1.16
For some of your answers to exercise 1.15 choose some specific circumstances and specific properties of actions and unroll your indefinite repetitions into particular sequences.

-=-=-=-=-=-=-=-=-=-=-=-

Sometimes sequences can be rolled up into repetitions. Some examples are obvious definite repetition: 'dig a well *and then* dig a well *and then* dig a well' is equivalent to 'dig three wells'. But although repetitions unroll into unique sequences, 'rolling up' isn't unique: 'dig a well *and then* dig a well *and then* dig a well *and then* dig a well *and then* dig a well *and then* dig a well' could be read as 'twice dig three wells', 'thrice dig two wells', 'dig six wells' or 'three times (dig a well *and then* dig a well)' or even '(five times dig a well) *and then* dig a well'.

1.8 PROCEDURES (ABSTRACTION)

When a plan calls for a particular action and that action requires explanation, there are various ways in which the action can be explained. One particularly useful way is to give the action a name, to refer to it by name in the plan and to explain it separately. So you might consider the indefinite repetition plan shown

> *to put up a fence:*
> *repeatedly insert a stake in the ground*
> **and then** *nail a fencing panel to it*
> *until the gap is filled*

program 1.2

in program 1.2 if you need to repair a gap in your garden fence.

Now there are various ways of inserting a stake in the ground. Program 1.3 shows one way which certainly works. But the plan for putting up a fence is independent of the technique for inserting a stake. We can change the staking technique without changing the fencing plan. We could use any of several different techniques (say one using metal post holders, or one using concrete to hold the base of the stake) and the fencing plan would still work.

> *to insert a stake in the ground:*
> *push a crowbar in the ground*
> **and then** *wiggle it about to make a small hole*
> **and then** *take the crowbar out*
> **and then** *put the point of a stake in the hole*
> **and then** *repeatedly hit the top of the stake*
> *until it is driven home*

program 1.3

Vice-versa, we can change the overall plan without changing the staking technique. The technique I have described is useful when putting up fences but could also be used in other kinds of plan: for example, in a plan for putting up a notice or a plan for putting up a bird table. I have described a particular *procedure* - a way of proceeding - which has a particular effect and can be used in different circumstances to produce that same effect for some other appropriate purpose.

Procedures are useful in planning because they describe separable pieces of a plan with identifiable goals and deducible effects. They are especially useful when they can be used in more than one plan and when they can be used more than once in the same plan. If your plan was to put up a fence *and then* to make a bird table on the same day you might naturally use the same *insert a stake* procedure in each part of your plan.

-=-=-=-=-=-=-=-=-=-=-=-

Exercise 1.17
Your activity on working days (weekdays) and rest days (weekends) will be different, yet many of your actions will be the same. For example, you eat meals on both kinds of day and you get out of bed on both kinds of day. Identify four procedures which are common to your day plan for a normal working day and a normal rest day. Identify two procedures which are similar but not identical (for example, you might eat a bigger or a smaller breakfast at weekends).

Exercise 1.18
In a typical day plan identify a procedure which is used more than once.

Exercise 1.19
The fencing plan above is a repetition within which there is a sequence (that is, it's a repetition of a sequence). What is the structure of the staking procedure? What structures does it contain? What structures do they contain?

-=-=-=-=-=-=-=-=-=-=-=-=-

Using the *insert a stake* procedure in the fence-building plan does more than give an activity a name. It also makes an abstraction. The procedure is being used for its effect: that is, because it achieves a useful sub-goal. It could be replaced by any other procedure which has the same effect. Indeed, in making the fence-building plan we don't care which procedure is eventually used to insert a stake, though we might want it to be one which doesn't take too much effort or cost too much money so that whoever puts up the fence doesn't get too tired or impoverished. All that matters is that there must be *some* effective procedure. It is even possible that we don't know how to insert a stake when we make the fence-building procedure but we have heard that it is possible: we know that we can make the overall plan and investigate stake insertion technology later.

Expanding procedure calls into sequences

If a plan calls upon a procedure then the actions of that procedure can be amalgamated into the plan by writing its description in the place that calls upon it, in place of its name. In this way a plan which uses procedures can be reduced to one which does not, and calculation of the detailed action of the plan is possible.

-=-=-=-=-=-=-=-=-=-=-=-=-

Exercise 1.20
If the staking procedure were incorporated into the fencing plan, what would be the structure of the whole plan? Describe the various structures and the way one encloses another in the manner of exercise 1.19.

Exercise 1.21
Both fencing plan and staking procedure use indefinite repetition. Consider a similar plan and procedure which use definite repetition to insert five stakes each of which requires seven hammer blows. Amalgamate the procedure into the plan and unroll the repetitions to calculate the sequence of actions which will be carried out if that plan is followed.

-=-=-=-=-=-=-=-=-=-=-=-=-

Parameterising a plan

A procedure makes a more powerful abstraction when it is able to adapt to various circumstances. A stake is hammered into place in the procedure above. Hammering a stake is something like hammering a nail. Hammering a large iron nail is very like hammering a small brass nail. We might describe the difference by saying that hammering a small nail is the same as hammering a big one except that for the small nail you use a lighter hammer and more rapid blows with a shorter stroke. The same principle covers other hammering tasks: there are concrete-piercing nails, which you mustn't hit too hard because they may shatter, and giant flat 'cut' nails, which you have to hit as hard as you can with a heavy hammer. A pointed fencing stake, from this point of view, is a very large wooden nail which you hit with a very big hammer.

In principle there ought to be a general hammering procedure which covers all eventualities. Its *parameters* - the things about it which can be varied to produce different effects - are the size of the nail, the weight of the hammer, the speed of the blow and the amount of nail you want to protrude after you've driven it in far enough. The procedure might be defined as in program 1.4.

> *to hammer a nail S until it sticks out distance D*
> *using blows of force B with hammer H*:
> *take S in left hand*
> ***and then** take H in right hand*
> ***and then** repeatedly make B blows*
> *until head of S protrudes D*

program 1.4

This definition makes it possible to give a very short description of how to nail a floorboard:

> *hammer cut 35 mm nail, 0 mm, medium–hard, 500 g*

or put up a nail in a concrete wall to hang a picture:

> *hammer hardened 25 mm nail, 10 mm, tapping, 500 g*

or insert a fence post (if you are strong enough to hold a sledgehammer in one hand!):

> *hammer 2 m wooden stake, 1.5 m, light, 7 kg sledge*

-=-=-=-=-=-=-=-=-=-=-=-=-

Exercise 1.22
Reconsider your working-day and rest-day plans: for two pairs of activities which are similar but not identical describe the parameters which characterise them. Hence give two procedures which cover each of the pairs of activities.

Exercise 1.23
Amalgamate the floorboard nailing plan and the hammering procedure. Write

down the sequence of actions this amalgamated plan describes.

Exercise 1.24
The hammering procedure only works for right-handed people. Parameterise it still further so that everybody can use it. [Hint: you need only one extra parameter.]

-=-=-=-=-=-=-=-=-=-=-=-=-

1.9 CHOICE

People don't like following method plans which other people have devised unless they have unusual faith in the planner (for example, the planner is a religious leader) or they have some other reason to obey without question (for example, the planner is their commanding officer). A person following someone else's method plan may complain 'it makes me feel like a cog in a machine' or 'they want me to be like a robot'. Most people feel that what distinguishes a human from a machine is that a human following a plan can respond flexibly to circumstances, even rejecting the plan if it seems inappropriate, whereas a machine must do precisely what it is told.

Programming is the preparation of plans for computing machines to carry out. It is certainly true that the kinds of plans/programs which are considered in this book don't allow the agent any freedom to reject the plan and invent another if unforeseen circumstances arise. But such a plan need not be completely inflexible because it can contain a description of how to respond to *foreseen* circumstances. For example, part of the plan of a walking journey might be as shown in program 1.5.

> *walk northeast five km to the old ford*
> ***and then*** *if the river is low cross on the stepping stones*
> > *but if the river is high go upstream 500 m to the bridge*
> > > ***and then*** *cross the bridge*
> > > ***and then*** *walk back to the ford*

program 1.5

This plan shows the characteristic structure of choice in programs. It lists every foreseen circumstance (eventuality, state of affairs, situation) and gives a separate action or sub-plan for each of them. In this plan there are two foreseen circumstances - either the river is low or the river is high. If a circumstance arises which isn't foreseen - if the river is so high that it has washed away the bridge, for example - then the plan is no use and must be rejected. At that point a human agent would be expected to improvise a new plan; a mechanical agent might be expected to sit by the river and wait for new orders. A careful person might notice that a completely absent river more or less fits the definition of a low river, but the machine would sit down and wait in all sorts of circumstances not *literally* described by the program.

-=-=-=-=-=-=-=-=-=-=-=-=-

Exercise 1.25
The walking plan above describes a sequence of actions in each of two circumstances. Say what those circumstances are and describe the sequence of actions which it plans for each of them. [Hint: the action *check the river level* is implicit in the choice plan; include it in your sequence description.]

Exercise 1.26
The walking plan above is a sequence of an action and a choice. What is the structure of the choice (that is, what structures does it contain and how are they linked together)?

-=-=-=-=-=-=-=-=-=-=-=-=-

Choices in a plan can allow a mechanical agent following that plan to take over tasks which seem at first sight to require human ingenuity and flexibility. For example, modern aircraft can land automatically using a radio beam projected along the ideal approach path to an airfield. One particular plan/program which describes how to use the beam is given in program 1.6. By repeatedly, rapidly and accurately following this plan the most inexperienced agent might be able to land a modern jet. No doubt real landing programs are more carefully designed than this example, but it shows in principle how the illusion of continuous control can be provided by a rapid sequence of discrete choices. Notice particularly that

> *repeatedly*
> > *if the beam is off–centre and error is static or increasing*:
> > > *if the beam is to the left*:
> > > > *turn to the left*
> > > *if the beam is to the right*:
> > > > *turn to the right*
> > > *if the beam is below*:
> > > > *drop the nose*
> > > *if the beam is above*:
> > > > *lift the nose*
> > *if there is no beam*:
> > > *blow the hooter, flash the PANIC light*
> > *if speed is low and either static or decreasing*:
> > > *apply more power*
> > *if speed is high and either static or increasing*:
> > > *reduce power*
> > *if the beam is centred or coming back to centre,*
> > > *and speed is ok or coming back to correct value*:
> > > *do nothing*
> *until the wheels are on the runway*

program 1.6

nothing in the example demands a computer or any other kind of machine to follow the plan. It's the sort of plan which could be used by you or me or might be used by a modern Doris Day after the cabin crew are all knocked out in a remake of one of those old aircraft disaster movies.

-=-=-=-=-=-=-=-=-=-=-=-=-

Exercise 1.27
What is the structure of the landing plan in program 1.6? [Hint: carefully examine the structure which deals with action when the beam is off-centre: there is more than one choice involved.]

-=-=-=-=-=-=-=-=-=-=-=-=-

Program 1.6 illustrates the way in which choice plans can allow an agent *real choice* in following a plan when circumstances in a choice structure overlap. Suppose that the landing beam is to the left and below the aircraft and that speed is too high. Then the program allows three possible choices: either turn left *or* drop the nose *or* decrease engine power. The program specifies that the choice plan should be followed repeatedly, and if this happens quickly enough the fact that the agent/pilot only does one thing at a time doesn't matter: in rapid succession first one of the controls will be adjusted, then a second and finally the third. A sequence of discrete actions based on discrete choices will look like continuous expert control. Speed of repetition in this case would depend on how quickly the agent (the air hostess or the machine) can assess the circumstances (measure airspeed and the apparent position of the beam) and carry out an action (adjust the controls).

The final alternative in program 1.6 specifies that under certain circumstances the agent should do nothing. If all foreseen circumstances are to be listed, one possible circumstance must be that everything is ok, and there is no need to do anything. Indeed when flying an aircraft it is important sometimes that you do nothing - 'keep your hands off the controls!'. The instruction to leave well alone is as important as any other in the program. Doing nothing, in the sense of leaving things as they are, takes no time at all, so the next repetition of the choice plan will follow immediately. If you could watch the plan being carried out when the plane is properly lined up you would see the landing agent continually assessing circumstances, then reassessing them immediately, then reassessing them once more, and so on indefinitely until either the plane lands or circumstances change. Machines are very good at that sort of eternal vigilance, which is comforting on a foggy night.   •

Choice and sequence

If a plan includes a choice between a number of actions then each time you make the choice you carry out just one of a number of actions. A repeated choice describes a sequence of actions, not all the same but chosen according to circumstances on each repetition. If you know the circumstances you can calculate which action will be chosen and, just as in the case of simpler repetition structures, the program can be reduced to a sequence of simple actions with the choices and decisions which led to them omitted.

Deciding what to do is an activity of the agent - it usually takes some effort, some skill and some time - but it doesn't change the state of affairs in the world outside the agent's calculating apparatus (head, central processor unit, calculator). Decisions are an example of *hidden* or *implicit* actions in a program.

-=-=-=-=-=-=-=-=-=-=-=-

Exercise 1.28
Suppose that when following program 1.6 the landing beam is above and to the left and the speed is too high. List all the different possible sequences of actions (including implicit actions) which the landing plan describes, up to the first *do nothing* action in each sequence.

Exercise 1.29
Aerodynamicists, trained pilots and skilled video games players will be aware of the fact that lifting an aircraft's nose reduces its speed. Repeat exercise 1.28 under each of three assumptions: (a) that nose-lifting reduces speed but still leaves it too high; (b) that it reduces speed to a level between minimum and maximum; (c) that it reduces speed to below minimum.

Exercise 1.30
The landing plan of program 1.6 may not be the best which could be devised. Which of the answers to exercise 1.29 suggest that this is so, and what changes in the plan do you think they call for?

-=-=-=-=-=-=-=-=-=-=-=-

1.10 MEMORY

I once had a cat which was afraid of beetles. As a kitten it had already killed a few flies when one day it tried its luck with a cockroach which crawled out from under a dustbin. One downward blow of the paw seemed to do the trick but just as Puss was about to pick up his prey it started to move. A second swipe seemed to have no effect. A third blow, this time a full-blooded wallop, only seemed to speed the thing up - it was heading at full speed for the dustbin and safety. This happened to take it straight towards the kitten, which fled in terror of its invincible opponent. In later life it killed rabbits, rats, mice, flies - even wasps, bees and spiders - and though I'm not sure it ever saw a cockroach again it always ran away from anything which looked a bit roachy.

Obviously that cat remembered its youthful experience. A cat must surely have a memory. But 'memory' is a more slippery word even than 'planning'. What do we mean when we say that somebody or something 'remembers' an occurrence or 'has a memory'? The everyday answer binds up memory with intelligence, reasoning, intellect and all sorts of other mental powers. If you strip away all other confusing considerations there is a very spare definition of memory, set out in definition 1.1. I know my cat had a memory according to this definition. I believe also that it had some flawed understanding of what had happened to it, though that is irrelevant to a discussion of whether or not it had a memory.

Something has a memory if its behaviour is influenced by its history.

definition 1.1

Now according to this definition a lot of very simple devices have a memory of a sort. The simplest one I can think of is the kind of clicking light switch which you press once for 'on' and press again for 'off'. It remembers very little, but it does remember whether it has been pressed an odd or an even number of times since it was assembled.

The simplest plans which include memory are conjuring tricks - see, for example, program 1.7. That sort of trick confuses most people at some time in their lives. Simple algebra shows how it works (but I shan't). The effect of such a program depends on the number it starts with (a parameter) and produces its effect because the agent remembers a number between steps of the plan.

> *Think of a number*
> *Double it*
> *Add ten*
> *Multiply by three*
> *Halve it*
> *Take away fifteen*
> *Divide by three*
> *– the answer is the number you first thought of*

program 1.7

The most common machine which obviously has a memory is a seat reservations computer. Suppose that on a particular day I book a seat on a particular airline flight. My travel agent asks me for various details - typically my name and my phone number - and types them into a computer console. The computer remembers me, it seems, because I can go back the next day to my agent, or even to a different travel agent who can connect to the same computer, and alter the date of my reservation or choose a vegetarian meal, for example. On the day of the flight I turn up at the airport and check in: I give my name and the flight number to the clerk, who types them in to the same computer, and I am allocated a seat. People who buy a ticket at the airport just before the plane leaves don't have reservations, so they aren't remembered by the computer and sometimes must wait till the last minute to get a seat.

The actions of the reservation computer are controlled by a program, and the part of the reservation program which controls seat allocation might look something like program 1.8. This program displays a classic memory technique: it

> *repeatedly*
> *accept an instruction from the desk clerk*
> **and then** *if the instruction is 'reserve':*
>   *if there's room: add details to list of people*
>   *if there isn't room: tell clerk to refuse*
>   *if the instruction is 'allocate seat':*
>   *if the person's details are in the list:*
>   *allocate a seat*
>   *if the details aren't in the list:*
>   *tell the clerk to attempt a reservation*
>   *if the instruction is 'cancel':*
>   *delete details from list of people*
> *until the flight takes off*

program 1.8

accumulates information, in this case lists of people booked on a flight, and carries out actions which depend on the *current state* of that information. For example, the action 'reserve' has different effects according to whether the plane is full or not; the action 'allocate' has different effects according to whether the information state records that a person with your name is booked on the flight or not. The same program will respond to the *same* request made at different times in many *different* ways, depending on the state of its memory of information at the time it receives the request. According to my definition it has a memory, but it certainly has no intelligence worth the name: most reservation systems would let me book on two simultaneous flights travelling in different directions, for example. Memory doesn't imply any sort of discretion or sense of purpose, or anything but sensitivity to history.

Reservation systems based on simpler technology also display memory. The book of tickets beside a theatre booking clerk is a memory of which seats have been booked. If the ticket has been ripped out, the seat has been booked. When the book is empty, the theatre is full.

Not every ticketing system has a memory. A railway booking office will sometimes issue an unlimited number of tickets for a particular route. Chaos often ensues, particularly on popular holiday weekends.

-=-=-=-=-=-=-=-=-=-=-=-

Exercise 1.31
List the ways in which a car displays a memory. List the ways in which the system car+road displays a memory.

Exercise 1.32
What should an airline reservation program do if told to cancel a reservation that was never made? Does the reservation program above cater for this possibility? If not, modify it so that it does what you think it should.

-=-=-=-=-=-=-=-=-=-=-=-

1.11 HOW MUCH DETAIL SHOULD A PLAN HAVE?

Plans which you make for yourself to carry out are often incomplete because you leave out bits which are just obvious to you. Part of a tomato-growing plan might cover when to prune the plant so as to get maximum production: if you are an experienced gardener you wouldn't bother to plan *how* to prune because you already know it so well. But if you were to give the plan to a novice gardener, perhaps saying 'here is a secret plan which will make you into a champion tomato grower' you would need to be more explicit. The more of a novice your agent is, the more detail you need to include.

In principle there is no limit to the amount of detail you need to include. The simplest of actions will require explanation to a person who has never carried out a similar action. If you make a plan for somebody else to carry out it is normal to try to discover just what background knowledge that other person has. If an agent's knowledge isn't enough to understand every detail of every part of your plan then the planner must put in more detail. For example, here are two published descriptions of how to stake and prune a tomato plant: the first is intended for the complete novice and is very detailed, the second is backed up by a television programme which gives some background knowledge. The second plan even neglects to point out that 'support' means tying the plant to the cane.

.. loosely tie the stem to the cane. Make the ties at 12 in. intervals as the plant grows. Side shoots will appear where the leaf stalk joins the stem. Cut or pinch them out when they are about 1 in. long.

   (*Vegetable Plotter*, Dr. D.G. Hessayon, pbi)

Use a single cane to support each plant and remove any side shoots which develop between the leaf and stem.

   ('*Dig This*' *Vegetable Guide*, Floraprint)

-=-=-=-=-=-=-=-=-=-=-=-

Exercise 1.33
Suppose that you travel to work by bus. Describe your route from home to the bus stop so that it can be understood by someone who has never been to your town.

Exercise 1.34
Describe how to get on a bus and find a seat to someone who has never been on a bus. Be careful to describe what to do if there are no empty seats.

Exercise 1.35
Suppose that someone has built an imitation human body with a separate motor controlling each articulating joint (hips, knees, elbows, and so on). Plan how this robot should stand up when it is sitting in a chair. Play robots: try out your plan (and be careful not to move bits that the plan doesn't tell you to move).

Exercise 1.36
Suppose that you have taught the robot to stand up and to walk forward and so on, but that it can't see or feel or hear. Plan its exit from the room you are sitting

in at the moment.

-=-=-=-=-=-=-=-=-=-=-=-=-

An agent who knows a lot about the way you live, think and plan your life doesn't need much instruction. 'Fetch my slippers' you might say to your faithful robot and it would do it. But *your* robot doesn't know where *my* slippers are kept nor even what they look like. It is specialised to the task of looking after you. The more general purpose the agent the more explanation it needs of our special goals and the more specific our plans and programs of instruction must be. Computers are very general purpose: you may at first be surprised at the amount of detail they require in programs which they are to follow.

1.12 BLIND OBEDIENCE AND MUTUAL UNDERSTANDING

Very occasionally a human may be asked to follow a plan without knowing its goal. Generals usually don't tell their armies what their orders are supposed to achieve: soldiers are expected to obey orders without question (and they aren't told because if they don't know the plan they can't give it away to the enemy). If soldiers were allowed to question orders they might disobey when the purpose of the orders is to sacrifice their lives for some political or military purpose. People in spy novels are told to go to secret rendezvous without being told why: usually they go, often with exciting results.

An agent who knows the goal of a plan might be trusted to replan if the original plan goes awry. But what if an agent isn't told or can't understand the goal of a plan? Question: how will such an agent behave if the plan steers away from the goal? Answer: 'like a machine', 'like a robot' she/he/it will continue to follow the plan no matter how absurd the consequences seem to those who do know or understand the goal.

It is here that computer programming and human planning most widely diverge. The agent, in the case of a computer program, is a computing machine whose every action can be controlled to whatever level of precision you desire. It never makes a mistake in following a program (though sometimes its components may fail, so that it breaks down and stops working). But we don't know any way of communicating the purpose of a program to a computer which isn't just another sort of program.

-=-=-=-=-=-=-=-=-=-=-=-=-

Exercise 1.37
Try to describe the purpose of a monster tomato-growing program in such a way that it could be understood by a computer or a robot. Make sure that the computer/robot isn't deluded into growing some other plant which grows in the plot by accident. Does your description eliminate giant red gooseberries? Strawberries? Apples? Plastic tomatoes? Triffids?

Exercise 1.38

If you instructed the robot controller of an agricultural research station, how would you tell it the difference between nice and nasty crops? For example, how would you describe the difference between 'tasty' and 'tasteless' tomatoes? How do you describe a tomato's taste to a robot?

-=-=-=-=-=-=-=-=-=-=-=-=-=-

The problem of communicating purposes between human and machine is just as much a problem between human and human. You never really know whether some other person understands you or not, no matter how well you know them. A machine doesn't share your life experience, doesn't have the same sense organs as you have, and in fact has very little in common with you. This book isn't the place to go into the complexities of the problem but it should be obvious that it would be very difficult to be confident that you had been understood by a machine.

The programming way around the difficulty is to communicate only with machines which you understand perfectly because they have been built to follow plans in a predictable and understandable way. Then it is possible to *calculate* what a machine will do when presented with a particular plan. It isn't necessary to communicate the purpose of a plan to the machine because it need not check whether the outcome of the plan corresponds to your purpose: you do that for yourself.

Chapter 2
SEQUENCES OF INSTRUCTIONS

Programming examples which draw on everyday experiences - getting dressed, going to work, eating a meal, hammering a stake into a vampire's heart - are useful up to a point but they are ultimately unconvincing. You can't try them out as programs because they are vague descriptions of behaviour and because present-day robots can't carry out most of the actions they call for. Perhaps very expensive robots could cope with some of the examples quoted so far, but certainly all of them are well beyond the capabilities of any robot which the average person could afford to buy.

For more convincing examples I have to look for problems which are clearly within the capabilities of everyday computing machinery. The example I have chosen is that of printing patterns in the style of a typewriter. The kind of printed pattern which I shall concentrate on is made up of asterisks and spaces. One example is a hollow square:

```
*******************
*******************
***             ***
***             ***
***             ***
***             ***
*******************
*******************
```

and another is a line of 'banner writing':

```
*     *    ********  *       *          *****
*     *    *         *       *         *     *
*******    *****,    *       *         *     *
*     *    *         *       *         *     *
*     *    ********  ******  ******   ******  *****
```

Many computers are equipped with printers which can produce these kinds of patterns on paper. Most can show them on a video screen, imitating the style of typewriter printing on an endlessly unrolling sheet of paper. Whether the marks appear more or less permanently on a piece of paper or evanescently on a screen makes no difference to a discussion of how to make a pattern of marks, so I shall discuss the problem without bothering about the picture medium.

2.1 TYPEWRITER STYLE PRINTING

On a typewriter there is usually a backspace key, or if there isn't one you can always push the carriage back with your hand. You can roll the paper up or down in small increments at any time during the typing activity. Backspacing, paper-rolling and crafty over-printing increase the range of arty patterns you can produce on an ordinary typewriter. But you can make interesting patterns even if you restrict yourself to use just the '*' key, the space bar and the RETURN key or the carriage-return lever.

This book is printed using characters of varying widths so that, for example, 'iiiii' is narrower than 'mmmmm'. Some computer printers and screens can print like that. Some can produce double-sized printing for emphatic display of headlines or program titles or advertising. Either kind of sophistication makes it difficult to describe some printed patterns, so I shall assume that each mark, whether letter, digit, punctuation or whatever, occupies a space on the paper or screen of the same width and height. This is how marks are printed on the average mechanical or cheap electric typewriter.

The problem, then, is to produce a program - a plan of action - which can be given to an automatic typewriter or a computer with a video screen to make it produce patterns like those above. The programs have to operate without intelligent intervention, using only actions which correspond to making a mark, leaving a blank space and moving to the next line.

2.2 BASIC INSTRUCTIONS

A program which is to print patterns in the style of a typewriter may use any of the structures and mechanisms introduced in chapter 1: sequence, repetition, procedures, choice, memory. It may use other structures and mechanisms which are outside the scope of this book. But ultimately it must produce a visible effect by carrying out a sequence of simple actions each of which makes a mark on the paper/screen/display medium, or moves the printhead/carriage, or both. For each of these simple actions I shall describe a *basic instruction* which commands the agent (computer, typewriter or whatever) to perform the simple action. My three basic instructions are *print**, *printspace* and *NL*.

The basic instruction *print** is pronounced 'print star' or 'print asterisk'. I intend that when this instruction is followed, or *executed*[†], an asterisk should be printed. An execution of the single-instruction program

*print**

must make an asterisk mark on the paper. That is, its effect should be the same as pressing the '*' key on a typewriter.

The *printspace* instruction is used to make blank marks on the paper. The effect is the same as pressing the space bar on a typewriter.

The *NL* instruction has the same effect as pressing the RETURN key on an electric typewriter, or pushing the carriage-return lever on a mechanical one.

2.3 CAREFUL DEFINITION

The definitions of the meanings of the basic instructions given above are far too casual. You can see that this is so, and also see what a more careful definition would be like, by considering the execution of a simple program which is a sequence of basic instructions.

The instructions 'Let there be light!' and 'Everybody out, we're closing!' have an effect which is independent of the state of things at the time the instruction is issued. In the first case, we are told, there was light; in the second, the effect is to produce an empty bar-room whether or not there was anybody there. But in general we can't say what the effect of an instruction will be unless we consider what the state of things might be before the instruction is executed. For example, consider how the effect of executing *print** varies according to circumstances.

First of all, and most obviously, the state produced depends on what is already on the paper. I might draw two before-after diagrams, one showing the final state if the paper already carries the word 'HELLO' and the other the state if it carries the word 'goodbye': figure 2.1 shows the sort of thing I mean. This example makes it obvious that the effect of executing *print** is to change the state of things so that an extra asterisk mark appears on the paper, not to produce a piece of paper which carries only a single asterisk.

But where should the asterisk appear? There isn't anything magnetic about either 'HELLO' or 'goodbye' so the asterisk doesn't have to appear right next to either of the words. I might have drawn the first part of figure 2.1 differently, perhaps as shown in figure 2.2.

[†] *Execute*: to follow, carry into effect, give effect to a command or an order or an instruction. Now an old-fashioned word in England, but still in use in the USA, and transmitted back to us under its original meaning. Outside the computing industry its common meaning has become 'to put to death' but originally it was the instruction of the judge - the death sentence - that was executed, not the prisoner.

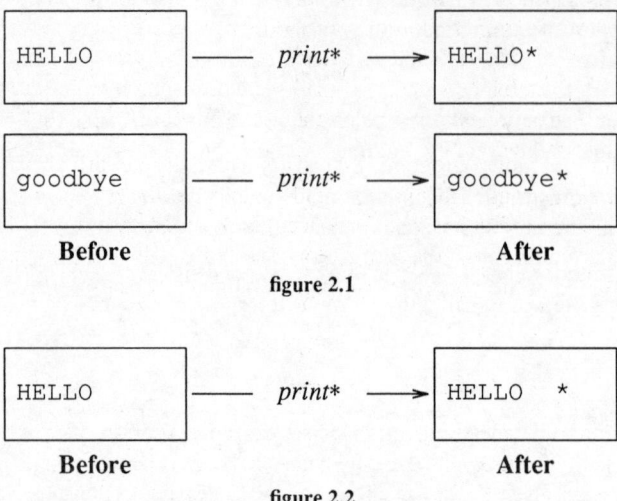

Before   **After**

figure 2.1

Before   **After**

figure 2.2

The differences in these diagrams seem to suggest that the effect of executing the *print** instruction is indeterminate: although the general effect is the same, the asterisk appears sometimes in one position, sometimes in another. If you have ever used a typewriter you know that this is misleading: there is a carriage and/or a printhead whose position determines where on the paper the next mark will be made. The state you produce when you press the '*' key on a real typewriter depends not only on what is already on the paper but also on the position of the carriage or the printhead relative to the paper. Most computer video screens use a flashing marker to show the position of an imaginary printhead. In either case there is a *cpp* (abbreviation for *C*urrent *P*rinting *P*osition) which defines where the next mark will be made if a printing key is pressed.

So a more complete definition of the effect of the *print** instruction is that executing it makes an asterisk mark at the cpp. If I show the position of the cpp with a '◊' mark in the before-after diagram then I can show the difference between the earlier two cases: figure 2.3 shows the sort of thing I mean.

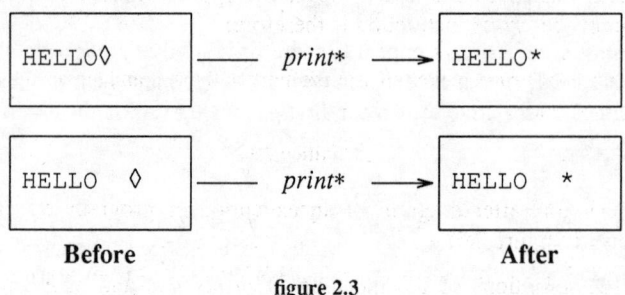

Before   **After**

figure 2.3

Still the diagram is incomplete: if the before state includes a cpp, so must the after state. How does execution of *print** affect the cpp? Since I am inventing a notation, I can decide to make whatever definition is convenient. Programs produce their effect by a sequence of printing actions, so it is helpful to consider sequences of instructions before making a final decision.

Consider, for example, program 2.1. This very simple program describes a sequence of executions. It should be read as: execute the *print** instruction once *and then,* when its effect has been produced, execute the *print** instruction again. Notice in particular how the semicolon symbol ';' is used in programming notation in place of the *'and then'* of English language descriptions.

*print**; *print**

program 2.1

I want to define the meaning of *print** so that an execution of program 2.1 will make two asterisk marks on the paper next to each other: after all, that is what two presses on the '*' key will do on a typewriter. Bearing in mind the discussion of sequence in chapter 1, which showed that when carrying out a sequence of actions each action takes place in the state which the previous one produced, an incomplete before-after diagram of an execution of program 2.1 can be drawn as in figure 2.4. The in-between state is both the after state of the first execution and the before state of the second. I want the second execution to put an asterisk to the right of the first one so by reasoning backwards you can see where the cpp must be in the in-between state. It must surely come after the first asterisk.

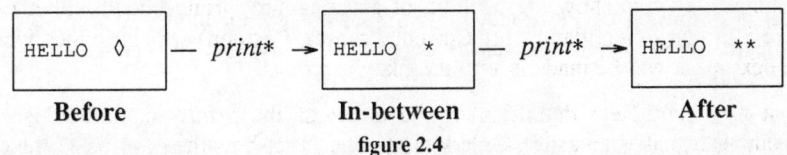

Before   **In-between**   **After**

figure 2.4

Now that you know what state is produced by the first execution of *print** in program 2.1, you should be persuaded that an execution of *print** has in general two effects: it makes a mark *and* it moves the cpp. A more complete definition of the effect of the *print** instruction is therefore:

> An execution of *print** makes an asterisk mark at the cpp and moves the cpp one place to the right.

definition 2.1

A complete before-after diagram of an execution of program 2.1 can now be drawn, shown in figure 2.5.

More careful definitions of the meaning of *printspace* and of *NL* can now be

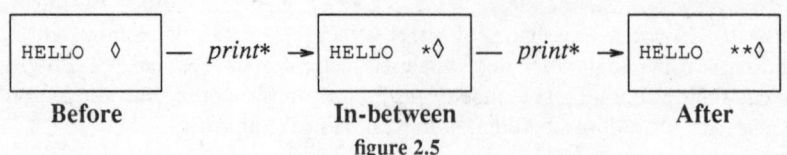

Before   **In-between**   **After**

figure 2.5

given:

>An execution of *printspace* moves the cpp one place to the right.

definition 2.2

An execution of *NL* moves the cpp down a line and to the left margin of the paper/screen.

definition 2.3

-=-=-=-=-=-=-=-=-=-=-=-=-

Exercise 2.1
Make a definition, in the style of the definitions above, of the final effect on the state of the paper and on the cpp of an execution of program 2.1.

Exercise 2.2
Make a definition, in the style of definition 2.1, of the effect of an execution of the program

>*print**; *print**; *print**; *print**

Exercise 2.3
Make a definition of the effect of two successive executions of program 2.1. Compare it with your answer to exercise 2.2; explain any similarities and differences.

Exercise 2.4
Make a definition, in the style of the definitions above, of the meaning of

>*NL*; *print**; *printspace*; *print**

Hence make a definition of the effect of one execution of this program.

Exercise 2.5
What is the effect of two successive executions of the program in exercise 2.4? Draw two before-after diagrams to illustrate your answer: one with one intermediate state, showing the effect of the two successive executions; one with seven intermediate states, showing the effect of each successive instruction execution.

-=-=-=-=-=-=-=-=-=-=-=-=-

2.4 CALCULATING MEANINGS

Definition 2.1 may at first seem rather pompously precise. Why should I spend so much time inventing a definition when I could just say that an execution of *print** has the same effect as pressing the asterisk key on a typewriter and then anyone who has ever seen a typewriter will understand? Why bother to work out the effect of a sequence from the effect of single executions when I could just define the effect of *print**; *print** to be that two asterisks are printed next to each other on the same line?

The difficulty with these more relaxed approaches to the meaning of instructions and programs is that neither of them corresponds to any of the ways in which we have been able to make machines that execute programs. Those machines work by following the defined meaning of program instructions very carefully, and by following rules which allow individual instruction executions to be composed into larger program executions. The rules can't appeal to 'what everybody knows' because machines don't know anything. The definitions of meaning have to be finite because the machines are finite and they have to be precise because we don't know how to be usefully imprecise.

In programming we make a virtue out of necessity and define everything as precisely as possible. The advantage we gain then is that we can *deduce* or *calculate* the effect of any program without necessarily having to try it out on a machine, and thereby save lots of frustrating trial and error. It is obviously possible to do so because a machine, stupidly and blindly following the same definitions, makes a similar calculation in order to produce the program's effect.

Normal and abnormal circumstances

Definition 2.1 is precise because it needs to be precise. But how can we tell when we have been precise enough? And what should happen when circumstances arise that we haven't considered?

For example, when you press the asterisk key on an ordinary typewriter the effect is normally just like that described by definition 2.1. But if you press the key and keep pressing it again you will print a line of asterisks. Eventually the line will grow long enough to approach the right-hand edge of the paper and a bell will ring because the cpp is a few places away from a margin; if you still keep going until the margin is reached then the keyboard mechanism will lock and pressing the key won't have any further effect. If our programs are to control automatic typewriters then all this detail must surely be in the definition of the effect of *print**. Definition 2.1 says nothing about margins or bells and doesn't say that sometimes nothing at all is printed. Is it precise enough? Is behaviour at the right margin its only omission, or are there yet further circumstances in which it is invalid?

One way to treat the question of precision is to say that definitions like definition 2.1 cover 'normal' conditions. There are sometimes abnormal circumstances in which an instruction is inapplicable; what happens in those circumstances is not covered in the definition. Under those circumstances action is undefined and anything at all might happen. So definition 2.1 applies in normal circumstances, which means circumstances in which there is paper in the machine, the cpp isn't next to the right margin or the bottom of the paper, there is plenty of typewriter ribbon left, the power is turned on, the asterisk type isn't broken, and so on.

A more convincing answer is to say that our definitions apply to an imaginary mathematical world with infinitely wide and infinitely long pieces of paper and that within that world our definitions are precise. We have abstracted away from the unnecessary and confusing detail required to deal with real-world machinery, which can be worn out, badly constructed or badly designed. Complete definitions can be given for any piece of real-world machinery that is working correctly, if they are needed.

-=-=-=-=-=-=-=-=-=-=-=-

Exercise 2.6
Suppose that a typewriter carriage has eight printing positions and that the margins are set at positions 5 and 75. The bell rings seven positions before the right margin. Define the effect of a depression of the asterisk key on this typewriter.

Exercise 2.7
Find out the effect of a depression of the asterisk key on the computer or the terminal you use for programming. Do so for at least two 'computing contexts': for example, when using an editor and when typing a command. [For hints about editors and commands see the end of this chapter.] Hence define the effect of an asterisk key depression on your machine.

-=-=-=-=-=-=-=-=-=-=-=-

2.5 NEWLINES AND THE CPP

Suppose that you have to write a program to draw a square pattern of asterisks next to the left margin of the paper:

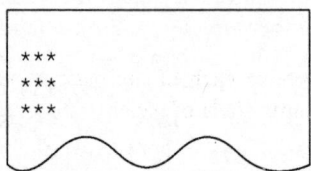

Counting asterisks tells you that your program must execute *print** nine times.

Since the pattern is printed on more than one line, it must include some executions of *NL*: since it has three lines it seems reasonable to execute *NL* three times. Each *NL* will then be grouped with three *print**s.

Another simple pattern is the three-by-three triangle of asterisks:

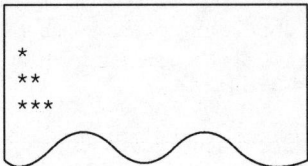

Here there are only six asterisks, but still three lines. Each *NL* will be grouped with a number of *print**s, but not all with the same number.

Last, consider the reversed three-by-three triangle, which may be the first programming puzzle you have seen:

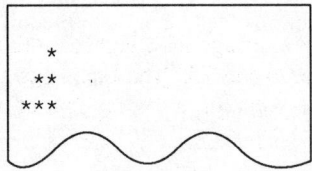

It looks very similar to the other triangle, and it contains exactly the same number of asterisks, but it can't be printed using *print** and *NL* alone. To see why this is so, consider how it is possible to print the first asterisk in the third position of the line. This can only be done with the basic instructions used in this chapter if a couple of *printspace*s first move the cpp to the right place. The pattern looks like a triangle of asterisks, but using the programming notation of this book makes it seem to be a square made up of visible asterisks and invisible spaces!

-=-=-=-=-=-=-=-=-=-=-=-

Exercise 2.8
Write programs which produce each of the patterns above.

Exercise 2.9
Write programs which produce each of the patterns above, spaced two positions away from the left margin.

Exercise 2.10
Write programs which produce each of the patterns above, hard up against the right margin of a forty-column sheet of paper.

Exercise 2.11
Take your program which prints the second triangle pattern shown above and rearrange its instructions (don't delete any of them) so that it prints the first

triangle pattern. The programs should leave the cpp in the same position.

Exercise 2.12
Estimate the number of different programs which could be correct answers to exercise 2.11.

-=-=-=-=-=-=-=-=-=-=-=-=-

Where should I put the newlines?

It seems reasonable to put three *NL* instructions into a program which is to print a pattern with three lines. It will always be possible to group the *NL* instruction with the *print** and *printspace* instructions in more than one way and usually some of the ways will be preferable to others. Consider, for example, programs 2.2 and 2.3. Each prints three newlines and nine asterisks, three to a line. Each is intended to produce a three-by-three square pattern of asterisks. Figure 2.6 shows that the two programs have similar but different effects when executed in one particular state of affairs. This is to be expected: although the programs are made up of the same instructions they have them in a different order.

NL; *print**; *print**; *print**;	*print**; *print**; *print**; *NL*;
NL; *print**; *print**; *print**;	*print**; *print**; *print**; *NL*;
NL; *print**; *print**; *print**	*print**; *print**; *print**; *NL*

program 2.2   **program 2.3**

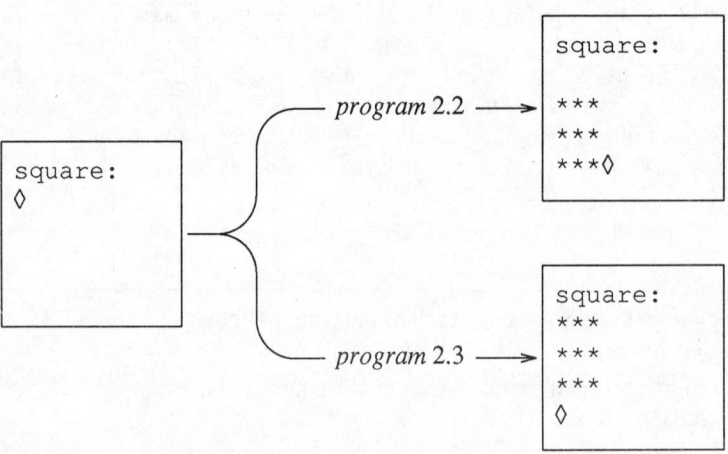

figure 2.6

Given identical initial conditions - a piece of paper with a one-line title on it and the cpp at the beginning of the second line - these two programs produce similar results with detail differences. They print their patterns on different lines of the paper: program 2.2 produces a blank second line and leaves the cpp on the fourth position of the fifth line, program 2.3 leaves the cpp at the start of a blank fifth line.

The differences seem remarkably trivial. Is there a more important distinction which can be made between these two programs, and is either to be preferred to the other? Yes there is, and so far as this book goes program 2.2 is to be preferred. The reason is that it is often necessary to reason about where on the page particular marks will appear. If a program starts printing with the *NL* instruction then it isn't necessary to assume anything about the initial position of the cpp, and this makes the reasoning more secure. To make the same point by example, consider figure 2.7, a before-after diagram which shows how the programs perform when the cpp is initially at the end of a title line. This diagram should help to convince you that whenever the lines below the cpp are blank, program 2.2 will always print a square pattern, but program 2.3 will only do so if the cpp is initially at the left margin. For the purpose of printing square patterns in unknown circumstances, program 2.2 is therefore to be preferred.

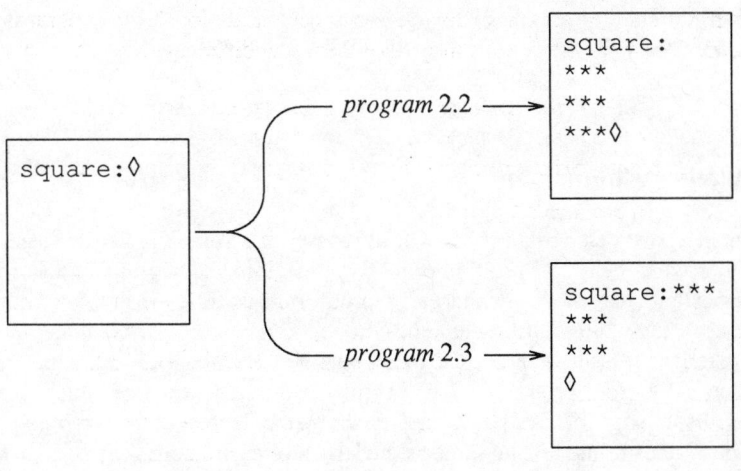

figure 2.7

-=-=-=-=-=-=-=-=-=-=-=-

Exercise 2.13
What is the pattern printed by two successive executions of program 2.2 in the two states of affairs indicated by the diagrams above?

Exercise 2.14
Repeat exercise 2.13, this time for program 2.3. In particular, how many lines of asterisks are printed in each case?

Exercise 2.15
Draw before-after diagrams for the execution of program 2.4 (see below) in the initial states described in figures 2.6 and 2.7. What is the essential difference between the final state left by program 2.3 and that left by program 2.4?

print*; print*; print*; NL;
print*; print*; print*; NL;
print*; print*; print*

program 2.4

Exercise 2.16
Draw before-after diagrams to show the effect of *two* successive executions of
program 2.4 in the same initial states as exercise 2.15.

Exercise 2.17
What is the difference in the effects of program 2.2 and program 2.5 (see below).
Draw before-after diagrams, if necessary, to illustrate your answer.

print*; print*; print*;
NL; print*; print*; print*;
NL; print*; print*; print*

program 2.5

Exercise 2.18
What is the difference in effect between programs 2.4 and 2.5?

-=-=-=-=-=-=-=-=-=-=-=-

Calculating with the cpp

I claimed above that program 2.2 will always print a square pattern of asterisks,
no matter what the initial position of the cpp. An informal argument, convincing
but somewhat short of the standard of a proof, runs as follows: first, program 2.2
doesn't print anything until the cpp has moved to a new line; second, each set of
three asterisks it prints is preceded by *NL* and hence will appear at the beginning
of a line. Therefore program 2.2 will print a pattern each line of which starts at
the left-hand edge of the paper and is the same length as every other. The
number of lines printed is the same as the length of each line.

The only printing instructions you know so far which can be used in a program
are *print** and *printspace*, each of which moves the cpp horizontally one position,
and *NL*, which moves it vertically one position and horizontally back to column
1. An execution of a program will consist of a certain number of horizontal
movements and a certain number of vertical movements. The final position of
the cpp will depend on its initial position and on the horizontal and vertical
motions. It will also depend on the order in which the vertical and horizontal
movements take place.

Suppose that an execution of a particular program executes the *NL* instruction k
times. Because each execution of *NL* moves the cpp back to column 1, the
horizontal positions which the cpp takes up during execution of the program
depend on the number of *print** and *printspace* instructions executed between
*NL*s. Suppose that initially the cpp is at position x of line y. Suppose that before

the first *NL* it moves the cpp horizontally, by executing *print** or *printspace*, h_0 places. Suppose that it moves the cpp horizontally h_1 positions after the first *NL*, h_2 positions after the second, .. and finally h_k positions after the last *NL*. In general it will move horizontally h_i positions between the *i*th and the (*i*+1)th *NL*. It is possible to use knowledge of *k*, *h*, *x* and *y* to calculate the position *x′* and *y′* of the cpp after execution of the program. For example, if *k*=1 then $x′=h_1+1$ and $y′=y+1$.

-=-=-=-=-=-=-=-=-=-=-=-=-

Exercise 2.19
Give a general formula for *x′* and *y′*, in terms of *x*, *y*, *h* and *k* when *k*>0.

Exercise 2.20
Give a general formula for *x′* and *y′*, in terms of *x*, *y* and *h* when *k*=0.

Exercise 2.21
Give values of *k*, h_0, .., h_k for programs 2.2, 2.3, 2.4 and 2.5 above.

Exercise 2.22
Give values of *k* and *h* for two successive executions of program 2.2. Likewise for two successive executions of programs 2.3, 2.4 and 2.5.

Exercise 2.23
Give values of *k* and *h* for an execution of program 2.2 followed by an execution of program 2.3. Likewise for an execution of program 2.3 followed by an execution of program 2.2.

Exercise 2.24
Under what initial conditions will an execution of program 2.3 produce the same visual effect as an execution of program 2.2, ignoring blank lines and the final position of the cpp?

-=-=-=-=-=-=-=-=-=-=-=-=-

2.6 COUNTER-EXAMPLES AND FINICKY DETAILS

In all the examples I have discussed, program 2.2 prints a square. I have shown one example where program 2.3 prints a square and one where it doesn't. You know that program 2.3 doesn't always work, but what should you believe about program 2.2? You have seen two states of affairs in which program 2.2 works: how many different states would you have to consider before you would stake your life that this program draws a square of asterisks? If that number is too large, how many before you would stake the price of a cup of coffee?

There is an old joke about a court case where a man is accused of a crime. The police bring a witness who saw him do it. The man wants to bring thousands of witnesses who *didn't* see him do it. Naturally his defence fails and he is found guilty.

Suppose that the first Martian you meet is a kind Martian. You can conclude that not all Martians are unkind, because you know there is at least one kind Martian. Suppose that you keep on meeting different Martians and they all turn out to be kind. It would be only natural to suppose that the next Martian you meet will be kind as well, but that is just a guess. You *cannot* conclude that every Martian is kind until you have met them all, and we still don't know for sure how many there are.

Universal assertions like 'all Martians are kind', 'everybody knows I'm innocent', 'honesty is the best policy', 'programming is easy', 'it always rains on my birthday', and so on present a simple logical stumbling-block. To prove a universal by example, you must check every example in the universe it describes. To *disprove* it takes only one *counter-example.* An infinite number of examples can be demolished by one counter-example.

Some universals are true and we know it. All equal-sided triangles have sixty-degree angles, for example. We know it not because anybody has measured them all but because we have seen a *proof* - a convincing argument that persuades us that it must be so. In this book I introduce one particular way of reasoning about programs and show some ways in which you can prove properties of programs.

Changing to negative statements doesn't make universals any easier to prove by example. Statements like 'there is no Santa Claus', 'there are no UFOs', 'nobody loves me', 'there are no mistakes in this program', are all impossible to prove but easy to disprove if only you can get one sighting of Santa Claus, see one UFO, find one true friend, find one mistake in your program.

This book isn't about rules of evidence or Santa Claus but it is concerned with constructing programs. How much trust should you put in 'evidence' that a program works as it should? Not much, because all it takes is one piece of evidence to the contrary, and your faith in the program will evaporate. Two examples do *not* prove that program 2.2 really does what it should. Proof requires more careful forms of argument. Careful argument is what mathematics is all about.

2.7 SOME SIMPLE MATHEMATICS

What does an algebraic equation mean? What do you learn if you have two formulas, $F1$ and $F2$, and somebody tells you that $F1=F2$? One thing that you learn is that in any formula where you write $F1$ you could write $F2$ instead, and vice-versa. This can serve as an explanation of what each of the formulas means in terms of the other. Alternatively, it can be used as a rule to calculate the meaning of a formula.

For example, suppose that you have the formula $x+39$, and you are told that $x=3$. You know immediately that your formula is equivalent to $3+39$, and your knowledge of arithmetic tells you that its value is 42. The equation has helped you to find the arithmetic value of the formula. Alternatively, your knowledge of arithmetic tells you that $39=13\times3$, so your formula could be written as $x+13\times3$. This time use the equation $x=3$ to write x in place of 3, and the formula becomes $x+13x$. Further manipulation would make it into $14x$, which could be more useful than its bald arithmetic value.

You learn more from a rule if it is parameterised: that is, if it contains names which can be replaced by formulas. For example, you might have a formula involving squaring - say y^2+6 - and you might not understand how to calculate the square of a number. You can understand squaring in terms of multiplication if you have a rule $F^2=F\times F$. This rule is intended to cover squaring of any formula: the name F is a *parameter* of the rule, a name which can be replaced by any formula. In particular the rule tells you, putting y in place of F, that $y^2 = y\times y$. Using this fact the original formula can become $y\times y+6$, and if you know that $y=5$ it can then become $5\times5+6$ and eventually 31.

The same squaring rule can help you to understand more complicated formulas. How should you calculate the value of $(x^2)^2$, knowing that $x=3$? There are two ways to solve the problem. One way is to take F to be x once more, which produces the formula $(xx)^2$; using the same rule again, but this time taking xx for F, gives $(xx)\times(xx)$; finally, using $x=3$, you get $3\times3\times3\times3$, which is 81. You get exactly the same result if the first step uses the squaring rule but puts x^2 in place of F: then the formula becomes $(x^2)\times(x^2)$; taking x to be F gives $(xx)\times(xx)$ as before and finally replacing x by 3 gives $3\times3\times3\times3$. There are several more ways to do the calculation! For example, start by replacing x by 3, giving $(3^2)^2$ first of all ..

-=-=-=-=-=-=-=-=-=-=-=-

Exercise 2.25
Complete the calculation started in the last paragraph. Do it two different ways. Don't calculate 3^2 or 9^2 directly.

-=-=-=-=-=-=-=-=-=-=-=-

To return to programming: a program can be treated as an algebraic formula. The effect of executing a program is to alter the state of affairs. Any two programs which produce the same change in the state of affairs are equivalent formulas, according to one view, because you might execute one in place of the other. When I write $P1=P2$, where $P1$ and $P2$ are programs, I mean that $P1$ and $P2$ have the same effect. It follows that wherever I write $P1$ I might write $P2$ instead, and vice-versa. It is just this technique of substituting equal program formulas for each other which is the foundation of the mathematical techniques used in this book.

Equal programs need not be identical programs, just as equal formulas need not be identical formulas. For example, if you know that $x=3$ then 81 and $(x^2)^2$ are equal formulas, though one of them gives you its value directly and the other requires you to calculate. If you execute a program *P1* you might find that it takes a great deal of huffing and puffing to produce its effect, whereas when you execute another program *P2* it produces the same effect very directly. Nevertheless the two programs are equal as formulas, so far as this book is concerned, if they always produce the same effect.

Calculating the effect of a sequence

Chapter 1 described the effect of a sequence of actions in the following terms:

> Each action takes place in the state produced by the previous action and in its turn produces the state in which the next action will take place. The first action takes place in an 'initial' state and the last action produces the 'final' state of affairs.

Clear enough but rather long-winded, like most definitions in English. It is a remark about states of affairs and instructions. It describes how a state of affairs is changed by a sequence of instructions, in terms of the changes produced by individual instructions. It can be stated much more economically. If I write

$$s \; tran \; i$$

(read as '*s* transformed by *i*') to mean 'the state of affairs produced by executing instruction *i* once, starting in state *s*', then I can define the effect of a two instruction sequence *p*; *q* as follows:

$$s \; tran \; p; q \; = \; (s \; tran \; p) \; tran \; q$$

definition 2.4

Read this definition as '*s* transformed by *p*; *q* is the same as' (*s* transformed by *p*) transformed by *q*'. It turns out that this is the only definition you need to find out the meaning of a sequence. It defines the meaning of the semicolon as an algebraic operator. You can deduce from it the definition given in chapter 1. But let me take those steps slowly, one at a time. First consider some simple calculations.

Suppose that the only effect of executing a program which interests you is the movement of the cpp. Then the position of the cpp is a complete statement of the state of affairs so far as you are concerned: I shall write it as $<x, y>$ to give position within a line and line number. The effect on the cpp of *print**, *NL* and *printspace* can be defined as in definition 2.5. It is immediately obvious that

$$<x, y> \; tran \; print* \; = \; <x+1, y>$$
$$<x, y> \; tran \; NL \; = \; <1, y+1>$$
$$<x, y> \; tran \; printspace \; = \; <x+1, y>$$

definition 2.5

according to this definition $print*=printspace$ just because for any state $<x,y>$, $<x,y>$ *tran print** = $<x,y>$ *tran printspace*.

-=-=-=-=-=-=-=-=-=-=-=-=-

Exercise 2.26
Prove that according to definitions 2.4 and 2.5

$$print*; print* = printspace; printspace$$
$$= print*; printspace = printspace; print*$$

Exercise 2.27
Prove that according to definitions 2.4 and 2.5, $print*; NL = NL$.

Exercise 2.28
'It is obvious that $NL=NL$. Considering only the position of the cpp, it is possible to prove that $print*; NL=NL$. Therefore $print*$ has no effect on the cpp.' What is the fallacy in this argument?

-=-=-=-=-=-=-=-=-=-=-=-=-

Definition 2.4 describes how to combine two executions into a sequence. You might fear that an unlimited number of definitions would be necessary to explain sequences of any length, describing how to join two actions with a third, three with a fourth, and so on. Not so, because the semicolon is an *associative* operator.

Addition in arithmetic is an associative operator: 1+(2+3)=(1+2)+3, and indeed in general for any a, b and c $(a+b)+c=a+(b+c)$. In the same way program brackets '⟨' and '⟩' can be used in an instruction sequence:

$$s\ \textbf{\textit{tran}}\ ⟨a; b⟩; c\ = s\ \textbf{\textit{tran}}\ a; ⟨b; c⟩$$

definition 2.6

You can deduce from this definition that however you bracket a sequence the effect is the same - just as the result is the same however you bracket an addition sum. You don't have to take this definition on trust because it can be proved. The proof requires one extra definition:

$$s\ \textbf{\textit{tran}}\ ⟨p⟩ = s\ \textbf{\textit{tran}}\ p$$

definition 2.7

which says that putting brackets round a program doesn't make any difference to its effect, and that taking them away doesn't make any difference either. In definitions 2.4, 2.6 and 2.7 the names p, q, a, b and c stand for *any* program: a single instruction, a sequence, a choice, a repetition, whatever you like.

As the first step in a proof I show how to convert the left-hand side of definition 2.6 into a form which doesn't include any program brackets, and leave it as an exercise for the reader to complete the proof.

$s \; tran \; (\!(a; b)\!); c = (s \; tran \; (\!(a; b)\!)) \; tran \; c$
          [by definition 2.4, taking $p = (\!(a; b)\!)$, $q = c$]
$= (s \; tran \; a; b) \; tran \; c$
          [by definition 2.7, taking $p = a; b$]
$= ((s \; tran \; a) \; tran \; b) \; tran \; c$
          [by definition 2.4 once more, taking $p = a$, $q = b$]

-=-=-=-=-=-=-=-=-=-=-=-=-

Exercise 2.29

Convert the right-hand side of definition 2.6 into a form without program brackets. Compare your formula with that above. The two formulas should be identical, which should enable you to conclude the truth of the definition.

-=-=-=-=-=-=-=-=-=-=-=-=-

It is possible to make a complete proof of definition 2.6 which shows that it doesn't matter how you bracket a sequence. I shan't do so yet because to do so requires an inductive proof (see chapter 7). You should already be able to see that the effect on any state s of a sequence $P_1; P_2; ..; P_n$ of programs, however it is bracketed, can be reduced to a formula

$$(.. ((s \; tran \; P_1) \; tran \; P_2) ..) \; tran \; P_n$$

and that the way you bracket a sequence therefore doesn't alter its meaning. This doesn't mean that program brackets are useless. Like brackets in arithmetic, they are useful when a formula contains more than one sort of operator. Just as use of brackets distinguishes between $(1+2)\times3$ and $1+(2\times3)$, so programming brackets fix the meaning of programs when operators other than the simple semicolon are used.

-=-=-=-=-=-=-=-=-=-=-=-=-

Exercise 2.30

Calculate the effect of programs 2.2, 2.3, 2.4 and 2.5 according to definition 2.5. Your calculations should correspond to those given as answers to the exercises in section 2.5.

Exercise 2.31

Calculate the effect of the following programs according to definition 2.5.

        p1: *printspace*; *printspace*; *print**
        p2: *printspace*; *print**; *print**
        p3: *print**; *print**; *print**

Hence confirm that an execution of *NL*, followed by an execution of *p1*, followed by another execution of *NL*, followed by an execution of *p2*, followed by a third execution of *NL*, followed finally by an execution of *p3* will print a shape whose visible right-hand edge is parallel to the margin of the paper or screen.

-=

APPENDIX 2.A TRYING OUT YOUR PROGRAMS ON A COMPUTER

The notation used in this book isn't that used by any programming system, so far as I am aware, although it shares ideas with most. In order to execute a program on a real machine using a real programming system it will be necessary to transcribe from programming notation to some form of notation that the programming system is designed to understand - a *mechanical code*.

The best way to program is to think and write in a notation *as abstract as possible*. Mechanical codes are too definite, too concrete. They restrict your thinking by forcing you to concentrate on confusing details of punctuation and description too soon. The notation used in this book is a little more abstract. I recommend that you design and write programs in this notation (until you can use something even more abstract) and transcribe your programs into a mechanical code only when you are sure they are correct. If your transcribed program doesn't work then you must have made an error in the transcription or in the original program. If it is the latter, go back to your programming notation and correct the program. Resist the temptation to 'debug' your coded transcription.

In order to transcribe a program from one notation into another all you need to know is an equivalent in the new notation for each instruction in the old and, similarly, an equivalent of each program structure. Occasionally genuine translation will be required, where there isn't a direct equivalent in the new notation of your ideas expressed in the original. This book gives a Pascal equivalent of every construct it introduces or tells you how to translate where that is absolutely essential. Friendly experts can show you how to transcribe into other codes (or see Part Five of this book).

For example: suppose that you have to transcribe the program

$$NL; print*; print*; print*$$

and that the equivalent of *print** in your mechanical code is the word BANG and the equivalent of *NL* is POP. Then one step towards a transcription is to write:

```
POP; BANG; BANG; BANG
```

The original program is a sequence of instructions. Suppose that in your mechanical code the elements of a sequence must be written in square brackets, separated by commas. Then a further step towards a transcription is to write:

```
[POP], [BANG], [BANG], [BANG]
```

There may be further steps. Perhaps you have to write a program title before the program and an epilogue after it. Perhaps the elements of the sequence must be numbered. There are all sorts of possibilities.

Submitting a program to a machine

A computer is a *programmable* machine because it is given a program of instructions which it executes without any other agent's intervention. A car, by contrast, is *continuously controlled*: you are constantly intervening to correct its course, its speed and the state of its external lighting. If you could give your car the details of your route and then sit back with folded arms while it drove you to your destination, it too would be a programmable machine.

A *programming system* is a collection of hardware and software which enables you to prepare programs and submit them for execution and which produces the effects described by those programs. A single computer will normally be capable of forming part of several different programming systems, often apparently simultaneously.

When you use any modern programming system there is a stage when you present your text - 'type it in' - followed by an instant when you somehow or other tell it to start work. Because it is tedious to type in a text and because you almost always make little mistakes when you do it, most programming systems keep a copy of your text which you can correct or *edit* when you notice those mistakes. Usually you type in your program, ask the system to execute it, notice a mistake, execute it again, edit it again, and so on until you are satisfied that it is correct. The details of how you type your program, how you refer to copies of different texts, how you edit a text, how you tell the system to use a text as a program, are details of your system. You have to learn how to do these minor miracles by reading the 'manual' or the 'documentation' of your system, or by asking some helpful and knowledgeable friend.

Command language and programming language

You will almost certainly construct and execute programs by using a computer 'interactively' - a word which means only that the machine is continuously controlled. Your use of the computer will be a sequence of large actions: you will type in a program text (action 1) and then ask the programming system to start work on it (action 2). When you see the results of action 2 you may not be satisfied, so you will alter the text by editing it (action 3) and then ask the programming system to consider the new version (action 4). This edit; execute; edit; execute; edit; .. sequence may be repeated as many times as you like until you are satisfied with the final effect. Perhaps you will intersperse it with other actions, like playing a video game or sending a message to a friend.

Your use of the computer will be 'interactive' in exactly the sense that the way you drive a car is 'interactive'. Just as you may change your route in a car because of the traffic you encounter, so you may change your program because of mistakes which your experience reveals to you. In a car you have a few controls which you manipulate to make the car do what you want. You might find buttons on the keyboard which do the same sort of thing (EDIT, EXECUTE, GAME buttons, for example) but more likely you will have to use some sort of notation misleadingly called a command language to instruct the computing system what to do next.

The notation in which you express your commands to execute, file away, edit, will almost certainly not be the same as the mechanical code into which you transcribe your programs. There are all sorts of reasons for the difference, some good and some bad, and this book isn't the place to discuss the design of command and programming notations. However, if you look back at your use of command notation during a session at the machine you will see that you have expressed a program of a kind - at the very least you have issued a sequence of commands. Some command notations can be used to express complicated programming ideas, but mostly they restrict themselves to simple sequences and very simple procedures.

APPENDIX 2.B BASIC INSTRUCTIONS AND SEQUENCES IN PASCAL

The basic instruction equivalences in Pascal are as follows:

This book	Pascal	Fussy Pascal
*print**	write('*')	write(output,'*')
printspace	write(' ')	write(output,' ')
NL	writeln	writeln(output)

Most Pascal systems will understand the instructions in the middle column. Any of them will accept the instructions in the right-hand column; some may be fussy and will accept only those instructions. You may learn enough from this book, in later chapters, to understand the purpose of the output decoration demanded by fussy Pascal systems, but it is enough at this stage to treat it as a sort of magic incantation.

Sequences in Pascal

Pascal uses semicolons in just the same way as the notation in this book. For example, the sequence

$$print*; print*; print*$$

transcribes into Pascal as the sequence

```
write('*'); write('*'); write('*')
```

A complete Pascal program text

A complete program text in Pascal always requires some special decoration. It has to start with the word `program`; you have to give the program a name; the instructions of the program have to be enclosed with the bracket words `begin` and `end` and the program has to end with a full stop (dot, period). Here, for example, is a program which prints three asterisks:

```
program first (input,output);
begin
    write('*'); write('*'); write('*')
end.
```

The first line is a pretty meaningless incantation. The *name* of your program is written after the word `program`: it should be different from any instruction name or any other name you use elsewhere. In the example I used 'first', but I could have used 'foo', 'richard', 'naomi', 'fred', 'jane', 'ahmed', 'silly', 'boring', 'nemo', 'thisisnotaname', .. After the program name you usually have to write the names `input` and `output`, bracketed together in that order and separated by a comma. At the end of it all you have to put a semicolon. Sometimes the Pascal system will let you leave out the `input` and `output` stuff, so you might be able to start your program with the line

```
program junk;
```

Program layout - the spacing of words within a line and breaks between lines - doesn't affect the meaning of a Pascal program provided you don't put spaces or line breaks in words like `program` or in names like `write`. Layout is irrelevant only so far as the programming system is concerned: spacing and layout matter a lot to the human reader so you should pay attention to them and always lay out your program so that it is clearly readable.

Punctuation words in Pascal

In Pascal the words `program`, `begin` and `end` are *punctuation words*: words which act like punctuation marks. These particular words are just fancy names for brackets. There are lots more of these punctuation words, which you can find listed in any description of the language. But `write`, `input` and `output` aren't punctuation words, they are *names*. You will begin to find out how to use names in a program in the next chapter. For the moment just notice that you can't use punctuation words as names. So you could never write

```
program begin (input,output);
```

because `begin` is a punctuation word, not a name. Your system might let you get away with

```
program write (input,output);
```

- `write` is a name, after all - but then it might become confused when it read the rest of the program because it could be seen as inconsistent to use `write` both as the program name and as the printing instruction name in the same program.

APPENDIX 2.C MAKING AND FINDING MISTAKES IN PROGRAMS

Sometimes when you transcribe a program into your chosen notation and submit it to a programming system everything will go well. At other times - to begin with it will seem more often than not - things will go badly. This will almost always be because *you* have made a mistake. Computing machines don't make mistakes, they just follow the wrong instructions. The kinds of mistakes you can make can be divided into several classes.

First, and most common, are transcription errors, when you don't type the program which you intended to. Second, and perhaps almost as common, are errors of consistency, where the program doesn't make sense because its parts don't fit together. Last, and most damaging, are errors of meaning: the program makes perfect sense but not the sense you thought it would.

When you submit your program to a programming system it will respond in different ways to your mistakes. The simplest kind of response is a complaint about the punctuation of your program. The famous English joke paragraph

> smith where jones had had had had had had had had had had the examiner's approval

makes a little more sense when punctuated correctly:

> Smith, where Jones had had 'had', had had 'had had'. 'Had had' had had the examiner's approval.

Programming systems get confused by very simple punctuation errors like missing out a comma or putting in too many brackets. A human can usually read your text, spot the mistake and understand the program nevertheless: in effect read what you *meant* to write rather that what you *actually* wrote. Programming systems have infinitely less intelligence than any human and their response to almost every punctuation error is to treat the program as unreadable and to display a remark, make a report, show a message, which announces their confusion.

Errors of consistency appear to the programming system as a program whose parts individually make sense but don't seem to fit together. Typically a programming system can read the program because it is correctly punctuated, but it makes as much sense as Chomsky's famous non-sentence:

> Colourless green ideas sleep furiously.

Programming systems presented with a nonsense program normally display remarks designed to point up its inconsistencies. Sometimes these remarks will help you to understand your mistake, sometimes not. Usually you can learn to interpret the runes with a bit of practice and a little help. Sometimes the only useful evidence is that the system is complaining about your program, so something must be wrong with it.

The third kind of mistake is the most serious and the one which takes up most of a programmer's time. You transcribe a program carefully and it all makes consistent sense to the programming system but when it is executed it doesn't have the effect you expect - or worse it *sometimes* doesn't have the effect you expect. Programming systems can't help much with this kind of mistake. The sort of reasoning which is discussed in this book in later chapters can help a lot.

APPENDIX 2.D COMPILERS AND INTERPRETERS

A programming system, faced with a new program which has to be executed, has two tasks. One is to find out what the program asks for; the other is to do what is asked. In order to find out what the program asks, the text must be analysed, instructions must be recognised, consistency must be confirmed. Once everything is recognised execution can commence.

Programming systems approach these tasks in two main ways. One way is to *interpret* the program text more or less as it is presented: to analyse and recognise each piece of the program just before it is executed. The other way is to *compile* the text, analysing it all in one go and at the same time transcribing it into a more internally convenient notation before executing it. Typically Pascal and FORTRAN are compiled, BASIC is interpreted.

Compiling

A *compiler* analyses, recognises and checks all of your text before any of it is executed. The transcription into another notation isn't important, so far as the novice is concerned. What is important is that the whole program text is carefully examined to see whether it is punctuated correctly and whether it seems to be self-consistent. If the compiler finds any mistakes then the program can't be executed at all: you have to correct the mistakes and start the compiler all over again.

Once a compiler accepts a program as correct the programming system can execute the version it has transcribed (though there may be further stages in preparing it for execution which take further effort and therefore make you wait a little longer). The only mistakes which can show up in your program now are mistakes of meaning: it might have the wrong effect or it might ask the machine to do something impossible - like printing a line of eighty-one asterisks on an eighty-column screen.

Interpreting

An *interpreter* analyses, recognises and checks all of your text in small pieces, each piece just before it is executed. When a mistake is found you must correct it and usually the interpreter must then start from the beginning of the program again - though if you are really lucky the interpreter might be able to carry on executing from where it left off.

Interpreters are more straightforward to use than compilers, especially for the novice. It is frustrating to wait while a compiler checks your program but it is equally frustrating when an interpreter finds a mistake in a program which has been executing for several minutes and has nearly finished!

APPENDIX 2.E SOME PROGRAMS TO TRY

Exercise 2.32
Write a program to print a square of asterisks:

```
***
***
***
```

Exercise 2.33
Write a program to print a hollow square of asterisks:

```
****
*  *
****
```

Exercise 2.34
Write a program to print a left-lower triangle of asterisks:

```
*
**
***
```

Exercise 2.35
Write a program to print a left-upper triangle of asterisks:

```
***
**
*
```

[Hint: you should be able to modify your answer to exercise 2.34 to produce this pattern.]

Exercise 2.36
Write a program to print a trapezium of asterisks:

```
*
**
***
***
***
***
***
**
*
```

[Hint: you should be able to use your answers to earlier exercises as parts of the answer to this one.]

Chapter 3
PROCEDURES

Suppose that you want to print a square pattern of asterisks next to the left edge of the paper, thus:

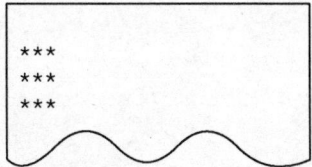

Program 3.1 will produce just that pattern. Program 3.2 will print one line of the pattern. Therefore program 3.3 is an alternative way of producing the whole square pattern, because it calls for three successive executions of program 3.2, each of which prints a single line of three asterisks; hence it prints three lines of three asterisks.

$$NL; print*; print*; print*;$$
$$NL; print*; print*; print*;$$
$$NL; print*; print*; print*$$

program 3.1

$$NL; print*; print*; print*$$

program 3.2

$$program\ 3.2;\ program\ 3.2;\ program\ 3.2$$

program 3.3

A program which is used as though it were an instruction, as program 3.2 is used by program 3.3, is termed a *procedure*. The program that uses it *calls for* or *calls upon* or just *calls* the procedure to produce an execution. The complete program is made up of the procedure definition (program 3.2, for example) and the text which calls upon that definition (program 3.3, for example).

3.1 PROCEDURES AS INVENTED INSTRUCTIONS

NL; print*; printspace; printspace; printspace; print*

program 3.4

NL; print*; print*; print*; print*; print*

program 3.5

program 3.5; *program* 3.4; *program* 3.4;
program 3.4; *program* 3.5

program 3.6

program 3.4; *program* 3.4; *program* 3.5;
program 3.4; *program* 3.4

program 3.7

Given definitions of programs 3.4 and 3.5, program 3.6 prints a hollow rectangle which looks very like a giant letter O:

```
*****
*   *
*   *
*   *
*****
```

The same definitions, called upon by program 3.7, can be used to print a giant letter-H pattern:

```
*   *
*   *
*****
*   *
*   *
```

Here the *same* procedures are being used in different programs to produce *different* effects. We call a procedure for its effect, just as we execute an instruction for its effect. A procedure is an invented instruction. Just as the basic instructions can be combined in various ways to make programs which write various kinds of patterns, so we can combine invented procedures. Although there is only a limited vocabulary of basic instructions, we can invent as many different procedures as our imagination will allow.

-=-=-=-=-=-=-=-=-=-=-=-

Exercise 3.1
A letter-E pattern might appear on the screen as shown in figure 3.1. Write a program to print this pattern, using any of the procedures defined already. [Hint: you may find it convenient to define one extra procedure.]

```
*****
*
*****
*
*****
```

figure 3.1

Exercise 3.2
Answer exercise 3.1 again, but this time for the letter-L pattern shown in figure
3.2.

```
*
*
*
*
*****
```

figure 3.2

Exercise 3.3
Write a program to print the word 'HELLO' in giant letters down the page (for
example, as in figure 3.3).

-=-=-=-=-=-=-=-=-=-=-=-

```
*    *
*    *
*****
*    *
*    *

*****
*
*****
*
*****

*
*
*
*
*****

*
*
*
*
*****

*****
*    *
*    *
*    *
*****
```

figure 3.3

The basic instructions were defined in chapter 2 by describing the effect of a single execution. Once the effect of a single execution is known the effect of a sequence of executions of the same instruction or of several different instructions can be calculated, using the definition of semicolon-combination (definition 2.4). The same goes for procedures. For example, the effect of program 3.2 can be defined as follows:

An execution of program 3.2 prints three asterisk marks at the beginning of the line following the cpp and moves the cpp to the fourth position of that line.

This definition follows from the definitions of *print**, *NL* and semicolon-combination given in chapter 2.

-=-=-=-=-=-=-=-=-=-=-=-=-

Exercise 3.4
Give definitions of programs 3.4 and 3.5 in the style of the definition above.

Exercise 3.5
Give a definition of program 3.6 in the style of the definition above.

-=-=-=-=-=-=-=-=-=-=-=-=-

Now if procedures can be given a meaning and used as instructions, then programs which use procedures can be given a meaning (as in exercise 3.4). In turn, those programs can be used as instructions themselves. If you agree that programs 3.6 and 3.7 have the effects illustrated above, then you must agree that program 3.8 will print a sort of letter-O above a sort of letter-H. To help convince you, figure 3.4 shows a diagram of the output of this program indicating which parts of it which are contributed by different procedures.

program 3.6; *NL*; program 3.7

program 3.8

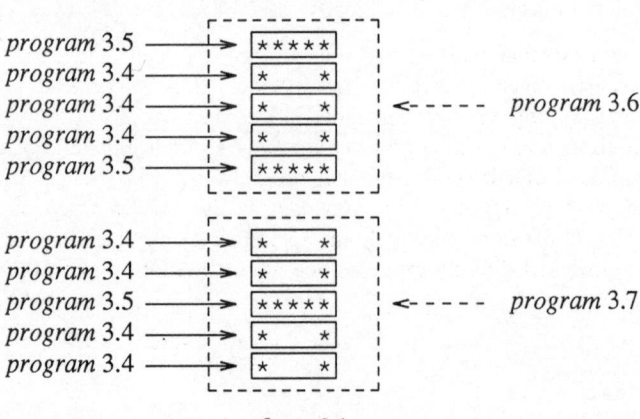

figure 3.4

-=-=-=-=-=-=-=-=-=-=-=-=-=-

Exercise 3.6
Draw a diagram similar to that in figure 3.4 for the 'HELLO' program you wrote
as answer to exercise 3.5.

Exercise 3.7
If your 'HELLO' program didn't make use of procedure calls within procedures
in the way that program 3.8 does - that is, if you didn't use a letter-H procedure, a
letter-E procedure, and so on - rewrite it to do so. Your program should get a lot
shorter (don't forget to notice that there will be two calls to your letter-L
procedure). Now answer exercise 3.6 again.

-=-=-=-=-=-=-=-=-=-=-=-=-=-

3.2 CONNECTING TEXTS AND EXECUTIONS

When a program calls upon procedures you can't count executions by counting
instructions as you can in the simpler programs of chapter 2. In calculating the
effect of a program it is important to distinguish between *textual* and *executional*
occurrences of an instruction. In the text of program 3.6 there are no *NL*
instructions at all. In the text of the procedures it calls upon, programs 3.4 and
3.5, the *NL* instruction occurs just twice. Yet an execution of program 3.6
executes the *NL* instruction five times in printing its five-line pattern. There are
two textual occurrences of *NL* and five executional occurrences of *NL* in the
complete program.

It is also important to distinguish between *direct* and *indirect* executions.
Program 3.6 doesn't execute *NL* directly, but programs 3.4 and 3.5 do, and
because program 3.6 calls for three executions of program 3.4 and two
executions of program 3.5, it indirectly calls for five executions of *NL*.

By recognising that indirect execution is possible and that textual occurrences
don't always match executional occurrences, it is possible to understand the
operation of a program which includes procedure calls. Quite simple calculations
can help to increase your confidence that a program has the effect you want. So,
for example, I can be confident that program 3.8 prints an eleven-line pattern
because: program 3.6 makes five procedure calls, each of which executes one *NL*
instruction; in the same way program 3.7 indirectly executes five *NL* instructions;
the program itself directly executes one *NL* instruction; five plus five plus one is
eleven.

-=-=-=-=-=-=-=-=-=-=-=-=-=-

Exercise 3.8
Your 'HELLO' program should print a twenty-nine-line pattern: check that you
have included the right number of *NL* instructions in the right places.

-=-=-=-=-=-=-=-=-=-=-=-=-

Dependency graphs

The *dependency graph* of a program shows the relationship between parts of a program and between programs or procedures and basic instructions. It doesn't even count textual occurrences. You draw a dependency graph by writing the names of the program and each of its procedures and basic instructions on a piece of paper, then drawing a line from the program to each of the procedures and basic instructions which it calls upon directly. Similarly for each of the procedures. For example, the dependency graph of program 3.3 is shown in figure 3.5 and the dependency graph of program 3.8 is shown in figure 3.6.

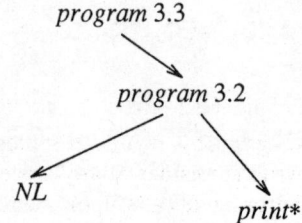

figure 3.5

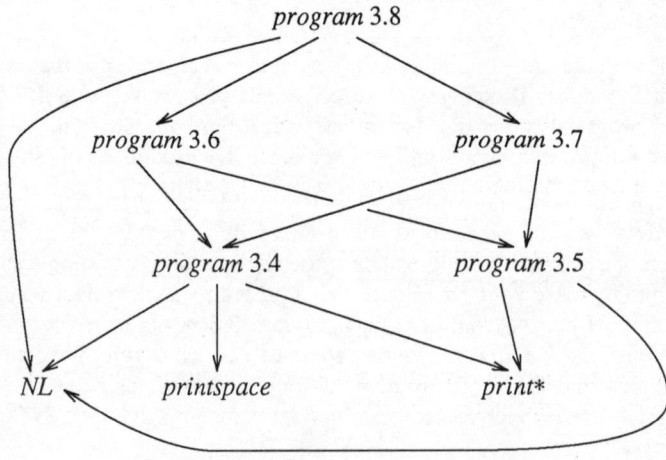

figure 3.6

The diagrams come straight from the text. They can be useful in determining just what definitions a program depends upon. Thus, though the text of program 3.8 calls directly on only *NL* and programs 3.6 and 3.7, the dependency graph shows that it depends indirectly on definitions of programs 3.4 and 3.5 and the basic instructions *print** and *printspace*.

-=-=-=-=-=-=-=-=-=-=-=-

Exercise 3.9
Draw dependency graphs for any procedures you used in the 'HELLO' program from the last section. Draw a dependency graph for the program itself.

-=-=-=-=-=-=-=-=-=-=-=-

Execution diagrams

When a program is executed and calls for execution of procedures or basic instructions the pattern of executions won't look anything like a dependency graph. It won't be a simple sequence either, although as always it will produce its effect by generating a sequence of basic instruction executions. An *execution diagram* shows the relationship between program execution, procedure executions (if any) and basic instruction executions. It shows how the internal actions of the program give rise to a sequence of external actions.

You draw an execution diagram by writing the program name on a piece of paper, then below it you write the names of any procedures or basic instructions which it calls upon, in the order it calls upon them, drawing a line from the program name to the thing it calls upon. Then you make similar execution diagrams below each procedure name, and so on until the only names at the tips of the tree are basic instruction names. For example, figure 3.7 shows the execution diagram of program 3.6.

-=-=-=-=-=-=-=-=-=-=-=-

Exercise 3.10
Draw an execution diagram for program 3.3.

Exercise 3.11
Draw an execution diagram for your 'HELLO' program.

Exercise 3.12
The following program prints O, then H, then O, then H, each shape separated from the last by a blank line:

$$program\ 3.8; NL; program\ 3.8$$

Draw its dependency graph; draw a diagram like figure 3.4 to show the way in which different procedures contribute the different parts of its output; draw an execution diagram.

-=-=-=-=-=-=-=-=-=-=-=-

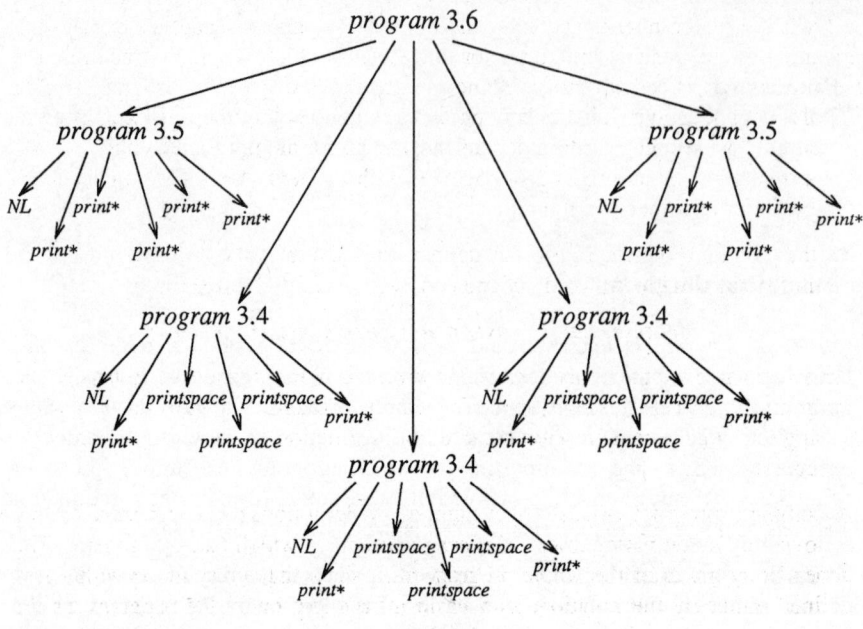

figure 3.7

3.3 A NOTATION FOR PROCEDURE DEFINITIONS AND PROCEDURE CALLS

A program which includes unexplained terms can't be understood and therefore can't be executed, no matter how carefully it is phrased. Unless the general level of anatomical understanding has risen enormously since I started writing this book, most people will have trouble executing the program

point to your liver

because most people don't know where their liver is. But if the program includes enough explanation

> *Your liver lies across your body, just behind the*
> *lower part of your breastbone*
> *Point to your liver*

then most of us have no difficulty because we know where our breastbone is (but if you don't then that term needs an explanation, and this could go on for ever). In stating the program I don't have to explain phrases like '*point to*' or how to comprehend the meaning of an English sentence from its parts, because those are basic items of knowledge which every reader can be presumed to possess.

When programming you can expect your readers to possess some basic knowledge of the notation. Each time I write a program I need not explain the meaning of the basic instructions nor the ways in which program structures like sequence and procedure call combine the meanings of parts of programs into a whole. But if I invent and call upon any procedures then I must explain them precisely. A complete program, like the liverish example above, must include the explanation of its procedures together with the text which calls upon them. One without the other will not do.

In the notation which I use throughout the rest of this book, a procedure definition starts with the word *def* and ends with *enddef.* For example:

def threestars() = NL; print*; print*; print* enddef

Here the name of the procedure is *threestars* and its meaning is given by the program *NL; print*; print*; print*.* The empty brackets '()' indicate that when calling on this procedure, no parameter information is required in order to execute it[†].

A complete program consists of a number of definitions - the **program head** - followed by some instructions - the **program body** - which call upon them. The dependency graph of the whole program must show that every name within it is defined either by the notation, as a basic instruction, or by the program, as the name of a procedure in the program heading.

Program 3.9 is a complete program which draws a square of asterisks. The body of the program is the sequence *threestars(); threestars(); threestars().* Each of the instructions in this sequence calls upon the procedure *threestars*: notice how the empty brackets in the definition of the procedure are echoed in the instructions which call upon it, indicating that no parameter information is provided in the call.

def threestars() = NL; print*; print*; print* enddef

threestars(); threestars(); threestars()

program 3.9

A procedure-calling instruction must always provide exactly the right amount of information and exactly the right kind of information. The information that is required is stated in the procedure definition: if no information is required then none should be supplied. Use of empty brackets when no parameter information is required allows an important distinction to be made between **naming** or **describing** a procedure and **calling for its execution** - a distinction which will be exploited in the next chapter.

[†] Recall the discussion of parameter information in chapter 1. The next chapter gives a fuller treatment of procedures with parameters.

68 PROCEDURES

Complete means *everything* must be included

The following program is *not* complete:

$$def\,H() = t1();\,t1();\,t2();\,t1();\,t1()\,enddef$$
$$def\,O() = t2();\,t1();\,t1();\,t1();\,t2()\,enddef$$
$$O();\,NL;\,H()$$

program 3.10

The program is supposed to have the same effect as program 3.8: that is, to print
an O-shape above an H-shape. The program body calls upon procedures H and
O, which are defined. But they in turn call upon procedures *t1* and *t2*, which are
not defined. The complete program must define every procedure whose name
appears in the dependency graph, so it must include definitions of the meaning of
t1 and *t2* as well. If the definitions of *t1* and *t2* call upon any procedures then
those must also be defined. Program 3.11 defines *t1* and *t2* in terms of basic
instructions only: this program is complete.

$$def\,H() = t1();\,t1();\,t2();\,t1();\,t1()\,enddef$$
$$def\,O() = t2();\,t1();\,t1();\,t1();\,t2()\,enddef$$
$$def\,t1() = NL;\,print*;$$
$$\qquad\qquad printspace;\,printspace;\,printspace;$$
$$\qquad\qquad print*$$
$$enddef$$
$$def\,t2() = NL;\,print*;\,print*;\,print*;\,print*;\,print*\,enddef$$
$$O();\,NL;\,H()$$

program 3.11

-=-=-=-=-=-=-=-=-=-=-=-

Exercise 3.13
Draw the dependency graph of program 3.11: hence satisfy yourself that the
program is complete.

-=-=-=-=-=-=-=-=-=-=-=-

Definitions within definitions

Program 3.11 prints a particular pattern. Suppose that for some reason I want to
print that pattern three times with blank lines separating the patterns one from
another. Then in the spirit of the examples at the beginning of this chapter I
would want to write program 3.12. But that isn't a complete program and it isn't
in the notation which I just introduced. In my new notation I would want to write
something like program 3.13.

program 3.11; *NL*; *program* 3.11; *NL*; *program* 3.11

program 3.12

def pattern( ) = .. *enddef*

pattern( ); *NL*; *pattern*( ); *NL*; *pattern*( )

program 3.13

This is a complete program provided that the text I write in place of '..' is itself a complete program - because then there can be nothing in the dependency graph which isn't defined. The program I want could be written as program 3.14.

def pattern( ) =
   def H( ) = *t1*( ); *t1*( ); *t2*( ); *t1*( ); *t1*( ) *enddef*
   def O( ) = *t2*( ); *t1*( ); *t1*( ); *t1*( ); *t2*( ) *enddef*
   def t1( ) = *NL*; *print**;
               printspace; *printspace*; *printspace*;
               print*
   enddef
   def t2( ) = *NL*; *print**; *print**; *print**; *print**; *print** *enddef*
   O( ); *NL*; *H*( )
enddef

pattern( ); *NL*; *pattern*( ); *NL*; *pattern*( )

program 3.14

If you accept that the meaning of program 3.11 is to print the OH pattern then you must agree that the meaning of program 3.14 is to print the same pattern three times, with a blank line separating each occurrence from the next. That must be so, because the body of the *pattern* procedure is identical to program 3.11. Plainly, there is no reason why the program which gives the meaning of a procedure definition should not itself include procedure definitions: equally plainly there is no reason why it must. I might have written instead program 3.15 and it would have had the same effect, as the next exercise demonstrates.

def H( ) = *t1*( ); *t1*( ); *t2*( ); *t1*( ); *t1*( ) *enddef*
def O( ) = *t2*( ); *t1*( ); *t1*( ); *t1*( ); *t2*( ) *enddef*
def t1( ) = *NL*; *print**;
            printspace; *printspace*; *printspace*;
            print*
enddef
def t2( ) = *NL*; *print**; *print**; *print**; *print**; *print** *enddef*
def pattern( ) = *O*( ); *NL*; *H*( ) *enddef*

pattern( ); *NL*; *pattern*( ); *NL*; *pattern*( )

program 3.15

-=-=-=-=-=-=-=-=-=-=-=-=-

Exercise 3.14
Draw the execution diagrams of programs 3.14 and 3.15: hence verify that the programs are equivalent.

-=-=-=-=-=-=-=-=-=-=-=-=-

Procedure names and consistency

Suppose that instead of program 3.9 I had written

> *def twostars*( ) = *NL*; *print**; *print**; *print** *enddef*
>
> *twostars*( ); *twostars*( ); *twostars*( )

program 3.16

Now this is *not* the same program as 3.9, in the sense that the texts are not identical. But the programs must surely have the same effect because the only difference is that where one has *threestars* the other has *twostars* and vice-versa. And, if you look carefully, an execution of the *twostars* procedure actually prints *three* asterisks. The meaning of a procedure comes from the text which defines it, not from its name.

Suppose now that I had written

> *def twostars*( ) = *NL*; *print**; *print**; *print** *enddef*
>
> *threestars*( ); *threestars*( ); *threestars*( )

program 3.17

- would this program have the same meaning as the other two? As before, the only difference is some change in the names used. This time the answer is no: if you look carefully the name used in the procedure definition isn't the same as the name used in the calling instruction. The program is incomplete, and therefore meaningless, without a definition of the meaning of *threestars*.

Suppose that I write

> *def twostars*( ) = *NL*; *print**; *print** *enddef*
> *def threestars*( ) = *NL*; *print**; *print**; *print** *enddef*
>
> *threestars*( ); *threestars*( ); *threestars*( )

program 3.18

This program is certainly complete, but there is a sense in which it is inconsistent to provide too much information in a program. It makes you suspect that there ought to be some instructions which connect the program to the *twostars* procedure. I shall avoid writing programs which have unnecessary definitions but, as you will see, calculating the meaning of a program can produce texts like this one. I don't want to say that calculation can change a consistent program into an inconsistent one, so I must allow redundant definitions in a program, provided that they don't get in the way of useful definitions.

Suppose that I change that redundant definition just a little:

> *def threestars*() = *NL*; *print**; *print* enddef*
> *def threestars*() = *NL*; *print**; *print**; *print* enddef*
>
> *threestars*(); *threestars*(); *threestars*()

program 3.19

Now the program is genuinely inconsistent. There are two definitions of *threestars* competing for our attention. Should the program print three lines of two asterisks or three lines of three asterisks: or should some lines have two asterisks and some lines have three? The program doesn't make it clear: the definitions and the program body don't fit together properly; the program is inconsistent.

Suppose that I had been a bit more careful, and I had written the program as

> *def threestars*() = *NL*; *print**; *print**; *print* enddef*
> *def threestars*() = *NL*; *print**; *print**; *print* enddef*
>
> *threestars*(); *threestars*(); *threestars*()

program 3.20

Now the definitions are identical, so it doesn't matter which you take. Is the program ok now, or is it still inconsistent? If you think it is ok, then how about the following program

> *def twostars*() = *print**; *print* enddef*
> *def threestars*() = *NL*; *print**; *twostars*() *enddef*
> *def threestars*() = *NL*; *print**; *print**; *print* enddef*
>
> *threestars*(); *threestars*(); *threestars*()

program 3.21

Here there are two different definitions which produce the same visible effect when executed. Is the program consistent, or inconsistent?

Consistency between definition and use of a procedure is an important matter. If a program contains obvious inconsistencies then it isn't clear what it means. Real-world programming systems, which only have a mechanical way of looking at things, must be given absolutely complete and self-consistent programs and are usually severe about shortcomings in what they receive. Because they have no idea about the meaning of most words you can give your procedures any names you like and the programming system will accept them. They will usually accept programs with unnecessary definitions. But I don't know any system which will accept alternative definitions, whether they are identical in effect or not.

3.4 CALCULATING MEANING BY SUBSTITUTION

Up to this point I have been relying on your intuition and good sense in introducing procedures and in discussing the meaning of programs which call upon procedures. In later chapters I shall make calculations using program texts which involve procedure definitions and procedure calls and it won't be enough to rely on common sense. Some formal means of calculating meaning is essential for sound reasoning.

A program text is a formula with a particular meaning; the meaning of a formula is found by combining in some way the meanings of its parts; if you replace some part of the formula by something with identical meaning then you don't change the meaning of the whole. It is just this technique of substitution of equals which is used in this book, and throughout I equate 'meaning of a program' with 'effect of its execution on the state of the world'.

One particularly simple description of the effect of a program is to give a sequence of basic instructions which have the same effect as the program when executed. So one way to discover the meaning of a program is to repeatedly replace parts of its text with other parts which have identical effects, until it is converted into a sequence of basic instructions.

Where a program includes procedure-calling instructions the substitution rule seems particularly obvious. The effect of a procedure-calling instruction is produced by executing the body of the procedure definition (the program which comes between '=' and 'enddef'): definition 3.1 shows how to produce an equivalent program.

> A procedure-calling instruction may be replaced with the body of the corresponding procedure definition.

definition 3.1

Surely if we make this sort of substitution in a program, the meaning of the whole formula, the whole program text, will not change. For example, the body of program 3.9 contains three calls to the procedure *threestars*. By replacing each procedure call with the body of the definition of *threestars* I produce program 3.22. The body of this program now consists only of basic instructions,

def threestars() = *NL*; *print**; *print**; *print** *enddef*

NL; *print**; *print**; *print** ; *NL*; *print**; *print**; *print** ; *NL*; *print**; *print**; *print**

program 3.22

A definition which is not referred to anywhere in a program may be deleted.

definition 3.2

NL; print*; print*; print* ; *NL; print*; print*; print** ; *NL; print*; print*; print**

program 3.23

and I can use a second rule (definition 3.2) to produce program 3.23.

In making the substitutions which converted program 3.9 into program 3.23 I have put in some extra space to separate the parts of the program, but in all other respects I have made a faithful substitution of procedure body for procedure-calling instruction. The two semicolons which separated the three instructions of the original program are still there and each copy of the procedure body is exactly like the original.

By substitution of one formula for an equal formula program 3.9 is proved to be equivalent to program 3.1, so far as visible effect is concerned. The substitution doesn't prove that either of the programs prints a square of asterisks but it does prove that if one does, then so does the other.

In my notation the layout of programs doesn't affect their meaning, so whether program 3.23 is written on one line or three or twelve or twenty-one or fifty it will have the same meaning. Layout *is* important to the human reader because, by giving different emphasis to different parts of a program you affect the way people read it. For example, program 3.24 contains the same instructions as program 3.23 and they are in the same order, but its layout doesn't help you to see that the programs are equivalent.

NL; print*; print*;
print*; NL; print*;
print*; print*; NL;
print*; print*; print*

program 3.24

-=-=-=-=-=-=-=-=-=-=-

Exercise 3.15
Given the following definition of procedure *X*:

def X( ) = print*; NL; print* enddef

show by substitution of procedure definition for calling instruction that the following program

NL; print*;
print*; X( );
print*; X( );
print*; print*

is equivalent to program 3.1.

Exercise 3.16
Show that the program in exercise 3.15 is equivalent to program 3.9. [Hint: very easy.]

Exercise 3.17
Find by text-substitution the sequence of basic instructions equivalent to program 3.7.

-=-=-=-=-=-=-=-=-=-=-=-=-

Bracketing and definitions

It is possible that in making substitutions you will have to insert brackets. For example, if you are told that $x=4+3$ and that $y=2x$ you cannot write $y=24+3$ nor even $y=2\times4+3$. Instead you must write $y=2(4+3)$ and deduce that $y=14$ rather than $y=27$ or $y=11$.

Consider program 3.25, which is yet another square-printing program. Each time procedure p is called a *program* is executed: the program is identical to program 3.26. This program defines a procedure q and executes instructions whose meaning depends on the meaning of q. So each time p is called a new meaning of q is used, identical to the others in every particular but a different individual, in the same way that your copy of this book is identical to all the others which have been printed but is still your own individual copy.

$def\,p() =$
$\quad def\,q() = print*; print*\ enddef$
$\quad NL; q(); print*$
$enddef$

$p(); p(); p()$

program 3.25

$def\,q() = print*; print*\ enddef$
$NL; q(); print*$

program 3.26

Now if I were to replace every procedure-calling instruction $p()$ in program 3.25 with the body of procedure p I would get a program which is a muddle of definitions and instruction sequences. I preserve the intended meaning of the program if I use program-brackets around the text which is being substituted to produce program 3.27.

$⟨def\,q() = print*; print*\ enddef\ NL; q(); print*⟩$;
$⟨def\,q() = print*; print*\ enddef\ NL; q(); print*⟩$;
$⟨def\,q() = print*; print*\ enddef\ NL; q(); print*⟩$

program 3.27

Execution of the whole program is a sequence of three *program* executions, just as it originally was. Each program defines and calls upon a procedure. The fact that there are three definitions of *q* within the whole program should cause no confusion: there is no possible inconsistency because each is being made in a different (sub-)program. The meaning of a definition extends only over the program in which it is made: each definition of *q* is private to its own bracketed program.

The effect of the first program can be found by substituting the definition of *q* for its call (definition 3.1) and removing the now redundant definition of *q* (definition 3.2) to produce program 3.28. The second and third programs can be similarly simplified to produce program 3.29. Then by definition 2.7 the brackets can be removed to give once again a text identical to program 3.1.

$$(\!(NL; print*; print*; print*)\!)$$
$$(\!(def\ q() = print*; print*\ enddef\ NL; q(); print*)\!) \quad ;$$
$$(\!(def\ q() = print*; print*\ enddef\ NL; q(); print*)\!)$$

program 3.28

$$(\!(NL; print*; print*; print*)\!);$$
$$(\!(NL; print*; print*; print*)\!);$$
$$(\!(NL; print*; print*; print*)\!)$$

program 3.29

-=-=-=-=-=-=-=-=-=-=-=-

Exercise 3.18
In the example above I first substituted the definition of *p*, then the definitions of *q*. Try it the other way around: substitute the definition of *q* to find the meaning of *p*, then substitute the definition of *p*. You should produce the same answer, but with rather less effort.

Exercise 3.19
Find by substituting definitions for calls the basic instruction sequence equivalent to program 3.14.

-=-=-=-=-=-=-=-=-=-=-=-

3.5 DEFINITIONS, EXECUTIONS AND ENVIRONMENTS

It is quite possible to make a programming system which calculates the effect of a program using substitution rules like those given in this book. It isn't usual to do so. Almost every programming system works with things called *executions* and things called *environments*. The very way we write and describe programs reflects this fact - or perhaps the influence has been the other way.

To execute program 3.30 means executing *print** three times in succession. Similarly, to execute program 3.31 means executing $f()$ three times in succession. Normally the fact that the instruction is $f()$ rather than $g()$ or $p()$ or *isadora*() or *fred*() is important. So to know how to execute $f()$ means that you must know the meaning of the name f and how to call upon that meaning. We say that to call upon a procedure **creates an execution** of that procedure. Therefore an execution of program 3.31 creates three executions of the meaning of f in succession, waiting for each to finish before starting to create the next.

$$\textit{print*}; \textit{print*}; \textit{print*} \qquad\qquad f();f();f()$$

program 3.30   **program 3.31**

You could execute program 3.31 if you were given the program text together with a description of the meaning of the name f. An **environment** is a dictionary of names and their associated meanings, organised so that you can look up the meaning of any particular name. Executing the definitions in a program creates an environment which gives meanings to the defined names; then the instructions can be executed 'in that environment': that is, taking account of the defined meanings.

$$\textit{def} f() = NL; \textit{print*}; \textit{print*}; \textit{print*}\ \textit{enddef}$$
$$f();f();f()$$

program 3.32

Program 3.32 gives a particular meaning to the name f and then executes the instruction $f()$ three times, each time calling upon the meaning it has just described. An **environment diagram** shows the way in which execution of the whole program relates to the procedure executions within it, and also how environments are set up during the execution. The diagram of an execution of the particularly simple program 3.32 is shown in figure 3.8. The diagram describes a sequence of actions or events and should be read as follows:

First, an execution of program 3.32 is created (the large box). This execution starts to follow the instructions of the program.

Second, the execution of the definition within program 3.32 creates a new environment. This environment is described as a variation of the basic environment: it contains the meanings of the basic instructions, plus the meaning defined for the name f.

Third, the execution of program 3.32 begins to obey its instructions. The first instruction is $f()$. The name f doesn't always have a meaning, but in the environment created by executing this program it does. This instruction is a procedure call and the meaning given to f is a procedure.

Fourth, an execution of f is created (the upper small box) and at the same time the execution of the calling instruction pauses. The execution of f starts to follow the instructions of the procedure definition.

Execute program 3.32 in an environment which contains
definitions of the basic instructions

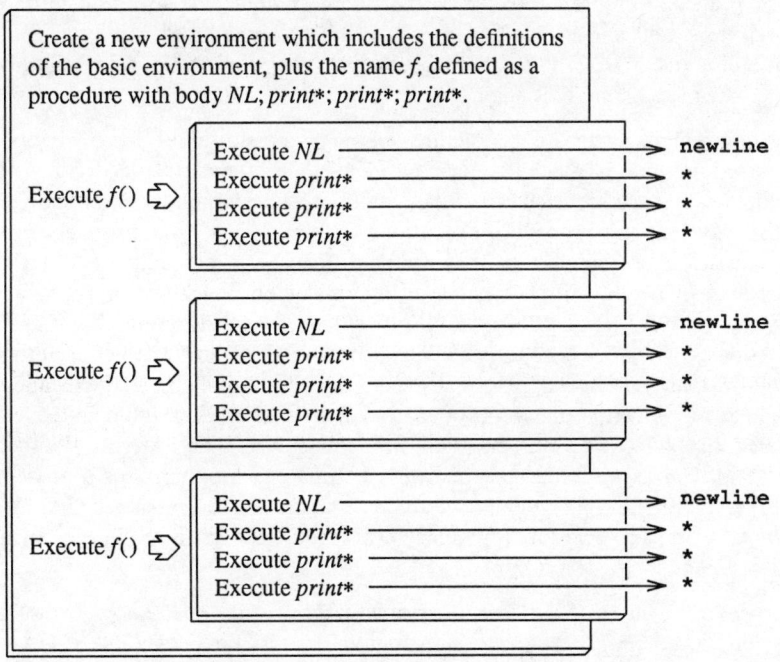

figure 3.8

Fifth, within the newly-created procedure execution there is an execution of *NL*,
which moves the cpp to the beginning of the next line.

Sixth, there is an execution of *print**, which makes an asterisk mark and moves
the cpp to the second position of the line.

Seventh and eighth, two more executions of *print** make two more asterisk marks
and move the cpp to the fourth position of the line.

Ninth, the procedure execution **terminates** (comes to an end) and disappears; so
does the execution of the instruction which created it.

Tenth, there is a second execution of the instruction *f*() which creates a second
procedure execution (the second small box) exactly like the one which just
terminated.

Eleventh, twelfth, thirteenth and fourteenth, the new procedure execution
executes *NL*, then *print**, then *print** and finally *print** once more.

Fifteenth, the second procedure execution terminates and along with it the
execution of the instruction which called it.

.. and so on until the third procedure execution terminates, and with it the third procedure-calling instruction.

Last of all, the program execution terminates. Whether or not the environment which it created is destroyed at the same time is a matter of tidiness within the computing machine: in this particular case it may as well be destroyed since there is no way of referring to it again.

The environment diagram is a picture of how patterns of execution evolve within a typical computing machine and how their environments relate. It shows how executions nest inside each other: the small boxes are within the larger one in the same way that the procedure executions are within the program execution. It emphasises that there is an environment for every procedure and program execution (and you will see in later examples that environments in a program do not always nest in exactly the same way as the executions within that program). It shows how many executions and environments there are in the entire program and how many are in progress at any one time. There are nineteen executions in all: one of the program, three of a procedure-calling instruction, three of the procedure body, three of *NL* and nine of *print**. The largest number of executions in existence at any one time is four: the program plus a procedure-calling instruction plus the procedure execution it creates plus either *NL* or *print**. There are five environments in all: one for each box plus the original environment.

The environment diagram description is carefully designed to give the same meaning to a program as the substitution description does (and vice-versa). Creating an execution of a procedure, following its instructions and finally terminating the procedure and the calling instruction executions is just like replacing a procedure-calling instruction with the body of the corresponding procedure definition, then executing the procedure body.

-=-=-=-=-=-=-=-=-=-=-=-=-=-

Exercise 3.20
Draw an environment diagram for program 3.11, as far as the end of the first call of procedure *t1*. Your diagram should have three levels of boxes: execution of the program, executions of procedure *O* and executions of procedures *t2* or *t1*.

-=-=-=-=-=-=-=-=-=-=-=-=-=-

Environment diagrams and environments

Environment diagrams like the one in figure 3.8 are nothing more than elaborate execution diagrams lying on their side. Environment diagrams become useful, as you will see in the next chapter, when computational environments become important. Program 3.14 is one in which a procedure execution creates an environment. The body of a procedure definition is, in general, a program so, in general, a procedure execution causes a program execution.

Execute program 3.14 in an environment which contains
definitions of the basic instructions

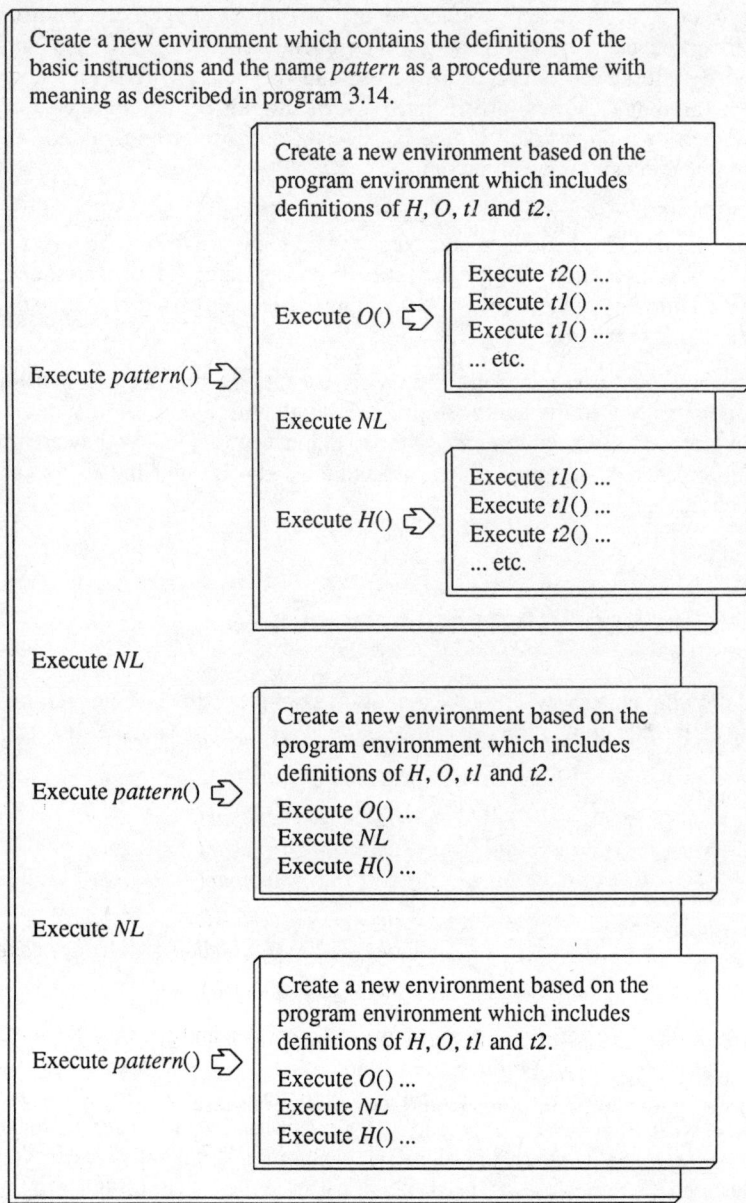

figure 3.9

The skeleton of an environment diagram of an execution of program 3.14 can be drawn as shown in figure 3.9. This diagram abbreviates the description of the environments which are created by calling procedure *pattern*. An environment, however created, is always based on another already existing. Each environment is a modified copy of an existing environment with some new and/or some altered definitions of names. But the old and the new environments are quite separate although the new one includes the definitions of the old one. Just as a photograph of a photograph is like but doesn't contain its original, so the new environment doesn't contain the old.

Execution of a program creates an environment. When the execution terminates that environment is abandoned and execution continues in the environment which called for the execution. Thus each time the execution of *H* terminates, and with it the execution of *pattern*, execution continues in the environment defined at the beginning of the program.

Notice how the use of environments in executions mirrors the substitution definition of procedure call (definition 3.1): the meanings of the definitions within a procedure execution are private to that execution, just as they are private to the bracketed program when procedure body is substituted for calling instruction.

3.6 PLANNING A SOLUTION WITH PROCEDURES

The following pattern, which appeared as an example in the last chapter, must be produced by executing a long sequence of *print**, *printspace* and *NL* instructions.

figure 3.10

If I write a program to produce the pattern using a straightforward sequence of basic instructions it even looks a little like the pattern, as program 3.33 illustrates. (I have written *pr** for *print** and *psp* for *printspace*, in order to make the program fit on the page and in order to emphasise the similarity between program and printed pattern). But it isn't necessary to write a monolithic program to produce this pattern because there are various regularities in the picture which can be exploited. For example, the first, second, seventh and eighth lines are identical, as are the third, fourth, fifth and sixth lines.

NL; *pr**; *pr**; *pr**; *pr**; *pr**; *pr**; *pr**; *pr**; *pr**; *pr**; *pr**; *pr**; *pr**; *pr**; *pr**; *pr**; *pr**; *pr**; *pr**;
NL; *pr**; *pr**; *pr**; *pr**; *pr**; *pr**; *pr**; *pr**; *pr**; *pr**; *pr**; *pr**; *pr**; *pr**; *pr**; *pr**; *pr**; *pr**; *pr**;
NL; *pr**; *pr**; *pr**; *psp*; *psp*; *psp*; *psp*; *psp*; *psp*; *psp*; *psp*; *psp*; *psp*; *psp*; *psp*; *psp*; *pr**; *pr**; *pr**;
NL; *pr**; *pr**; *pr**; *psp*; *psp*; *psp*; *psp*; *psp*; *psp*; *psp*; *psp*; *psp*; *psp*; *psp*; *psp*; *psp*; *pr**; *pr**; *pr**;
NL; *pr**; *pr**; *pr**; *psp*; *psp*; *psp*; *psp*; *psp*; *psp*; *psp*; *psp*; *psp*; *psp*; *psp*; *psp*; *psp*; *pr**; *pr**; *pr**;
NL; *pr**; *pr**; *pr**; *psp*; *psp*; *psp*; *psp*; *psp*; *psp*; *psp*; *psp*; *psp*; *psp*; *psp*; *psp*; *psp*; *pr**; *pr**; *pr**;
NL; *pr**; *pr**; *pr**; *pr**; *pr**; *pr**; *pr**; *pr**; *pr**; *pr**; *pr**; *pr**; *pr**; *pr**; *pr**; *pr**; *pr**; *pr**; *pr**;
NL; *pr**; *pr**; *pr**; *pr**; *pr**; *pr**; *pr**; *pr**; *pr**; *pr**; *pr**; *pr**; *pr**; *pr**; *pr**; *pr**; *pr**; *pr**; *pr**

program 3.33

It is normal to plan a program by inventing actions which can be combined to make up the effect you want, then to write the program *as if* there were procedures to carry out those actions and finally to consider how to write those procedures. It is also normal to make mistakes: sometimes you will find the actions you invent in the first stage aren't appropriate or won't fit together nicely to make a satisfactory program; sometimes you just don't like your first attempt at a solution ánd you go back to the beginning and start planning all over again. But in any case the first stage of planning is to invent the actions you want to use (in the present case the printing of two types of line); the second stage is to consider in detail how to fit those actions together to produce the effect you want; the third stage is to define how those actions are to be carried out.

Part of the second stage activity is to refine and clarify your ideas of what the effect of each action should be. You will often find that you will need to invent new sorts of actions, or change your mind about the ones you've already invented, and then you will have to start the design process again. In the present case there's not much scope for refinement or additional actions because the solution is so obvious, but in later examples in this book and in your programming life you will find plenty of room for intuition and inspiration in the allegedly 'logical' and 'systematic' world of program design. Programming is *not* a mechanical activity.

In the first stage of planning I decide that I require two procedures, one to print lines like the first line in the pattern, the other to print lines like the third line. I call these procedures *type1* and *type2*. The second stage of planning produces an 'as if' program, which in the current case would be:

```
type1(); type1();
type2(); type2(); type2(); type2();
type1(); type1()
```

program 3.34

At this point it might occur to you to check that the program will print an eight-line pattern. Since there are no *NL* instructions in the program but there is one procedure call per line of the pattern, either we must include an *NL* before each procedure call, or each procedure call must execute the *NL* instruction once. I choose to include the *NL*s in my procedure definitions and with this minor

82 PROCEDURES

alteration to what was my original intention the design survives.

Now to the third stage of planning, writing the procedures. The *type1* procedure must print a line of nineteen asterisks, which seems fairly straightforward. There is some regularity in the *type2* line: it consists of three asterisks, then thirteen spaces, then three asterisks. It just about makes sense to invent a *threestars* procedure which prints three asterisks and to define it and the *type2* procedure as in program 3.35.

> *def threestars*() = *print**; *print**; *print* enddef*
>
> *def type2*() = *NL*; *threestars*();
> > *printspace*; *printspace*; *printspace*; *printspace*;
> > *printspace*; *printspace*; *printspace*; *printspace*;
> > *printspace*; *printspace*; *printspace*; *printspace*;
> > *printspace*;
> > *threestars*()
> > *enddef*

program 3.35

Last of all, the *type1* procedure. There are now two 'obvious' ways to define it. The first is with an *NL* followed by nineteen *print**s. The second is to use the definition of the *threestars* procedure and to define *type1* as an *NL* followed by six *threestars*() and one *print**. But because there is no six-way or three-way regularity in the original picture, this second definition would be misleading to the reader: even though it would be textually shorter than the nineteen *print** definition I reject it.

There is, though, still some regularity in the problem which I haven't exploited in my solution. An alternative way to look at *type1* lines is that they are the same as *type2* lines except that they have asterisks where *type2* lines have spaces. A helpful definition for the *type1* procedure, then, would be as shown in program 3.36, in which I have further emphasised the similarity between the procedures by using the same layout as in the *type2* definition.

> *def type1*() = *NL*; *threestars*();
> > *print**; *print**; *print**; *print**;
> > *print**; *print**; *print**; *print**;
> > *print**; *print**; *print**; *print**;
> > *print**;
> > *threestars*()
> > *enddef*

program 3.36

The definition of *type1* shown in program 3.36 is preferable both to the nineteen *print** and to the six *threestars* plus one *print** solution, just because it is more obviously similar to the definition of *type2*. It is more clearly and transparently a solution to the problem than either of the other candidates.

In the last analysis questions of clarity and transparency become issues of style and are susceptible to personal prejudice, and I do not claim that my solution to this problem is indisputably the best. However much we argue about our programming styles, we should never forget that programs are documents meant to be read and understood by human beings. Small changes which present the same computational information in different ways can make all the difference between a program which just seems to work and one which can be seen to work, both by yourself and by others.

In the end the best program is the most beautiful program, and the most beautiful is the best. The way to program successfully is to design a beautiful program first of all and only then, when you are satisfied that you have found the best and most beautiful solution to your problem, transform it systematically into one which is acceptable to your programming system.

3.7 PROGRAMS FIT FOR EXECUTION

Pascal demands that procedure definitions come in a particular order: my notation doesn't. Many codes (for example, BASIC) won't allow a procedure definition to contain subsidiary definitions: my notation will. There are lots of programs - program 3.14, for example - which can't be transcribed directly into some mechanical codes because definitions are in the wrong order or because definitions are nested.

The wrong response to this problem would be to write programs only in the way which the mechanical code prefers: that is, only to write programs which can be transcribed directly and automatically. The correct response is to realise that the programs you write can be manipulated to fit the mechanical code before you transcribe them.

Ordering definitions

Some programming systems demand that a procedure definition must come before the first textual occurrence of an instruction which calls on the procedure. In program 3.14 this isn't the case because the definitions of procedures H and O contain calls to $t1$ and $t2$. But the definitions can be simply re-ordered, as shown in program 3.37.

This is still a perfectly sensible program and it still has the same meaning as the original, but now every definition precedes its first call. Pascal demands that definitions are ordered in this way: the program is now *Pascal-fit* and can be transcribed directly into Pascal.

$$def\ pattern(\ ) =$$
$$def\ t1(\ ) = ..\ enddef\ \ def\ t2(\ ) = ..\ enddef$$
$$def\ H(\ ) = ..\ enddef\ \ def\ O(\ ) = ..\ enddef$$
$$O(\ ); NL; H(\ )$$
$$enddef$$
$$pattern(\ ); NL; pattern(\ ); NL; pattern(\ )$$

program 3.37

Unpacking definitions

Some programming systems don't understand nested procedure definitions like those of program 3.14. In simple cases it is possible to *unpack* the definitions, converting them to a single-level set of definitions: see, for example, program 3.38. After unpacking, the definitions which were originally inside the procedure *pattern* have been moved outside. Previously they described part of the environment created on each procedure execution and were available for use only during procedure executions. Now they form part of the program environment, and are available for use throughout the program execution. BASIC and FORTRAN don't allow definitions within definitions: the program is now *BASIC-fit* and *FORTRAN-fit*.

$$def\ H(\ ) = ..\ enddef\ \ def\ O(\ ) = ..\ enddef$$
$$def\ t1(\ ) = ..\ enddef\ \ def\ t2(\ ) = ..\ enddef$$
$$def\ pattern(\ ) = O(\ ); NL; H(\ )\ enddef$$
$$pattern(\ ); NL; pattern(\ ); NL; pattern(\ )$$

program 3.38

Usually unpacking is a straightforward transformation but sometimes it may make the program inconsistent. In the sort of programs discussed so far, this can only be because one of the procedure names is already in use in the program environment. When this happens you must systematically alter the name of the unpacked procedure in the definition and in every instruction which depends upon it. For example, I might have changed the names *t1* and *H* when unpacking the definitions, producing program 3.39. This program has the same effect as the original: only the names have been changed in unpacking it.

$$def\ HX(\ ) = t1X(\ ); t1X(\ ); t2(\ ); t1X(\ ); t1X(\ )\ enddef$$
$$def\ O(\ ) = t2(\ ); t1X(\ ); t1X(\ ); t1X(\ ); t2(\ )\ enddef$$
$$def\ t1X(\ ) = ..\ enddef\ \ def\ t2(\ ) = ..\ enddef$$
$$def\ pattern(\ ) = O(\ ); NL; HX(\ )\ enddef$$
$$pattern(\ ); NL; pattern(\ ); NL; pattern(\ )$$

program 3.39

The transformations described here to make Pascal-fit or BASIC-fit or FORTRAN-fit or C-fit programs are rather trivial. You should be able to do them in your head. You may feel at first that I am being a little perverse in not choosing a mechanical code X and writing X-fit programs in the first place, or even in not programming in mechanical code X. That objection will be answered in later chapters when I begin to use ideas and structures which aren't included in most codes.

3.8 TRANSCRIBING BASIC INSTRUCTIONS: A QUICKER WAY

Now that you know how to write programs which include procedure definitions and procedure calls you can use a very simple trick to shorten the transcribed versions of your program. In most mechanical codes the equivalents of *print** and *printspace* are tedious to type, but by defining a procedure whose effect is equivalent to a basic instruction this difficulty can easily be overcome. For example, the procedure definition

$$def\ ast(\ ) = print*\ enddef$$

can easily be transcribed. Then instead of having to transcribe every *print** in your program into a complicated instruction you can transcribe each one into a procedure call and transcribe *print** only once. A similar sort of thing can be done for *printspace* if necessary, and program 3.11 could be changed into program 3.40. This alternative version of the program is much easier to transcribe into a mechanical code, especially for the one- or two-fingered typist.

$$def\ ast(\ ) = print*\ enddef$$
$$def\ psp(\ ) = printspace\ enddef$$

$$def\ H(\ ) = t1(\ );\ t1(\ );\ t2(\ );\ t1(\ );\ t1(\ )\ enddef$$
$$def\ O(\ ) = t2(\ );\ t1(\ );\ t1(\ );\ t1(\ );\ t2(\ )\ enddef$$
$$def\ t1(\ ) = NL;\ ast(\ );\ psp(\ );\ psp(\ );\ psp(\ );\ ast(\ )\ enddef$$
$$def\ t2(\ ) = NL;\ ast(\ );\ ast(\ );\ ast(\ );\ ast(\ );\ ast(\ )\ enddef$$

$$O(\ );\ NL;\ H(\ )$$

program 3.40

-=

APPENDIX 3.A PROCEDURE DEFINITIONS AND CALLS IN PASCAL

Pascal procedure definitions are like miniature Pascal programs. They use the word procedure rather than program and there isn't all that stuff about input and output. The most important differences between my notation and Pascal, so far as this chapter is concerned, is that you don't need (indeed, can't use) empty parameter brackets when a procedure has no parameters.

It is simplest to illustrate transcription into Pascal by giving an example. Program 3.9 transcribes into Pascal as shown in figure 3.11. The procedure definition in the Pascal transcription comes before the program body, just as it does in my notation. I have changed the name of the procedure from *threestars* to `three` because it is a good idea, when using most Pascal programming systems, to use names which are no longer than eight characters. Six other points to notice are:

(a) the definition starts with the word `procedure`;

(b) it doesn't use the empty parameter brackets of my notation;

(c) there is a semicolon rather than an equals sign before the body of the procedure;

(d) the instruction sequence in the body of the procedure is enclosed with `begin` and `end` brackets just like the body of a program;

(e) the definition is followed by a semicolon;

(f) the procedure-calling instructions don't have empty parameter brackets, and thus match the definition.

The instructions of the procedure body have been transcribed according to the rules given in chapter 2.

```
program X(input,output);
procedure three;
begin
  writeln; write('*'); write('*'); write('*')
end;
begin three; three; three end.
```

figure 3.11

Order of definitions

When a program has several procedure definitions they all come before the instruction sequence (between the `program..` heading and the `begin` of the program body). Pascal has an infuriating rule that procedure definitions must be given in order so that each definition textually precedes the first call upon it. You may have to re-order the definitions, as discussed in section 3.7 above, before transcribing a program into Pascal. For example, program 3.11, once its definitions have been re-ordered, can be written in Pascal as shown in figure 3.12 (check the six points given above against each of the procedure definitions in this program). Notice that it is a good idea to use blank lines and indentation to distinguish or emphasise different parts of your program. Notice also how wordy

```
program Y(input,output);
  procedure t1;
  begin writeln;
    write('*'); write(' '); write(' '); write(' ');
    write('*')
  end;

  procedure t2;
  begin writeln; write('*'); write('*'); write('*');
    write('*'); write('*')
  end;

  procedure H; begin t1; t1; t2; t1; t1 end;
  procedure O; begin t2; t1; t1; t1; t2 end;
begin O; writeln; H end.
```

figure 3.12

Pascal is, like most notations designed for machines to recognise.

It isn't always as easy to re-order definitions as this example suggests. In fact it is the procedure *heading* which must precede any procedure calls, rather than the whole definition. It is sometimes possible, therefore, to solve the ordering problem by nesting definitions within definitions. Pascal has a special .forward notation for use when all else fails: look it up in a Pascal book if you think you need to use it.

```
program Z(input,output);
  procedure pattern;
    procedure t1;
    begin writeln;
      write('*'); write(' '); write(' '); write(' ');
      write('*')
    end;

    procedure t2;
    begin writeln; write('*'); write('*'); write('*');
      write('*'); write('*')
    end;

    procedure H; begin t1; t1; t2; t1; t1 end;
    procedure O; begin t2; t1; t1; t1; t2 end;
  begin O; writeln; H end;
begin pattern; writeln; pattern; writeln; pattern end.
```

figure 3.13

Definitions within definitions

Pascal has no problem with nested definitions. You can write procedure definitions between the procedure heading and the instructions of the procedure body, just as you can between the program heading and the instructions of the program body. The definitions come between the procedure.. bit and the begin which is the opening bracket round the instructions of the procedure body. Program 3.14, for example, can be transcribed to give figure 3.13.

APPENDIX 3.B SOME PROGRAMS TO TRY

Many of the following exercises are very similar to those at the end of chapter 2. Often you may be able to answer them just by including one of the programs you wrote then in a procedure definition. Also read section 3.8 above, if you haven't already done so: it should simplify the transcription of your programs.

-=-=-=-=-=-=-=-=-=-=-=-

Exercise 3.21
Write a definition of a procedure *three* so that the instruction *three*() prints a line of three asterisks:

                                    ***

Exercise 3.22
Check that the program *three*(); *three*() actually prints the pattern

                                    ***
                                    ***

Hence construct a program which prints a square.

Exercise 3.23
Write and test four procedures, each of which can be used to print one of the following four triangle-patterns:

```
    *         ***              *         ***
    **        **               **        **
    ***       *                ***       *
```

Exercise 3.24
Write a program which prints a trapezium and one which prints a parallelogram of asterisks standing on end:

```
        *                     *
        **                    **
        ***                   ***
        ***                   ***
        ***                   ***
        ***                   ***
        ***                   ***
        **                    **
        *                     *
```

Exercise 3.25
Write a program which prints a trapezium and one which prints a parallelogram lying down:

```
    *****            *******
   *******           *******
  *********           *******
```

Exercise 3.26
Write a procedure which prints a left bracket:

```
        *
       *
      *
      *
      *
       *
        *
```

and one which prints a right bracket.

Exercise 3.27
Write a procedure which prints a left arrow:

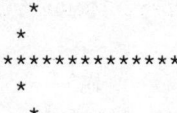

```
      *
     *
  **************
     *
      *
```

and one which prints a right arrow.

Exercise 3.28
Write a program which prints the following shape, made up of brackets and arrows:

```
      *                   *
     * *               * *
    *   *             *   *
   *  ********** **********  *
    *   *             *   *
     * *               * *
      *                   *
```

[Hint: your *bracket* and *arrow* procedures won't be much use here.]

Exercise 3.29
Write a program which prints your name (or any other words you like) in vertical
banner-writing like that in figure 3.14. Resist the temptation to print the result of
your program on paper too often: think of the forests you would be helping to
kill.

figure 3.14

Chapter 4
PROCEDURES WITH PARAMETERS

Few real-world programming systems have basic instructions which mimic *print**. In Pascal you have to use `write('*')` and in Basic `PRINT;"*";`. You may already have experimented with your system and have successfully used instructions like

```
write('hello')     PRINT "GOODBYE"
write('*** ***')   PRINT "X=3"
```

The basic printing instruction in most programming systems prints anything you give to it. It can be *parameterised* to produce many different visible effects.

The procedure definitions of chapter 3 make abstractions. They each make a single instruction out of a program so that we can call for the effect of that program without having to write it down every time we require it. But that is a very limited form of abstraction because every one of the procedure's executions is exactly like every other. If a procedure, or an instruction, can express a range of possible executions, controlled by some parameter or parameters, then it becomes a more powerful abstraction. This chapter is all about the use of procedures which accept parameter information.

4.1 PARAMETERS AND ENVIRONMENTS

I pointed out in chapter 3 that the meaning of a sequence like $p();p();p()$ depends on the meaning ascribed to the name p. Put another way, the effect of this program depends on the environment in which it is executed. However, the shape of the program puts some constraint on the meanings that an environment can sensibly ascribe to p: in this specific case it is clear that the meaning must be a procedure because p occurs in the program only as a procedure name.

Chapter 3 showed one way to create an environment in which p has a meaning, by giving a *def..enddef* definition of the name p. Program 4.1 incorporates the $p();p();p()$ sequence and with a suitable definition of p prints three asterisks.

$$def\ p() = print*\ enddef$$
$$p();p();p()$$

program 4.1

$$def\ p() = NL;print*;print*;print*\ enddef$$
$$p();p();p()$$

program 4.2

With the same program body but a different definition of p, program 4.2 prints a square pattern of nine asterisks. This sort of thing could go on indefinitely, producing program after program which uses the same program body, but none of those programs would fully exploit the abstraction which the sequence offers. It is a description of 'doing something three times' and the name p is a *parameter* of the original sequence, in the sense that by providing different meanings for p we get different effects: that is, by substituting different formulas for p we get different programs[†].

In programs 4.1 and 4.2 the meaning of p is fixed throughout the program, which is by no means necessary. An extension of the notation of chapter 3 allows me to exploit the sequence much more effectively. I make the same $p();p();p()$ sequence the body of a procedure which has the name p as a parameter. Then I can call upon that procedure as many times as I wish, so long as each time I do so I provide a sensible meaning to be ascribed to p.

$$def\ r3(p) = p();p();p()\ enddef$$
$$def\ one() = print*\ enddef$$
$$def\ two() = NL\ enddef$$
$$def\ three() = NL;print*;print*;print*\ enddef$$
$$r3(one);r3(two);r3(three)$$

program 4.3

In program 4.3 the $p();p();p()$ sequence is the body of procedure $r3$. Each of the procedure-calling instructions $r3(one)$, $r3(two)$ and $r3(three)$ specifies an execution of $r3$ - that is, an execution of the sequence $p();p();p()$ - and each gives a meaning which is to be ascribed to the name p throughout its particular execution. For example, the instruction $r3(one)$ effectively calls for an execution of the sequence $one();one();one()$ and since $one()$ prints a single asterisk, the effect of $r3(one)$ is to print three asterisks. Similarly the effect of $r3(two)$ is to execute three NLs and the effect of $r3(three)$ is to print three lines of three asterisks. Figure 4.1 shows the output which this program would produce if the cpp was initially at the start of a line.

[†] Note that p isn't a parameter of program 4.1 or program 4.2: each of these examples provides a meaning for p and is a complete program.

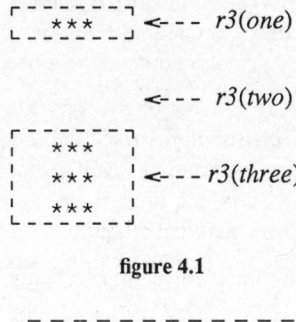

figure 4.1

-=-=-=-=-=-=-=-=-=-=-=-=-

Exercise 4.1
Construct a definition of a procedure *alpha* such that a procedure call *r3*(*alpha*) prints the pattern

```
        *
        *
        *
```

[Hint: each execution of *alpha* should print a third of this pattern. Don't forget the *NL* instructions. It may help if you write out the instruction sequence which would print this pattern and divide it into three equal parts.]

Exercise 4.2
Construct a definition of a procedure *beta* such that a procedure call *r3*(*beta*) prints nine asterisks in a vertical line. [Hint: your answer to exercise 4.1 may help to produce a compact solution.]

Exercise 4.3
Suppose that the definition of *r3* had been written

$$def\ r3(x) = x(); x(); x()\ enddef$$

What difference would this change have made to the effect of program 4.3? To your answers to exercises 4.1 and 4.2?

Exercise 4.4
Suppose that the definition of *r3* had been written

$$def\ r3(p) = p(); p(); p(); p()\ enddef$$

- that is, with four *p*() instructions in its body instead of three. Would program 4.3, *r3*(*alpha*) and *r3*(*beta*) still make sense? If not, why not? If so, would there be any change in the effect of these programs? If so, what change and why? If not, why not?

-=-=-=-=-=-=-=-=-=-=-=-=-

Some points of notation are worth attention. First, in the definition of *r3* in program 4.3 a ***parameter name*** *p* appears in brackets in the head of the procedure definition, and the same name is used in the body of the definition as if it was the name of a procedure. The appearance in the procedure head signals that when the procedure is executed some extra information must be provided. Because of the way the name *p* is used in the procedure body, you can deduce that the extra information that must be provided should describe a procedure.

Second, a single procedure name - *one* or *two* or *three* - is written between the parameter brackets in any instruction which calls upon *r3*. This **argument formula** matches the parameter name: the value (meaning) of the formula is supplied as the extra information required in the procedure call. During an execution of the procedure the parameter name *p* stands for the value of the argument formula. Thus each procedure-calling instruction in the body of program 4.3 names a procedure to be executed - in each case *r3* - and a procedure to be provided as argument to the execution - either *one* or *two* or *three*.

Third, the argument formula in each of the instructions of program 4.3 is just a procedure name without any parameter brackets. That is because a procedure name - the name *one*, for example - is a formula which describes a particular procedure. That procedure is not to be executed immediately but is to be provided as an argument to an execution, possibly to be executed at some later stage. It would be wrong to write *r3(one())* because the formula *one()* is an instruction formula calling for an execution of the procedure named *one*. Naming a procedure is one thing; calling for its execution is quite another.

-=-=-=-=-=-=-=-=-=-=-=-

Exercise 4.5
Define procedures *x*, *y* and *z* such that the sequence *NL; r3(x); NL; r3(y); NL; r3(z)* prints the pattern

```
  *     *     *
 **    **    **
***   ***   ***
```

Exercise 4.6
Define procedure *r4* such that, given the definitions of *x*, *y* and *z* from exercise 4.5, the sequence *NL; r4(x); NL; r4(y); NL; r4(z)* prints the pattern

```
  *     *     *     *
 **    **    **    **
***   ***   ***   ***
```

Exercise 4.7
The procedure call *r3(one)*, given the definition of procedure *one* from program 4.3, prints three asterisks. Given the definition

$$def\ A() = r3(one); r3(one); r3(one)\ enddef$$

how many asterisks are printed by *r3(A)* ?

Exercise 4.8
The *r3* procedure can be used in such a way that the single instruction *r3(C)* can print a 27-by-27 square, yet in all of the procedure definitions of the program there is only one *print** instruction and only one *NL* instruction. Write that program. [Hint for the totally innumerate: 27=3×9; 9=3×3. Hint 2: if you find

this hard, try it first for a 9-by-9 square, and look at exercise 4.7.]

Exercise 4.9

Answer exercise 4.8 again, this time for a 243-by-243 square. [243=9×27.]

-=-=-=-=-=-=-=-=-=-=-=-

4.2 DIAGRAMS OF PROCEDURES

In program 4.3 the program body calls directly for three procedure executions, each an execution of procedure *r3*. Indirectly it calls for three executions of procedure *one*, three of procedure *two* and three of procedure *three*. Still more indirectly it calls for twelve executions of *print** and six of *NL*. The execution diagram is shown in figure 4.2.

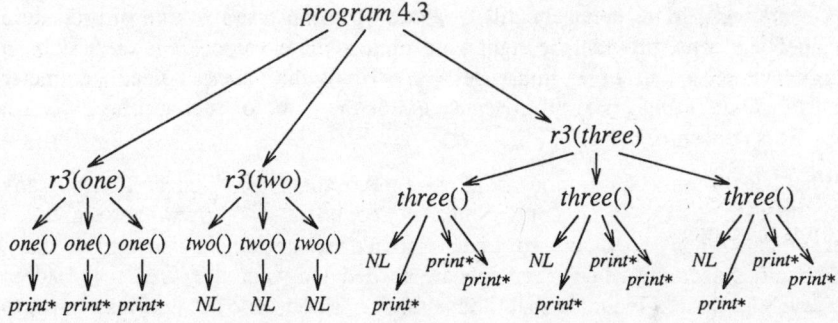

figure 4.2

The dependency graph, shown in figure 4.3, is straightforward to draw but perhaps a little surprising when you first see it. The meaning of the body of the program depends on the meanings of the names *r3*, *one*, *two* and *three*. The body of *r3* depends on nothing but *p*, which is a parameter of the procedure, so the

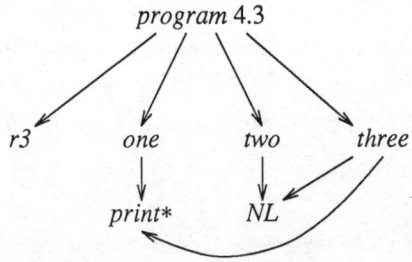

figure 4.3

definition of *r3* is complete and self-supporting. The body of *one* depends on *print**, the body of *two* on *NL* and the body of *three* on *NL* and *print** together.

The next chapter deals in more detail with the matter of what depends on what, and why and how, under the heading of 'Free, Bound and Binding Occurrences'.

4.3 CONSISTENT DEFINITIONS

The body of *r3* in program 4.3 is the sequence $p(); p(); p()$, which doesn't have a definite meaning unless a meaning is provided for *p*. It follows that the instruction *r3()* is meaningless nonsense because it doesn't provide a meaning for *p*. Just providing a meaning isn't enough: we can't provide any sort of meaning we like, because the procedure body won't have a meaning unless the right kind of meaning is provided for *p*. We must provide a procedure value: you can't write *r3(print*)* because *print** is an instruction; you can't write *r3(7)* because 7 is a number[†]. More precisely still, you can't provide just any kind of procedure value: you must provide the right kind of procedure value. It is clear that an argument to a call of *r3* must be a procedure that doesn't need parameter information: *r3(one)* is alright because one is the name of such a procedure, but *r3(r3)* is nonsense.

What about the instruction *one(two)*? Procedure *one* doesn't need any parameters, so the argument formula is redundant. Is it wrong to give an argument when none is required? Novice programmers sometimes have difficulties deciding when arguments are needed and when they aren't, so I adopt a severe attitude: I maintain that the instruction is nonsense because it attempts to provide an argument to an execution which can't accept it. Procedure executions must be provided with exactly as many arguments as the procedure definition provides parameter names. Providing too many or too few arguments shows that you are confused, either about what a procedure call instruction means or about the meaning of the procedure being called.

The next chapter goes into the question of fitting argument formulas to procedure definitions in much greater detail.

[†] Strictly speaking - and it is an important distinction which has an effect on the way we write programs - *print** is the *name* of an instruction and 7 is the *name* of a number. I return to this topic later in this chapter.

4.4 CALCULATING MEANING BY SUBSTITUTION

Careful readers will have noticed that definition 3.1, which explains how the meaning of a procedure call can be calculated by substituting the procedure body for the procedure-calling instruction, is not adequate to explain program 4.3. If you replace $r3(one)$ by $p(); p(); p()$ you don't get a sequence which necessarily prints three asterisks or even one which has any defined meaning. An expanded explanation is required, one which takes account of the relationship between parameter name and argument formula in a procedure call:

> A procedure-calling instruction is equivalent to a copy of the body of the procedure definition in which each occurrence of the parameter name has been replaced by the argument formula.

definition 4.1

Notice that definition 3.1 is a special case of definition 4.1: with no parameter name and no argument formula there can be no alterations in the procedure body and the copy will be the same as the original.

In the definition of $r3$ in program 4.3, p is the parameter name. In the procedure-calling instruction $r3(one)$, one is the argument formula. So the effect of the procedure call, according to definition 4.1, can be found by replacing every occurrence of the name p in $p(); p(); p()$ by the formula one: that is, the effect of $r3(one)$ is the same as the effect of the sequence $one(); one(); one()$.

In this case calculation transforms a single procedure call into a sequence of three calls. The effect of the transformed sequence can be calculated by following definition 4.1 three times more, each time replacing the instruction $one()$ by the body of procedure one, unaltered because there is no parameter name and no argument formula. The final result of the calculation is the sequence $print*; print*; print*$, a program which evidently prints three asterisks.

-=-=-=-=-=-=-=-=-=-=-=-

Exercise 4.10
Use definition 4.1 to show that the second and third procedure-calling instructions in program 4.3 produce the effect described in figure 4.1.

Exercise 4.11
Use definition 4.1 to show that the effects of procedure calls $r3(alpha)$ and $r3(beta)$, where $alpha$ and $beta$ are the procedures you defined in answer to exercises 4.1 and 4.2, are to print a vertical line of three asterisks and a vertical line of nine asterisks, in each case converting the program to a sequence of NLs and $print*$s, then counting newlines and asterisks.

Exercise 4.12
Use definition 4.1 to find the meaning of the instruction $r3(x)$, taking the definition of procedure $r3$ and procedure one from program 4.3 and the definition of x as

$$def\ x() = NL;\ r3(one)\ enddef$$

[Hint: calculating the meaning of *r3(one)* might simplify your answer.]

-=-=-=-=-=-=-=-=-=-=-=-=-

4.5 ARGUMENTS, PARAMETERS AND ENVIRONMENTS

Definition 4.1 didn't arise out of the air or by accident. The definitions we give to programming constructs must make sense in mechanical terms: that is, we must be able to build machines which can imitate those definitions. Vice-versa, the machines we build must follow what we think are sensible definitions. Either way, we must be able to give a mechanical explanation of a procedure-calling instruction which corresponds to definition 4.1 and which gives programs an equivalent meaning. An explanation of the meaning of a procedure call as a mechanism runs as follows:

(a) Find the value of the argument formula, if any.

(b) Create a new computational environment, based on the one in which the procedure was *defined*, in which the parameter name identifies the value of the argument formula.

(c) Execute the procedure body in the new environment.

(d) Continue execution in the old environment.

definition 4.2

Just as when an environment is created when definitions are executed, the environment created in step (b) of this definition is based on an existing environment. That is, the new environment is a copy of the one in which the procedure is defined, apart from the fact that in the new environment the parameter name has a particular value. If the parameter name had a meaning in the original environment, then it has a new one in the copy. If it had no meaning in the original, it has one in the copy. A procedure call which doesn't have an argument creates a new environment which is an exact copy of the one in which it was defined.

You should be able to see that the mechanical explanation given in definition 4.2 has been carefully designed to produce the same effect as the substitution explanation given in definition 4.1. If you replace every occurrence of a parameter name by the argument formula and then execute the **changed** procedure body, you produce the same effect as if you were to execute the *original* text in an environment set up so that the parameter name identifies the argument value.

It is step (c) of the mechanical definition that produces the effect of the procedure call, by executing the procedure body in the new environment. But steps (b) and (d) are crucially important because first of all the new environment must be constructed and last of all it must be abandoned so that execution continues in the calling instruction's environment. Step (a) is needed because to execute a particular procedure call we must find out what meaning is to be ascribed to the parameter name.

An important feature of definition 4.2 is that the environment which is created in step (b) depends on the one in which the procedure is *defined,* which is not necessarily the same as the environment from which it is *called.* Very soon you will see several program examples which exploit just this point.

A diagram of part of the execution of program 4.3 is shown in figure 4.4. In this diagram the outermost box describes an execution of the whole program. The program's procedure definitions create a variation of the basic environment, then its instruction sequence begins to produce the program's effect. The first instruction of the sequence is *r3(one).*

According to definition 4.2 this creates a new environment (the second box in the diagram). The new environment is a copy of the first-box environment with the addition of a meaning for the name *p.* Then the sequence $p(); p(); p()$ is executed within the new environment (note that this sequence would be meaningless in either of the earlier environments env-0 or env-1).

The first instruction in the sequence calls for an execution of the procedure identified by *p*: in the inner-box environment this means the same thing as the procedure identified by *one* in the outer-box environment. So the effect is as if to call procedure *one.*

Calling procedure *one* creates yet another environment, shown as the third box of the diagram. Because the procedure definition has no parameters the new environment is exactly like env-1, the environment in which procedure one was defined. Execution of the body of procedure *one* in this environment prints an asterisk[†].

When the last instruction in the execution of procedure *one* terminates the execution also terminates. The environment it created is abandoned and the instruction which called it terminates. Execution of the next instruction in the calling execution starts: this is another call on procedure *p*, shown as the fourth box, which has just the same effect as the previous call. The third instruction is yet another call of procedure *p* and is shown as the fifth box.

[†] The *print*∗ instruction would produce the same effect in *any* environment, but programming definitions are constructed to be taken literally and computers follow them precisely: in this case a new environment is created even though it is not needed. Part of the business of programming is knowing when to overlook and when to exploit such literal obedience to orders. At this stage it is safest to overlook nothing.

Execute program 4.3 in an environment which contains
definitions of the basic instructions. Call this environment
env-0.

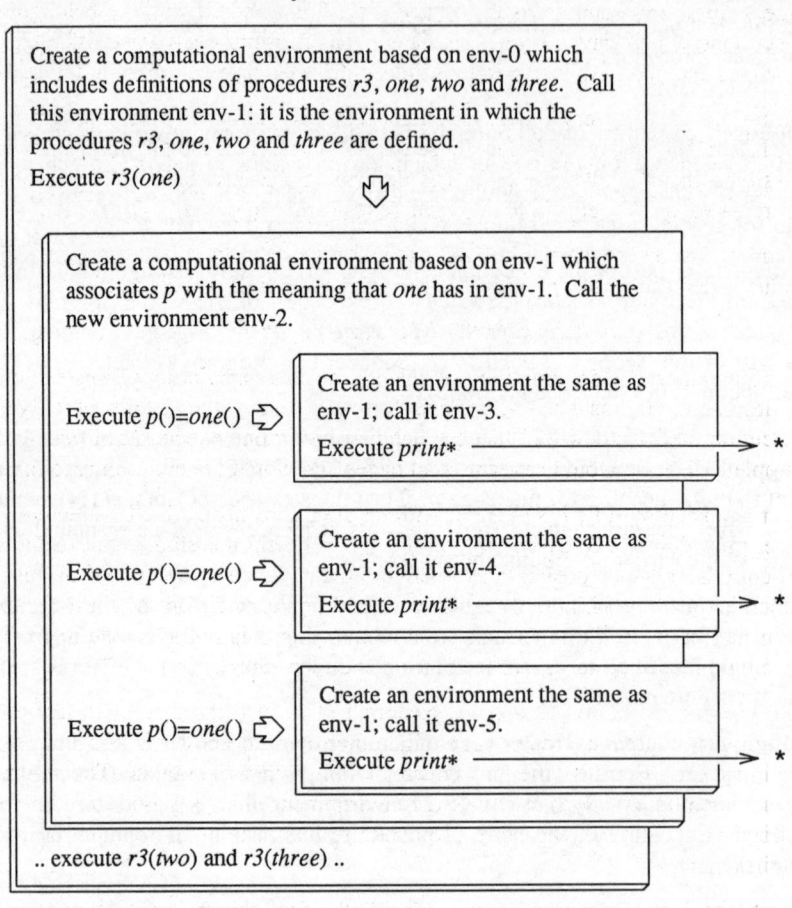

figure 4.4

Finally, the execution of *r3* terminates, and with it the execution of the
instruction *r3(one)*. The rest of the action of the program is not shown in this
diagram.

-=-=-=-=-=-=-=-=-=-=-=-

Exercise 4.13
Draw the missing part of figure 4.4 which shows the execution of *r3(two)*.
Include all the executions caused by this instruction, directly or indirectly.

Exercise 4.14
Draw the missing part of figure 4.4 which shows the execution of *r3(three)*.

-=-=-=-=-=-=-=-=-=-=-=-=-

From figure 4.4 and the answers to exercises 4.13 and 4.14 you should be able to verify that execution of program 4.3 creates thirteen environments; that at any time a single environment is in use and there are at most two more belonging to executions which haven't yet terminated; that it prints twelve asterisks and six newlines and that in doing so it does indeed print the pattern shown in figure 4.1.

Figure 4.4 gives a very full description of the execution of part of program 4.3 but it is rather wordy. It makes sense to abbreviate environment diagrams where possible. In particular the sentences describing the environments can often be abbreviated, and repetition of identical boxes can be avoided.

Figure 4.5 shows a diagram of the execution of $r3(x)$ in an environment which includes definitions of $r3$ and one as in program 4.3, and x is defined by

$$def\, x() = NL;\, r3(one)\ enddef$$

The diagram has been simplified by leaving out the description of this enclosing environment. It has been simplified further to show the details of only one execution of $x()$ and within that the details of only one execution of $one()$. The complete diagram would cover several pages and would be tediously repetitive.

First an execution of $r3$ is created, with an environment in which p identifies the outer procedure x. To execute $p()$ in this environment therefore is to execute $x()$. When x is called it creates a new environment which is a copy of the one in which it was defined: note that it is *not* based on the one from which it is called, even indirectly, and that therefore the meaning of p is not available to it. This execution first executes an NL instruction and then $r3(one)$.

The $r3(one)$ instruction creates an execution of $r3$ just like the one in figure 4.4, but this time it does so as part of another execution of $r3$. As before the environment created is based on the one in which $r3$ was defined. The argument value is obtained from the calling environment: this is based on the outer environment and so the value provided is the meaning of one in the outer environment.

The second execution of $r3$ is nested inside the first, shown in the diagram by the way the third box is enclosed by the second which is in turn enclosed by the first. There is no confusion about which execution to follow - the machine simply follows the last one created until it terminates and then it goes back to the calling execution. There is no confusion either about the meaning of p in either of the executions since each of them uses its own particular environment. In the environment created and used by the inner execution p means the same as one, in the environment created and used by the outer execution it means the same as x.

When the instruction $p()$ is executed within the environment created by the second execution the effect is to call procedure one rather than procedure x. Three executions of $p()$ in that environment therefore print three asterisks, just as they did in figure 4.4.

Execute *r3(x)*

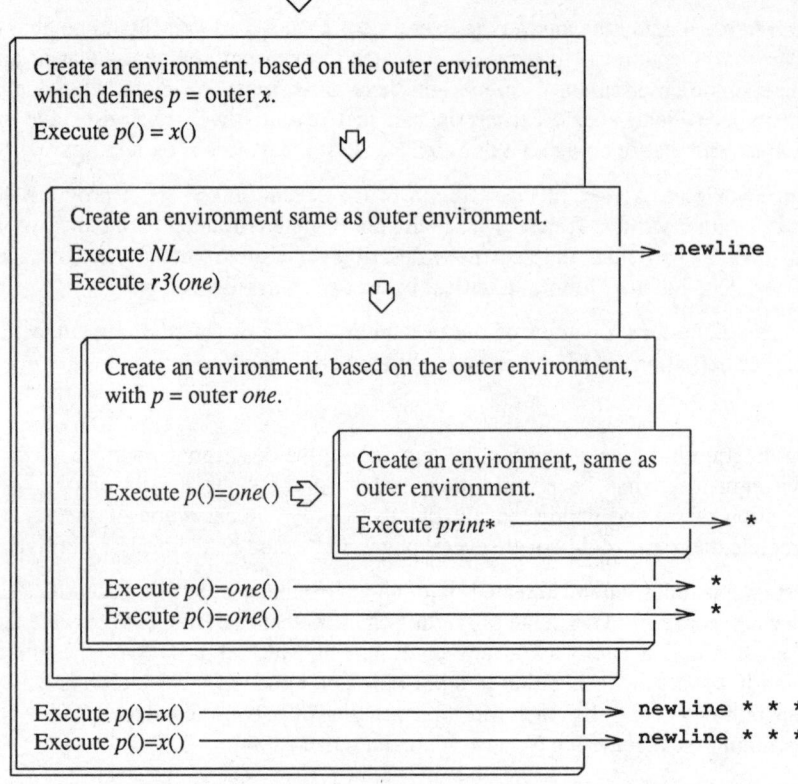

figure 4.5

When the last execution of *one()* terminates so does the execution of *r3(one)* and with that the execution of *x()*. Then *p()* is executed again in the outermost box: this is the fifth time this instruction has been executed but only the second time in the environment in which *p* identifies *x*. This procedure call has the same effect as the previous call of *x*: an execution of *NL* followed by three executions of *print**. The final execution of *p()* calls *x* again, produces the same effect again, and the overall effect of the program is to print a three-by-three square of asterisks.

-=-=-=-=-=-=-=-=-=-=-=-

Exercise 4.15
Given the following definition of procedure y, assumed to be made in an environment which includes *r3* and *x*:

$$def\ y() = r3(x)\ enddef$$

(a) construct as much of the environment diagram of *r3(y)* as necessary to verify that this instruction prints a three-by-nine rectangle of asterisks (three across, nine down); (b) use definition 4.1 to convert $r3(y)$ into an instruction sequence which prints a three-by-nine rectangle of asterisks.

Exercise 4.16
Construct a definition of procedure *gamma* so that $r3(gamma)$ prints a nine-by-nine square of asterisks. Try to use as few instructions as possible in your definition, by using procedure $r3$ as much as possible. Check your procedure definition using substitution according to definition 4.1 and by drawing an environment diagram.

-=-=-=-=-=-=-=-=-=-=-=-

4.6 PROCEDURE NAMES AND PROCEDURE VALUES

Definition 4.2 demands that in the environment created by a procedure execution the parameter name must identify the argument value. In the instruction $r3(one)$, *one* is the argument *formula*. What, then, is the argument *value*? I glossed over the problem in figures 4.4 and 4.5, making remarks like 'p has the same meaning as *one* in the outer environment'.

The distinction between a procedure formula and a procedure value is the same as that which can be made between the formula $x+y$ and the value - say 7 - which it might deliver given some particular values of x and y. *One* is the name of a procedure, and we know the effect of an execution of the instruction *one*(), so we might describe the procedure value as 'that procedure which, when called with no parameters, prints an asterisk'. We might further agree, looking at the definition of procedure *one*, that the procedure produces its effect by executing *print**. So the value of the formula *one* is 'the procedure which takes no parameters and which executes *print** once and nothing more'.

Definitions of values as 'the procedure which ..' are long-winded and prone to error because English isn't a notation designed to be concise or precise. There is a notation in widespread use, called the lambda notation, which conveys the same information precisely and far more concisely. The formula

$$\lambda().print*$$

describes 'the procedure which takes no parameters and executes *print**'. Notice the use of empty parameter brackets to indicate the fact that this procedure requires no parameter information. This formula could be used to describe the value of the formula *one* in program 4.3. The value of the formula $r3$ in the same program can be written as $\lambda(p).(p(); p(); p())$: note the use of program brackets '(' and ')' to enclose the body of the procedure. It might equally well be written as $\lambda(q).(q(); q(); q())$. Either formula means 'the procedure which, given a parameterless procedure as argument, will call that argument three times in succession'.

Substitution of procedure values

The principle of the substitution of equals is that one formula can be substituted for another of equal meaning. In a program where *one* is a formula with the same meaning as λ().*print*∗ it must be possible to replace either formula by the other. That is, substitution could convert *r3(one)* into *r3*(λ().*print*∗). Then substitution of argument for parameter according to definition 4.1 will give the sequence

$$(\lambda().print*)(); (\lambda().print*)(); (\lambda().print*)()$$

I have bracketed the procedure formulas in this example to make it clear what is the structure of the program and of each instruction. Substitution has produced a sequence of three procedure-calling instructions, each of which describes its procedure directly with a lambda formula rather than indirectly via a defined name.

Just as the instruction *one*() means 'call the procedure described by *one*', so the instruction (λ().*print*∗)() means 'call the procedure described by λ().*print*∗'. Using definition 4.1 and replacing the procedure call by a copy of the procedure body with every occurrence of the parameter name replaced by the argument formula, (λ().*print*∗)() converts into *print*∗, so a sequence of three similar instructions can be replaced by *print*∗; *print*∗; *print*∗, giving the same result as before.

Environments and procedure values

The value of a formula depends not only on its text but also on the environment in which it is calculated. Some formulas, like '*print*∗' or '2+2', have the same meaning in every environment. Some, like '*x+y*' or 'λ().《*x*(); *y*()》', combine unknown values and depend on the environment to supply information about those values.

Basic instructions like *print*∗ are constants, as are numerals like 2, 3 or 99. Formulas made up only from constants are themselves constants: this covers program formulas like '*print*∗; *print*∗' as well as procedure formulas like 'λ().*print*∗' and arithmetic formulas like '2+2'. Then there is no difficulty in giving the value of *one* in program 4.3: it is the constant λ().*print*∗.

If *x* has the value of the formula λ().《*NL*; *r3(one)*》, is it enough to give just that formula to describe the value of *x*? Certainly not, because the formula refers to the names *r3* and *one* and its meaning depends on the meanings of those names. Those meanings are in turn procedure formulas which could require still more meanings from the environment, and so on. In the end the simplest thing is to regard a procedure value as a pairing of the lambda formula with its defining environment, which gives the meanings of all the names which can validly appear within the procedure formula. And since when a name is defined to be a procedure name, the name and the procedure formula have the same meaning in the environment in which the definition was made, a pairing of the procedure name and that environment would do as well.

Unfortunately I don't know a concise formal notation which describes environments. Because neither the procedure name nor the lambda formula is enough on its own and because names are usually shorter than the lambda formula, I shall continue with the subterfuge of describing procedures in phrases like 'x from env-16' or 'one from env-1'. Which is right back where I started.

I beg your pardon?

What was all the fuss about? If my first attempt was good enough, why give any other explanation? Why introduce the notion of procedure values when we already have procedure names? Who needs procedure formulas anyway? One answer is: see the definition of procedure *square* in the next chapter. Another answer is more philosophical.

The discussion of procedure names, procedure formulas and procedure values uncovers an important distinction between things-themselves and names-of-things which will appear several times more in this book. It is a vital distinction, not only in programming but also more generally in mathematics. Lewis Carroll joked about it in *Through the Looking Glass*, where Humpty Dumpty uses words to mean just what he chooses them to mean. In the same book the White Knight offers to sing a song to Alice, and Carroll makes a joke about names of names (of names of names ..). The song's name is called Haddock's Eyes; its name *is* The Aged Aged Man. But that is only the name: the song is called Ways and Means. Again that is only what it is *called*: it really *is* A-sitting on a Gate. Then he sings the song ..

This sort of difficulty doesn't only arise in programming and mathematical joke books. The names 'that man there' and 'Private Bornat' may at some time be alternative names for the same person. He may also be known as '4578321176'. This last name is called his service number. From some point of view I might insist that he *is* my father and that 'Private Bornat' is merely one of his names. That name is called his rank.

Learning about programming makes you more than usually aware of the need for a distinction between names and meanings, shows you that there can be names of names and different ways of naming things, and helps you to understand the intricate structures which can arise when names and meanings are manipulated. It is a real and worthwhile distinction, as the examples in the rest of this book will demonstrate.

4.7 OTHER KINDS OF VALUE

So far the only kind of argument values considered have been procedures, and only parameterless procedures at that. There are lots of other kinds of values which are useful and interesting. *Numbers* are an obvious example, though I shall wait until I introduce counting repetition in chapter 6 before I make much use of them. *Characters* - the marks that we type and which the computer prints, like x, +, &, £, and so on - are very useful for producing different visible effects. Sequences of characters, called *strings,* like "hello", "The Third Policeman", "+−*/", and so on, are equally useful. Procedures which take parameters can themselves be used as arguments.

Single-character arguments

In order to deal with single-character values I need to expand the basic vocabulary of my notation. To make use of single-character values I need at least to be able to make marks on the screen by printing them. The basic procedure *printchar* - a procedure whose definition is included in the basic environment - is provided with a character as its argument, makes a corresponding mark on the paper or the screen and moves the cpp. Thus, for example, *printchar*('*') has the same effect as *print**; *printchar*('+') prints a plus sign; *printchar*('R') prints the first letter of my name. I use single quotation marks to bracket the character being described[†]. Note that space is a printable character and that therefore *printchar*(' ') has the same effect as *printspace*.

In most real-world programming systems there is a character-value which, if you print it, moves the cpp to a new line. You can't easily write such a value enclosed in quotation marks, so usually it has a special name or there is some very system-specific way of obtaining the value. I shall name that value, when I need it, by writing *newline*, so that *printchar*(*newline*) will have the same effect as *NL*. There are usually several other layout characters which affect the position of the cpp: *newpage* and *tab*, for example.

Character values are values. They can be named indirectly if names stand for them, just like any other value. For example, what does the following sequence mean?

$$printchar(c); printchar(c); printchar(c)$$

Just as the meaning of the sequence $p(); p(); p()$ depends on the meaning of p, so the meaning of this sequence depends on what you mean by c. To put it another way, it depends on the environment in which the sequence is executed. If c

---

[†] Experienced programmers should ask at this point: how do you describe the quoting characters? The answer is that if I need to describe those characters themselves I shall write ''' or ''', so that, for example, *printchar*(''') will make an opening-quote mark on the paper.

stands for the value '*' then this program prints three asterisks; if c stands for '+' it prints three plus signs[†]; if c stands for $\lambda().print*$ the sequence is meaningless.

You can create environments by procedure call. Make the sequence the body of a procedure of which c is the parameter name: for example, you can write

$$def\ threec(c) = printchar(c); printchar(c); printchar(c)\ enddef$$

Then *threec*('9') will print 999 because parameter-substitution makes the procedure body into the sequence

$$printchar('9'); printchar('9'); printchar('9')$$

-=-=-=-=-=-=-=-=-=-=-=-

Exercise 4.17
Draw an environment diagram of an execution of *threec*('*').

Exercise 4.18
Write a definition of procedure *square* so that a procedure call *square*('*') prints a three-by-three square of asterisks, *square*('+') a similar figure of plus signs.

Exercise 4.19
What is printed by *square*(' ')? How does it differ from an execution of *NL*; *NL*; *NL*? If it is different, is an execution of the sequence *square*(' '); *NL* different in final effect from an execution of *NL*; *NL*; *NL*; *NL*?

Exercise 4.20
Which of the instructions in the following program are sense and which are nonsense, and why? What is the meaning of the sensible ones?

$$def\ quote(c) = NL; printchar(''); printchar(c); printchar('')\ enddef$$
$$def\ x() = print*\ enddef$$

$$quote('x'); quote('*'); quote('c'); quote(c); quote(x)$$

-=-=-=-=-=-=-=-=-=-=-=-

String arguments

A string is a sequence of character values. Printing a string is a matter of printing its characters one at a time, in order. I define the basic procedure *printstring*, which should be provided with a character sequence and will print the elements of the sequence one-by-one, moving the cpp after each character. For example, *printstring*("hello") prints h, then e, then l, then l again and finally o. In total it moves the cpp five positions to the right. This single instruction is equivalent to the sequence

---

[†] Notice: we are already sitting on the White Knight's gate. + is the name of the addition operation in arithmetic and in my notation as well. '+' is the name of the name of the addition operation. If c stands for '+' then c is the name of the name of the name of the addition operation.

printchar('h'); *printchar*('e'); *printchar*('l'); *printchar*('l'); *printchar*('o')

Strings can be of any length from zero up. The empty string "" contains no characters: if it is printed then no mark is made and the cpp doesn't move.

-=-=-=-=-=-=-=-=-=-=-=-

Exercise 4.21
Give a sequence of *printchar* instructions equivalent to *printstring*("goodbye").

Exercise 4.22
Give the *printstring* instruction equivalent to the sequence

$$printchar('N'); printchar('o'); printchar('!')$$

Exercise 4.23
What is the single-instruction equivalent of

$$printstring("good"); printspace; printstring("morning")$$

Exercise 4.24
Direct-mail canvassing often uses spuriously 'personal' letters produced by computer. For example:

Dear Mr Donald Duck,

You have been selected to take part in our Mystery Challenge. Just fill in the attached form and return it to our office to get four chances to win a plastic chicken. Just think how nice it would be to show off to your neighbours by walking your plastic chicken with Mrs Donald Duck on a Sunday morning. Or do you like to play in the bath, Donald Duck? Your own chicken will be carefully engraved 'property of Donald Duck' ..

- and so on, rapidly ad nauseam. Write a definition of a procedure *letter* which is given a string - for example, "Mickey Mouse", "Isaac Newton", "Queen Elizabeth" - and produces one of these unnecessary missives.

-=-=-=-=-=-=-=-=-=-=-=-

Procedure values which take arguments

Up to now the procedures which have been given as arguments in procedure calls have all been parameterless. This has been convenient but it's by no means necessary. For example, consider the following definition

$$def\ twice(x) = x('*'); x('+')\ enddef$$

Twice(one) - given the definition of *one* from program 4.3 - wouldn't make sense because *one*('*') and *one*('+') don't make sense. But *twice(printchar)* would be ok - it would print "*+". And *twice(quote)* - see exercise 4.20 - would be alright: it would print the six-character sequence " "*"'+'" ". *Twice(square)* - see exercise 4.18 - would print a rectangular pattern of asterisks and plus signs.

You can tell, by looking at the definition of *twice*, that the argument corresponding to *x* must be a procedure. But you can tell also that it must be a procedure which accepts a character value as its own argument. So *twice(r3)* - see program 4.3 again - won't do because although *r3* does accept an argument, it needs a procedure and not a character value as argument. And *twice(letter)* - see exercise 4.24 - won't do because *letter* needs a string argument.

-=-=-=-=-=-=-=-=-=-=-=-

Exercise 4.25
Is the instruction *twice(twice)* meaningful? Justify your answer.

Exercise 4.26
Define a procedure *thrice*, similar to *twice* but with the modification suggested by its name. Use it to define a program which prints a three-by-three square of asterisks but does not contain an instruction *printchar*(..) or an instruction *print**. Check carefully that every procedure-calling instruction is meaningful. [Hint: try calling *printchar* indirectly.]

Exercise 4.27
Repeat exercise 4.26 for a nine-by-nine pattern, then an eighty-one-by-eighty-one pattern. [Hint: *r3* will probably be useful. And don't forget to check that you are providing the right kind of argument to every procedure.]

-=-=-=-=-=-=-=-=-=-=-=-

4.8 MORE THAN ONE PARAMETER

Consider the following procedure definition:

def sandwich(jam, bread) = bread(); jam(); bread() enddef

program 4.4

This procedure requires *two* argument values, each a procedure, in order to be executed. Given definitions of *px* and *pO*: say, for example,

def pO() = printchar('O') enddef
def px() = printchar('x') enddef

the procedure call *sandwich(px, pO)* prints "OxO" and the call *sandwich(pO, px)* prints "xOx". The procedure needs two arguments, but they don't have to be different: *sandwich(pO, pO)* prints "OOO".

How does it all work? You have seen definitions with zero and with one parameter name, and in this case there are two. Definitions may have three, four, five, or any number of parameter names, provided only that they are all different. The procedure call must include the same number of argument formulas as the definition gives parameter names. Then the first argument formula gives a meaning for the first parameter name, the second formula a meaning for the second parameter name, and so on. Thus the substitution explanation of the procedure call *sandwich(px, pO)* makes it equivalent to the sequence *pO(); px(); pO()* and the definitions of *pO* and *px* make it clear that this sequence prints "OxO", just as I claimed above.

-=-=-=-=-=-=-=-=-=-=-=-=-

Exercise 4.28
Draw an environment diagram of *sandwich(pO, px)*, executed in an environment which includes the definitions of *sandwich*, *pO* and *px* given above; hence show that this instruction is equivalent to *printstring*("xOx").

-=-=-=-=-=-=-=-=-=-=-=-=-

Procedure definitions can have any number of parameters. The following definition has three:

> *def doubledecker (fill1, fill2, bread) =*
>   *bread(); fill1(); bread(); fill2(); bread()*
> *enddef*

program 4.5

-=-=-=-=-=-=-=-=-=-=-=-=-

Exercise 4.29
Either by substitution or by drawing an environment diagram, find the meaning of *doubledecker(one, px, pO)* where procedure *one* is defined as in program 4.3.

Exercise 4.30
Given definitions of *sandwich* and *doubledecker* as above, find the meaning of the following program:

> *def a() = printchar('a') enddef*
> *def b() = printchar('b') enddef*
> *def c() = printchar('c') enddef*
>
> *def one() = sandwich(a, b) enddef*
> *def two() = doubledecker(c, a, b) enddef*
>
> *sandwich(one, two)*

[Hint: try finding the meanings of *one* and *two* first.]

Exercise 4.31
Why is the following definition nonsense?

> *def p(a, b, a) = a(); b(); a() enddef*

Exercise 4.32
Given the following definition:

> *def q(a, b) = a(); a(); a() enddef*

comment on the sense or nonsense of the following instructions: $q(pO, px)$, $q(pO, ' ')$, $q(' ', pO)$, $q(pO, ' ', "xyz")$. Is the procedure definition nonsense? If so, why? If not, why not?

Exercise 4.33
Pseudo-personal letters are usually produced by a procedure with more than one parameter. For an example, see figure 4.6. How many arguments would the procedure which produced this letter require? [Hint: more than two.] What kind of value is required for each of the arguments - a character, a procedure, a number, a string?

Donald Duck
1642 Ocean Boulevard
Hollywood

Dear Mr Duck (or may we call you Donald?)

We note that you haven't replied to our earlier letter. Don't you like plastic chickens? Don't you want to walk yours down Ocean Boulevard with Mrs Duck and all the little Ducks? Donald, this is your last chance. Send the money now!

.. squiggle ..
J. F. Hackenburger
Plastic Chicken Corp.

figure 4.6

-=-=-=-=-=-=-=-=-=-=-=-

4.9 PLANNING A SOLUTION

Suppose that you were shown the pattern

```
  *
 **
***
****
  *
 **
***
****
  *
 **
***
****
```

figure 4.7

and were asked to write a program to produce it, together with a strong hint that the solution has something to do with the procedure *sandwich*. It doesn't take much imagination to look at the pattern and notice the bread, jam, bread pattern it makes:

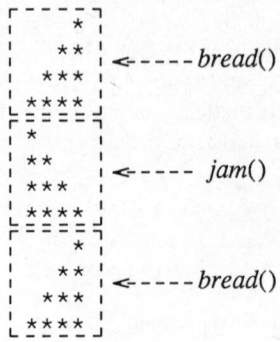

figure 4.8

The regularity in the pattern almost shouts at you. The first step in planning the program which prints this pattern is to suppose that there are two procedures which produce the two parts of the pattern and to write down the solution as the single instruction

$$sandwich(middle, outside)$$

Notice that the *as if* style of programming introduced in chapter 3 is still the one I use: design the program as if the procedures had been written, satisfy yourself that the program uses the procedures properly, finally write the procedures. In this case the *middle* and *outside* procedures are very easy to write, so there isn't much left to do to solve the problem.

-=-=-=-=-=-=-=-=-=-=-=-

Exercise 4.34
Define the *middle* and *outside* procedures so that *sandwich(middle, outside)* prints the pattern shown in figure 4.7.

Exercise 4.35
Assuming the definitions of *middle* and *outside* from exercise 4.34, what would be printed by the following program?

> *def inner*() = *outside*(); *middle*(); *outside*()
> *def outer*() = *printstring*("")
>
> *sandwich(inner, outer)*

Exercise 4.36
Answer exercise 4.35 for the following program:

> *def a*() = *sandwich(middle, outside)*
> *def b*() = *printstring*("")
>
> *sandwich(a, b)*

-=-=-=-=-=-=-=-=-=-=-=-

Suppose now that you were asked to write a program which prints the sequence 'ABDCDAB', with a strong hint that this problem too has something to do with sandwiches. You might reasonably guess that the pattern is a sandwich of 'DCD' inside a pair of 'AB's, and your solution might look like program 4.6. But you should remember the programmer's maxim 'First thoughts are rarely best' and look again. You might then notice that the jam in program 4.6 is itself a sandwich, and produce a more intricate solution like program 4.7. You probably wouldn't notice at first (though the exercises above hint at it) that there is a family of other solutions all of which depend on the fact that printing an empty string has no effect. It is possible, using this fact, to surround a filling with any number of infinitely thin pieces of bread: program 4.8 gives an example of what I mean.

$$sandwich(\lambda().printstring(\text{``DCD''}), \lambda().printstring(\text{``AB''}))$$

program 4.6

$$sandwich(\lambda().sandwich(\lambda().printchar(\text{`C'}), \lambda().printchar(\text{`D'})), \\ \lambda().printstring(\text{``AB''}))$$

program 4.7

$$sandwich(\lambda().printstring(\text{``ABDCDAB''}), \lambda().printstring(\text{``''}))$$

program 4.8

-=-=-=-=-=-=-=-=-=-=-=-

Exercise 4.37
Draw environment diagrams for an execution of each of programs 4.6, 4.7 and 4.8. Hence verify that each prints the same pattern.

Exercise 4.38
Check each of the three programs 4.6, 4.7 and 4.8 again, this time using substitution.

-=-=-=-=-=-=-=-=-=-=-=-

In a competition for the most sandwichy *sandwich* program which prints 'ABDCDAB', program 4.7 would probably win. Program 4.6 isn't so deeply nested, and program 4.8 or anything like it would be immediately disqualified for cheating.

But consider now the pattern 'BABACABAB'. This doesn't have a unique best-sandwich pattern, so far as I can see. One solution has ACA as the jam and BAB as the bread: each of these is an obvious sandwich so you finish up with the program

$$sandwich(\lambda().sandwich(\lambda().printchar(\text{`C'}), \lambda().printchar(\text{`A'})), \\ \lambda().sandwich(\lambda().printchar(\text{`A'}), \lambda().printchar(\text{`B'})))$$

But there are other ways of doing it: the pattern is a C inside As, inside Bs, inside As, inside Bs. Or is it a C inside ABAs, inside Bs (in which case the ABA-bread is another sandwich)? Or what?

-=-=-=-=-=-=-=-=-=-=-=-=-=-

Exercise 4.39
Write programs which correspond to the two solutions suggested above.

-=-=-=-=-=-=-=-=-=-=-=-=-=-

The moral of all this discussion is that, although programming often requires you to seek a systematic structure in a problem, there is never a unique systematic structure and sometimes not even a structure which is obviously 'best'. This implies several things:

(a) You should continue to look for alternative structures even though you think you have found one that fits: there may be a better structure which you haven't found yet.

(b) You will have to decide between structures. Choices may be based on which yields the shortest program, which yields the clearest program, which yields the most economical execution, which you find easiest to understand, and so on.

(c) Learn when to stop looking for new solutions. Novices usually stop too early, but we all have to stop sometime.

(d) If you think the problem may have been solved already by someone else, don't re-invent the wheel: look for a solution in books and in magazines and in learned journals.

4.10 PROCEDURES WHICH CALCULATE AND DELIVER VALUES

So far I have dealt with instruction procedures - procedures which structure the execution of instruction sequences. There are also value-delivering procedures - procedures which structure the calculation of formulas.

Consider, for example, the formula

$$x \times a + (y-3)/z$$

The value delivered by a calculation of this formula depends on the meanings given to the names x, a, y and z. If we are given the particular meanings $x=4$, $a=10$, $y=9$ and $z=3$ then we can easily calculate the meaning of the formula by substitution:

$$x \times a + (y-3)/z = 4 \times 10 + (9-3)/3 = 40+2 = 42$$

Formulas are often used to give a mathematical expression to theories about the world. For example, you can construct formulas which express theories about the way furnace temperature varies with fuel input or how a child's height at a given age is related to its parents' income and height, or how the incidence of cancer relates to temperature, food intake and the price of tomatoes. Suppose that the formula above expresses such a theory: then you might want to write a program which prints out the value it delivers for various different values of x, a, y and z. One such program might be program 4.9.

$$def\ printvalue(x, a, y, z) = printnumber(x{\times}a+(y{-}3)/z)\ enddef$$
$$printvalue(4, 10, 9, 3); printvalue(5, 11, 4, 7); printvalue(3, 3, 4, 4)$$

program 4.9

-=-=-=-=-=-=-=-=-=-=-=-

Exercise 4.40
Assuming the definition of *printvalue* from program 4.9, why is *printvalue*$(0, 0, 0, 0)$ a meaningless instruction? Why isn't *printvalue*$(0, 0, 0, 3)$ meaningless and what would it print? How about *printvalue*$(0, 0, 3, 0)$?

-=-=-=-=-=-=-=-=-=-=-=-

Execution of program 4.9 causes some numerals to be printed. Hidden in the execution will be a number of calculations - multiplications, additions, subtractions and divisions - which are used to compute the values of the numerals that are eventually printed. Program 4.10 produces the same visible effect as program 4.9 but uses a value-delivering procedure: one whose execution causes a calculation and delivers the value calculated.

$$def\ f(x, a, y, z) = x{\times}a+(y{-}3)/z\ enddef$$
$$printnumber(f(4, 10, 9, 3)); printnumber(f(5, 11, 4, 7));$$
$$printnumber(f(3, 3, 4, 4))$$

program 4.10

A call on a value-delivering procedure has a similar effect to a call on an instruction procedure: in execution terms, it creates a new environment in which the parameter names have the meanings given by the argument formulas, performs a calculation in that environment, then delivers the calculated value to be used in the calculation which called the procedure; in substitution terms, the procedure call can be replaced by a copy of the procedure body in which parameter names have been replaced by the corresponding argument formulas.

Just as instruction procedures are like invented instructions, so value-delivering procedures are like invented operators or functions. They can structure calculations by factoring out important parts of the calculation for special emphasis. For example, program 4.11 prints several numbers whose calculation depends on a formula but which aren't simply values of the formula.

$def\,f(x, a, y, z) = x{\times}a{+}(y{-}3)/z\ enddef$

$printnumber\,(f(4, 10, 9, 3));\,printnumber\,(f(5, 11, 4, 7){-}12);$

$printnumber\,(5{\times}f(3, 3, 4, 4))$

program 4.11

Value-delivering procedures can manipulate more than just numbers. Any of the other sorts of values introduced in this chapter - strings, characters, procedures - can be an argument to a value-delivering procedure or delivered as its result. Extensive examples must wait until later chapters have introduced other program structures.

-=

APPENDIX 4.A PROCEDURE DEFINITIONS AND CALLS IN PASCAL

Argument formulas transcribe fairly directly from my notation into Pascal. The major difference between Pascal procedure definitions and my notation is that in Pascal each parameter name must be decorated with a description of the kind or *type* of argument formula which corresponds to it. In my notation you are expected to deduce this information from the way the parameter name is used in the procedure body; in Pascal you must give the information explicitly.

Pascal can't handle all of the kinds of value described in this book. In particular, programs which manipulate strings are notoriously difficult to transcribe into Pascal. The transcription is tedious and you will need to be patient and careful.

Printchar and *printstring* in Pascal

The basic procedures *printchar* and *printstring* can be imitated by the Pascal write instruction. Both *printchar*(F) and *printstring*(F) transcribe to the Pascal instruction write(F).

Character and string constants in Pascal

Pascal string constants are enclosed in prime (single-quote) characters rather than the double quotes used in this book. Where I write "**+**" Pascal programming systems require ′**+**′. Character constants are enclosed in primes as well: where I write '+' Pascal requires ′+′. The similarity in notation means that a character value and a one-element character sequence are described identically in Pascal.

Parameter descriptions

In my notation a procedure definition starts with the word *def*, followed by a procedure heading which gives the name of the procedure and the names of any parameters. Next comes an equals sign, followed by a procedure body and a closing *enddef*. Pascal procedure definitions have almost the same structure but a slightly different punctuation. They start with `procedure` rather than *def*, there is a semicolon in place of the equals sign, the body must be enclosed in `begin`-`end` brackets and there is a closing semicolon in place of *enddef*. The heading gives not parameter names but parameter *descriptions*. Each parameter description gives the parameter name and states the kind of argument formula which can be provided in its place: I give examples below for all the kinds of value discussed in this chapter. Parameter descriptions are separated by semicolons rather than commas.

Character arguments

If a parameter name is intended to correspond to a character-valued argument formula, the fact must be indicated by writing `:char` after the parameter name in the procedure heading. For example, the procedure definition

> *def bracket*(*c*) =
> *printchar*('('); *printchar*(*c*); *printchar*(')')
> *enddef*

transcribes into Pascal as:

```
procedure bracket(c:char);
begin write('(');write(c);write(')') end;
```

Number arguments

If a parameter name is intended to correspond to a whole-number argument then you must write `:integer` after the parameter name in the parameter heading. Fractions like 1.345 or 3.1412 need the description `:real`, but none of the examples in this book need fractional numbers.

Procedure values as arguments

If an argument is to be a procedure value the corresponding parameter entry must be written as if the procedure were being defined. For procedure arguments which take no parameter, you must write the word `procedure` before the parameter name because that makes a description like the head of a parameterless procedure definition in Pascal. For example, the definition

$$def\, r3(p) = p();p();p()\ enddef$$

transcribes into Pascal as:

```
procedure r3(procedure p); begin p;p;p end;
```

Note that as always in Pascal, parameterless procedures are called without parameter brackets.

If the argument is to be a procedure which takes arguments itself then the parameter description must include parameter descriptions. For example, the definition

$$def\, X(a,b) = printchar(a); b(a)\ enddef$$

transcribes into Pascal as

```
procedure X(a:char; procedure b(z:char));
begin write(a);b(a) end;
```

Some very old-fashioned Pascal systems accept only the 'procedure N' form of parameter entry, whatever kind of procedure value is to be given as argument.

Value-delivering procedures in Pascal

In Pascal a value-delivering procedure is called a *function*. The word function replaces the word procedure in the heading, and the type of value delivered by the calculation is described just before the semicolon. The body of the procedure contains a single instruction[†]

$$<name> := <formula>$$

where *<name>* is the procedure name and *<formula>* is the calculation to be performed. For example, the procedure of programs 4.10 and 4.11 can be written as

```
function f(x,a,y,z:integer):integer;
begin f := x*a + (y-3)/z end;
```

Note the way in which several parameter descriptions can be run into one. Note the result-type description :integer between the closing bracket and the semicolon of the heading.

Strings as arguments

Strings are tricky in Pascal. You need to do quite a lot to transcribe even a simple program which uses strings. It is impossible to write your program so that

---

[†] You can have many more instructions than one in the body of a Pascal function but so far as this chapter is concerned you only need one.

strings of any length can be given to a procedure: instead you must always fix on a maximum length. Then you can write your program so that every string is the maximum length (solution number 1 below) or so that some strings are treated as if they were shorter than the maximum (solution number 2 below).

String arguments (solution 1)

Each procedure must be given string arguments of a fixed length. The length may differ between procedures but not between calls of the same procedure. The first step is to make all string arguments the same length. You can do this by cutting bits off the strings that are too long, but it is more usual to add spaces to those that are too short. For example, in the following program

$$def\ tw(s) = NL; printstring(s); NL; printstring(s)\ enddef$$

$$tw(\text{``hello''}); NL; tw(\text{``goodbye''})$$

program 4.12

the procedure *tw* is called once with an argument which is a string of five characters and once with a string of seven characters. It is made Pascal-fit if the first string is extended to seven characters:

$$def\ tw(s) = NL; printstring(s); NL; printstring(s)\ enddef$$

$$tw(\text{``hello\ \ ''}); NL; tw(\text{``goodbye''})$$

program 4.13

The Pascal transcription must include the information that each argument to a procedure will be a string of a particular length. You have to do this in two stages. First you must invent a *type name* and make a separate *type definition* which associates that name with the description of strings of a particular length. Each type definition is written:

<type name> = packed array[1..*<length>*] of char;

In place of *<type name>* you put the name you invented and in place of *<length>* you write the number of characters in strings of this type. Between the 'program..' stuff and the first procedure definition you write the word 'type', followed by all your type definitions (don't forget that each type definition ends with a semicolon!). Finally, you write : *<type name>* after each parameter name which requires arguments of that type. For example, in transcribing program 4.13 you might choose the type name *str* to describe strings of seven characters. Then your program could read

```
program P(input,output);
type str = packed array[1..7] of char;
procedure tw(s:str);
begin writeln;write(s);writeln;write(s) end;
begin tw('hello  ');writeln;tw('goodbye') end.
```

String arguments (solution 2)

To make an accurate transcription you must rewrite your program so that every string argument is represented by *two* values: one a sequence of characters and the other a number which says how many of those characters are to be noticed. You make all the sequences the same length, as in the earlier technique. The pair S and n are taken to mean that the first n characters of string S are important and the rest (if any) can be ignored.

You make this change to every string argument, even the argument to *printstring*. Thus, for example, program 4.13 becomes

$def\ tw(s, n) = NL; printstring(s, n); NL; printstring(s, n)\ enddef$

$tw(\text{"hello   "}, 5); NL; tw(\text{"goodbye"}, 7)$

program 4.14

Then you transcribe *printstring*(S, n) into Pascal write(S:n), an instruction which prints only the first n characters from string S. Program 4.14 transcribes into Pascal as:

```
program P(input,output);
type str = packed array[1..7] of char;
procedure tw(s:str;n:integer);
begin writeln;write(s:n);writeln;write(s:n) end;
begin tw('hello  ',5);writeln;tw('goodbye',7) end.
```

Consider another example. In program 4.15 the *double* procedure has two string parameters. The first step is to make this Pascal-fit by extending every string argument so that all are the same length (program 4.16). The second step is to make every string argument into two arguments (program 4.17). Finally, this

$def\ double(a, b) = printstring(a); NL; printstring(b)\ enddef$

$double(\text{"hello"}, \text{"and goodbye"})$

program 4.15

$def\ double(a, b) = printstring(a); NL; printstring(b)\ enddef$

$double(\text{"hello   "}, \text{"and goodbye"})$

program 4.16

$def\ double(a, an, b, bn) = printstring(a, an); NL; printstring(b, bn)\ enddef$
$double("hello\ \ \ \ \ \ \ ", 5, "and\ goodbye", 11)$

program 4.17

```
program A(input,output);
type str = packed array[1..11] of char;
procedure double(a:str;an:integer;b:str;bn:integer);
begin write(a:an);write(b:bn) end;
begin double('hello      ',5,'and goodbye',11) end.
```

figure 4.9

program transcribes into Pascal as in figure 4.9.

APPENDIX 4.B SOME PROGRAMS TO TRY

Many of the exercises in this chapter make interesting examples to transcribe into a mechanical code. You might try some of the following exercises: 4.1, 4.2, 4.5, 4.6, 4.8, 4.20-4.24 and 4.26.

Some exercises ask you to calculate the effect of a program. You can gain confidence that your calculation and your transcription are correct if you execute the program and see if you get the right sort of effect. Try exercises 4.29, 4.30, 4.34 and 4.39.

-=-=-=-=-=-=-=-=-=-=-=-

Exercise 4.41
Many Edward Lear limericks have the form:

> There was an old <*thing*> of <*bimbam*>
> Who <*mumbletygrumbletyslam*>
> When they said "<*diddleypom*>"
> <*he/she*> replied "<*twiddleydom*>"
> That <*something*> old <*thing*> of <*bimbam*>

Write a procedure which takes seven parameters and prints a limerick of this form. It will be your responsibility to ensure that the limerick is funny, scans, is or isn't obscene, and so on.

Exercise 4.42
Given the following definition of procedure bracket:

$def\ bracket(p) = printchar('('); p(); printchar(')')\ enddef$

write a program which prints the formula $(x+y)$.

Exercise 4.43

Repeat exercise 4.42 for the formula $(x+y+(z \times a))$. Do it by using the *bracket* procedure as intensively as possible.

Exercise 4.44

Write programs which print the formulas $(x+y)/(x+y+(z \times a))$, $((x+y)/(x+y+(z \times a)))-(x+y)$ and $(((x+y)/(x+y+(z \times a)))-(x+y))$, still using the *bracket* procedure intensively.

Chapter 5
NAMES AND ENVIRONMENTS

As programmers we always try to produce as beautiful and elegant a solution to a problem as we can. We are rarely satisfied with our first attempt and we usually produce several solutions before settling on one of them. One way to invent elegant and beautiful programs is to generalise a particular solution and to make it more abstract. This can uncover the structure of the program and separate essential parts of the design from the accidental.

Programs can often be generalised by using procedure parameters. For example, the program $p(); p(); p()$, where p is a parameter, is a generalisation of all the programs like *one()*; *one()*; *one()* or *two()*; *two()*; *two()* or *Hello()*; *Hello()*; *Hello()*. In chapter 4 I plucked the $p(); p(); p()$ program out of the air in order to illustrate a mechanism. I might instead have generalised, abstracted from, *parameterised* a program which called a procedure three times and invented the sequence that way.

Programming notation works according to precise rules. In order to make the most effective generalisations we may sometimes need to exploit notations and definitions to the limit. This chapter examines the use of parameters in more complicated circumstances than those covered in chapter 4. As a result it refines the substitution explanation and reinforces the execution explanation of procedure call.

5.1 FITTING ARGUMENTS TO PARAMETERS

Programs have to make sense. Demanding that the arguments to a procedure calling instruction fit with the parameters isn't a fussy matter of notation because arguments which don't fit make nonsense of a procedure call. An explanation of why a procedure-call instruction is sense or nonsense can appeal either to the substitution or to the execution explanation or to both. For example, program 5.1 is nonsense. It is nonsense because to execute it you must execute a nonsense instruction. $r3('+')$ is nonsense under the substitution explanation because

$$def\ r3(p) = p();p();p()\ enddef$$
$$r3(`+`)$$

program 5.1

'+'(); '+'(); '+'() is a nonsense program. It is nonsense under the execution explanation because you can deduce from the definition of *r3* that its argument must be a procedure value but the instruction provides a character value.

In the same way, but for different reasons, *r3*() is a nonsense instruction: under the substitution explanation it doesn't provide a formula to be substituted for the parameter name *p*; under the execution explanation it doesn't describe a value to be the meaning of *p* in the environment created by its execution.

r3(*r3*) is yet another nonsense instruction, even though its argument is a procedure value. It is nonsense both because substitution leads to the sequence *r3*(); *r3*(); *r3*() which contains three nonsense instructions, and because we can deduce from the definition of *r3* that an execution of *r3* requires a parameterless procedure but the instruction *r3*(*r3*) provides a procedure which has a parameter.

The fault isn't always in the procedure-calling instruction. Sometimes a procedure definition is written so that no procedure call could fit it. Consider the following definition of *A*:

$$def\ A(x) = x();printchar(x)\ enddef$$

You can't write an argument formula which could be used in a call to *A* because no possible formula could be substituted *both* for a procedure name *and* for a character name. No possible value could serve *both* as a procedure value *and* as a character value. The definition is nonsense.

Where procedure arguments are involved, nonsense definitions can be a little harder to spot. For example, what is wrong with the following definition?

$$def\ B(x,y,z) = x(`+`);y(x);z();x(`-`);y(z);z()\ enddef$$

From the first instruction we can deduce that *x* must name a procedure. Further, it must name a procedure which takes a character value as argument. Possible arguments corresponding to *x* could be *printchar* or something like $\lambda(c).\langle printchar(c);printchar(`.`)\rangle$. The second instruction tells us that the argument corresponding to *y* must also be a procedure: knowing something about *x* enables us to say further that *y* must take as argument a procedure which takes a character-valued argument. The next instruction tells us that *z* must also be a procedure, but this time a procedure which has no parameters. The fourth instruction confirms what we already know about *x* (so far so good!). But the fifth instruction is inconsistent with the second: it tells us that *y* is a procedure which takes a parameterless procedure as argument. Therefore the definition of *B* is nonsense.

-=-=-=-=-=-=-=-=-=-=-=-

Exercise 5.1
Is the following program sense or nonsense, and why?

$$def\,x() = printchar(\text{'}x\text{'})\;enddef$$
$$printchar(x)$$

Exercise 5.2
What if the body of the program in exercise 5.1 was *printchar(x())*?

Exercise 5.3
Write a definition of *x* such that the instruction *printchar(x())* does make sense. [Hint: value-delivering procedure.]

Exercise 5.4
For each of the following definitions, say whether it is sense or nonsense, and why.

$$def\,A(x, y, z) = x(y); y(z); z(x)\;enddef$$
$$def\,B(u, v, w) = u(\text{'}+\text{'}); v(u); w(\text{''}+\text{''}); v(w)\;enddef$$
$$def\,C(j, k) = j(i); k(i); j(\text{'}+\text{'})\;enddef$$

Exercise 5.5
Describe an environment in which the definition of *C* in exercise 5.4 wouldn't fit, and one in which it would fit.

Exercise 5.6
Say why the following definition isn't nonsense, assuming my usual definition of *r3*:

$$def\,infin(x) = r3(x); infin(x)\;enddef$$

What would be printed by a procedure call *infin(λ().(NL; print*))*?

-=-=-=-=-=-=-=-=-=-=-=-

$$def\,r3(p) = p(); p(); p()\;enddef$$
$$def\,one() = print*\;enddef$$
$$def\,two() = NL; r3(one)\;enddef$$
$$r3(one); r3(two)$$

program 5.2

$$def\,r3(q) = q(); q(); q()\;enddef$$
$$def\,one() = print*\;enddef$$
$$def\,two() = NL; r3(one)\;enddef$$
$$r3(one); r3(two)$$

program 5.3

5.2 CHOOSING A PARAMETER NAME

The parameter name you choose when you parameterise a program is a place-holder. You intend to substitute an argument formula for it later on, or to give a meaning for it as part of an environment when the program is executed. Provided that you choose a name which doesn't appear anywhere else in the program it doesn't matter how you choose. Programs 5.2 and 5.3 are the same except for the parameter name chosen for *r3*: I claim that they should have the same effect. The substitution and execution explanations of chapter 4 show that they do. Indeed the definition of *r3* in either program might have been any of the following:

> *def r3(six) = six(); six(); six() enddef*
> *def r3(nothing) = nothing(); nothing(); nothing() enddef*
> *def r3(stop) = stop(); stop(); stop() enddef*
> *def r3(no) = no(); no(); no() enddef*

and the meaning of *r3*, and hence of the whole program, would be unaffected.

-=-=-=-=-=-=-=-=-=-=-=-

Exercise 5.7
Show, by substitution and by environment/execution diagrams, that programs 5.2 and 5.3 have the same effect.

-=-=-=-=-=-=-=-=-=-=-=-

Programming definitions, like any mathematical explanation, are intended to be taken literally and it often helps to consider extreme examples to be sure that you really understand the definition. For example, what should we make of program 5.4? In my notation this program has the same meaning as programs 5.2 and 5.3, because the definition of *r3* in each case makes it equivalent to $\lambda(name).(name(); name(); name())$. Each of the definitions describes a value which is complete and self-supporting, a value that is not affected by what is written in the rest of the program. Choice of parameter name shouldn't affect the meaning of a parameterised formula.

> *def r3(one) = one(); one(); one() enddef*
> *def one() = print* enddef*
> *def two() = NL; r3(one) enddef*
>
> *r3(one); r3(two)*

program 5.4

The problem is to show that the substitution and execution explanations give programs like program 5.4 the meaning I require. They must also cope with extreme cases like program 5.5, which I shall show to have the same meaning as the other three examples.

$def\ r3(r3) = r3(\ );\ r3(\ );\ r3(\ )\ enddef$
$def\ one(\ ) = print*\ enddef$
$def\ two(\ ) = NL;\ r3(one)\ enddef$
$r3(one);\ r3(two)$

program 5.5

5.3 SUBSTITUTION AND PARAMETER NAMES

The substitution explanation treats all four programs 5.2-5.5 identically. When the formula giving the effect of a procedure call is calculated the parameter name is replaced by the argument formula and disappears, so the result isn't affected by what the parameter name used to be. For example, program 5.5 can be treated as follows:

$def\ r3(r3) = r3(\ );\ r3(\ );\ r3(\ )\ enddef$
$def\ one(\ ) = print*\ enddef$
$def\ two(\ ) = NL;\ r3(one)\ enddef$
$r3(one);\ r3(two)$

$= \quad def\ r3(r3) = r3(\ );\ r3(\ );\ r3(\ )\ enddef$
$def\ one(\ ) = print*\ enddef$
$def\ two(\ ) = NL;\ r3(one)\ enddef$
$one(\ );\ one(\ );\ one(\ );\ r3(two)$

$= \quad def\ r3(r3) = r3(\ );\ r3(\ );\ r3(\ )\ enddef$
$def\ one(\ ) = print*\ enddef$
$def\ two(\ ) = NL;\ r3(one)\ enddef$
$print*;\ print*;\ print*;\ r3(two)$

$= \quad def\ r3(r3) = r3(\ );\ r3(\ );\ r3(\ )\ enddef$
$def\ one(\ ) = print*\ enddef$
$def\ two(\ ) = NL;\ r3(one)\ enddef$
$print*;\ print*;\ print*;\ two(\ );\ two(\ );\ two(\ )$

$= \quad def\ r3(r3) = r3(\ );\ r3(\ );\ r3(\ )\ enddef$
$def\ one(\ ) = print*\ enddef$
$print*;\ print*;\ print*;$
$NL;\ r3(one);\ NL;\ r3(one);\ NL;\ r3(one)$

$= \quad def\ one(\ ) = print*\ enddef$
$print*;\ print*;\ print*;$
$NL;\ one(\ );\ one(\ );\ one(\ );$
$NL;\ one(\ );\ one(\ );\ one(\ );$
$NL;\ one(\ );\ one(\ );\ one(\ )$

$$= print*; print*; print*;$$
$$NL; print*; print*; print*;$$
$$NL; print*; print*; print*;$$
$$NL; print*; print*; print*$$

-=-=-=-=-=-=-=-=-=-=-=-

Exercise 5.8
When one formula is replaced by an equal formula the meaning of a program doesn't change; therefore the order in which substitutions are carried out doesn't matter. Show that this is true of program 5.5 by carrying out a substitution in which the formula *r3(one)* within the definition of procedure *two* is changed before any occurrence of the formula *two()* is altered.

Exercise 5.9
Show that the meaning of program 5.4 is the same as that of program 5.5. [Hint: it isn't necessary to reduce them to a sequence of basic instructions.]

Exercise 5.10
Show that all four programs 5.2-5.5 have identical meaning under the substitution explanation.

-=-=-=-=-=-=-=-=-=-=-=-

Simultaneous substitution

You must be careful when substituting argument formulas for parameter names if more than one substitution needs to be done. Consider, for example, program 5.6. This program certainly prints the message "hello, hello". The definition of *sandwich* is as self-supporting as the definition of *r3*. Since I can choose parameter names freely I might rewrite it as in program 5.7, and the rewritten program will surely have the same effect as the original. Substitution gives the

> *def sandwich(jam, bread) = bread(); jam(); bread() enddef*
>
> *def a() = printstring("hello") enddef*
> *def b() = printstring(", ") enddef*
>
> *sandwich(b, a)*

program 5.6

> *def sandwich(a, b) = b(); a(); b() enddef*
>
> *def a() = printstring("hello") enddef*
> *def b() = printstring(", ") enddef*
>
> *sandwich(b, a)*

program 5.7

meaning which I require provided that substitution of the first argument formula for the first parameter name happens *simultaneously* with substitution of the second argument formula for the second parameter name, changing $b()$; $a()$; $b()$ instantaneously into $a()$; $b()$; $a()$.

-=-=-=-=-=-=-=-=-=-=-=-

Exercise 5.11
Show that if the substitution of parameter names were carried out in sequence instead of all at once - that is, if the first parameter name were replaced *and then* the second, or vice-versa - program 5.7 would be given the wrong meaning.

Exercise 5.12
If some of the as are replaced, then some of the bs, then some more of the as, and so on, you can make program 5.7 print any combination of "hello"s and ", "s. Define an incorrect substitution which would make it print "hello, ,".

-=-=-=-=-=-=-=-=-=-=-=-

5.4 ENVIRONMENTS AND PARAMETER NAMES

The execution explanation introduces environments to associate names in programs with values (meanings). The explanation has been designed so that there is no difficulty with examples like program 5.5 or even program 5.7, but it is still necessary to use some care when constructing the diagrams.

Consider, for example, the execution of the instruction $r3(two)$ during an execution of program 5.5. Figure 5.1 shows the relevant parts of the execution diagram. This diagram shows that although executions may be contained one within another, their environments need not be related in the same way. It is precisely because a procedure call creates an environment based on the one in which the procedure was *defined* that the execution explanation produces the answer I require. Env-2 in figure 5.1 is based on env-1; env-3 is created by a procedure call executed in env-2 but it is based on env-1 and has no connection with env-2. Therefore the name $r3$ can have one meaning in env-2, given to it because $r3$ is a parameter of the definition which was called upon, but another meaning in env-3, inherited from env-1 where $r3$ was defined.

-=-=-=-=-=-=-=-=-=-=-=-

Exercise 5.13
Draw environment diagrams of programs 5.6 and 5.7: hence show that these two programs have the same effect.

-=-=-=-=-=-=-=-=-=-=-=-

Execute program 5.5 in an environment env-0 which
includes the basic instruction names with their usual
meanings

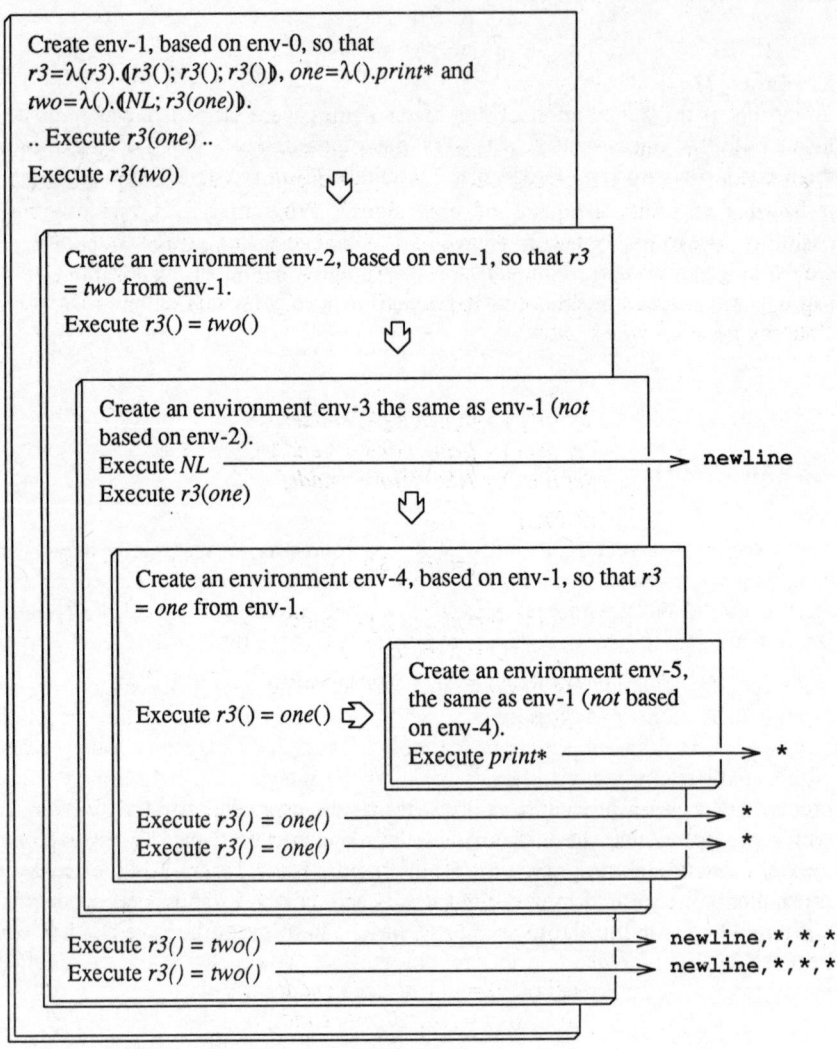

Create env-1, based on env-0, so that
$r3=\lambda(r3).(r3(); r3(); r3())$, $one=\lambda().print*$ and
$two=\lambda().(NL; r3(one))$.

.. Execute $r3(one)$ ..

Execute $r3(two)$

Create an environment env-2, based on env-1, so that $r3$
= *two* from env-1.

Execute $r3() = two()$

Create an environment env-3 the same as env-1 (*not*
based on env-2).
Execute NL ─────────────────────────→ `newline`
Execute $r3(one)$

Create an environment env-4, based on env-1, so that $r3$
= *one* from env-1.

Execute $r3() = one()$

Create an environment env-5,
the same as env-1 (*not* based
on env-4).
Execute *print** ───────────→ *

Execute $r3() = one()$ ────────────→ *
Execute $r3() = one()$ ────────────→ *

Execute $r3() = two()$ ─────────────────→ `newline,*,*,*`
Execute $r3() = two()$ ─────────────────→ `newline,*,*,*`

figure 5.1

5.5 PARAMETERISING PROGRAMS

Program 5.8 prints a square of asterisks. I would like to generalise this program,
to parameterise it so that it isn't tied to printing asterisks. Then I could use my
generalised version as the body of a procedure *square* which would print squares

$def\ r3(p) = p();p();p()\ enddef$
$def\ one() = print*\ enddef$
$def\ line() = NL;r3(one)\ enddef$
$r3(line)$

program 5.8

of whatever character I choose.

Before you can generalise it is essential to see some more examples in order to get an idea of what the general case is. How, for example, can I change program 5.8 so that it prints a square of plus signs? Program 5.9 is one obvious possibility, but to make it work I have had to change *print* into *printchar('+')*. One valid generalisation from these two examples would be to say that both programs are particular cases of program 5.10, whose parameter is the instruction X, but my notation won't allow it[†].

$def\ r3(p) = p();p();p()\ enddef$
$def\ one() = printchar('+')\ enddef$
$def\ line() = NL;r3(one)\ enddef$
$r3(line)$

program 5.9

$def\ r3(p) = p();p();p()\ enddef$
$def\ one() = X\ enddef$
$def\ line() = NL;r3(one)\ enddef$
$r3(line)$

program 5.10

An alternative generalisation is to observe that the parameter is the definition of procedure *one*, so that the program is naturally generalised just by leaving out that definition, giving program 5.11. This program is too general for my purpose. In programs 5.8 and 5.9, some character is printed three times after each *NL*. That detail has been lost in program 5.11, which doesn't seem to have much to do

$def\ r3(p) = p();p();p()\ enddef$
$def\ line() = NL;r3(one)\ enddef$
$r3(line)$

program 5.11

[†] It would be possible to change my notation so that it allowed the substitution of instruction formulas and so that the execution explanation covered the use of instruction values. To do so would complicate things so much that I have decided not to consider it.

with squares of characters.

The generalisation I am looking for is shown in program 5.12. If I write '+' in place of c, program 5.12 turns into program 5.9. If I write '*' in place of c, program 5.12 doesn't quite become program 5.8, but I do get a program with the same effect since *print** is equivalent to *printchar*('*'). All I am interested in is the effect of the program, so program 5.12 is an adequate generalisation.

$$def\ r3(p) = p(); p(); p()\ enddef$$
$$def\ one() = printchar(c)\ enddef$$
$$def\ line() = NL; r3(one)\ enddef$$
$$r3(line)$$

program 5.12

Now I can define the square procedure. Program 5.13 has the same effect as program 5.8. *Square*('+') prints a square of plus signs, *square*('@') a square of at signs, *square*('*') a square of asterisks, *square*(' ') a square of spaces.

$$def\ square(c) = def\ r3(p) = p(); p(); p()\ enddef$$
$$def\ one() = printchar(c)\ enddef$$
$$def\ line() = NL; r3(one)\ enddef$$
$$r3(line)$$
$$enddef$$
$$square('*')$$

program 5.13

-=-=-=-=-=-=-=-=-=-=-=-

Exercise 5.14
What would be printed by *square*('+') if the definition of *one* in program 5.13 was altered to read *def one*() = *printchar*('c') *enddef*?

Exercise 5.15
By substituting procedure bodies for procedure-calling instructions, prove that the procedure call *square*('x') is equivalent to the program

$$NL; printchar('x'); printchar('x'); printchar('x');$$
$$NL; printchar('x'); printchar('x'); printchar('x');$$
$$NL; printchar('x'); printchar('x'); printchar('x')$$

-=-=-=-=-=-=-=-=-=-=-=-

5.6 MORE ON ENVIRONMENT DIAGRAMS

So far I have described two ways in which an environment can be created. An environment is created when the procedure definitions within a program are

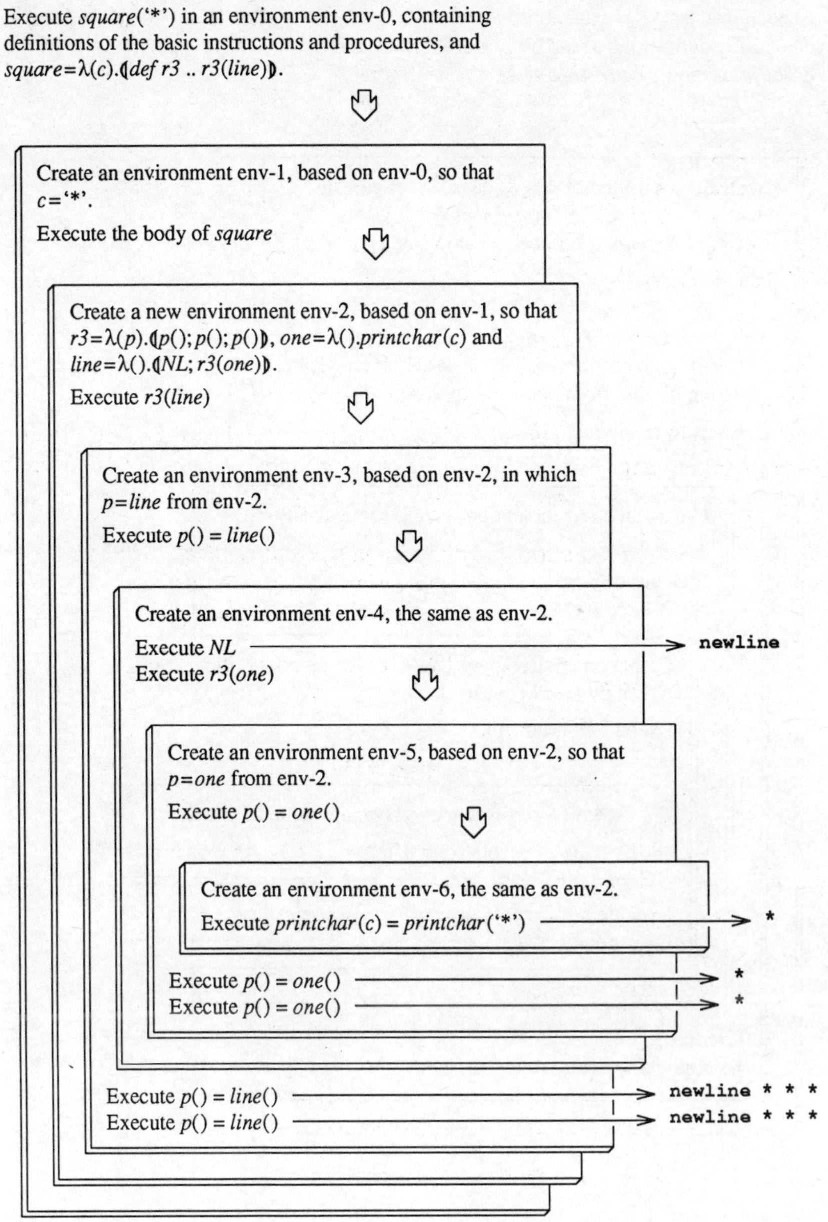

Execute *square*('*') in an environment env-0, containing definitions of the basic instructions and procedures, and *square*=λ(*c*).《*def r3* .. *r3*(*line*)》.

Create an environment env-1, based on env-0, so that *c*='*'.

Execute the body of *square*

Create a new environment env-2, based on env-1, so that *r3*=λ(*p*).《*p*(); *p*(); *p*()》, *one*=λ().*printchar*(*c*) and *line*=λ().《*NL*; *r3*(*one*)》.

Execute *r3*(*line*)

Create an environment env-3, based on env-2, in which *p*=*line* from env-2.

Execute *p*() = *line*()

Create an environment env-4, the same as env-2.

Execute *NL* ⟶ **newline**

Execute *r3*(*one*)

Create an environment env-5, based on env-2, so that *p*=*one* from env-2.

Execute *p*() = *one*()

Create an environment env-6, the same as env-2.

Execute *printchar*(*c*) = *printchar*('*') ⟶ *

Execute *p*() = *one*() ⟶ *
Execute *p*() = *one*() ⟶ *

Execute *p*() = *line*() ⟶ **newline** * * *
Execute *p*() = *line*() ⟶ **newline** * * *

figure 5.2

Execute *square*('*') in an environment env-0,
containing definitions of the basic instructions and
procedures, and *square*=λ(*c*).⟨*def r3* .. *r3*(*line*)⟩.

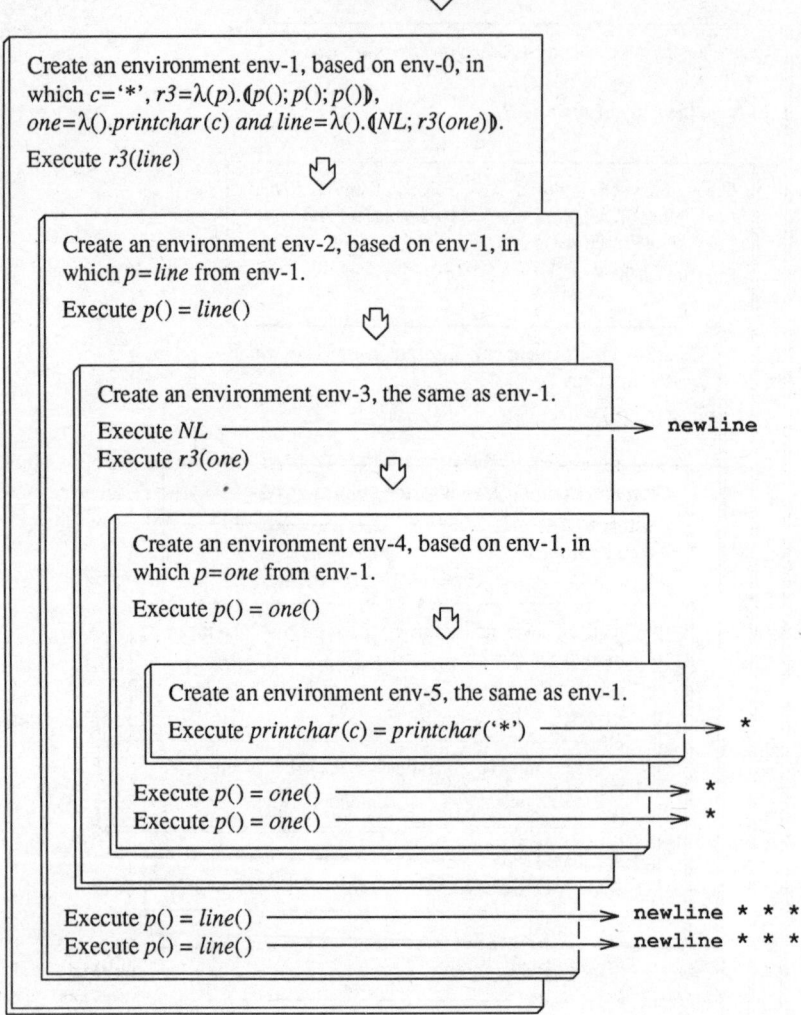

figure 5.3

executed; an environment is created when a procedure is called. Calling procedure *square* in program 5.12 causes both of these things to happen, one after the other, as illustrated in figure 5.2.

The diagram follows the execution explanation precisely, and is all very well as it stands, but it is unnecessarily precise in making a distinction between environments env-2 and env-1. Env-1 is created by the procedure call *square*('*'), which provides the meaning '*' for *c*. Execution of the body of *square* in env-1 immediately creates env-2 by adding meanings of *r3*, *one* and *line*. The instructions of *square* are executed within env-2; once they terminate env-2 is discarded and then env-1 is immediately discarded as well.

A simplified environment diagram of the same execution, shown in figure 5.3, glosses over the distinction between the environment created on procedure call and the one created by execution of definitions within a procedure body. This is a worthwhile simplification and in future diagrams I shall adopt the convention illustrated in figure 5.3.

5.7 FREE, BOUND AND BINDING OCCURRENCES

So far I have used the word **parameter** rather loosely as a description of a place-holder in a formula: that is, a name whose meaning isn't fixed or defined by some other part of the formula. In the execution explanation the meanings of parameters must be found in the environment. In the substitution explanation parameter names can be replaced by some other formula. In chapter 3 I discussed whether a program was complete and self-supporting or not, which is clearly a question of whether or not every name in the program has a definition. It is time to make these distinctions more definite and more precise, so that I can describe how to carry out substitutions on every program no matter how complicated its structure.

In computer science we say that a name for which no definition is provided within a formula is *free* within that formula. Names which are defined by a formula are **bound**. Every occurrence of a name is either free, bound or **binding** - the last reserved for occurrences of names used to define their meaning. Free names have been called 'parameters' in the informal discussions so far. The idea is that by substitution the bound and binding occurrences of names can be entirely eliminated, but the free occurrences will remain. Consider an example from ordinary algebra:

$$x \times y \ where \ y = 7$$

This formula contains three obvious names (*x*, *y* and 7) and three symbols which I shall treat as punctuation (*where*, ×, =). Only *y* is given a meaning within the formula. Therefore *x* and 7 are free. The whole formula is equivalent to *x*×7, making a substitution to eliminate the bound name *y*. The first occurrence of *y* in this formula is a bound occurrence - one that is given meaning by the definition - and the second is a binding occurrence - one that gives meaning.

One important distinction between free occurrences on the one hand, and bound and binding occurrences on the other, is that you can always rewrite a formula changing the bound and binding occurrences. For example, the formula above could be rewritten as

$$x \times z \ where \ z=7$$

and its meaning would be unchanged. It's still equivalent to $x \times 7$.

If you change one of the bound occurrences of a name, you must make the same change to its binding occurrence and all the other occurrences it binds because they are all bound together. The example formula is *not* equivalent to

$$x \times z \ where \ y=7$$

nor is it equivalent to

$$x \times y \ where \ z=7$$

You can't change the free occurrences in a formula at all or you change the meaning of the formula. For example,

$$z \times y \ where \ y=7$$

doesn't have the same meaning as the original formula above. This one means $z \times 7$.

If you want to rewrite a formula, altering the bound names, you don't have an absolutely free choice in choosing a new bound name. You can't change a bound name to be the same as a free name. For example, the formula

$$x \times x \ where \ x=7$$

is not a valid rewriting of the original formula: this one has the constant value 49. In general it is best to pick a new name which isn't used anywhere else in the formula you are rewriting: then nothing can go wrong.

A name which is free in a formula may be bound in an enclosing formula. For example, x is bound in the formula

$$(x \times y \ where \ y=7) \ where \ x=2$$

The first occurrence of x is bound; its binding occurrence is the second one. The first occurrence of y is bound by the second occurrence of y. But the formula in brackets is just the one which I have already discussed and x is free in that formula. Only 2 and 7 are free in the whole formula and since they are constant names the value of the whole formula is fixed: it is 2×7, which is 14.

A name may have more than one binding occurrence in a single formula. For example:

$$(x \times y \ where \ y=7) + (x/y \ where \ y=2)$$

This formula is evidently equivalent to $(x \times 7)+(x/2)$. The brackets control the range or *scope* of the definitions of y so that it can have two separate meanings in one single formula. Program brackets '$($ $)$' have the same function in program texts.

A name may be bound more than once in formulas which enclose one another. For example:

$$(x \times y \text{ where } y{=}7){+}y \text{ where } y{=}2$$

This formula is equivalent to $x \times 7{+}2$. The bracketed formula can be rewritten in various ways, but in particular as $x \times 7$ or as $(x \times z \text{ where } z{=}7)$, and neither of these forms takes any account of y, which shows that the first and second occurrences of y aren't bound by the fourth.

The meaning of y in the examples above is given by a constant formula, but that isn't an essential feature. For example:

$$x \times y \text{ where } y{=}z{+}t$$

This formula is equivalent to $x \times (z{+}t)$, again making the obvious substitution to eliminate y. The name y is bound in this formula despite the fact that its definition is given in terms of another formula which contains free names. To find the value of this formula you have to find the values of the free names x, z and t.

Enough of examples based on non-programs! Consider the following program:

$$def\ a() = printchar(b); printchar(b)\ enddef$$
$$a(); a()$$

program 5.14

Three names occur in this program: a, b and *printchar*. *Printchar* is a constant name, so the program doesn't have to explain it; a is bound by the procedure definition; b is free, and a meaning must be provided for it whenever the program is executed. If you execute program 5.14 in an environment in which b means '+' you get four plus signs; in an environment in which b means '*' you get four asterisks. Giving a meaning to free names makes a program complete, means that we can execute it.

But suppose that you execute program 5.14 in an environment in which b means '+' and a means "***". Does the meaning given to a by the environment make any difference? The answer is surely: No, it doesn't make any difference. The program can be rewritten so that the name a is removed - changing it to X, for example, to produce program 5.15 - and therefore the meaning of the program can't be affected by the meaning of a in the environment.

$$def\ X() = printchar(b); printchar(b)\ enddef$$
$$X(); X()$$

program 5.15

$$(\lambda().\langle\!| printchar(b); printchar(b) |\!\rangle)(); (\lambda().\langle\!| printchar(b); printchar(b) |\!\rangle)()$$

program 5.16

Another way of rewriting program 5.14 is to replace a by the formula $\lambda().\langle\!| printchar(b); printchar(b) |\!\rangle$, changing the program body into program 5.16.

This formula also makes no mention of a. All three versions of the program convert according to normal substitution rules into

$$printchar(b); printchar(b); printchar(b); printchar(b)$$

Parameter names are bound in the body of a procedure definition. For example, in the procedure definition

$$def\, x(a) = y(a); printchar(a)\ enddef$$

there are four names: x, a, y and *printchar*. As always *printchar* is a constant name; the only occurrence of x is a binding occurrence; y is free. Concentrate on the name a: the first occurrence is a binding occurrence which makes it clear that a is a parameter name of the program which follows; the other two occurrences of a are bound by the first. The effect of an execution of this procedure is determined not by the meaning of the name a in its environment but instead by the argument formula which is provided in the procedure call.

In my notation names become bound when they are introduced as procedure or parameter names[†]. That is, if a program defines procedures $N_1, N_2, .., N_m$:

$$def\, N_1\ ..\ enddef\, def\, N_2\ ..\ enddef\, ..\ def\, N_m\ ..\ enddef$$
$$S_1; S_2; ..; S_n$$

then the names N_1, N_2, .., N_m are bound in that program. If a procedure definition or a procedure formula introduces parameter names $p_1, p_2, .., p_k$:

$$def\, N(p_1, p_2, .., p_k) = program\ enddef$$
$$\text{or}$$
$$\lambda(p_1, p_2, .., p_k).program$$

then the names $p_1, p_2, .., p_k$ are bound in the body of that procedure (and note that the name N is bound as well because of the earlier rule).

-=-=-=-=-=-=-=-=-=-=-=-

Exercise 5.16
Which names are free in each of the following formulas?
> 1. $printchar(c)$
> 2. $printchar('c')$
> 3. $printstring(\text{"printchar"})$
> 4. x
> 5. $x()$
> 6. $x(a)$
> 7. $x(a, b, x)$

Exercise 5.17
Which names are free in the following formulas?
> 1. $def\, q(c) = printchar(c)\ enddef$

[†]   There are other ways of binding names, which will be introduced in Part Two and Part Four.

$$2.\ def\ r(c) = printchar(`c`)\ enddef$$
$$3.\ (\!(\ def\ p() = r3(x)\ enddef$$
$$def\ x() = r3(y)\ enddef$$
$$r3(p); r3(c)$$
$$)\!)$$

Exercise 5.18

For each occurrence of the name x in the following formulas, say whether it is free, bound, binding or some other sort of occurrence; in the case of bound occurrences indicate the binding occurrence.

$$1.\ x$$
$$2.\ def\ r(x) = printchar(x)\ enddef$$
$$3.\ def\ x(y) = printchar(y)\ enddef$$
$$4.\ (\!(\ def\ a(x) = def\ r(x) = printchar(x)\ enddef$$
$$NL; r(x)$$
$$enddef$$
$$def\ b(c) = printchar(c); printchar(x)\ enddef$$
$$a(`x`); a(x)$$
$$)\!)$$

-=-=-=-=-=-=-=-=-=-=-=-

5.8 DEFINITIONS WITHIN DEFINITIONS (1)

Consider program 5.17, which prints a line of three asterisks. It has no free names except *printchar*, *NL* and '*', which are all constants. Names are bound in this program at four levels: in the program itself *pat* is bound; in the definition of *pat* the name c is bound; the body of *pat* is a program in which *r3* and x are bound; in the definition of *r3*, p is bound.

$$def\ pat(c) = def\ r3(p) = p(); p(); p()\ enddef$$
$$def\ x() = printchar(c)\ enddef$$
$$NL; r3(x)$$
$$enddef$$
$$pat(`*`)$$

program 5.17

The definition of *r3* binds p, but of course that definition can be rewritten to use any parameter name we wish. Suppose that it is rewritten using the name c to give program 5.18. This program is more confusing to read than program 5.17, just because of its multiple use of the name c. Confusing programs are bad programs, but not necessarily meaningless programs. Is this particular bad program meaningless? Certainly not, and clearly this program must have the same meaning as program 5.17 because one definition of *r3* has been replaced by

$$def\,pat(c) = def\,r3(c) = c(); c(); c()\ enddef$$
$$def\,x() = printchar(c)\ enddef$$
$$NL; r3(x)$$

.   *enddef*

pat('')*

program 5.18

another which has identical meaning.

-=-=-=-=-=-=-=-=-=-=-=-

Exercise 5.19

Show by drawing environment diagrams that programs 5.17 and 5.18 have identical effect. [Hint: be sure that the environment created when *r3* is called is the same as the one in which it was defined, except that *c* has the meaning given by the argument formula.]

-=-=-=-=-=-=-=-=-=-=-=-

Exercise 5.19 shows that the execution explanation has no difficulty when bound names are altered. What about the substitution explanation? Definition 4.1 talks about 'replacing every occurrence' of the parameter name in the procedure body by the argument formula. If you made such a substitution for the procedure call *pat('*')* in program 5.18 you would produce a nonsense program. In particular part of that program would be the nonsense definition

$$def\,r3('*') = '*'(); '*'(); '*'()\ enddef$$

which is not at all what is required.

The solution is to alter definition 4.1. It should read:

> A procedure-calling instruction is equivalent to a copy of the body of the procedure definition in which each free occurrence of each parameter name has been replaced by the corresponding argument formula.

definition 5.1

Only *free* occurrences are to be replaced: this makes sense because all other occurrences are either binding, giving a new meaning to the parameter name for a portion of the procedure body, or bound, given a meaning by a binding occurrence elsewhere in the procedure body.

The body of *pat* in program 5.18 is the program

$$def\,r3(c) = c(); c(); c()\ enddef$$
$$def\,x() = printchar(c)\ enddef$$
$$NL; r3(x)$$

In this program the first occurrence of *c* is a binding occurrence which binds the next three: none of these four occurrences of *c* is free. The fifth occurrence is

free, however, and according to definition 5.1 it should be replaced by '*' to find
the meaning of the procedure call pat('*'). The result is the program

$$def\ r3(c) = c(); c(); c()\ enddef$$
$$def\ x() = printchar('*')$$
$$NL; r3(x)$$

Replacing procedure calls by suitably modified procedure bodies, this converts
into

$$NL; printchar('*'); printchar('*'); printchar('*')$$

which is as it should be.

5.9 DEFINITIONS WITHIN DEFINITIONS (2)

Consider program 5.19, another variation on program 5.17. This time the
definition of *pat* is written within a definition of a new procedure *p1*. Despite this
alteration, program 5.19 has the same effect as programs 5.17 and 5.18.

$$def\ p1(a) =$$
$$def\ pat(c) = def\ r3(p) = p(); p(); p()\ enddef$$
$$def\ x() = printchar(c)\ enddef$$
$$NL; r3(x)$$
$$enddef$$
$$pat(a)$$
$$enddef$$
$$p1('*')$$

program 5.19

When formulas are substituted for names in program 5.19 there can be only one
result when all the bound names have been eliminated. That result must be the
formula

$$NL; printchar('*'); printchar('*'); printchar('*')$$

as the following exercises show.

-=-=-=-=-=-=-=-=-=-=-=-=-

Exercise 5.20
Take program 5.19 and replace procedure calls by procedure bodies in the
following order: first calls of *p1*, then calls of *pat*, then calls of *r3* and finally
calls of *x*.

Exercise 5.21
Substitute formulas for names in program 5.19 in the order *x*, *r3*, *pat*, *p1*. [Hint: *x*
can be replaced by the formula $\lambda().printchar(c)$.]

Exercise 5.22
Repeat exercise 5.21 with another order of substitution.

-=-=-=-=-=-=-=-=-=-=-=-

Substitution works on the principle of replacing one formula with an equal formula and it is essential that the original and the modified program should always produce the same effect. My rules must be worded so that the order in which substitutions are made doesn't affect the final result. Your answers to the exercises above show that for some programs any order of substitution will give the same answer: now I must show that *any* order of substitution in *any* program will do. It turns out that the substitution rules need refinement if they are to cope with some extreme examples. Consider, for example, program 5.20, which is just program 5.19 rewritten so that the parameter name a is changed to x.

$$def\,p1(x) =$$
$$def\,pat(c) = def\,r3(p) = p();p();p()\;enddef$$
$$def\,x() = printchar(c)\;enddef$$
$$NL; r3(x)$$
$$enddef$$
$$pat(x)$$
$$enddef$$
$$p1(\text{`*'})$$

program 5.20

-=-=-=-=-=-=-=-=-=-=-=-

Exercise 5.23
Replace procedure call by procedure body in program 5.20 in the order $r3$, x, *pat*, *p1* and show that the result is the sequence $NL; printchar(\text{`*'})$; $printchar(\text{`*'}); printchar(\text{`*'})$

-=-=-=-=-=-=-=-=-=-=-=-

Exercise 5.23 shows that with at least one order of substitution you can produce the same answer as before. But for this example it appears that order of substitution does matter. In particular if I first replace the call on procedure *pat* in the body of procedure *p1* I get the nonsense program 5.21. This is the wrong answer because the argument to *printchar*, which was originally c and was free in

$$def\,p1(x) = def\,r3(p) = p();p();p()\;enddef$$
$$def\,x() = printchar(x)\;enddef$$
$$NL; r3(x)$$
$$enddef$$
$$p1(\text{`*'})$$

program 5.21

the program '*def r3* .. *r3(x)*', has been replaced by *x*, which is bound by a definition in that program!

This sort of problem often occurs when there is more than one binding occurrence of a name. In program 5.21 a free occurrence of *c* in the body of procedure *pat* has been replaced by a formula *x* which includes names that are bound by that same body. The *x* in the substituted formula should not be associated with the *x* in the procedure body: they have different binding occurrences but the substitution hasn't taken this into account.

To avoid the problem I need a new rule:

> A formula *F* may be substituted into a formula (for example, a program) *P* only when *P* does not bind any of the names in *F*.

definition 5.2

This rule makes it clear that I can't substitute *x* for the parameter name *c* in program 5.20. There are two strategies I can follow to solve the problem: I can change the argument formula so that it isn't the name *x*; or I can change the body of *pat* so that it doesn't bind *x*. I can change the argument formula in two ways: because it is a bound occurrence I might change it and its binding occurrence to *a*, say, thus regenerating program 5.19; or I might eliminate it by substituting for the call of procedure *p1*, producing program 5.22. Using the other strategy, I can change the body of *pat* if I replace the binding and all bound occurrences of *x* by *z*, say, producing program 5.23.

$$def\, pat(c) = def\, r3(p) = p(); p(); p()\ enddef$$
$$def\, x() = printchar(c)\ enddef$$
$$NL; r3(x)$$
$$enddef$$
$$pat('*')$$

program 5.22

$$def\, p1(x) = def\, pat(c) = def\, r3(p) = p(); p(); p()\ enddef$$
$$def\, z() = printchar(c)\ enddef$$
$$NL; r3(z)$$
$$enddef$$
$$pat(x)$$
$$enddef$$
$$p1('*')$$

program 5.23

In general, then, when a formula *F* cannot be substituted into a program *P* because *P* binds some of the names in *F*, there are three possible courses of action, set out in definition 5.3. Any of the three solutions shown in definition 5.3 will work. Which you pick is a matter of taste and convenience. For

(a) Simplify F by substitution so that it doesn't contain the offending name, by replacing that name with a formula describing its meaning.

(b) Change the names in the program which includes F so that F contains a different name.

(c) Rename P so as to change the offending bound name before making the replacement. Choose a new name t and replace the binding and every bound occurrence in P of the offending name by t.

definition 5.3

example, in program 5.20 the argument formula x could be converted into the formula '*', following rule (a) from definition 5.3. Alternatively, the parameter name of $p1$ could be changed to a or b or $hello$, following rule (b). Or perhaps every occurrence of x in the definition of pat could be changed to z, following rule (c). Any of these modifications would produce a program in which argument formula may be freely substituted for parameter name.

-=-=-=-=-=-=-=-=-=-=-=-=-

Exercise 5.24
Supposing that $printnum(F)$ prints the numerical value of F and that + and × indicate addition and multiplication, what will be printed by the following program if x means 2 and y means 3? Justify your answer by substituting formula for name until you produce a single *printnumber* instruction.

$$def\ triple(y) = def\ thrice(x) = printnum(3 \times x)\ enddef$$
$$def\ x() = thrice(y)$$
$$r3(x)$$
$$enddef$$
$$triple(x+y)$$

[Hint: don't forget to use bracketing, where necessary, during substitution.]

Exercise 5.25
In your answer to exercise 5.24 you used one of the techniques a, b or c from definition 5.3. Repeat the exercise twice more using each of the other techniques.

-=-=-=-=-=-=-=-=-=-=-=-=-

5.10 EXECUTIONS VERSUS SUBSTITUTIONS

The environment diagram explanation requires that it is the *value* of an argument formula which is provided to help create the environment of a procedure execution. The substitution explanation just deals with the replacement of names by equal formulas and, since the name and the formula have the same meaning, the order of substitution doesn't matter.

The execution explanation corresponds to substitution performed in a particular order: always replace the names in an argument formula by their meanings, and continue to do so until you have calculated a constant formula (the argument value); then replace the parameter name by that constant formula. There is a theorem in the lambda-calculus which states that, provided the substitution terminates, you always get the same answer as you would with any other order of substitution. Proof, or indeed any further explanation, is outside the scope of this book.

The problems discussed (and solved) in this chapter all come about because of the multiple use of names within programs; because a single name, at different points of the text or at different times during an execution, can have different meanings. You might think you would be able to avoid these problems by carefully choosing the names you use, but that's not so. The programming mechanisms of recursion and of assignment, introduced in the next part of this book, make them real problems whatever you do.

5.11 UNPACKING DEFINITIONS

It is usually possible to *unpack* programs which have definitions within definitions so that the program has just a single-level set of definitions, as the *pattern* procedure of program 3.27 was unpacked to produce program 3.28.

It isn't always so easy to unpack a program. For example, consider program 5.13. Execution of that program relies on the fact that an execution of *square* creates an environment in which the name c has a meaning and the fact that the procedure *one* is defined in that environment. Figures 5.2 and 5.3 make it clear what is going on. The body of procedure *one* refers to *printchar* and to c; c is not a constant so that in any execution of *one* a meaning must be provided for c; the environment created by a call of procedure *one* is based on the environment in which it is defined; since c is defined in that environment all is well.

$$def\ r3(p) = p();\ p();\ p()\ enddef$$
$$def\ one() = printchar(c)\ enddef$$
$$def\ line() = NL;\ r3(one)\ enddef$$
$$def\ square(c) = r3(line)\ enddef$$
$$square('*')$$

program 5.24

Consider program 5.24, which is a faulty atttempt to unpack program 5.13. Substituting the body of procedure *square* for the calling instruction *square*('*') in this program shows immediately that it doesn't have the right meaning: *square*('*') is replaced by *r3(line)*: but *square*('+') would produce the same result, as would *square*('@'), as would any other call of *square* no matter what

Create an environment env-0, in which
$r3 = \lambda(p).(p(); p(); p())$, $one = \lambda().printchar(c)$,
$line = \lambda().(NL; r3(one))$ and $square = \lambda(c).r3(line)$

Execute $square('*')$

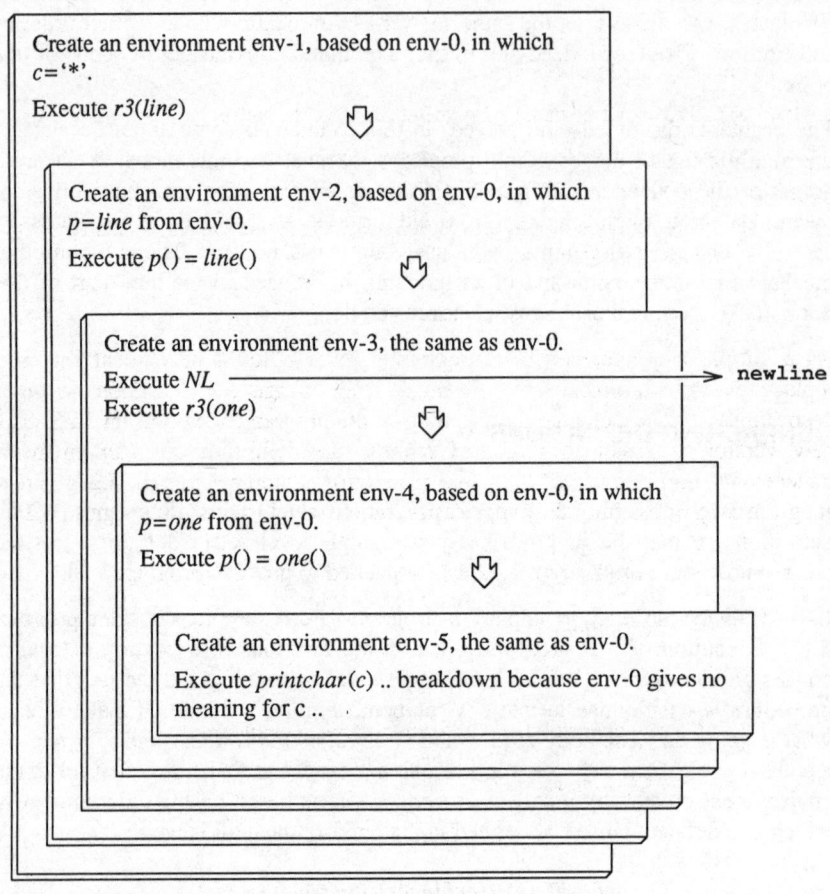

Create an environment env-1, based on env-0, in which
$c = '*'$.

Execute $r3(line)$

> Create an environment env-2, based on env-0, in which
> $p = line$ from env-0.
>
> Execute $p() = line()$
>
> > Create an environment env-3, the same as env-0.
> >
> > Execute NL ─────────────────────────────► newline
> > Execute $r3(one)$
> >
> > > Create an environment env-4, based on env-0, in which
> > > $p = one$ from env-0.
> > >
> > > Execute $p() = one()$
> > >
> > > > Create an environment env-5, the same as env-0.
> > > >
> > > > Execute $printchar(c)$ .. breakdown because env-0 gives no
> > > > meaning for c ..

figure 5.4

the argument formula. The best that can be done with this program is to reduce it
to

$$NL; printchar(c); printchar(c); printchar(c);$$
$$NL; printchar(c); printchar(c); printchar(c);$$
$$NL; printchar(c); printchar(c); printchar(c);$$

Evidently program 5.24 isn't complete without a definition of c. Exactly the
same defect shows up in the environment diagram, shown in figure 5.4: execution
reaches the point where a meaning of c is required, and it can't proceed any
further without one.

When unpacking programs like 5.13 there is a uniform technique which solves the problem. If an enclosed procedure (such as *one*) has a free occurrence of a name (such as *c*) which is bound in the enclosing definition but is not the procedure name in a *def* definition, then proceed as described in definition 5.4, which converts the program into one in which only defined procedure names are free.

    To unpack procedure definitions:

    (a) make every free name a parameter of the procedure;

    (b) include values for every free name as arguments in every call to that procedure;

    (c) when the value of that procedure is passed as an argument, include the values of the free names as well.

definition 5.4

As a simple example, consider program 5.25. It should be evident that if I replace every call *inner*() with *inner*(*x*) and change the definition of *inner* accordingly, I do not change the meaning of the program: see program 5.26. The new version is easier to read if I rename the definition of *inner* to avoid unnecessary multiple use of the name *x*: see, for example, program 5.27. Either program 5.26 or program 5.27 may easily be unpacked to produce program 5.28.

$$def\ outer(x) = def\ inner() = r3(x)\ enddef$$
$$inner();\ inner()$$
$$enddef$$

program 5.25

$$def\ outer(x) = def\ inner(x) = r3(x)\ enddef$$
$$inner(x);\ inner(x)$$
$$enddef$$

program 5.26

$$def\ outer(x) = def\ inner(y) = r3(y)\ enddef$$
$$inner(x);\ inner(x)$$
$$enddef$$

program 5.27

$$def\ outer(x) = inner(x);\ inner(x)\ enddef$$
$$def\ inner(y) = r3(y)\ enddef$$

program 5.28

-=-=-=-=-=-=-=-=-=-=-

Exercise 5.26
Unpack the program

$$def\,X(a,b,c) = def\,U() = p(a); p(a)\ enddef$$
$$def\,V() = b(); b()\ enddef$$
$$def\,W() = c(a); c(b)\ enddef$$
$$U(); V(); U(); U(); W()$$
$$enddef$$

Be sure that none of the procedure definitions in your answer has free occurrences of *a*, *b* or *c*.

Exercise 5.27
Unpack the following program so that it includes only a single-level set of procedure definitions:

$$def\,A(x) = def\,B(y) = x(y)\ enddef$$
$$def\,C(z) = def\,D() = z(x)\ enddef$$
$$D(); D()$$
$$enddef$$
$$B(x); C(x)$$
$$enddef$$

-=-=-=-=-=-=-=-=-=-=-=-

Unpacking program 5.13 is a little more tricky than the examples above, but it can be carried out as follows. First, the definition of *one* must be changed to

$$def\,one(c) = printchar(c)\ enddef$$

- a definition in which only *printchar* occurs free. *One* is actually called from *r3*, so it is necessary to redefine *r3* also. To avoid confusion I define a new procedure *r3c*:

$$def\,r3c(p) = p(c); p(c); p(c)$$

- but this also has free occurrences of *c* so it also must be changed to:

$$def\,r3c(p,c) = p(c); p(c); p(c)$$

Now the call of *r3* in *line* can be changed to *r3c(one, c)* - but this makes *c* occur free in *line* so that also must be redefined:

$$def\,line(c) = NL; r3c(one, c)\ enddef$$

(notice that although *r3c* occurs free in this definition, that is ok because it is bound by a *def* definition).

Next, I change *r3(line)* inside procedure *square* to *r3c(line, c)*. This produces program 5.29 - a program which can be unpacked without difficulty. The definition of *r3* is redundant in this program and can be deleted, thus finally producing program 5.30.

$$def\ square(c) = def\ r3(p) = p();p();p()\ enddef$$
$$def\ one(c) = printchar(c)\ enddef$$
$$def\ r3c(p,c) = p(c);p(c);p(c)\ enddef$$
$$def\ line(c) = NL;r3c(one,c)\ enddef$$
$$r3c(line,c)$$
$$enddef$$
$$square('*')$$

program 5.29

$$def\ r3c(p,c) = p(c);p(c);p(c)\ enddef$$
$$def\ one(c) = printchar(c)\ enddef$$
$$def\ line(c) = NL;r3c(one,c)\ enddef$$
$$def\ square(c) = r3c(line,c)\ enddef$$
$$square('*')$$

program 5.30

Notice that in program 5.30 the free names in procedure bodies are either constants or procedure names defined by *def* elsewhere in the program. The aim of unpacking a program is to produce a text in which there is a single level of procedure definition, in which each procedure call will produce an extension of the single environment in which the meanings of all the procedure names are defined.

-=-=-=-=-=-=-=-=-=-=-=-

Exercise 5.28
Draw execution diagrams of programs 5.29 and 5.30: hence show that these programs are equivalent to program 5.13.

Exercise 5.29
Show by substitution that programs 5.13, 5.29 and 5.30 are equivalent.

-=-=-=-=-=-=-=-=-=-=-=-

Why not change the explanation?

My response to the difficulty introduced by program 5.24 and illustrated in figure 5.4 is to show how programs can be rewritten so that they can be unpacked. An alternative response would be to change our ideas about what programs mean: that is, to change the substitution and execution explanations. In one alternative execution explanation, sometimes used as the basis of real-world programming systems, a procedure call creates an environment based on the one in which the procedure call is made. I reject that explanation for two reasons: first because it makes a substitution explanation difficult; second because it makes a distinction between programs which I want to define as equal. Specifically, it requires that $\lambda(x).p(x)$ and $\lambda(y).p(y)$ are formulas with *different* meanings, as the exercises below demonstrate.

-=-=-=-=-=-=-=-=-=-=-=-=-

Exercise 5.30
By drawing environment diagrams in which the environment created on procedure call is based on the one in which the call is made, show that under this explanation programs 5.13 and 5.24 have identical effect.

Exercise 5.31
Repeat exercise 5.30 after replacing the definition of *r3* in programs 5.13 and 5.24 by *def r3(c) = c(); c(); c() enddef.* Show that this time the alternative execution explanation makes the programs meaningless.

Exercise 5.32
Repeat exercise 5.31, this time with the definition *def r3(one) = one(); one(); one() enddef.*

-=-=-=-=-=-=-=-=-=-=-=-=-

Why nest definitions?

Nested definitions enable us to make packages of sets of definitions and to parameterise them in a simple way. Program 5.13 packages the things which have to do with making squares made up of a character *c* and provides the name *square* for the package. Perhaps *r3* doesn't belong in the package - it has nothing to do with squares - but both *line* and *one* certainly do. Program 5.30, though it has the same effect, isn't so nicely put together.

Programs which package together related parts and hide them from the rest of the program are easier to understand than programs which don't, just because they come apart into relatively independent pieces. It is always possible to unpack definitions in order to satisfy an unhelpful programming system, but it isn't a good idea to do so otherwise.

Part Two
STRUCTURED INSTRUCTIONS

The programs of Part One all describe straightforward sequences. Programs would be very boring if they always executed exactly the same instructions in the same order. This part introduces the *structured instructions* which allow repetition and choice to be introduced into programs. It contains a great deal of information, giving both execution and substitution definitions of the meaning of each new instruction. Some of the explanations may seem rather arbitrarily chosen, but the examples in Parts Three and Four will justify those choices.

The first instructions described are the *counting repetition* instructions: instructions which require the repetition of some program a fixed number of times, perhaps while systematically varying a parameter. The next structures are the *choice* instructions, which allow a program to decide between courses of action depending on circumstances. Both of these kinds of instructions have fairly straightforward substitution and execution definitions.

Next come the *assignment* instructions, which are structure-breakers. They allow a program to alter the state of affairs as it executes so as to affect the future calculation of the value of formulas. They have a deceptively simple execution definition and a rather long-winded substitution definition. It is essential to understand them before moving on to understand *unlimited repetition* instructions, which allow repeated execution of some program until the state of affairs has changed in some prescribed way.

Last of all come the *termination* instructions, which allow a sequence to stop execution before it reaches its normal end. They fit reasonably well with other structured instructions, bending the structure of a program a little but not destroying it.

As soon as you get away from the simplest sequences it is easy to design a program which has an infinite range of behaviours, or at least one which has such an enormous range that it is impossible to try it out in every circumstance. The reasoning introduced in Part One, based on substitution of one formula for another, is used in this Part to allow *proof by induction* of some programs. This technique allows you to make finite proofs about infinite sets of procedure executions, and thus to build up confidence that the programs and procedure definitions you write will have the effect you want them to have.

Chapter 6
COUNTING REPETITION

Chapter 4 introduced the abstraction of three-times repetition, via a particular procedure definition. That is ingenious but it is by no means the most general abstraction of repetition. This chapter introduces two more general abstractions: repetition a fixed number of times and repetition a fixed number of times with a parameter.

6.1 TWO AUXILIARY DEFINITIONS

In order to be able to give definitions of structured instructions, I need some auxiliary definitions. The *donothing* instruction allows me to describe null executions and the *let* definition allows me to describe bindings of names to simple formulas.

The *donothing* instruction

The simplest instruction of all is *donothing*. It does absolutely nothing and it does it very quickly. Its execution definition is:

An execution of *donothing* has no effect upon anything and takes no time at all.

definition 6.1

You can include *donothing* in the middle of any sequence without affecting its meaning in any way. That fact is expressed by its substitution definition:

donothing; $X = X$; *donothing* = X

definition 6.2

This definition tells you that you can insert *donothing*s into a sequence or delete

152

them from a sequence whenever you like. The meaning of a sequence isn't affected by how many *donothing*s it contains.

The substitution definition of *donothing* is very like the algebraic definition of addition with zero:

$$0+x = x+0 = x$$

Donothing in programming notation is just as useful as zero in arithmetic or algebra.

The *let* definition

The *let* definition allows me to associate names with values in the same way that parameter names are associated with argument values, but without needing to write a procedure definition and a procedure call. For example, the program *printchar(c)* contains a free occurrence of *c*. If I write it as the body of a procedure definition and provide an argument formula which corresponds to *c* then I have made it into a complete program:

$$(\lambda(c).printchar(c))('+')$$

This program, according to the substitution rules of chapters 4 and 5, is equivalent to *printchar('+')*. But it is a very clumsy definition. Consider the alternative notation:

$$let\ c = '+'$$

$$printchar(c)$$

The intention is that this program also should be equivalent to *printchar('+')*. This is a consequence of the following substitution definition:

$$let\ x_1 = F_1\ ..\ let\ x_n = F_n\ P$$
$$= (\lambda(x_1, .., x_n).P)\ (F_1, .., F_n)$$

definition 6.3

Note some important consequences of this definition:

(a) the names $x_1..x_n$ are bound in the program P but not in the formulas $F_1..F_n$;

(b) the program can be rewritten without those definitions but with every free occurrence of the names x_i simultaneously replaced by the corresponding formula F_i;

(c) the order of *let* definitions in a program doesn't matter.

Point (c) is a consequence of simultaneous substitution: the program

$$let\ x=7\ let\ y=3\ printnumber(x+y)$$

is equivalent in every way to the program

$$let\ y=3\ let\ x=7\ \ printnumber(x+y)$$

Simultaneous substitution means that one *let* definition can't affect another. The program

$$let\ y=3\ let\ x=y+1\ \ printnumber(x+y)$$

is equivalent to *printnumber*$((y+1)+3)$. It is *not* in general equivalent to *printnumber*(7) unless $y=3$ in the enclosing environment. Note also that y occurs free in this program: the free occurrence of y in the second definition is not bound by the first definition.

Let definitions allow you to simplify a program by factoring out a frequently-occurring formula. You replace every occurrence of a particular formula F by a name x and include *let* $x = F$ in the program's definitions. Because such a definition does not bind x in the formula F, it is possible to write things like *let* $x=x-5$ which are meaningful but somewhat confusing. Consider, for example, the program:

$$let\ a=41$$
$$(\!|\ let\ a=a+1$$
$$printnumber(a)$$
$$|\!)$$

This program prints 42. To show this using definition 6.3, one possible order of substitution is:

$$let\ a=41\ (\!|\ let\ a=a+1\ printnumber(a)\ |\!)$$

$= let\ a=41\ (\!|\ printnumber(a+1)\ |\!)$ [by definition 6.3 in the inner program]

$= let\ a=41\ printnumber(a+1)$ [by definition 2.7]

$= printnumber(41+1)$ [by definition 6.3]

Another possible order is:

$$let\ a=41\ (\!|\ let\ a=a+1\ printnumber(a)\ |\!)$$

$= (\!|\ let\ a=41+1\ printnumber(a)\ |\!)$ [by definition 6.3 in the outer program]

$= (\!|\ printnumber(41+1)\ |\!)$ [by definition 6.3]

$= printnumber(41+1)$ [by definition 2.7]

If any of the names in the formula F of a *let* definition are bound in the program, then by definition 5.3 you can't make the substitution. When this happens, you must use one of the techniques described in definition 5.4 to eliminate the offending name from F or P. For example, program 6.1 also prints 42.

-=-=-=-=-=-=-=-=-=-=-=-=-

$$let\ a=13$$
$$(\ let\ b=a\times3$$
$$def\ a(x) = printnumber(x)\ enddef$$
$$a(b+3)$$
$$)$$

program 6.1

Exercise 6.1

Prove that program 6.1 really does print 42. Do it in two ways, using different techniques.

-=-=-=-=-=-=-=-=-=-=-=-

6.2 VERY SIMPLE REPETITION

Consider once again that old friend, a program which prints a three-by-three square of asterisks. The most straightforward program which does the job is a sequence:

NL; print*; print*; print*;
NL; print*; print*; print*;
NL; print*; print*; print*

program 6.2

You might object that by using *printstring*("***") you could produce a still simpler program, but please suspend that objection for a page or two.

The *r3* procedure of chapter 4 allowed a very neat solution to this particular problem:

$$r3(\lambda().(NL; r3(\lambda().print*)))$$

That solution is all very well, but it doesn't help me with the problem of printing squares of any other size - four-by-four or two-by-two or whatever. To provide different varieties of repetition I would have to write procedures which repeat twice, four times, five times, six times, and so on.

N-times repetition is such a useful and ubiquitous program structure that I need a notation which allows me to express it directly. My notation is the *times-do* instruction. It contains a number formula and a program formula. For example,

times 3 *do print* od

prints three asterisks. And

times 4 *do NL; print* od

prints a column of four asterisks. In general:

$$times\ F\ do\ P\ od$$

is an instruction which executes program *P* exactly *F* times. The *do* and *od* punctuation words bracket the program which is to be repeated.

Thus an alternative solution to the three-by-three square problem is program 6.3. But that program itself is a three-times repeated sequence, so it can be further contracted to program 6.4. Notice the nested bracketing of this example: the whole program is a three-times repetition of a sequence, which includes a three-times repetition of a single instruction.

NL; *times* 3 *do print* * *od*;
NL; *times* 3 *do print* * *od*;
NL; *times* 3 *do print* * *od*

program 6.3

times 3 *do*
        NL; *times* 3 *do print* * *od*
od

program 6.4

-=-=-=-=-=-=-=-=-=-=-=-=-

Exercise 6.2
Program 6.4 prints nine asterisks and three newlines which make a three-by-three square. How many asterisks and newlines are printed by the following instruction?

times 3 *do times* 3 *do print* *; *NL od od*

[Hint: draw boxes round the parts of the instruction to find what is repeated, and how many times it is repeated.] What shape of figure does this program print?

Exercise 6.3
Repeat exercise 6.2 with the program

times 3 *do times* 3 *do print* * *od od*; *NL*

Exercise 6.4
What do you think should be printed by the instruction *times* 0 *do print* * *od*?

-=-=-=-=-=-=-=-=-=-=-=-=-

Substitution definition of *times-do*

Definition 6.4 gives the meaning of *times-do* in terms of the number formula *F* and the program formula *P* which it contains. It gives three alternative meanings for the instruction. One meaning applies when the formula *F* delivers zero, the

$$times\ F\ do\ P\ od = \text{(when } F=0\text{)}\quad donothing$$
$$\text{(when } F>0\text{)}\quad P;\ times\ F{-}1\ do\ P\ od$$
$$\text{(when } F>0\text{)}\quad times\ F{-}1\ do\ P\ od;\ P$$

definition 6.4

others when it delivers a value greater than zero. The definition gives no meaning at all when F is negative, because *times* -3 *do print* od* can't possibly print a negative number of asterisks and *times* -6 *do p() od* can't create a negative number of procedure executions. Instructions with negative F are undefined: that is, they are silently defined to be meaningless.

At first it may seem that this definition doesn't tell you what a *times-do* means when F is greater than zero because it passes the buck: it gives the meaning in terms of a sequence containing another *times-do*. For example, it tells you that *times* 8 *do P od* is equivalent to P; *times* $8{-}1$ *do P od*. But that *times-do* has a formula F with a smaller value than the original instruction. You can repeat the same substitution, to give P; P; *times* $8{-}2$ *do P od*, and so on, converting each *times-do* into a sequence involving a smaller repetition, until you finally come up with a long sequence in which the only repetition is *times* $8{-}8$ *do P od*. That you can replace with *donothing*, which you can throw away according to definition 6.2. So in the end definition 6.4 really does tell you what *times F do P od* means, provided you know what F and P mean.

-=-=-=-=-=-=-=-=-=-=-

Exercise 6.5
According to definition 6.4, can a *times-do* instruction have a meaning even though F and P are both meaningless? Can it have a meaning when F has a meaning but P does not?

Exercise 6.6
If you answered 'yes' to either part of exercise 6.5, give an example instruction which proves that you are correct. Give the meaning of your example instruction, and check it against definition 6.4.

Exercise 6.7
Can a *times-do* be meaningless even though F and P are both meaningful? If your answer is 'yes', give an example which proves you correct.

-=-=-=-=-=-=-=-=-=-=-

The advantage of a formal definition like 6.4 is that it can be used to prove what a *times-do* instruction means by reducing it to a sequence of simpler instructions: **unrolling** the repetition in the terminology of chapter 1. For example, I can prove the extremely obvious equivalence

$$print*;\ print*;\ print* = times\ 3\ do\ print*\ od$$

The proof can be made by transforming either formula: I shall prove it by expanding the *times-do* instruction.

times 3 *do print* od*
= *print**; *times* 3−1 *do print* od*   [by definition 6.4]
= *print**; *times* 2 *do print* od*
= *print**; *print**; *times* 2−1 *do print* od*   [by definition 6.4 again]
= *print**; *print**; *times* 1 *do print* od*
= *print**; *print**; *print**; *times* 1−1 *do print* od* [by definition 6.4 a third time]
= *print**; *print**; *print**; *times* 0 *do print* od*
= *print**; *print**; *print**; *donothing*   [by definition 6.4 once more]
= *print**; *print**; *print**   [by definition 6.2]

Because the reasoning in this example uses substitution of equal formulas, it can be read equally well in reverse. In that direction it shows one way to convert *print**; *print**; *print** into *times* 3 *do print* od*.

-=-=-=-=-=-=-=-=-=-=-=-=-

Exercise 6.8
The derivation above used only the first and second lines of definition 6.4. Construct the proof which uses only the first and third lines of that definition.

Exercise 6.9
Repeat exercise 6.8, but this time make a proof which uses every line of definition 6.4.

Exercise 6.10
Prove the equivalence of programs 6.2 and 6.4.

Exercise 6.11
There are two ways to answer exercise 6.10, according to whether you treat the inner or the outer *times-do* instruction in program 6.4 first. Whichever way you did it, now do it the other way.

Exercise 6.12
You might have answered exercises 6.10 and 6.11 either by expanding program 6.4 or by contracting program 6.2. Whichever way you did it, now do it the other way. [Hint: very easy.]

Exercise 6.13
Use *times-do* in a program which prints a five-by-four rectangle:

```
*****
*****
*****
*****
```

In this program should the *times* 4 be inside the *times* 5 or vice-versa? Use definition 6.4 to check that you haven't made a mistake, by proving that your program executes exactly 4 *NL* instructions: that is, prove that your program is equivalent to

NL;.. some *print*s* ..;
NL;.. some *print*s* ..;
NL;.. some *print*s* ..;

$$NL;.. \text{ some } print*s ..;$$

-=-=-=-=-=-=-=-=-=-=-=-=-=-

Times-do and non-constant formulas

So far so good, but not yet good enough. The instruction *times* 3 *do P od* is not much more convenient than $(\lambda(q).(\!(q(); q(); q()))\!)(\lambda().P)$. Each repeats execution of program *P* three times, and to change either we must edit the instruction. But the *times-do* instruction includes a number formula and you might expect that we could play the usual tricks with the environment. For example, I might write the following:

> *times n do*
> *NL; times m do print* od*
> *od*

program 6.5

Now if this program is executed in an environment in which *n* and *m* each mean three, you get a three-by-three square. In an environment in which *n* means four and *m* means five, it prints the five-by-four rectangle of exercise 6.13. One easy way to find such an environment is to create it with a procedure call. I can define the procedure *rect* as follows:

> *def rect(n, m) = times n do*
> *NL; times m do print* od*
> *od*
> *enddef*

program 6.6

-=-=-=-=-=-=-=-=-=-=-=-=-=-

Exercise 6.14
Assuming the definition of *rect* from program 6.6, write a procedure call which produces the five-by-four rectangle of exercise 6.13. Does the 4 come before the 5 in the arguments or vice-versa? Check you haven't made a mistake by proving that your program executes exactly four *NL* instructions.

Exercise 6.15
Repeat exercise 6.14, but this time for a pattern which is a vertical line of four asterisks:

$$*$$
$$*$$
$$*$$
$$*$$

Exercise 6.16
Repeat exercise 6.14 again, this time for a pattern which is a horizontal line of
four asterisks:

$$****$$

-=-=-=-=-=-=-=-=-=-=-=-=-

6.3 LAYOUT AND PROGRAM STRUCTURE

Chapter 4 introduced you to the way that programs can be written with
definitions inside definitions. Once you start using structured instructions, of
which the *times-do* is only the first example, program structure can become quite
intricate.

Intricate structures can be understood - indeed can sometimes be easier to
understand than coarser structures - provided that they are properly presented to
the reader. In chapter 4 I was careful to lay out my program examples in such a
way that the parts of the program could be easily seen. For example, in the
following program

> *def pat(c) = def once() = printchar(c) enddef*
>   *def line() = NL; r3(once) enddef*
>
>   *r3(line)*
> *enddef*
> *pat('+'); pat('*'); pat(x)*

program 6.7

I have used blank lines to separate definitions from program body, blank space to
indent the program inside the definition of *pat* and lined up *enddef* with *def* when
a definition won't fit all on one line. Surely that version of the program is easier
to understand than this one:

> *def pat(c) = def once() = printchar(c)*
> *enddef def line() = NL;*
> *r3(once) enddef r3(line) enddef pat('+')*
> *; pat('*'); pat(x)*

program 6.8

The *times-do* introduces a new form of bracketing, to join (..), *def..enddef* and
(..). When you have a lot of brackets in a single formula it can easily get
confusing. Layout can help to clarify the program. Consider yet another
example, and compare program 6.9 with the more carefully-laid-out version
program 6.10.

times 2 do NL; times 40 do NL; times 20 do print* od od od

program 6.9

 times 2 do
  NL; times 40 do
   NL; times 20 do print* od
   od
 od

program 6.10

I prefer to lay my programs out so that I can draw a *rectangular* box round any instruction, and draw it in such a way that the box doesn't take in part of any other instruction. The same goes for the components of a structure: I want to be able to draw a rectangular box round each component so that the box doesn't take in part of any other component. For an example, see figure 6.1.

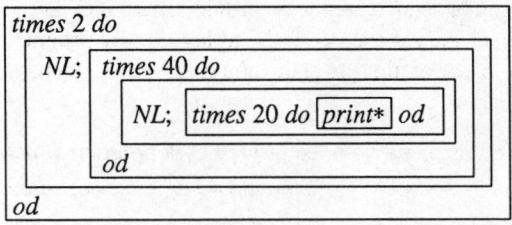

figure 6.1

Indentation is probably more important than bracketing in indicating the structure of a program to the eye. Bad indentation can be misleading, tending to make the reader believe that the structure of the program is what it isn't: for example, the first two lines in program 6.8 [†].

Preferences about layout are, in the end, a matter of taste. You may find that where you work or study there is a 'house style' which you are encouraged or compelled to follow. There may be several alternative styles. Whether or not you have a convention imposed on you, careful layout is an essential aid to clear thinking. It certainly helps you to answer questions like those which follow.

-=-=-=-=-=-=-=-=-=-=-=-

Exercise 6.17
There are several places where a *printspace* instruction might be inserted into program 6.10. For example, after the first *NL*; after the second *NL*; before the first *print**; after the first *print**. For each of these positions say (a) how many

---

[†] At least one modern programming code, called occam, has been designed with this lesson in mind and uses indentation in place of brackets. If you write in occam you have to lay your programs out moderately nicely.

times a *printspace* instruction in that position would be executed; (b) what the effect will be of the program which includes the *printspace* in that position.

Exercise 6.18

Find each of the other six positions in which a *printspace* might be inserted into program 6.10 and answer the questions in exercise 6.17 about each of them.

-=-=-=-=-=-=-=-=-=-=-=-=-

6.4 REPETITION IN A SEQUENCE OF ENVIRONMENTS

Simple 'do this instruction a fixed number of times' repetition can be useful, but it certainly doesn't cover all eventualities. It doesn't even cover all counting eventualities. For example, consider the problem of printing a triangular pattern of asterisks, in which each line of the pattern has a different number of asterisks:

```
    *
   **
  ***
 ****
*****
```

Now of course this picture *can* be printed by a program which uses a sequence of *times-do* instructions. For example:

> *NL; print**;
> *NL; times* 2 *do print** *od*;
> *NL; times* 3 *do print** *od*;
> *NL; times* 4 *do print** *od*;
> *NL; times* 5 *do print** *od*

program 6.11

This program has an obvious repetitive structure: most lines consist of

> *NL; times n do print** *od*

with just a different value of *n* in each case: first 2, then 3, then 4 and finally 5. Even the first line can be included in this structure if you realise that *print** means the same as *times* 1 *do print** *od*. I might define a procedure and call it five times, as in program 6.12.

> *def tn(n) = NL; times n do print** *od enddef*
> *tn*(1); *tn*(2); *tn*(3); *tn*(4); *tn*(5)

program 6.12

This program is certainly more concise than program 6.11 but it isn't definite enough in imposing the structure I require. The program should go systematically through the sequence <1,2,3,4,5> and program 6.12 does so only by accident. If I had happened to write the procedure calls down in a different order it would still be a meaningful program but no longer the sort of triangle-printing program I want.

The *for-do* instruction is designed to solve this difficulty and to impose the sort of structure I am looking for. It produces a sequence of environments, each of which gives a meaning to a particular name and within each of which a particular instruction is executed. The instruction which is to be executed, the name which is to be given a meaning and the sequence of meanings are each defined as part of the instruction. For example, an instruction which prints the triangle I want is:

$$for\ n\ runningthrough\ 1..5\ do$$
$$NL;\ times\ n\ do\ print*\ od$$
$$od$$

program 6.13

or indeed:

$$for\ n\ runningthrough\ 1..5\ do\ tn(n)\ od$$

program 6.14

Informally, the *for-do* contains a name (*n* in this example), a sequence formula (1..5 in this example) and a program formula (*NL; times n do print* od* in program 6.13, *tn(n)* in program 6.14). Normally the name in the *for-do* is free in the program formula. The *for-do* executes the program in each of a sequence of environments. In each environment the name takes one of the values listed in the sequence-formula. In effect the name is used as a parameter to the repeatedly-executed program.

In program 6.13 the effect is to execute *NL; times n do print* od* first in an environment in which *n* means 1, then to execute that same program in an environment in which *n* means 2, then in an environment in which *n* means 3, then in an environment in which *n* means 4 and finally in an environment in which *n* means 5. The overall effect is to print a line of one asterisk, a line of two asterisks, and so on until a line of five asterisks is printed and the triangle is complete.

I write *for-do* instructions in several slightly different forms, but always with the same three components. The sequence-formula can be written in various ways and since *runningthrough* is such a long word I usually abbreviate it as *rt*. Some examples:

$$for\ n\ rt\ 1..5\ do\ NL;\ times\ n\ do\ print*\ od\ od$$
$$for\ n\ rt\ <1, 2, 3, 4, 5>\ do\ NL;\ times\ n\ do\ print*\ od\ od$$

Each of these instructions is equivalent to program 6.13.

There is no reason why the sequence-formula in a *for-do* should always identify a sequence of numbers. If, for example, I were to relax my notation so as to allow formulas with instructions as their value, I could write an instruction which prints a line of three asterisks in a very unusual way:

$$for\ i\ rt\ <NL, print*, print*, print*>\ do\ i\ od$$

That example is a bit of a joke, but certainly the following program prints the message 'Hello!', treating a string as a sequence of characters in a manner which will be exploited in Part Four of this book:

$$for\ c\ rt\ ``Hello!"\ do\ printchar(c)\ od$$

There is no reason why the program formula in a *for-do* should have only one parameter. Why not an instruction which varies several names at once? Such an instruction might look like

$$for\ x, y, z\ rt\ <(0, 1, 2), (4, 6, 9)\ ..etc..>\ do\ ..etc..\ od$$

The nice thing about making up your own notation is that you don't have to beg a machine's permission to invent some more! In this book I shall rely heavily on the simpler forms of the *for-do* instruction, but it is nice to be able to call on the other forms when necessary.

Substitution definition of *for-do*

Definition 6.5 gives the meaning of the *for-do* in terms very like the definition of *times-do*. A *for-do* is equivalent to *donothing* when its controlling sequence S is empty (like *times* 0); a *for-do* can be unrolled in either direction, in very much the same way as the *times-do*. One unrolling corresponds to 'do the first step first of all, then do everything else', the other to 'do everything but the last step, then do the last step'. Notice that it is implicit in definition 6.4 that the name N is bound in the body of a *for-do*.

> $for\ N\ rt\ S\ do\ P\ od =$
> (when S = the empty sequence <>)   *donothing*
> (when $S = <S_1, .., S_n>$) $(let\ N=S_1\ P)$; $for\ N\ rt\ <S_2, .., S_n>\ do\ P\ od$
> (when $S = <S_1, .., S_n>$) $for\ N\ rt\ <S_1, .., S_{n-1}>\ do\ P\ od$; $(let\ N=S_n\ P)$

definition 6.5

Using this definition, the first steps in proving program 6.13 to be equivalent to program 6.11 might be:

> $for\ n\ rt\ 1..5\ do\ NL;\ times\ n\ do\ print*\ od\ od$
>
> $= (\ let\ n=1\ NL;\ times\ n\ do\ print*\ od\ )$;
> $for\ n\ rt\ 2..5\ do\ NL;\ times\ n\ do\ print*\ od\ od$ [by definition 6.5]
>
> $= (\ NL;\ times\ 1\ do\ print*\ od\ )$;
> $for\ n\ rt\ 2..5\ do\ NL;\ times\ n\ do\ print*\ od\ od$ [by definition 6.3]

= (*NL*; *print**); *for n rt* 2..5 *do NL*; *times n do print* od od*
             [by definition 6.4 twice, then by definition 6.2]

= *NL*; *print**; *for n rt* 2..5 *do NL*; *times n do print* od od*
                                  [by definition 2.7]

The last steps in the proof could be:

= *NL*; *print**; *NL*; *print**; *print**; *NL*; *print**; *print**; *print**;
NL; *print**; *print**; *print**; *print**;
for n rt 5..5 *do NL*; *times n do print* od od*

= *NL*; *print**; *NL*; *print**; *print**; *NL*; *print**; *print**; *print**;
NL; *print**; *print**; *print**; *print**;
(*let n=5 NL*; *times n do print* od*);
for n rt <> *do NL*; *times n do print* od od*   [by definition 6.5]

= *NL*; *print**; *NL*; *print**; *print**; *NL*; *print**; *print**; *print**;
NL; *print**; *print**; *print**; *print**;
(*NL*; *times 5 do print* od*);
for n rt <> *do NL*; *times n do print* od od*   [by definition 6.3]

= *NL*; *print**; *NL*; *print**; *print**; *NL*; *print**; *print**; *print**;
NL; *print**; *print**; *print**; *print**;
NL; *times 5 do print* od*; *donothing*   [by definitions 2.7 and 6.5]

= *NL*; *print**; *NL*; *print**; *print**; *NL*; *print**; *print**; *print**;
NL; *print**; *print**; *print**; *print**;
NL; *times 5 do print* od*   [by definition 6.2]

= *NL*; *print**; *NL*; *print**; *print**; *NL*; *print**; *print**; *print**;
NL; *print**; *print**; *print**; *print**;
NL; *print**:*print**; *print**; *print**; *print**
             [by definitions 6.4 and 2.7, several times each]

-=-=-=-=-=-=-=-=-=-=-=-=-

Exercise 6.19
Fill in the missing steps in the proof that programs 6.13 and 6.11 are equivalent.

Exercise 6.20
The proof above unrolls the *for-do* at the front and uses only the first and second parts of definition 6.5. Give the first and last steps in a proof which uses the first and third parts of the same definition, unrolling the *for-do* instruction at the back.

-=-=-=-=-=-=-=-=-=-=-=-=-

Using the name in the *for-do* instruction

You can use the name introduced in a *for-do* instruction in more ways than I have illustrated so far. The name can appear in a formula together with other names (rather than on its own, as a formula, as it has so far). For example, you can print an upside-down triangle with program 6.15.

$$for\ n\ rt\ 1..5\ do$$
$$NL;\ times\ 6-n\ do\ print*\ od$$
$$od$$

program 6.15

-=-=-=-=-=-=-=-=-=-=-=-=-

Exercise 6.21
Satisfy yourself that the pattern printed by program 6.15 is an upside-down version of that printed by program 6.11, by satisfying yourself that the ith line printed by program 6.11 is identical to the $(6-i)$th line printed by program 6.15, and vice-versa.

Exercise 6.22
Prove, using definition 6.5, that the first line printed by program 6.11 is identical to the last line printed by program 6.15, and vice-versa.

-=-=-=-=-=-=-=-=-=-=-=-=-

Empty sequences and counting backwards

We often use sequences which aren't just numerically ascending. Descending sequences are just as useful as ascending sequences. For example, the program

$$for\ n\ rt\ <5,4,3,2,1>\ do$$
$$NL;\ times\ n\ do\ print*\ od$$
$$od$$

prints an upside-down version of a triangle. It does so more obviously (more clearly, more transparently) than does program 6.15 and is therefore a better program.

I haven't yet introduced a shorthand notation which describes descending sequences. It might seem obvious that if 1..5 is shorthand for $<1,2,3,4,5>$ then 5..1 should be shorthand for $<5,4,3,2,1>$, but that interpretation has a disadvantage. If $i=1$ and $j=5$ then $i..j$ means $<1,2,3,4,5>$, which is a sequence with five components. It seems reasonable that $i+1..j$ should represent a sequence with four components: that is, $<2,3,4,5>$ or $i..j$ with the first element missed out. If $i=j$ then the sequence $i..j$ has only one component: surely $i+1..j$ must have one fewer component still, and must be the empty sequence, written as $<>$. Under that interpretation, which is the one I choose in this book, the formula 5..5 means $<5>$ and 6..5 means $<>$.

But what can 7..5 mean? It should have one less component than 6..5 according to the argument I have made so far, but no sequence can have less components than the empty sequence, so either 7..5 is a meaningless formula or it too must mean the empty sequence. In this book I choose the empty-sequence interpretation, so 5..1, 100..43, 9..–48 or indeed any formula *a..b* where *a* is greater than *b*, are each a way of specifying the empty sequence. Then, for example, the program

> *for n rt* 5..1 *do*
> > *NL*; *times n do print* *od*
> *od*

is just a wordy way of writing *donothing* - in particular it does *not* print an upside-down five-by-five triangle.

This leaves me with the problem of describing programs that use downwards counting sequences. I shall use a form of the *for-do* instruction which runs backwards through a sequence of environments. When I need to write an instruction which runs through a descending numerical sequence, I shall write it using *runningbackthrough* (*rbt* for short). For example:

> *for n runningbackthrough* <1, 2, 3, 4, 5> *do*
> > *NL*; *times n do print* *od*
> *od*

> *for n rbt* 1..5 *do*
> > *NL*; *times n do print* *od*
> *od*

In each of these examples the sequence-formula describes an ascending sequence but the instruction specifies that execution should run backwards through the values in the sequence.

-=-=-=-=-=-=-=-=-=-=-=-

Exercise 6.23
Construct a version of definition 6.5 for the instruction

> *for N rbt S do P od*

Exercise 6.24
Program 6.11 prints a 'left triangle'. Write a program that prints a 'right triangle' of the same size:

> ```
>     *
>    **
>   ***
>  ****
> *****
> ```

[Hint: think how you would type such a triangle on a typewriter, using the space bar and the asterisk key. Then observe that there is a simple arithmetic relationship between the number of spaces and the number of asterisks on each line.]

Exercise 6.25
Prove that your solution to exercise 6.24 prints a figure which has a vertical right-hand edge (that is, the last asterisk is on the same position in every line).

Exercise 6.26
Choose one of the 'left triangle' programs from this chapter and prove that your 'right triangle' program prints a mirror image of the figure produced by the 'left triangle' program.

Exercise 6.27
Write a program which prints an upside-down right triangle. Prove that it prints a mirror image of the figure printed by a program which prints an upside-down left triangle.

-=-=-=-=-=-=-=-=-=-=-=-

6.5 ENVIRONMENT DIAGRAMS AND *for-do* INSTRUCTIONS

The *for-do* instruction creates a sequence of new environments. When you draw an environment diagram of the execution of a program which includes a *for-do*, your diagram should in principle indicate the environments which that instruction creates. But you should avoid cluttering your diagrams with too much information. The environments created by a *for-do* are based straightforwardly on the environment in which the *for-do* itself is executed: for example, figure 6.2 shows the environment diagram of an execution of program 6.13. Even that much detail can be confusing: figure 6.3 shows an alternative which is quite acceptable in such a simple case.

6.6 CONVERTING BETWEEN *times-do* AND *for-do*

There is a strong similarity between *times-do* and *for-do* repetition. Many mechanical codes don't have a *times-do* instruction. That is because you can always convert a *times-do* into a *for-do*. The conversion is very simple:

$$times\ F\ do\ P\ od =$$
$$(if\ F \geq 0\ and\ n\ isn't\ free\ in\ P)\quad for\ n\ rt\ 1..F\ do\ P\ od$$

definition 6.6

You invent a name n and use it to count F environments. It is simplest if n is a brand-new name which doesn't appear anywhere else in your program, but it is enough that n isn't free in P. Although the instruction creates a sequence of environments, each different from the one before, the effect of P is the same in each of them just because the value of n has no effect on P.

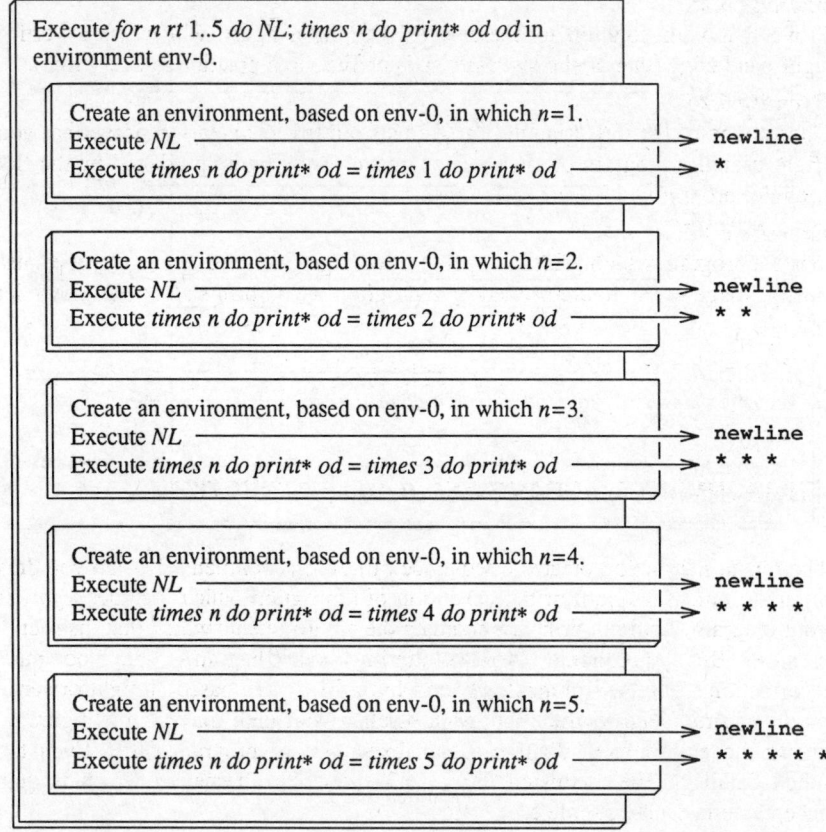

Execute *for n rt* 1..5 *do NL*; *times n do print* od od* in environment env-0.

Create an environment, based on env-0, in which *n*=1.
Execute *NL* ────────────────────────────> newline
Execute *times n do print* od* = *times* 1 *do print* od* ──> *

Create an environment, based on env-0, in which *n*=2.
Execute *NL* ────────────────────────────> newline
Execute *times n do print* od* = *times* 2 *do print* od* ──> * *

Create an environment, based on env-0, in which *n*=3.
Execute *NL* ────────────────────────────> newline
Execute *times n do print* od* = *times* 3 *do print* od* ──> * * *

Create an environment, based on env-0, in which *n*=4.
Execute *NL* ────────────────────────────> newline
Execute *times n do print* od* = *times* 4 *do print* od* ──> * * * *

Create an environment, based on env-0, in which *n*=5.
Execute *NL* ────────────────────────────> newline
Execute *times n do print* od* = *times* 5 *do print* od* ──> * * * * *

figure 6.2

Translation from *for-do* to *times-do* is a little trickier. You can do it using the assignment instruction, but that isn't introduced until chapter 10; otherwise you can only do it when the name used in the *for-do* isn't free in the repeated program *P*. If you are using the shorthand notation *x..y* to describe the sequence of values in the *for-do*, defining the length of the sequence by subtracting the lower limit from the upper limit is tricky (how many elements in the sequence 7..5?).

Definition 6.7 tells you how to translate, but it's fairly useless because most *for-do* instructions use the name *n* to systematically vary the effect of executing *P*: that is, in general the name *n* is a parameter of the repeated program *P*. Indeed if you write a program which uses a *for-do* whose name isn't a parameter of the program it executes then you are guilty of spreading confusion. Your program has a simpler structure than it seems to have: you should be using a *times-do* instruction instead!

There is always an overriding obligation to write a clearly understandable program. Anyone who reads a *for-do* instruction reasonably expects it to create a

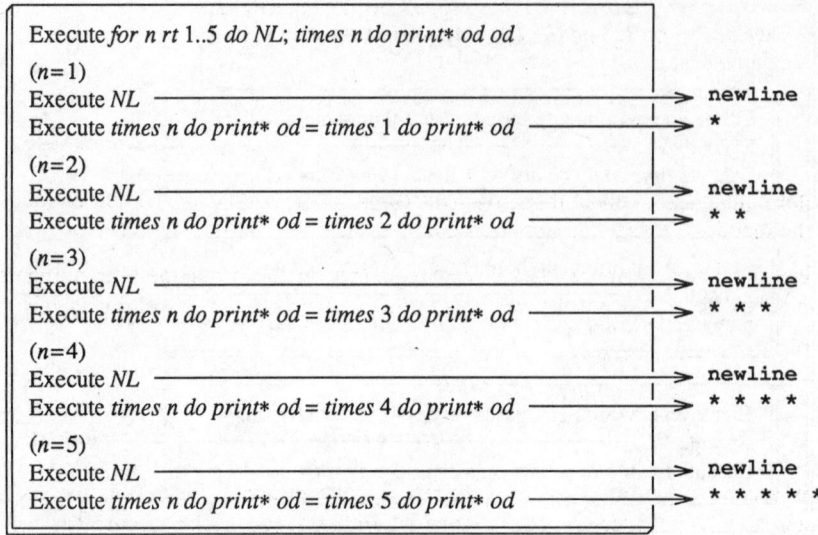

figure 6.3

$$for\ n\ rt\ <S_1,..,S_k>\ do\ P\ od =$$
$$(when\ n\ is\ not\ free\ in\ P)\quad times\ k\ do\ P\ od$$

$$for\ n\ rt\ F..F+k-1\ do\ P\ od =$$
$$(when\ n\ is\ not\ free\ in\ P\ and\ k \geq 0)\quad times\ k\ do\ P\ od$$
$$(when\ k \leq 0)\quad donothing$$

definition 6.7

sequence of executions each systematically different from the last; anyone who reads a *times-do* instruction expects it to create a sequence of identical executions. Using one instruction for the other's purpose is misleading and therefore should be avoided. Just as you can't jump into the same river twice, so a program can't be read by the same person twice. The person you will confuse will be yourself, reading the program tomorrow.

6.7 FINDING A SEQUENCE FORMULA FOR A *for-do*

Suppose that you had to write a program to print the sequence of numbers 1, 4, 9, 16, 25, 36, 49, 64, 81, 100. The most basic solution to the problem would be the sequence *printnumber*(1); *printstring*(", "); *printnumber*(4); *printstring*(", "); ..; *printnumber*(100). But there is an obvious regularity in the problem which can be exploited to make a solution using a *for-do* instruction: see, for example, program 6.16. Because there are ten numbers but only nine commas to be printed, every number except the last is printed by the *for-do* in this program - I

for i rt <1, 4, 9, 16, 25, 36, 49, 64, 81> *do*
  printnumber(*i*); *printstring*(", ")
od;
printnumber(100)

program 6.16

might equally have made it repeat *printstring*(", "); *printnumber*(*i*) and included in the repetition every number but the first.

There is still some more unexploited regularity in the problem. The numbers printed are the squares of the numbers from 1 to 10. So a better solution is

for i rt 1..9 *do printnumber*(i^2); *printstring*(", ") *od*;
  printnumber(10^2)

program 6.17

This second program is to be preferred for two reasons. First, it is the most systematic of the three solutions I have presented. Second, the mechanical code of your programming system may not permit *for-do* instructions which contain explicit sequences like the one in program 6.16. Some demand that a sequence formula describes only integer (whole number) sequences. Some demand sequences of consecutive integers. Often the problem is to find a formula which relates a sequence of integers to the sequence of values required in the problem.

-=-=-=-=-=-=-=-=-=-=-=-

Exercise 6.28
Figure 6.4 is part of the graph of the function $y=x \times x$, shown from $x=-5$ to $x=+5$, drawn 'lying on its side'. Define a program P such that the instruction *for x rt* $-5..+5$ *do P od* will draw this graph.

```
                                        *
                             *
                      *
               *
            *
          *
          *
            *
               *
                      *
                             *
                                        *
```

figure 6.4

Exercise 6.29
The answer to exercise 6.28 creates eleven environments. Define *P1* such that the instruction *for x rt* 1..11 *do P1 od* will draw the same pattern.

Exercise 6.30
Repeat exercise 6.29 for the program *P2* and the instruction *for x rt* 0..10 *do P2 od*.

Exercise 6.31
Write an instruction *for x rt* 1..5 *do Q od* which prints the series 2, 4, 6, 8, 10
without the separating commas.

Exercise 6.32
Repeat exercise 6.31 for the series 1, 3, 5, 7, 9.

Exercise 6.33
Write an instruction *for y rt* 0..8 *do R od* which prints (again without the
commas) the series 13, 23, 33, 43, .., 93.

-=-=-=-=-=-=-=-=-=-=-=-=-

The exercises above show that provided there is a systematic relationship
between the elements of a series you can usually find it and construct a formula
which connects it to an ascending sequence of integers starting from 1 or from 0.
This is an essential skill when transcribing into restricted programming codes.

Sometimes the relationship is there but you can't see it. For example, the series
477, 602, 698, 778, 845 can be generated systematically, but you'd be lucky to
spot the formula. In fact each element in the sequence is the first three digits of
log_{10} of the numbers 3, 4, 5, 6 and 7 (at least my home micro says they are). So
you might print this series with the instruction

  for i rt 3..7 *do* .. *printnumber(integerpartof*(1000×*log10(i))) .. od*

Some series are completely impenetrable. For example, what connects 142, 77,
81, 160? Nothing sensible, I think. For a programming solution to problems
based on unsystematic series you must wait a couple of chapters.

6.8 PLANNING A SOLUTION WITH COUNTING REPETITION

So far in this book I have discussed two program structures:

   Sequence
   Counting Repetition

plus the use of procedures to invent new kinds of instructions and to make
parameterised abstractions. If you are presented with a programming problem
you always have to choose a structure for your program. When you know only
two structures the choice is usually quite easy.

With the structures discussed so far, the choice lies between sequence and
repetition. You have to decide whether the solution will be a sequence of very
different executions - in which case you must just describe that sequence - or a
sequence of executions which are systematically related in some way - in which
case you can use repetition. You use procedures essentially to package
executions so as to invent novel instructions and, via the use of parameters, to
connect executions which are systematically related but which don't occur in

sequence. And in particular you use procedures to ensure that your structure has relatively few parts.

Once you have chosen the overall structure of your program you must make the same choice for every instruction which that structure contains. You don't have to choose the same structure at every level of the hiearchy: you can have a sequence of repetitions, a repetition of sequences, a sequence of procedure calls and repetitions or whatever you like. Then you make the same choice about the parts of the parts of the structure, and keep going until you have divided the problem into pieces which can be imitated by basic instructions.

All that sounds very cerebral and very systematic. You may already have discovered that it isn't always that way for you. You are not alone: it isn't always like that for me, or for anybody else. In reality we think of a structure, try it out and fail, try again with another structure, fail again, try again perhaps with a different version of the first structure, and so on, learning about the problem as we go until at last we find something that works. Sometimes we find a partial solution and try to generalise it to cover the whole problem. Sometimes we guess the answer (and we often guess wrong). Sometimes we think of the kernel of a solution - part of the program right inside the structure we have to build - and for a time we work outwards towards the problem rather than inwards towards the solution.

But when we have found a solution, or something we think is a solution, then we should always be cerebral and systematic. Then is the time to analyse the structure of the solution, to check and to prove if possible that it does what we want it to do. And then sometimes we have to go back to square one because what we thought was a 'solution', wasn't.

If you guess or are told or deduce that the structure of a solution is a repetition, what do you do next? For example, suppose that you have to write a procedure which prints an n-by-n 'hollow triangle'. Figure 6.5 shows a seven-by-seven example: since this is a chapter about counting repetition, I shall develop a repetitive program to print this picture. The development proceeds in several stages.

```
* * * * * * *
*           *
 *         *
  *       *
   *     *
    * *
     *
```

figure 6.5

Step 1: Find some pieces of the series

A repetition is shorthand for a sequence of instructions. It is a repetition because the elements of the sequence are systematically related. When you don't know what to write in a repetition, the first step is to find some typical elements of that sequence. In the present example you might reasonably decide that the figure is printed by a repetition each element of which prints one line. What instructions would actually print the lines of this figure?

The first line could be printed by

NL; *times 7 do print* od*

The second line is a bit different. It could be printed by

NL; *printspace*; *print**; *times 4 do printspace od*; *print**

The third line is rather like the second, but the spaces are differently distributed. It needs

NL; *times 2 do printspace od*; *print**; *times 3 do printspace od*; *print**

By now you should be able to spot the general case but if not, keep looking. The fourth line needs

NL; *times 3 do printspace od*; *print**; *times 2 do printspace od*; *print**

It is now clear that the second, third, fourth and fifth lines of the seven-by-seven pattern can be printed by a *for-do* repetition. Only the distribution of five spaces differs between these lines.

Notice that already it is necessary to retract the original design decision. The program which prints figure 6.5 isn't a counting repetition. Instead the solution is a sequence:

print the first line;
print the middle lines using for-do repetition;
print the last line

It's quite normal when planning a program to find that your first guess at the structure isn't the overall structure but is contained in something else. Programming is by no means 'top-down reasoning'.

Step 2: Find the formulas which make the general case

I continue, then, to develop the bit of the program which is a *for-do* repetition. The middle lines of figure 6.5 can each be printed by the sequence

NL; *times F1 do printspace od*; *print**; *times F2 do printspace od*; *print**

with different values of *F1* and *F2* in each case. We know that *F1* and *F2* must add up to five, because each line contains five spaces and two asterisks, making seven characters in all and ensuring that the program prints a seven-by-seven figure. In the first of the middle lines (the second line of the figure) $F1 = 1$; in the second of those lines $F1 = 2$; and so on. I am led immediately to conclude that if the repetition uses the instruction *for i rt* 1..5 *do* .. *od* then in place of $F1$ I can write *i*. Since $F1$ and $F2$ add up to five, I know that in place of $F2$ I can write $5-i$. The complete program for a seven-by-seven hollow triangle is shown in program 6.18.

> *NL*; *times* 7 *do print* od*
> *for i rt* 1..5 *do*
>   *NL*; *times i do printspace od*; *print**;
>   *times* 5–*i do printspace od*; *print**
> *od*
> *NL*; *times* 6 *do printspace od*; *print**

program 6.18

And if, finally, I want to generalise this to an *n*-by-*n* hollow triangle procedure I need only alter a few numbers to formulas involving *n*. In the first *times-do*, 7 can be replaced by *n*; in the *for-do* and in the second *times-do*, 5 can be replaced by $n-2$; in the third *times-do*, 6 can be replaced by $n-1$. The result is the procedure shown in program 6.19.

> *def hollowtriangle*(*n*) = *NL*; *times n do print* od*
>   *for i rt* 1..*n*–2 *do*
>   *NL*; *times i do printspace od*; *print**;
>   *times n*–2–*i do printspace od*; *print**
>   *od*;
>   *NL*; *times n*–1 *do printspace od*; *print**
>   *enddef*

program 6.19

-=-=-=-=-=-=-=-=-=-=-=-

Exercise 6.34
If the *for-do* in program 6.18 had used the sequence 2..6 rather than 1..5, what would the formulas $F1$ and $F2$ have been? Construct the program and generalise it to make a procedure definition for printing *n*-by-*n* triangles.

-=-=-=-=-=-=-=-=-=-=-=-

6.9 PLANNING A SOLUTION: RASTER PRINTING

So far you have been able to write procedures which draw triangles and you can use these procedures to draw columns of triangles. Each triangle is drawn systematically by a *for-do* repetition. The column is constructed by a *times-do*.

It is easy to construct a definition of a procedure *column* so that the instruction *column*(*n*, *k*) will draw a column of *k* triangles, each *n*-by-*n*.

-=-=-=-=-=-=-=-=-=-=-=-

Exercise 6.35
Construct the *column* procedure.

-=-=-=-=-=-=-=-=-=-=-=-

But how can we define a procedure *row* so that *row*(*n*, *k*) will draw a row of *k* triangles, each *n*-by-*n*? For example, here is a row of three triangles, each four-by-four, with a blank column separating adjacent triangles:

```
         ****  ****  ****
          ***   ***   ***
           **    **    **
            *     *     *
```

figure 6.6

Evidently the program which prints this pattern could be a repetition. Just as before, the first step in planning a programming solution is to describe some typical elements of the sequence of executions which produce this picture. The first line could be printed by

> *NL*; *times* 4 *do print** *od*; *printspace*;
> *times* 4 *do print** *od*; *printspace*;
> *times* 4 *do print** *od*

the second line by

> *NL*; *printspace*; *times* 3 *do print** *od*;
> *times* 2 *do printspace od*; *times* 3 *do print** *od*;
> *times* 2 *do printspace od*; *times* 3 *do print** *od*

and the third line by

> *NL*; *times* 2 *do printspace od*; *times* 2 *do print** *od*;
> *times* 3 *do printspace od*; *times* 2 *do print** *od*;
> *times* 3 *do printspace od*; *times* 2 *do print** *od*

The second and third lines suggest a generalisation: each line is printed by

> *NL*; *times* *F1*–1 *do printspace od*; *times* *F2* *do print** *od*;
> *times* *F1* *do printspace od*; *times* *F2* *do print** *od*;
> *times* *F1* *do printspace od*; *times* *F2* *do print** *od*

or, if we are prepared to print an extra space before the first triangle we can use *times-do* repetition:

>   *NL*; *times* 3 *do times* *F1* *do printspace od*;
>   *times* *F2* *do print** *od*
>   *od*

Or it might be better to add the extra space to the end of the line:

NL; *times* 3 *do times F1*–1 *do printspace od*;
  times F2 do print* od;
  printspace
od

For the sake of simplicity I shall choose the first of these alternative solutions, putting the extra space at the beginning of the line.

Now, what should be written in place of *F1* and *F2*? If the *for-do* is based on the sequence 1..4 then *F1* must be *i* and *F2* must be 5–*i*. But because I am printing upside-down triangles I want to run backwards through the sequence 1..4[†]. Then *F2*, which describes the number of asterisks in each row of each triangle, can be *i* and *F1* can be 5–*i*; the program which produces a row of three four-by-four triangles can be written as in program 6.20.

for i rbt 1..4 *do*
  NL; *times* 3 *do times* 5–*i do printspace od*;
    times i do print* od
  od
od

program 6.20

This program uses the technique of **raster-printing,** so called because it works like the raster scan of a television picture: in order to draw a row of figures it draws a line which contains the first lines of each, then a line which contains the second lines of each, and so on until the last line of the picture is drawn. It isn't possible, in raster scanning or in typewriter-style printing, to draw all the lines of one figure before starting on the next.

The next step is to generalise from four rows and three columns to *n* rows and *k* columns. In program 6.20, '*for i rbt* 1..4' comes from the fact that we must print four lines in a four-by-four triangle; '*times* 3' from the fact that the row contains three triangles, and '*times* 5–*i*' prints just one space more than the size of the triangle. Then the procedure which prints a row of *k* upside-down *n*-by-*n* triangles can be written as in program 6.21.

It is possible to push this example quite a lot farther. The pattern printed by program 6.21 is a repetition of a particular shape. The program has parameters which control the size of the shapes used and their number. How can the program be parameterised to print rows of other shapes?

As usual it is helpful to consider other examples before generalising. In appendix 6.B below I classify the shapes printed by program 6.20 as 'pattern B triangles'. Using one of the other shapes from that classification, what would the program

---

[†] This will turn out to be a bad decision. Programming is not always a matter of careful and accurate deduction.

```
def row(n, k) =
   for i rbt 1..n do
      NL; times k do times n+1-i do printspace od;
                       times i do print* od
            od
   od
enddef
```

be like which printed rows of pattern D triangles, as in figure 6.7, for example? As before, this requires a four-times repetition of a three-times repetition, but - see program 6.22 - it seems more natural in this case to count forwards in the *for-do* rather than backwards.

```
  *      *      *
 **     **     **
***    ***    ***
****   ****   ****
```

figure 6.7

```
for i rt 1..4 do
   NL; times 3 do times i do print* od;
                 times 5-i do printspace od
         od
   od
```

Notice that leaving redundant spaces at the end of every line simplifies the structure of the program and emphasises its similarity to program 6.20. Notice also that although pattern D triangles printed one at a time don't need spaces following the asterisks on each line, in this program the spaces *are* required. The raster-printing technique requires each repeated shape to be rectangular, and program 6.22 prints spaces to make a square pattern out of a triangle.

It seems sensible, even without considering other patterns, to conclude that my original decision to count backwards was wrong and that the general solution to the problem would be:

```
for i rt 1..n do
   NL; times k do .. print spaces and asterisks .. od
   od
```

It is possible to generalise much farther. Each line printed by program 6.20 and by program 6.22 contains repeated parts of an n-by-n triangle pattern. Every execution of the larger *times-do* in these programs must print one row of a triangle pattern, without executing any *NL*s. Suppose that the procedure call $Brow(x, y)$ prints the yth row of an x-by-x pattern B triangle. Then the procedure which prints a pattern B triangle could be written as:

$$def\,B(n) = for\ i\ rt\ 1..n\ do\ NL;\ Brow(n,i)\ enddef$$

and the procedure which prints a row of k triangles, each n-by-n, could be as shown in program 6.23. Note the *printspace* which follows the call to procedure *Brow*, separating the triangle patterns in the row.

> *def row*$(n, k) =$
> *for i rt* 1..n *do*
>   *NL*; *times k do Brow*(n, i); *printspace od*
> *od*
> *enddef*

program 6.23

This procedure definition shows a systematic way of drawing B-pattern triangles in a row. It can be parameterised to print a row of k n-by-n patterns of any kind by using a parameter which is a procedure: see program 6.24, for example. Now *prow*$(4, 3, Brow)$ will draw figure 6.6 and *prow*$(4, 3, Drow)$ will draw figure 6.7.

> *def prow*$(n, k, pat) =$
> *for i rt* 1..n *do*
>   *NL*; *times k do pat*(n, i); *printspace od*
> *od*
> *enddef*

program 6.24

-=-=-=-=-=-=-=-=-=-=-=-=-

Exercise 6.36
Define procedure *Brow*. Note that the first row of an n-by-n pattern B triangle contains n asterisks only and that the nth row contains one asterisk and $n-1$ spaces.

Exercise 6.37
Define procedures *Arow*, *Crow* and *Drow* (see appendix 6.C). Don't forget the spaces which make the patterns rectangular.

Exercise 6.38
Define a procedure *spacerow* so that *spacerow*(n, k, pat, s) prints a row of k n-by-n *pat*-patterns separated by s blank spaces.

Exercise 6.39
What would be printed by *spacerow*$(4, 3, Arow, 0)$?

Exercise 6.40
Is *spacerow*$(x, y, p, -1)$ meaningful, whatever the meanings of x, y and p? If so, why? If not, why not?

Exercise 6.41
Define a procedure *Srow* so that *Srow*(n, j) draws the lines (rows) of an n-by-n square: then *prow*$(5, 3, Srow)$, for example, will draw a row of three five-by-five squares separated by spaces.

Exercise 6.42
Why wouldn't it be sufficient in exercise 6.41 to define *Srow* so that *Srow*(*n*) draws one row of an *n*-by-*n* square of asterisks? [Hint: fitting arguments to parameters!]

Exercise 6.43
Prove that *prow*(3, 1, *Srow*) draws a square of asterisks.

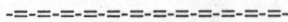

You now know a systematic way of drawing a row of identical figures systematically. Consider the following pattern:

figure 6.8

The problem is to write a program to draw this pattern systematically, using the technique of raster-printing.

The first step in the solution is to find structure in the pattern which can be exploited in the programming solution. You can see the structure if I add some extra blank columns:

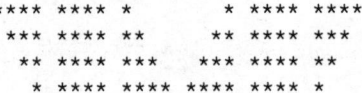

figure 6.9

This reveals the pattern to be a row consisting of a pattern B triangle, next to a square, next to a pattern D triangle, next to a pattern C triangle, next to a square, next to a pattern A triangle. The first line of figure 6.8 could be printed by the sequence

   NL; *Brow*(4, 1); *Srow*(4, 1); *Drow*(4, 1); *Crow*(4, 1); *Srow*(4, 1); *Arow*(4, 1)

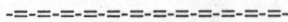

Exercise 6.44
Write the program which draws figure 6.8, based on procedures *Arow*, *Brow*, *Crow*, *Drow* and *Srow*.

Exercise 6.45
Figure 6.8 is the top third of a letter V. Add a couple more rows of squares and triangles to complete the picture. [Hint: you will probably need to invent a procedure *Irow*, which draws the rows of an 'invisible' square of spaces. Another hint: there probably isn't a useful systematic relationship between the three thirds of the whole picture.]

Exercise 6.46
Your answer to exercise 6.45 draws a letter V based on four-by-four figures. Generalise it to define a procedure *V* so that *V(n)* draws a pattern of the same shape, but made up of *n*-by-*n* figures.

-=

APPENDIX 6.A COUNTING REPETITION IN PASCAL

There are four ways in which Pascal counting repetition differs from mine. First, Pascal has no direct equivalent of the *times-do* instruction, so you have to convert *times-do*s into *for-do*s using definition 6.6. Second, Pascal *for-do*s can contain only a single instruction rather than a program, so you may have to unpack definitions and/or use `begin-end` bracketing. Third, Pascal *for-do*s only count in consecutive sequences, so you may have to convert your program to use only those kinds of sequences. Fourth, Pascal *for-do*s don't bind a name, so you have to bind the names in *for-do* instructions at the beginning of the procedure or program in which they occur.

(a) [Convert *times-do* into *for-do*.] Follow definition 6.6. For example, the program

times 4 do NL; times 5 do print* od od

can become the program

for x rt 1..4 do NL; for y rt 1..5 do print* od od

Note that because of rule (e) below, it is sensible to choose different parameter names for nested *for-do*s.

(b) [Convert the body of a *for-do* into an instruction sequence.] If the body of a *for-do* contains any definitions, unpack them in the manner of chapter 5. For example, convert the program

for i rt 1..5 do
  def asp() = print*; printspace enddef
  asp(); asp(); asp()
od

into

def asp() = print*; printspace enddef
for i rt 1..5 do asp(); asp(); asp() od

(c) [Convert the body of a *for-do* into a single instruction.] If the body of any *for-do* instruction is a sequence rather than a single instruction, use ⟮-⟯ program brackets, which transcribe into Pascal as `begin-end` brackets, to make it into a single instruction. For example, convert the program above into

$$def\ asp() = print*; printspace\ enddef$$
$$for\ i\ rt\ 1..5\ do\ (\!(asp(); asp(); asp())\!)\ od$$

(d) [Convert any sequences in *for-do*s into integer sequences.] Use the techniques illustrated in section 6.6 above.

(e) [Make nested *for-do*s use different parameter names.] If one *for-do* contains another, make sure that they use different names. If not, change the name used in one of them and change its bound occurrences. For example, change

$$for\ i\ do\ ..i..$$
$$for\ i\ do\ ..i..\ od$$
$$..i..$$
$$od$$

either by renaming the inner *for-do*:

$$for\ i\ do\ ..i..$$
$$for\ j\ do\ ..j..\ od$$
$$..i..$$
$$od$$

or else by renaming the outer one:

$$for\ j\ do\ ..j..$$
$$for\ i\ do\ ..i..\ od$$
$$..j..$$
$$od$$

(f) [Direct transcription.] Transcribe *for n rt a..b do I od* into Pascal:

```
for n:=a to b do I
```

Transcribe *for n rbt a..b do I od* into Pascal:

```
for n:=b downto a do I
```

Note that there is no need for a closing *od* bracket in a Pascal *for-do* because *I* is always a single instruction.

(g) [Name binding.] Include in the program or procedure which contains a *for-do* instruction the 'variable declaration'

```
var n:integer;
```

Put all your variable declarations after any type declarations (see appendix 4.A) but before any procedure definitions. For example, you might transcribe program 6.6 into Pascal as figure 6.10.

```
procedure rect(n:integer; m:integer);
   var i:integer; j:integer;
   begin for i:=1 to n do
           begin writeln; for j:=1 to m do write('*') end
   end;
```

figure 6.10

APPENDIX 6.B SOME PROGRAMS TO TRY

Exercise 6.47
Transcribe and execute the answers to exercises 6.13-6.16.

Exercise 6.48
Define four procedures *A*, *B*, *C* and *D* which each print an *n*-by-*n* version of one of the following triangle-patterns:

```
****           ****              *               *
***            ***             **              **
**             **             ***             ***
*              *             ****            ****


A(4)           B(4)            C(4)            D(4)
```

Exercise 6.49
What is printed by *A*(0)? Is it sensible? Modify your procedure if necessary to make it so.

Exercise 6.50
What is printed by *A*(−1)? Modify your procedure, if possible, to produce what you think is a sensible effect (or non-effect).

Exercise 6.51
Pattern A and pattern B are related in an obvious fashion: each is a mirror-image of the other. Prove from your procedure definitions (before they have been transcribed into mechanical code) that the *n*th line of pattern A has the same number of asterisks as the *n*th line of pattern B. And that pattern A has a vertical left-hand edge. And that pattern B has a vertical right-hand edge because each line it prints has the same number of characters. Hence you can conclude that the procedures print mirror-images of each other.

Exercise 6.52
Repeat exercise 6.51 for patterns C and D.

Exercise 6.53
Repeat exercise 6.51 for patterns A and D (the mirror is above A, below D).

Exercise 6.54
Repeat exercise 6.51 for patterns B and C, or show that it follows from what you have already proved.

Exercise 6.55
Transcribe and execute answers to exercises 6.28-6.33.

Exercise 6.56
Transcribe and execute answers to exercises 6.35-6.38, 6.41, 6.44-6.46.

Chapter 7
PROOF BY INDUCTION

Whenever you write a program or a procedure definition you want it to work: you want it to have the effect you designed it to have. When you are a novice programmer you check your programs by trying them out in lots of different circumstances, hoping to include every possible case so that you can be sure you have succeeded in writing a reliable program. But it isn't always easy to tell whether you have succeeded, especially when a procedure will accept a wide range of parameters. There can be just too many circumstances - too many possible parameter values - for you to test them all. You may already know of programs which display a wide range of behaviours depending on what information you type on the keyboard - you may have come across calculators, formatting printers, databases, spread sheets, compilers, interpreters - and you may already suspect that it would be difficult to test that sort of program in every possible circumstance.

Ideally you would like to try out your program or your procedure on a few well-chosen cases and then be able to reason from what you find that it will work in every other possible circumstance. A convincing argument is called a *proof* in mathematics. This chapter is about one technique of making a proof.

7.1 SPECIFICATION AND PROOF

Suppose that you need to prove that a program does what you want it to do. First you must write down what you want the program to do: you must write a *specification* of the program. The specification will be a statement of what you require of the program, in terms of its behaviour or its output or both, written to be as precise as possible. The proof must then show that *any* execution of the program meets the specification, or if it can't do that then it must show just *which* executions will meet the specification.

Sometimes a proof can show you exactly what you want, but other times you may have to prove a result indirectly by showing that the program has certain properties from which you can conclude that the specification is satisfied. For example, a car is a generalised tool for getting people from any point A on a road to any point B on any connected road. If you want to travel between some particular points X and Y you won't find a car built to make just that journey. But all you need to do is to find out if they are connected by road: if they are then you need a driver, a map and enough petrol and you can do the job. It doesn't matter that a tool or a program is not designed precisely to satisfy some particular specification, so long as it satisfies a general specification of which the one you are interested in is a special case or a provable consequence.

7.2 PROOF BY COUNTING UPWARDS

Up to now the proofs which you have been able to make have always been about particular instances of particular instructions. You can prove, for example, that *times* 3 *do print*∗ *od* is equivalent to *print*∗; *print*∗; *print*∗ and therefore prints three asterisks. You will have generalised from this experience and concluded that, to take another example, *times* 56 *do print*∗ *od* prints fifty-six asterisks. What you have decided is that in general *times* k *do print*∗ *od* prints k asterisks (and if you are a careful sort of person you may have added the proviso that k mustn't be negative). That generalisation is correct and it is possible to prove it so.

To prove something about a program will often require a generalisation to an infinite number of cases because even simple programs may have an infinite number of possible executions. For example, a procedure which adds together two numbers has an infinite number of possible pairs of arguments and therefore an infinite number of possible executions[†]. The technique of mathematical induction provides a way of proving the general properties of infinite sets of things.

You can get a clue about how mathematical induction works if you consider how you would proceed to discover the effect of *times* 56 *do print*∗ *od*, when you had already proved what the effect of *times* 55 *do print*∗ *od* is. The proof would have very few steps:

[†] You may object that a computer can represent only a finite number of these possible inputs, but in practice that number can be so large that it might as well be infinite for the purposes of testing. For example: some microcomputer programming systems calculate with 32-bit numbers; the part of the programming system which adds together two numbers must deal correctly with every possible pair of numbers; there are 2^{64} possible pairs of 32-bit numbers, or about eighteen million million million different possible executions of that tiny part of the programming system. Testing such a number of executions is practically impossible: if each test took only a thousandth part of a second, trying every case would take nearly six hundred million years. Even if you could speed up the test a hundred million times it still wouldn't be a practical way of finding out whether that part of the programming system works or not.

    times 56 *do print* od*
= *print**; *times* 55 *do print* od*   [by definition 6.4]
= *print**; an instruction which prints 55 asterisks
                                  [by what you have already proved]
= a sequence which prints 56 asterisks

Now that you know the effect of *times* 56 *do print* od* you can calculate the effect of *times* 57 *do print* od*; knowing that you can calculate the effect of *times* 58 *do print* od*; knowing that you can calculate the effect of *times* 59 *do print* od*; and so on as far as you like for any number greater than fifty-five. But to prove that *times k do print* od* always prints *k* asterisks would seem to require an infinite series of proofs each standing on the shoulders of the one before. Proofs about infinite sets can't be infinitely long or you could never live to write them down and you would have gained nothing.

Mathematical induction works by observing the similarity between counting upwards and the proof technique sketched above. We learn in primary school that 'numbers go on for ever'. The argument which eventually convinces us is that from any number it is possible to reach a number just slightly larger, so there can't ever be a largest possible number. Inductive arguments have the same sort of structure. You number the things you are talking about - procedure executions, formulas, whatever - and you show that they all share a particular property by showing that the first one has the property and whichever one you pick, the property is passed on from it to the next in line. It is like climbing a staircase: if you can get on to the bottom step and if you are confident that from any step you can reach the next then, given time and strength, you can climb the stairs.

A parable of simple induction

Imagine an infinite featureless desert, with an infinite line of soldiers stretching across it waiting to advance on the word of command. The soldiers are numbered, as in any good army: soldier number 1 stands at the edge of the desert; next to him is soldier number 2; next to soldier number 2 is soldier number 3; and so on. In general soldier number i stands between soldier $i-1$ and soldier $i+1$. Next to soldier number 1 is the sergeant-major, who has a very loud, but not an infinitely loud voice. The sergeant-major would like to bellow 'ADVANCE!' and see the whole infinite army move into battle, but he realises that even his voice can't reach the end of an infinite line.

Suppose, though, that the sergeant-major knows that his army comes from a warrior race. They have been bred to fight and if any man advances, the man next to him will advance as well. Then the sergeant-major can save his voice for the coming battle and merely whisper 'advance' to soldier number 1. He trusts soldier number 1 to obey; he knows that if any soldier i moves forward then soldier $i+1$ will follow him; he can conclude that any soldier he likes to name will move forward eventually. His conclusion is valid, based on counting: if soldier 1 moves then 2 will follow, 3 will follow 2, 4 will follow 3, and so on for ever. As soon as the sergeant-major speaks the army will start to move across the desert in a long diagonal line.

The army contains an infinite number of soldiers, so in answering the question 'will soldier k eventually move?' the sergeant-major's proof has covered an infinite number of possibilities. His answer is in every case 'yes, given enough time for the order to reach him'. If each soldier moves one tenth of a second after the one before, the billionth soldier will move after about a thousand days, which is about three years. The ten billionth soldier will move after thirty years. The trillionth soldier won't move for three thousand years, so I must presume that this warrior race is very long-lived if that many soldiers are required to join the battle.

Although the sergeant-major has answered an infinite number of questions, each is a question about a particular soldier with a particular finite number. The question about infinity isn't answered and indeed there never will be a time when the *whole army* has moved. But if there is any finite number which is large enough to win the battle and if the sergeant-major can wait long enough, that number of soldiers will arrive.

As it is with infinite lines of soldiers, so it is with infinite sets of objects of any kind provided that you can number them 1, 2, 3 .. or 0, 1, 2, .. or with any ascending sequence of consecutive integers. The technique of proof based on counting upwards is called *simple induction*. A simple induction proof has two parts: you must prove that the first of the set of objects (the one with the lowest number) has some property and you must prove that each object passes on the property to its neighbour (the one with the next higher number). When you have made both parts of the proof you may conclude that every object has the property. The parts of the proof correspond to the sergeant-major's trust in the first soldier and his faith in his warrior race. The conclusion corresponds to his confidence that the advance will continue indefinitely.

An easy proof

In programming the objects which we number are executions of programs, procedures or instructions: the properties are the behaviours or outputs which we specify for that program, procedure or instruction. As a first example I shall prove an obviously true statement:

> P0: *times k do print* od* is an instruction which prints exactly k asterisks provided that $k{\geq}0$.

This kind of statement is called a *proposition* about a program. It is an English sentence whose parameter is k. Particular instances of the proposition are found by replacing k with some particular value. For example, P0(2) is the English sentence '*times 2 do print* od* is an instruction which prints exactly 2 asterisks provided that $2{\geq}0$'. It is certainly true that $2{\geq}0$, so this sentence is true if and only if *times* 2 *do print* od* prints exactly two asterisks.

The executions I want to consider are simply numbered by the value of the formula *k*. I need to prove that P0(*k*) is a true statement for any *k* - or rather for any non-negative *k* because I am not interested in the negative cases. I can start by observing that *times* 0 *do print* od* is by definition equivalent to *donothing*, an instruction which prints no asterisks at all; this proves P0(0). This is the *base case* of the proof or the *basic step*: it corresponds to the sergeant-major's whispered confidence in soldier number 1, or your belief that you can reach the first step on a staircase.

The second part of the proof is the *inductive step* or the *inductive case*. I choose some particular case P0(*K*)[†] and must prove that P0(*K*+1) follows logically from it: that *if* P0(*K*) is a true statement *then* P0(*K*+1) is also true. In mathematical terms I must prove that P0(*K*) *implies* P0(*K*+1), which is written P0(*K*) => P0(*K*+1). P0(*K*) is the particular remark:

> *times K do print* od* is an instruction which prints exactly *K* asterisks provided that $K \geq 0$.

- that is, it is proposition P0 with every *k* replaced by *K*. P0(*K*+1) is a very similar remark:

> *times K+1 do print* od* is an instruction which prints exactly *K*+1 asterisks provided that $K+1 \geq 0$.

To prove that P0(*K*) => P0(*K*+1), therefore, I must prove that *if times K do print* od* prints *K* asterisks, **then** *times K+1 do print* od* certainly prints *K*+1 asterisks. This step in the proof is like the sergeant-major's faith that every soldier will follow his neighbour, or your belief that from any arbitrary step on a staircase you can reach the next one. In the present proof it goes as follows:

(a) Suppose that P0(*K*) is true for some $K \geq 0$: that is, assume that *times K do print* od* prints *K* asterisks. This assumption is called the *inductive hypothesis*.

(b) Show that P0(*K*+1) follows logically from P0(*K*). P0(*K*+1) is a remark about *times K+1 do print* od* so it seems reasonable to try substitution on that instruction:

> *times K+1 do print* od*
>
> = *print**; *times* (*K*+1)−1 *do print* od*
> [because $K \geq 0$ it follows that $K+1 > 0$;
> then definition 6.4 applies]

[†] It is conventional in inductive proofs to use a lower-case letter (for example, *k*) as the parameter of the proposition and to use an upper-case letter (for example, *K*) to stand for the particular case on which the inductive step is based. *k* stands for all cases; *K* may be chosen freely but stands for some particular case.

= *print*; times K do print* od*

Note that the decomposition of *times K+1* into a sequence depends critically on the fact that $K \geq 0$: it wouldn't be valid, for example, if K was equal to -1.

(c) At this point in the proof the inductive hypothesis comes into play. I have proved that *times K+1 do print* od* is the same as *print*; times K do print* od* when $K \geq 0$. The inductive hypothesis is that *times K do print* od* is an instruction with a particular sort of effect, and the proof is trying to show that *times K+1 do print* od* has the effect it does because of what I assumed about *times K do print* od*. The next step of the proof is to say that under the inductive hypothesis:

> *print*; times K do print* od*
> = *print*;* an instruction which prints K asterisks
> = a program which prints $K+1$ asterisks

The inductive step has shown that *if times K do print* od* prints K asterisks, **then** *times K+1 do print* od* must print $K+1$ asterisks: *if* you stand on that step, *then* you can reach the next; *if* soldier K moves, *then* soldier $K+1$ will follow. The base step showed that *times 0 do print* od* prints 0 asterisks: you *can* reach the base of the stair, soldier 1 *will* hear the order. The conclusion is that by counting upwards you can show that any one of the numbered instructions has the property: you *can* reach any step you like, any soldier you choose *will* eventually move forward. P0(k) is proved true for any $k \geq 0$.

Making mistakes

Proofs by induction can go wrong, just as programs can go wrong. The easiest way to make a wrong proof is to make one in which the proof doesn't rest on the base case. Suppose that I could prove that P0($K+1$) followed from P0(K), but only when I assumed that $K > 0$. Then my proof would be in trouble: remarks about *times 1 do print* od* would then *not* necessarily follow from remarks about *times 0 do print* od*. The sergeant-major would have this difficulty if soldier number 2 hates soldier number 1: then telling number 2 to move makes the rest of the army move but telling number 1 to move has no effect on number 2 and, therefore, has no effect on any other soldier either.

Another way to make an invalid proof is to skip some cases. For example, suppose that I proved that P0($K+2$) follows from P0(K). Then P0 would be true for even cases only: remarks about *times 2 do print* od* would follow from remarks about *times 0 do print* od*, remarks about *times 4 do print* od* from remarks about *times 2 do print* od*, and so on, but that proof wouldn't help you to be certain about what *times 1* or *times 3* or *times 5 do print* od* might do.

I have proved that any execution of *times k do print* od* has a particular property but like the sergeant-major I haven't proved much about a program which contains *every* execution. In fact you have good reason to suppose that such a program would never finish execution no matter how (finitely) fast it printed asterisks.

You might object that my simple induction proof is a sledgehammer to crack a nut, that such an obvious property of the *times-do* instruction doesn't really need a proof. The answer to the first objection is that indeed induction is a powerful technique used here to prove something rather simple, but proofs aren't like sledgehammers: you need to practise on small examples. The answer to the second objection you know already from experience: whenever you make a mistake in writing a program, what is 'obvious' to you turns out to be false. Proofs help to ensure that only what is true is obvious.

7.3 DOUBLE INDUCTION

Quite often we need to prove something about a set of things which we can't number simply 0,1,2,.. but we need to number with pairs of numbers (0,0),(0,1),(0,2),...,(1,0),(1,1),.. Consider, for example, the following program:

times m do NL; times n do print* od od

program 7.1

This program certainly prints an *m*-by-*n* rectangle of asterisks whenever $m \geq 0$ and $n \geq 0$. How can this be proved? The formal proposition might be

> P1: An execution of program 7.1 prints a sequence of *m* lines, each consisting of *n* asterisks, whenever $m \geq 0$ and $n \geq 0$.

I want to establish the truth of $P1(m, n)$ for any *m* and *n*. There are two different ways in which I might proceed.

I might first establish $P1(0,0)$ and then show that $P1(M+1, 0)$ follows from $P1(M, 0)$: that would be a simple induction proof like the proof of P0 in section 7.2 and it would enable me to conclude $P1(m, 0)$ for any *m*. Then if I could show that $P1(M, N+1)$ follows from $P1(M, N)$ I would have completed the proof[†]. The idea can be illustrated by a diagram, shown in figure 7.1. You can reach any particular *M* by moving along the bottom line, using the proof that $P1(m,0)$ is true for any *m*, and then up to the *N* you want, using the proof that $P1(M, n)$ leads to $P1(M, n+1)$.

Alternatively, you can do the same thing in the other dimension, proving $P1(0, n)$ first - see figure 7.2 - and there are other ways as well, such as moving along

---

[†] From $P1(m,0)$ I have, in particular, $P1(M, 0)$. From $P1(M, 0)$ and $P1(M, N) => P1(M, N+1)$ I have $P1(M, n)$ for any $n \geq 0$. And since *M* was chosen arbitrarily I have $P1(m, n)$ for any $m, n \geq 0$.

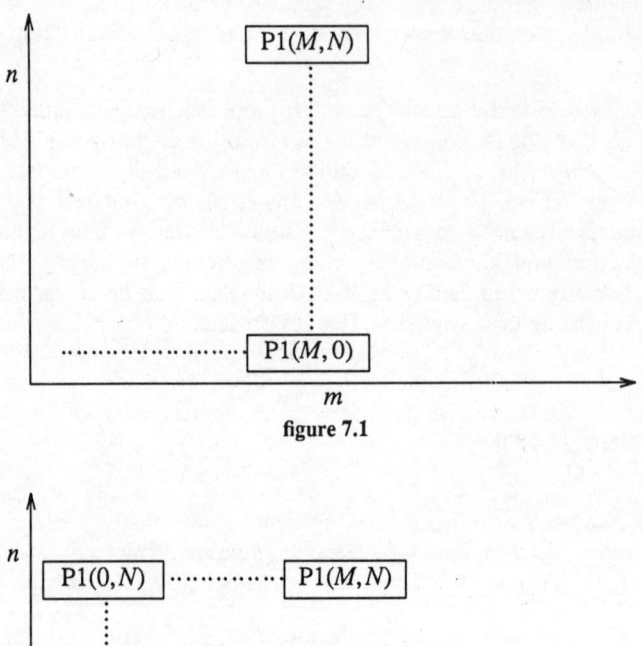

figure 7.1

figure 7.2

diagonals, which I shan't bother to illustrate here.

In the present case the technique of figure 7.2 seems appropriate, just because *times* 0 *do NL*; *times n do print* od od* is equivalent to *donothing* whatever the value of *n*: the proof of P1(0, *n*) for any *n* is completed and doesn't even involve the assumption that $n \geq 0$. To move across the diagram the inductive hypothesis is P1(M, N) for some $M, N \geq 0$: that is, that *times M do NL*; *times N do print* od od* prints *M* lines each of *N* asterisks for some $M, N \geq 0$. The next step is to show that P1($M+1, N$) follows: because that is a proposition about *times M+1 do .. od* it is sensible to start with that instruction:

   times M+1 do NL; *times N do print* od od*

= *NL*; *times N do print* od*;
      times M do NL; *times N do print* od od*   [since $M+1 > 0$,
                                                                              definition 6.4 applies]

= NL; *times N do print* od*;
   print M lines of N asterisks   [by inductive hypothesis]

= NL; *print N asterisks*;
   print M lines of N asterisks   [since $N \geq 0$ and by proof
                                                    of P0 above]

= print M+1 lines of N asterisks

If I had tried the figure 7.1 approach instead, I could certainly prove that *times* 0 *do NL*; *times* 0 *do print* od od* is *donothing*, which proves P1(0,0). I could assume P1(M,0): that is, that *times M do NL*; *times* 0 *do print* od od* prints M lines each consisting of 0 asterisks. Then by an argument like that which proved P0 above, I can show that P1(M+1,0) follows: that is, that *times M+1 do NL*; *times* 0 *do print* od od* prints M+1 lines of 0 asterisks. But if I assume P1(M,N) for some $M, N \geq 0$ just as in the proof above, I cannot easily transform

times M do NL; *times N+1 do print* od od*

into anything which includes

times M do NL; *times N do print* od od*

so this proof won't go through.

-=-=-=-=-=-=-=-=-=-=-=-

Exercise 7.1
Prove that the program *times m do P od*; *times n do P od* is equivalent to the program *times m+n do P od* whenever $m \geq 0$ and $n \geq 0$. [Hint: either of the techniques will do in this case.]

Exercise 7.2
Prove that *times n do P od*; *times n do P od* = *times 2n do P od*. [Hint: easy after you have done exercise 7.1.]

Exercise 7.3
Prove that *times m do times n do P od od* = *times m×n do P od* whenever $m, n \geq 0$.

Exercise 7.4
Prove that *times n×n do P od* = *times n do times n do P od od*. [Hint: see exercise 7.3.]

-=-=-=-=-=-=-=-=-=-=-=-

Exercises 7.1-7.4 show how it may sometimes be necessary to prove a general result in order to establish something simple. Take exercises 7.3 and 7.4: you can't easily transform *times N+1 do times N+1 do P od od* into anything involving *times N do times N do P od od*: but if you have proved that *times m do times n do P od od* is equivalent to *times m×n do P od* - a straightforward double induction - then the case when m=n is an immediate consequence.

7.4 CARE WITH PROPOSITIONS

Programmers, as you will already have learnt, must be very careful in what they write because a programming system takes account of *exactly* what a program says. Proofs must also be exact but at present there are no widely available mechanical proof-followers which can scrutinise our proofs in the way that programming systems scrutinise our programs. This means that unfortunately you may make mistakes in a proof without knowing it[†]. The place where care is most essential is in phrasing the proposition which you hope to prove. Often when making a proof you will find that your first attempt at a proposition isn't good enough and you have to alter it a bit. For example, consider the proof of P1 above. In that proof I appealed to your understanding to say that the sequence

$$NL; \text{ print } N \text{ asterisks; print } M \text{ lines of } N \text{ asterisks}$$

prints $M+1$ lines each of N asterisks. But it might not: the discussion of programs 2.2 and 2.3 in chapter 2 shows that this conclusion might not be true. For example, suppose that the M lines were printed by the instruction

$$\textit{times } M \textit{ do times } N \textit{ do print* od; NL od}$$

Then the conclusion wouldn't be justified, because the whole program would print M lines, the first of which would contain $2N$ asterisks. But of course that instruction isn't the one which is used and the proof should say so.

It would have been better if the proposition had been worded:

P1a: An execution of program 7.1 prints a sequence of m lines, each consisting of n asterisks, *starting on the line below the cpp*, whenever $m \geq 0$ and $n \geq 0$.

This more precise definition makes it clear that the original conclusion really *is* justified: the inductive hypothesis P1a(M,N) allows me to conclude that:

$$\textit{times } M+1 \textit{ do NL; times } N \textit{ do print* od od}$$

$$= NL; \text{ print } N \text{ asterisks;}$$
$$\quad \text{print } M \text{ lines of } N \text{ asterisks starting on the line below the cpp}$$

$$= \text{ print } M+1 \text{ lines of } N \text{ asterisks starting on the line below the cpp}$$

Although the original conclusion was true, the argument I made didn't completely justify it. I picked a hole in that proof and then plugged it up by revising the proposition.

[†] Don't be disheartened - lack of mechanical support has its advantages! Proofs can be written in a more relaxed way than programs in a mechanical code: for example, you can miss out intermediate steps which are just obvious. And you can invent new notation because no mechanical (=stupid, mindless) agent has to be persuaded of its worth.

A slightly harder proof

Consider another example. The procedure definition

> *def A(n) =*
> *for i rbt 1..n do NL; times i do print* od od*
> *enddef*

program 7.2

describes a procedure which prints an *n*-by-*n* triangle pattern. For example, the procedure call *A*(5) prints the pattern

```
*****
****
***
**
*
```

How can I prove that any execution of the procedure prints an *n*-by-*n* triangle? I might start by writing down the obvious proposition:

> P2: An execution of *A*(*k*), where *k*≥0, prints a *k*-by-*k* triangle pattern.

The proof starts out reasonably enough:

> *A*(0) = *for i rbt 1..0 do NL; times i do print* od od*
> = *donothing* [because 1..0 is the empty sequence]

So *A*(0)=*donothing*: does that prove P2(0)? In order to move my proof along, I would like to say that to print nothing is to print a zero-by-zero triangle pattern - but I think I have to be more honest than that. An *n*-by-*n* triangle pattern, as printed by procedure *A*, is a sequence of *n* lines. Certainly *A*(0) prints a pattern of 0 lines, so P2(0) is a true statement according to that definition. But not every *n*-line pattern is a triangle, and sooner or later I must say something about the number of asterisks on each line. What makes the pattern a triangle is that each line overlaps the next by exactly one position. I can rephrase the proposition:

> P2a: An execution of *A*(*k*), where *k*≥0, prints a sequence of *k* lines in which each line is exactly one asterisk shorter than the one before.

Notice that this proposition says nothing about triangles. Rather it describes a pattern which you can deduce is a triangle: that is, if P2a(*j*) is true then A(*j*) prints a pattern which we can recognise as a *j*-by-*j* triangle pattern. Notice also that P2a(0) is true because *A*(0)=*donothing* and the elements of a zero-length sequence each have every property you can think of.

The next step in my proof is to make an inductive hypothesis that P2a(*K*) is true for some arbitrary *K*≥0 and to show that if that were so then P2a(*K*+1) would follow.

(a) Assume P2a(*K*) for some *K*≥0: that is, assume that *A*(*K*) prints a sequence of *K* lines in which each line is exactly one asterisk shorter than the one before.

(b) Show that P2a(K+1) follows from the hypothesis. As usual this means transforming the instruction which P2a(K+1) makes a remark about:

$A(K+1) = for\ i\ rbt\ 1..K+1\ do\ NL;\ times\ i\ do\ print*\ od\ od$

$= ([let\ i=K+1\ NL;\ times\ i\ do\ print*\ od]);$
  $for\ i\ rbt\ 1..(K+1)-1\ do\ NL;\ times\ i\ do\ print*\ od\ od$
  [$K{\geq}0$, therefore $K+1{>}0$, therefore $1..K+1$ is not
  the empty sequence; then the rbt version of
  definition 6.5 applies]

$= NL;\ times\ K+1\ do\ print*\ od;$
  $for\ i\ rbt\ 1..K\ do\ NL;\ times\ i\ do\ print*\ od\ od$

$= NL;\ times\ K+1\ do\ print*\ od;\ A(K)$
  [applying the definition of procedure call in reverse]

To complete the inductive step I must show that the sequence $NL;\ times\ K+1\ do\ print*\ od;\ A(K)$ makes P2a(K+1) true: to do that I must show that it prints a sequence of K+1 lines in which each line is one asterisk shorter than the one before. By inductive hypothesis $A(K)$ prints K lines, so the sequence seems to print K+1 lines. Every line printed by $A(K)$ is one shorter than the one before. Substitution has shown that the pattern printed by $A(K+1)$ starts with a line of K+1 asterisks (by P0 above); to polish off the proof I need to show that the first line printed by $A(K)$ is exactly $(K+1)-1 = K$ asterisks long. But the inductive hypothesis doesn't say anything about the actual lengths of the lines printed by $A(K)$, only that each is shorter than the one before. The proof is stuck.

The solution to the problem is to change the proposition once again. You should know perfectly well that in the pattern printed by $A(k)$ the first line has k asterisks, the next has $k-1$ asterisks, and so on until the last line, which has just one asterisk. If the proposition says so, then the proof can go through:

P2b: An execution of $A(k)$, where $k{\geq}0$, prints a sequence of k lines in which the first line has exactly k asterisks and each subsequent line is exactly one asterisk shorter than the one before.

P2b(0) is still trivially true. The substitution above is still valid (it uses only the definition of A, not any propositions about it). The final step in the proof observes that $A(K+1)$ prints a line of K+1 asterisks and then (by the new inductive hypothesis P2b(K)) a pattern of K lines which starts with a line of K asterisks and continues with each line one asterisk shorter than the one before. This is evidently a pattern which satisifies P2b(K+1), and the inductive proof is completed.

On picking holes

A proof is a logical argument justifying an assertion. It is addressed by one human being to another. In the last analysis a proof is acceptable if the person giving it and the person receiving it both believe in it. Some people might have believed the proof based on proposition P2. I feel that to print $K+1$ asterisks followed by a 'K-by-K triangle pattern' isn't obviously a '$(K+1)$-by-$(K+1)$ triangle pattern' so I didn't like that proof and refined it. I don't think that many people would be convinced by an inductive proof based on proposition P2a because the inductive proof doesn't go through in the final step, but most people are convinced by the proof based on proposition P2b.

Notice that formal substitutions on programs can only convert one program into another, demonstrating their equality but not telling you what either of the programs *mean*. For example, I can convert *times* 3 *do print* * *od* into *print* *; *print* *; *print* *, but I rely on your good sense to convince yourself that this sequence prints three asterisks. The proof that *times k do print* * *od* prints *k* asterisks relied on a hand-waving argument in the end, and the proof of proposition P2b above rested on that proof. My proof of proposition P2b is therefore not as 'formal' as it might appear, but your faith in it shouldn't be shaken by a certain amount of informality.

Your faith in a proof can be destroyed by a counter-example. Suppose it could be shown that for some particular positive value of i, executing $A(i)$ doesn't print a triangle. Then the proof would necessarily be wrong and you could conclude that I must have made a slip somewhere. In this case I don't think I have made such a slip and I believe that the conclusion is true: I believe that the program really does print triangle patterns.

Proposition P2b has the same deficiency that P1 had. It doesn't say that $A(k)$ starts printing on the line below the cpp: so a malicious opponent might propose that although $A(3)$ prints the pattern:

```
***
**
*
```

and although $A(4)$ is equivalent to the sequence *NL*; *times* 4 *do print* * *od*; $A(3)$, the instruction $A(4)$ might print:

```
*******
**
*
```

This pattern is, after all, four asterisks 'followed by' the $A(3)$ pattern. But I know that this isn't the pattern which $A(4)$ prints and I must make the proposition more definite so as to make that point precisely:

P2c: An execution of $A(k)$, where $k \geq 0$, prints a pattern of k lines in which the first line has k asterisks and is printed on the line below the cpp and every subsequent line is one asterisk shorter than the one before.

The inductive proof goes through just as before, and this time the step in the reasoning which says that $A(K+1)$ prints a $K+1$ line pattern can be a little more definite.

Proposition P2c doesn't deflect all criticism of the proof. How can we show that $A(3)$ prints the pattern shown above, and not the following pattern?

```
*  *    *
   *  *
      *
```

This is a pattern in which the first line 'contains three asterisks' and each line is 'one asterisk shorter' than the one before. To meet this objection, the proposition must be strengthened still further to make it clear that each line consists *only* of asterisks.

Is it helpful to pick holes in proofs which seem acceptable, or is it only something which teachers do to students? The answer must be that it is a very useful thing to do. Deflecting criticism by improving the standard of reasoning in a proof increases your confidence that what it asserts is really true. It makes sure that you know what you are talking about. And of course, sometimes the pernickety criticisms turn out to be justified, showing you that your 'proof' is wrong, that what it asserts isn't so.

-=-=-=-=-=-=-=-=-=-=-=-=-

Exercise 7.5
Write the improved proposition suggested above, and write out the steps in the improved proof that $A(k)$ prints a k-by-k triangle pattern.

Exercise 7.6
Prove that the instruction *for i rt* 1..*n do NL; times i do print* od od* prints an n-by-n triangle pattern. [Hint: you will have to 'unroll' this repetition at the latter end and your proposition should define where the instruction leaves the cpp.]

Exercise 7.7
Prove that the instruction

> *for i rbt* 1..*n do NL; times n–i do printspace od;*
> > *times i do print* od*
> *od*

prints an n-by-n triangle pattern. [Hint: if you make a proposition $Q(k)$ you will probably find that $Q(K+1)$ doesn't depend on $Q(K)$ and you will have to do a double induction on a more complicated proposition which allows spaces at the start of a line.]

Exercise 7.8
Prove that the instruction

> *for i rt* 1..*n do NL; times n–i do printspace od;*
> > *times i do print* od*
> *od*

prints an n-by-n triangle pattern.

-=-=-=-=-=-=-=-=-=-=-=-=-

7.5 AN INTRICATE EXAMPLE

Consider the effect of an execution of procedure X, defined by:

> $def X(n) =$
> $\quad for\ i\ rt\ 1..n\ do\ X(i-1);\ print*\ od$
> $enddef$

program 7.3

This procedure definition is intricate, but by no means too intricate to execute - see, for example, figure 7.3 at the end of this chapter - and it is a fact that an execution of $X(n)$ prints 2^n-1 asterisks. Some examples:

$X(0) = for\ i\ rt\ 1..0\ do\ ..\ od = donothing$ $\qquad [2^0-1 = 1-1 = 0]$

$X(1) = for\ i\ rt\ 1..1\ do\ X(i-1); print*\ od = X(0); print*$
$\quad = donothing; print* = print*$ $\qquad [2^1-1 = 2-1 = 1]$

$X(2) = for\ i\ rt\ 1..2\ do\ ..\ od = X(0); print*; X(1); print*$
$\quad = donothing; print*; print*; print*$
$\quad = print*; print*; print*$ $\qquad [2^2-1 = 4-1 = 3]$

-=-=-=-=-=-=-=-=-=-=-=-=-

Exercise 7.9
Calculate the effect of $X(3)$, $X(4)$, $X(5)$, $X(6)$ and $X(7)$.

-=-=-=-=-=-=-=-=-=-=-=-=-

I wish to prove the following proposition:

> P3: An execution of $X(k)$ when $k \geq 0$ will print exactly 2^k-1 asterisks.

The base step considers $X(0)$:

> $X(0) = for\ i\ rt\ 1..0\ do\ X(i-1); print*\ od$
> $\quad = donothing = $ print 0 asterisks
> $\quad = $ print 1-1 asterisks = print 2^0-1 asterisks

The base case is proved: $X(0)$ does print 2^0-1 asterisks. The inductive hypothesis is to assume P3(K) for some $K \geq 0$: that is, assume that $X(K)$ prints 2^K-1 asterisks. The inductive step must show that P3($K+1$) follows from this assumption. As usual I start by transforming the instruction which P3($K+1$) describes:

> $X(K+1) = for\ i\ rt\ 1..K+1\ do\ X(i-1); print*\ od$

$= for\ i\ rt\ 1..(K+1)-1\ do\ X(i-1); print*\ od;$
$(let\ i=K+1\ X(i-1); print*)$
  [since $K \geq 0$, $K+1 \geq 1$; then $1..K+1$ isn't empty
  and definition 6.5 applies]

$= for\ i\ rt\ 1..K\ do\ X(i-1); print*\ od;\ X((K+1)-1); print*$

$= for\ i\ rt\ 1..K\ do\ X(i-1); print*\ od;\ X(K); print*$

$= X(K); X(K); print*$

Now by inductive hypothesis $X(K)$ prints 2^K-1 asterisks, so $X(K); X(K); print*$ prints $2^K-1 + 2^K-1 + 1$ asterisks = $2\times(2^K)-2+1$ asterisks = $2^{K+1}-1$ asterisks.

Notice how this proof depended on unrolling the *for-do* at the back to produce *for* $i\ rt\ 1..K$, and notice also how the shortened *for-do* was replaced by a procedure call, using definition 5.1 'in reverse'.

-=-=-=-=-=-=-=-=-=-=-=-=-

Exercise 7.10
Given the definition

$$def\ Y(n) = NL; for\ i\ rt\ 1..n\ do\ Y(i-1); print*\ od\ enddef$$

prove that $Y(k)$, when $k \geq 1$, prints a 2^n-line pattern in which alternate lines are blank.

-=-=-=-=-=-=-=-=-=-=-=-=-

7.6 STRONG INDUCTION

How can the sergeant-major know that the soldiers are all warlike and will advance with their neighbours? He has an infinite population and he can't have interviewed them all. Even if he made every third soldier a corporal and every tenth soldier a sergeant and delegated the intervewing to his NCOs he could never listen to their infinite number of reports. Again he must trust to mathematical induction: he must *prove* that they will fight.

Suppose that the warrior race reproduces asexually, parthenogenetically like aphids or dandelions. This of course means that the sergeant-major is female, and all of her soldiers female too. Suppose that a warlike mother gives birth only to warlike babies. Then if the sergeant-major can prove that every soldier is the daughter of a warlike mother the whole army will be proved warlike and will fight.

A simple induction proof, like the one which shows that her army will advance on command, wouldn't do. If she numbers the children in order of birth she certainly won't find that soldier number $K+1$ is always the daughter of soldier number K. Even warriors don't reproduce like that, all in a line. Soldier number

$K+1$ is likely to be the daughter of soldier number $K-1000$ or $K-1\,000\,000$ or perhaps even soldier number 1.

Suppose that she knows that, bee-like, the whole population has sprung from the loins of one warrior, the sergeant-major herself. (Which of course means that she and I must stop pretending that the population is infinite because she hasn't been alive for ever.) She knows for sure that there was a time when the whole population was as warlike as herself, because once the whole population *was* herself. This is her base case. She knows also that *if* at any time the whole population is warlike (her inductive hypothesis) *then* any child which is born must come from a warlike mother and therefore will be warlike. That is her inductive step. She can conclude, standing beside her line of soldiers which has shrunk to finite length but is growing with every birth, that it will indeed advance on the whisper of command.

As always she can be frustrated and fail to make a proof. If daughters can be created out of the air, as presumably she once was, if originally she wasn't the only mother alive, or if foreign peace-loving mothers ever infiltrate (perish the thought!) then her proof will break down. And in any case she will never breed the infinite army that she dreams of and I once described.

As it is with warrior-daughters, so it is sometimes with program executions. Consider the executions of procedure $Z^\dagger$ and the proposition P4:

$$def\, Z(n) =$$
$$print*;\, for\ i\ rt\ 1..n\ do\ Z(i \div 2);\, Z(i \div 2)\ od$$
$$enddef$$

P4: An execution of $Z(k)$, where $k \geq 0$, prints an odd number of asterisks.

The base case is just as you might expect:

$$Z(0) = print*;\, for\ i\ rt\ 1..0\ do\ Z(i \div 2);\, Z(i \div 2)\ od$$
$$= print*;\, donothing$$
$$= print\ 1\ asterisk$$

Next I assume P4(K) and try to show that it implies P4($K+1$):

$$Z(K+1) = print*;\, for\ i\ rt\ 1..K+1\ do\ Z(i \div 2);\, Z(i \div 2)\ od$$
$$= print*;\, for\ i\ rt\ 1..K\ do\ Z(i \div 2);\, Z(i \div 2)\ od;\, Z((K+1) \div 2);\, Z((K+1) \div 2)$$
$$[\text{since } K \geq 0 \text{ definition 6.5 applies}]$$
$$= Z(K);\, Z((K+1) \div 2);\, Z((K+1) \div 2)$$

Here the simple inductive argument breaks down: P4($K+1$) depends on P4(K), certainly, but it depends on P4($(K+1) \div 2$) as well. This is a funny kind of staircase, where you need to stand on more than one step to climb it. But it is like the sergeant-major's problem, because certainly $Z((K+1) \div 2)$ is an ancestor of $Z(K)$.

$\dagger$ '$\div$' means division keeping only the whole-number part: for example, $4 \div 2 = 5 \div 2 = 2$.

To make a *strong inductive* proof I have to assume that *every* procedure call $Z(0)$, $Z(1)$, $Z(2)$, .., $Z(K)$ prints an odd number of asterisks: then I can show that $Z(K+1)$ also prints an odd number. The base case is P4(0), just as before. This time the inductive hypothesis assumes P4(0), P4(1), .., up to and including P4(K) (in mathematical notation $\forall i: 0 \leq i \leq K: \text{P4}(i)$). I transform $Z(K+1)$ just as before

$$Z(K+1) = Z(K); Z((K+1)\div 2); Z((K+1)\div 2)$$

Now since $K+1 > 0$ I know that $(K+1)\div 2 \geq 0$ because a positive number doesn't become negative when you halve it. And from the same premise it follows that $(K+1)\div 2 < K+1$ because a number which is bigger than zero must get smaller when you halve it. From these facts you can deduce that $0 \leq (K+1)\div 2 \leq K$ when $K \geq 0$, and then by the inductive hypothesis:

$$Z(K+1) = Z(K); Z((K+1)\div 2); Z((K+1)\div 2)$$
$$= \text{print an odd number of asterisks;}$$
$$\text{print an odd number of asterisks;}$$
$$\text{print an odd number of asterisks}$$

If you add three odd numbers you get an odd number; therefore $Z(K+1)$ prints an odd number of asterisks.

This example strains a little to make its point. Later chapters will pose more realistic problems which can be solved by the strong induction technique.

7.7 SIMPLE INDUCTION EQUALS STRONG INDUCTION

Some people find simple induction easy to understand but can't get a grasp on strong induction. It may help to know that under the skin the techniques are the same. One of them proves things about a sequence of objects (soldiers lined up in the desert) and the other proves things about sequences of sets-of-objects (successive populations of warriors after each birth).

The induction problem is to show that in an infinite set of objects every object has a particular property P. In either induction technique we number the objects 1, 2, 3, .. or whatever. Then in *simple* induction we show that object number 1 has property P and that any object $K+1$ inherits it from K, so that 2 inherits it from 1, 3 from 2, and so on for every object, counting upwards, climbing the staircase. In *strong* induction we consider the sets of objects $\{1\}$, $\{1,2\}$, $\{1,2,3\}$, .. - sets of size i containing every object 1..i - and try to show inheritance between sets-of-objects rather than objects. That is, we try to show that if the Kth set has property P then the $K+1$th set will inherit it.

The property P we want to prove in a strong induction proof can always be stated as 'every element of the kth set has property P1', for example, 'every member of the kth population is warlike'. To prove the base case we must show that the set $\{1\}$ has property P - which means in practice, just as in a simple induction proof, proving that the object numbered 1 has property P1. The inductive hypothesis is that every member of the set $\{1, 2, .., K\}$ has property P1 and the inductive step must show that if this is so, then every member of the set $\{1, 2, .., K, K+1\}$ has the property too. But the only difference between these sets is the element $K+1$, and the inductive hypothesis has assumed that all the common members have the property, so all that is needed is to prove that the $K+1$th object inherits property P1 from the objects numbered $1, 2, .., K$.

Simple induction and strong induction are the same in principle: one is induction on sequences of numbers, the other is induction on sequences of (numbered) sets-of-numbers. The surface difference between the techniques comes from the short cut in the argument: if you assume every element of the Kth set has a particular property, you don't have to prove it again when the same elements appear in the $K+1$th set.

7.8 ENVIRONMENT DIAGRAMS REVISITED

The substitution explanation gives a meaning to instructions which call procedure X (see section 7.5 above) or procedure Z (see section 7.6). Yet they are fairly intricate definitions and in particular they are *recursive*: the body of X calls for a sequence of executions of X, for example. Are they too intricate to execute? Certainly they are not and the fact that these definitions can be transcribed into a suitable mechanical code and then executed should persuade you that they are indeed sensible and that they do produce the effects described in the proofs[†].

An environment diagram shows how it is done - see figure 7.3 for example. Within the programming system environments and executions are piled up ('stacked') in the same way as the boxes of the diagram are drawn one on top of the other.

-=-=-=-=-=-=-=-=-=-=-=-

Exercise 7.11
Figure 7.3 is abbreviated. It doesn't show the environments created by *for-do*s as boxes. It only shows a complete description of one execution of $X(0)$, $X(1)$ and $X(2)$. Draw the complete diagram.

Exercise 7.12
Draw the abbreviated environment diagram of $Z(5)$.

[†] They normally produce the effects described but sometimes limitations of the programming system may be shown up. For example, my microcomputer BASIC can cope with $X(10)$ but not with $X(20)$.

Execute $X(3)$ in environment env-0 which defines the basic
instructions and $X = \lambda(n).($for i rt $1..n$ do $X(i-1)$; $print*$ $)$.

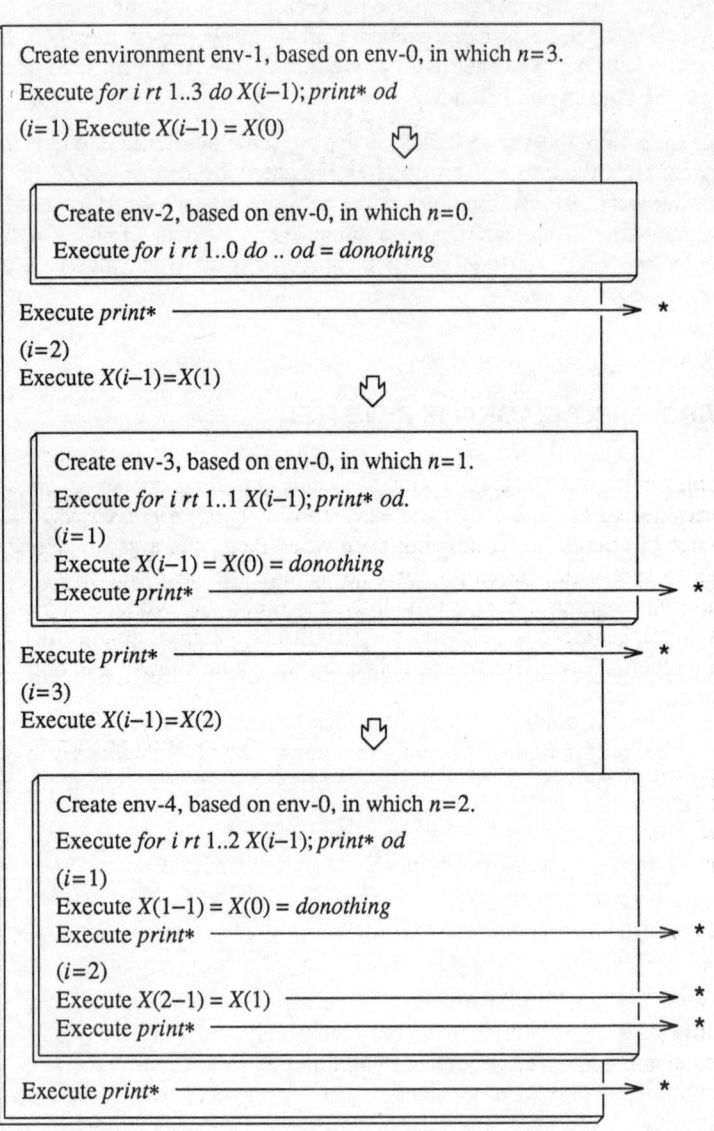

figure 7.3

Chapter 8
CHOICE

Programs which use procedures and counting repetition as their structuring mechanisms can be remarkably intricate but at bottom they are just predictable sequences. They do what the average person would expect of a 'robot' or a 'machine' because when set on a course they follow it no matter what. An example of such a program could be seen controlling robots in car assembly factories during the late 1970s and early 1980s. Those robots blindly followed a sequence of operations, continuing even when there was a gap in the line of car bodies to spot-weld the empty air. To venture too near was to risk your life, because the welding arm moved rapidly, forcefully and without warning to each of its welding positions. The machine handled anything that got in its way with no more feeling or understanding than a runaway train shows to an obstruction on its track.

When programs can choose between different courses of action they lift computing machinery away from the everyday conception of what machines must be like. Linked with the ability to take in information from the outside world, choice structures in a program enable a machine to respond flexibly to circumstances, producing behaviour quite unlike what the average person would expect of a mechanical device. The behaviour can appear so complicated that some people may begin to believe the machine has become intelligent - but that is quite another story.

As I write this book in the mid-1980s, car assembly robots have already become 'intelligent' enough to distinguish between trolleys carrying different types of car bodies and to vary their sequence of welding actions accordingly. It is still very difficult to make the things sensitive to human presence so as to stop them braining unwary humans (plugging the robot in to a TV camera doesn't help because it is so hard to process the flood of information that comes in from the camera).

This chapter is about choice, about making use of information to affect the course of an execution. I leave input - how the execution gets hold of the information - until chapters 10 and 11.

8.1 COMPLETE AND INCOMPLETE CHOICES

The program for a mid-1980s welding robot will normally include a choice between actions. If there are two types of car then there would seem to be a choice between two actions. The choice is probably most easily signalled by a machine-readable label such as a magnetic stripe or a supermarket-style bar code on each assembly-line trolley, sensed by some device attached to the robot. It would seem reasonable that the program should make its choice based on what is on the label:

> *repeatedly*
>   *if* "type1" *on label*:
>   *perform welding sequence* 1
>   *if* "type2" *on label*:
>   *perform welding sequence* 2
> *until switched off*

program 8.1

This program specifies a choice between two actions, but it is unsatisfactory because it doesn't specify what to do in every possible circumstance. The label on the trolley may not read either "type1" or "type2". It may read "type3", there may be no label, it may be so badly damaged that it is unreadable, there may even be a gap in the line so that there is no trolley to carry a label. In any of these circumstances the program is inapplicable and therefore meaningless: a robot using it would be unable to make a choice and would have to stop operating. In order to keep going, the program must consider a third possibility, in this case a simple catch-all for every other circumstance:

> *repeatedly*
>   *if* "type1" *on label*:
>   *perform welding sequence* 1
>   *if* "type2" *on label*:
>   *perform welding sequence* 2
>   *if neither* "type1" *nor* "type2" *on label*:
>   *donothing*
> *until switched off*

program 8.2

This describes a robot which treats type1 and type2 bodies differently *and* leaves unrecognisable body types alone *and* stands still if there is a gap in the line. It is a robot which doesn't damage type3 bodies if it comes across one. This is a true paragon of robotic virtue. (Just wait until it misreads a label, though ..)

It is always necessary to make sure that a choice-structure specifies an action for every circumstance which can arise and it is often the case (see, for example, program 1.6 in chapter 1) that one of the actions turns out to be *donothing*.

Binary choices aren't always adequate

Most mechanical programming codes don't provide a full choice-structuring instruction. Instead they provide a binary choice instruction which allows the program to choose between two courses of action, one if some condition applies and the other if it doesn't. This encourages programmers to overlook the fact that choice-structures should be made to consider every possible circumstance and therefore to write programs which are often absurd and sometimes dangerous. For example, a bad program for the welding robot might be:

> *repeatedly*
> *if* "type1" *on label*:
>   *perform welding sequence* 1
> *otherwise*:
>   *perform welding sequence* 2
> *until switched off*

program 8.3

This program is complete in that it specifies an action for every circumstance but the fundamental error in it is to assume that the only possible circumstances are a type1 label and a type2 label: to assume that if the robot is not standing on an assembly line faced with a type1 trolley then it must be standing on an assembly line faced with a type2 trolley. Unless you can prove that those alternatives are the only possible ones, and I suppose that an assembly line is sufficiently unpredictable to ensure that you never could, this program is not what is required. A robot based on this program could do a lot of damage, confronted with a type1 car on an unlabelled trolley.

In the early days of the BART train system in San Francisco the same sort of programming mistake nearly led to a nasty accident. The story goes[†] that a sensor beside the track was supposed to listen for a signal from a transmitter on each train and switch the points accordingly. A signal received meant 'switch points left' and no signal meant 'switch points ahead'. The line ahead led nowhere because it wasn't yet completed, so every train sent the sensor a signal and was switched safely left - until one day either the sensor or the transmitter was slightly out of adjustment .. The error was corrected by the human driver who managed to stop the train before the end of the tracks ahead. The story illustrates all sorts of lessons, but among them is the lesson that not seeing A doesn't mean that B is there instead.

[†] I *think* this is a true story. I certainly read it in a reputable British magazine. Even if it is only an urban legend, it makes a good point.

Choices can be ambiguous

Many problems have mutually exclusive sets of circumstances, like the welding
problem above - the robot 'sees' either a type1 or a type2 trolley or neither, and
the action in each case is different. Not every problem is like that: for example,
the aircraft-landing program 1.6 of chapter 1 chooses between different actions to
correct the speed, the height and the direction of an aircraft. It is quite reasonable
to suppose that at some instants all three may be slightly out of line and that it
doesn't matter much which of the adjustments the program makes first. The
choice of action in those circumstances is arbitrary and the aircraft-landing
program expresses that arbitrariness with an intentionally ambiguous choice-
structure. You can't predict, and don't care, which of the possible alternatives
the program will select. If you *do* care which alternative is selected, perhaps
because one sequence of actions is safer than another, you must alter the program
to make it select between alternatives more carefully.

Ambiguity in a choice-structure is in general a good thing when it expresses an
arbitrary decision. A program is misleading if it seems to require more careful
choice than is absolutely necessary. The classical example of an ambiguous
choice occurs in a program which prints out the smaller of two numbers. A
programmer weaned on the binary-choice mechanisms of the average
programming code might write:

$$select\ a \leq b\colon printnumber(a)$$
$$b < a\colon printnumber(b)$$
endselect

program 8.4

But the division of action between the two alternatives when $a = b$ is quite
arbitrary. The program might as well be

$$select\ a < b\colon printnumber(a)$$
$$b \leq a\colon printnumber(b)$$
endselect

program 8.5

The first program insists that when $a = b$, it is the value of a that must be printed;
the second insists that it must be the value of b. But when $a = b$ it genuinely
doesn't matter which of them is printed because then *printnumber(a)* and
printnumber(b) have the same effect. It is generally agreed that the most elegant
solution to this problem uses an ambiguous choice: see program 8.6, for example.
This version doesn't specify what it needn't specify. It doesn't say how an agent
should choose between the alternatives when $a = b$ because it doesn't need to.

> select $a≤b$: *printnumber*(a)
> $b≤a$: *printnumber*(b)
> *endselect*

program 8.6

8.2 THE *select* INSTRUCTION

The *select* instruction is the programming-notation description of choice between actions. It starts with the word *select* and ends with *endselect* (I sometimes abbreviate these to *sel* and *es*) and contains a number of **arms**. Each arm consists of a program labelled with a **condition-formula** - a formula which delivers, calculates or is equivalent to the value true or the value false.

An example *select* instruction is shown in the following program, which prints one of two messages.

> select
> $a>b$: *printstring*("a is bigger than b")
> $a<b$: *printstring*("b is bigger than a")
> *endselect*

program 8.7

The effect of a *select* instruction is to execute the program in just *one* of its arms, choosing an arm depending on the values of the various condition-formulas. In program 8.7 the conditions are simple comparisons between number-values a and b, the programs single *printstring* instructions.

Execution of a *select* instruction proceeds as follows:

(a) The condition-formulas are evaluated: if any of them is meaningless, the whole *select* is meaningless.

(b) If any of the condition-formulas delivers true, the program labelled by one of the true conditions is executed.

(c) If all of the condition-formulas deliver false, the whole *select* is meaningless.

definition 8.1

So program 8.7 is meaningful provided that a and b identify different numbers. Program 8.8 shows a similar instruction, constructed so that it is meaningful even when $a=b$.

Note that according to definition 8.1 the order of the arms within a *select* doesn't matter - it contains a *set* of arms, not a sequence.

-=-=-=-=-=-=-=-=-=-=-=-

```
select
   a>b: printstring("a is bigger than b")
   a<b: printstring("b is bigger than a")
   a=b: printstring("both the same")
endselect
```

program 8.8

Exercise 8.1

Define a procedure *fig* so that *fig*(*x*, *n*) prints either squares or triangles of size *n*-by-*n* according to whether *x* is 'S' or 'T'. For example, *fig*('S', 3) should print a three-by-three square.

Exercise 8.2

Given your answer to exercise 8.1, what is printed by *fig*('H', 4)? What is printed by *fig*('S', −1)? [Hint: in at least one of these cases the procedure will probably be equivalent to a sequence which contains a meaningless instruction.]

Exercise 8.3

Modify your procedure definition so that a message is printed if the size of the figure is negative or outside the capacity of your screen, and a different message if the identifying letter is neither 'S' nor 'T'.

Exercise 8.4

Check that in your answer to exercise 8.3 only one of the condition-formulas is true under each of the following circumstances:

a. x='S', n=4
b. x='S', n=−1
c. x='H', n=4

Exercise 8.5

With your modified procedure definition, what would be printed by *fig*('H', −1)? One or two messages? Is your *select* instruction ambiguous in this circumstance? If so, does it matter?

-=-=-=-=-=-=-=-=-=-=-=-=-

8.3 MANIPULATING CONDITION-FORMULAS

Arithmetic formulas calculate and deliver numbers. Condition-formulas calculate and deliver one of the two logical values true or false. Comparisons, like $a=b$, $a<b$, $a \geq b$, and so on, are simple condition-formulas. More complicated formulas can be made by combining simpler formulas using the operations '∧' ('and') and '∨' ('or'), in much the same way as × and / combine numerical formulas. $F1 \wedge F2$ delivers true when both $F1$ and $F2$ deliver true and delivers false when either or both of them deliver false. $F1 \vee F2$ delivers false when both $F1$ and $F2$ deliver false, and delivers true when either or both of them deliver true. $\neg F$ ('not' F) is inversion or logical negation: it delivers true when F

delivers false, false when F delivers true.

When reasoning about choice instructions and choice formulas it is usually necessary to manipulate the condition-formulas they contain. The technique is very like manipulating ordinary arithmetic-algebra formulas. Just as there are rules of equivalence which apply to formulas containing arithmetic operators, so there are rules for condition-formulas, which I state below. In understanding these formulas it may help to observe that there is an arithmetical analogy: *true* behaves like 1, *false* like 0, $a \wedge b$ is like multiplication $a \times b$. $a \vee b$ is like addition $a+b$, but it sticks at 1 (that is, $1+1+1=1$). $\neg f$ is like $1-f$.

The simplest rules are very like those of arithmetic:

$$
\begin{aligned}
a \vee true &= true & (1+1=1,\ 0+1=1) \\
a \vee false &= a & (a+0 = a) \\
a \vee a &= a & (1+1=1,\ 0+0=0) \\
a \vee b &= b \vee a & (a+b = b+a) \\[4pt]
a \wedge true &= a & (a \times 1 = a) \\
a \wedge false &= false & (a \times 0 = 0) \\
a \wedge a &= a & (1 \times 1=1,\ 0 \times 0=0) \\
a \wedge b &= b \wedge a & (a \times b = b \times a) \\[4pt]
\neg true &= false & (1-1=0) \\
\neg false &= true & (1-0=1) \\
\neg(\neg a) &= a & (1-(1-a)=a)
\end{aligned}
$$

A condition is either true or it isn't, and it can't be both at once:

$$
\begin{aligned}
a \vee \neg a &= true & (1+0=1,\ 0+1=1) \\
a \wedge \neg a &= false & (1 \times 0=0,\ 0 \times 1=0)
\end{aligned}
$$

Lots more rules can be derived from those above, but it is convenient to give some of them explicitly. When formulas with '$\wedge$' or '$\vee$' are negated the operations change as well as the operated-on values:

$$
\begin{aligned}
\neg(a \vee b) &= \neg a \wedge \neg b \\
\neg(a \wedge b) &= \neg a \vee \neg b
\end{aligned}
$$

In algebra multiplication 'distributes over' addition, so that $a \times (b+c) = (a \times b)+(a \times c)$. In Boolean algebra both '$\wedge$' and '$\vee$' distribute:

$$
\begin{aligned}
a \vee (b \wedge c) &= (a \vee b) \wedge (a \vee c) \\
a \wedge (b \vee c) &= (a \wedge b) \vee (a \wedge c)
\end{aligned}
$$

Because a formula is always either true or false, some simplifications are possible:

$$
\begin{aligned}
a \vee (a \wedge b) &= a \\
a \wedge (a \vee b) &= a
\end{aligned}
$$

-=-=-=-=-=-=-=-=-=-=-=-

Exercise 8.6
Check the last six definitions by calculating the value of each side for all four possible combinations of values of a and b.

-=-=-=-=-=-=-=-=-=-=-=-=-

Many programs can be simplified by simplifying formulas which involve the inequalities ≥, >, <, ≤, ≠. There are several helpful rules which can all be derived from one single rule. In comparing two numbers one is less than the other, or vice-versa, or they are equal:

$$a<b \lor a=b \lor a>b$$

Equality has an inverse and so does every inequality:

$\neg(a=b)$	$=$	$a \neq b$
$\neg(a<b)$	$=$	$a \geq b$
$\neg(a \leq b)$	$=$	$a>b$
$\neg(a \geq b)$	$=$	$a<b$
$\neg(a>b)$	$=$	$a \leq b$
$\neg(a \neq b)$	$=$	$a=b$

Some inequalities are obviously combinations:

$a \leq b$	$=$	$a<b \lor a=b$
$a \geq b$	$=$	$a>b \lor a=b$

from which it follows that they all are:

$a>b$	$=$	$\neg(a \leq b)$
	$=$	$\neg(a<b \lor a=b)$
	$=$	$\neg(a<b) \land \neg(a=b)$
	$=$	$a \geq b \land a \neq b$

-=-=-=-=-=-=-=-=-=-=-=-=-

Exercise 8.7
Prove that:

$a<b$	$=$	$a \leq b \land a \neq b$
$a=b$	$=$	$a \geq b \land a \leq b$
$a \neq b$	$=$	$a<b \lor a>b$

-=-=-=-=-=-=-=-=-=-=-=-=-

Because of the preceding rules, some combinations of inequalities can be simplified. For example:

$a<b \land a \geq b$	$=$	$a<b \land \neg(a<b)$
	$=$	*false*

-=-=-=-=-=-=-=-=-=-=-=-=-

Exercise 8.8
Prove that:

$a<b \land a>b$	$=$	*false*
$a \leq b \lor a \geq b$	$=$	*true*

Exercise 8.9

Construct the simplest inverse of

$$K \geq n \wedge (n=1 \vee n>1)$$

-=-=-=-=-=-=-=-=-=-=-=-=-

8.4 SUBSTITUTION DEFINITION OF *select*

Definition 8.1 shows how execution of a *select* instruction is broken down into a sequence of calculations and executions. The substitution definition of the *select* instruction shows how to produce the same effect by replacing a choice-structure by one of its arms. In principle you do this by calculating the value of the condition-formulas and throwing away any arms labelled by false. If this leaves a *select* which contains only a single arm, labelled by true, you can replace the *select* with that arm.

First, then, you can delete any false-labelled arm from a *select*, or vice-versa insert a false-labelled arm into any *select* without affecting its meaning (definition 8.2). Second, you can replace a *select* which consists of only a true-labelled arm by the program of that arm, or vice-versa replace any program by a *select* with a single true-labelled arm (definition 8.3). A *select* instruction with more than one true-labelled arm is not meaningless but it is ambiguous. Its effect is to make an arbitrary choice between the true-labelled arms and to execute the chosen program.

$$select \, C_1{:}P_1 \, .. \, C_{i-1}{:}P_{i-1} \, false{:}P_i \, C_{i+1}{:}P_{i+1} \, .. \, C_n{:}P_n \, endselect$$
$$= \, select \, C_1{:}P_1 \, .. \, C_{i-1}{:}P_{i-1} \, C_{i+1}{:}P_{i+1} \, .. \, C_n{:}P_n \, endselect$$

definition 8.2

$$select \, true{:}P \, endselect = P$$

definition 8.3

In definition 8.1 the order of the arms in the *select* instruction doesn't matter. Execution ignores all the arms labelled false and chooses one of the arms labelled true, in principle choosing at random. There are several rules which exploit this order-independence. First, because the order of arms in a *select* doesn't matter, re-ordering them doesn't affect its meaning (definition 8.4). Second, you can combine copies of any arm (definition 8.5). Notice that this means that a *select*

$$select \, .. \, C_i{:}P_i \, .. \, C_j{:}P_j \, .. \, endselect$$
$$= \, select \, .. \, C_j{:}P_j \, .. \, C_i{:}P_i \, .. \, endselect$$

definition 8.4

$$\text{if } P_i = P_j \text{ then}$$
$$select .. C_i{:}P_i \ .. \ C_j{:}P_j .. endselect$$
$$= select .. C_i{\lor}C_j{:}P_i .. endselect$$

definition 8.5

which consists of several identical true-labelled arms has a clearly-defined meaning.

-=-=-=-=-=-=-=-=-=-=-=-=-

Exercise 8.10
Prove that the instruction

$$select\ a{<}b{:}\ printnumber(a)$$
$$b{<}a{:}\ printnumber(b)$$
$$a{=}b{:}\ printnumber((a{+}b){\div}2)$$
$$endselect$$

prints 10 when $a=10$ and $b=30$, 6 when $a=10$ and $b=6$, 13 when $a=13$ and $b=13$.

Exercise 8.11
Prove that in general when $a{\le}b$ the instruction in exercise 8.10 prints a, but when $b{\le}a$ it prints b.

Exercise 8.12
Prove that the instruction in exercise 8.10 is equivalent to

$$select\ a{\le}b{:}printnumber(a)\ \ a{\ge}b{:}printnumber(b)\ endselect$$

Exercise 8.13
What is the instruction sequence equivalent to the following instruction[†]

$$select\ n{<}10{:}\ printdigit(n)$$
$$n{\ge}10{:}\ printnumber(n{\div}10);\ printdigit(n\ rem\ 10)$$
$$endselect$$

(a) when $n=9$? (b) when $n=44$? (c) when $n=436$? (d) when $n=-436$?

Exercise 8.14
Prove that when $n{\ge}0$ the instruction in exercise 8.13 is equivalent to the sequence

$$select\ n{\ge}10{:}\ printnumber(n{\div}10)$$
$$n{<}10{:}\ donothing$$
$$endselect;$$
$$printdigit(n\ rem\ 10)$$

[Hint: consider separately the cases $n{\ge}10$ and $n{<}10$: show that the two programs

---

[†] '*rem*' is remaindering, calculating what is 'left over' after integer division. For example, $13\,rem\,2 = 1$, $12\,rem\,2 = 0$, $44\,rem\,9 = 8$.

are equivalent in each case.]

-=-=-=-=-=-=-=-=-=-=-=-=-

Choice-completeness and choice-ambiguity

If in a *select* instruction

$$select\ C_1{:}P_1\ \ C_2{:}P_2\ ..\ C_n{:}P_n\ endselect$$

the condition-formulas add up to true (that is, if $C_1 \vee C_2 \vee .. \vee C_n = true$) then the choice gives an alternative for every circumstance because there must always be at least one condition-formula which is true. If they add up not to true but to a formula F then whenever F is true, so is one of the condition-formulas: that is, the instruction has an alternative for every circumstance in which F delivers true.

If no two conditions are ever simultaneously true (that is, if $C_i \wedge C_j = false$ whenever $i \neq j$) then each arm will be selected unambigously because whenever one of them is true all the rest must be false.

-=-=-=-=-=-=-=-=-=-=-=-=-

Exercise 8.15
What is the sum of the conditions in the instruction

> *select* $k{=}1$: *printnumber*(n)
> $n{<}k$: *printstring*("sequence impossible")
> $k{>}1$: *printnumber*(1); *printspace*; *printseq*$(n{-}1, k{-}1)$
> *endselect*

Simplify your formula as far as possible; find some values of n and k for which the formula is false; hence conclude that this instruction does not specify an action under all circumstances.

Exercise 8.16
Repeat exercise 8.15 for the instruction

> *select* $k{=}1 \wedge n{>}0$: *printnumber*(n)
> $k{\leq}0 \vee n{<}k$: *printstring*("sequence impossible")
> $k{>}1 \wedge n{>}0$: *printnumber*(1); *printspace*; *printseq*$(n{-}1, k{-}1)$
> *endselect*

but this time show that your formula is true for any combination of values of k and n. [Hint: consider positive, negative and zero values of k and of n; hence conclude that this instruction specifies an action for every circumstance.]

-=-=-=-=-=-=-=-=-=-=-=-=-

Removing common instructions

If a *select* instruction is followed by a program X then no matter which arm is selected, X will be executed when the *select* finishes. So you can move X inside the *select*, adding it at the tail of every arm. Vice-versa you can factor out a common ending from the arms of a *select* instruction (definition 8.6).

$$select\ C_1{:}P_1\ \ C_2{:}P_2\ ..\ C_n{:}P_n\ endselect;\ X$$
$$=select\ C_1{:}P_1;X\ \ C_2{:}P_2;X\ ..\ C_n{:}P_n;X\ endselect$$

definition 8.6

Factoring and expanding *select* instructions

The program in the arm of a *select* instruction can quite reasonably be another *select* instruction. This structure can be used to factor out common parts of several condition-formulas. Vice-versa, a factored *select* can be simplified into a single *select* instruction. For example, program 8.9 chooses between three alternative actions. Evidently b is printed by this instruction only if $a>0$ and $b<0$; a is printed only if $a>0$ and $b>0$; it does nothing if $a<0$; if $a=0$ the instruction is meaningless. Program 8.10 expresses exactly the same choice.

$$select\ a>0{:}\ select\ b<0{:}\ printnumber(b)$$
$$b>0{:}\ printnumber(a)$$
$$endselect$$
$$a<0{:}\ donothing$$
$$endselect$$

program 8.9

$$select\ a>0{\wedge}b<0{:}\ printnumber(b)$$
$$a>0{\wedge}b>0{:}\ printnumber(a)$$
$$a<0{:}\ donothing$$
$$endselect$$

program 8.10

Factoring and expanding must be done with care because you can quite easily change the meaning of a program. For example, program 8.11 chooses what to

$$select\ b>0{:}\ select\ a/b>c{:}\ printstring(\text{``c is smaller''})$$
$$a/b{\le}c{:}\ printstring(\text{``c isn't smaller''})$$
$$endselect$$
$$b=0{:}\ printstring(\text{``can't divide by 0''})$$
$$endselect$$

program 8.11

print depending on the values of a, b and c, and never tries to divide a by zero. Program 8.12 is an attempt to expand program 8.11 which is unsuccessful because it may sometimes try to divide by zero. In general you can only expand a factored *select* if the condition-formulas inside the inner *select* are always meaningful.

> *select* $b>0 \wedge a/b>c$: *printstring*("c is smaller")
> $b>0 \wedge a/b \leq c$: *printstring*("c isn't smaller")
> $b=0$: *printstring*("can't divide by 0")
> *endselect*

program 8.12

A *select* can only be factored if there is a clean break between the arms which are included in the inner *select* and the ones which are left outside: that is, if there is no ambiguity in choice between the arm which is a *select* and all the other arms of the outer *select*. For example, program 8.13 has a choice for every circumstance but program 8.14 does not. The problem is that when $n>0$ it might also be less than k: there is an ambiguous choice in program 8.14 between the inner *select* and the *printstring*. If $n>0$ and $k<0$, program 8.13 will print "sequence impossible", but program 8.14 may choose the first arm of the *select* (because $n>0$) and will then reduce to a *select* in which neither condition-formula is true, and which is therefore meaningless. It is necessary to do more than find common formulas in order to be able to factor a *select* instruction. The complete rule is shown in definition 8.7 [†].

> *select* $k=1 \wedge n>0$: *printnumber*(n)
> $k>1 \wedge n>0$: *printnumber*(1); *printspace*; *printseq*(n−1, k−1)
> $k \leq 0 \vee n<k$: *printstring*("sequence impossible")
> *endselect*

program 8.13

> *select* $n>0$: *select* $k=1$: *printnumber*(n)
> $k>1$: *printnumber*(1); *printspace*; *printseq*(n−1, k−1)
>   *endselect*
> $k \leq 0 \vee n<k$: *printstring*("sequence impossible")
> *endselect*

program 8.14

-=-=-=-=-=-=-=-=-=-=-=-

[†] I am grateful to my student Mr Arshad Mahmood for pointing out errors in my earlier version of this definition.

$select\ C_x{\wedge}C_1{:}P_1\ \ C_x{\wedge}C_2{:}P_2\ ..\ C_x{\wedge}C_i{:}P_i\ \ C_{i+1}{:}P_{i+1}\ ..\ C_n{:}P_n\ endselect$

$=\ select\ C_x{:}\ select\ C_1{:}P_1\ C_2{:}P_2\ ..\ C_i{:}P_i\ endselect$

$\qquad C_{i+1}{:}P_{i+1}\ ..\ C_n{:}P_n$

$endselect$

provided that

(a) when C_x is false, all of $C_1..C_i$ are meaningful (so that both instructions are meaningful under identical circumstances); and

(b) when C_x is true, all of $C_{i+1}..C_n$ are false (so that both instructions select their alternatives in exactly the same way).

definition 8.7

Exercise 8.17

Factor the *select* instruction

$select\ size{>}0\ \wedge\ letter{=}\text{'S'}:\ printsquare(size);\ NL;\ NL;\ NL$

$\qquad size{>}0\ \wedge\ letter{=}\text{'T'}:\ printtriangle(size);\ NL;\ NL$

$\qquad size{>}0\ \wedge\ letter{\neq}\text{'S'}\ \wedge\ letter{\neq}\text{'T'}:\ printstring(\text{"wrong letter"});\ NL$

$\qquad size{<}0:\ printstring(\text{"negative size impossible"})$

$\qquad size{=}0:\ donothing$

$endselect$

Exercise 8.18

Expand the *select* instruction

$\qquad select\ w{\geq}0:\ select\ n{<}10:\ times\ w\ do\ printspace\ od$

$\qquad\qquad\qquad\qquad\quad n{\geq}10:\ printnumber(n{+}10,w{-}1)$

$\qquad\qquad\qquad endselect;$

$\qquad\qquad\qquad printdigit(n\ rem\ 10)$

$\qquad\qquad w{<}0:\ donothing$

$\qquad endselect$

[Careful! The first arm is a sequence.]

-=-=-=-=-=-=-=-=-=-=-=-

8.5 SHORTHAND CHOICE INSTRUCTIONS

Sometimes a *select* makes a rather long-winded description of a choice. Sometimes the description can be shortened because the choice is being made in a particularly simple way. There are several shorthand choice-description forms in common use in programming codes: two which are particularly useful are the *case* and the *if-then-else*.

The *case* instruction

The *case* instruction allows you to abbreviate a choice which is being made on the basis of the different possible values of some formula. For example, the instruction

$$select\ letter = 'S': square()\ \ letter = 'T': triangle()\ \ letter = 'C': circle()\ endselect$$

is equivalent to the *case* instruction

$$case\ letter\ of\ 'S': square()\ \ 'T': triangle()\ \ 'C': circle()\ endcase$$

The formulas in a *case* instruction can be as complicated as you like. The definition is as follows:

$$case\ F\ of\ G_1: P_1\ G_2: P_2\ ..\ G_n: P_n\ endcase$$
$$= select\ F = G_1: P_1\ F = G_2: P_2\ ..\ F = G_n: P_n\ endselect$$

definition 8.8

Using a *case* instruction rather than a *select* may improve a program in two ways. First, it will probably shorten it by taking out repeated instances of the formula F. Second, it emphasises that the choice depends always on the value of F, information which may be obscured in the more wordy *select* version.

A *case* instruction can be incomplete or ambiguous if the *select* instruction from which it is derived is incomplete or ambiguous. To make a *case* instruction complete I allow an arm to be labelled with '*otherwise*':

$$case\ F\ of\ G_1: P_1\ \ G_2: P_2\ ..\ G_n: P_n$$
$$otherwise: P_{n+1}$$
$$endcase$$
$$= select\ F = G_1: P_1\ \ F = G_2: P_2\ ..\ F = G_n: P_n$$
$$F \neq G_1 \wedge F \neq G_2 \wedge .. \wedge F \neq G_n: P_{n+1}$$
$$endselect$$

definition 8.9

The '*otherwise*' notation is sometimes essential in a *case* instruction, but there is no similar notation for *select*. The reason is that it is important to be able to calculate the circumstances under which any arm can be chosen. To allow '*otherwise*' in *select* instructions would allow the programmer to brush too much under the carpet.

-=-=-=-=-=-=-=-=-=-=-

Exercise 8.19
Give the *case* instruction equivalent of programs 8.1 and 8.2.

Exercise 8.20
Using the equivalences

$$x<y \quad = \quad (x<y)=true \quad = \quad (x\geq y)=false$$
$$x\geq y \quad = \quad (x\geq y)=true \quad = \quad (x<y)=false$$
.. etc.

give the *case* instruction equivalent of programs 8.4 and 8.5.

Exercise 8.21
Use *case* in a procedure *name*, defined so that *name*(n) prints the name in English (or any other human language you wish) of the single-digit number *n*. For example, if your procedure works in English *name*(6) should print "six" and *name*(4) should print "four".

-=-=-=-=-=-=-=-=-=-=-=-

The *if-then-else* instruction

Sometimes a *select* is used to express a binary choice between condition and not-condition. For example, the *select* instruction in program 8.15 expresses a binary choice between $x=0$ and $\neg(x=0)$. Such an instruction can be converted into an alternative notation (definition 8.10). The *if-then-else* notation shortens a program and usually clarifies it by making it clear that a binary choice is being made.

$$select\ x=0:\ pn(-1) \quad x\neq 0:\ pn(x+1)\ endselect$$

program 8.15

$$if\ F\ then\ P_1\ else\ P_2\ fi \quad = \quad select\ F:\ P_1\ \neg F:\ P_2\ endselect$$

definition 8.10

-=-=-=-=-=-=-=-=-=-=-=-

Exercise 8.22
Give the *if-then-else* equivalent of program 8.15.

Exercise 8.23
Give the *if-then-else* equivalent of the *select* instruction from exercise 8.13.

-=-=-=-=-=-=-=-=-=-=-=-

When a *select* specifies a hierarchy of mutually-exclusive choices it can be converted into an *if-then-else–if-then-else..* structure. For example, the *select* instruction

$$select\ a=0:\ P_1$$
$$a\neq 0 \wedge b=0:\ P_2$$
$$a\neq 0 \wedge b\neq 0 \wedge c<5:\ P_3$$
$$a\neq 0 \wedge b\neq 0 \wedge c\geq 5:\ P_4$$
$$endselect$$

can be converted into an *if-then-else* structure by following several steps. First, factor the *select* into several nested instructions:

$$select \ a{=}0 {:} \ P_1$$
$$a{\neq}0 {:} select \ b{=}0 {:} \ P_2$$
$$b{\neq}0 {:} select \ c{<}5 {:} \ P_3 \ c{\geq}5 {:} \ P_4 \ endselect$$
$$endselect$$
$$endselect$$

then convert each into an *if-then-else*:

$$if \ a{=}0 \ then \ P_1$$
$$else \ select \ b{=}0 {:} \ P_2$$
$$b{\neq}0 {:} select \ c{<}5 {:} \ P_3 \ c{\geq}5 {:} \ P_4 \ endselect$$
$$endselect$$
$$fi$$

$$= if \ a{=}0 \ then \ P_1$$
$$else \ if \ b{=}0 \ then \ P_2$$
$$else \ select \ c{<}5 {:} \ P_3 \ c{\geq}5 {:} \ P_4 \ endselect$$
$$fi$$
$$fi$$

$$= if \ a{=}0 \ then \ P_1$$
$$else \ if \ b{=}0 \ then \ P_2$$
$$else \ if \ c{<}5 \ then \ P_3 \ else \ P_4 \ fi$$
$$fi$$
$$fi$$

-=-=-=-=-=-=-=-=-=-=-=-

Exercise 8.24
Give the *select* equivalent of the instruction

$$if \ x{<}y \ then \ P_1 \ else \ if \ x{>}y \ then \ P_2 \ else \ P_3 \ fi \ fi$$

Simplify the condition-formulas in your answer.

Exercise 8.25
Give the *if-then-else* equivalent of the instructions from exercises 8.17 and 8.18.

-=-=-=-=-=-=-=-=-=-=-=-

I'm not especially fond of the *if-then-else* shorthand because it makes implicit the conditions under which instructions get executed, whereas a *select* makes those conditions explicit.

If-then: a bad shorthand

Quite often one of the alternative actions in a binary choice is *donothing*. Many programming codes have a notation which is used to shorten such choices: definition 8.11 gives the meaning of the *if-then* notation. This notation has

$$if\ F\ then\ P\ fi$$
$$=\ if\ F\ then\ P\ else\ donothing\ fi$$
$$=\ select\ F:\ P\ \ \neg F:donothing\ endselect$$

definition 8.11

nothing to recommend it except its conciseness. I rarely find any advantage in being able to miss out the *else* part of an *if-then-else*. Indeed I find positive advantages in being made to recognise the existence of a *donothing* alternative if there is one. Don't use this notation unless you are forced to!

8.6 REASONING WITH SHORTHANDS IS TRICKY

I prefer the *select* notation to the more conventional *if-then-else* because it makes reasoning about programs much simpler. Put another way, *select* instructions make it easier to see what a program will do when it is executed and therefore make programs easier to understand. Consider by way of illustration the following instruction:

$$if\ a<0\ then\ P_1$$
$$else\ if\ b\neq0\ then\ P_2$$
$$else\ if\ a=b\ then\ P_3$$
$$else\ if\ a=0\ then\ P_4\ fi$$
$$fi$$
$$fi$$
$$fi$$

program 8.16

This program uses the technique of nested *if-then-else* instructions, following the *else* with another *if-then-else*. You will have to do this if you need to describe a multiple choice in a mechanical code which only provides a binary-choice instruction. There is no reason to do so when you don't have to, because you can very easily confuse yourself.

Suppose that you are asked: under what conditions will program 8.16 execute P_4? The very naive programmer might answer: when $a=0$. In fact the answer is that P_4 can *never* be executed. To calculate what the program does, and to confirm my claim, it is helpful to convert it into a *select* instruction:

$select\ a<0: P_1$
$a{\geq}0: select\ b{\neq}0: P_2$
$b=0: select\ a=b: P_3$
$a{\neq}b: select\ a=0: P_4$
$a{\neq}0: donothing$
$endselect$
$endselect$
$endselect$
$endselect$

This is a faithful transcription of the original instruction using definitions 8.10 and 8.11. Notice that there is an explicit *donothing* alternative in the *select* version: the danger of using *if-then* without the *else* is that it makes it easy to overlook the fact that *donothing* is always a possible action.

The next step is to use definition 8.7 to eliminate the nested *select* instructions. It doesn't matter in what order they are eliminated. A first step might be to eliminate the innermost one:

$select\ a<0: P_1$
$a{\geq}0: select\ b{\neq}0: P_2$
$b=0: select\ a=b: P_3$
$a{\neq}b \wedge a=0: P_4$
$a{\neq}b \wedge a{\neq}0: donothing$
$endselect$
$endselect$
$endselect$

The other enclosed *select* instructions can be eliminated in a similar way, giving eventually:

$select\ a<0: P_1$
$a{\geq}0 \wedge b{\neq}0: P_2$
$a{\geq}0 \wedge b=0 \wedge a=b: P_3$
$a{\geq}0 \wedge b=0 \wedge a{\neq}b \wedge a=0: P_4$
$a{\geq}0 \wedge b=0 \wedge a{\neq}b \wedge a{\neq}0: donothing$
$endselect$

This transformation is interesting in itself, revealing how much information is bound up in the *if-then-else* version. But the picture is still rather confused and the condition-formulas can be simplified to show more clearly the circumstances under which different arms are selected. In the third arm, for example: $b=0{\wedge}a=b$ clearly implies $a=0$ and then because the formula already includes $a{\geq}0$, $a{\geq}0{\wedge}a=0$ just means $a=0$. In the fourth arm it is impossible that $b=0$ and $a=0$ and $a{\neq}b$: the whole condition is always false no matter what the values of a and b. Simplifying the formulas and using definition 8.2 to remove the false-labelled arm gives the instruction

$select\ a<0: P_1\ \ a{\geq}0{\wedge}b{\neq}0: P_2\ \ b=0{\wedge}a=0: P_3\ \ a>0{\wedge}b=0: donothing\ endselect$

This instruction has some surprising features when you compare it with the original *if-then-else*. In particular it is interesting that one of the original alternatives has been eliminated, that the condition-formula labelling P_3 doesn't look much like the one in the original and that the condition-formula labelling *donothing* is much more prominent than you might have expected.

A single example does not prove that every *if-then-else* should be rewritten as a *select*, and should not even be taken as evidence for such a mistaken conclusion. It does illustrate the fact that it can often be difficult to calculate the effect of complicated *if-then-else* instructions.

-=-=-=-=-=-=-=-=-=-=-=-

Exercise 8.26
Transform program 8.17 into a *select* instruction and simplify it. [Hint: combine the two '*P*' arms, at least!]

$$
\begin{aligned}
&if\ a{\leq}b\ then \\
&\quad if\ y{>}b\ then\ P \\
&\qquad else\ if\ x{<}a\ then\ P \\
&\qquad\quad else\ if\ y{\geq}a \wedge x{\leq}b\ then\ Q\ else\ R\ fi \\
&\qquad\quad\ fi \\
&\quad\ fi \\
&fi
\end{aligned}
$$

program 8.17

Exercise 8.27
Convert your answer to exercise 8.26 back into the simplest *if-then-else* you can manage.

Exercise 8.28
Convert program 8.18 into the simplest possible *select* instruction.

$$
\begin{aligned}
&if\ a{<}b\ then\ if\ b{<}0\ then\ P\ fi \\
&\quad else\ if\ a{=}b\ then\ if\ b{=}0\ then\ Q\ fi \\
&\qquad\quad else\ if\ b{>}0\ then\ R\ fi \\
&\qquad\quad\ fi \\
&\quad\ fi
\end{aligned}
$$

program 8.18

Exercise 8.29
Convert your answer to exercise 8.28 into the simplest possible *if-then-else* instruction.

-=-=-=-=-=-=-=-=-=-=-=-

8.7 PLANNING A SOLUTION WITH CHOICE INSTRUCTIONS

You now know three program structures:

Sequence
Counting repetition
Choice

plus the use of procedure definitions to make a hierarchy of instruction definitions. When you are faced with a programming problem, you should ask yourself 'which of these structures is appropriate?' If it looks as though the problem requires a sequence of different actions, use sequence. If it looks like a sequence of similar actions, use repetition. If it looks like a choice between different actions, use choice.

Choice is especially useful when you need a solution to a problem for a wide range of circumstances but you can't find a general formula which covers every circumstance, just a jumble of formulas which fit in different situations. This is illustrated in each of the examples which follow.

An example: 'verbalising' a number

The rules of the English language which describe the way we name numbers are sort-of systematic. They are sort-of systematic rather than completely systematic because although there are some rules about the way we name numbers - for example, twenty-one and twenty-two are related in the same way as one and two are and so, in a different way, are one hundred and two hundred - there isn't a systematic connection between the names (two plus one = three?), the rules for naming decades don't follow the same rules as the simple numbers (twenty not twoty, forty not fourty) and there is a relic, in the use of teen-names (thirteen, fourteen) of the time when Europeans used to count in scores rather than tens.

It is an interesting illustration of the use of choice in programming to write a program which will print out the English name of a number: a procedure *verbalise* can be defined so that, for example, *verbalise*(416) prints

four hundred and sixteen

and *verbalise*(299) prints

two hundred and ninety-nine

The difficulty is to get all the spaces and dashes in the right place and to spell everything correctly.

The system of English number-names is based on the decimal system. It contains words which correspond to single-digit decimal numbers. As a first step in a solution, I propose the procedure *singlev*, defined so that *singlev*(n) will verbalise a single-digit number *n*. My definition is shown in program 8.19.

def singlev(n) =
   printstring(*case n of* 0: "zero" 1: "one"   2: "two"
                              3: "three" 4: "four"   5: "five"
                              6: "six"   7: "seven" 8: "eight"
                              9: "nine"
       endcase)
  enddef

program 8.19

Notice that this program uses a *case formula* rather than a *case* instruction. Choice formulas aren't mysterious in any way: their evaluation is very similar to the execution of a choice instruction in that an arm is chosen and then that arm is evaluated; their substitution definition is exactly like that of choice instructions. In this program the use of a *case* formula factors out what would otherwise be repeated occurrences of *printstring* in every arm of a *case* instruction. Notice also that there is no *otherwise* arm in program 8.19: if *singlev* is given a number which it can't verbalise, like 14 or -1, it should be treated as a meaningless instruction.

You see that English number-names are by no means simply decimal when you try to use the *singlev* procedure straightforwardly in the definition of a *twov* procedure which verbalises two-digit numbers [†]:

def twov(n) = *singlev*($n \div 10$); *printstring*("ty-");
               singlev(*n rem* 10)
  enddef

program 8.20

Sometimes program 8.20 gives the right answer: for example, *twov*(67) prints "sixty-seven" and *twov*(94) prints "ninety-four". But it can't spell forty or eighty (it prints fourty and eightty, which might sound right but look wrong); it prints twoty, threety and fivety, which don't even sound right; it prints sixty-zero rather than just plain sixty. It has difficulties with the teen-numbers: *twov*(16) would print onety-six instead of sixteen. And it prints zeroty-six when it should print six. Evidently a *twov* procedure must be more complicated than that.

A complete solution to the problem isn't difficult, just a little bit more intricate than program 8.20. In program 8.21 I define a *teenv* procedure so that *teenv(n)* prints the name of any number between ten and nineteen, and I call on this procedure in a new definition of *twov* which attempts to handle all the difficulties shown up by program 8.20.

[†] The operations '+' and '*rem*' perform integer division: '$a \div b$' calculates the whole-number quotient (the 'answer' of the division); '*a rem b*' calculates the remainder (what is 'left over' after division). So $64 \div 10$ is 6 and $64 \, rem \, 10$ is 4, because when you divide 64 by 10 the answer is 6, with 4 left over.

```
def teenv(n) =
    printstring(case n of 10: "ten"          11: "eleven"
                         12: "twelve"        13: "thirteen"
                         14: "fourteen"      15: "fifteen"
                         16: "sixteen"       17: "seventeen"
                         18: "eighteen"      19: "nineteen"
                endcase)
enddef

def twov(n) =
    select 0≤n≤9: singlev(n)
           10≤n≤19: teenv(n)
           20≤n≤99: printstring(case n÷10 of 2: "twenty" 3: "thirty"
                                            4: "forty"   5: "fifty"
                                            6: "sixty"   7: "seventy"
                                            8: "eighty"  9: "ninety"
                            endcase);
                    select (n rem 10)=0: donothing
                           (n rem 10)≠0: printchar('-'); singlev(n rem 10)
                    endselect
    endselect
enddef
```

program 8.21

The new *twov* procedure contains three alternative actions, the first two of which
are single instructions, the third a sequence. It discriminates between single-digit
numbers, ..teen numbers and ..ty numbers. The ..ty numbers are handled by the
sequence which consists of a *printstring* followed by a *select*: the *printstring*
prints the decade-name (one of twenty, thirty, or whatever) and then the *select*
decides whether to print a digit-name or not, so as to avoid the sixty-zero
problem of program 8.20.

It is easy to convince yourself that this definition does what is expected of it: it
works provided that *singlev* and *teenv* correctly verbalise single-digit numbers
and teen numbers respectively. It spells decade names correctly. It avoids the
sixty-zero problem. So it seems to work.

-=-=-=-=-=-=-=-=-=-=-=-

Exercise 8.30
By substitution or drawing environment diagrams, show that the procedure calls
twov(5), *twov*(37) and *twov*(17) print the correct verbalisation of their arguments.

-=-=-=-=-=-=-=-=-=-=-=-

An aside on 'specification', 'testing' and 'proof'

You can informally satisfy yourself that program 8.21 correctly verbalises numbers. But informality ought to make you uneasy: perhaps you have overlooked something. Even when you convince yourself that there is nothing left unchecked, what if you have misunderstood the rules of English and misspelt one of the names? What if there is a special rule of English which writes 55 as fifty-fif - a rule you have never heard of before?

In the case of a procedure like *twov*, you might expect to test the procedure by exhaustively trying every possible input: after all there are only a hundred numbers to consider. The complete *verbalise* procedure, which handles numbers of any size, wouldn't be so easy to test. Just printing the names of all the integer numbers which your programming system can represent might take several hours. Checking the list would be so tedious that you could never be sure that you hadn't made a mistake.

What you really need is a *proof* that your procedure definition is correct. But a proof can only establish that your procedure definition corresponds to some specification of the effect of a procedure call. You must write the specification, it must be precise if the proof is to establish anything, but the requirement 'print the names of English numbers' is rather vague.

It would be possible to write a reasonably precise specification. I haven't explicitly stated what the specification of *twov* should be, but implicitly my comments require that the digit- and decade-names should be spelt as in English, that special consideration should be given to the numbers ten to nineteen and that both leading zeros (zeroty-five) and trailing zeros (twenty-zero) should be silent.

A program which provably meets its specification is 'correct' in a certain mathematical sense. But it may not be correct in the engineering sense that it meets the purpose for which it was designed. If there really were a rule in English that 55 should be verbalised as 'fifty-fif' my *twov* procedure would be correct according to its specification (which doesn't take notice of such a rule) but incorrect as a verbalising device. I believe that there is no such rule, and therefore that my procedure is correct in both senses.

-=-=-=-=-=-=-=-=-=-=-=-

Exercise 8.31
Define a *verbalise* procedure which handles numbers in the range 0..999. Your procedure can use the definitions of *twov* and *singlev*: be careful to handle leading and trailing zeros correctly.

Exercise 8.32
Extend your definition of *verbalise* to handle numbers in the range 0..9999.

Exercise 8.33
Construct a specification for a procedure *Roman* which Roman-verbalises numbers in the range 0..999: for example, *Roman*(14) might print "XIV". Construct a procedure which conforms to your specification.

-=-=-=-=-=-=-=-=-=-=-=-

Systematic generation versus exhaustive listing

Program 8.19 prints number-names by selecting a name from an exhaustive listing, whereas program 8.21 prints number-names by generating them more or less systematically. These are very different techniques of description: when should you use one rather than the other?

You can see the relative advantages of the techniques if I construct a systematic-generation solution to the teen-number problem. The *teenv* procedure in program 8.21 factors out the use of *printstring* in each arm, but ignores the fact that seven of the strings it prints end with "teen". Also, some of the "teen" strings contain single-digit number-names like "four", "seven", and so on. An alternative definition might try to exploit this regularity in the problem: see program 8.22. Which procedure definition is clearer: *teenv* from program 8.21 or from program 8.22? One measure of program clarity is how easy it is to read the program and be sure that it is right. On this measure the first procedure definition scores over the second: it is about half as long and much more simply structured.

> *def teenv*(*n*) =
>   *select n*≤12: *printstring*(*case n of* 10: "ten"   11: "eleven"
>   12: "twelve"
>   *endcase*)
>
>   *n*>12: *case n of* 13: *printstring*("thir")
>   15: *printstring*("fif")
>   18: *printstring*("eigh")
>   14, 16, 17, 19: *singlev*(*n rem* 10)
>   *endcase*;
>   *printstring*("teen")
>   *endselect*
>   *endselect*

program 8.22

When there are very few possibilities or the different possibilities aren't easily generated systematically, then exhaustive listing is attractive. Program 8.22 seems long-winded because the rules of English number naming in this area are hardly systematic at all and because we know there is a shorter-winded version. The regularity in the solution is hardly 'systematic' at all, especially when you see that some teen-number names use single-digit names and some do not. Where is the sense in that? Better just to give a list of the silly things.

When there are more possibilities or when there is more structure in the problem definition then the balance shifts. An exhaustive listing of the number-names between zero and ninety-nine would not be attractive, both because it would be hard to check so many alternatives and because there is enough structure in the number-naming rules at that level to make systematic generation relatively straightforward. Exercise 8.31 shows that for numbers from one hundred to nine hundred and ninety-nine the rules are so simple that to consider anything other than systematic generation would be ridiculous.

Programs and procedure definitions aren't cast in stone: we invent them and we must expect to have to alter them to cope with changes in the specification, either to correct our mistakes or to make a program which does something similar to but different from the original. The balance of advantages depends on whether the change is systematic or arbitrary. Suppose that you found a population which said 'tiddleypom' instead of 'seventeen'. The exhaustive-listing *teenv* procedure definition in program 8.21 could be changed easily by altering just one string, but program 8.22 would present more difficulty. On the other hand, if the change is systematic then the systematic definition wins. Suppose you find another isolated population which speaks perfect English except that everybody says 'toot' where we say 'teen'. It would be easy to change program 8.22 to fit their almost-English rules but tedious to change program 8.21.

8.8 RASTER PRINTING OF IRREGULAR SHAPES

Chapter 6 illustrated raster printing of regular shapes like triangles and rectangles. If *A*, *B* and *C* are procedures which print rows of particular *n*-by-*k* shapes then the instruction

>   *for i rt* 1..*n do*
>   *NL*; *Arow*(*i*); *printspace*; *Brow*(*i*); *printspace*; *Crow*(*i*)
>   *od*

will print a row consisting of an *A*-shape next to a *B*-shape next to a *C*-shape.

The shapes illustrated in chapter 6 are all regular because it is necessary to calculate what should be printed as the *i*th row of any particular shape and the only means available at that point in the book was straightforward arithmetic. So shapes which have *i* asterisks and *k*−*i* spaces on their *i*th row could be catered for, but a letter A - see figure 8.1 - was then impossible because there isn't any

```
          ***
         *   *
        *     *
        *     *
        *******
        *     *
        *     *
```

figure 8.1

systematic arithmetic relationship between the row-number and the shape on the row.

What is unsystematic is a matter of arbitrary choice! It is relatively simple to write a procedure which prints the ith row of a letter A: program 8.23 does the job, for example. Procedures can easily be constructed for other letters and horizontal raster printing of text messages is within your grasp!

```
def Arow(i) = printstring(case i of 1: "   ***   "
                                  2: "  *   *  "
                                  3: " *     * "
                                  4: " *     * "
                                  5: " ******* "
                                  6: " *     * "
                                  7: " *     * "
                          endcase)
        enddef
```

program 8.23

This problem illuminates an important point of programming style and shows that the shortest procedure definition is not always the best. Consider programs 8.24 and 8.25, each of which is intended to print a letter P. The *Prow1* procedure is written so that it obviously draws the parts of a letter P. If I had made a mistake then it would show up on the page: I don't have to test this procedure to know that it works. And with the humblest computer text editor it is easy to write. But the *Prow2* procedure tries to exploit an unsystematic regularity in the

```
def Prow1(i) = printstring(case i of 1: "*****  "
                                   2: "*    * "
                                   3: "*    * "
                                   4: "*    * "
                                   5: "*****  "
                                   6: "*      "
                                   7: "*      "
                           endcase)
        enddef
```

program 8.24

```
def Prow2(i) = printstring(case i of 1, 5: "*****  "
                                   2, 4: "*    * "
                                   3: "*    * "
                                   6, 7: "*      "
                           endcase)
        enddef
```

program 8.25

problem definition and thereby sacrifices clarity for conciseness. You would have to test this procedure, either on a computer or with pencil and paper, to be sure that it works. You might even be tricked by its peculiar layout into thinking that there are the wrong number of spaces and asterisks on some of the lines, and be forced to count them using a ruler. In this case at least, concise definition does not lead to clarity.

-=-=-=-=-=-=-=-=-=-=-=-

Exercise 8.34
Write definitions of enough letter-procedures to print your name horizontally. The letters should all be the same height but need not all be the same width. Write a program which calls those procedures, in the style of program 8.23 above.

Exercise 8.35
Using the definitions from exercise 8.34, write a program which prints your name upside-down: for example, see figure 8.2. [Hint: it is all to do with the formulas you use in the calls to the letter-procedures.]

```
N       N  A      A  N      A  CCCC        Y
N      NN  A      A  N     NN  C     C      Y
N     N N  A      A  N    N N  C             Y
N    N  N  AAAAAAA N  N    N  C             Y
N N     N  A      A N N    N  C           Y Y
NN      N  A    A   NN     N  C     C   Y     Y
N       N  AAA      N      N  CCCC    Y         Y
```

figure 8.2

Exercise 8.36
Write a program, still using the same definitions, which prints your name on the slant: for example, see figure 8.3. [Same hint as in previous exercise.]

```
DDDD
D    D   I
D    D   I  N      N
D    D   I  NN     N      AAA
D    D   I  N N    N     A   A   H       H
D    D   I  N  N N  A       A  H       H
DDDD     I  N    N N  AAAAAAA  H       H
         I  N     NN  A       A  HHHHHHH
         N       N  A       A  H       H
                     A       A  H       H
                                H       H
```

figure 8.3

Exercise 8.37
Wallpaper designers often use a pattern which is repeated diagonally, as in figure 8.3. The design will contain several rows one above the other. Write a program which prints an *n*-line by *k*-column wallpaper pattern containing as many copies and partial copies of your name as possible across the sheet. [Hint: it is easier if all your letters are the same width. Choose *n* and *k* to fit your terminal screen.]

-=-=-=-=-=-=-=-=-=-=-=-

8.9 CLASSIFYING TRIANGLES

Triangles have three angles. The largest one can be a right angle (90°), acute (sharper or less than 90°) or obtuse (blunter or greater than 90°).

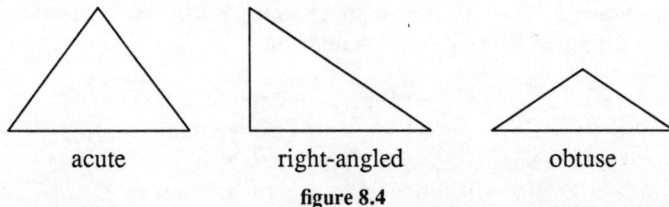

acute   right-angled   obtuse

figure 8.4

Given three numbers a, b and c in descending order of size, describing the lengths of the sides of a triangle, it is possible to write a program which tells you what sort of triangle they describe. There are actually four possibilities because some triplets don't describe a triangle at all: consider, for example, $<13,2,2>$ and think of joining together three straws, one length 13 cm and two of length 2 cm.

A program which solves this problem must be able to print one of four messages and is an obvious choice instruction: program 8.26 shows its structure. The problem is to devise formulas for the conditions C_1, C_2, C_3 and C_4.

> *select* C_1: *printstring*("acute")
> C_2: *printstring*("right-angled")
> C_3: *printstring*("obtuse")
> C_4: *printstring*("not a triangle at all")
> *endselect*

program 8.26

One at least of these formulas is easy to invent. If a describes the longest side and b and c describe sides too small to reach from one end to the other of a, then a, b and c don't describe a triangle. I have assumed that a, b and c are given in descending order of size, so C_4 can be $a>b+c$. Following Pythagoras everybody knows something about C_2: if $a^2=b^2+c^2$ then you have a right-angled triangle. If a is shorter then a^2 is smaller, the angle is smaller and therefore the triangle is classified as 'acute'; if a is longer it can be classified as 'obtuse'. So you might guess at the solution shown in program 8.27.

But this instruction is ambiguous. For example, if $a=13$, $b=3$ and $c=2$ program 8.27 might print "obtuse" or it might print "not a triangle at all". Clearly my C_1, C_2 and C_3 aren't precise enough: they must ensure that the triangle-

$select\ a^2<b^2+c^2:\ printstring(\text{``acute''})$
$\qquad a^2=b^2+c^2:\ printstring(\text{``right-angled''})$
$\qquad a^2>b^2+c^2:\ printstring(\text{``obtuse''})$
$\qquad a>b+c:\ printstring(\text{``not a triangle at all''})$
$endselect$

program 8.27

describing messages are printed only when a, b and c actually do describe a triangle.

A more accurate solution is shown in program 8.28, which can be factored according to definition 8.7 to give program 8.29.

$select\ a\leq b+c \wedge a^2<b^2+c^2:\ printstring(\text{``acute''})$
$\qquad a\leq b+c \wedge a^2=b^2+c^2:\ printstring(\text{``right-angled''})$
$\qquad a\leq b+c \wedge a^2>b^2+c^2:\ printstring(\text{``obtuse''})$
$\qquad a>b+c:\ printstring(\text{``not a triangle at all''})$
$endselect$

program 8.28

$select\ a\leq b+c:\ select\ a^2<b^2+c^2:\ printstring(\text{``acute''})$
$\qquad\qquad\qquad a^2=b^2+c^2:\ printstring(\text{``right-angled''})$
$\qquad\qquad\qquad a^2>b^2+c^2:\ printstring(\text{``obtuse''})$
$\qquad\qquad endselect$
$\qquad a>b+c:\ printstring(\text{``not a triangle at all''})$
$endselect$

program 8.29

-=-=-=-=-=-=-=-=-=-=-=-

Exercise 8.38
What would be printed by program 8.29 if $a=3$, $b=0$ and $c=-3$? Modify the program so that it prints "not a triangle at all" in that and all similar circumstances.

Exercise 8.39
What would be printed by program 8.29 if $a=5$, $b=3$ and $c=2$? Modify the program to make the message more specific in this case.

Exercise 8.40
What would be printed by program 8.29 if a, b and c are not in ascending order: for example, if $a=3$, $b=4$ and $c=5$? Consider cases $a<b$, $a<c$ and $b<c$ and say which of these leads to wrong behaviour. Hence write a program in which program 8.29 is the body of a procedure. The program should print out the correct message no matter what the order of the triplet of numbers it finds.

-=-=-=-=-=-=-=-=-=-=-=-

8.10 CHOICE FORMULAS

So far this chapter has concentrated on choice instructions which choose between one program and another, and therefore between one course of execution and another. There are equally useful choice *formulas,* which choose between one formula and another and therefore between one calculation and another. These formulas are particularly useful when performing non-systematic calculations.

For example: the lengths of months in the European calendar are non-systematic. The assignment of thirty days to some months, thirty-one to others and twenty-eight days to February has to do with Roman politics of almost two thousand years ago. We have to learn the Emperor Augustus's scheme by heart, using mnemonic rhymes or counting on our knuckles. Lots of programs have to deal with the problem: payroll programs, tax programs, timetabling programs, programs which just print a calendar of the year. A formula which calculates and delivers the number of days in any particular month M could be as follows:

$$case\ M\ of\ 1,3,5,7,8,10,12:\ 31$$
$$4,6,9,11:\ 30$$
$$2:\ 28$$
$$endcase$$

program 8.30

-=-=-=-=-=-=-=-=-=-=-=-

Exercise 8.41
Program 8.30 is wrong in every leap year. Augustus's correction to this formula gave February 29 days in each year whose number is divisible by four. Write a formula which expresses Augustus's algorithm. [Hint: two parameters.]

Exercise 8.42
The present-day Gregorian calendar gives February 28 days if the year-number is divisible by 100 but *not* by 400: thus 1900 was not a leap year but 2000 will be. Write a formula which calculates whether a year is leap (29 days in February) or not (28 days).

Exercise 8.43
Write a definition of a procedure *max* so that *max(a, b)* delivers the larger of two numbers a and b.

Exercise 8.44
Write a definition of a procedure *max3* so that *max3(a, b, c)* delivers the largest of three numbers a, b and c.

-=-=-=-=-=-=-=-=-=-=-=-

The verbalising programs of section 8.7 above are based on instruction procedures. They calculate and then print the string which is the English-language name of a number. If the calculation of the string were separated from the printing, then we could use the calculated string in various different ways.

For example, there are programs which 'speak' telephone numbers (spies use them in thriller movies). Suppose there is a basic procedure *speak* which is given a string representing an English word and which uses a speech-synthesing chip to generate electrical impulses which drive a loudspeaker to make a sound rather like the word. London telephone numbers have a three-digit exchange code and a four-digit number. Queen Mary College's number is 980 4811, which can be spoken in English style as

> *nine, eight, oh, (pause), four, eight, one, one*

Program 8.31 might be used to speak London telephone numbers.

```
def digitname(n) =
    case n of 0: "oh"   1: "one"   2: "two"   3: "three"   4: "four"
              5: "five"  6: "six"   7: "seven"  8: "eight"  9: "nine"
    endcase
enddef

def speaktelenum(E, N) =
    speak(digitname(E+100)); speak(digitname((E+10) rem 10));
    speak(digitname(E rem 10));
    pauseabit();
    speak(digitname(N+1000)); speak(digitname((N+100) rem 10));
    speak(digitname((N+10) rem 10)); speak(digitname(N rem 10));
enddef
```

program 8.31

-=-=-=-=-=-=-=-=-=-=-=-

Exercise 8.45
Satisfy yourself that all the '+' and '*rem*' operations in program 8.31 produce the effect which I claim for them.

Exercise 8.46
What would be said by *speaktelenum*(0, 0)?

Exercise 8.47
The true English style runs together pairs of identical digits, so it would say

> *nine, eight, oh, (pause), four, eight, double-one*

See if you can write a procedure which can do that!

-=-=-=-=-=-=-=-=-=-=-=-

8.11 ENCODING CHOICES

The reason why this book doesn't describe all its programs in one of the many mechanically acceptable codes is that those codes restrict your thinking. For example, the notion of choice is fundamental to programming but for all sorts of reasons no widely available mechanical code provides a completely general choice instruction like the *select*. Instead they provide *if-then-else*, which is a sequenced choice: try this test, if it succeeds perform this action but if it fails try that test, if that succeeds perform that action but if that also fails .. and so on.

Now a sequential choice is always *un*ambiguous because it always considers the tests in the same order and stops at the first one which comes out true. And in almost every mechanical code the choice instruction has an implicit *donothing* alternative which is chosen if every test in the sequence fails. It is very difficult - so difficult as to be practically impossible - to encode an ambiguous choice in a code which only gives sequential choice. When it includes an implied *donothing* alternative a sequential choice doesn't express the implied '*stop execution*' alternative of the *select* instruction.

This all boils down to the bad news that though it is always easy to express an *if-then-else* instruction as a *select*, it is sometimes hard to encode a *select* instruction as an *if-then-else*. Nil desperandum ..

Encoding *select* as *if-then-else*

An ambiguous *select* instruction can't be encoded exactly by an *if-then-else* instruction. The implied '*stop execution*' alternative of a *select* must be expressed explicitly in the *if-then-else*.

Suppose that there is a basic instruction *ERROR* which, when executed, stops execution dead in its tracks. If you like you can view *ERROR* as a different kind of *donothing*, the kind which makes nothing happen and which takes forever about it. Or if you like you can view it as an instruction which stops the program and prints some message like "horror!". You can convert an unambiguous *select* into a sequential choice with *ERROR* as the final explicit alternative: that is, convert

$$select\ C_1{:}P_1\ C_2{:}P_2\ ..\ C_n{:}P_n\ endselect$$

into

$$if\ C_1\ then\ P_1\ else\ if\ C_2\ then\ P_2\ else$$
$$..\ else\ if\ C_n\ then\ P_n\ else\ ERROR\ fi\ ..\ fi\ fi$$

The potential ambiguity of the original *select* has been lost, because the *if-then-else* is equivalent to

$$select\ C_1{:}\ P_1\ \neg C_1{\wedge}C_2{:}P_2\ \neg C_1{\wedge}\neg C_2{\wedge}C_3{:}P_3\ ..$$
$$\neg C_1{\wedge}\neg C_2{\wedge}\ ..\ {\wedge}\neg C_{n-1}{\wedge}C_n{:}P_n$$
$$endselect$$

but any *select* instruction which already expresses an unambiguous choice will of course be translated accurately.

Encoding choice formulas as choice instructions

Program 8.19 includes a choice formula inside a *printstring* instruction but it could as easily have been written as a choice instruction by **distributing** the procedure call operation over the arms of the choice formula. It would then become:

> *case n of* 0: *printstring*("zero")   1: *printstring*("one")
> 2: *printstring*("two")   3: *printstring*("three")
> 4: *printstring*("four")   5: *printstring*("five")
> 6: *printstring*("six")   7: *printstring*("seven")
> 8: *printstring*("eight")   9: *printstring*("nine")
> *endcase*

This technique of distributing operations over the arms of a choice formula can be used repeatedly until what is left is a choice instruction. Take another example - an instruction which contains a choice formula so as to avoid division by zero:

> *printnumber*(a+(*if* b=0 *then* 1 *else* b))

This can be converted into a choice instruction in two stages. First, distribute the '+' operation:

> *printnumber*(*if* b=0 *then* a+1 *else* a+b)

then distribute the *printnumber* call:

> *if* b=0 *then* printnumber(a+1) *else* printnumber(a+b)

This program can be simplified still further because a+1=a, but that isn't the point of the example.

-=

APPENDIX 8.A CHOICE STRUCTURES IN PASCAL

Pascal has *if-then* and *if-then-else* instructions and a form of *case* instruction. It has no choice formulas at all.

Transcribing condition-formulas into Pascal

Pascal has '<>' (less than or greater than) for '≠'. It has 'and' for '∧' and 'or' for '∨', but beware! - when combining formulas with 'and' or with 'or', bracket the formulas you are combining. That is, transcribe

$$x = \text{‘a’} \lor q \leq r \lor y \neq \text{‘c’}$$

into Pascal as

```
(x='a') or (q<=r) or (y<>'c')
```

Transcribing choice formulas into Pascal

Convert choice formulas into choice instructions as described in section 8.11 above, then transcribe the choice instruction.

Transcribing *select* instructions into Pascal

Convert *select*s into *if-then-else* instructions, then transcribe those instructions. Don't forget to include an *ERROR* alternative unless your *select* is provably complete (and perhaps include one even then: you might make a mistake somewhere in the proof or in your transcription). A possible transcription of *ERROR* in Pascal is:

```
begin write('error in select in procedure X'); write(1/0) end
```

The attempt to divide one by zero should force the program to stop with a bang. Your system may have a more convenient instruction than `write(1/0)` - examples are `halt` and `terminate`. Look it up in the manual, or ask a friend.

Transcribing *if-then-else* instructions into Pascal

Pascal *if-then-else* instructions don't have a closing *fi* bracket and as usual with Pascal structured instructions they contain single instructions rather than programs. So if either alternative in an *if-then-else* is a program, unpack its definitions and enclose its body with `begin-end` brackets to make it a single instruction. If the instruction following *then* is itself an *if-then-else*, `begin-end` bracket that alternative as well (it reduces confusion when you make a transcription error). *Donothing* can always be imitated by the empty bracketed instruction `begin end`.

Finally, transcribe *if F then I_1 else I_2 fi* into Pascal as

$$\text{if F then } I_1 \text{ else } I_2$$

That is, just leave off the *fi* bracket.

Transcribing *case* instructions into Pascal

Pascal `case` instructions may only contain *constant* formulas labelling each arm. For example, you can transcribe

$$case \ x \ of \text{'S'}:.. \ \text{'T'}:.. \ \text{'U'}:.. \ endcase$$

into Pascal, but you can't necessarily transcribe

$$case \ a \ of \ b+1:.. \ x \times 2:.. \ y+c:.. \ endcase$$

If your *case* instruction uses non-constant label formulas, convert it into a *select* and proceed as above.

Pascal `case` allows only single instructions instead of programs in each arm, so if your *case* includes programs, unpack the definitions and then bracket instruction sequences with ⦗ and ⦘ (which convert to `begin` and `end`). *Donothing* can be imitated by `begin end`. Finally, transcribe

$$case \ F \ of \ C_1:I_1 \ C_2:I_2 \ .. \ C_n:I_n \ endcase$$

into Pascal as

```
case F of C₁:I₁; C₂:I₂; ..; Cₙ:Iₙ end
```

That is, use 'end' rather than '*endcase*' and insert semicolons to separate the arms. Don't put a semicolon between the last arm and the 'end' or you might confuse the programming system (and if so it will certainly return the favour).

Pascal `case` instructions don't allow an *otherwise* alternative, so you have first to construct an *if-then-else* which encloses the *case* and picks out the relevant values. For example, convert

$$case \ x \ of \text{'S'}:I_1 \ \text{'T'}:I_2 \ \text{'U'}:I_3 \ otherwise:I_4 \ endcase$$

into

$$if \ x=\text{'S'} \vee x=\text{'T'} \vee x=\text{'U'} \ then$$
$$case \ x \ of \text{'S'}:I_1 \ \text{'T'}:I_2 \ \text{'U'}:I_3 \ endcase$$
$$else \ I_4 \ fi$$

and then continue as above. Since the labels on the arms of the Pascal `case` must all be constants, the choice can often be neatly expressed with a Pascal `set` formula. For example, the program above can be expressed in Pascal as:

```
if x in ['S','T','U'] then
    case x of 'S':I₁; 'T':I₂; 'U':I₃ end
else I₄
```

APPENDIX 8.B SOME PROGRAMS TO TRY

Several of the programs in the exercises in this chapter make interesting programs. Exercise 8.1 is a very simple introduction (and you should answer the questions in exercises 8.2-8.5 and test your program to be sure that it agrees with your answers). Exercises 8.31-8.33 on verbalising numbers give some more extended practice, as do exercises 8.34-8.37 on raster printing.

Chapter 9
CHOICE AND RECURSIVE PROCEDURES

Inductive proofs have a base case and an inductive step. A recursive procedure which uses choice can often be written so that it mimics the structure of its own inductive proof.

9.1 SIMPLE INDUCTION WITH CHOICE AND RECURSION

Consider the following procedure definition:

$$def\ A(n,p) = select\ n=0:\ donothing$$
$$n>0:\ p();A(n-1,p)$$
$$endselect$$
$$enddef$$

program 9.1

It should be obvious that an execution of $A(k,q)$ will call procedure q exactly k times, that it is equivalent to *times k do q() od*. For example, if $q()$ prints an asterisk then $A(k,q)$ will be equivalent to *times k do print* od* and will print k asterisks. Calculation gives evidence that the procedure does do what I say it does:

$A(0,q) = select\ 0=0:donothing\ 0>0:q();A(0-1,q)\ endselect = donothing$

$A(1,q) = select\ 1=0:donothing\ 1>0:q();A(1-1,q)\ endselect$
$= q();A(0,q) = q();donothing = q()$

$A(2,q) = select\ 2=0:donothing\ 2>0:q();A(2-1,q)\ endselect$
$= q();A(1,q) = q();q()$

$A(3,q) = select\ 3=0:donothing\ 3>0:q();A(3-1,q)\ endselect$
$= q();A(2,q) = q();q();q()$

The proof is straightforward because the structure of the procedure gives a base

242

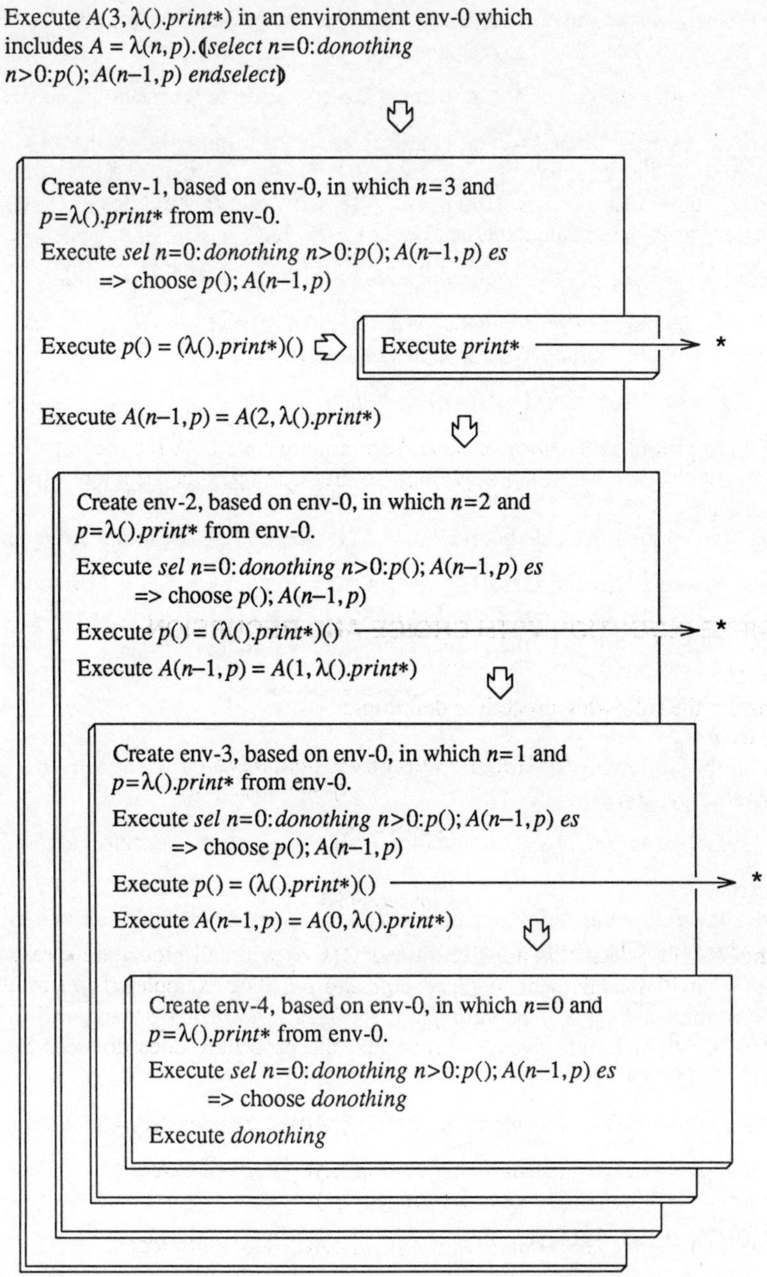

Execute $A(3, \lambda().print*)$ in an environment env-0 which
includes $A = \lambda(n,p).(select\ n=0: donothing$
$n>0:p();\ A(n-1,p)\ endselect)$

Create env-1, based on env-0, in which $n=3$ and
$p=\lambda().print*$ from env-0.

Execute *sel* $n=0: donothing\ n>0:p();\ A(n-1,p)\ es$
$\Rightarrow$ choose $p();\ A(n-1,p)$

Execute $p() = (\lambda().print*)()$ ⟹ | Execute *print* ————————→ *

Execute $A(n-1,p) = A(2, \lambda().print*)$

> Create env-2, based on env-0, in which $n=2$ and
> $p=\lambda().print*$ from env-0.
>
> Execute *sel* $n=0: donothing\ n>0:p();\ A(n-1,p)\ es$
> $\Rightarrow$ choose $p();\ A(n-1,p)$
>
> Execute $p() = (\lambda().print*)()$ ————————————→ *
>
> Execute $A(n-1,p) = A(1, \lambda().print*)$
>
> > Create env-3, based on env-0, in which $n=1$ and
> > $p=\lambda().print*$ from env-0.
> >
> > Execute *sel* $n=0: donothing\ n>0:p();\ A(n-1,p)\ es$
> > $\Rightarrow$ choose $p();\ A(n-1,p)$
> >
> > Execute $p() = (\lambda().print*)()$ ————————→ *
> >
> > Execute $A(n-1,p) = A(0, \lambda().print*)$
> >
> > > Create env-4, based on env-0, in which $n=0$ and
> > > $p=\lambda().print*$ from env-0.
> > >
> > > Execute *sel* $n=0: donothing\ n>0:p();\ A(n-1,p)\ es$
> > > $\Rightarrow$ choose *donothing*
> > >
> > > Execute *donothing*

figure 9.1

case (when $n=0$) and an inductive case (when $n>0$). The proposition is as follows:

P1: An execution of $A(k, q)$ where $k \geq 0$ is equivalent to *times k do q() od.*

The base case is when $k=0$: straightforward substitution shows that $A(0, q) =$ *donothing.* The inductive hypothesis is P1(K): that is, that $A(K, q)$, for some $K \geq 0$, is equivalent to *times K do q() od.* To show that this implies P1($K+1$) it is necessary as usual to calculate the effect of $A(K+1, q)$:

$A(K+1, q) = select\ K+1=0:donothing\ K+1>0:q(); A(K+1-1, q)\ endselect$

$= select\ false:donothing\ true:q(); A(K, q)\ endselect$
[since $K \geq 0$, it follows that $K+1>0$ and then $K+1 \neq 0$]

$= select\ true:q(); A(K, q)\ endselect$

$= q(); A(K, q)$

$= q();\ times\ K\ do\ q()\ od$ [by inductive hypothesis]

$= times\ K+1\ do\ q()\ od$ [since $K+1>0$ definition 6.4 applies]

I have proved P1(0) and that P1(K), when $K \geq 0$, implies P1($K+1$). I can conclude that P1(k) is true for every $k \geq 0$. Environment diagrams of calls to procedure A confirm the conclusion of the proof. For example, see figure 9.1.

-=-=-=-=-=-=-=-=-=-=-=-

Exercise 9.1
Given the following definition of procedure B, prove that a call $B(k, q)$ is equivalent to $A(k, q)$.

$def\ B(n, p) = select\ n=0:donothing\ n>0:B(n-1, p); p()\ endselect\ enddef$

Exercise 9.2
Given the following definition of procedure C, under what circumstances is a procedure call $C(k, q)$ equivalent to $A(k, q)$?

$def\ C(n, p) = select\ n=1:p()\ n>1:p(); C(n-1, p)\ endselect\ enddef$

Exercise 9.3
Prove the proposition you framed in answering exercise 9.2.

-=-=-=-=-=-=-=-=-=-=-=-

9.2 FINDING A FORMULA

The technique used on procedure A above - try some examples until you see a pattern emerging, guess a formula, try to prove it - will work just as well on more complicated examples. For example, consider program 9.2. The problem is to find and prove a formula *count(k)* which calculates the number of executions of

$$def\ D(n,p) = select\ n{=}0{:}\ donothing$$
$$n{>}0{:}\ p();D(n{-}1,p);D(n{-}1,p)$$
$$endselect$$
$$enddef$$

program 9.2

$q()$ which will be caused by $D(k,q)$. Obviously $D(0,q)$ is *donothing*, so
$count(0){=}0$. Some other examples:

$D(1,q) = select\ 1{=}0{:}donothing\ 1{>}0{:}q();D(1{-}1,q);D(1{-}1,q)\ endselect$
$\quad = q();D(0,q);D(0,q) = q()$
$\quad [count(1){=}1]$

$D(2,q) = select\ 2{=}0{:}donothing\ 2{>}0{:}q();D(2{-}1,q);D(2{-}1,q)\ endselect$
$\quad = q();D(1,q);D(1,q) = q();q();q()$
$\quad [count(2){=}3]$

$D(3,q) = select\ 3{=}0{:}donothing\ 3{>}0{:}q();D(3{-}1,q);D(3{-}1,q)\ endselect$
$\quad = q();D(2,q);D(2,q)$
$\quad [count(3) = 1{+}count(2){+}count(2) = 1{+}3{+}3 = 7]$

$D(4,q) = select\ 4{=}0{:}donothing\ 4{>}0{:}q();D(4{-}1,q);D(4{-}1,q)\ endselect$
$\quad = q();D(3,q);D(3,q)$
$\quad [count(4) = 1{+}7{+}7 = 15]$

$D(5,q) = q();D(3,q);D(3,q)$
$\quad [count(5) = 1{+}15{+}15 = 31]$

$count(6) = 1{+}31{+}31 = 63$
$count(7) = 1{+}63{+}63 = 127$

No programmer should fail to recognise the series 0, 1, 3, 7, 15, 31, 63, 127 ..: it
is just the series of the powers of two - 1, 2, 4, 8, 16, 32, 64, 128, .. - with one
subtracted from each component. It seems clear that $D(k,q)$ causes $2^k{-}1$
executions of $q()$. In the base case $D(0,q)$ is *donothing*, which causes no
executions of $q()$, and $0 = 1{-}1 = 2^0{-}1$. How many executions of $q()$ are caused
by $D(K{+}1,q)$ if $D(K,q)$ causes $2^K{-}1$ executions and $K{\geq}0$?

$D(K{+}1,q) = select\ K{+}1{=}0{:}donothing$
$\quad\quad K{+}1{>}0{:}q();D(K{+}1{-}1,q);D(K{+}1{-}1,q)$
$\quad endselect$

$\quad = select\ false{:}donothing\ true{:}q();D(K,q);D(K,q)\ endselect$
$\quad [since\ K{\geq}0\ it\ follows\ that\ K{+}1{>}0]$

$\quad = q();D(K,q);D(K,q)$

- a program which causes (by inductive hypothesis) $1 + 2^K{-}1 + 2^K{-}1 =
2{\times}2^K{+}1{-}2 = 2^{K+1}{-}1$ executions of $q()$.

-=-=-=-=-=-=-=-=-=-=-

Exercise 9.4
Draw an environment diagram of the execution of $D(3, \lambda().print*)$.

Exercise 9.5
Given the following definition of procedure E, find and prove a formula for the number of executions of $q()$ caused by $E(k, q)$.

$$def\ E(n,p) = select\ n=0:\ donothing$$
$$n>0:\ p();\ E(n-1, \lambda().(\!(p();\ p()\!)\!))$$
$$endselect$$
$$enddef$$

[Hint: powers of 2 again.]

Exercise 9.6
Find and prove a formula for the number of executions of $q()$ caused by $F(k, q)$.

$$def\ F(n,p) = select\ n=0:\ donothing$$
$$n>0:\ p();\ F(n-1, \lambda().A(2,p))$$
$$endselect$$
$$enddef$$

Exercise 9.7
Draw environment diagrams of the execution of $E(3, \lambda().print*)$ and $F(3, \lambda().print*)$.

Exercise 9.8
Find and prove a formula for the number of executions of $q()$ caused by $G(k, q)$.

$$def\ G(n,p) = select\ n=0:\ donothing$$
$$n>0:\ p();\ G(n-1, \lambda().(\!(p();\ p();\ p()\!)\!))$$
$$endselect$$
$$enddef$$

[Hint: powers of 3 this time.]

Exercise 9.9
Find and prove a formula for the number of executions of $q()$ caused by $H(k, q)$.

$$def\ H(n,p) = select\ n=0:\ donothing$$
$$n>0:\ p();\ H(n-1, \lambda().(\!(p();\ p();\ p();\ p()\!)\!))$$
$$endselect$$
$$enddef$$

Exercise 9.10
Keep going: find and prove a formula in terms of k and i for the number of executions of $q()$ caused by $I(k, q, i)$.

$$def\ I(n,p,m) = select\ n=0:\ donothing$$
$$n>0:\ p();\ I(n-1, \lambda().A(m,p),\ m)$$
$$endselect$$
$$enddef$$

[Hint: a generalisation of the last few exercises; powers of j.]

Exercise 9.11

Repeat exercise 9.10 for procedure J and executions of $J(k, q, i)$.

$$def\ J(n, p, m) = select\ n{=}0:\ donothing$$
$$n{>}0:\ p();\ J(n{-}1,\ \lambda().J(m, p, 1), m)$$
$$endselect$$
$$enddef$$

[Hint: this formula is a bit difficult to calculate. Try guessing a formula and proving it. It has a great deal to do with the answer to exercise 9.10.]

-=-=-=-=-=-=-=-=-=-=-=-

9.3 WHAT COULD POSSIBLY GO WRONG WITH A PROOF?

Lots. The procedure definitions given above are intentionally very simple so that they have simple proofs. The purpose of proofs in programming is to convince yourself (and others) that a particular program has particular properties, usually because you wrote it and you want to be sure you got it right. The property isn't always as simple to prove as any of those in this chapter. When you fail to make a convincing proof, the problem can be either in your proving or in your programming. You may have chosen the wrong proposition, you may have made a mistake in the proof, you may have made a mistake in the program or perhaps the program just doesn't have the property you think it has. Experience is the only way to find out which sort of problem you have, so you must practise until you get the feel of things.

For example, the proof of the effect of a procedure call $A(k, q)$ above is valid only when $k{\geq}0$. Suppose that I had the misguided aim of trying to prove the proposition that some formula $F(k)$ gives the number of executions of $q()$ caused by $A(k, q)$ when k is zero or negative (the proposition can't be proved because there is no such formula F). The base case isn't too hard: $F(0) = 0$ because $A(0, q) = donothing$. But when I try the inductive step I might make the hypothesis that $A(K, q)$ causes $F(K)$ executions of $q()$ for some $K{<}0$ and try to show that this implies something about $A(K{+}1, q)$:

$$A(K{+}1, q) = select\ K{+}1{=}0:\ donothing\ K{+}1{>}0{:}q();\ A(K, q);\ A(K, q)\ endselect$$

Now if $K{=}{-}1$ then $K{+}1{=}0$ and the procedure call is equivalent to *donothing*. But if $K{<}{-}1$ then $K{+}1{<}0$ and the procedure call is equivalent to a meaningless *select* instruction. My 'proof' can go no further. If I tried to count the other way - that is, to show that $F(K{-}1)$ depended on $F(K)$ - I wouldn't have any more success. My failure fits perfectly well with the observation that $A(k, q)$ is meaningless when k is negative.

Suppose, though, that the procedure had been defined differently. Consider procedure $A2$, defined in program 9.3. $A2({-}1, q)$ isn't obviously meaningless.

$$def\ A2(n,p) = select\ n=0:\ donothing$$
$$n \neq 0:\ p();A2(n-1,p)$$
$$endselect$$
$$enddef$$

program 9.3

Give definition and call to a real programming system and it will do its best to produce an infinite sequence of executions of $q()$:

$$A2(-1,q) = select\ -1=0:donothing\ \ -1 \neq 0:q();A2(-1-1,q)\ endselect$$
$$= q();A2(-2,q)$$
$$= q();\ select\ -2=0:donothing\ \ -2 \neq 0:q();A2(-2-1,q)\ endselect$$
$$= q();q();A2(-3,q)$$
$$= q();q();\ select\ -3=0:donothing\ \ -3 \neq 0:q();A2(-3-1,q)\ endselect$$
$$= q();q();q();A2(-4,q)$$

We say that execution of $A2(-1,q)$ will never terminate[†], but a program that doesn't terminate isn't necessarily a meaningless program. Nevertheless I could not construct a formula $F(k)$ which counts the number of executions of $q()$ caused by $A2(k,q)$ when $k<0$ because that number is infinite - literally uncountable.

$$def\ A3(n,p) = select\ n=0:\ donothing$$
$$n>1:\ p();A3(n-1,p)$$
$$endselect$$
$$enddef$$

program 9.4

There are still more ways in which an inductive proof can go wrong. Consider procedure $A3$, defined in program 9.4. If you try to prove that $A3(k,q)$ causes k executions of $q()$ when $k \geq 0$ you would certainly fail. If you choose $k=0$ as the base case then the basic step works fine but in the inductive step you must assume $K \geq 1$ (or, if you like, $K>0$) because only then can you conclude that $K+1>1$ and that the second arm of the *select* is activated. This makes the hoped-for conclusion invalid because it *doesn't rest on the base case*. In the inductive step you must assume $K \geq 1$ and therefore you can't conclude that $A3(1,q)$ has anything to do with $A3(0,q)$, so you can't ascend the inductive ladder.

This all fits nicely with the observation that $A3(1,q)$ is meaningless and that all executions with $n>1$ count downwards towards $n=1$, so all are equivalent to a

---

[†] Execution of $A2(-1,q)$ will never terminate 'normally' in the sense of coming to a proper and designed end, but in a real programming system it will probably terminate 'abnormally' because eventually the environments it creates exhaust the system's capacity, or repeated subtraction reaches the largest negative number that the system can represent, or somebody turns the power off, or the computer wears out ..

sequence which ends with a meaningless instruction. If you sloppily imagine that $K \geq 1$ means the same as $K \geq 0$ then your 'proof' would be no proof at all, as you might discover if you tried to execute a program which contained a call to this procedure. The moral is that you must be careful when making proofs: if you make an invalid step then your proof is invalid.

$$def\ A4(n,p) = select\ n=0:\ donothing$$
$$n>0:\ p();A4(n-2,p)$$
$$endselect$$
$$enddef$$

program 9.5

Consider procedure $A4$, defined in program 9.5. Forewarned that there might be something strange about this procedure, you should notice that it counts downwards in twos so that $A4(k,q)$ depends on $A4(k-2,q)$. Therefore $A4(1,q)$ depends on $A4(-1,q)$, which is meaningless and, because all odd-numbered executions count downwards finally to reach $A4(1,q)$, every odd-numbered execution is meaningless. Even-numbered executions are ok because $A4(2k,q)$ depends on $A4(2k-2,q) = A4(2(k-1),q)$, which depends on $A4(2(k-2),q)$, .. and so on: they all depend eventually on $A4(0,q)$, which is *donothing*.

All executions of $A4(k,q)$ in which k is an odd number are meaningless because they are equivalent to a sequence which ends with a meaningless instruction. A proof which attempted to justify a formula $F(k)$ which counted executions of $q()$ caused by $A4(k,q)$ for any $k \geq 0$ would have a parallel difficulty: all you could prove would be that if $A4(2K,q)$ caused K executions of $q()$ for some $K \geq 0$ then $A4(2(K+1),q)$ would cause $K+1$ executions: that is, your proof would work for even numbers only, just like the calls on the procedure.

$$def\ A5(n,p) = select\ n=0:\ donothing$$
$$n>0:\ p();A5(n,p)$$
$$endselect$$
$$enddef$$

program 9.6

Or consider procedure $A5$, defined in program 9.6. No formula can say how many executions of $q()$ are caused by $A5(k,q)$ when $k>0$ because $A5(K+1,q)$ depends on $A5(K+1,q)$. In a real-world programming system $A5(k,q)$ would be another version of an infinite sequence for any positive non-zero k.

-=-=-=-=-=-=-=-=-=-=-=-

Exercise 9.12
Prove that $L(k,q)$ - see program 9.7 -will cause k executions of $q()$ when $k \geq 0$. [Hint: nothing wrong with the procedure definition but you might need to consider odd and even K separately in the inductive step, or you might need to use strong induction, or something else.]

$$def\,L(n,p) = select\ n=0:\ donothing$$
$$n=1:\ p()$$
$$n>1:\ p();p();L(n-2,p)$$
$$endselect$$
$$enddef$$

program 9.7

Exercise 9.13
Suppose that program 9.7 were altered so that $L(n,p)$ depended on $L(n-3,p)$. For what values of k would $L(k,q)$ terminate? How many executions of $q()$ in those cases? If you tried to prove that formula in general, how and where would your proof break down?

-=-=-=-=-=-=-=-=-=-=-=-

9.4 SOMETIMES YOU MUST USE STRONG INDUCTION

Sometimes you can't complete an inductive proof because you have chosen the wrong induction scheme. Consider the procedure *threepower* defined in program 9.8. Provided that $n\geq1$, *threepower*(n) prints "yes!" if n is a power of three, "no" otherwise [†].

$$def\,threepower(n) = select\ n=1:\ printstring(\text{“yes!”})$$
$$(n\,rem\,3)=0:\ threepower(n+3)$$
$$n\neq1\ \wedge\ (n\,rem\,3)\neq0:\ printstring(\text{“no”})$$
$$endselect$$
$$enddef$$

program 9.8

-=-=-=-=-=-=-=-=-=-=-=-

Exercise 9.14
Draw environment diagrams for procedure calls *threepower*(3), *threepower*(6), *threepower*(18) and *threepower*(27) to convince yourself that the *threepower* procedure prints the right answer in those cases at least.

-=-=-=-=-=-=-=-=-=-=-=-

[†] Readers without a mathematical training should observe that there can be zero and negative powers of three. Since $3\times(3^i) = 3^{i+1}$ it follows that $3^{i-1}= (3^i)/3$. So from the fact that $3^2=3\times3=9$ you know that $3^1=9/3=3$ and from that you can see that $3^0=3/3=1$. The number 1 *is* a power of three: in fact it is the zeroth power of any number. If you carry on down you find that negative powers of three are fractions: $3^{-1}= 1/3$; $3^{-2}= 1/9$; and so on.

The proposition which must be proved about *threepower* can be phrased as follows:

P2: An execution of *threepower*(*k*) when *k*≥1 prints "yes!" if *k* is a power of three (that is, if *i* exists such that *k*=3^i) or prints "no" if *k* is not a power of three.

The base case here is *k*=1. 3^0=1 so the proposition is satisfied if *threepower*(1) prints "yes!":

> *threepower*(1) = *select* 1=1: *printstring*("yes!")
> (1 *rem* 3)=0: *threepower*(1÷3)
> 1≠1 ∧ (1 *rem* 3)≠0: *printstring*("no")
> *endselect*
>
> = *select* 1=1: *printstring*("yes!")
> 1=0: *threepower*(0)
> 1≠1 ∧ 1≠0: *printstring*("no")
> *endselect*
>
> = *select true*: *printstring*("yes!")
> *false*: *threepower*(0)
> *false* ∧ *true*: *printstring*("no")
> *endselect*
>
> = *select true*: *printstring*("yes!") *endselect*
>
> = *printstring*("yes!")

The base case at least is proved. Now make the normal simple induction hypothesis that *P2*(*K*) is true for some *K*≥1. To prove *P2*(*K*+1), try to establish the meaning of *threepower*(*K*+1):

> *threepower*(*K*+1) = *select K*+1=1: *printstring*("yes!")
> ((*K*+1) *rem* 3)=0: *threepower*((*K*+1)÷3)
> *K*+1≠1 ∧ ((*K*+1) *rem* 3)≠0: *printstring*("no")
> *endselect*
>
> = *select false*: *printstring*("yes!")
> ((*K*+1) *rem* 3)=0: *threepower*((*K*+1)÷3)
> *true* ∧ ((*K*+1) *rem* 3)≠0: *printstring*("no")
> *endselect*
> [since *K*≥1 it follows that *K*+1>1 and then *K*+1≠1]
>
> = *select* ((*K*+1) *rem* 3)=0: *threepower*((*K*+1)÷3)
> ((*K*+1) *rem* 3)≠0: *printstring*("no")
> *endselect*

To proceed further in the proof I must consider two cases, one for each of the two arms of the *select*. If *K*+1 divided by three gives a remainder which isn't zero, then *K*+1 isn't a multiple of three. And if it isn't a multiple of three it can't be a power of three (unless it is one or a fraction of one: but *K*+1>1 so that can't be so). Therefore the procedure should print "no" if (*K*+1) *rem* 3 isn't zero, and it does, so in that case at least the procedure does the right thing.

The other case to consider is when $K+1$ is a multiple of three. In this case $(K+1)\div3=x$ — that is, $K+1=3x$ - and x will be a power of three when $K+1$ is a power of three, and vice-versa. But the effect of $threepower(K+1)$ depends on $threepower((K+1)\div3)$ ($=threepower(x)$), which is by no means certain to be the same thing as $threepower(K)$. I can't show that the effect of $threepower(K+1)$ can be deduced from the effect of $threepower(K)$ and my simple induction proof has broken down.

It remains to try strong induction. The strong inductive hypothesis is $P2(1)..P2(K)$: that is, that every procedure call $threepower(1)$, $threepower(2)$, .., $threepower(K)$ prints "yes!" or "no" appropriately. If $K+1>1$ and $K+1$ is a multiple of three it follows that $K+1\geq3$; then certainly $(K+1)\div3\leq K$ and equally certainly $(K+1)\div3\geq1$. Thus the transformation above can be used as the basis of a strong induction proof.

The case when $(K+1)$ rem 3 is non-zero goes through as before. In the other case, if $K+1$ is a power of three and $K+1>1$ then $(K+1)\div3$ is a power of three and vice-versa; conversely, if $K+1$ isn't a power of three then $(K+1)\div3$ isn't a power of three and again vice-versa. Since $(K+1)\div3$ must be a number in the range $1..K$, under the strong inductive hypothesis $P2(1)..P2(K)$ it follows that $threepower((K+1)\div3)$ must print "yes!" or "no" appropriately.

I have now proved both cases to complete a proof that $(P2(1)..P2(K)) => P2(K+1)$ when $K\geq1$. Because I already have $P2(1)$, I can conclude that $P2(k)$ is true whenever $k\geq1$.

9.5 PROOFS WITH AMBIGUOUS CHOICES

To those used to choice mechanisms in other programming notations, the conditions in the *select* instruction in the *threepower* example above may seem surprisingly complicated. Many people, asked to design a solution, construct the procedure definition shown in program 9.9, unaware that when $n=1$ both the first and the third conditions are true, and then the instruction might either print "yes!" or print "no", in principle choosing at random[†].

This kind of programming mistake arises perhaps because the condition '$n=1$' appears to be much more specific than '$(n\,rem\,3)\neq0$'. When we give instructions to humans we expect specific instructions to over-rule general ones, but the definition of the *select* instruction makes no distinction between specific and non-specific conditions.

[†] If you believe in the possibility of intelligent computers then it might choose maliciously always to print "no" - intelligence doesn't imply benevolence!

$$def\ tp(n) = select\ n=1:\ printstring(\text{“yes!”})$$
$$(n\ rem\ 3)=0:\ tp(n+3)$$
$$(n\ rem\ 3)\neq0:\ printstring(\text{“no”})$$
$$endselect$$
$$enddef$$

program 9.9

The *select* in the definition of *tp* is a potentially ambiguous instruction. The ambiguity should show up in the proof if it is important, and it does because it is. In the base case:

$$tp(0) = select\ 1=1:\ printstring(\text{“yes!”})$$
$$1=0:\ tp(0)$$
$$1\neq0:\ printstring(\text{“no”})$$
$$endselect$$

$$= select\ true:printstring(\text{“yes!”})\ \ true:printstring(\text{“no”})\ endselect$$

With two true-labelled arms each with a different effect the proof can go no further.

Consider an intentionally ambiguous instruction, the one I introduced at the beginning of chapter 8:

$$select\ a\geq b:printnumber(a)\ \ b\geq a:\ printnumber(b)\ endselect$$

program 9.10

Suppose this instruction is executed when $a=b=5$. Then it becomes

$$select\ 5\geq5:printnumber(5)\ \ 5\geq5:printnumber(5)\ endselect$$

$$= select\ true:printnumber(5)\ \ true:printnumber(5)\ endselect$$

No problem this time: the instruction contains two true arms with identical effect. No matter how malevolently demonic the choice made by the machine, it must print 5. Formally, by definition 8.5 the arms can be combined, leaving a *select* instruction with a single arm labelled by *true∨true* (*=true*).

9.6 RECURSIVE CALCULATIONS

Often a formula is self-referential or recursive. Then it is possible to write a recursive value-delivering procedure, using the same techniques as are used in recursive instruction procedures. The classic examples of this technique are to be found in formulas defined by recurrence relations.

The example of examples is the Fibonacci series. Signor Fibonacci discovered the series named after him in attempting to describe the rate at which a population of rabbits increases, which as everybody knows is by no means linear. His series described the number of pairs in a population in which each pair produces two children each month and in which a newborn pair doesn't reproduce for its first two months of life:

$$1, 1, 2, 3, 5, 8, 13, 21, 34, ..$$

The series is characterised by the fact that each number after the second is the sum of the previous two. It has been a favourite mathematical puzzle ever since it was invented.

A classical way of defining this series is by means of a recurrence relation:

$$Fib_1 = 1$$
$$Fib_2 = 1$$
$$Fib_{n+2} = Fib_n + Fib_{n+1}$$

Writing $k=n+2$ (that is, replacing n by $k-2$) this relation can be imitated by a recursive procedure definition:

$$def\ Fibr(k) = select\ k=1 \lor k=2:\ 1$$
$$k>2:\ Fibr(k-2)+Fibr(k-1)$$
$$endselect$$
$$enddef$$

program 9.11

-=-=-=-=-=-=-=-=-=-=-=-

Exercise 9.15
Draw an execution tree for *Fibr*(5): count the number of procedure executions required to calculate this value.

Exercise 9.16
How many procedure executions are needed to calculate *Fibr*(6)?

-=-=-=-=-=-=-=-=-=-=-=-

Program 9.11 has a disadvantage, which exercises 9.15 and 9.16 hint at and which later chapters will expand upon. There are several more 'efficient' ways to calculate this series, all of which make less demands upon a computing machine's calculating effort. But program 9.11 has a compensating advantage: it corresponds so closely to the original definition that it is easy to write it down correctly; indeed it is hard to make a mistake. It might not be very useful if you want to know the millionth Fibonacci number, but it will do very nicely in many other circumstances.

-=-=-=-=-=-=-=-=-=-=-=-

Exercise 9.17
The factorial series is calculated by multiplying numbers together. Thus $1!=1$, $2!=1\times2=2$, $3!=1\times2\times3=6$, .. $n!=1\times2\times..\times n$. This series can also be described by a recurrence relation:

$$Fac_1 = 1$$
$$Fac_{n+1} = (n+1) \times Fac_n$$

Write a recursive procedure definition $Facr(k)$ which computes and delivers the value of Fac_k.

Exercise 9.18

Exponential powers of a number can be calculated by repeated multiplication: $x^n = x \times x \times .. \times x$ ($n-1$ multiplications in all). They can also be defined by a recurrence relation:

$$x^0 = 1$$
$$x^{n+1} = x \times x^n$$

Write a recursive procedure $power(x, k)$ which calculates x^k.

Chapter 10
MEMORY, INPUT AND ASSIGNMENT

Your experience with computers must by now have convinced you that they can remember things. For example, when you type a program which is stored in a file, execute it and then edit the program to change its effect, the programming system can be said to remember your program text between executions. It certainly fits the definition of memory given in chapter 1 because its present behaviour is affected by its past experience.

Computer memory is of enormous economic significance. Many of the largest computer systems in the world are databases - repositories of information stored in computer memory. Computer memory is of enormous historical significance. Computers which can remember programs long enough to execute them are easily programmable and their development led eventually to miniature calculators, digital watches, talking cars, computer-controlled washing machines (and more useful things like wordprocessors, databases, machines which supervise intensive care patients, ..).

Memory has to do with time, with the order in which things happen. If something hasn't happened yet, you can't be expected to remember it. Memory in programming has to do with sequences of actions. An action produces a state of affairs; subsequent actions take place in that state of affairs and are affected by it; memories are part of the state of affairs and can thereby affect actions.

The simplest memories are passive accumulations of effects. Iron bars rust away, your teeth wear out, coastlines erode by passage of time. The wear on a carpet records the effect of all the feet that have walked across it since it was made. Less simply, the position of a typewriter's printing head is a memory of the cumulative effect of all the motions that it has undertaken in the past; the contents of your trouser pockets record the cumulative effect of insertion and extraction of things since you bought the trousers.

Active *remembering*, as humans do it, is a recording of present circumstances so that we can refer to our records at some future time. Records can be stored in our heads, or on paper, or in our pockets, or in a wordprocessor, or wherever. What we remember is intended to affect what we do: when we resolve to remember something we make a note and at the same time we make a plan to refer to that note in future and to take actions which depend on what we find recorded there.

Some sort of memories can be actively forgotten, as we tear up a notebook or erase a videotape or burn a photograph. Some memories can be forgotten because they are overwritten by others, as when we record a new song on a cassette tape or paint a new picture on a canvas or put new wallpaper on the wall of our bedroom.

The programming description of memory mimics active remembering and forgetting. The *assignment* instruction is used to remember part of the present state of affairs; instructions which are subsequently executed may refer to the retained memory and their action can be affected by what is found; memories can be discarded or rewritten.

Input to a program can be treated as a sort of remembering. A program which can remember what was presented to it - typed or signalled or however - and then later act on that memory is sensitive to the outside world. In this way we can make *interactive* programs which permit continuous control - eventually wordprocessors, databases, calculators, computer games, ..

10.1 CONTAINERS AND REMEMBERING

The value of a formula depends on the values ascribed to the names it contains. The effect of a program depends on the values of the formulas it contains. In this book so far the values of names, and hence the effects of programs, have been fixed within an environment. To produce programs which can remember circumstances and later act upon what was remembered, there must be formulas whose effect is variable and affected by memory.

In my notation and in almost every mechanical code names can be introduced which refer to memory *containers*. Containers hold values in the way that a bucket holds water, a bag holds shopping or a box holds whatever you put in it. When a container name is used in a formula, the value of the formula depends on what value is found in the container. Memories can be rewritten, like recordings on magnetic tape, and therefore the value of the formula must depend on what was *last written* in the container. Repetitive calculation of the same formula in different circumstances may therefore deliver different values: this is at once the great advantage and the great disadvantage of program memory.

It is an advantage because it permits the extremely useful program structure called 'indefinite repetition', which is the subject of chapter 12 and is the reason for introducing assignment in the first place. It is a disadvantage when calculating the effect of a program. The substitution rules given in earlier chapters have all replaced formulas with other formulas, and have all relied implicitly on an assumption that the meaning of a formula depends only on the environment in which it is calculated and not on when the calculation takes place. Once active memory is introduced that assumption is no longer valid and we have to reconsider every rule so as to decide when calculation should take place. For that reason there are lots of substitution rules in this chapter, showing how formulas which include memory containers must be treated. (Programs which don't use container names can of course continue to use the old substitution rules.)

10.2 THE INITIALISE DEFINITION

Container names aren't like the names introduced by *def* and *let* definitions. A container name directly identifies a container: only indirectly and transiently does it identify the value which that container happens to hold. For that reason I use a special definition for container names in my notation. The *initialise* definition introduces the name and defines a value which should be placed in the container, to remain there until it is replaced. For example, the definitions

$$initialise\ x := 3$$
$$initialise\ y := \text{'h'}$$
$$initialise\ z := \text{"hello"}$$
$$initialise\ p := \lambda().print*$$

introduce the names x, y, z and p as container names and put different values in each of the containers they name. In my notation any container can hold any sort of value: numbers, characters, procedures, ..

Initialise definitions, like *let* and *def* definitions, are executed at the beginning of a program to create a new environment. In the new environment the container name can be used in formulas and will be replaced on calculation by the value which is held in the container. For example, program 10.1 prints 3.

$$initialise\ x := 3$$

$$printnumber(x)$$

program 10.1

Like *let* definitions, the idea is that the order of *initialise* definitions doesn't matter. In principle the calculations take place all at once, the containers are created and the values placed in them all at once.

10.3 THE ASSIGNMENT INSTRUCTION

The *assignment* instruction $x:=e$, pronounced 'x becomes e', calculates the value of formula e - a property of the current state of affairs - and remembers it in container x. Subsequent occurrences of the container name in formulas will be replaced by the remembered value, unless and until the memory is obliterated by a fresh assignment to the same container. For example, the following program prints 3 and then 4:

initialise $x:=2$

printnumber $(x+1); x:=25; printnumber((x+5)-1)$

program 10.2

In execution terms:

The assignment instruction $x:=e$ first calculates the value of formula e and then puts that value in container x.

definition 10.1

This definition necessarily makes the execution of an assignment instruction a mini-sequence: *first* do the calculation, *second* remember what was calculated. This order of action is exploited in almost every program which uses assignment. For example, the most commonly used assignment instructions have the form

$$a:=a+1$$

This instruction has the effect of adding one to the number in container a. It calculates the value of the formula $a+1$, which means looking in the container a and calculating the successor of the number found; then it puts the calculated number into the container a, obliterating what is found there[†].

In substitution terms the assignment instruction affects every formula up to the next assignment to the same container. The instruction $x:=e$ can be read as 'replace future occurrences of x by e'. The notation $F[a\backslash b]$ means a copy of formula F with every occurrence of name a replaced by formula b. The fundamental substitution rule of assignment is:

If program P doesn't contain an assignment to container x nor to any container named in formula e, then

$$..x:=e; P; .. = ..P[x\backslash e]; x:=e; ..$$

definition 10.2

This definition moves an assignment instruction forward one place in a sequence,

---

[†] Note that the calculation of the formula $a+1$ has *no effect* on the container a: it is the assignment to a, after the calculation, that changes the state of affairs.

making a substitution in the instruction it moves past. The same rule can then be used on the next instruction in the sequence, and so on until it no longer applies. When P, or an instruction within P, does alter the value in x or does affect the meaning of e then other rules apply; these are described later in this chapter.

Notice that the substitution definition copes effortlessly with the assignment $a:=a+1$ and all its variations. For example:

$$x:=7; printnumber(x+3); x:=x-2; printnumber(5 \times x)$$
$$= printnumber(7+3); x:=7; x:=x-2; printnumber(5 \times x)$$
$$= printnumber(10); x:=7; printnumber(5 \times (x-2)); x:=x-2$$
$$= printnumber(10); printnumber(5 \times (7-2)); x:=7; x:=x-2$$
$$= printnumber(10); printnumber(25); x:=7; x:=x-2$$

Both the assignment instructions in this example reach the end of the program and can be removed entirely. Rules for doing so are given later in this chapter.

An assignment instruction may put a value into more than one container at a time. The instruction $x, y := e, f$ calculates the values of e and of f and places them in x and y respectively. So, for example, $a, b := 1, 2$ puts 1 into a and 2 into b[†]. In general the instruction

$$x1, x2, .. , xn := e1, e2, .. , en$$

first simultaneously calculates the values of formulas $e1..en$ and then simultaneously stores those values in the containers $x1..xn$. The substitution definition of this instruction, which I will give later in this chapter, relies on simultaneous substitution of $e1$ for $x1$, $e2$ for $x2$, .., en for xn.

Multiple assignment instructions are particularly useful for exchanging the values held in containers: for example, the instruction $x, y := y, x$ exchanges the values held in containers x and y, and the instruction $a, b, c := b, c, a$ rotates the values held in the three containers a, b and c.

10.4 SHARING CONTAINERS BETWEEN ENVIRONMENTS

When an environment is created - by a call to a procedure, for example - the new environment usually retains some of the name$\rightarrow$meaning mappings of the one on which it is based. Those mappings might as well be shared between the original and the new environment. When the meaning of a name is a value - a number, a character, a string, or whatever - then sharing meanings between environments causes no difficulty. When the meaning of a name is a container, sharing

---

[†] In each case not strictly into a or b but into the container named by a or the container named by b. The abbreviation, equating the name with the container it identifies in the current environment, helps to reduce the length of my sentences but you should keep in mind the fuller and more correct version.

between environments means that an assignment instruction executed in either environment can be used to affect that container. That is, the effect of assignments executed in the created environment can be felt in the environment on which it is based and, perhaps, in the environment on which that is based, and so on. For example, program 10.3 prints first 3, then 4 and finally 5. Figure 10.1 shows an environment diagram which traces the history of container x in this program.

$$initialise\ x := 12$$
$$def\ puzzle(a) = printnumber(x); x := a\ enddef$$

$$printnumber(x+4);$$
$$x := 4; puzzle(7);$$
$$printnumber(x-2)$$

program 10.3

Execute program 10.3 in an environment env-0 containing the basic instruction and procedure names with their normal meanings.

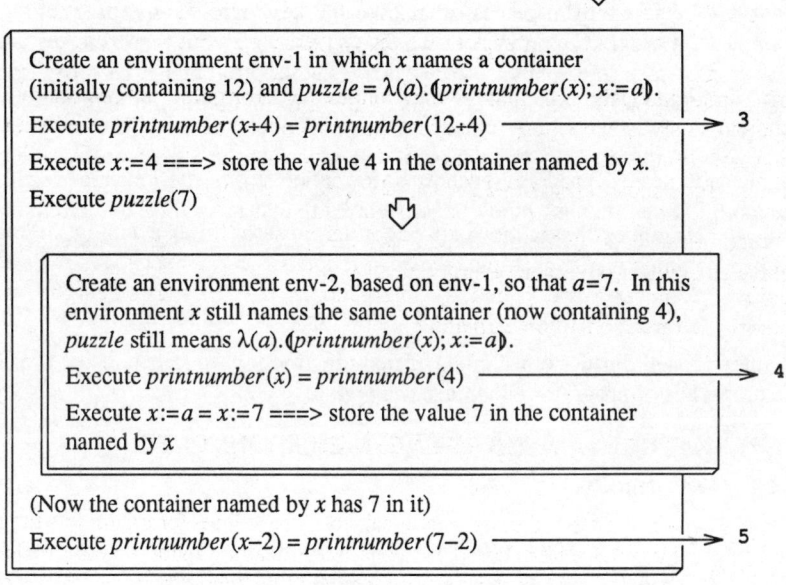

Create an environment env-1 in which x names a container (initially containing 12) and $puzzle = \lambda(a).\langle printnumber(x); x := a\rangle$.

Execute $printnumber(x+4) = printnumber(12+4)$ ⎯⎯⎯⎯⎯⎯→ 3

Execute $x := 4$ ===> store the value 4 in the container named by x.

Execute $puzzle(7)$

Create an environment env-2, based on env-1, so that $a=7$. In this environment x still names the same container (now containing 4), $puzzle$ still means $\lambda(a).\langle printnumber(x); x := a\rangle$.

Execute $printnumber(x) = printnumber(4)$ ⎯⎯⎯⎯⎯⎯→ 4

Execute $x := a = x := 7$ ===> store the value 7 in the container named by x

(Now the container named by x has 7 in it)

Execute $printnumber(x-2) = printnumber(7-2)$ ⎯⎯⎯⎯⎯→ 5

figure 10.1

-=-=-=-=-=-=-=-=-=-=-=-

Exercise 10.1

Show that the substitution of procedure body for procedure call in program 10.3 produces a program which has the effect described in figure 10.1.

-=-=-=-=-=-=-=-=-=-=-=-

10.5 INPUT INSTRUCTIONS

Up to this point the programs you have written, no matter how intricately they have been constructed, have been deaf to the outside world. Every program, once started, runs through its little performance without variation, and each performance is the same as the last. That sort of program can be very useful when you must make a complicated calculation: for example, of some formula which describes the future state of the weather, or the electron potential around a deuterium nucleus, or whatever. But as always we like to generalise, to parameterise our programs so that we don't have to edit them to produce slightly different effects or to alter the initial conditions in the formula.

Programs which accept information from a keyboard, nowadays called *interactive* programs, are interesting to use because they allow some continuous control. The information you type alters the program's course while it is executing. Video games are interactive programs, as are text editors and some programming-system interpreters. Most useful programs nowadays are interactive to some extent.

Input can be taken from places other than the keyboard. Some programs - for example, the programming system which you use to try out the exercises in this book - can take information from files. These programs aren't necessarily interactive but their behaviour depends on the information in the files which they are given.

In my notation a program accepts information from the outside world by executing a particular kind of assignment instruction. The *readnumber* instruction accepts numerals typed on the keyboard, and *readnumber x* is equivalent to the assignment instruction

x := whatever is typed, interpreted as a numeral

Chapter 11 will discuss other kinds of input instruction. In this chapter I explore the properties of programs which use *readnumber*.

A simple example

Consider a program which prints out triangles (still the same n-by-n pattern as before), but which asks you what size of triangle you want to see. Two examples of interaction with such a program are shown in figures 10.2 and 10.3. In these illustrations the *input* - what you might type on the keyboard - is shown in bold italic script while the *output* - what the program would print on the screen - is shown normally.

Program 10.4 can produce this sort of effect. It uses familiar techniques to print its messages and the triangular pattern. Its novel feature is a *readnumber* instruction used to accept information from the keyboard and assign it to a container called *size*. Use of the name *size* in the formula controlling a repetition

```
What size of triangle would you like to see? 5

*
**
***
****
*****

That's all!
```

figure 10.2

```
What size of triangle would you like to see? 7

*
**
***
****
*****
******
*******

That's all!
```

figure 10.3

initialise size := 0

printstring("What size of triangle would you like to see? ");
readnumber size;

for n rt 1*..size do NL*; *times n do print* od od*;
NL; *printstring*("That's all!"); *NL*

program 10.4

produces a triangle with the right number of asterisks. The stages of execution of program 10.4 are:

(a) Acquire a container, called *size* and containing zero.

(b) Print the first message (although it looks like a question to our eyes, it is just a sequence of characters to be printed).

(c) Inspect what is typed on the keyboard and calculate the value of the number described; put this number into the container called *size*, obliterating whatever is in it at the time (in this case zero).

(d) Execute *for n rt* 1*..size do* .. *od*. This means finding out what is in the container called *size*, calculating the sequence described by '1..what is found' (that is, 1..what was just put there) and then executing the body of the *for-do* in the appropriate sequence of environments.

(e) Print the final message.

The effect of program 10.4 can't be calculated at all without knowing what is to be typed in response to the program's printed question, which will be interpreted as the number to be assigned to the container called *size*. If in fact '14' is typed on the keyboard, I can rewrite program 10.4 as follows:

> *initialise size*:=0;
>
> *printstring*("What size of triangle would you like to see? ");
> *size*:=14;
> *for n rt* 1..*size do NL*; *times n do print* od od*;
> *NL*;*printstring*("That's all!");*NL*

program 10.5

According to the substitution explanation of assignment, the instruction *size*:=14 should be understood as 'in place of *size*, read 14 until you find an instruction to the contrary'; definition 10.2 shows how this reading can be put into effect.

The aim of the substitution explanation is to eliminate container names from the program entirely, replacing occurrences of the name by the value which it holds. The replacement can validly take place only between one assignment and the next. In program 10.5 this means replacing every occurrence of *size* between the initialise instruction and the first assignment with the formula 0 (in this case there aren't any to replace, but I would do so if necessary)[†] and replacing every occurrence between the assignment and the end of the program with the formula 14. This produces program 10.6, which prints a fourteen-by-fourteen triangle.

> *initialise size*:=0
>
> *printstring*("What size of triangle would you like to see? ");
> *for n rt* 1..14 *do NL*; *times n do print* od od*;
> *NL*;*printstring*("That's all!");*NL*;
> *size*:=14

program 10.6

When assignment instructions are used in more complicated programs the explanation gets a little more involved but the principle stays the same: eliminate every occurrence of a container name by replacing each one with the value which is certain to be found in the container at the time the assignment is executed.

An example with more than one container

There can quite reasonably be several input instructions in a single program. For example, program 10.7 asks how many triangles you want to see, then for each

---

[†] The rules for treating *initialise* definitions are given later in this chapter: for the moment I am treating the definition as another kind of assignment statement, as the rules permit.

initialise size:=0, *count*:=0

NL; *printstring*("How many triangles do you want to see? ")
readnumber count;

for i rt 1..*count do*
    NL; *printstring*("What size should triangle number ");
    printnumber(*i*); *printstring*(" be? ");
    readnumber size;

    NL; *for n rt* 1..*size do NL*; *times n do print* od od*
od;

NL; *printstring*("That's all!"); *NL*

program 10.7

```
How many triangles do you want to see? 3

What size should triangle number 1 be? 4

      *
      **
      ***
      ****

What size should triangle number 2 be? 19

      *
      **
      ***
      ****
      *****
      ******
      *******
      ********
      *********
      **********
      ***********
      ************
      *************
      **************
      ***************
      ****************
      *****************
      ******************
      *******************

What size should triangle number 3 be? 0


That's all!
```

figure 10.4

initialise size:=0, *count*:=0

NL; *printstring*("How many triangles do you want to see? ")

for i rt 1..3 *do*
  NL; *printstring*("What size should triangle number ");
  printnumber(*i*); *printstring*(" be? ");
  readnumber size;
  NL; *for n rt* 1..*size do NL*; *times n do print* od od
od;

NL; *printstring*("That's all!"); *NL*;
count:=3

program 10.8

initialise size:=0, *count*:=0

NL; *printstring*("How many triangles do you want to see? ")

❲ *let i*=1
  NL; *printstring*("What size should triangle number ");
  printnumber(*i*); *printstring*(" be? ");
  size:=4;
  NL; *for n rt* 1..*size do NL*; *times n do print* od od
❳;
❲ *let i*=2
  NL; *printstring*("What size should triangle number ");
  printnumber(*i*); *printstring*(" be? ");
  size:=19;
  NL; *for n rt* 1..*size do NL*; *times n do print* od od
❳;
❲ *let i*=3
  NL; *printstring*("What size should triangle number ");
  printnumber(*i*); *printstring*(" be? ");
  size:=0;
  NL; *for n rt* 1..*size do NL*; *times n do print* od od
❳;

NL; *printstring*("That's all!"); *NL*;
count:=3

program 10.9

triangle asks how large you want it to be.

Suppose that the typed reply to the first question is '3'. Then the *readnumber* instruction will place 3 in the container called *count*; therefore the formula 1..*count* means 1..3, and it follows that you will be asked three times what size triangle you want. If the first time your answer is '4' then the formula 1..*size* will come to mean 1..4 and you get a four-by-four triangle; the second time you could answer '19' and get a nineteen-by-nineteen triangle; by the third time you might *initialise size*:=0

NL; *printstring*("How many triangles do you want to see? ")

NL; *printstring*("What size should triangle number ");
printnumber(1); *printstring*(" be? ");
size:=4;
NL; *for n rt* 1*..size do NL*; *times n do print* od od*

NL; *printstring*("What size should triangle number ");
printnumber(2); *printstring*(" be? ");
size:=19;
NL; *for n rt* 1*..size do NL*; *times n do print* od od*

NL; *printstring*("What size should triangle number ");
printnumber(3); *printstring*(" be? ");
size:=0;
NL; *for n rt* 1*..size do NL*; *times n do print* od od*

NL; *printstring*("That's all!"); *NL*;
count:=3

program 10.10

initialise size:=0

NL; *printstring*("How many triangles do you want to see? ")

NL; *printstring*("What size should triangle number ");
printnumber(1); *printstring*(" be? ");
size:=4;
NL; *for n rt* 1*..size do NL*; *times n do print* od od*

NL; *printstring*("What size should triangle number ");
printnumber(2); *printstring*(" be? ");
size:=19;
NL; *for n rt* 1*..size do NL*; *times n do print* od od*

NL; *printstring*("What size should triangle number ");
printnumber(3); *printstring*(" be? ");
NL; *for n rt* 1*..0 do NL*; *times n do print* od od*

NL; *printstring*("That's all!"); *NL*;
size:=0; *count*:=3

program 10.11

be bored and answer '0', making 1*..size* mean the empty sequence so you get nothing but a blank line. Finally the program prints its mindless but cheerful goodbye message. The overall effect is illustrated in figure 10.4.

The substitution explanation of program 10.7 is only a little more complicated than that of program 10.4. If I suppose once again that the numbers typed are 3, 4, 19 and 0 then the first *readnumber* instruction is equivalent to *count*:=3 and occurrences of *count* can be replaced immediately to give program 10.8. The *initialise size*:=0

NL; *printstring*("How many triangles do you want to see? ")

NL; *printstring*("What size should triangle number ");
printnumber(1); *printstring*(" be? ");
NL; *for n rt* 1..4 *do NL*; *times n do print* od od*

NL; *printstring*("What size should triangle number ");
printnumber(2); *printstring*(" be? ");
NL; *for n rt* 1..19 *do NL*; *times n do print* od od*

NL; *printstring*("What size should triangle number ");
printnumber(3); *printstring*(" be? ");
NL; *for n rt* 1..0 *do NL*; *times n do print* od od*

NL; *printstring*("That's all!"); *NL*;
size:=4; *size*:=19; *size*:=0; *count*:=3

program 10.12

for-do now has to be unrolled to make sense of the assignments to the container called *size*. Unrolling gives program 10.9. Next, simplifying by replacing occurrences of *i* and removing program brackets gives program 10.10. Now I use definition 10.2 to move *size*:=0 to the end of the program, producing program 10.11, and then I use the same definition to move the other two assignment instructions, first moving *size*:=19 and then moving *size*:=4, to produce program 10.12.

The complete substitution has replaced every occurrence of *size* between the *initialise*, and the first assignment by 0, every occurrence between the first and the second assignment instructions by 4; every occurrence between the second and third assignment instructions by 19; every occurrence between the third assignment instruction and the end of the program by 0.

-=-=-=-=-=-=-=-=-=-=-=-

Exercise 10.2

Write a program which asks what character you want your triangles printed with, then how many triangles you want and then what size each triangle should be: that is, a version of program 10.7 which will print '+' triangles or '£' triangles or even invisible ' ' triangles. Use the *readchar* instruction to read a character value into a container: for example, use *readchar x* to find out what character to print, then use *printchar*(*x*), as many times as necessary, to print it. [Hint: it will probably be easiest to read the character first, before any of the numbers - explanation must wait until chapter 11.]

-=-=-=-=-=-=-=-=-=-=-=-

10.6 WHEN SHOULD CONTAINERS BE SHARED?

In program 10.7 the container *size*, created by the *initialise* definition at the beginning of the program, is shared between the program environment and the subsidiary environments created by execution of the *for-do* (four environments in all - see program 10.9). In itself this creates no difficulty, either for the execution explanation or for the substitution explanation of assignment. There is, however, a powerful argument that container-sharing shouldn't happen unless it is absolutely necessary, because it can be confusing when effects produced in one part of the program silently and unexpectedly affect another part.

The container called *size* need not be shared between the different environments of program 10.7, because we can produce the same effect with a program which doesn't share: program 10.13, for example. (Note that the container *count* is still shared between all the environments, but since the only instructions which alter it are executed in the outer environment no confusion need be caused[†].) In this program each repetition of the the *for-do* executes a program which includes an *initialise* definition. Each execution of that program creates a new environment and acquires a container called *size*; when the execution terminates the environment is abandoned and with it the container; the next execution creates a new environment and acquires a new container.

> *initialise count*:=0
>
> *NL*; *printstring*("How many triangles do you want to see? ")
> *readnumber count*;
>
>   *for i rt* 1..*count do*
>   *initialise size*:=0
>
>   *NL*; *printstring*("What size should triangle number ");
>   *printnumber*(*i*); *printstring*(" be? ");
>   *readnumber size*;
>
>   *NL*; *for n rt* 1..*size do NL*; *times n do print** *od od*
>   *od*;
>
> *NL*; *printstring*("That's all!"); *NL*

program 10.13

In some circumstances it is essential to share containers between environments. For example, see program 10.14 below.

[†] In my explanation of program execution each new environment is based on an existing one, inheriting all those parts of the original environment which aren't replaced by new name→meaning mappings. It would be possible to define environment creation in such a way that mappings which identify containers weren't automatically inherited in this way, and in many ways it would be preferable to do so, but it would be an unacceptable complication in an introductory text.

10.7 WHAT IS *REALLY* IN A CONTAINER?

What does it mean to say that a container holds the number one? Does it hold it in the sense that a security officer holds the keys to a bank? Obviously not, or you could lock up the number one in your computer and nobody else in the world could count their sheep, or play dice, or have their first birthday, or go on a number one bus, or anything.

In our world the number one and every other number is an abstraction. All you can ever have is a picture or name of it which other people (or other computers or other programs) will recognise. We call these pictures and names *numerals*. 'Four' is a numeral, so is '4', so is '////', so is 'IV', so are 'quatre', 'vier', 'quattro' and lots more in languages I don't know and/or can't type on my wordprocessor.

The pictures or *representations* of numbers which are used inside computers can be patterns of electrical charge, or patterns of magnetic force, or patterns of circulating audio energy, or almost anything. What they are doesn't matter, provided that some pattern can be *seen as* a numeral: that is, if there is some code which tells how to calculate the value of the number which the pattern represents. Then a value-container can 'hold' that number by actually holding a copy of that pattern.

A program text may contain the same numeral more than once - program 10.7 has two instances of 0 and two of 1, for example. In just the same way a program execution may hold in its value-containers many copies of a representation of a number (or, as we often say with decreasing precision, many copies of a number, the same number many times). A great part of the work of a machine consists of calculating with representations, making copies of representations and putting representations in different containers.

If you look inside a computer you won't see anything you recognise as a number or even a conventional numeral. Nowhere in the machine would you see a pattern which looks like

42

no matter how hard you look with what electromagnetic machinery. Computer-pictures aren't the same as printed numerals. And in a sense machines can't even add up, subtract, multiply, or whatever. What they 'actually' do is to perform algebraic operations on numerals (strings of bits) which produce other numerals (strings of bits): the algebra is carefully designed to imitate adding up, subtracting, multiplying .. But what 'actually' happens is hard to pin down: a computer engineer will tell you that 'actually' the algebra is imitated by moving voltage levels. And a quantum physicist would tell you how the moving voltages 'actually' happen.

Luckily what 'actually' happens isn't important - at least most of the time - and I shall continue to talk as if computer representations were really the things they represent.

What's in an empty container?

A bucket can be empty of water. A bank account can be empty of money. A political program can be empty of purpose. A head can be empty of ideas (or so they say). Perhaps a value-container can be empty of any value. If so, how would you tell?

Take the bank account example. My own account has often been empty. More than once it has been *less* than empty. Clearly bank accounts aren't like buckets. I suspect that my bank account is 'actually' a number written somewhere in the bank's records. When the number written down is zero then the bank and I both agree that the account is empty. But since the genius who invented zero also invented negative numbers I can owe the bank money and it must sometimes roar and gnash its teeth to show its fury as the number gets more and more negative. My bank has large teeth and a terrible fury so I stop spending as soon as I hear it roar, and do my best to make my bank account at least empty again.

You might suppose that a value-container would be empty if it contained zero. The bank account example shows that this is not so: zero is an extremely useful number, as respectable as any other. If you ask me how many lettuces I grew last year and I don't speak I have told you nothing: but if I tell you 'zero' then I have certainly told you something. Zero isn't the same as nothing.

Lewis Carroll made a classic joke about this subject. Alice was questioned by the White King in *Through the Looking Glass*:

> ".. Just look along the road and tell me whether you can see either of them."
>
> "I see nobody on the road", said Alice.
>
> "I only wish *I* had such eyes", the King remarked in a fretful tone. "To be able to see Nobody! And at that distance too! Why, it's as much as *I* can do to see real people, by this light!"

Certainly you could look into a container and see Nothing. Nothing is a picture of nothing. The bank looks into its records of my account, sees zero - which so far as it is concerned is a picture of nothing - and says the account is empty. I look into my larder, see some dust and some air - which is a picture of no food - and say the cupboard is empty.

So a value-container might contain Nothing, although it couldn't reasonably contain nothing. Some systems make Nothing a dangerous value which stops the program if you try to use it in any way: a sort of computational crocodile, not to be touched. Some systems just pick a value you are unlikely to need in the hope that you might recognise it as Nothing. Some systems have no Nothing: you find an accidental value in any container it creates for you, which stays there until you explicitly store a new value.

P -J

In the programs above every value-container acquired by an *initialise* definition was given a value. But in many examples it doesn't matter what formula appears in the *initialise* definition, because there are no occurrences of the container name between the *initialise* and the first assignment to the container. For example, program 10.4 could reasonably have been written with any number as the initial value for the container *size*:

> *initialise size*:=97
>
> *printstring*("What size of triangle would you like to see? ");
> *readnumber size*;
>
> *for n rt* 1..*size do NL*; *times n do print* od od*
> *NL*; *printstring*("That's all!"); *NL*

program 10.14

Since I can choose any number I might even have chosen Nothing:

> *initialise size*:=?
>
> *printstring*("What size of triangle would you like to see? ");
> *readnumber size*;
>
> *for n rt* 1..*size do NL*; *times n do print* od od*
> *NL*; *printstring*("That's all!"); *NL*

program 10.15

The question mark can be read as allowing the execution to use any convenient value, or even Nothing if that is more convenient. In substitution terms the question mark should be substituted for every free occurrence of *size* between the initialisation and the first assignment; since there aren't any, the fact that a question mark is a meaningless formula doesn't have any effect on the interpretation of the program.

In my notation the *initialise* definition requires that you either give an initial value to every container that a program creates or say explicitly that you don't care what value is used. Some mechanical codes (for example, Pascal) don't have any notation which allows you to describe the initial value of a container. In effect those codes always use the question mark. You should take great care, when transcribing programs into such a code, to include an extra assignment instruction when it is necessary to give a container an initial value.

-=-=-=-=-=-=-=-=-=-=-=-=-

Exercise 10.3
Find out if your programming system demands initial values for every container. If not, has it a representation of Nothing? Does it act as a computational crocodile? Is there a different Nothing for each kind of value (numbers, characters, texts, procedures ..)?

-=-=-=-=-=-=-=-=-=-=-=-=-

10.8 PLANNING A SOLUTION WITH ASSIGNMENT

Suppose that you have to write a program which reads a sequence of a hundred numbers typed on the keyboard and prints their sum and their average. Really the only problem is how to calculate the sum, because you already know about the *printnumber* instruction and you should know that the average of a sequence of a hundred numbers is just the sum divided by one hundred.

There is an 'obvious' solution which uses a hundred different containers, a hundred separate *readnumber* instructions and an enormous formula:

readnumber a; *readnumber b*; .. ; *readnumber cv*;
printnumber(*a+b+c+* .. *+z+aa+* .. *+az+ba+* .. *+bz+ca+* .. *+cv*)

That program is easy to imagine but would be tedious to write down in detail. It would be even more tedious if what is required is the sum and average of a thousand numbers, or a million. Clearly something more systematic is required.

A systematic solution might be either repetitive or recursive. I choose repetition because the problem seems so naturally to fit the *times-do* instruction. Immediately the question arises: how many times to repeat and what to repeat? As so often with assignment programs, the answer is discovered by arguing backwards from a finishing point.

I suppose that at the end of the program there are a number of printing instructions:

NL; *printstring*("total="); *printnumber*(*tot*);
NL; *printstring*("average="); *printnumber*(*tot*/100)

This immediately simplifies the problem: the program must produce an environment in which *tot* names the sum of one hundred numbers. I intend it to produce this environment as the result of a repetition which assigns a value to a container called *tot*.

When I introduced repetitions in chapter 6 I explained their meaning by describing how they can be unrolled. To invent them it is often helpful to think the other way, inductively inventing the loop and rolling it up. In this case consider how to add the last action to the repetition. Consider: what should *tot* name just before the hundredth number is read? One reasonable answer would be: the sum of the first ninety-nine numbers. Then the program which leads from the ninety-nine-number state to the final one-hundred-number state could be

initialise N:=?
readnumber N; *tot*:=*tot+N*

This program will read the hundredth number into a container *N*, calculate the sum of the first ninety-nine and the new number and finally place the sum in the container *tot*. With just a twitch of the inductive imagination you can see that repeating this program one hundred times may be the solution I require. Careful, though! What is the base case: what should *tot* contain before the first number is read? Plainly it must contain zero, because then

$$0+N_1+N_2+..+N_{100} = N_1+N_2+..+N_{100}$$

All of this leads to program 10.16.

> *initialise tot*:=0
>
> *times* 100 *do initialise N*:=?
> > *readnumber N*; *tot*:=*tot+N*
>
> *od*;
>
> *NL*; *printstring*("total="); *printnumber*(*tot*);
> *NL*; *printstring*("average="); *printnumber*(*tot*/100)

program 10.16

Before I leave this example I can wring one more lesson out of it. The non-repetitive solution uses one hundred different containers and one hundred *readnumber* instructions, but its final formula has only ninety-nine addition symbols (count them!). Program 10.16 makes one hundred additions, the first of which adds zero and the first number, with predictable result.

What would a program based on *times* 99 be like? The final step of the program would be just as before, adding the hundredth number to the sum of the previous ninety-nine. But since the *times-do* will now only read ninety-nine numbers, the value of *tot* before the first repetition must be the value of the first number - which leads to an alternative repetitive solution, program 10.17.

> *initialise tot*:=?
>
> *readnumber tot*;
> *times* 99 *do initialise N*=?
> > *readnumber N*; *tot*:=*tot+N*
>
> *od*;
>
> *NL*; *printstring*("total="); *printnumber*(*tot*);
> *NL*; *printstring*("average="); *printnumber*(*tot*/100)

program 10.17

-=-=-=-=-=-=-=-=-=-=-=-=-

Exercise 10.4
Replace '100' and '99' in programs 10.16 and 10.17 by '10' and '9' respectively. Then by pencil-and-paper execution with input sequences of your own choosing, satisfy yourself that the two programs print the same output.

-=-=-=-=-=-=-=-=-=-=-=-=-

Notice that in either of these example programs it is essential that the container called *tot* is shared between the main environment and those created by execution of the *times-do*. Container-sharing isn't always a bad thing.

10.9 PARAMETERISING ASSIGNMENT INSTRUCTIONS

Quite often you want to write a procedure which has an effect on memory containers. Sometimes this is because the procedure definition encapsulates a sequence of often-repeated assignment instructions. For example:

$$initialise\ count:=?,\ sum:=?$$

$$def\ setup() = count:=0;\ sum:=0\ enddef$$

$$..\ setup();\ ..\ setup();\ ..\ setup();\ ..$$

program 10.18

The normal substitution rules and the usual execution explanation cover programs like this without difficulty.

Sometimes you will want to parameterise a procedure so that you can control the container, or containers, which it alters. For example, I might wish to parameterise program 10.17 so that it can compute the total of a sequence into any container I choose. I would like to write the parameterised program as the body of a procedure: program 10.19 gives an example.

$$def\ readsequence(n, t) = readnumber\downarrow t;$$

$$times\ n-1\ do\ initialise\ x:=?$$

$$readnumber\ x;\ \downarrow t:=\downarrow t+x$$

$$od$$

$$enddef$$

$$initialise\ tot:=?$$

$$readsequence(100, @tot)$$

program 10.19

$$initialise\ t1, t2, t3\ :=\ ?, ?, ?$$

$$readsequence(30, @t1);\ NL;\ printnumber(t1);$$

$$readsequence(40, @t2);\ readsequence(100, @t3);$$

$$NL;\ printnumber(t2\times t3)$$

program 10.20

In this procedure the parameter t corresponds to an argument value which describes a container. Such values are called *addresses of*, *references to* or *pointers to* a container: I shall call them *references*. A reference value indicates (indexes, identifies, describes) one of the collection of containers in use in a program. The formula $\downarrow r$, where r is a reference formula, means 'the container indicated by r'.

Arguments in a call of *readsequence* must describe the length of the sequence to be read (a number) and the container in which the result is to be remembered (a reference). The execution of program 10.19 proceeds according to the environment diagram shown in figure 10.5. The formula *@tot* provides a description of the container named *tot*; the formula ↓*t*, where *t* is a container description, accesses the described container. Program 10.20 shows how the *readsequence* procedure can be applied to several container-describing

Execute program 10.19 in an environment env-0 containing the
basic instruction and procedure names with their normal meanings.

Create an environment env-1 in which *readsequence* =
λ(*n*, *t*).(*readnumber* ↓*t*; *times n*−1 *do..od*) and *tot* names a container
(initially containing *Nothing*).
Execute *readsequence*(100, *@tot*)

Create an environment env-2, based on env-1, in which *n* = 100
and *t* = a value which describes the container named by *tot* in
env-1.
Execute *readnumber* ↓*t* ===> *tot* from env-1 := what is typed
Execute *times* 99 *do .. od*

Create an environment env-3, based on env-2, in which *x* names a
container (initially containing *Nothing*).
Execute *readnumber x* ===> *x* := what is typed
Execute ↓*t*:=↓*t*+*x* ===> *tot* from env-1 := *tot* from env-1 + *x*

Create an environment env-4, based on env-2, in which *x* names a
container (initially containing *Nothing*).
Execute *readnumber x* ===> *x* := what is typed
Execute ↓*t*:=↓*t*+*x* ===> *tot* from env-1 := *tot* from env-1 + *x*

And so on until ..

Create an environment env-101, based on env-2, in which *x* names
a container (initially containing *Nothing*).
Execute *readnumber x* ===> *x* := what is typed
Execute ↓*t*:=↓*t*+*x* ===> *tot* from env-1 := *tot* from env-1 + *x*

figure 10.5

arguments.

$$\downarrow@x = x$$

definition 10.3

The substitution explanation uses one single rule, given in definition 10.3. This rule can be used to show that programs 10.17 and 10.19 are equivalent:

> *def readsequence*(*n, t*) = *readnumber* $\downarrow t$;
>> *times n*−1 *do initialise x*:=?
>>> *readnumber x*; $\downarrow t$:=$\downarrow t$+*x*
>>
>> *od*
>
> *enddef*
> *initialise tot*:=?
> *readsequence*(100, @*tot*)

> = *initialise tot*:=?
> *readnumber* $\downarrow@tot$;
> *times* 100−1 *do initialise x*:=?
>> *readnumber x*; $\downarrow@tot$:=$\downarrow@tot$+*x*
>
> *od*

> = *initialise tot*:=?
> *readnumber tot*;
> *times* 99 *do initialise x*:=?
>> *readnumber x*; *tot*:=*tot*+*x*
>
> *od*

Similarly *readsequence*(40, @*t2*) expands to

> *readnumber t2*;
> *times* 39 *do initialise x*:=?
>> *readnumber x*; *t2*:=*t2*+*x*
>
> *od*

The '$\downarrow$' operation makes sense only if it is applied to a container description, and the '@' operation makes sense only if it is applied to a container formula. Break either of these rules and you get nonsense. For example:

> *def silly*(*x*) = $\downarrow x$:=0 *enddef*
> *silly*(@1)

converts by substitution to 1:=0, and assignment to numbers is nonsense. Similarly:

> *def silly*(*x*) = $\downarrow x$:=0 *enddef*
> *silly*('a')

converts to $\downarrow$'a':=0, which is nonsense because characters don't identify containers.

10.10 THE SUBSTITUTION DEFINITION OF ASSIGNMENT

Substitution is used in this book for two purposes. One purpose is to show that two programs are equivalent, by transforming one into the other or by transforming both into a common form. The second purpose is to calculate the effect of a program, reducing it to a sequence of basic instructions and eliminating structure from the program. Replacing procedure call by procedure body eliminates procedure definitions; deleting false-labelled arms and selecting true-labelled arms eliminates choice instructions; unrolling counting repetition eliminates loops.

An assignment instruction $x:=e$ can be understood in various ways:

(a) as an instruction to remember the present value of formula e in container x;

(b) as an instruction to replace future occurrences of x by formula e;

(c) as an alteration to the state of affairs, of which the value held in container x is a part.

It is the second of these interpretations which gives rise to the substitution rules for assignment. It tells us when assignment instructions can be eliminated, because if there are no future occurrences of x then the instruction is irrelevant and might as well not be there. Therefore we need substitution rules which show how to move assignments forward in a program to the point where there are no future occurrences of the container name.

Because we are dealing with 'future occurrences' of a container name not in a textual sense but in the sense of the order of execution of instructions, a program must be converted into a sequence of instructions before we can decide what is a 'future occurrence' and what isn't. For example, in a counting repetition the textual order of the instructions in the repeated program doesn't correspond to the executional order. The assignment substitution rules cut across the structures imposed by procedure definitions, counting repetition and choice instructions: that is what makes them a little tricky.

Individually the substitution rules for assignment instructions are very simple, but collectively there are rather a lot of them. I can resolve some problems by making certain simplifications. First, I assume that evaluating a formula never has an effect on the state of affairs (see chapter 14 for an example which shows how this assumption can be invalidated). Second, I assume that when substituting a formula e for a container name x in a program formula P there are no 'hidden occurrences' of x: that is, P doesn't contain any procedure calls which can be expanded to give extra free occurrences of x. Third, the rules don't apply to instructions and formulas that mention containers indirectly via reference formulas, which must be eliminated using definition 10.3 before they can be treated properly. Fourth, special rules apply to *terminate* and *deliver* instructions (see chapter 14) to stop you inventing or destroying instructions in a program.

The aim of the rules is to produce a situation in which an instruction $x:=e$ is equivalent to *donothing* because there are no future occurrences of x in the program which includes the instruction and the *initialise* definition which binds x. It should be clear what is meant by 'future occurrence' in a sequence of instructions: the definition of what it means for a program to 'mention' a container name below is as close as I come to a precise definition.

Substitution in sequences of instructions

If a program is just a sequence of simple instructions, substitution can be straightforward. For example, it is obvious that $x:=3$; *print** means the same as *print**; $x:=3$. A little more generally, $x:=3$; *printnumber*$(x+1)$ means the same as *printnumber*$(3+1)$; $x:=3$.

In execution terms the sequence $x:=e$; P tells us first to calculate the value of formula e and remember it in container x, then to execute program P. If P contains any formula which refers to the container x then the remembered value of formula e will be used: so it is reasonable to suppose that P would produce the same effect if it was rewritten with every occurrence of x replaced by e. Rewriting P won't in general eliminate the assignment instruction because P may not be the last thing in the whole program: therefore the equivalent program is $P[x\backslash e]$; $x:=e$.

Now this rule can't apply if P contains an assignment instruction $x:=f$. For example, suppose that P is *printnumber*(x); $x:=x+1$. The program

$$x:=e; printnumber(x); x:=x+1; printnumber(x)$$

prints e and then $e+1$; the program

$$(printnumber(x); x:=x+1)[x\backslash e]; x:=e; printnumber(x)$$
$$= printnumber(e); e:=e+1; x:=e; printnumber(x)$$

is nonsense unless e is a container name, and even if it makes any sense it alters container e as well as x, which makes it quite a different program from the original. Plainly, we cannot move an assignment instruction straight past an assignment to the same container: it is the second assignment which must affect the rest of the program, not the first.

Equally, if formula e includes a container name y and program P alters container y then executing P changes the meaning of formula e and $x:=e$; P won't have the same effect as $P[x\backslash e]$; $x:=e$, even if the substitution doesn't change the meaning of P. For example, suppose that e is y and that P is *printnumber*(y); $y:=g$. Consider the program

$$y:=d; x:=y; printnumber(y); y:=g; printnumber(x)$$

This program prints d and then d once more but the program

$$y:=d;\ (printnumber(y);y:=g)[x\backslash y];\ x:=y;\ printnumber(x)$$
$$=\ y:=d;\ printnumber(y);\ y:=g;\ x:=y;\ printnumber(x)$$

will print d and then g.

-=-=-=-=-=-=-=-=-=-=-=-

Exercise 10.5
Verify, by pencil-and-paper execution, that the programs above have the effect I claim they have.

-=-=-=-=-=-=-=-=-=-=-=-

The fundamental rule of assignment is as follows (restating definition 10.2):

If program P doesn't alter x or any container name included in formula e, then

$$x:=e;P\ =\ P[x\backslash e];x:=e$$

This definition is all very well, but what if P *does* alter x or the meaning of e: how should we proceed then? One way is to treat P as a sequence, apply definition 10.2 to as many instructions of the sequence as possible, then think again. For example, if P is

$$printnumber(x+1);printnumber(y-2);x:=x+1$$

then I can convert the program in stages:

$$x:=e;printnumber(x+1);printnumber(y-2);x:=x+1$$
$$=\ printnumber(e+1);x:=e;printnumber(y-2);x:=x+1$$
$$=\ printnumber(e+1);printnumber(y-2);x:=e;x:=x+1$$
$$=\ printnumber(e+1);printnumber(y-2);x:=e+1$$

The last of these steps uses a new rule. In execution terms it is easily justified: if you first remember e then remember what you just remembered plus 1, you might as well just remember $e+1$. Definition 10.4 states that two consecutive assignments to a container can always be combined into one.

$$x:=e;x:=f\ =\ x:=f[x\backslash e]$$

definition 10.4

-=-=-=-=-=-=-=-=-=-=-=-

Exercise 10.6
Write a justification of definition 10.4 (a) in terms of execution; (b) in terms of replacing every occurrence of x by e in a sequence of instructions to which definition 10.2 applies.

-=-=-=-=-=-=-=-=-=-=-=-

Definition 10.4 applies to consecutive assignments to a single container. What if two consecutive assignment instructions refer to *different* containers? Sometimes the order of the instructions doesn't matter, other times it matters a great deal. For example, $x:=3;y:=4$ clearly means the same as $y:=4;x:=3$, but $x:=y;y:=z$

clearly doesn't always mean the same as $y:=z; x:=y$.

-=-=-=-=-=-=-=-=-=-=-=-=-

Exercise 10.7
Why not? Define circumstances in which the programs $x:=y; y:=z$ and $y:=z; x:=y$ are equivalent and circumstances in which they are not.

-=-=-=-=-=-=-=-=-=-=-=-=-

The next rule (definition 10.5) converts two consecutive assignments to different containers into a multiple assignment. It asks you to read the second assignment in the light of the first, then perform them both at once. For example:

$$x:=3; y:=4 \quad = \quad x,y:=3,4 \quad = \quad y:=4; x:=3$$
$$x:=7; y:=x+1 \quad = \quad x,y:=7,7+1 \quad = \quad y:=8; x:=7$$

In each of these substitutions the last step is made by applying definition 10.5 backwards (right to left).

$$x:=e; y:=g \quad = \quad x,y:=e, g[x\backslash e]$$

definition 10.5

-=-=-=-=-=-=-=-=-=-=-=-=-

Exercise 10.8
By finding a counter-example, show that the following equation is false:

$$i:=i+1; j:=i+2 \ = \ i,j:=i+1, i+2$$

Exercise 10.9
Show that if e doesn't mention y, then $x:=e; y:=f$ is equivalent to $y:=f[x\backslash e]; x:=e$.

Exercise 10.10
Give an example which shows that the equivalence in exercise 10.9 is *not* valid when e mentions y.

Exercise 10.11
Definitions 10.2 and 10.5 can't be applied to programs which mention reference values. To see that this is so, consider the following procedure definition:

$$def\ trick(x) = y:=4; \downarrow x:=7; y:=y+1\ enddef$$

What procedure call would *not* have the effect of assigning 5 to y? What effect would it have? [Hint: which of the two definitions should be applied to the first two instructions in this procedure?]

-=-=-=-=-=-=-=-=-=-=-=-=-

Initialise definitions

Initialise definitions introduce a container name and give it a value. They bind the name in the same way as *let* definitions: the rule is given in definition 10.6.

If the definitions of a program include *initialise x:=e* then the name x is bound in
that program but not in the formula e nor in the formulas of the other *let* and
initialise definitions of that program.

definition 10.6

The value given in the *initialise* definition affects the instructions of the program
up to the first assignment instruction to the container. Definition 10.7 shows how
to incorporate that initial value into the program: it says that an *initialise*
definition has the same effect as an initial assignment instruction.

If none of the definitions $D_1..D_m$ of a program bind any of the names in formula
e, then

$$D_1 .. D_{i-1} \ \ initialise \ x:=e \ \ D_{i+1} .. D_m \ \ S_1; ..; S_n$$
$$= \ \ D_1 .. D_{i-1} \ \ initialise \ x:=f \ \ D_{i+1} .. D_m \ \ x:=e; S_1; ..; S_n$$

definition 10.7

If the definitions of a program do happen to bind any of the names in e then
definition 10.7 doesn't apply. In that case, as was described in chapter 5, you
must either simplify formula e to get rid of the offending names or systematically
alter bound and binding occurrences of names in the program to produce the
same effect.

-=-=-=-=-=-=-=-=-=-=-=-

Exercise 10.12
In definition 10.7 *any* formula f may be introduced: justify this feature of the rule
by appealing to earlier rules.

-=-=-=-=-=-=-=-=-=-=-=-

If instructions $S_{j+1}..S_n$ don't mention container x then

$$D_1 .. D_{i-1} \ \ initialise \ x:=e \ \ D_{i+1} .. D_m \ \ S_1; ..; S_{j-1}; x:=f; S_{j+1}; ..; S_n$$
$$= D_1 .. D_{i-1} \ \ initialise \ x:=e \ \ D_{i+1} .. D_m \ \ S_1; ..; S_{j-1}; S_{j+1}; ..; S_n$$

definition 10.8

If instructions $S_1..S_n$ don't mention container x, then

$$D_1 .. D_{i-1} \ \ initialise \ x:=e \ \ D_{i+1} .. D_m \ \ S_1; ..; S_n$$
$$= D_1 .. D_{i-1} D_{i+1} .. D_m \ \ S_1; ..; S_n$$

definition 10.9

The next two rules show how to get rid of assignment instructions and *initialise*
definitions. Informally, an instruction or a formula 'mentions' a container name
x if it contains a free occurrence of x or a call to a procedure whose body
'mentions' x (notice that this is a recursive definition). Definition 10.8 shows
how to get rid of assignment instructions. When every reference to a container
has been eliminated from the program, definition 10.9 shows how even the

initialise definition can be removed.

-=-=-=-=-=-=-=-=-=-=-=-=-

Exercise 10.13
Prove that the sequence $ta:=a; tb:=b; a:=tb; b:=ta$ is equivalent to $ta:=a; a:=b; b:=ta$ if it occurs in a program which doesn't mention *tb* anywhere else.

Exercise 10.14
Prove that the sequence $tb:=b; b:=a; a:=tb$ is equivalent to the sequences in exercise 10.13 when it occurs in a program which doesn't mention *ta* or *tb* anywhere else.

-=-=-=-=-=-=-=-=-=-=-=-=-

Assignment and the *select* instruction

Most of the time definition 10.2 can be used with structured instructions (*times-do*, *for-do*, *select*, *iterate*). It is only when the execution of the structured instruction includes an assignment instruction which affects x or e that we need a more complicated rule. The main rule connects assignment and *select* instructions: other rules are built in terms of this one.

Execution of a *select* instruction calculates the values of the condition-formulas, chooses an arm and executes that arm. Preceded by an assignment instruction the calculation, choice and execution will all take place in the changed state of affairs produced by the assignment. Definition 10.10 states that the same effect is achieved when the calculations are first performed as if the assignment had taken place and then the assignment is always performed whatever arm is chosen, just before that arm is executed.

$$x:=e; select \ C_1:P_1 \ \ C_2:P_2 \ .. \ C_n:P_n \ endselect$$
$$= \ select \ C_1[x\backslash e]:x:=e; P_1 \ \ C_2[x\backslash e]:x:=e; P_2 \ .. \ C_n[x\backslash e]:x:=e; P_n \ endselect$$

definition 10.10

For example, consider

$$x:=y+1; \ select \ x=0:printnumber(x) \ \ x\neq0:donothing \ endselect$$

By definition 10.2 this program is equivalent to

$$select \ y+1=0:printnumber(y+1) \ \ y+1\neq0:donothing \ endselect; \ x:=y+1$$

I can produce the same effect by a more roundabout route using definition 10.10:

$$x:=y+1; \ select \ x=0:printnumber(x) \ \ x\neq0:donothing \ endselect$$
$$= \ select \ y+1=0:x:=y+1; printnumber(x) \ \ y+1\neq0:x:=y+1; donothing \ endselect$$
$$= \ select \ y+1\neq0:printnumber(y+1); x:=y+1 \ \ y+1\neq0:x:=y+1 \ endselect$$
$$= \ select \ y+1\neq0:printnumber(y+1) \ \ y+1\neq0:donothing \ endselect; \ x:=y+1$$

Another example, which this time can't use definition 10.2, is:

$x:=48$; *select* $x<50:x:=x+1$ $x>50:x:=x-1$ *endselect*
= *select* $48<50:x:=48; x:=x+1$ $48>50:x:=48; x:=x-1$ *endselect*
= *select true*:$x:=48; x:=x+1$ *false*:$x:=48; x:=x-1$ *endselect*
= $x:=48; x:=x+1$ = $x:=48+1$ = $x:=49$

-=-=-=-=-=-=-=-=-=-=-=-

Exercise 10.15
Show that if $n<b^{K-1}<b^K$, the program

$$i:=K; \text{ } select \text{ } n<b^{i-1}: i:=i-1$$
$$b^i\leq n: i:=i+1$$
$$n\geq b^{i-1} \wedge b^i>n: donothing$$
$$endselect$$

is equivalent to $i:=K-1$.

Exercise 10.16
Show that if $b^{K-1}<b^K<n$, the program in exercise 10.15 is equivalent to $i:=K+1$.

-=-=-=-=-=-=-=-=-=-=-=-

Assignment and counting repetition

I haven't yet given a description of the interaction of assignment and counting repetition which is adequate to explain the meaning of the Problem Program 10.21. One possible reading of this program is that it prints three asterisks and leaves the container x holding the number 6, since after the assignment $x:=3$, the instruction *times x do .. od* should mean *times 3 do ..od*.

$$x:=3; \text{ } times \text{ } x \text{ } do \text{ } print*; x:=x+1 \text{ } od$$

program 10.21

An alternative reading would be that it prints an unlimited number of asterisks, based on the following argument:

$x:=3$; *times x do print*; $x:=x+1$ *od*
= $x:=3$; *print*; $x:=x+1$; *times x–1 do print*; $x:=x+1$ *od*
= *print*; $x:=3$; $x:=x+1$; *times x–1 do print*; $x:=x+1$ *od*
= *print*; $x:=4$; *times x–1 do print*; $x:=x+1$ *od*
= *print*; $x:=4$; *print*; $x:=x+1$; *times x–2 do print*; $x:=x+1$ *od*
= *print*; *print*; $x:=5$; *times x–2 do print*; $x:=x+1$ *od*
= *times N do print* *od*; $x:=3+N$; *times x–N do print*; $x:=x+1$ *od*

Each of these readings is supportable but I have designed my definition to support the first of them. That is, I have decided that the Problem Program 10.21

should print three asterisks and not an unlimited number[†].

If the number formula which controls the number of executions of a *times-do* instruction includes container names whose value is affected by execution of the instruction, then a straightforward use of definition 6.4 would substitute the number formula into a program which alters its meaning. This problem is avoided if I define an order of calculation: first calculate the value of the number formula, second execute the program formula that number of times. Definition 10.11 ensures that this is so by introducing a new container t (which therefore cannot be altered by any instruction of the program) to remember the value of the number formula[‡].

When F includes container names whose value is altered by execution of P, then definition 6.4 no longer applies. However:

$times\ F\ do\ P\ od\ =\ t:=F;\ select\ t=0:\ donothing$
$\qquad\qquad\qquad\qquad\qquad t>0:\ P;\ times\ t-1\ do\ P\ od$
$\qquad\qquad\qquad\qquad\qquad t>0:\ times\ t-1\ do\ P\ od;\ P$
$\qquad\qquad\qquad\qquad\quad endselect$

where t is a new container name.

definition 10.11

This new definition makes the meaning of the Problem Program 10.21 perfectly clear, although it takes a little labour to show it:

$\qquad x:=3;\ times\ x\ do\ print*;\ x:=x+1\ od$

$=x:=3;\ t:=x;$
$\qquad select\ t=0:\ donothing;$
$\qquad\qquad t>0:\ print*;\ x:=x+1;\ times\ t-1\ do\ print*;\ x:=x+1\ od$
$\qquad\qquad t>0:\ times\ t-1\ do\ print*;\ x:=x+1\ od;\ print*;\ x:=x+1$
$\qquad endselect$

$=\ x,t:=3,3;$
$\qquad select\ t=0:\ donothing;$
$\qquad\qquad t>0:\ print*;\ x:=x+1;\ times\ t-1\ do\ print*;\ x:=x+1\ od$
$\qquad\qquad t>0:\ times\ t-1\ do\ print*;\ x:=x+1\ od;\ print*;\ x:=x+1$
$\qquad endselect$

[†] Historically this was a real issue: various language descriptions were unclear about which of these two readings they supported. Things seem to have settled down nowadays.

[‡] In this rule and in the two which follow I have omitted the program brackets and *initialise* definition required to introduce a new container to a program, in order to simplify the presentation.

$= x:=3; t:=3;$
    select $t=0$: *donothing*;
        $t>0$: *print**; $x:=x+1$; *times* $t-1$ *do print**; $x:=x+1$ *od*
        $t>0$: *times* $t-1$ *do print**; $x:=x+1$ *od*; *print**; $x:=x+1$
    endselect

$= x:=3;$
    select $3=0$: *donothing*;
        $3>0$: *print**; $x:=x+1$; *times* $3-1$ *do print**; $x:=x+1$ *od*
        $3>0$: *times* $3-1$ *do print**; $x:=x+1$ *od*; *print**; $x:=x+1$
    endselect;
    $t:=3$

$= x:=3;$
    select false: *donothing*;
        true: *print**; $x:=x+1$; *times* 2 *do print**; $x:=x+1$ *od*
        true: *times* 2 *do print**; $x:=x+1$ *od*; *print**; $x:=x+1$
    endselect;

$= x:=3;$
    select true: *print**; $x:=x+1$; *print**; $x:=x+1$; *print**; $x:=x+1$
        true: *print**; $x:=x+1$; *print**; $x:=x+1$; *print**; $x:=x+1$
    endselect;

$= x:=3$; *print**; $x:=x+1$; *print**; $x:=x+1$; *print**; $x:=x+1$
$=$ *print**; *print**; *print**; $x:=6$

There is a very similar rule for *for-do* instructions: I give it in definition 10.12 but its notation is not explained until the next chapter.

Where formula S mentions container names whose value is altered by execution of P, definition 6.5 does not apply. However:

    for N rt S do P od $=$
        $T:=S$; *select* $T=<>$: *donothing*
                $T\neq<>$: $($*let* $N=T_1$ $P)$; *for N rt* $T_{2..n}$ *do P od*
                $T\neq<>$: *for N rt* $T_{1..n-1}$ *do P od*; $($*let* $N=T_n$ $P)$
        endselect
    where T is a new container and $n=length(S)$.

definition 10.12

Assignment, procedure call and *let* definitions

Consider the Problem Program 10.22. Under the execution explanation of procedure call, this program creates an environment in which the name a means 7 and the name b means 8, and then executes the body of q in that environment. The first action of q is to needlessly alter the container x which it shares with the calling environment; then it similarly alters the container y; then it prints the *initialise* $x := 6, y := 9$

def $q(a, b) =$
 $x := x+1; y := y-1; printnumber(a); printnumber(b)$
enddef

$q(x+1, y-1)$

program 10.22

value named by a, which is 7; then it prints the value named by b, which is 8.

At least one order of substitution of formula for name gives the same answer as execution. If 6 is substituted for x and 9 for y in the argument formulas, and then arguments are substituted for parameters as usual, the program prints 7 and then 8. Some other orders give a different result: first substitute $x+1$ for a and $y-1$ for b to make the body of the procedure into

$$x := x+1; y := y-1; printnumber(x+1); printnumber(y-1)$$

When this sequence is substituted for the procedure call I get a program which prints first 8, then 7 - the opposite order to that predicted by the pure execution explanation.

I have to face once more the problem of substituting a formula that includes container names into a program which alters the values of those containers. One solution is to use substitution to remove the offending container name from the argument formula; the other solution is to calculate the value of the argument and remember it in a new container t, created for the purpose just as in definitions 10.11 and 10.12 above. Definition 10.13 gives the new rule.

> If formula e contains container names which may be altered by execution of the body of procedure p, then substitution of a procedure call containing formula e may not be made. However:
>
> $$p(.., e, ..) = t := e; p(.., t, ..)$$
>
> where t is a new container.

definition 10.13

Assignments and program bindings

The interaction between assignment instructions and programs which include definitions provides the final substitution rules for assignment. In many cases when P is a program with *let*, *initialise* and *def* definitions, definition 10.2 will apply. In other cases the program will contain conflicting assignment instructions. For example, the following program is equivalent to $x:=15$:

$$x:=12; \; (\!(let \; y=3 \; \; x:=x+y)\!)$$

program 10.23

One way to show the equivalence is to replace y by 3 and remove the brackets, giving $x:=12; x:=x+3$. Another way is to insert the assignment instruction into the bracketed program, giving $(\!(let \; y=3 \; \; x:=12; x:=x+y)\!)$, and then to replace y by 3, giving the same result as before.

It is sometimes necessary to move an assignment instruction which precedes a program to the beginning of the program's instruction sequence, then move it through the sequence step by step, in order to calculate the final effect of the program on that container. Definition 10.14 describes how to do this.

If definitions $D_1..D_m$ do not bind the name x nor any of the names in formula e, then

$$x:=e; \; (\!(\; D_1 \; .. \; D_m \; \; S_1; ..; S_n \;)\!) \; = \; (\!(\; D_1[x?e] \; .. \; D_m[x?e] \; \; x:=e; S_1; ..; S_n \;)\!)$$

where $D[x?e]$ is   *initialise* $y:=g[x\backslash e]$ if $D = initialise \; y:=g$

          let $a=f[x\backslash e]$ if $D = let \; a=f$

          D otherwise

definition 10.14

The rule expresses no more than a common-sense reading of the execution definition: calculations in *let* and *initialise* definitions must take account of the assignment; procedure bodies must be left unaltered because, in execution terms, their bodies take effect when they are called. The rule can't be used if there is a clash of names between the assignment instruction and the program, and in such a case you must either simplify e or systematically alter names in the program to remove the difficulty. Once you have moved an assignment instruction through a program, you can take it out from the other end: see definition 10.15.

If definitions $D_1..D_m$ do not bind x nor any of the names in e, then

$$(\!(D_1 \; .. \; D_m \; \; S_1; ..; S_n; x:=e)\!) \; = \; (\!(D_1 \; .. \; D_m \; \; S_1; ..; S_n)\!); x:=e$$

definition 10.15

$$x:=7; \; (\!(\; let \; a=x+10 \; \; x:=x\times10; printnumber(a) \;)\!)$$

program 10.24

Since the formula in a *let* definition is associated with a name in just the way that an argument formula is associated with a parameter name, you might expect that assignment instructions cause trouble there as well. Indeed it is so: consider the Problem Program 10.24, which prints '17' and not '70' and certainly not '170'. Evidently the formula in a *let* definition can't be substituted into a program which alters the meaning of that formula, and as usual the solution is either to simplify the formula if possible or else to remember its value in a new container: see

If in a program

$$D_1 \; .. \; D_{i-1} \; let \; a{=}e \; D_{i+1} \; .. \; D_m \; S_1; ..; S_n$$

formula e contains container names which may be altered by execution of instructions $S_1..S_n$, then definition 6.3 does not apply. However, the program is equivalent to

$$t{:=}e; \; (\!| D_1 \; .. \; D_{i-1} \; let \; a{=}t \; D_{i+1} \; .. \; D_m \; S_1; ..; S_n |\!)$$

where t is a new container.

definition 10.16

definition 10.16.

10.11 IMITATING MULTIPLE ASSIGNMENT INSTRUCTIONS

Multiple assignment instructions like $x,y{:=}e,f$ are extremely useful, both in the design of a program and in calculating its effect. You should use them even though most mechanical codes don't provide a direct equivalent, because they are very easy to imitate.

In execution terms a multiple assignment

$$x1,x2,..,xn{:=}e1,e2,..,en$$

requires the calculation of a number of formulas and then their assignment to several containers. The calculations go on all together, and then the assignments happen all at once. The calculations and assignments can't be interleaved because in general assigning a new value to xi might affect the calculation of formula ej. In substitution terms the instruction describes a simultaneous replacement of names by formulas, just like the replacement of parameter names by argument formulas.

The key to the imitation is to realise that assignment of a value to a container which isn't referred to anywhere else can't affect the rest of the program. An assignment $t1{:=}e1$, where $t1$ is a new container invented for the purpose, can be put anywhere in the program without any effect[†]. Thus the sequence of single assignment instructions

$$t1{:=}e1; \; t2{:=}e2; ..; tn{:=}en$$

calculates and remembers the values of the formulas $e1..en$ in the new containers $t1..tn$. Assigning these remembered values to the containers $x1..xn$ has the required effect:

[†] I assume as usual that calculating the value of a formula doesn't affect the state of affairs - see chapter 14 for an example which shows that this isn't always so.

$$x1, x2, .., xn := e1, e2, .., en$$
$$= t1 := e1; t2 := e2; ..; tn := en; x1 := t1; x2 := t2; ..; xn := tn$$

Since all the names $t1..tn$ are distinct the order of the first group of assignments doesn't matter. Provided that $x1..xn$ are also distinct, the order of the second group doesn't matter either. For example:

$$x, y := y, x \quad = \quad tx := x; ty := y; x := tx; y := ty \quad = \quad ty := y; tx := x; y := ty; x := tx$$
.. etc.

-=-=-=-=-=-=-=-=-=-=-=-

Exercise 10.17
Prove that $x, y = y, x \quad = \quad tx := x; x := y; y := tx \quad = \quad ty := y; y := x; x := ty$ where tx, ty are new containers.

-=-=-=-=-=-=-=-=-=-=-=-

10.12 IMITATING REFERENCE ARGUMENTS

Some codes don't provide a mechanism which allows procedures to be parameterised on container names, so it is difficult to describe sharing of containers between calling and called environments. It is possible, up to a point, to produce the same effect by sharing containers in another way.

Consider, for example, program 10.25. The effect of the procedure calls shown is to add three to the values stored in containers x, y and z.

$$def\ p3(a) = \downarrow a := \downarrow a + 3\ enddef$$
$$..\ p3(@x)\ ..\ p3(@y)\ ..\ p3(@z)\ ..$$

program 10.25

Program 10.26 produces the same effect by a more roundabout technique. Here the calling and the called environments share a container Ga. Use of the container-describing parameter a has been replaced by use of Ga. Each procedure call has been replaced by an initial assignment from the argument container to Ga (so that when execution starts, Ga holds the starting value of the argument container), followed by a procedure call without any container argument, followed by an assignment from Ga back into the argument container (so that the argument container now holds the value left in Ga after the procedure

$$initialise\ Ga := ?$$
$$def\ p3() = Ga := Ga + 3\ enddef$$
$$..\ Ga := x; p3(); x := Ga\ ..\ Ga := y; p3(); y := Ga\ ..\ Ga := z; p3(); z := Ga\ ..$$

program 10.26

call). Obviously the value put into the argument container records what happened to Ga, the surrogate parameter, during execution of the procedure.

The technique illustrated in program 10.26 must be refined a little to cope with calls to recursive procedures that have reference arguments. Each call will normally introduce a new sharing between calling and called environments. In order to imitate this using a single globally-shared container it is necessary to remember the value in that container before the call (which represents the current sharing) and to restore it afterwards. The technique is therefore to rewrite the procedure definition

$$def\, proc(n_1, n_2, .., n_{i-1}, R, n_{i+1}, ..) = P\; enddef$$

where R corresponds to a reference argument, as the pair of definitions

$$initialise\; GC := ?$$
$$def\, proc(n_1, n_2, .., n_{i-1}, n_{i+1}, ..) = P[R\backslash @GC]\; enddef$$

and to replace every procedure call

$$proc(a_1, a_2, .., a_{i-1}, @x, a_{i+1}, ..)$$

by the program

$$\begin{array}{l} (\!\!(\; let\; t := GC \\ \quad GC := x; proc(a_1, a_2, .., a_{i-1}, a_{i+1}, ..); x := GC; \\ \quad GC := t \\ )\!\!) \end{array}$$

This imitation doesn't produce quite the right effect when the body of the procedure assigns to x directly as well as indirectly via R. But nowadays that sort of thing - it's called *aliasing* - is frowned upon, so the imitation is good enough to be used in practice.

-=

APPENDIX 10.A ASSIGNMENT AND INPUT IN PASCAL

Pascal assignment instructions look just like those in my notation, but its equivalent of *initialise* doesn't let you define the initial value of a container. It has an equivalent of *readnumber* and of the other input instructions to be discussed in chapter 11.

Creating new containers

First, convert your program using definition 10.7 so that every *initialise* definition
stores Nothing in its new container. Then imitate *initialise* x:=? by a `var`
declaration (like those you used to introduce the names for *for-do* instructions).
The type of the values which can be stored in the container (`integer`, `boolean`,
or whatever) must be described. You can create containers only at the beginning
of a procedure execution or the beginning of the program execution. See the
example below.

Basic input instructions

The Pascal instruction `read` applies to all types of container (just as `write`
applies to all types of value). If `x` is a container which is introduced by
`var x:integer`, `read(x)` is the Pascal equivalent of *readnumber x*.

An example

Program 10.15 can be transcribed into Pascal as:

```
program trinp(input,output);
var size:integer; n,n1:integer;
begin write('What size of triangle would you like to see? ');
      read(size);
      for n:=1 to size do
          begin writeln; for n1:=1 to n do write('*') end;
      writeln; write('That's all!'); writeln
end.
```

References to containers

Pascal doesn't have an operator which corresponds to the @ of my notation.
However, it is possible to use the qualification `var`, attached to a parameter name
in the definition of a procedure, to produce the effects illustrated in this chapter.
If in a procedure call `p(.., a, ..)` the corresponding parameter name in the
definition is qualified with the word `var` - for example,

> procedure p(..; var r: <*some type*>; ..);

- then

 (a) the corresponding argument formula `a` must describe a container (for
     example, be a container name);

 (b) occurrences of the parameter name `r` in the body of the procedure refer
     to the container named by `a`.

For example, program 10.19 can be transcribed into Pascal as follows:

```
program X(input,output);
var tot:integer;
procedure readseq(n:integer; var t:integer);
  var x:integer; i:integer;
  begin read(t);
        for i:=2 to n do begin read(x); t:=t+x end
  end;
begin readsequence(tot) end.
```

In this transcription ↓*t* has been replaced by t, which is declared to be a var parameter.

Two points to note about this program. A single container x must be created at the beginning of the procedure execution, which is shared between executions of the *for-do*: you can't have a new one each time unless you define an auxiliary procedure and make the body of the loop call upon it. The readseq procedure isn't exactly equivalent to *readsequence* when *n* is negative, because a *for-do* doesn't exactly imitate a *times-do*, but in this case I suppose that it doesn't make any difference.

Ordinary parameters in Pascal

Ordinary parameters (non-var parameters) in Pascal can be assigned a value. The effect of a Pascal procedure call is to set up a new environment in which the ordinary parameter names describe new containers which are initialised with the corresponding argument values. If you mistakenly assign them new values these will obliterate the argument values.

APPENDIX 10.B SOME PROGRAMS TO TRY

The most interesting programs based on assignment use input instructions, which are explained in chapter 11, and unlimited repetition, which is introduced in chapter 12. To make the exercises as interesting as possible it is necessary to delay until the end of the next chapter.

Chapter 11
THE INPUT SEQUENCE AND THE CRP

The *readnumber* instruction introduced in chapter 10 is by no means the most basic input instruction. The most basic input instructions, so far as this book is concerned, work in terms of character values. Input to a program, like output from it, can be viewed as a sequence of character values.

In every programming system, the treatment of input as a straightforward sequence is modified when programs are connected to keyboards. It is convenient to see what you are typing, and it is convenient to be able to change your mind or correct mistakes. What is presented to a program is normally an cleaned-up version of a typed input sequence.

11.1 OUTPUT AND INPUT SEQUENCES

In chapter 2 I described the action of *print** as making a mark on paper or on a screen, and in other chapters I gave the same sort of description to other output instructions. You may have discovered already that the output from one of your programs can be remembered in a file and printed later: that is, output can be described in a way which doesn't seem to be dependent on program execution. Similarly, the program text which you prepare is input to a programming system but it can often be printed on a screen or on paper: that is, it can be treated as if it was the output of a program, and indeed it is the output of your programming system's editor.

When you type on a keyboard you press keys. Normally the order in which you press those keys is as important as the identity of the keys you choose. You can think of what you are doing as generating a sequence of key-pressing events, with varying intervals of time between events. On a typewriter there would be a corresponding sequence of printing events, each making a mark on paper, or moving the carriage, or both. Simplify the problem by ignoring the speed of typing, and ignore the possibility that you might sometimes accidentally press more than one key at once: then because there is only a finite number of keys, the sequence you generate can be described by a sequence of coded values, one per key. We can allow for some intentional double-key presses if we say that the event of pressing the A key at the same time as SHIFT is a single event, different to pressing the A key without SHIFT: after all, those events cause different marks on the typewriter paper.

This description makes an immediate connection between input and output. Execution of a program will normally produce a sequence of character codes which describe marks to be made on a screen or on paper. Typing on the keyboard produces a sequence of character codes. Considered as sequences of character codes the input and output sequences are very similar.

11.2 BASIC INPUT INSTRUCTIONS

When you type at a keyboard you generate a sequence of character codes. If a program takes notice of what you type, it must do so by examining that sequence of codes. I specify which part of the sequence to examine by defining a *C*urrent *R*eading *P*osition: *crp* for short. The basic input instructions are *readchar* and *movecrp* and there is a basic formula *crp*^.

The *readchar* instruction

The *readchar* instruction assigns the character code at the crp to its argument and moves the crp to the next position in the input sequence ready to read the next character: that is, *readchar x* is equivalent to

$$x := whatever\ character\ code\ is\ typed;\ move\ the\ crp$$

For example, program 11.1 reads six characters, printing the first, the third and the fifth.

> *initialise c*:=?
>
> *printstring*("Type six characters now: ")
> *times* 3 *do readchar c*; *printchar*(*c*); *readchar c od*

program 11.1

Evidently the *readnumber* instruction can be imitated by a sequence of *readchar* instructions. Chapter 12 discusses just how to do this.

Looking at the character in the Current Reading Position

Readchar isn't the most basic input instruction in my notation. A program may examine the character at the crp by calculating the formula *crp*^: its value is the character code at the crp but the crp doesn't move. For example, if the only key you press on the keyboard is the 'A' key (without SHIFT), then program 11.2 will print 'Ta Ra!'. Note that examining the character at the crp doesn't change anything: in particular the crp doesn't move.

$$printchar(\text{'T'}); printchar(crp\hat{}); printstring(\text{" R"}); printchar(crp\hat{}); printchar(\text{'!'})$$

program 11.2

The *movecrp* instruction

Movecrp moves the crp to the next position in the input sequence but doesn't take any account of what code is at either position. It is often convenient to use *crp*̂ and *movecrp* together to produce the same effect as *readchar*, in particular when reading variable-length items such as numerals or personal names from the input sequence.

$$readchar\, x \;=\; x := crp\hat{}; movecrp$$

definition 11.1

The beginning and the end of the input sequence

What should happen if a program tries to calculate the value of *crp*̂ when the input sequence is empty: that is, before you type anything on the keyboard? The value of the formula is **undetermined** and only becomes determined when you type something. I assume that the program must wait until you type something before it can proceed and I have based my examples in this chapter and subsequent chapters on that assumption. Some programming systems deliver a special 'Nothing' code to distinguish an empty input sequence.

I assume that the input sequence is potentially infinitely long, but that it has a first element. I don't provide any instructions which allow a program to move backwards in the input sequence, so it is possible to think of *movecrp* and *readchar* as destroying the first element of the sequence and *crp*̂ as always referring to the first element. That view is particularly helpful when reasoning about programs which use the input sequence - see section 11.3 below. If you type five characters and the program executes five *movecrp*s or five *readchar*s then it is as if the program is at the beginning of an empty input sequence. At that point the program behaves as any program must when the input sequence is empty: that is, a calculation of *crp*̂ must wait until something more is typed before it can deliver a result.

I assume that if a program executes *movecrp* when the input sequence is empty then the program must wait until a code has been typed (so that the crp contains some value) before it can move to the next position. I find it convenient to assume that *movecrp* can move the crp to the first position which is still empty, but that if a program calculates *crp^* or executes *movecrp* when the crp is empty then it must wait. For example, if you type one character to program 11.3 then it will print 'ready' and wait for you to type another. The first *movecrp* instruction must wait until the first position of the input sequence contains a character code, so this program doesn't print anything until you type the first character.

$$movecrp; printstring(\text{"ready"}); printchar(crp\hat{\ })$$

program 11.3

As a simplification I assume that when a program starts to execute its input sequence is empty, and I don't concern myself with what should happen to the input sequence of a program when it finishes execution. You may find that on your programming system neither of these assumptions is exactly true. In particular you may find that you can 'type ahead' whilst one program is executing, placing characters in the input sequence which will eventually be examined by another program.

11.3 REASONING WITH THE INPUT SEQUENCE AND THE CRP

Most interesting programs are parameterised by their input: that is, they produce different effects depending on what they read. As a very simple example, consider

$$printchar(crp\hat{\ }); movecrp; printchar(crp\hat{\ }); movecrp; printchar(\text{'!'})$$

program 11.4

This program obviously prints the first two characters in the input sequence followed by an exclamation mark: if you type 'H' followed by 'a' it will print "Ha!". It also moves the crp forward by two positions, so it is sensible to repeat it several times:

> *times* 5 *do*
> $printchar(crp\hat{\ }); movecrp; printchar(crp\hat{\ }); movecrp; printchar(\text{'!'})$
> *od*

program 11.5

I claim that this program takes the first ten characters from the input sequence and prints them two at a time, each pair followed by an exclamation mark, and that it also moves the crp forward ten positions. You may find this claim to be obviously true or you may feel that it requires explanation. My explanation is based on an argument about the effect of the program on the input sequence *I*. Before I can give that explanation I must introduce some new notation.

Indexing and sub-sequencing

A *sequence* is a collection of elements which are *indexed* (identified, distinguished, selected) by number. In this book my convention is that the first element of any sequence S is S_1, the element indexed by 1. There is no element indexed by 0, nor are there any elements indexed by negative numbers -1, -2, .. A sequence can be split into sub-sequences: for example, a sequence of length 10 can be split into the sub-sequences $S_{1..5}$ and $S_{6..10}$, or into the sub-sequences $S_{1..4}$ and $S_{5..10}$, or into many other possibilities.

A sub-sequence is a sequence, and its elements are also indexed from 1. Thus, for example, $(S_{7..9})_2$ selects the second element of $S_{7..9}$, which is S_8. Similarly, sub-sequences can be sub-divided: $(S_{7..19})_{3..8}$ selects the third to the eighth elements of $S_{7..19}$: that is, $S_{9..14}$.

It is possible to have sequences of any length from zero to infinity. The only zero-length sequence is the empty sequence[†]. $S_{1..0}$, for example, is the empty sequence because 1..0 is the empty sequence (recall the discussion in chapter 6). The empty sequence is a sub-sequence of anything, so it is possible to split $S_{1..10}$ into $S_{1..0}$ and $S_{1..10}$, or $S_{1..3}$, $S_{3..2}$, $S_{4..10}$, and so on. A sequence length n can be indexed by any of the numbers 1..n (and therefore the empty sequence can't be indexed at all). The formula S_a is only meaningful if S has an ath element: that is, if the length of S is greater than or equal to a.

As a shorthand I permit the formula $S_{a..}$ to mean $S_{a..length(S)}$: a sub-sequence extending from the ath element of S to the last; in effect a copy of S with the first $a-1$ elements thrown away. This formula is meaningful even if $a>length(S)$, when it describes the empty sequence.

Definitions of *crp^* and *movecrp*

$$crp^\wedge \; = \; I_1$$

definition 11.2

$$movecrp \; = \; I:=I_{2..}$$

definition 11.3

The input sequence I is normally best thought of as an infinite sequence, with its first element I_1 the character delivered by *crp^*. The *movecrp* instruction can then be thought of as moving the input sequence one place forward, replacing I_1 by I_2, I_2 by I_3, and in general replacing I_n by I_{n+1}. This can be modelled by an assignment instruction $I:=I_{2..}$. As an example, consider program 11.4:

[†]   There is only one empty sequence, but there are many formulas which describe it.

$printchar(crp^\wedge); movecrp; printchar(crp^\wedge); movecrp; printchar('!')$

$= printchar(I_1); I:=I_{2..}; printchar(I_1); I:=I_{2..}; printchar('!')$
 [by definition of $crp^\wedge$ and $movecrp$]

$= printchar(I_1); printchar((I_{2..})_1); I:=I_{2..}; I:=I_{2..}; printchar('!')$
 [by definition of assignment]

$= printchar(I_1); printchar(I_2); I:=(I_{2..})_{2..}; printchar('!')$
 [by definition of indexing and of assignment]

$= printchar(I_1); printchar(I_2); I:=I_{3..}; printchar('!')$
 [by definition of sub-sequencing]

This proof shows that the program does indeed have the effect I claimed for it.

-=-=-=-=-=-=-=-=-=-=-=-=-

Exercise 11.1
Prove that the program *times k do printchar*$(crp^\wedge)$; *movecrp od* is equivalent to the program *for i rt* $1..k$ *do printchar*(I_i) *od*; $I:=I_{k+1..}$. [Hint: $I_{1..} = I$.]

-=-=-=-=-=-=-=-=-=-=-=-=-

The definitions of $crp^\wedge$ and of $movecrp$ will be exploited in future chapters.

11.4 ECHOING, EDITING AND CONFIRMATION

A direct connection between keyboard and program would allow you to type an input sequence to your program, but only in the very crudest of programming systems is that all that is provided. Almost every system makes marks on the screen as you press keys so that you can see what input sequence you have generated. They usually allow you to change your mind a bit or to rub out mistakes as you go along. In computer user's jargon the system *echoes* what you type by making marks on the screen and, by taking notice of special key-presses, allows you to *edit* the input sequence before it is presented to the program.

Suppose that a program prints the message

What size of triangle would you like to see?

and then executes a *readnumber* instruction. Imagine that I intend to have a twelve-line triangle, so first I press the key marked '1'. The programming system will show me a 1 on the screen, echoing what I typed. Then I press the key marked '2' and the system obligingly shows me a 2 next to the 1. Nothing else happens, and nothing will happen unless I press a special *confirmation* key, signalling that the input can be passed to the program. In most systems the confirmation key is the RETURN key, but in principle it could be any other key at all.

But I don't have to press the confirmation key next, because most systems let me change my mind about what should be presented to the program. Suppose that I decide that I would prefer a fifteen-line triangle.· I press a special key, marked DELETE or BACKSPACE or something like that, and the 2 vanishes from the screen; I press the key marked '5' and a 5 mark appears in place of the vanished 2. Since this as much messing about as I feel is appropriate in this case, I press the confirmation key to confirm what I have typed.

Up to this point the input sequence generated by key-pressing has been input to the programming system, not to the program it is executing. The input sequence now presented to the program is an edited version of what I typed. In the example above, the sequence <'1', '2', delete, '5', confirm> would be converted into <'1', '5', confirm> and the program will print a fifteen-line triangle.

Echoing and editing are provided by a programming system as an aid to the human. Even the best typist makes typing mistakes. The echoing and editing program itself processes the input sequence you actually type. The program-text editor in your programming system may be equally privileged (or equally condemned) to view your keystrokes and to construct a plausible text from them. Programs executing under the control of the programming system normally see only an edited, cleaned-up version of the input sequence.

Multi-line inputs and confirmation codes

The editing mechanism of your programming system will almost certainly work line-by-line, the end of each line signalled by pressing the confirmation key. Each time you press the confirmation key the edited version of the sequence generated by the keys you pressed since the last confirmation will be passed to whatever program is running, or shelved away to be presented to a program later if there isn't one running or if the running program isn't looking at the input sequence.

Programming systems differ according to whether or not the confirmation (end of line) code appears in the input sequence presented to the program. Suppose that it *does* appear in the input sequence, and that you have to write a program which prints four three-line triangles, asking you in each case what character you want the triangle to be printed with. Then program 11.6, for example, won't have the right effect. The input sequence presented to this program might be

<'*', confirm, '&', confirm, '£', confirm, '1', confirm, ..>

Given this input, the program will print a triangle of asterisks, then a 'triangle' of confirmation codes, then a triangle of ampersands, then another confirmation-code 'triangle'.

This effect isn't at all what was intended, and program 11.7 would be a better solution to the problem. The *movecrp* instruction in this program (which might have been another *readchar* with identical effect in this particular case) skips

def triangle(*c*) =
  for i rt 1..3 *do NL*; *times i do printchar*(*c*) *od*
enddef

times 4 *do*
  initialise x:=?
  printstring("what character do you want this time? ");
  readchar x; *triangle*(*x*)
od

program 11.6

def triangle(*c*) =
  for i rt 1..3 *do NL*; *times i do printchar*(*c*) *od*
enddef

times 4 *do*
  initialise x:=?
  printstring("what character do you want this time? ");
  readchar x; *movecrp*; *triangle*(*x*)
od

program 11.7

over the confirmation code which you must type after each character to signal
that the program can receive its input.

11.5 *Readnumber* AND THE CRP

The instruction *movecrp* and the formula *crp^* are basic tools for manipulating the
input sequence; *readchar* is less basic. *Readnumber* is not even so basic an
instruction as *readchar* because it must interpret a sequence of character codes as
a description of a number: to describe twelve in decimal notation, for example,
you must press at least two keys. The equivalent of *readnumber* in most
programming systems will accept as a description of a number a sequence of
digit-character codes, possibly prefixed by an indefinitely long sequence of space
and/or *newline* character codes: that is, a numeral prefixed by as much blank
space and as many blank lines as you wish. Usually the length of the numeral
isn't fixed, so in order to signal that you have finished typing the numeral you
must type something that isn't a digit - space, *confirm*, an '&' sign, or whatever.

The best-designed programming systems make their *readnumber* instruction a
sort of generalised *readchar*. In those systems *readnumber* consumes the spaces
and digit characters which describe the number, leaving the crp pointing to the
character which follows the number description: that is, pointing at the space, the
confirm, the '&' sign or whatever it was you typed. Less scrupulous designers
make their systems consume the terminating character as well. You may need to

experiment in order to find out what sort of programming system you have (see appendix 11.B below).

Even with the best-designed programming systems there can still be a difficulty. How do you write a program which reads first a number and then a character? For example, consider the design of a program which asks you what size of triangle you want and what character you want it printed with. Program 11.8 won't necessarily have the right effect.

```
def triangle(n, c) =
  for i rt 1..n do NL; times i do printchar(c) od
enddef

initialise size, char := ?, ?

printstring("Type size of triangle and printing character: ");
readnumber size; readchar char;

NL; triangle(size, char);
NL; NL; printstring("That's all!");
```

program 11.8

If you have been used to writing and using programs which include a *readnumber* instruction, the natural way to respond to this program's prompting message would be to type a number followed by *confirm* and then type the character asked for, followed by *confirm*. If the description of the triangle's size takes up N positions in the input sequence, you would have typed $N+3$ characters. Given to a programming system which uses the 'best' sort of *readnumber* instruction, the *readnumber* in program 11.8 will move the crp by N positions and the *readchar* will assign the character in the $N+1$th position to x: so if you typed *confirm* to end the number, it will try to print a triangle of confirmation codes. You might get over this problem by leaving out the *confirm* between the number and the printing character, but then it would be impossible to make the program print a triangle made up of 1s or 0s or any other digit character.

Program 11.8 might be 'fixed' or 'de-bugged' by including a *movecrp* between the *readnumber* and the *readchar* instructions, but it would be hard to explain to an average person that it is necessary to press a key after typing the size-number and before typing the triangle-character. The best solution to this sort of problem is to redesign the program: make it ask two questions, so that the two input values appear on different lines; make sure that the first instruction consumes every character typed in response to its question. So program 11.9 is a better solution to the original problem.

def triangle(*n, c*) =
    for i rt 1..*n do NL*; *times i do printchar*(*c*) *od*
enddef

initialise size, char := ?, ?

printstring("Type size of triangle, followed by *confirm*: ");
readnumber size; *movecrp*;
printstring("Type character, followed by *confirm*: ");
readchar char; *movecrp*;

NL; *triangle*(*size, char*);
NL; *NL*; *printstring*("That's all!");

program 11.9

11.6 IMITATING BASIC INPUT INSTRUCTIONS

Every programming system, so far as I know, has a *readchar* equivalent. Not every one has an equivalent of *crp^* or of *movecrp*. These more basic instructions can be imitated by *readchar*, as follows. At the head of your program put

initialise crpm=?

and before any other input instructions, execute *readchar crpm*. Then replace the formula '*crp^*' by '*crpm*'; replace the instruction '*movecrp*' by '*readchar crpm*'.

If you mix *crp^* formulas and *movecrp* instructions with *readchar* or *readnumber* instructions in the same program, this trick won't work.

-=

APPENDIX 11.A INPUT INSTRUCTIONS IN PASCAL

The Pascal instruction `read` applies to all types of container (just as `write` applies to all types of value). For *crp^* write `input^`. For *movecrp* write `get(input)`, or sometimes just `get`. In some very old-fashioned Pascal systems `input^` is nonsense (garbage, undefined, Nothing, a computational crocodile) when the program starts executing: in which case you need to execute `get(input)` before you make your first inspection of the input sequence.

Space bars, RETURN keys and `eoln`

Pascal is a notation of a certain age. It was invented at a time when most programs were punched onto cards and most output was produced on line-printers. There were no microcomputers and precious few computer terminals. It was a time when ASCII, the now almost universal character code, was still a bit of a novelty.

Punched cards hold eighty characters. If the input is a sequence of cards, how does a program tell where one card ends and the next begins? Counting in eighties doesn't always work - some operating systems throw away trailing spaces at the end of a card. Pascal contains in its heart a fossilised solution to this ancient and long-departed problem, a rock which waits to trip up every novice programmer. At the end of a card/line, it says, comes an extra space. But it isn't an ordinary space: you can distinguish it from ordinary spaces by using the formula `eoln(input)`. This formula (whose name is short for *end of line*) is true just when `input`^ is an end-of-line space.

It isn't hard to transcribe the formula *crp^=newline* into Pascal - it just becomes `eoln(input)`. But it is unfortunately rather hard to transcribe into Pascal the formula *crp^=' '*. It isn't enough to write `input^=' '`, because that formula is also true when *crp^=newline*. The correct transcription is the rather fearsome formula

```
(input^=' ') and (not eoln(input))
```

Note the brackets round the terms being combined with 'and', required because Pascal has so much trouble with expressions which combine comparisons - one of its other little quirks.

APPENDIX 11.B SOME PROGRAMS TO TRY

Exercise 11.2
Write a program which executes a *readnumber* instruction followed immediately by two *readchar*s. Find out what the effects of *readnumber* and *readchar* really are on your system by executing this program with lots of different inputs. In each case record the effect, which may include the program not executing properly because the system considers that you typed the input incorrectly, or the program not terminating because the system is waiting for you to type something more. Try at least the following inputs:

> 123 ab*confirm*
> 123ab*confirm*
> 12.3ab*confirm*
> 123*confirm*ab*confirm*
> 123a*confirm*
> 123 a*confirm*

Generalise from the results of your experiment (and any others you might like to invent) to make an exact definition of the effect of executing your system's equivalent of the *readnumber* and *readchar* instructions.

Exercise 11.3
Write a program which reads first a number, followed by an arithmetic operation character like +, * or /, followed by a second number and prints the corresponding arithmetic value. For example, given input '123+456' it should print '579'; given '123*456' it should print '56088'.

Exercise 11.4
Write a program which reads a number N followed by a sequence of N numbers and prints their sum.

Exercise 11.5
Write a program which reads a number N followed by an operation character *op* and a sequence $S_{1.N}$ of numbers and prints the value of S_1 *op* S_2 *op* .. *op* S_N. For example, if $N=40$ and *op*='+' it should print the sum of forty numbers; if $N=25$ and *op*='*' it should print the product of twenty-five numbers. Make up your own meanings for other operation characters.

-=-=-=-=-=-=-=-=-=-=-=-=-

Many interesting programs which use assignment do so as part of an unlimited repetition: further exercises are therefore left until chapter 12.

Chapter 12
UNLIMITED REPETITION

Often an activity is repetitive but you can't say in advance exactly how many repetitions it will take to achieve your goal. Chapter 1 used the example of driving in a fencing stake with a sledgehammer. It is difficult to tell in advance how many blows it will take to drive in a stake. If you are very experienced you can make a good guess by looking at the ground and knowing your own strength, but even the most experienced guess can be wrong if just under the surface the ground is wetter or drier or stonier or crumblier than you expect. Pre-calculation is impossible: you can't dig a trial hole because that would disturb the structure of the ground where the stake is to go. The only way to do it is to hit the stake as many times as necessary, stopping when it reaches the correct depth.

This form of repetition - keep doing something until you reach a satisfactory situation - is a very common form of planning. Some more examples:

Walk north till you reach the white tree, dig where its shadow falls at noonday.

Turn the knob until the gas ceases to flow.

Stir the sauce until it thickens.

Keep right on to the end of the road.

A characteristic of this form of description is that you can't say in advance how long it will take to reach your goal. You don't know how many paces it is to the white tree nor how deep you must dig. You don't know how far the knob must be turned to stop the gas. You don't know how many times you must stir the sauce. Nobody knows how far it is to the end of the road. Hence the name *unlimited* or *unbounded* repetition, to contrast it with the counting repetition of chapter 6, where the action of the system is calculated before repetition starts.

The problem with unlimited repetition is that carelessly used it may never reach its goal. If there is a concrete block under the ground no number of blows with a sledgehammer will drive a wooden stake through it; if you were to give the staking program of chapter 1 to a very stupid person or to a robot in such circumstances they would keep hitting the stake for ever, perhaps even after it split into fragments. If the white tree has died or burnt down you will never reach it. If the gas isn't lit the sauce will never thicken. If you are facing the wrong way you will never reach the end of the road. Hence the need in general to *prove* that in some particular range of circumstances an unlimited repetition will truly reach its goal.

12.1 THE *iterate* INSTRUCTION

There are two ways of describing the final situation or state of affairs which a repetition is intended to reach. It can be described *positively* as: stop when you reach this state of affairs. Or it can be described *negatively* as: keep going as long as the state of affairs is like this. ('As long as' is 'while' in most English-speaking areas, with the famous exception of Yorkshire.) Some negative-description examples are:

Stir the sauce as long as it is lumpy.

Fight on while a single invader remains in our country.

As long as you can see the lights of the city keep going north.

Pull the lashing tight: if the beams move it isn't tight enough so pull it tighter and try again.

Enlisted for the duration of hostilities.

The negative form describes an undesirable feature of the current state of affairs and gives an action which, if repeatedly carried out, should remove that feature. You can describe several undesirable features at once, giving an action for each one. For example, if you are tuning a piano you may find that adjusting one string puts others slightly out of tune. If the piano frame isn't too rickety a large alteration to one string tension affects other strings only a little, so you can repeatedly adjust the tension of any out-of-tune string, keeping going as long as any string is out of tune, and you can be sure that you will eventually finish. Again, if you are tidying up a garden different weeds need different actions: some can be hoed, some must be dug, some may be poisoned. You probably wouldn't weed the garden in strict sequence: more likely you would repeatedly slaughter the plants you dislike in whatever order you notice them - a genuinely unlimited repetition with many alternative actions.

The programming notation for unlimited repetition is the *iterate* instruction. It uses negative description and it can describe repetitions which have alternative actions. In form it looks rather like a *select*. For example, an instruction which re-orders the contents of three containers a, b and c so that eventually $a \geq b \geq c$ is

$$\text{iterate } a < b: a, b := b, a$$
$$b < c: b, c := c, b$$
$$\textit{enditerate}$$

program 12.1

shown in program 12.1. An instruction which moves the crp to the first non-space character in the input sequence is shown in program 12.2.

iterate crp^=' ': movecrp enditerate

program 12.2

Execution of *iterate* instructions

Iterate instructions, like *select* instructions, consist of a number of arms each with a condition-formula and a program. Execution proceeds in three stages, described in definition 12.1. Note that an *iterate* instruction terminates immediately - that is, it is equivalent to *donothing* - if all its condition-formulas evaluate to false.

  (a) All the condition-formulas are evaluated.

  (b) If any of the formulas delivers true then one of the true-labelled arms is chosen, its program is executed and then execution of the *iterate* instruction is repeated.

  (c) If all the formulas deliver false then execution of the *iterate* instruction terminates.

definition 12.1

Executing an *iterate* means evaluating its formulas, executing a program, re-evaluating the formulas, executing a program, re-evaluating the formulas, and so on. If the execution is ever to terminate, the values of the formulas must be changeable - that is, they must depend on values stored in containers - and each program executed must change the value of some container or other. This also means that when, or rather *if* execution of an *iterate* instruction terminates, the state of affairs will be such that every one of its formulas delivers the value false.

Consider the execution of program 12.1. This program is provided with three containers a, b and c and must sort their contents into order: this would be useful as a preamble to the triangle-classifying program of chapter 8, where the numbers have to be in descending order or the program may print the wrong message.

Suppose that initially the numbers are in quite the wrong order: for example, a might contain 3, b contain 4 and c contain 5. Then both $a<b$ and $b<c$ deliver true and either arm might be chosen. Suppose that the first arm is chosen: the instruction $a,b:=b,a$ produces a state in which a contains 4, b contains 3 and c still contains 5. Now the *iterate* instruction repeats: only $b<c$ delivers true this time so $b,c:=c,b$ is executed, producing a state in which a still contains 4, b now contains 5 and c contains 3. Once again the instruction repeats and this time only $a<b$ delivers true, so $a,b:=b,a$ produces the state in which a contains 5, b contains 4 and c contains 3. The instruction repeats again: this time both

condition-formulas deliver false so the execution terminates, producing the desired state of affairs.

-=-=-=-=-=-=-=-=-=-=-=-=-

Exercise 12.1
Using definition 12.1, trace the execution of program 12.1 again with the same initial conditions but this time choosing the second arm on the first repetition.
Exercise 12.2
Trace the execution of program 12.1 when initially the numbers are in the right order: for example, $a=10$, $b=2$, $c=1$.

-=-=-=-=-=-=-=-=-=-=-=-=-

Non-terminating repetition

One, two or even three examples don't make a proof. We know from definition 12.1 that *if* program 12.1 terminates it must produce the right effect because both formulas will then deliver false, therefore $a \geq b$ and $b \geq c$. But will its execution terminate? Not every *iterate* execution terminates: for example,

$$iterate\ a \geq 0:\ print*\ enditerate$$

is an instruction which does nothing if a is negative but otherwise prints an endless sequence of asterisks and doesn't terminate. The most famous example of a non-terminating repetition is McCarthy's joke make-yourself-rich program:

> As long as you have less than a million dollars walk along looking at the ground, picking up every dollar bill you see.

In fact program 12.1 will always terminate no matter what the initial value of a, b or c and there is a very simple and elegant proof of that fact. Think of the numbers a, b and c as the digits of a numeral abc. The value of the numeral abc is largest when $a \geq b \geq c$. Executing either arm of program 12.1 increases the value of the numeral abc and there are only nine possible arrangements of the three digits. Hence it must terminate in at most eight repetitions. (Actually it takes at most three, but a proof of that is a little more complicated.)

Substitution definition of the *iterate* instruction

Iterate instructions generate a sequence of executions. The sequence they unroll into depends on the circumstances in which they are executed. It is reasonable therefore to define unlimited repetition in terms of choice. Definition 12.2 makes an *iterate* instruction R equivalent to a *select* instruction which includes every arm of R extended by R itself, plus an an extra arm whose program is *donothing* and whose condition-formula is true when every condition-formula of R is false. That is, if any condition-formula of R is true, execute the corresponding arm and

$iterate\ C_1{:}P_1\ \ C_2{:}P_2\ ..\ C_n{:}P_n\ enditerate$

$= select\ C_1{:}P_1; iterate\ C_1{:}P_1\ C_2{:}P_2\ ..\ C_n{:}P_n\ enditerate$
$\quad\ \ C_2{:}P_2; iterate\ C_1{:}P_1\ C_2{:}P_2\ ..\ C_n{:}P_n\ enditerate$

$\quad\ \ ..$
$\quad\ \ C_n{:}P_n; iterate\ C_1{:}P_1\ C_2{:}P_2\ ..\ C_n{:}P_n\ enditerate$
$\quad\ \ \neg C_1 \wedge \neg C_2 \wedge .. \wedge \neg C_n{:}donothing$
$endselect$

definition 12.2

then execute R again, but if every condition-formula is false, do nothing.

This is a recursive definition: an *iterate* instruction is defined in terms of itself surrounded by a *select* instruction. Recursive definitions should give you no particular difficulty after chapter 9. You won't be surprised to learn that proofs about unlimited repetition are usually inductive. The base case will obviously be a state of affairs in which the *donothing* alternative of the *select* is chosen.

12.2 REASONING WITH THE *iterate* INSTRUCTION

Consider the *iterate* instruction shown in program 12.3. If this *iterate* is executed when n contains forty-eight, then its condition-formula will deliver true and the instruction $n{:}{=}n{+}1$ will be executed: this will make n contain forty-nine; the condition-formula will be evaluated again, once more it will deliver true and $n{:}{=}n{+}1$ will be executed, this time making n contain fifty; the condition-formula will be evaluated a third time and this time will deliver false so that execution of the *iterate* instruction will terminate. A moment's thought should convince you that if this program is executed when n contains any number less than fifty then $n{:}{=}n{+}1$ will be repeatedly executed to increase n until it contains fifty, but that if it is executed when n contains fifty or any number larger than fifty then the condition-formula will deliver false and the repetition will never start because the *iterate* will immediately terminate.

$iterate\ n{<}50{:}\ n{:}{=}n{+}1\ enditerate$

program 12.3

That kind of reasoning is perfectly valid but it is rather wordy. *Iterate* instructions have a recursive definition and proofs about *iterate* instructions can be inductive. In general the idea is to prove that the *iterate* is equivalent in certain circumstances to an assignment instruction. The 'certain circumstances' can be most easily described by an initial assignment instruction: for example, it is possible to prove that when $k{\geq}0$ program 12.4 is equivalent to the single assignment instruction $n{:}{=}50$. The proposition makes it clear that we are talking about circumstances in which the container named n holds a number which may be any number less than or equal to fifty, and the introduction of the parameter k

$$n:=50-k;\ iterate\ n<50:\ n:=n+1\ enditerate$$

program 12.4

into the problem makes the proposition much easier to state. The use of an assignment instruction links together with the assignment in the body of the *iterate*.

In making proofs of this kind it is always useful if the program is first of all transformed into a *select* using definition 12.2 and the definitions of assignment instructions:

$$n:=50-k;\ program\ 12.3$$

$$= n:=50-k;\ select\ n<50:\ n:=n+1;\ program\ 12.3$$
$$n\geq50:\ donothing$$
$$endselect$$

$$= select\ 50-k<50:\ n:=50-k;\ \hbar:=n+1;\ program\ 12.3$$
$$50-k\geq50:\ n:=50-k;\ donothing$$
$$endselect$$

$$= select\ k>0:\ n:=50-k+1;\ program\ 12.3$$
$$k\leq0:\ n:=50-k$$
$$endselect$$

With this transformation the base case is easily proved: when $k=0$ the whole program is equivalent to $n:=50-0$ which is $n:=50$. And a hypothesis that the program is equivalent to $n:=50$ when $k=K$ for some $K\geq0$ enables me to establish its effect when $k=K+1$:

$$select\ K+1>0:\ n:=50-(K+1)+1;\ program\ 12.3$$
$$K+1\leq0:\ n:=50-(K+1)$$
$$endselect$$

$$= n:=50-(K+1)+1;\ program\ 12.3$$

$$= n:=50-K;\ program\ 12.3$$

which by inductive hypothesis is equivalent to $n:=50$; hence the proposition is proved.

Note that program 12.3 counts upwards towards fifty, but by introducing the formula $50-k$ it was possible to convert this into a counting downwards towards zero, which best fits the sort of induction proofs I have been using so far in this book.

-=-=-=-=-=-=-=-=-=-=-=-

Exercise 12.3
Prove that the program

$$n:=x;\ iterate\ n<50:n:=n+1\ \ n>50:n:=n-1\ enditerate$$

is equal to $n:=50$ whatever number x might be. [Hint: convince yourself, using definition 12.1 and some well-chosen examples, that the program really is equivalent to $n:=50$. Do this perhaps by transforming the program into a single *select* instruction using definition 12.2; then consider separately the cases $x=50-k$ and $x=50+k$; finally convince yourself that there are no other possibilities.]

-=-=-=-=-=-=-=-=-=-=-=-

Non-terminating *iterate* instructions

An *iterate* instruction implicitly describes the state of affairs it will produce *if* it terminates: in that case every one of the condition-formulas must have delivered false, which often describes the state of affairs very precisely. For example, if program 12.3 terminates then it must be the case that $n \geq 50$. The proof given above shows that program 12.3 will terminate when $n=50-k$ and $k \geq 0$; you don't need induction to prove that it will terminate when $n=50+k$ and $k \geq 0$; therefore it will always terminate.

Not every *iterate* instruction will always terminate in the nice tidy way of program 12.3. Most *iterate* instructions terminate only under certain conditions, and one of the easiest programming mistakes is to write an *iterate* which won't terminate under any circumstances - a so-called 'infinite loop'. Naturally it is only a mistake to write an infinite loop if you didn't intend to!

Consider, for example, program 12.5. It is possible to prove that this program has the same effect as program 12.3 whenever n contains a number less than or equal to fifty.

$$iterate\ n \neq 50:\ n:=n+1\ enditerate$$

program 12.5

-=-=-=-=-=-=-=-=-=-=-=-

Exercise 12.4
Go ahead and prove it. [Hint: don't forget to include $n:=50-k$ in the program whose properties you prove.]

-=-=-=-=-=-=-=-=-=-=-=-

When n contains fifty both program 12.3 and program 12.5 have the same effect: the condition-formula is evaluated, delivers false and the *iterate* instruction terminates. But the two programs do not have the same effect when n contains a number larger than fifty: say fifty-two, for example. Program 12.3 is equivalent to *donothing* because $52<50$ is false. But $52 \neq 50$ delivers true, so program 12.5 executes $n:=n+1$, thereby making n contain fifty-three; then $53 \neq 50$ again delivers false, $n:=n+1$ makes n contain fifty-four, .. and so on as long as the machine supporting the execution continues in existence. Evidently program

12.5 will not terminate if *n* initially contains a number greater than 50.

The argument that program 12.5 will not terminate is an informal argument, but it isn't the less convincing for that. I can't prove, in the system of reasoning used in this book, that program 12.5 will fail to terminate when *n*>50. Not being able to prove something doesn't make it false: for example, I can't prove that the sun will rise tomorrow and I can't remember how to prove Pythagoras's theorem. But I am as sure that Pythagoras's theorem is true and that the sun will rise tomorrow as I am of any of the propositions I have proved in this book.

-=-=-=-=-=-=-=-=-=-=-=-=-

Exercise 12.5
Under what initial conditions will each of the following instructions terminate?

>a. *iterate n≠50*: *n*:=*n*−1 *enditerate*
>b. *iterate n≠a*: *n*:=*n*+1 *enditerate*
>c. *iterate n≠a*: *n*:=*n*+b *enditerate*
>d. *iterate n≠a*: *n*:=*n*+a *enditerate*

[Hint: be careful to consider the possibility that *b* or *a* might be negative.]

Exercise 12.6
Repeat exercise 12.5 with the instructions

>a. *iterate n<50*: *n*:=*n*+1 *enditerate*
>b. *iterate n<50*: *n*:=*n*−1 *enditerate*

Exercise 12.7
Repeat exercise 12.5 again with the instructions

>a. *iterate n>50*: *n*:=*n*+1 *enditerate*
>b. *iterate n>50*: *n*:=*n*−1 *enditerate*
>c. *iterate n>a*: *n*:=*n*+1 *enditerate*
>d. *iterate n>a*: *n*:=*n*+b *enditerate*
>e. *iterate n>a*: *n*:=*n*+a *enditerate*

-=-=-=-=-=-=-=-=-=-=-=-=-

It is sometimes possible to prove properties of *iterate* instructions by indirect reasoning: if this instruction ever terminated, then it would establish such-and-such a state of affairs. Consider, for example, the *iterate* instruction shown in program 12.6. This instruction will obviously terminate if *n*=50 initially, but not at all otherwise. Why not? The instruction which is repeated is an *iterate* instruction which itself may or may not terminate. If it does terminate then it must establish a state of affairs in which *n*>100; if it doesn't terminate then

>*iterate n≠50*:
> *iterate n≤100*: *n*:=*n*+1 *enditerate*
>*enditerate*

program 12.6

neither does the whole of program 12.6. To make n bigger than one hundred will certainly not make it equal to fifty, so repeatedly executing the inner instruction will never bring about the state of affairs in which the enclosing iterate instruction will terminate. Therefore unless $n = 50$ initially, the example program will never terminate.

-=-=-=-=-=-=-=-=-=-=-=-=-

Exercise 12.8
Under what initial conditions will the following instructions terminate?

> *a. iterate n≠50: iterate n>100: n:=n+1 enditerate enditerate*
> *b. iterate n>50: iterate n<100: n:=n+1 enditerate enditerate*
> *c. iterate n>50: iterate n<100: p(n) enditerate enditerate*

Exercise 12.9
How about these two-armed *iterate* instructions?

> *a. iterate n<50: n:=n+1 n>50: n:=n−1 enditerate*
> *b. iterate n<50: n:=n+2 n>50: n:=n−2 enditerate*
> *c. iterate n<50: n:=n+2 n>50: n:=n−3 enditerate*
> *d. iterate n<a: n:=n+b n>a: n:=n−c enditerate*

-=-=-=-=-=-=-=-=-=-=-=-=-

A proof that an *iterate* instruction is equivalent to an assignment instruction is of course enough to show that execution of the *iterate* will terminate. For example, program 12.7, which moves the value of n upwards or downwards until it reaches the value j, can be proved equivalent to the single instruction $n := j$ using an argument similar to the proof about program 12.3 given above. It doesn't matter whether j is positive or negative.

> $n := i$; *iterate* $n < j: n := n+1$ $n > j: n := n-1$ *enditerate*

program 12.7

-=-=-=-=-=-=-=-=-=-=-=-=-

Exercise 12.10
Prove that program 12.7 is equivalent to $n := j$.

-=-=-=-=-=-=-=-=-=-=-=-=-

Reasoning with *iterate* instructions and the crp

It isn't always trivial to reduce an *iterate* instruction to an assignment instruction. Consider, for example, program 12.2. Clearly this instruction terminates when the input sequence doesn't have a space character at the current reading position. It is fairly obvious that it terminates with the crp at the *first* non-space position in the input sequence. But how to prove that?

The method of reasoning with the input sequence introduced in the last chapter makes *movecrp* equivalent to an assignment instruction which alters the input sequence I. Using this method, it is possible to prove that program 12.2 is equivalent to $I:=X$ where X_1 isn't a space. As usual, the effect of the *iterate* depends on the state of affairs in which it is executed. So, the first step is to describe that state of affairs. Program 12.8 uses a sequence J to describe the initial state of the input sequence.

$$I:=J;\ iterate\ crp\hat{\ }=`\ ':\ movecrp\ enditerate$$

program 12.8

My proposition makes the whole program equivalent to a single assignment instruction:

P0: An execution of program 12.8, where $J_{1..k}$ are all spaces, J_{k+1} is not a space and $k\geq 0$, is equivalent to the instruction $I:=J_{k+1..}$.

Now by definition 12.2, program 12.8 is equivalent to:

$$I:=J;\ select\ crp\hat{\ }=`\ ':\ movecrp;\ iterate\ crp\hat{\ }=`\ ':\ movecrp\ enditerate$$
$$crp\hat{\ }\neq`\ ':\ donothing$$
$$endselect$$

$$=\ I:=J;\ select\ I_1=`\ ':\ I:=I_{2..};\ iterate\ crp\hat{\ }=`\ ':\ movecrp\ enditerate$$
$$I_1\neq`\ ':\ donothing$$
$$endselect$$

$$=\ select\ J_1=`\ ':\ I:=J;\ I=I_{2..};\ iterate\ crp\hat{\ }=`\ ':\ movecrp\ enditerate$$
$$J_1\neq`\ ':\ I:=J;\ donothing$$
$$endselect$$

$$=\ select\ J_1=`\ ':\ I:=J_{2..};\ iterate\ crp\hat{\ }=`\ ':\ movecrp\ enditerate$$
$$J_1\neq`\ ':\ I:=J$$
$$endselect$$

The base case is when $k=0$: $J_{1..k}$ is the empty sequence and $J_{k+1}=J_1$ isn't a space; program 12.8 is therefore equivalent to $I:=J$, which is the same as $I:=J_{1..}$, which is the same as $I:=J_{k+1..}$; hence the base case is proved.

Make the usual inductive hypothesis, that P0(K) is true for some $K\geq 0$: that is, that when $J_{1..K}$ is a sequence of spaces and J_{K+1} isn't a space, execution of program 12.8 is equivalent to $I:=J_{K+1..}$. Then to show that P0(K+1) follows I must show that program 12.8, executed when $J_{1..K+1}$ is a sequence of spaces and J_{K+2} isn't a space, is equivalent to $I:=J_{K+2..}$. Since $K+1\geq 1$ I know that J_1 must be a space, and then:

$$select\ J_1=`\ ':\ I:=J_{2..};\ iterate\ crp\hat{\ }=`\ ':\ movecrp\ enditerate$$
$$J_1\neq`\ ':\ I:=J$$
$$endselect$$

$$=\ I:=J_{2..};\ iterate\ crp\hat{\ }=`\ ':\ movecrp\ enditerate$$

Now if $J_{1..K+1}$ is a sequence of spaces, $K+1 \geq 1$ and J_{K+2} isn't a space, it follows that $(J_{2..})_{1..K} = J_{2..K+1}$ is a sequence of spaces and that $(J_{2..})_{K+1} = J_{K+2}$ isn't a space. Thus by inductive hypothesis:

$$I := J_{2..}; \; iterate \; crp\hat{\ } = `\; ': movecrp \; enditerate \; = I := (J_{2..})_{K+1} = I := J_{K+2..}$$

and $P0(K) => P0(K+1)$ is proved.

12.3 PLANNING A SOLUTION: READING A NUMERAL

Suppose that your programming system doesn't have the ability to read numbers but can read single characters. That is, suppose that it doesn't have a *readnumber* instruction but that it does have *readchar* or *crp^/movecrp*. How could you program a system like that to imitate *readnumber*?

Whenever you are presented with a programming problem you must choose a program structure for your solution. You now know notation for all the structures which are introduced in this book. You must decide which of the following will solve your problem: is your program

   (a) a *sequence* of different actions,

   (b) a *choice* between different actions,

   (c) a *repetition* of similar actions (and then you have to decide whether to use *counting* repetition or *unlimited* repetition),

   (d) a *recursive application* of a procedure call.

You should also be aware that for every repetitive solution there is a similar recursive solution and vice-versa, but there will be more about that in Part Three.

To read a numeral is to read a sequence of digit characters. Calculating the value of the numeral means doing something with the values described by each character in the sequence. The solution is obviously either repetitive or recursive and since this is a chapter on repetition I reject recursion out of hand.

Why is reading a numeral unlimited rather than counting repetition? Consider what a program must do with the input sequence after it has printed the message

what size of triangle would you like to see?

Suppose that in the input sequence the crp points to the character '2'. Should the program print a two-by-two triangle? Perhaps it should or perhaps it should not. The next character in the input sequence might be '0', for example. Then should the program print a twenty-by-twenty triangle? Again perhaps it should, but if the character after the zero is '7' it looks as though the triangle should have two hundred and seven rows. Still it might not have finished - the fourth character might be yet another digit, and so might the next, and the next, and on and on for as long as the person at the keyboard keeps strumming on the top line of keys.

You might use counting repetition to calculate the value of a numeral typed on the keyboard, but you would have to demand that every numeral typed must have the same number of digits - say three digits, for example. This would make life tedious when typing small numbers - to get a two-by-two triangle you would have to type '002'; to get a fifteen-by-fifteen triangle you would have to type '015' - and it would put an immediate maximum limit on the values of numerals that can be recognised.

It should be obvious that unless you use a fixed-length straitjacket, reading a numeral is a job for unlimited repetition. Having justified the choice, now to plan the program.

Calculating the value of a numeral

Most people have so much practice manipulating decimal numerals - adding them up, subtracting them, multiplying and dividing them - that the ability has become second nature. We all do our mental arithmetic with decimal numerals. Most people think decimal numerals *are* numbers and numbers *are* decimal numerals. Thinking yourself back to a time when you didn't know about numerals or even numbers is a little difficult. Here goes with an attempt to strip away some of those layers of education.

In a decimal numeral each digit represents a value which is partly determined by its own character-identity, partly by its position in the numeral - units, tens, hundreds, thousands, and so on. Decimal numerals are a particular example of a general *positional* numeral notation. You may know that most computers actually do their stuff with 'binary numerals': positional numerals in which there are only two possible digit values and the digit positions are units, twos, fours, eights, .. You may have met other positional notations: base 5 seems to be a very popular illustration with position values units, fives, twenty-fives, ..

Stick notation - scratches on prison walls, pictures on the side of World War II planes, notches on a Western villain's gun - is non-positional because every scratch, notch or picture has the same value no matter where it appears in the sequence. Positional notation can be described in terms of sticks: in decimal numeral notation a number xyz describes a pile of x hundreds of sticks plus y tens of sticks and z more sticks. In base five notation (quinqual?) a numeral xyz means x twenty-fives of sticks, y fives and z more sticks. In binary notation it means x fours, y twos and z.

Decimal notation is based on tens and therefore needs ten different digit values. Consider the notation which would be used if there were thirteen digit values. To make things as unfamiliar as possible I shall use letters of the alphabet to name the thirteen possible values and I shall describe those values in stick notation:

> a means no sticks, b means /, c means //, d means ///,
> e means ////, f means /////, g means ///// /,
> h means ///// //, i means ///// ///, j means ///// ////,

k means ///// /////, l means ///// ///// /,
m means ///// ///// //.

Then I can ask: how many sticks does the numeral 'ej' describe? Recall that in decimal notation the numeral '39' means 3×ten+9. Then in my new notation 'ej' must mean e×thirteen+j, or (////)×(///// ///// ///) + (///// ////) sticks. I might draw it as

///// ///// ///
///// ///// ///   + ///// ////
///// ///// ///
///// ///// ///

which I am sure you can calculate to be

///// ///// ///// ///// ///// ///// ///// /////
///// ///// ///// ///// /

In decimal terms 'ej' is 4×13+9 = 61 sticks. You can calculate the value of any funny numeral in just the same sort of way that you calculate the value of a decimal numeral, but instead of counting ones, tens, hundreds, thousands, ten thousands, .. the positions of a funny numeral count as ones, thirteens, hundred and sixty-nines, two thousand one hundred and ninety-sevens, twenty-eight thousand five hundred and sixty-ones, ...[†].

Calculating the value of a funny numeral like 'elabk' looks pretty horrible, involving lots of very long multiplications and additions. In fact it is easy to calculate it left-to-right, in the order it is read. Going back to decimal for a moment:

$$39841 = 3×10^4 + 9×10^3 + 8×10^2 + 4×10 + 1$$
$$= (((3×10 + 9)×10 + 8)×10 + 4)×10 + 1$$

See the first digit and think 'three'; see the second digit, multiply by ten, add and think 'thirty-nine'; see the third digit, multiply by ten, add and think 'three hundred and ninety-eight'; see the fourth digit, multiply by ten, add and think 'three thousand, nine hundred and eighty-four'; see the last digit, multiply by ten, add and think 'thirty-nine thousand eight hundred and forty-one'.

Mental, or pencil and paper, or electronic calculator conversion of the funny numeral 'elabk' can follow a similar course. See the first digit and think either '/////' or more likely 'four'. Multiply by thirteen and add l=eleven: think 'sixty-three'. Multiply by thirteen and add a=zero: think 'eight hundred and nineteen'. Multiply by thirteen and add b=one: think 'ten thousand six hundred and forty-eight'. Multiply by thirteen and add k=ten: think 'one hundred and thirty-eight thousand, four hundred and thirty-four'.

[†] Of course those are the *decimal* names of the position values - if we had six and a half fingers on each hand we might have invented nice short names for the powers of thirteen.

So if I want to write a program which reads funny numerals and calculates their value I can use the technique of repeatedly multiplying by thirteen and adding the value of the next digit until the end of the number is reached.

-=-=-=-=-=-=-=-=-=-=-=-

Exercise 12.11
Calculate the decimal equivalents of

> ek
> aa
> ba
> baa
> kkkl
> kkkla
> bkd

-=-=-=-=-=-=-=-=-=-=-=-

The program at last

To design an unlimited repetition instruction it is necessary to answer three questions:

(a) What should be repeated?

(b) When should it stop? (Or alternatively, when should it continue?)

(c) In what initial states of affairs is it supposed to work?

You already know part of the answer to the first question for the problem of reading a funny numeral: it has something to do with multiplying by thirteen and adding a digit value. The second question has an obvious answer: stop when the repetition reaches the end of the numeral, when you see a character like a full stop, a comma or a letter 'z' which can't form part of the numeral. It is easiest to do this using the *crp^/movecrp* basic instructions, producing a repetition which stops when the crp points to the character just *past* the end of the numeral, so that the funny numeral program consumes every character of the input relevant to its purpose, no more and no less.

Programming in the familiar 'as if' style leads to program 12.9, in which every repetition moves the crp one position forward. I can prove that this program will terminate, using an argument similar to the proof of program 12.2 given above.

> *iterate crp^ is a funny digit character:*
> *calculate and move the crp*
> *enditerate*

program 12.9

Deciding whether or not *crp*^ is a digit character means deciding whether it is a character in the set {'a', 'b', .., 'm'}. In the notation of this book that can be done by making a lot of separate comparisons: to clarify the structure of the program I introduce a procedure to make the decision. Program 12.10 shows what I mean.

$$def\ isadigit(c) = c='a' \lor c='b' \lor c='c' \lor c='d' \lor c='e' \lor$$
$$c='f' \lor c='g' \lor c='h' \lor c='i' \lor c='j' \lor$$
$$c='k' \lor c='l' \lor c='m'$$

enddef

iterate isadigit(crp^): calculate with crp^; movecrp enditerate

program 12.10

Now suppose that the purpose of the program is to place the value of the funny numeral it has read in a container *N*. Using the 'multiply by thirteen, then add' technique described above, the *calculate* instruction in program 12.10 could be

$$N := N{\times}13 + digit\ value\ described\ by\ crp^$$

To answer the third design question, it is helpful to consider the last and the first repetitions of this instruction and argue inductively. If the last repetition is to have the right effect, *N* must hold the value of the numeral up to the digit before the last. For example, if the number is 'elabk', *N* must hold the value of 'elab'; multiplying this by thirteen and adding the value of 'k' will then give the right answer. Before the first repetition *N* must evidently hold zero.

It only remains to write a procedure which translates from input character to digit value to make the program complete. Program 12.11, for example, reads a funny numeral and prints the equivalent decimal numeral.

$$def\ isadigit(c) = c='a' \lor c='b' \lor c='c' \lor c='d' \lor c='e' \lor$$
$$c='f' \lor c='g' \lor c='h' \lor c='i' \lor c='j' \lor$$
$$c='k' \lor c='l' \lor c='m'$$

enddef

def digitvalue(c) = case c of 'a':0 'b':1 'c':2 'd':3 'e':4
                                'f':5 'g':6 'h':7 'i':8 'j':9
                                'k':10 'l':11 'm':12

endcase

enddef

initialise N:=0

iterate isadigit(crp^): N:=N×13+digitvalue(crp^); movecrp enditerate;

printnumber(N)

program 12.11

-=-=-=-=-=-=-=-=-=-=-=-=-

Exercise 12.12
Supposing that the input sequence is <'b', 'a', 'k', '.',..>, trace the effect of executing program 12.11.

Exercise 12.13
Repeat exercise 12.12 with the input sequence <'a', 'a', 'x', 'l', 'a',..>.

Exercise 12.14
Repeat 12.12 with the input sequence <'x','e','l','.',..>.

Exercise 12.15
What would be the change in effect of program 12.11 if the body of the *iterate* was changed to

$$movecrp; \ N:=N{\times}13+digitvalue(crp\hat{\ })$$

[Hint: consider your answers to exercises 12.12 and 12.13.]

Exercise 12.16
Assuming that executions of *isadigit* and *digitvalue* perform as they should, prove the following proposition:

If $J_{1..k}$ is a sequence of funny digits (characters in the set {'a'..'m'}), J_{k+1} is not a funny digit and $k{\geq}0$, execution of

$I,N:=J, x;$ *iterate isadigit*$(crp\hat{\ })$: $N:=N{\times}13+digitvalue(crp\hat{\ });$ *movecrp enditerate*

is equivalent to

$$I,N := J_{k+1..}, x{\times}13^k+valueof(J_{1..k})$$

-=-=-=-=-=-=-=-=-=-=-=-=-

Exercise 12.14 hints at a flaw in the design of program 12.11. The definition of the meaning of an *iterate* instruction is such that if initially every condition-formula delivers false, the whole instruction is equivalent to *donothing*. So if the first character in the input sequence isn't a digit character, program 12.11 doesn't move the crp and prints '0', which is not exactly what I would have hoped for. The body of the program would express my wishes better if it were written as in program 12.12.

```
select isadigit(crp^): iterate isadigit(crp^):
                    N:=N×13+digitvalue(crp^); movecrp
            enditerate;
            printnumber(N)
        ¬isadigit(crp^): printstring("Where's the number?")
endselect
```

program 12.12

12.4 SHORTHAND FORMS OF THE *iterate* INSTRUCTION

The multi-armed *iterate* is quite a modern invention in programming and I don't know of any widely available mechanical code which includes it. Lots of codes have the older *while-do* or *repeat-until* instruction.

The *while-do* instruction

While-do is a single-armed *iterate* instruction. Its definition in terms of *iterate* is given in definition 12.3. Conversion from *while-do* to *iterate* is trivial; conversion from *iterate* to *while-do* can be trickier, because a multi-armed *iterate* instruction offers the machine a choice of actions.

$$while\ C\ do\ P\ od\ =\ iterate\ C{:}P\ enditerate$$

definition 12.3

If the choice is made inside the repetition then it can be converted into a single-armed *iterate* containing a multi-armed *select* according to the rule set out in definition 12.4. In execution terms the two instructions are clearly equivalent: each terminates only when all the condition-formulas $C_1..C_n$ are false; each chooses a program to execute in the same way[†]. This equivalence can be proved by substitution (see exercise 12.21 below).

$$iterate\ C_1{:}P_1\ \ C_2{:}P_2\ ..\ \ C_n{:}P_n\ enditerate$$
$$=\ iterate\ C_1{\vee}C_2{\vee}\ ..\ {\vee}C_n{:}$$
$$\qquad select\ C_1{:}P_1\ \ C_2{:}P_2\ ..\ \ C_n{:}P_n\ endselect$$
$$enditerate$$

definition 12.4

-=-=-=-=-=-=-=-=-=-=-=-

Exercise 12.17
Convert the multi-armed *iterate*

$$iterate\ crp\hat{\ }='\ ':\ movecrp$$
$$crp\hat{\ }=newline{:}\ NL;\ movecrp$$
$$enditerate$$

into a single-armed *iterate* instruction.

,

[†] The equivalence would be falsified if evaluating a formula twice in the same environment could give different results. You can produce that sort of bizarre effect by playing around with value-delivering procedures and assignment instructions - see chapter 14 for an example - but I refuse to contemplate such nastiness in my definitions.

Exercise 12.18
Repeat exercise 12.17 with the instruction

> *iterate crp^=' ': movecrp*
>   *crp^=newline: NL; movecrp*
>   *crp^≠' '∧crp^≠newline∧crp^≠'.': printchar(crp^); movecrp*
> *enditerate*

[Hint: you can simplify the condition of the single-armed instruction quite a bit.]

Exercise 12.19
Convert

$$while \ n<b \ \lor \ crp^=' \ ' \ do$$
$$if \ n<b \ then \ n:=n+1 \ else \ movecrp \ fi$$
$$od$$

into a multi-armed *iterate* instruction.

Exercise 12.20
Repeat exercise 12.19 with the instruction

$$while \ a>0 \ \lor \ a+x>y \ do$$
$$if \ a+x>y \ then \ x:=x-1 \ fi; \ a:=a-1$$
$$od$$

Exercise 12.21
Suppose that Y is the single-armed *iterate* instruction in definition 12.4. Then by using definition 12.2 and the definition of the *select* instruction, prove that

$$Y = select \ C_1: P_1; Y \quad C_2: P_2; Y \quad .. \quad C_n: P_n; Y$$
$$\neg C_1 \wedge \neg C_2 \wedge .. \wedge \neg C_n: donothing$$
$$endselect$$

This equivalence proves definition 12.4.

-=-=-=-=-=-=-=-=-=-=-=-=-

Definition 12.4 doesn't describe the only possible way of transcribing a multi-armed *iterate*. Definition 12.5 gives an alternative rule which at first sight looks rather unlikely: it makes a multi-armed *iterate* equivalent to a single-armed *iterate* instruction which contains a *sequence* of single-armed *iterate* instructions.

> *iterate $C_1: P_1$ $C_2: P_2$.. $C_n: P_n$ enditerate*
>
> can be transcribed as
>
> *iterate $C_1 \lor C_2 \lor .. \lor C_n$:*   *iterate $C_1: P_1$ enditerate;*
>   *iterate $C_2: P_2$ enditerate;*
>   *..;*
>   *iterate $C_n: P_n$ enditerate*
> *enditerate*

definition 12.5

In execution terms the transcription makes sense. The single-armed version executes each instruction sequence only under the same conditions as the multi-armed version, and if the single-armed version terminates, every condition-formula of the multi-armed version will be false. Every effect produced by the single-armed version is also an effect which can be be produced by the multi-armed version. The rule does not describe an equivalence because the single-armed version makes an unambiguous choice when deciding which of the original Ps to execute, but the multi-armed version is potentially ambiguous.

The *repeat-until* instruction

Repeat-until is an alternative form of unlimited repetition. It is a single-armed instruction in which each repetition takes place *before* the condition-formula is evaluated and in which the termination condition is stated positively (instead of negatively as in the *iterate* instruction). Definition 12.6 gives its meaning in terms of *iterate*. Converting from a single-armed *iterate* to *repeat-until* is straightforward (definition 12.7).

$$repeat\ P\ until\ C \quad = \quad P;\ iterate\ \neg C{:}P\ enditerate$$

definition 12.6

$$iterate\ C{:}P\ enditerate$$
$$= select\ C{:}\ repeat\ P\ until\ \neg C$$
$$\neg C{:}\ donothing$$
$$endselect$$

definition 12.7

-=-=-=-=-=-=-=-=-=-=-=-

Exercise 12.22
Repeat exercises 12.17-12.20, this time converting into *repeat-until* instructions.
Exercise 12.23
Assuming definition 12.6, prove definition 12.7.

-=-=-=-=-=-=-=-=-=-=-=-

If you can prove that the formula C in a single-armed *iterate* is always true it is obviously much simpler to transcribe it into *repeat-until*. Also, the *select* instruction of definition 12.7 maps straightforwardly into an *if-then-else* (or even, perish the thought, an *if-then*).

12.5 TRANSLATING BETWEEN CHARACTER AND DIGIT VALUES

Program 12.11 uses *case* formulas both to enumerate the possible digit characters in its peculiar numeral notation and to calculate their equivalent values. It's an adequate technique and it helps to emphasise that the mapping from character to digit value is completely arbitrary: for example, I chose to name the digit values in alphabetical order but I need not have done so.

The normal decimal-digit alphabet is equally arbitrary. There is no reason why a picture of an egg standing on its end should mean zero or an egg standing on a tail should mean nine - it's just a convention. But it's such a well-established convention that it finds an echo in the way that computing machinery manipulates character values.

Computers recognise a limited set of characters. Most machines in the mid-1980s recognise and manipulate the one hundred and twenty-eight characters defined in the ASCII code. By pressing keys on your keyboard you signal one out of one hundred and twenty-eight possibilities. Some of these correspond to printable characters: pressing the A key, for example, signals a printable 'a' or 'A' character. Some correspond to layout characters: RETURN and TAB, for example. Some are control signals: pressing a letter key at the same time as pressing the CTRL key, for example, will send a signal to your computer but what it means depends on the particular system.

Whatever the code used - and ASCII isn't the only one - if there are a limited number of possibilities there is nothing more natural than to number them[†]. If you are numbering the characters the pressure of history is so strong that you would almost certainly do it in alphabetical order - thus if you number the character 'a' as 62 you would naturally number 'b' as 63, 'c' as 64, .., 'z' as 87. Likewise if '0' is character number 18 then '1' would probably be number 19, '2' would be number 20, .., '9' would be number 26. The numbering scheme is part of the code so that on every computing system which uses the ASCII code, for example, the asterisk character is number 42 (truly a cosmic coincidence).

In most programming systems there are ways of finding out the code-number of a character or the character corresponding to a particular number. So you might write

printchar(encode(42))

- an instruction which on an ASCII-code machine would be equivalent to *print**.

[†] Present-day computers represent everything with patterns of ones and zeros (high and low voltage, left and right magnetisation, charge and no charge, or whatever). A binary numeral is a sequence of ones and zeros. A particular character is represented as a sequence of ones and zeros. So from a certain point of view close to the hardware, character-representations and numbers are the same. Every numeral can be seen as a pattern of ones and zeros, every pattern of ones and zeros can be seen as a numeral. But from the programming point of view characters and numbers remain as different as chalk and cheese.

Or you might write

$$printnumber(decode(`*')+6)$$

- an instruction equivalent to *printnumber*(7) on an ASCII machine.

If the code-numbering on your machine is done in a straightforward way you can play some simple tricks to simplify numeral-to-number translation. You might find that the alphabetic characters are numbered sequentially, so that, for example, 'b' is numbered one greater than 'a'. Then the formula

$$decode(`a')+1$$

is the code number for 'b', and the instruction

$$printchar(encode(decode(`a')+1))$$

(read it carefully!) is equivalent to *printchar*('b'). More to the point, so far as this chapter is concerned, is the reverse translation: the formula

$$decode(`b')-decode(`a')$$

will deliver 1, and if *x* describes a character from the set {'a'..'m'} the formula

$$decode(x)-decode(`a')$$

will tell you where in the range your character is. That is, the formula is equivalent to *digitvalue*(*x*) from program 12.11.

Similar tricks work with decimal digit characters. If *x* describes a character from the set {'0', '1', .., '9'}, the formula

$$decode(x)-decode(`0')$$

usually gives the equivalent decimal digit value.

You will have to discover whether your particular programming system codes digit and letter characters conveniently or not. You can usually find out by looking in the system manual. If you can't get hold of the manual or you can't understand it, try writing a program which prints out the code value of every character you are interested in.

-=

APPENDIX 12.A *Iterate* INSTRUCTIONS IN PASCAL

Pascal has *while-do* and *repeat-until* instructions. First of all, then, you must convert multi-armed *iterate* instructions into single-armed ones. The Pascal *while-do* instruction is written

```
while C do I
```

- no closing *od* bracket and I is as usual a single instruction. If the body of your *iterate* instruction is a program you must unpack the definitions and begin–end bracket its body.

Pascal *repeat-until* is just the one in my notation, except that 'repeat' and 'until' can only bracket an instruction or a sequence of instructions (that is, not programs in general):

```
repeat S until C
```

Encode and *decode* in Pascal

Pascal ord(x) imitates *decode(x)* if *x* is a character formula. Pascal chr(n) is equivalent to *encode(n)*.

Sets of characters

Pascal has a notation for sets of values. For nasty mechanical reasons the use of this notation is limited but it is nevertheless useful. You can construct sets by writing values in square brackets '[' and ']', calculate union using '+', intersection using '-' and test for set membership using 'in'. One particularly useful formula is

```
c in ['0','1','2','3','4','5','6','7','8','9']
```

which tests whether a character value c is a decimal digit character or not. This formula can be abbreviated to

```
c in ['0'..'9']
```

There are other very useful set constant formulas: for example, ['0'..'9','a'..'f'] is the set of hexadecimal digit characters. Look up sets in a book on Pascal for more details.

An awful reminder

If you are trying the examples in appendix 12.B, don't forget the fact that *crp^='* ' transcribes into Pascal as

```
(input^=' ') and (not eoln(input))
```

that *crp^=newline* transcribes into eoln(input) and that there is no character-code representation in Pascal for the *newline* character. This lack of a character representation gives real difficulty: for example, the rather simple instruction

> *iterate crp^=' ': movecrp*
> *crp^≠' ' ∧ crp^≠'.': printchar(crp^); movecrp*
> *enditerate*

which skips over characters, printing the non-space ones and terminating when it reaches a full stop, must be made Pascal-fit as something like program 12.13 before you transcribe it into Pascal. It often helps if you simplify the instruction before you transcribe it: for example, by expanding the inner *select* instruction this example can become program 12.14.

$$iterate\ crp\hat{\ }=`\ '\wedge crp\hat{\ }\neq newline: movecrp$$
$$(crp\hat{\ }\neq`\ '\vee crp\hat{\ }=newline)\wedge crp\hat{\ }\neq`.':$$
$$select\ crp\hat{\ }=newline: NL;\ movecrp$$
$$crp\hat{\ }\neq newline: printchar(crp\hat{\ });\ movecrp$$
$$endselect$$
$$enditerate$$

program 12.13

$$iterate\ crp\hat{\ }=`\ ': movecrp$$
$$crp\hat{\ }=newline: NL;\ movecrp$$
$$crp\hat{\ }\neq`\ '\wedge crp\hat{\ }\neq`.'\wedge crp\hat{\ }\neq newline:$$
$$printchar(crp\hat{\ });\ movecrp$$
$$enditerate$$

program 12.14

APPENDIX 12.B SOME PROGRAMS TO TRY

Exercise 12.24
Write a program which reads the characters you type on the keyboard, terminating when it reaches a full stop (period) and printing every character which isn't a space, including the full stop. The crp should finish at the position after the full stop. For example, given the input

```
    h   e   low o     r l            d      . .xyz
```

the program should print

```
            helloworld.
```

and if given the input

```
            hello   you
            rs  e   l  f.that's it.
```

it should print

```
            helloyou
            rself.
```

[Hint: what is typed and what is printed may sometimes be muddled up on the screen: blame your programming system, not the exercise.]

Exercise 12.25
Write a program which reads characters up to a full stop, printing only the decimal digit characters it reads.

Exercise 12.26
Write a program which reads characters up to a full stop, printing only the alphabetic characters it reads.

Exercise 12.27
Write a program which reads characters up to a full stop, printing only the odd-valued decimal digit characters it reads: that is, printing 1s, 3s, 5s, 7s and 9s but ignoring 0s, 2s, 4s, 6s and 8s.

Exercise 12.28
Execute program 12.11 and use it to check your answers to exercise 12.11 (and vice-versa, use your answers to check your program).

Exercise 12.29
Write a version of program 12.11 which works for normal decimal numerals.

Exercise 12.30
Write a version of program 12.11 which works for hexadecimal numerals. [Hexadecimal notation is base-sixteen and has sixteen digit characters: digit characters 0-9 have their usual meaning and then

a means ///// /////, b means ///// ///// /,
c means ///// ///// //, d means ///// ///// ///,
e means ///// ///// ////, f means ///// ///// /////

So, for example, 2a (2×sixteen+a) in hexadecimal notation names the same number as 42 in decimal; ff (f×sixteen+f) is decimal 255.]

Exercise 12.31
Write a program which reads in (using your system's equivalent of *readnumber*) a base or radix in the range 2..10, then reads a sequence of characters representing digits in that base (optionally preceded by spaces and newlines), stops when the first character which isn't a valid digit is reached and finally prints out the decimal equivalent of the numeral it has read. For example, given the input

4 32599x

it should stop with the crp on the '5' and print '14'.

Exercise 12.32
Repeat exercise 12.31, this time without using *readnumber*.

Chapter 13
REPETITIVE FORMULAS

Chapters 6, 7 and 8 introduced recursive executions and recursive calculations. Since there are repetitive executions you should expect there would be repetitive calculations. I have delayed their discussion until this point in the book because their imitation in a mechanical code normally requires the use of assignment instructions. Repetitive calculations are important, which is why they get a chapter on their own, and very easy to understand, which is why this chapter is so short.

13.1 CALCULATING POWERS OF X

Consider the calculation of x^n, the nth power of an integer x. Chapter 8 defined x^n with a recurrence relation and the program which corresponds naturally to that definition is recursive. But anybody who is asked to calculate such a formula without a calculator or a computer to help them would perform a repetitive calculation. Most people would calculate in the way of program 13.1. Those with a mathematical training would perhaps use program 13.2, because they know of the possibility that n might be zero or negative, and they know what x^n means in either of those circumstances. Those with both a mathematical and a programming training might use program 13.3, because they know that no

> *start with x*
> *times n−1 do multiply by x od*

program 13.1

> *start with* 1
> *when n≥0: times n do multiply by x od*
> *when n<0: times n do divide by x od*

program 13.2

start with 1
when n≥0: times n do multiply by x od
when n≤0: times n do divide by x od

program 13.3

divisions is just as sensible as no multiplications and that either will produce the same result.

To perform a repetitive calculation you must know what to start with (the base value) and what to do at each step. The repetition can reasonably be a *times-do* or a *for-do*. Landin's notation uses '*initially*' to describe the base value and ordinary algebraic notation to describe what to do at each step. For example, program 13.4 is equivalent to 1×2×2×2×2 and calculates 2^4, which is 16. I leave the substitution definition of this notation as an exercise for the reader.

initially 1
times 4 *do* ×2 *od*

program 13.4

-=-=-=-=-=-=-=-=-=-=-=-

Exercise 13.1
Write a repetitive calculation of $x!$ = 1×2×3×..×x, using *for-do* rather than *times-do*[†].

Exercise 13.2
Give the substitution definition of

initially x   times F do op y od

where *op* is any binary operation (+, −, ×, /, ∧, ∨, ..). Check that your definition gives the right meaning to program 13.4. Check that it gives the correct meaning to a program which includes '*times* 0 *do* .. *od*'.

Exercise 13.3
The meaning of

initially x   for N rt S do op y od

is intended to be x *op* $y[N\backslash S_1]$ *op* $y[N\backslash S_2]$ *op* .. *op* $y[N\backslash S_{length(S)}]$. Give a substitution definition which makes this so. Check that your definition gives the correct meaning when $length(S)=0$. Check that it gives the right meaning to your factorial calculation from exercise 13.1.

-=-=-=-=-=-=-=-=-=-=-=-

[†] Note for non-mathematicians: 0! = 1, for much the same reason that x^0 = 1.

13.2 QUANTIFIED FORMULAS

Repetitive calculations are especially useful when dealing with quantified logical formulas. The formula

$$\forall i: a \leq i \leq b: F$$

is pronounced 'for all i such that $a \leq i \leq b$, the formula F holds'. It is a naturally repetitive description: F will in general depend on i, and the formula says that $F[i \backslash a]$ holds (is true) and so does $F[i \backslash a+1]$ .. and so does $F[i \backslash b]$. It is in effect a repeated calculation with '$\wedge$', so you may immediately jump to the conclusion that the formula is equivalent to

initially true
for i rt a..b do $\wedge F$ *od*

Why *initially true*? Well, if every one of the Fs is true we get *true*$\wedge$*true*$\wedge$..$\wedge$*true*, which is true. If any of them is false we get *true*$\wedge$..$\wedge$*false*$\wedge$.., which is false. If the calculation started with *false* the answer would always be *false*, which would be a complete waste of time. Notice that if *a..b* is empty - that is, if b is less than a - the calculation delivers true, which is just what a mathematician requires of the '$\forall$' formula.

There are other quantified formulas. One very useful one is

$$\exists i: a \leq i \leq b: F$$

This formula says 'there exists an i such that $a \leq i \leq b$ for which F holds'. It is true if $F[i \backslash a]$ holds (is true) or $F[i \backslash a+1]$ holds .. or $F[i \backslash b]$ holds, and is evidently equivalent to

initially false
for i rt a..b do $\vee F$ *od*

13.3 IMITATING REPETITIVE CALCULATIONS

The mechanical code of your programming system will almost certainly not allow you to describe repetitive calculations directly. One way to imitate them is by using memory and assignment. If container a holds the value of the calculation so far, then the sub-calculation '*op y*' can be imitated by the instruction '$a := a$ *op y*'. For example, program 13.5 assigns x^n to container z, so

$z := 1;$
times n do $z := z \times x$ *od*

program 13.5

long as n isn't negative.

-=-=-=-=-=-=-=-=-=-=-=-=-

Exercise 13.4
Prove that when $n=4$ and $x=2$, program 13.5 is equivalent to $z:=16$.

-=-=-=-=-=-=-=-=-=-=-=-=-

We can always replace repetitive calculations by programs which assign the calculated value to a container. If a formula or an instruction contains a repetitive calculation we can replace it by a sequence which first calculates the value in a container, then an instruction which uses the container name in place of the original repetitive formula. For example, a program which prints a power of 5:

> *printnumber (initially* 1 *times* 13 *do* ×5 *od)*
>
> = *initialise* $z:=1$
> *times* 13 *do* $z:=z\times5$;
> *printnumber* (z)

Chapter 14
TERMINATION, FAILURE AND SEARCHING

Not every program execution succeeds. We often mistakenly write programs that call for recursions which never end, or give negative execution counts in *times-do* repetitions, or print lines which are too long for the screen. Sometimes failure can be predicted by pre-calculating the effect of the program, but in general we can't predict everything because programs interact with an unpredictable world. Consider a program which imitates a desk calculator by reading two numbers a and b and printing the quotient $a \div b$. If we ask it to divide one by zero it might reasonably fail to do so: is its failure caused by an incorrect design or by what it has been required to do?

In programming terminology we say that an execution *terminates* if it follows all of its finite sequence of instructions. Programs which follow infinite sequences clearly don't terminate. We say that a program *fails to terminate* if it doesn't reach the end of its sequence, either because something goes wrong or because the sequence is infinite. Termination is defined in the sense of a train journey reaching its terminal station: a train which is shunted into a circular siding will never reach its terminus; a train which crashes has certainly stopped moving but it hasn't 'terminated'.

Programmers, like train drivers, can often anticipate difficulties. A program execution can choose between alternatives just as a train can be switched between tracks. The desk calculator program might refuse to divide a by b when b is 0 and instead print a warning message. But then suppose that this calculation forms part of a long sequence of calculations: what should the calculator program do after it has printed the message? One very reasonable answer is: nothing; it should terminate immediately. This is rather like letting the passengers off at an intermediate station: the execution has *terminated prematurely*.

Instructions which describe premature termination enable us to short-circuit executions. They permit descriptions of programs which normally execute a sequence to its conclusion, but which sometimes terminate prematurely. This means that the program's sequence of actions can be described with repetitions, choices, procedure calls, recursions - all the usual structures - plus premature termination instructions which are modifiers of the normal execution structure.

Premature termination has more constructive uses than coping with program failure. In this book it is used to describe programs which search for a solution. One way of searching is to enumerate every candidate solution, testing each one as it arises and stopping as soon as a satisfactory candidate has been found. In such a program normal termination corresponds to failure of the search, premature termination to success. Failure and success of a search don't necessarily correspond to failure and success of the program, since you often hope that a search will fail - say when you are searching for counter-examples to a novel and exciting conjecture.

14.1 THE *terminate* INSTRUCTION

Premature termination applies only to sequences of executions. As with assignment instructions, you have to think of an execution as a sequence to make sense of premature termination. Consider, for example, program 14.1, which is bracketed with '*A:* ' and '*:A*'. Bracketing a program in this way provides a name with which its executions can be terminated. The program is described as an infinite loop and normally we expect execution to go on for ever, because *true* is always true. It prints a message, reads two numbers into containers *a* and b, prints *a+b*, prints a message, reads two numbers, .. and so on. But as soon as it reads a number *b* which is zero it prints a different message and terminates the execution of the sequence *A*. This short-circuits the infinite loop, and the execution stops.

```
A:  iterate true:
            initialise a,b :=?,?
            NL; printstring("type numbers to be divided");
            readnumber a; readnumber b;
            select b≠0: NL; printnumber(a+b)
                   b=0: NL; printstring("whoops!"); terminate A
            endselect
        enditerate
    :A
```

program 14.1

Premature termination short-circuits whatever structures are imposed on a sequence of executions. The *terminate* instruction of program 14.1 is within a sequence within a *select* within a sequence within a program within an *iterate*: premature termination cuts through them all.

Any *terminate X* instruction within brackets *X:* and *:X* will stop execution of the whole bracketed sequence no matter where it occurs. Program 14.2 is a rewriting of program 14.1 just to make that point. Although in this program *terminate A* is executed within a sequence within a procedure call within a *select* within a

A: *def main() = initialise a, b:=?, ?*
      NL; printstring("type numbers to be divided");
      readnumber a; readnumber b;
      select b≠0: NL; printnumber (a+b)
          b=0: crash()
          endselect
  enddef
  def crash() = NL; printstring("whoops!"); *terminate A enddef*
  iterate true: main() enditerate
  :A

program 14.2

sequence within a program within a procedure call within an *iterate* (puff!), the effect is just the same as that of program 14.1.

14.2 SUBSTITUTION DEFINITION OF *terminate*

The meaning of a *terminate* instruction is given in terms of the bracketed program within which it occurs. The *terminate* instruction and every instruction which follows it can be deleted (definition 14.1). Note from the definition that the *terminate* must occur in the body of a bracketed program: if it appears in a procedure definition then you must use substitution to bring it out into the body of the program. The bracketing names can be removed from a program once there are no more *terminate* instructions which refer to them (definition 14.2).

$$B: S_1; .. ; S_{i-1}; terminate\ B; S_{i+1}; .. :B$$
$$= B: S_1; ..; S_{i-1} :B$$

$$B: D_1 .. D_m \quad S_1; .. ; S_{i-1}; terminate\ B; S_{i+1}; .. :B$$
$$= B: D_1 .. D_m \quad S_1; .. ; S_{i-1} :B$$

definition 14.1

if B is not mentioned in P, then

$$B: P :B \ = \ P$$

definition 14.2

Because a *terminate* instruction deletes everything which follows it up to the closing bracket it is necessary to be careful about assignment instructions. An assignment which is moved over a *terminate* is lost from the program. This is alright, provided that the *initialise* definition which acquired the container affected by the assignment is one of the definitions of the bracketed program: then there can be no subsequent instructions which could take account of the assignment (definition 14.3).

Normally an assignment instruction cannot be moved past a *terminate* instruction. However:

> B: *initialise* $x:=f$ .. $x:=e$; *terminate* B .. :B
> = B: *initialise* $x:=f$ .. *terminate* B; $x:=e$ .. :B

definition 14.3

14.3 SHORT-CIRCUITING CALCULATIONS WITH *terminate-delivering*

Suppose that you have to write a procedure to discover whether a number k is prime or not: that is, to find out whether it has any factors other than k and one. This is naturally a repetitive calculation, and a good first guess would be to calculate the value of the formula

$$\forall i: 2 \leq i \leq k-1: i \text{ doesn't divide } k \text{ exactly}$$

This formula is the definition of what it is to be a prime number, and is true when k is prime, false when it isn't. To decide whether i divides k or not, it is only necessary to look at the remainder on division: if $k \, rem \, i$ is zero then i divides k exactly but if there is a non-zero remainder, it doesn't. So a repetitive calculation of whether k is prime or not could be as shown in program 14.3.

> *initially true*
> *for i rt* $2..k-1$ *do* $\wedge$ $(k \, rem \, i \neq 0)$ *od*

program 14.3

Now program 14.3 does far too much work, because there are well-known ways of getting the same answer with much less effort. It tests too many numbers: if k is divisible by i then $k \div i = j$ and k is also divisible by j; if i is larger than j then by the time program 14.3 gets to i, it must already have discovered that k is divisible by j. When i is larger than the square root of k then j is smaller and vice-versa. Therefore it is only necessary to check numbers on one side or the other of the square root. In general there are far fewer numbers below the square root than above, so a more sensible prime-number check is program 14.4.

> *initially true*
> *for i rt* $2..\sqrt{k}$ *do* $\wedge$ $(k \, rem \, i \neq 0)$ *od*

program 14.4

You can do better still: the program need test only odd numbers in the range $3..\sqrt{k}$, and only numbers divisible neither by two nor by three in the range $5..\sqrt{k}$, and so on. If you have a list of the prime numbers smaller than the square root of k then the program can be speeded up enormously. That is the technique of the

Sieve of Erastosthenes.

Ignore Erastosthenes's invention for the moment, and consider the question 'is $100\,000\,001$ a prime?'. The answer is no, because it has the factors 17 and $5\,882\,353$ (looks unlikely but it's true). The square root of the number is about ten thousand, so program 14.4 would do about ten thousand divisions in calculating an answer. Even if the repetition was based on a prime sieve it would still check more than a thousand primes between two and ten thousand. But of course the calculation can be short-circuited as soon as it is discovered that the number divides by seventeen, after only sixteen divisions in the brute force program or only seven in the case of the sieved program. Most numbers aren't prime - half of them are even! - so short-circuiting will make an enormous difference to the execution of the program.

Now it is a fact about the formula '$a \wedge b \wedge c \wedge .. \wedge z$' that its value is false so long as any of its component values is false, and true only if every component is true. Therefore we can think of calculating the value of a $\forall$-formula as a search for a false component: if we find one, we can terminate the search and deliver false; if we can't find any, we must deliver true. This is just the method of looking for a counter-example. Consider program 14.5, in which the calculation is expressed in terms of searching for a counter-example. The program presumes the answer is true until it is proved otherwise. Each time the program unsuccessfully divides k by i it does nothing more (since $x \wedge true$ is always the same as x); if once the division succeeds then the calculation terminates prematurely and delivers false.

> *initially true*
> *for i rt* $2..\sqrt{k}$ *do*
>   *select k rem i = 0: deliver false*
>   *k rem i ≠ 0: ∧ true*
>   *endselect*
> *od*

program 14.5

It is often very convenient to express short-circuited calculations in terms of instruction executions. Program 14.5 delivers false prematurely or delivers true if none of the divisions succeeds: program 14.6 expresses the same thing by using

> *B: for i rt* $2..\sqrt{k}$ *do*
>   *select k rem i = 0: terminate B delivering false*
>   *k rem i ≠ 0: donothing*
>   *endselect*
> *od;*
> *terminate B delivering true*
> *:B*

program 14.6

a sequence of instructions. This program looks even more like a search than the one before. It gratefully delivers a value if it can do so prematurely and immediately abandons its computation; it delivers a final value only if it has to, when all searches have failed to find a factor. That is what searching is about: you know you haven't found something until you find it; once you find it you can give up and stop searching; you know it isn't there only after you have looked in every possible place and failed to find it in any of them.

In program 14.6 the instruction sequence B: .. :B is turned into a formula by use of the *terminate-delivering* instruction. The program is a formula because if you execute it, it delivers a value rather than producing an effect. So you might reasonably write

$$printboolean(B: .. :B)$$

which would print either 'true' or 'false' according to whether k is prime or not. You might write the formula as the body of a procedure definition

$$def\,prime(k) = B: .. :B\ enddef$$

so that *prime*(x) delivers either true or false according to whether or not x is a prime number. You could write the formula as a condition-formula in a *select* instruction, and so on.

The *deliver* instruction

Programs like program 14.6 are a little unwieldy and it is often most convenient to write them as the body of a procedure definition. In such a case my notation permits a shorthand: *deliver F* in the body of a procedure definition means terminate the execution of the procedure body and deliver the value of the formula *F*. The complete rule is shown in definition 14.4. Thus I can miss out the brackets B: and :B, and I may define a procedure which calculates whether or not k is prime as in program 14.7.

$$B: .. \text{ terminate } B \text{ delivering } F .. :B \ = \ (\!(.. \text{ deliver } F ..)\!)$$

definition 14.4

$$def\,prime(k) = for\ i\ rt\ 2..\sqrt{k}\ do\ select\ k\,rem\,i = 0:\ deliver\,false$$
$$k\,rem\,i \neq 0:\ donothing$$
$$endselect$$
$$od;$$
$$deliver\ true$$
$$enddef$$

program 14.7

14.4 SHORT-CIRCUITING RECURSIVE CALCULATIONS

The examples above are based on a repetitive definition of the meaning of a $\forall$-formula. There are alternative recursive definitions, very reminiscent of those given in chapter 6 for the *for-do* instruction. For example:

$$\forall i: a{\leq}i{\leq}b: F = \text{(when } a{>}b) \quad true$$
$$\text{(when } a{\leq}b) \quad F[i\backslash a] \wedge (\forall i: a{+}1{\leq}i{\leq}b: F)$$
$$\text{(when } a{\leq}b) \quad (\forall i: a{\leq}i{\leq}b{-}1: F) \wedge F[i\backslash b]$$

Using part of this definition, plus the facts that $x{\wedge}true = x$, $x{\wedge}false = false$, I can construct the *prime* procedure shown in program 14.8.

```
def prime(k) = indivisible(k, 2, √k) enddef
def indivisible(x, a, b) =
    select a>b: true
           a≤b: select x rem a = 0: false
                       x rem a ≠ 0: indivisible(x, a+1, b)
                endselect
        endselect
    enddef
```

program 14.8

The definition of *indivisible* in program 14.8 isn't an attractive recursive procedure definition. It exhibits what is called *tail recursion*. An execution of *indivisible* either delivers true, delivers false, or delivers what a recursive execution of the same procedure delivers. It is unnecessary to have one execution depending on another in this way, and tail recursion can always be removed, replacing it with an *iterate* instruction.

The recursive call is replaced by an assignment to some variables which track the values of the arguments: see program 14.9, for example. Here $a1$ and $b1$ represent the arguments a and b; the call $indivisible(x, a{+}1, b)$ is replaced by $a1:=a1{+}1$; the *iterate* terminates normally if the search fails and then the program delivers true.

```
def indivisible(x, a, b) =
    initialise a1, b1 := a, b
    iterate a1≤b1: select x rem a1 = 0: deliver false
                          x rem a1 ≠ 0: a1:=a1+1
                   endselect
        enditerate;
        deliver true
    enddef
```

program 14.9

14.5 SUBSTITUTION DEFINITION OF *terminate-delivering*

The definition of the *terminate-delivering* instruction (and via that definition, of the *deliver* instruction) is very similar to the definition of the *terminate* instruction. It applies to bracketed sequences of instructions or bracketed programs, and it eliminates instructions which follow it in the sequence (definition 14.5). You can eliminate a *terminate-delivering* instruction and the brackets around the program in which it occurs when the program has been reduced to a single *terminate-delivering* instruction (definition 14.6). Assignment instructions may be moved past a *terminate-delivering* in order to produce a single-element instruction sequence but, as with *terminate*, you can only do this with assignments whose definitions are entirely included in the bracketed program (definition 14.7).

$$B: S_1; \, .. \, ; S_{i-1}; \textit{ terminate B delivering } F; S_{i+1}; \, .. \, ; S_n : B$$
$$= B: S_1; \, .. \, ; S_{i-1}; \textit{ terminate B delivering } F : B$$

$$B: D_1 \, .. \, D_m \quad S_1; \, .. \, ; S_{i-1}; \textit{ terminate B delivering } F; S_{i+1}; \, .. \, ; S_n : B$$
$$= B: D_1 \, .. \, D_m \quad S_1; \, .. \, ; S_{i-1}; \textit{ terminate B delivering } F : B$$

definition 14.5

$$B: \textit{ terminate B delivering } F : B \; = \; F$$

definition 14.6

Normally an assignment instruction cannot be moved past a *terminate-delivering* instruction. However:

$$B: \textit{ initialise } x := f \, .. \, x := e; \textit{ terminate B delivering } F \, .. : B$$
$$= B: \textit{ initialise } x := f \, .. \, \textit{ terminate B delivering } F[x \backslash e]; x := e \, .. : B$$

definition 14.7

-=-=-=-=-=-=-=-=-=-=-=-=-

Exercise 14.1
Prove that when $k=9$, program 14.6 is equivalent to *false*.

Exercise 14.2
Prove that when $k=11$, program 14.6 is equivalent to *true*.

-=-=-=-=-=-=-=-=-=-=-=-=-

Formulas with side effects

def silly(k) $=$ *printstring*("the answer is "); *deliver k+3 enddef*
for i rt $1..10$ *do NL; printnumber(silly(i)) od*

program 14.10

What sense are you to make of program 14.10? If you transcribe and execute this program, its effect in any programming system that I have ever come across will be to print a sequence of lines:

```
the answer is 4
the answer is 5
          . .
the answer is 13
```

The program doesn't make sense at all, according to definitions 14.5, 14.6 and 14.7. The instruction *printnumber*(*silly*(1)) requires that *silly*(1) should be replaced by a number formula. Substituting the body of *silly* produces the instruction formula

printstring(*S*:*printstring*("the answer is "); *terminate S delivering* 1+3:*S*)

which doesn't fit any of the definitions so far.

In execution terms there is no difficulty in explaining what happens. To execute *printnumber*(*silly*(1)) first the value of *silly*(1) must be calculated. To do this an environment is created in which *k* means 1, then the body of *silly* is executed within that environment. The instructions of *silly* are first of all *printstring*, which prints a message "the answer is", followed by a *deliver* instruction which delivers *k*+3: in that environment this is 1+3, which is 4. The value 4 is therefore delivered as the result of *silly*(1) and *printnumber*(4) is executed.

The difficulties with program 14.10 could be overcome (see, for example, definition 14.8 below). The real problem with the definition of *silly* is that it breaks the basic principle of substitution, that replacing one sub-formula with an equal sub-formula doesn't change the meaning of the whole. Consider programs 14.11 and 14.12. In execution terms the procedure call *silly*(2) certainly delivers 10, so each certainly prints 10. But how many times will they print "the answer is "? In most programming systems program 14.11 will print it once and program 14.12 will print it twice[†]. Yet definition 6.3 makes it clear that programs 14.11 and 14.12 are equivalent.

> *let n*=*silly*(2)
> *printnumber*(*n*+*n*)   *printnumber*(*silly*(2)+*silly*(2))
>
> **program 14.11**   **program 14.12**

Silly(*x*) is an example of a formula calculation which has a **side effect**: an effect on the state of things. In general side effects are unhelpful things, as you will see. The *silly* procedure is dangerous to reasoning!

I do not intend to present a complete solution to the *silly* problem in this book. The outline of a solution would be as follows: a formula like *silly*(2) whose

---

[†] Some very clever 'optimising' programming systems may take program 14.12 and deduce that, since *silly*(2) is a number formula there can be no justification for calculating its value twice. Such a system might well convert program 14.12 into program 14.11!

calculation affects the state of affairs must be *simplified* before it is substituted. Simplification involves the replacement of procedure calls by procedure bodies and the use of definitions like 14.8. That rule enables you to calculate the effect of a procedure call like *silly*(2) in just the same way that a programming system does.

If

    (a) definitions D_1 .. D_m do not bind any of the names in formula p;

    (b) those definitions, together with instructions S_1 .. S_n, do not mention B;

    (c) none of the instructions S_1 .. S_n affect the value of p;

then the instruction formula

$$p(B: D_1 .. D_m \ S_1; ..; S_n; terminate \ B \ delivering \ F:B)$$

is equivalent to the program

$$D_1 .. D_m \ S_1; ..; S_n; p(F)$$

definition 14.8

Definition 14.8 shows how the meaning of program 14.10 could be incorporated into the substitution scheme. This definition only covers value-delivering formulas used as arguments in procedure calls: a more general definition could cover the use of formulas in *times-do*, *for-do*, *select* and *iterate* instructions as well as formulas on the right-hand side of assignment instructions.

The third condition in definition 14.8 says that the bracketed program shouldn't alter the meaning of formula p. You may not yet have encountered programs which alter the meaning of procedure formulas (they certainly exist, although there are none of them in this book) but you are familiar with programs which alter the meanings of other sorts of formulas and they too have a bearing on the meaning of *terminate-delivering* instructions.

Consider, for example, program 14.13. In execution terms, to calculate the value of the formula *a+nasty*(1) it is necessary to find out the values of its components and to combine them according to the rules of calculation of my notation. Most programming systems work from left to right: that is, they would find out the value of *a*, which is a container name, so they would look in the container called *a* and find zero. To find out the value of *nasty*(1) it is necessary to find out the values of *nasty* and of 1 (both are constants in this program, so there is nothing to do there), to create an environment in which $n=1$ and to execute the body of *nasty* within it. That program first alters the value held in container *a* (in this

> *initialise a:=?;*
> *def nasty(n) = a:=a+1; deliver a+n enddef*
>
> *a:=0; NL; printnumber(a+nasty(1));*
> *a:=0; printchar(','); printnumber(nasty(1)+a);*

program 14.13

case making it hold one) and then delivers $a+n$, which in this case will be two. Finally the program adds together the numbers it has calculated and prints 2.

The truly nasty thing about program 14.13 is that, although we believe that in general $x+y$ should mean the same as $y+x$, left-to-right calculation means that the second *printnumber* instruction prints 3.

-=-=-=-=-=-=-=-=-=-=-=-=-=-

Exercise 14.3
Show that with left-to-right calculation, the second *printnumber* in program 14.13 would print 3.

Exercise 14.4
Show that if program 14.13 was executed by a programming system which calculates the value of a formula from right to left, it would print '3' followed by '2'.

Exercise 14.5
Find out what your own programming system would print given a transcription of program 14.13.

-=-=-=-=-=-=-=-=-=-=-=-=-=-

Programming systems don't have to decide on a fixed order of calculation. Some calculate left to right, some right to left, some whichever way is convenient in particular circumstances. So you might see '2,2' or '2,3' or '3,2' or '3,3' if you were to execute program 14.13. This program is truly ambiguous and that sort of ambiguity is not to be applauded.

If

    (a) definitions $D_1 .. D_m$ do not bind any of the names in formula g;

    (b) those definitions, together with instructions $S_1 .. S_n$, do not mention B;

then the formula

$$g+(B: D_1 .. D_m \ S_1; ..; S_n; \text{ terminate } B \text{ delivering } F:B)$$

is equivalent to either of the formulas

$$B: \text{initialise } t:=g \ D_1 .. D_m \ S_1; ..; S_n; \text{ terminate } B \text{ delivering } t+F:B$$
$$B: D_1 .. D_m \ S_1; ..; S_n; \text{ terminate } B \text{ delivering } g+F:B$$

definition 14.9

Definition 14.9 gives more of the horrible story and uncovers the ambiguity in program 14.13. It gives two alternative meanings for a calculation which involves a *terminate-delivering* instruction: one in which the value of formula g is remembered in a container t (that equivalence corresponds to left-to-right calculation) and the other in which g is calculated at the end of the bracketed program (which corresponds to right-to-left calculation). Although this definition applies only to addition calculations it should be obvious that a more general definition could be written which would extend the same principle to all other formula calculations (other operators, value-delivering procedure calls, and so on).

-=-=-=-=-=-=-=-=-=-=-=-

Exercise 14.6
Verify that definition 14.9 can give by substitution all the answers that execution of program 14.13 can.

Exercise 14.7
Definition 14.8 does not apply when the bracketed program alters the value of formula *p*. Construct a definition, similar to definition 14.9, which does apply in such a case; make sure that your version allows for pre- and post-calculation of the value of *p*.

-=-=-=-=-=-=-=-=-=-=-=-

Programs like 14.10 and 14.13 are in doubtful taste. We don't expect the calculation of a formula to affect the state of the world - to print something on a screen or to alter the values of some containers within a program. You can be unpleasantly surprised if you write such a program unwittingly. The surprise is most painful if there is any ambiguity in the program's meaning because the programming system may often find an interpretation which surprises you. Worse, different systems on different machines may find different interpretations.

Definitions 14.8 and 14.9 are only part of the truth. The complete set of substitution rules would take so long to state and explain that I do not hesitate to omit them from this book. For the sake of simple substitutions I have restricted myself to value-delivering procedures which have no side effects and I suggest that you do likewise.

Hacking out more of the truth

Every computing machine is a designer's attempt to imitate an ideal computing machine and for all sorts of reasons the attempt is bound to fail: for example, computers are finite whereas an ideal machine might be infinite. The detailed definition of a mechanical code will always leave a loophole somewhere where the real machinery doesn't exactly match the ideal machine. If 'programming' is the activity of design and 'coding' is the activity of forcing programs into a mechanical straitjacket then 'hacking' is the business of finding loose places in the straitjacket[†]. It is a nasty business if done for real and the knowledge you gain is treacherous and unsure. But it is harmless if you treat it just as fun: a sort of problem-solving, finding and exploiting accidental features of a programming

---

[†] Newspapers and television have recently adopted the word 'hacking' to describe the business of finding your way into other people's computers and getting at their secret data. I use the term in another sense, to describe the activity of laying about yourself with sharpened knowledge of lots of programming instructions. In any case it has a much more innocent meaning in its original American English.

system. When programs go wrong a programming system may produce odd results and often those results can only be completely explained if you know every nook and cranny of the system. For example, the crannies explored by the following exercises.

-=-=-=-=-=-=-=-=-=-=-=-=-

Exercise 14.8
By defining two procedures f and g and evaluating the formula $f(0)+g(0)$ you should be able to find out whether your system evaluates formulas from left to right or from right to left.

Exercise 14.9
Write a program which investigates the order of evaluation of bracketed expressions within a formula.

Exercise 14.10
In evaluating the formula $f(0)+f(0)$ a programming system might decide to evaluate $f(0)$ twice and add the results together, or it might equally reasonably evaluate it only once and double the answer. Find out which strategy your system follows.

-=-=-=-=-=-=-=-=-=-=-=-=-

Hacking is a grubby business. It has its place: like the people who keep old car engines going using bits of bent wire and glue in place of the proper parts, hacking is sometimes the only way to get what you want. But who wants to rely on a program design held together with logical safety pins?

14.6 IMITATING PREMATURE TERMINATION WITH *goto*

Many mechanical codes have an equivalent of the *deliver* instruction for value-delivering procedures. Some have an equivalent of *terminate* for procedures and some repetitions. Really old-fashioned ones don't have either, and you have to fall back on the more primitive mechanism which they usually offer.

Goto instructions apply to the position of execution within a sequence, and use labels which mark positions within sequences. The instruction '*goto L*', where both the label L and the *goto* instruction appear within the same instruction sequence, means

abandon execution of the sequence and restart at the position labelled L.

Terminate instructions apply to executions of sequences. If an instruction sequence X is a sub-sequence of another sequence, then the effect of executing *terminate X* is to move on to the instruction which follows X in the larger sequence. If the position after X is labelled L then *goto L* has the same meaning as *terminate X*.

Therefore, to make your program fit a code which doesn't include *terminate* transcribe

$$T: S_1; .. S_n :T$$

into

$$S_1; .. S_n; <label\ T> donothing$$

and replace every instance of *terminate T* by *goto T*.

Reading programs which include *goto* instructions

You may at some time in your career be confronted by a program which is written using *goto* instructions and be asked to make sense of it. If the *goto* instructions have been used carefully to imitate normal programming constructs then the program won't be too hard to understand. Unfortunately it is very easy to misuse the *goto* instruction, which is why hardly anybody defends its use any more.

Goto instructions are used to imitate repetition and termination and sometimes to describe choices. The way to understand a program which includes *goto* instructions is to construct the program which it imitates. Unfortunately again, there is no mechanism which can transcribe programs that use *goto* instructions into programs which don't. Instead you have to attempt a translation.

*Goto*s used to implement repetition usually have something to do with *if-then* instructions and always refer to a label placed in the sequence before the *goto* itself. For example, the program

$$i:=1; <label\ L> if\ i\leq 3\ then\ print*; i:=i+1; goto\ L\ fi$$

is imitating a repetition: the *goto* instruction causes execution of the *if-then* to be abandoned and then a new execution created. Each time it restarts it is equivalent to *donothing* if *i* is greater than 3. So this program is equivalent to

$$i:=1; iterate\ i\leq 3: print*; i:=i+1\ enditerate$$

which in its turn is equivalent to

$$times\ 3\ do\ print*\ od;\ i:=3$$

*Goto*s are sometimes used to describe choices when a code demands choice between single instructions and doesn't provide any means of bracketing programs to make single instructions. For example, the program

$$if\ i\neq 0\ then\ goto\ L1\ fi;$$
$$print*; NL; goto\ L2;$$
$$<label\ L1>\ NL; printchar('x');$$
$$<label\ L2>$$

describes a choice between two sequences. Either *print*; *NL* is executed, and then the program terminates, or *NL*; *printchar*('x') is executed and then the program terminates. It is obviously equivalent to

> *select i=0*: *print**; *NL*
> *i≠0*: *NL*; *printchar*('x')
> *endselect*

*Goto*s which imitate termination, including termination which is used to imitate a *terminate-delivering* instruction, will be recognisable because they use the techniques described above.

It may take quite a lot of effort and not a little inspiration to unravel the tangle of a program based on *goto* instructions, but never despair: it can always be done.

14.7 IMITATING *deliver* AND *terminate-delivering*

If your mechanical code doesn't have an equivalent of *terminate-delivering* or *deliver*, it is possible to imitate them using assignment and a *terminate* instruction. Then if it doesn't have a *terminate* instruction you can in turn imitate that with a *goto*.

> *printnumber*(*X*: *for i rt a..b do select p(i)*: *terminate X delivering i*
> ¬*p(i)*: *donothing*
> *endselect*
> *od*;
> *terminate X delivering b+1 :X*)

program 14.14

> *X*: *for i rt a..b do select p(i)*: *t:=i*; *terminate X*
> ¬*p(i)*: *donothing*
> *endselect*
> *od*;
> *t:=b+1*
> :*X*;
> *printnumber(t)*

program 14.15

Suppose that your program includes a formula which is a bracketed instruction sequence using *terminate-delivering* instructions. This can always be replaced by a program which first assigns the value of the offending formula to a container *t* and then uses a formula which has *t* in place of the original bracketed sequence. Usually *t* will be a new container not used elsewhere in the program. For example, program 14.14 prints the first number in the range *a..b* for which *p* delivers true, or else prints *b+1* if it can't find such a number. It is equivalent to program 14.15, which first assigns the value of the number which would be printed by program 14.14 into a container *t* and then prints what was placed in *t*.

-=-=-=-=-=-=-=-=-=-=-=-

Exercise 14.11
Write the *goto* equivalent of program 14.15.

-==

APPENDIX 14.A PREMATURE TERMINATION IN PASCAL

Pascal has no premature termination instructions.

Imitating *terminate* in Pascal

Terminate must be imitated with *goto*, as described in section 14.6 above. Labels are written in Pascal as sequences of decimal digits followed by a colon - for example, 1:, 2:, 3:, 105:, 99:. The labels are just tags: they don't have any numerical significance.

If the body of a program or a procedure definition includes a label I then that label must be 'declared' at the beginning of the program or procedure. Before any type, variable, procedure or function definitions you write

```
label I;
```

For example, the transcription into Pascal of a program which reads two numbers and then performs like program 14.15 might be as shown in figure 14.1.

```
program findit(input,output);
  label 99;
  var i,a,b,t:integer;
  function p(i:integer):boolean; begin ..<some action>.. end;

  begin read(a); read(b);
    for i := a to b do
      if p(i) then begin t:=i; goto 99 end
            else begin end;
    t:=b+1;
  99:
    write(t)
  end.
```

figure 14.1

Imitating *deliver* in Pascal

Values are delivered from Pascal functions by writing the pseudo-assignment
instruction N:=F, where N is the name of the function and F is the formula
whose value is to be delivered. The value delivered is always the latest value to
be 'assigned' in this way. *Deliver F* may therefore be imitated as N:=F followed
by a *goto* instruction which terminates execution of the procedure body. For
example, first transcribe program 14.7 into the Pascal-fit program 14.16, which
can then be transcribed into Pascal as in figure 14.2.

$$def\ prime(k) = for\ i\ rt\ 2..\sqrt{k}\ do\ select\ k\ rem\ i = 0:\ t:=false;\ goto\ 99$$
$$k\ rem\ i \neq 0:\ donothing$$
$$endselect$$
$$od;$$
$$t:=true$$
$$<label\ 99>\ deliver\ t$$
$$enddef$$

program 14.16

```
function prime(k:integer):boolean;
  label 99;
  var i: integer;
  begin for i := 2 to sqrt(k) do
          if (k mod i) = 0 then begin prime:=false; goto 99 end
                           else begin end;
       prime:=true;
     99:
  end;
```

figure 14.2

APPENDIX 14.B SOME PROGRAMS TO TRY

Exercise 14.12
Try the *silly, nasty* and hacking examples of section 14.5.

Exercise 14.13
Write a procedure *forall* so that *forall*(a, b, p) delivers the value of the formula

$$\forall i:\ a \leq i \leq b:\ p(i)$$

Exercise 14.14
Write a procedure *exists* so that *exists*(a, b, p) delivers the value of the formula

$$\exists i:\ a \leq i \leq b:\ p(i)$$

Exercise 14.15
Write a program which calculates and prints the value of the formula

$$\exists i:\ 25 \leq i \leq 30:\ prime(i)$$

Exercise 14.16
Write a program which calculates and prints the value of the formula

$$\exists i:\ 25 \leq i \leq 40:\ prime(i)$$

Exercise 14.17
Write a program which calculates and prints the value of the formula

$$\forall x:\ a \leq x \leq b:\ \exists y:\ a \leq y \leq b:\ y\ divides\ x\ exactly$$

Choose some interesting numbers a and b to test your program.

Part Three
SOME EXTENDED EXAMPLES

Programming is a kind of problem-solving and almost any problem has more than one solution. The novice programmer sometimes expects that it must be possible to see the best solution to a problem and that experienced programmers never experiment with alternative solutions. Not so: we all make experiments when programming novel problems.

Making experiments isn't the same as proceeding blindly. We are helped because there are relatively few *shapes* or *structures* of program that we can recognise, and any solution we propose must conform to one of these shapes. For the kind of programming described in this book the structures are:

(a) *Sequence*: the program is a sequence of instructions, each with different effect.

(b) *Choice*: the program is a choice between alternative actions, each with different effect.

(c) *Repetition*: the program is a repetition of the same instruction, each execution being systematically related to the last.

(d) *Recursion*: the program is a parameterised sequence, choice or repetition in which some of the actions call upon the same program.

Any solution to a programming problem must be a sequence, a choice, a repetition or a recursive definition. There are other kinds of control structure, outside the scope of this book, and no doubt others will be invented as computer science develops. But there will always be a limited number, and you will always have to use one of the structures which you know and which your programming notation allows. Therefore the first step in finding a programming solution to a problem is to choose a structure for your program.

A program will normally contain many smaller structures within its overall structure - typically there will be structures within structures within structures .. When you design a program you will have to take many separate decisions about which structure to use and they will often be inter-related. It is normal to repeat the process more than once!

It is usually possible to envisage alternative solutions to a problem which use alternative structures. This is most often the case with repetition and recursion:

what you can do with a repetition you can always do with a recursion and vice-versa.

Programming is a creative activity and creation is sometimes a painful business, especially when you make mistakes and have to correct them. There is in the end no substitute for experiment, but as far as possible the experimenting should be conducted away from the pressures of computer systems because computer systems force you to concentrate on detail and ignore questions of design. When you are very experienced experiments can happen inside your head without anything being written down, but you must expect at first to experiment laboriously, writing down lots of different solutions and rejecting all but the best of them.

Chapter 15
PRINTING A NUMERAL WITH REPETITION

A numeral is a sequence of digits. To print a numeral a computer must print a sequence of digit characters. Suppose that your computer system could print characters but had no equivalent of *printnumber*. How could you program it to imitate *printnumber*?

15.1 CHOOSING A PROGRAM STRUCTURE

The first step in planning a solution is to choose a program structure. A program which uses the typewriter style of printing must print the digits of a numeral left-to-right in order. Printing a sequence of digits is clearly a repetition: perhaps the program might have the structure

> *for j rt <.. some sequence ..> do*
> *.. print the jth digit of the numeral ..*
> *od*

program 15.1

If I choose this structure - and it is very attractive - there is an immediate problem. Designing a *for-do* program includes deciding the sequence of values it will run through: in making that decision I am defining the number of digits in any numeral which will be printed by my program. This is a drawback of the design, and recognising it immediately makes program 15.1 much less attractive. If I choose a short sequence, so that the program always prints three digits, for example, then large numbers will be cut short: instead of printing 14783 the program might print 147, or perhaps 783, or even 478, none of which is a correct numeral representation of the number. If I choose a long sequence, so that the program prints, say, ten digits, then small numbers will be elongated: instead of printing 231 the program might print 0000000231, which is a correct representation but unnecessarily confusing to read.

Perhaps program 15.1 might be useful as part of a solution. If the program first
calculates how many digits ought to be printed and then uses an instruction like
program 15.1, the difficulty is avoided. This structure of this alternative solution
is a sequence:

> *Find out how many digits must be printed;*
> *for j rt <.. a sequence of the length decided ..> do*
> *.. print the jth digit of the numeral ..*
> *od*

program 15.2

The rest of this chapter explores the consequences of this design decision, which
does actually point to a useful program.

You should notice that the design shown in program 15.2 wasn't entirely the
product of rational argument. The need for a sequence structure was a fairly
rational choice, once I had decided to use a *for-do* instruction to print the digits of
the numeral, but the choice of a *for-do* - even the choice of repetition - was
nothing more than a guess. It would be best at this stage to consider other
solution structures and to see which of the possible ones seems preferable. In this
chapter I develop program 15.2 into a finished definition without considering any
other structure. In real programming life it is better to proceed more carefully,
considering various alternative solutions before undertaking a detailed
investigation of any of them.

15.2 PRINTING THE *J*TH DIGIT

The second stage in constructing a programming solution is to fill in the parts of
the structure. Program 15.2 has two parts, which can be tackled in either order. I
choose to construct first a program which prints a numeral, assuming that the
length of the numeral - the number of digits it contains - has already been
calculated.

In any positional numeral notation - decimal, binary, octal, hexadecimal, the base
thirteen funny numerals of chapter 12, and so on - the quantity represented by a
digit symbol in a numeral depends on its position in the numeral. Although '2'
means two and in the decimal numeral '12' it stands for the quantity two, in the
decimal numeral '24' it stands for twenty and in the decimal numeral '248' it
stands for two hundred. In binary numerals each digit symbol stands for its own
value multiplied by a power of two which depends on its position:

$$\text{binary } 111001 = 1{\times}2^5{+}1{\times}2^4{+}1{\times}2^3{+}0{\times}2^2{+}0{\times}2^1{+}1{\times}2^0$$
$$= \text{thirty-two + sixteen + eight + one}$$
$$= \text{fifty-seven}$$

Similarly in quintal (base five) the digit values are multiplied by powers of five:

quintal $3124 = 3 \times 5^3 + 1 \times 5^2 + 2 \times 5^1 + 4 \times 5^0$

$\qquad\qquad\quad$ = three hundred and seventy-five + twenty-five + ten + four

$\qquad\qquad\quad$ = four hundred and fourteen

and in decimal (base ten) they are multiplied by powers of ten:

$\qquad$ decimal $817 = 8 \times \text{ten}^2 + 1 \times \text{ten}^1 + 7 \times \text{ten}^0$

$\qquad\qquad\qquad\quad$ = eight hundred + ten + seven

$\qquad\qquad\qquad\quad$ = eight hundred and seventeen

The way in which we calculate the value represented by a numeral using powers of two, five, ten (or whatever the base happens to be) which increase from right to left suggests strongly that we might number the digits in a numeral from right to left even though we print them from left to right. The rightmost digit is number 0, the one before it digit number 1, the one before that digit number 2, and so on. In an i-digit numeral they can be numbered from 0 to $i-1$:

$$d_{i-1} d_{i-2} .. d_1 d_0$$

The value described by the numeral is

$$\sum_{j=0}^{j=i-1} d_j b^j$$

where b is the number base of the numeral. We can use this numbering scheme to make the calculation of a particular digit value precise: it is the value d_j which should be represented in position j of the numeral.

How might a program calculate the value of a particular digit? The formula above gives a clue, and the same clue is given by the number-reading program 12.9. That program multiplies the number by the numeral base (thirteen in its case) before adding the next digit. If you take the number after a particular repetition and divide by the base b the remainder will be the digit just added in. That is, the formula $n \, rem \, b$ gives the value of d_0, the *last* digit of the numeral. The value which should be given to d_1 might be calculated in several ways. Two of them are as follows:

$\qquad (n \div b) \, rem \, b \qquad$ [the last digit of the numeral $d_{i-1}..d_1$]

$\qquad (n \, rem \, b^2) \div b \qquad$ [the first digit of the numeral $d_1 d_0$]

The value which should be given to d_2 might be calculated in a similar way

$\qquad (n \div b^2) \, rem \, b \qquad$ [the last digit of the numeral $d_{i-1}..d_2$]

$\qquad (n \, rem \, b^3) \div b^2 \qquad$ [the first digit of the numeral $d_2 d_1 d_0$]

and d_3 is either $(n \div b^3) \, rem \, b$ or $(n \, rem \, b^4) \div b^3$, and so on for d_4, d_5, .., d_{i-1}. In general d_j is $(n \div b^j) \, rem \, b$ or $(n \, rem \, b^{j+1}) \div b^j$. In this pair of formulas I prefer the first just because it is simpler to calculate.

Just as the number-reading program 12.9 had to calculate a digit value given a digit character, so the number-printing program must calculate a digit character given a digit value. This can be done by exhaustive comparison, as usual. Then if i is the number of digits to be printed, a program which prints the funny numeral notation of chapter 12 might be

$def\ digchar(n) = case\ n\ of$ 0:'a'   1:'b'   2:'c'   3:'d'   4:'e'
                        5:'f'   6:'g'   7:'h'   8:'i'   9:'j'
                        10:'k'   11:'l'   12:'m'
                    $endcase$
$enddef$
$def\ digval(n,j) = (n+13^j)\ rem\ 13\ enddef$
$for\ j\ rbt\ 0..i-1\ do\ printchar(digchar(digval(n,j)))\ od$

program 15.3

Provided that you know i, the number of digits in the numeral to be printed, this program is quite adequate. Notice that it uses *runningbackthrough* to generate the digits from left to right in the correct order.

As an example execution of program 15.3, suppose that n is three hundred and two and i is 3. This will lead to the sequence of executions

$printchar(digchar(digval(302, 2)))$
$= printchar(digchar((302+13^2)\ rem\ 13))$
$= printchar(digchar((302+169)\ rem\ 13))$
$= printchar(digchar(1\ rem\ 13))$
$= printchar(digchar(1))$
$= printchar('b')$

$printchar(digchar(digval(302, 1)))$
$= printchar(digchar((302+13^1)\ rem\ 13))$
$= printchar(digchar((302+13)\ rem\ 13))$
$= printchar(digchar(23\ rem\ 13))$
$= printchar(digchar(10))$
$= printchar('k')$

$printchar(digchar(digval(302, 0)))$
$= printchar(digchar((302+13^0)\ rem\ 13))$
$= printchar(digchar((302+1)\ rem\ 13))$
$= printchar(digchar(302\ rem\ 13))$
$= printchar(digchar(3))$
$= printchar('d')$

The program thus prints 'bkd'.

-=-=-=-=-=-=-=-=-=-=-=-

Exercise 15.1
Check that 'bkd' is a correct funny numeral representation of three hundred and two.

-=-=-=-=-=-=-=-=-=-=-=-=-

Program 15.3 is rather strange because it doesn't print in a familiar notation. Program 15.4 is a little more reasonable: *printn(x, w, r)* prints a number *x* as *w* digits in any base *r* up to twenty, and for bases up to ten it uses the conventional decimal digit notation.

> *def printn(n, i, b)* =
> > *def digchar(n)* = *case n of*   0: '0'   1: '1'   2: '2'   3: '3'   4: '4'
> >   5: '5'   6: '6'   7: '7'   8: '8'   9: '9'
> >   10: 'A'   11: 'B'   12: 'C'   13: 'D'   14: 'E'
> >   15: 'F'   16: 'G'   17: 'H'   18: 'I'   19: 'J'
> >   *endcase*
> > *enddef*
> >
> > *def digval(n, j)* = $(n \div b^j)$ *rem b enddef*
> >
> > *for j rbt* 0..*i*−1 *do printchar(digchar(digval(n, j))) od*
> > *enddef*

program 15.4

-=-=-=-=-=-=-=-=-=-=-=-=-

Exercise 15.2
Verify that *printn*(302, 9, 2) prints '100101110', the correct binary numeral representation of three hundred and two.

Exercise 15.3
Find out what is printed by *printn*(302, 2, 20). Verify that it is a correct base twenty representation of three hundred and two.

Exercise 15.4
Verify that *printn*(302, 3, 10) prints '302', that *printn*(302, 4, 10) prints '0302', that *printn*(302, 5, 10) prints '00302'.

Exercise 15.5
Verify that *printn*(302, 2, 10) prints a sequence which is a decimal numeral but is *not* a correct decimal representation of three hundred and two.

-=-=-=-=-=-=-=-=-=-=-=-=-

15.3 CALCULATING THE LENGTH OF A NUMERAL

Exercises 15.2-15.5 should persuade you that the *printn* procedure of program 15.4 gives a correct answer provided that the number *i*, which controls the length of the numeral printed, is not too small. It gives the most pleasing answer provided that *i* is not too large. If *i* is too large the procedure prints some 'leading zeros' in front of the numeral, printing 00065 rather than 65, for example. The zeros are distracting but they don't affect the meaning of the numeral. The original design decision to use a *for-do* seems to have paid off, but to make a complete solution I must find out how to calculate the value of *i*.

The value of *i* clearly has something to do with powers of *b*, the base in which the numeral is to be printed. The smaller the base, the larger the value of *i* in most cases. To print three hundred and two in binary notation *i* must be at least ten; to print it in decimal it need only be three.

The largest number which can be printed as a three-digit decimal numeral is nine hundred and ninety-nine ($999=\text{ten}^3-1$); the largest number which can be printed as a three-digit binary numeral is seven ($111=\text{two}^3-1$). It is an obvious generalisation to say that the largest number which can be printed as an *i*-digit numeral in base *b* is b^i-1. The smallest non-negative number which can be printed in *i* digits is zero in any base, but the smallest number which *needs i* digits (that is, which can't be printed in *i*-1 digits) is b^{i-1}. For example, in decimal numerals the smallest number which needs three digits is one hundred ($100=\text{ten}^2=\text{ten}^{3-1}$); in binary numerals it is four ($100=\text{two}^2=\text{two}^{3-1}$).

So the value of *i* we require is the one which makes the following formula true:

$$b^{i-1} \le n < b^i$$

How can the program calculate this number? Normally you might use some pre-calculated tables (for example, logarithms) or some program designed by someone else (for example, a calculator). I want to design an instruction which calculates *i* using only the simple arithmetic operations +, −, ×, / and exponentiation.

I take 'calculate a value of *i*' to mean 'assign a value to a container *i*'. So my procedure definition will read:

> *def printn2* (*n, b*) =
> .. *define digchar and digval* ..
> *initialise i* := .. *something* ..
> .. *assign a value to i somehow* ..
> *for j rbt* 0..*i*−1 *do printchar* (*digchar* (*digval* (*n, j*)))
> *enddef*

The instruction I choose to assign a value to *i* could be a single assignment instruction - but if I knew the formula to put in that instruction there would be no problem and I wouldn't need the instruction at all! I reject that alternative and try instead to find a sequence, a repetition, a choice or a recursive definition. I reject sequence. Choice would be appropriate if I knew a maximum value for *i*. Then I could write a *select* instruction, each arm of which tested for one particular value of *i*:

> *select* $0 \le n < b$:*i*:=1 $b \le n < b^2$:*i*:=2
> .. $b^8 \le n < b^9$:*i*:=9 $b^9 \le n < b^{10}$:*i*:=10 ..
> *endselect*

If I knew that my procedure would never be asked to print a numeral longer than twenty digits I could write a *select* instruction with twenty arms; if I knew that it would never be asked to print a numeral longer than five digits I would only need five arms. But I reject that solution also: I want something more systematic and less tedious to write.

I might choose recursion or repetition. I choose once more to investigate repetition. But what kind of repetition? Again, if I knew the number of times to repeat I wouldn't need to write the instruction, so it can't be counting repetition and it must be unlimited repetition. The instruction must terminate in a state of affairs which makes the formula $b^{i-1} \le n < b^i$ true: that is, it must continue as long as the formula is false. Any number i is either too large, too small or just right. If i is too large then n will be below the range $b^{i-1}..b^i-1$. If i is too small then n will be above this range. Which leads to the instruction

$$iterate \ n<b^{i-1}: i:=i-1$$
$$b^i \le n: i:=i+1$$
$$enditerate$$

program 15.5

To complete the solution, the program requires some initial value of i: a guess at the number of digits that need to be printed. The *iterate* instruction above has the useful property that it doesn't matter how wild the guess is because each repetition will move i towards the right value. My numeral-printing program is now as shown in program 15.6 - I assume the definition of *digchar* as in program 15.4. I have decided (with no supporting evidence) that on average the numerals which this procedure will print will be about five digits long. Hence the initial value of i will be five, and if I am wrong the effect isn't too important because the *iterate* instruction will correct my error.

$$def \ printn2(n, b) =$$
$$def \ digval(n, j) = (n \div b^j) \ rem \ b \ enddef$$
$$initialise \ i:=5$$
$$iterate \ n<b^{i-1}: i:=i-1$$
$$b^i \le n: i:=i+1$$
$$enditerate;$$
$$for \ j \ rbt \ 0..i-1 \ do \ printchar(digchar(digval(n,j))) \ od$$
$$enddef$$

program 15.6

This procedure indeed prints the correct numeral representation for very many positive integers in very many bases. Very seductive, but slightly flawed, as the following exercises show.

-=-=-=-=-=-=-=-=-=-=-=-

Exercise 15.6
Trace the execution of *printn2*(302, 7) and show that it prints '611': show that *printn2*(302, 2) prints '100101110'.

Exercise 15.7
Show that *printn2*(0, 10) will never terminate.

Exercise 15.8
Show that *printn2*(302, 1) will never terminate.

Exercise 15.9
Show that *printn2*(15, 0) will never terminate.

Exercise 15.10
Show that program 15.6 *will* terminate if initially $n=302$, $b=-10$, $i=5$. [Hint: $-10 \times -10 = 100$; $-10 \times 100 = -1000$, and so on. There are two alternatives in the *iterate*: consider them both.]

-=-=-=-=-=-=-=-=-=-=-=-

15.4 FINDING AND CORRECTING MISTAKES

Exercises 15.6-15.10 show that with certain values of n and b an execution of *printn2*(n, b) won't terminate, and that when b is negative very strange results can be expected. In all these cases the problem lies in the *iterate* instruction: either it doesn't terminate or it terminates with ludicrous effect. You might expect that the problem would have shown up if I had tried to prove that the *iterate* instruction terminates before confidently presenting the solution. Certainly that is true, but proofs can be as subtle as programs and a careless proof can miss all the difficult points. I can illustrate this by showing how I might try to construct a proof that program 15.5 will terminate giving the correct value of i.

> P0: An execution of the sequence '$i:=x$; *program* 15.5' is equivalent to execution of the instruction '$i:=W$', where $b^{W-1} \le n < b^W$.

My proof will be by induction on the difference between the final value W and the initial value x: that is, I shall consider cases $x=W+k$ and $x=W-k$. Because I know that *printn2* doesn't work when $b=0$ or $b=1$ I shall assume throughout that $b \ge 2$.

First, as always, it is convenient to convert the combination of *iterate* and assignment into a *select*:

$$i:=x; \; iterate \; n<b^{-1}:i:=i-1 \; b^i \le n:i:=i+1 \; iterate$$

$$= i:=x; \; select \; n<b^{i-1}: \; i:=i-1; iterate \; .. \; enditerate$$
$$b^i \le n: \; i:=i+1; iterate \; .. \; enditerate$$
$$n \ge b^{i-1} \wedge b^i > n: donothing$$
$$endselect$$

$$= select\ n<b^{x-1}: i:=x; i:=i-1; iterate\ ..\ enditerate$$
$$b^x \le n: i:=x; i:=i+1; iterate\ ..\ enditerate$$
$$n \ge b^{x-1} \wedge b^x > n: i:=x; donothing$$
$$endselect$$

$$= select\ n<b^{x-1}: i:=x-1; iterate\ ..\ enditerate$$
$$b^x \le n: i:=x+1; iterate\ ..\ enditerate$$
$$n \ge b^{x-1} \wedge b^x > n: i:=x$$
$$endselect$$

Considering $x=W\pm k$, the base case is clearly when $k=0$, that is, when $x=W$. Remembering that $b^{W-1} \le n < b^W$:

$$select\ n<b^{W-1}: i:=W-1; iterate\ ..\ enditerate$$
$$b^W \le n: i:=W+1; iterate\ ..\ enditerate$$
$$n \ge b^{W-1} \wedge b^W > n: i:=W$$
$$endselect$$

$$= select\ false: i:=W-1; iterate\ ..\ enditerate$$
$$false: i:=W+1; iterate\ ..\ enditerate$$
$$true \wedge true: i:=W$$
$$endselect$$

$$= i:=W$$

As an inductive step I shall assume P0 where $x=W+K$ for some $K \ge 0$ and consider execution of the program when $x=W+(K+1)$:

$$select\ n<b^{W+K+1-1}: i:=W+K+1-1; iterate\ ..\ enditerate$$
$$b^{W+K+1} \le n: i:=W+K+1+1; iterate\ ..\ enditerate$$
$$n \ge b^{W+K+1-1} \wedge b^{W+K+1} > n: i:=W+K+1$$
$$endselect$$

$$select\ n<b^{W+K}: i:=W+K; iterate\ ..\ enditerate$$
$$b^{W+K+1} \le n: i:=W+K+2; iterate\ ..\ enditerate$$
$$n \ge b^{W+K} \wedge b^{W+K+1} > n: i:=W+K+1$$
$$endselect$$

In order that the proof should go through, I would like the first condition-formula in this *select* to be true, the second and the third to be false. To show that this is so requires some discussion of the properties of numbers which are powers of b.

I know that $b^{y+1} = b \times b^y$ and I have assumed that $b \ge 2$. It follows that $b^{y+1} > b^y$ and that in general, when $z>y$, $b^z > b^y$. I know that $b^{W-1} \le n < b^W$; I know that $K \ge 0$ and that therefore $W+K+1 > W+K \ge W$; it follows that $n < b^W \le b^{W+K} < b^{W+K+1}$. From that I know that I can rewrite the *select* instruction:

$$select\ true: i:=W+K; iterate\ ..\ enditerate$$
$$false: i:=W+K+2; iterate\ ..\ enditerate$$
$$false \wedge true: i:=W+K+1$$
$$endselect$$

$$= i := W + K; iterate \;.. \;enditerate$$

which by inductive hypothesis is equivalent to $i := W$. This completes the proof when $x = W + k$; the proof when $x = W - k$ is similar.

-=-=-=-=-=-=-=-=-=-=-=-

Exercise 15.11
Complete the proof of the proposition P0 when $x = W - k$, $k \geq 0$.

-=-=-=-=-=-=-=-=-=-=-=-

Your experience with exercises 15.6-15.10 will have shown you that program 15.5 doesn't behave properly in all sorts of circumstances. Those difficulties should have shown up in the proof of proposition P0 but they didn't - or rather, not all of them did. That should make you uneasy. Is there anything wrong with the argument I gave above? Well, yes there is.

Let me try to make you a little more uneasy. Part of the proof purported to stand on the observation that since $b \geq 2$, $b^{y+1} > b^y$. But in fact all that is required is to assume that $b \geq 0$: then $b^{y+1} \geq b^y$, which is a weaker relationship, but the argument seems to stand up: from $n < b^W \leq b^{W+K} \leq b^{W+K+1}$ I can still prove that only the first condition-formula in the *select* is true. Yet your answers to exercises 15.8 and 15.9 show that program 15.5 doesn't terminate when $b = 1$ or $b = 0$. The 'proof' seems to suggest - or at least not to contradict - something that is empirically untrue.

The solution to this problem lies not in the proof but in the proposition I chose to try to prove: the lesson I expect you to draw is that the design of a proposition (that is, specification of a program's effect) is at least as important as the argument which asserts the proposition's truth. Buried in proposition P0, and used in the argument above, is the assumption that $b^{W-1} \leq n < b^W$. This implicitly assumes that $b^{W-1} < b^W$. This is certainly not so when $b = 0$ or $b = 1$: whatever the value of W, $0^{W-1} = 0^W = 0$ and $1^{W-1} = 1^W = 1$. In effect the proposition should have included the phrase 'provided that W exists such that $b^{W-1} \leq n < b^W$'.

Still I haven't finished: what about exercise 15.7, which shows that program 15.5 doesn't terminate when $n = 0$? Where does that show up in the proof? The answer in this case is that induction works only on finitely long executions. There is no finite value of W which is small enough so that $b^{W-1} \leq 0^\dagger$, and therefore it is impossible to count to W starting a finite distance from it. It is as if the sergeant-major is standing at the wrong side of the infinite desert, faced with an infinite walk before she can whisper 'advance' to her beloved soldier number 1. An infinite walk will never end so the advance will never start. It is the same with program 15.5 when $n = 0$: i is always too large no matter how much you reduce it and the program trudges for ever towards an infinitely negative i.

$\dagger$ Remember that negative powers of b are fractions $1/b$, $1/b^2$, $1/b^3$, .. When $b > 0$ b^y is always positive and never quite zero no matter how negative y might be.

A careful proof will always confirm what you find by examining test cases. Program 15.5 works if n is greater than zero and b is greater than one. You shouldn't find any difficulty in persuading yourself that a value of W exists which validates the assumption made in proposition P0 in those cases. When b is negative the program behaves erratically, just because there are infinitely many possible values of W which will do.

15.5 A CORRECTED VERSION

An obvious 'fix' for the $n=0$ problem is to make it a special case, as in program 15.7. An obvious 'fix' for the problems of negative n and bases b less than two is to ignore them because the program was never intended to work in those cases.

```
def printn(n, b) =
  select n=0: printchar('0')
         n>0: def digval(n, j) = (n÷bʲ) rem b enddef
              initialise i:=5
              iterate n<bⁱ⁻¹: i:=i–1
                      bⁱ≤n: i:=i+1
              enditerate;
              for j rbt 0..i–1 do printchar(digchar(digval(n, j))) od
  endselect
enddef
```

program 15.7

Notice how the structure of the solution has changed as it has been developed. First I thought of repetition (the *for-do*); then I had to make the solution a sequence so that the parameters of the *for-do* could be calculated; finally I had to make it a choice to cater for one difficult situation. In this solution the *for-do* instruction which started the whole thing off isn't even particularly prominent.

15.6 ON NOT WASTING EFFORT

The *printn* procedure of program 15.7 was developed as the result of a rational argument, with just a little guesswork at the beginning. It was developed with an eye to correct operation rather than rapid operation, except that when designing the *digval* procedure I chose between mechanisms on the basis that one would lead to an easier calculation than the other.

Yet program 15.7 is by no means the most *efficient* solution to the numeral-printing problem. Efficiency of a program relates to the computational effort which is required to produce its effect. If one program produces the same effect as another, calling on only half as many calculations or on the same number of calculations each of which is only half as difficult, it is clearly twice as efficient. The visible effect of efficiency is often increased speed of execution: efficient programs give computers less work to do, so efficient programs run faster and therefore give results faster.

One of the main concerns of programmers has always been to produce the most efficient programs possible because the amount of computing you want to do always seems to exceed the capacity of the machinery you can afford. Before I attempt to show any more efficient solutions to the number-printing problem, I should like to emphasise two points: (a) intellectual effort is costly; (b) correct programs can be efficient. Neither point is controversial but both are too often disregarded by too many programmers.

The desire for efficiency arose when computing was young and machines were enormously expensive: when there was too much computing work to do it was cheaper to pay programmers to make programs more efficient than to buy more computers to run inefficient programs. The same logic rules even now that machines have become much cheaper. The economic balance may have altered - you can buy a lot more computing power and a lot less programming effort for the money you would have spent twenty years ago - but all that's happened is that people nowadays use lots more computing power. They use as much as they can get and they use it as efficiently as possible because no matter how cheap computers become you can never afford an infinite amount of them.

But there is still a balance. Programs cost money to *write* - either you have to pay programmers to do it or you have to spend time of your own which you could use to do something more enjoyable or more profitable - and they cost money to *run* - you have to buy computers to run them. You might pay for £x of programming effort to save £y of computing effort. If $x>y$ you're losing: buy a new computer. The same economic balance applies to your own programming effort. You may not cost your own time in money terms as you slave over a hot terminal or a warm micro, but it's your life-time and you could be spending it doing something else.

Put 'program efficiency' in its place and don't worship it. But when an efficient program *is* required, how do you go about building one? Landin contrasted two strategies in his famous diagram, reproduced as figure 15.1. One strategy moves downwards and then to the right: find out fast mechanisms which seem relevant to your problem, build a partial solution which is fast, then work at making it complete. The trouble with this strategy is that it is often very difficult to make the rightward jump and you finish up with a fast partial solution. Partial programming solutions are sometimes worse than useless. Half a loaf may be better than none, but half a table won't stand up: I'd rather put my plate on my lap.

The other solution, which Landin advocated and which I support in this book, is to move rightwards and then down in the diagram. Concentrate first on making a

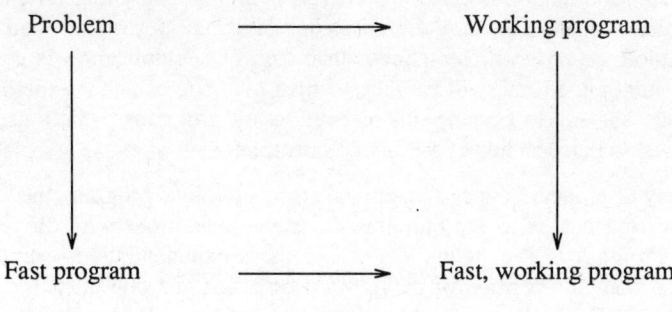

Problem   ⟶   Working program

Fast program   ⟶   Fast, working program

figure 15.1

working program - never mind how inefficient it is in detail - and then work on speeding it up. Perhaps you will finish up with a solution which is slower than you hoped, but if you proceed carefully you can be sure that it will work. Your table may have more legs than you expected, but at least it holds up the meal.

Better structures make faster programs

The Landin diagram doesn't give the whole picture. There are always lots of fast partial solutions, all different, and there are lots of correct slow solutions. That is, there are lots of horizontal and vertical lines: many different squares laid on top of each other. If you are interested in a 'reasonably fast' program you may construct one correct solution, speed it up a bit and leave it at that. If you want a really fast program you would do better to consider several correct solutions and find which of them will speed up most effectively, because some solutions are just naturally more efficient than others. Structure-polishing, concentrating on the details of a solution's operation, is only worthwhile when you have persuaded yourself that you have the best possible structure to start with.

Chapter 16 will discuss an alternative structure for the numeral-printing program, one which seems more naturally efficient according to some measures. Before I display that solution I shall spend some time structure-polishing program 15.7.

15.7 A MORE EFFICIENT REPETITIVE SOLUTION

You may already know that computing machines don't perform their basic operations with equal speed. Some operations are 'cheaper' to use because they take less machine effort, and therefore take less time to perform than others. For example, some of the arithmetic operations used in calculating the value of a formula cost more than others. On many small machines addition is a simpler calculation than multiplication, so that $a+b$ will be a shorter, cheaper calculation than $a \times b$. Subtraction is easier than division, and on many machines $a-b$ will be far quicker than a/b, $a+b$ or $a \, rem \, b$. Division is simpler than logarithm calculation, so $a+b$ will be quicker than $log_b a$. Multiplication is cheaper than exponentiation, so $a \times b$ will be cheaper than a^b. You can check these things out on your system by timing the execution of programs which use counting repetition to perform lots of arithmetic operations.

One way of reducing the computational effort used by a program, thereby making it more efficient, is to replace slow expensive operations with quicker cheaper ones. Program 15.7 contains lots of expensive exponentiation operations: there are two in each repetition of the *iterate* instruction and one in each repetition of the *for-do*. This program would execute faster if I could remove these operations or at least reduce their number. There must be several ways in which it can be done: I show the ways which occur to me.

First, it turns out that I don't really need both of the exponentiations in the *iterate*. instruction. If I could be sure that my first guess for i was always just right or too large, I could get away with an *iterate* which only reduces i; if I could be sure that my first guess was just right or too small I need only increase it. In principle there is no finite value of i which is bound to be large enough: if I pick $i=M$ then the program won't work when $n \geq b^M$. But $i=1$ is guaranteed never to be too large, since a numeral must have at least one digit. Therefore I can use an *iterate* which only increases i:

$$initialise \; i := 1$$
$$iterate \; b^i < n: \; i := i+1 \; enditerate$$

program 15.8

This decreases the number of exponentiation operations in each execution of the *iterate*: whether it reduces the number of exponentiations overall compared with program 15.5 depends on the length of the numeral. Program 15.8 is clearly better when the numeral needs only one digit and program 15.5 is better when it needs five.

-=-=-=-=-=-=-=-=-=-=-=-=-

Exercise 15.12
Assuming that each stage of execution of program 15.8 performs one exponentation and that each stage of execution of program 15.5 performs two exponentiations, calculate the number of exponentiations performed by each instruction for numerals of lengths one to ten characters, assuming that in program 15.5 the initial guess is $i := 5$.

Exercise 15.13
Construct a formula which relates $i0$, the initial guess at the length of the numeral and W, the length of the numeral to be printed, to $E5$, the number of exponentiations performed by program 15.5. Construct a similar formula $E8$ for program 15.8. Hence compare the efficiency of the two programs in different circumstances.

-=-=-=-=-=-=-=-=-=-=-=-

Observe now that the value which is compared with n in program 15.8 varies systematically. The first time the condition-formula is calculated n is compared with b^1, the next time with b^2, after that with b^3, and so on. The value used increases by a factor of b in each repetition, so it is possible to replace the exponentiation by a multiplication, provided that the program retains some memory of the value it used in the previous repetition and multiplies it by b each time around the loop. This means that I need a container which can hold that value. It is important to realise that in the *first* repetition there is no previous value to remember, so the container must be initialised to some appropriate value.

In program 15.9 each repetition of the instruction calculates the value to be compared in the *next* repetition: this fits smoothly with the way that an *iterate* instruction works. Before and after each repetition the value in container bi is equal to b^i: since initially $i=1$ the initial value chosen is b ($=b^1$) and each time i is increased, so is bi[†].

> *initialise* $i, bi := 1, b$;
> *iterate* $bi < n$: $i, bi := i+1, bi \times b$ *enditerate*

program 15.9

Notice that programs 15.8 and 15.9 *will* terminate when $n=0$, and will do so leaving $i=1$. This accidental effect means that I can simplify the *printn* procedure quite a lot, leaving out the discrimination between $n=0$ and $n>0$: see program 15.10. This version carries out a single multiplication where program 15.7 would carry out two exponentiations. Provided that multiplications are much faster than exponentiations, which they usually are, the program will execute measurably faster.

> *def printn*$(n, b) =$
>   *def digval*$(n, j) = (n \div b^j) \, rem \, b \, enddef$
>   *initialise* $i, bi := 1, b$;
>   *iterate* $bi < n$: $i, bi := i+1, bi \times b$ *enditerate*;
>   *for* j *rbt* $0..i-1$ *do printchar*(*digchar*(*digval*(n, j))) *od*
> *enddef*

program 15.10

The next step in my search for efficiency is to remove exponentiation from the *for-do*. Each repetition of the *for-do* instruction calls the procedure *digval*, and each execution of *digval* involves an exponentiation. If I expand the procedure

---

[†] The technique used in inventing this program has general application but I don't have space to go further into it in this book.

call the situation is a little clearer:

$$for\ j\ rbt\ 0..i-1\ do\ printchar(digchar((n+b^j)\ rem\ b))\ od$$

program 15.11

The technique used with the *iterate* works with the *for-do* as well, because the value used to divide n decreases systematically with each repetition. On the first repetition it is b^{i-1}, on the next it is b^{i-2}, and so on until on the last repetition it is b^0, which is 1. Each value is just the previous one divided by b. As before, the program must provide a value to be used in the first repetition, and this might seem to require an instruction $X:=b^{i-1}$. Not so: after the *iterate* instruction terminates, which is just before the first repetition of the *for-do*, the container bi holds the value b^i, which is only a factor of b too large. If each repetition of the *for-do* reduces the value in bi just before using it, the right effect is achieved:

$$for\ j\ rbt\ 0..i-1\ do$$
$$bi := bi \div b;$$
$$printchar(digchar((n \div bi)\ rem\ b))$$
$$od$$

program 15.12

This instruction need no longer run j backwards through a sequence $0..i-1$, because its body makes no use of j at all. It can and should be changed to a *times-do*, which leads to the definition shown in program 15.13.

$$def\ printn(n, b) =$$
$$initialise\ i, bi := 1, b;$$
$$iterate\ bi < n:\ i, bi := i+1, bi \times b\ enditerate;$$
$$times\ i\ do$$
$$bi := bi \div b;$$
$$printchar(digchar((n \div bi)\ rem\ b))$$
$$od$$
$$enddef$$

program 15.13

This chapter is intended to illustrate the slogan that it is reasonable *first* to construct a program considering only its faithful operation but without considering the efficiency of its individual parts; *second* to massage that program into a more execution-efficient program. Sometimes you can be surprised by the result: it is possible that program 15.13 might occur to you in a flash but it is more probable that, like me, you have to develop it by polishing a more long-winded program which you do understand.

Structure-polishing can go on for ever. Program 15.13 isn't the end of the road by any means: for example, you might find that it is possible to speed it up still further if the *digchar* procedure were to use the *encode/decode* tricks of chapter

12, section 12.5.

-=

APPENDIX 15.A SOME EXAMPLES TO TRY

Exercise 15.14
Investigate the cost of arithmetic operations on your system: use a stopwatch or, better, some measure of calculating execution times which is internal to the system. Your programs should use counting repetition to repeat particular operations a large number of times, so as to make the execution times large enough to measure accurately.

Exercise 15.15
Transcribe program 15.13 into a mechanical code and execute it. You may have some difficulty in checking its output, so I provide the following list, showing the output of a program which called this procedure several times, each time with *n* five hundred and forty-seven and *b* a number between two and twenty:

base	numeral
2	1000100011
3	202021
4	20203
5	4142
6	2311
7	1411
8	1043
9	667
10	547
11	458
12	397
13	331
14	2b1
15	267
16	223
17	1f3
18	1c7
19	19f
20	177

Exercise 15.16
If your programming system has an exponentiation operation, compare execution times for sample calls to programs 15.7 and 15.8 (you may need to call each procedure a few hundred times to make the execution times large enough to

measure). If your programming system doesn't have an exponentiation operation, there's no contest.

Chapter 16
PRINTING A NUMERAL WITH RECURSION

The basis of the numeral-printing procedure of chapter 15 is the observation that the digits of a numeral must be printed in sequence from left to right. The first visible effect of the program is to print the leftmost digit, and the *for-do* instruction is an obvious choice for printing the digits in left-to-right order. That choice turns out to require an additional repetition which counts the digits. Eventually a reasonably simple program was developed, but with some difficulty. In particular it was tricky to construct an *iterate* instruction which counts the digits in the numeral and which is guaranteed to terminate.

When designing a program it doesn't pay to consider a single structure. In general it is best to look for other structures and to play around with several possibilities before settling on one of them. In particular every programmer should be aware that repetition and recursion are two sides of a coin: any repetitive solution can be matched by a recursive one, any recursive solution by a repetition.

16.1 PRINTING THE LAST DIGIT LAST

In the case of numeral-printing the recursive solution grows out of a search for simplicity. The difficulties encountered in developing a repetitive solution in chapter 15 arose in calculating the value of the *j*th digit and in counting the digits of the numeral. Only the last digit value, the value of d_0, was easy to calculate. All the solutions in chapter 15 derived from an initial decision to print the first digit first. What would a program be like which prints the last digit last and leaves the rest up to some other program? It would be a sequence:

print the numeral $d_{i-1}..d_1$ somehow; *print the digit d_0*

Chapter 15 showed a formula which calculates the value of d_0 and by the way a formula which calculates the value of the numeral $d_{i-1}..d_1$. If n is represented by the numeral $d_{i-1}..d_0$ in base-b notation then $n\,rem\,b$ is represented by d_0 and $n \div b$

374   PRINTING A NUMERAL WITH RECURSION

by $d_{i-1}..d_1$. *If n is less than b then $n \div b$ is zero and you don't need to print it.*

I now have the basis of a recursive solution, which I can write immediately as a procedure definition:

> *def printnr(n, b) =*
>   *select $n < b$: printchar(digchar(n))*
>   *$n \geq b$: printnr$(n \div b, b)$; printchar(digchar$(n$ rem $b)$)*
>   *endselect*
>   *enddef*

program 16.1

This definition is so simple that it is beautiful - compare it with the complexities of program 15.13[†]. It handles any positive number: even zero.

-=-=-=-=-=-=-=-=-=-=-=-=-=-

Exercise 16.1
Draw environment diagrams for sample calls of the *printnr* procedure, such as *printnr*$(57, 2)$, *printnr*$(10, 10)$, *printnr*$(0, 5)$. Satisfy yourself that in each case it produces the correct printed output.

-=-=-=-=-=-=-=-=-=-=-=-=-=-

16.2 HOW DOES IT WORK?

I give two proofs about the *printnr* procedure. The first, which is very simple, shows that the sequence of digits which it prints doesn't have any unnecessary leading zeros. The second proof has the same shape but it is a little more complicated: it shows that the numeral printed by *printnr*(n, b) is a correct representation of the number n. Other proofs are asked for in the exercises.

P0: A procedure call *printnr*(k, x), where $k \geq 1$ and $x \geq 2$, prints a sequence of i digits $d_{i-1} d_{i-2}..d_0$ in which d_{i-1} is not the digit zero.

The base case is when $k = 1$:

> *printnr*$(1, x)$ = *select* $1 < x$: *printchar(digchar(1))*
> $1 \geq x$: *printnr*$(1 \div x, x)$; *printchar(digchar$(1$ rem $x)$)*
>   *endselect*

Now $x \geq 2$, therefore $1 < x$, and therefore:

[†] I first saw this procedure definition when I had just started to teach computer science. My best effort at numeral printing had been a mess, about thirty lines long and by no means as simple even as program 15.13. I was shocked to find that everything my program was capable of could be matched by a three-line recursive definition.

$$printnr(1,x) = select\ true:\ printchar(digchar(1))$$
$$false:\ printnr(1÷x,x); printchar(digchar(1\ rem\ x))$$
$$endselect$$

$$= printchar(digchar(1))$$

$$= printchar('1')$$

This is an instruction which prints a sequence of digits of length 1, in which $d_{1-1} = d_0 = 1$ is not the digit zero.

As inductive hypothesis I assume that $P0(k)$ is true for every k, $1 \le k \le K$ and some $K \ge 1^\dagger$. Then to show $P0(K+1)$ I must investigate $printnr(K+1,x)$:

$$printnr(K+1,x) = select\ K+1 < x:\ printchar(digchar(K+1))$$
$$K+1 \ge x:\ printnr((K+1)÷x,x);$$
$$printchar(digchar((K+1)\ rem\ x))$$
$$endselect$$

I must consider two cases: either $K+1 < x$ or $K+1 \ge x$. In the first case the procedure call is evidently equivalent to $printchar(digchar(K+1))$, an instruction sequence which obviously prints a single digit, and since $K+1 > 1$, that digit isn't zero. When $K+1 \ge x$ I have

$$printnr(K+1,x) = select\ false:\ printchar(digchar(K+1))$$
$$true:\ printnr((K+1)÷x,x);$$
$$printchar(digchar((K+1)\ rem\ x))$$
$$endselect$$

$$= printnr((K+1)÷x,x); printchar(digchar((K+1)\ rem\ x))$$

Now $K+1 > 0$ and $x \ge 2$, therefore $(K+1)÷x < K+1$ (when you divide $K+1$ by x it must get smaller). Also $K+1 \ge x$, and therefore $(K+1)÷x \ge 1$. Thus I know that $1 \le (K+1)÷x \le K$. Then by inductive hypothesis:

$$printnr(K+1,x) = an\ instruction\ which\ prints\ a\ sequence\ length\ i\ in$$
$$which\ d_{i-1}\ is\ not\ the\ digit\ zero;\ printchar(digchar((K+1)\ rem\ x))$$

This is evidently an instruction which prints a sequence (length $i+1$) in which d_i is not the digit zero: hence $P0(K+1)$ is proved.

Thus the sequence printed by a call $printnr(k,x)$ doesn't start with a zero, provided that $k > 0$. It remains to prove that it prints a correct numeral representation of the number k. The proof is the same shape as the one above (except that this time it includes the case when $k = 0$), but the proposition is necessarily more complicated:

$\dagger$ Note that strong induction is used here.

P1: A call of $printnr(k,x)$ when $k \geq 0$ and $x \geq 2$, prints a correct numeral representation of k in base x: that is, it prints a sequence of digits $d_{i-1}d_{i-2}..d_1d_0$ such that

$$k = \sum_{j=0}^{j=i-1} d_j x^j$$

This time the base case is when $k=0$:

$$
\begin{aligned}
printnr(0,x) = &\ select\ 0{<}x{:}\ printchar(digchar(0)) \\
&\quad\quad\quad\ 0{\geq}x{:}\ printnr(0{\div}x,x); \\
&\quad\quad\quad\quad\quad\quad printchar(digchar(0\ rem\ x)) \\
&\ endselect \\
\\
= &\ select\ true{:}\ printchar(digchar(0)) \\
&\quad\quad\quad false{:}\ printnr(0{\div}x,x); \\
&\quad\quad\quad\quad\quad\ printchar(digchar(0\ rem\ x)) \\
&\ endselect \\
\\
= &\ printchar(digchar(0)) \\
\\
= &\ printchar(`0\text{'})
\end{aligned}
$$

Evidently "0" is a sequence of digit characters which is a correct representation of zero $(0 \times x^0 = 0 \times 1 = 0)$.

The inductive hypothesis is that P1(k) holds for all k such that $0 \leq k \leq K$, and for some $K \geq 0$. To show that P1($K+1$) follows I must consider $printnr(K+1,x)$:

$$
\begin{aligned}
printnr(K+1,x) = &\ select\ K+1{<}x{:}\ printchar(digchar(K+1)) \\
&\quad\quad\quad\ K+1{\geq}x{:}\ printnr((K+1){\div}x,x); \\
&\quad\quad\quad\quad\quad\quad printchar(digchar((K+1)\ rem\ x)) \\
&\ endselect
\end{aligned}
$$

As before I must consider two cases. If $K+1{<}x$, $printnr(K+1,x)$ is evidently equivalent to $printchar(digchar(K+1))$, which is equally evidently an instruction which prints a correct single-digit representation of $K+1$ and which satisfies P1 $((K+1) \times x^1 = (K+1) \times 1 = K+1)$. If $K+1 \geq x$ I have as before:

$$printnr(K+1,x) = printnr((K+1){\div}x,x); printchar(digchar((K+1)\ rem\ x))$$

Just as in the proof of P0 above, I know that $0 \leq (K+1){\div}x \leq K$ and that therefore $printnr((K+1){\div}x,x)$ is an instruction covered by the inductive hypothesis. Therefore it will print a correct representation of $(K+1){\div}x$. Suppose that the numeral it prints is $d_{i-1}..d_0$. By inductive hypothesis I have:

$$(K+1){\div}x = \sum_{j=0}^{j=i-1} d_j x^j$$

and the two instructions in sequence print a numeral $d_{i-1}..d_0 D$, whose value is

$$(K+1)\ rem\ x + \sum_{j=0}^{j=i-1} d_j x^{j+1}$$

$$= ((K+1)\ rem\ x) + x \times ((K+1){\div}x)$$

$$= K+1$$

My proofs of the propositions P0 and P1 show that the procedure call $printnr(k,x)$, when $k{\geq}0$ and $x{>}1$, prints a sequence of digits which doesn't have unnecessary leading zeros and which is a correct numeral representation of the number k.

-=-=-=-=-=-=-=-=-=-=-=-=-

Exercise 16.2
Where exactly in the proofs did it matter that $x{>}1$?

Exercise 16.3
Prove that when $x^{W-1}{\leq}k{<}x^W$, $k{\geq}1$ and $x{>}1$, a procedure call $printnr(k,x)$ prints exactly W digits.

-=-=-=-=-=-=-=-=-=-=-=-=-

16.3 PRINTING A COLUMN OF NUMERALS

Suppose that you want to print a sequence of numerals in a column, perhaps with their total at the bottom. Figure 16.1 shows what such a column would look like if you used $NL;printnr(n,10)$ to print each component. Certainly you would get a column of numerals, one above the other. But the column is printed so that the leftmost digits of the numerals line up one above the other, and this makes it useless for certain purposes. If the numerals represent amounts of money, as they do in a bank statement, then it would be much more pleasing to print them so that the rightmost digits are aligned, as in figure 16.2, because that way you can add them up more easily by eye.

```
   15                     15
   35                     35
   0                       0
   156                    156
   3865                   3865
   2                       2
   1944                   1944
   6017                   6017
   -----                  -----
   12034                  12034
```

figure 16.1   figure 16.2

Your experience with triangle-printing should teach you that in order to print a pattern which has a vertical right-hand edge, every line must contain the same number of characters. So we need a procedure which prints a number of spaces followed by a numeral, and which ensures that the total number of characters printed is the same each time. The procedure will require three parameters: n the number to be printed, b the number-base and w the width of the column (that is, the total number of characters to be printed).

It is easy to see how the repetitive *printn* procedure of program 15.13 could be adapted to this specification: once the number *i* of digits in the numeral has been calculated, print *w−i* spaces, then print *i* digits as before. It is equally easy to see that the task is impossible when *w<i*, because the program can't print a negative number of spaces.

It is hardly more difficult to see how *printnr* could be adapted. Each arm of the *select* must be made to print exactly *w* characters: the non-recursive arm (the 'base case') already prints one character which should be preceded with *w−1* spaces; the recursive arm (the 'inductive case') prints a numeral followed by a single digit and if the total is to be *w* characters that numeral must be *w−1* characters long. The new version of the procedure is therefore:

$$def\ printnrw(n, b, w) =$$
$$select\ n<b:\ times\ w-1\ do\ printspace\ od;$$
$$printchar(digchar(n))$$
$$n \geq b:\ printnrw(n+b, b, w-1);$$
$$printchar(digchar(n\ rem\ b))$$
$$endselect$$
$$enddef$$

program 16.2

This procedure hardly seems to need a formal proof: it is just *obvious* that the procedure prints *w* characters in the inductive case because *w−1+1=w*. Unfortunately what is obvious isn't always true: this procedure doesn't always work.

-=-=-=-=-=-=-=-=-=-=-=-

Exercise 16.4
Trace the execution of *printnrw*(3468, 10, 15): show that it prints exactly 15 characters.

Exercise 16.5
Trace the execution of *printnrw*(341, 2, 12): show that it prints exactly 12 characters.

Exercise 16.6
What is the effect of *printnrw*(3468, 10, 3)? Of *printnrw*(341, 2, 5)?

Exercise 16.7
Prove that a procedure call *printnrw*(k, x, j), where $k \geq 0$, $x \geq 1$, $x^{W-1} \leq k < x^W$ and $j \geq W$, prints a sequence of characters of length *j*.

Exercise 16.8
Continuing exercise 16.7: prove that the sequence of characters consists of *j−W* spaces followed by *W* digits.

Exercise 16.9
Continuing exercises 16.7 and 16.8: what would be the effect of *printnrw*(k, x, j) if $x^{W-1} \leq k < x^W$ and $j < W$?

-=-=-=-=-=-=-=-=-=-=-=-=-

Your answers to exercises 16.6 and 16.9 show that $printnrw(n, b, w)$ prints w characters only if n can be represented as a numeral of no more than w digits in base b - which is what you should have expected, because the repetitive version would have the same difficulty. If n requires more than w digits the procedure call is equivalent to a sequence which contains an invalid *times-do* instruction and therefore will not terminate.

-=-=-=-=-=-=-=-=-=-=-=-≭-=-

Exercise 16.10
If w is negative *printnrw* can't do what is asked. But as long as w is positive or zero it might reasonably try to print exactly w characters, no matter whether they are a correct representation of n or not. By modifying the definition of *printnrw*, or otherwise, define a procedure *printnrw2* such that $printnrw2(n, b, w)$ prints exactly w characters whenever $w \geq 0$ and prints a correct representation of n whenever w is large enough.

-=-=-=-=-=-=-=-=-=-=-=-=-

16.4 PRINTING NEGATIVE NUMERALS

A procedure which prints positive or negative numerals in base b within a column of width w must obey the following proposition:

P2: A call of $printnrws(n, b, w)$ where $b \geq 2$, $w \geq 0$, $0 \leq b^{W-1} \leq n < b^W \leq b^w$, will print $w-W$ spaces followed by W digits; when $0 \leq b^{W-1} \leq -n < b^W \leq b^{w+1}$ it will print $w-W-1$ spaces followed by a minus sign followed by W digits.

That is, the procedure must print a W-digit representation of the magnitude of the number n preceded, if n is negative, by a minus sign. I don't specify what it should do if w is too small to hold what must be printed. It goes without saying that the W digits it prints should be a correct representation: the proofs of propositions P0 and P1 should carry over in any case.

When you are designing a recursive procedure definition it helps to know what the complete proposition is. Proposition P2 suggests two base cases immediately:

$0 \leq n < b$: *times* $w-1$ *do printspace od*; *printchar*$(digchar(n))$

$-b < n < 0$: *times* $w-2$ *do printspace od*; *printchar*$('-')$; *printchar*$(digchar(-n))$

The inductive case for positive n is the same as it always was:

$n \geq b$: *printn*$(n \div b, b, w-1)$; *printchar*$(digchar(n\ rem\ b))$

In the inductive case for negative n you need to be a little careful. What exactly are the values of $n \div b$ and $n\ rem\ b$ when n is negative?

Everybody agrees that the remainder is the bit 'left over' after division - that is, that $x = (x \div y) \times y + x \, rem \, y$ - but that is where agreement ends. You might hear from a mathematician that $\div$ and rem should mimic 'modulo arithmetic' and that the quotient $x \div y$ must not be larger than the true fractional answer. This implies that the remainder must always be the same sign as the divisor (y, the number which does the dividing). Since $-17/10$ is -1.7, it follows from this definition that $-17 \div 10$ should be -2 and $-17 \, rem \, 10$ must then be 3. Lots of computing machine designers have decided to follow an alternative definition of integer division which in effect treats negative numbers as decorated positive numbers and makes the sign of the remainder the same as the sign of the dividend (x, the number which is divided): under this definition $-17 \div 10$ is -1, $-17 \, rem \, 10$ is -7.

I haven't defined what $\div$ and rem should do with negative numbers and I have only vaguely defined what they should do with positive numbers. You will often, unfortunately, come across this sort of vague definition in your programming life. When you encounter such vagueness, what should you do about it? One thing you might do is to find out by experiment which definition your programming system really uses and to base your program on that definition. An alternative is to write your program so that whatever definition is used it will get the right result. That is what I have chosen to do in defining my own solution to this problem: see program 16.3. I have forced this program to divide only positive numbers.

> *def printnrws* $(n, b, w) =$
>   *select* $0 \le n < b$: *times* $w{-}1$ *do printspace od*; *printchar*(*digchar*(n))
> $n \ge b$: *printn*($n \div b, b, w{-}1$); *printchar*(*digchar*($n \, rem \, b$))
>
> $-b < n < 0$: *times* $w{-}2$ *do printspace od*; *printchar*('-');
>   *printchar*(*digchar*($-n$))
> $n \le -b$: *printn*($-((-n) \div b), b, w{-}1$); *printchar*(*digchar*(($-n$) *rem b*))
>   *endselect*
> *enddef*

program 16.3

-=-=-=-=-=-=-=-=-=-=-=-

Exercise 16.11
A call to *printnrws* won't terminate if w is too small. Modify the procedure so that it prints the correct representation of n if possible but otherwise always prints exactly w characters (provided w isn't negative).

-=

APPENDIX 16.A SOME EXAMPLES TO TRY

Exercise 16.12
Transcribe programs 16.1, 16.2 and 16.3 into a mechanical code and execute
them. The sequence of numerals given in appendix 15.A might confirm that you
have done it properly.

Exercise 16.13
Transcribe the procedure definitions of programs 15.13 and 16.1 into the notation
of your programming system. Compare execution times for calls of each
procedure; hence discover which is more time-efficient.

Exercise 16.14
Construct and prove a formula for the number of '+' and '*rem*' operations which
will be performed by a call of *printnr* with arguments $k \geq 0$ and $x \geq 2$. Similarly
for *printn* (program 15.13). Does your answer help to explain the comparison
you made in exercise 16.13? If not, what *does* explain the differences in
execution-time between the two procedures? [Hints: how long does it take to
make a comparison? to create an environment? to decide to repeat an instruction?
Are the procedures comparable in all these respects?]

Chapter 17
A NUMERICAL CALCULATOR

Your programming system will certainly be able to calculate the value of formulas like

$$(a+14)\times62+47-y$$

If you make a mistake in typing a formula in a program, most programming systems will print helpful error messages which indicate the sort of mistake you have made and where in your program it occurs. This chapter discusses how to write a program which can calculate the value of a formula typed on the keyboard and can respond helpfully when the formula is meaningless.

17.1 CALCULATING WITH TWO NUMBERS

You already know how to write a procedure which can read and calculate the value of a numeral expressed in any base. The simplest formulas are a pair of numbers separated by a single arithmetic operator: + for addition, - for subtraction, * for multiplication, / for integer division, ^ for exponentiation (a^b means a^b). Some sample formulas are:

$$46-42$$
$$1354/9$$
$$2^{\wedge}31$$

The simplest program which can read and calculate the value of such a formula must surely be a sequence:

> *read the first number;*
> *read the operator;*
> *read the second number;*
> *calculate 'first op second' and print it*

There is no difficulty in translating this design into a complete program:

> *initialise a, op, b := ?, ?, ?*
>
> *readnumber a; readchar op; readnumber b;*
> *printnumber(case op of '+':a+b '-':a−b '*':a×b*
> $$'/':a÷b \verb|'^'|:a^b$$
> *endcase)*

program 17.1

-=-=-=-=-=-=-=-=-=-=-=-

Exercise 17.1

The *readchar* instruction moves the crp one position forward. Assume that if the crp is over the first character of a numeral, the *readnumber* instruction moves the crp to the character after the numeral. What then will be the effect of program 17.1 given each of the following input sequences?

> a. <'1', '2', '-', '3', 'a', ..>
> b. <'1', '2', '-', '3', ' ', 'a', ..>
> c. <'1', '2', '.', '3', 'a', ..>
> d. <'1', '2', ' ', '-', '3', 'a', ..>
> e. <'1', '2', '-', ' ', '3', 'a', ..>
> f. <' ', '1', '2', '-', '3', 'a', ..>
> g. <' ', '1', '2', ' ', '-', ' ', '3', ' ', 'a', ..>

In each case say whether the program will terminate normally. If so, give the final position of the crp and describe the output sequence produced. If not, say why not.

Exercise 17.2

Define the effect in general of an execution of program 17.1.

-=-=-=-=-=-=-=-=-=-=-=-

Program 17.1 is very simple. Indeed it is too simple to be 'helpful' or what is nowadays called 'user-friendly'. It operates correctly only if the input sequence is perfectly constructed. If there are spaces before the first numeral or between the operation character and either numeral it won't work properly; nor will it produce a meaningful result if the operation character isn't one of the ones it recognises. If the input sequence doesn't meet its requirements it 'blows up', 'crashes', fails to terminate, which isn't very helpful.

It's unreasonable to design a calculator program which is so fussy when the mistakes you might make in typing a formula are so easily anticipated. Consider first the matter of the spaces. The *skipspaces* procedure of program 17.2 moves the crp to the first non-space character. By employing this procedure at all the necessary places in my program it immediately becomes less sensitive to the layout of the formula it reads.

-=-=-=-=-=-=-=-=-=-=-=-

def skipspaces( ) = *iterate crp^='* ': *movecrp enditerate enddef*

initialise a, op, b := ?, ?, ?

skipspaces( ); *readnumber a*;
skipspaces( ); *readchar op*;
skipspaces( ); *readnumber b*;

printnumber(*case op of '+': a+b '-': a−b '*': a×b*
$$\qquad\qquad\quad '/': a+b \ \ '\hat{\ }': a^b$$
$\qquad\qquad endcase$)

program 17.2

Exercise 17.3
Describe the effect of program 17.2 given each of the input sequences from exercise 17.1.

Exercise 17.4
Describe the effect of program 17.2 given each of the following input sequences:

a. < ' ', ' ', '1', ' ', ' ', 'x', ' ', ' ', '3', ' ', 'a', ..>
b. < ' ', ' ', 'x', ' ', ' ', '+', ' ', ' ', '4', ' ', 'a', ..>
c. < ' ', ' ', '1', ' ', ' ', '+', ' ', ' ', 'x', ' ', 'a', ..>

-=-=-=-=-=-=-=-=-=-=-=-

There are still various ways in which program 17.2 can 'crash'. If the first non-space character isn't a digit the first *readnumber* instruction won't work; if the non-space character between the numerals isn't one of the operation characters which it recognises then the *case* formula is meaningless; if the first non-space character after the operation isn't a digit the second *readnumber* will crash. Programs which crash aren't nice to use: I'd much rather have a program which points out my mistake and invites me to try again.

The first problem is to detect mistakes in what is typed. The most obvious 'fix' for this problem is to use lots of choice instructions which look to see if there is a digit when a numeral should occur and check the operation character when it's read. But this makes the program into a nasty tangle, illustrated in program 17.3.

As so often happens, including a 'fix' destroys the structure of the program. Most of the original sequence has been fragmented and the pieces buried in a nested *select* within *select* structure. If I extend the problem to allow three, or four, or an indefinite number of numerals in a formula there would need to be more *selects* within *selects*. Clearly program 17.3 isn't a sufficiently systematic solution. One way to proceed towards a better solution is to investigate what an extended formula-reading program would look like before attempting to write down a complete design.

def skipspaces ( ) = *iterate crp^='* *': movecrp enditerate enddef*
initialise a, op, b := ?, ?, ?

skipspaces ( );
select isdigit(crp^):
    readnumber a; skipspaces ( );
    select crp^='+' ∨ *crp^='-'* ∨ *crp^='*'* ∨
        crp^='/' ∨ *crp^='^':*
        readchar op; skipspaces ( );
        select isdigit(crp^):
            readnumber b;
            printnumber (case op of '+': $a+b$ '-': $a-b$ '*': $a \times b$
                                    '/': $a+b$ '^': a^b
                    endcase)
        ¬*isdigit(crp^):*
            print("no second number")
        endselect
    crp^≠'+' ∧ *crp^≠'-'* ∧ *crp^≠'*'* ∧
        crp^≠'/' ∧ *crp^≠'^':*
        print("dud operation symbol")
    endselect
¬*isdigit(crp^):*
    print("no first number")
endselect

program 17.3

17.2 CALCULATING WITH SHORTER AND LONGER FORMULAS

The two-numeral formulas handled by program 17.3 are a special case of an *n*-numeral formula. A formula can contain just one numeral or as many as ten, twenty, a hundred - as many as you like. As with the numeral-reading problem of chapter 12, formula-reading can be carried out by a repetition which keeps going until it reaches something which isn't part of the formula. Or, remembering chapter 16, it might be better expressed as a recursion.

The systematic way of planning a repetition is to investigate different executions and to search for some regularity in a series of executions, following the style of chapter 6. A single-numeral formula might be read by a sequence:

        skipspaces ( ); *readnumber a*

and a two-numeral formula by a sequence:

        skipspaces ( ); *readnumber a;*
        skipspaces ( ); *readchar op;*
        skipspaces ( ); *readnumber b;*
        calculate with a and b and op

It seems plausible that to read an *n*-numeral formula would require *skipspaces*();
readnumber a followed by *n* repetitions of *skipspaces*(); *readchar op*;
skipspaces(); *readnumber b*; *calculate with a and b and op*. Plausible, but there's
a flaw. How can the program tell whether you have typed a single-numeral or a
two-numeral formula or a three-numeral formula in the input sequence? In other
words, how can the program decide when to stop? The number-reading program
of chapter 12 (program 12.9) keeps reading digits until it reaches a character that
doesn't form part of a numeral. The *readformula* program must behave
similarly. Faced with the input sequence

$$< ' \ ', ' \ ', '1', '2', ' \ ', ' \ ', .. >$$

it must read the 1 and the 2 as the number twelve; then it must keep reading when
it finds the space after '2' because if the next non-space character is '+' then
there must be a two- (or three- or four- or more-) numeral formula; if the first
non-space character is ',' or *newline* or a digit or anything except an operation
symbol, there is only a one-numeral formula in the input.

To read a one-numeral formula, then, requires a sequence:

>   *skipspaces*(); *readnumber a*; *skipspaces*()

and to read a two-numeral formula:

>   *skipspaces*(); *readnumber a*; *skipspaces*();
>   *readchar op*;
>   *skipspaces*(); *readnumber b*; *skipspaces*();
>   *calculate with a and b and op*

and a three-numeral formula:

>   *skipspaces*(); *readnumber a*; *skipspaces*();
>   *readchar op*;
>   *skipspaces*(); *readnumber b*; *skipspaces*();
>   *calculate with a and b and op*;
>   *readchar op*;
>   *skipspaces*(); *readnumber b*; *skipspaces*();
>   *calculate with a and b and op*

I summarise the design in program 17.4.

>   *skipspaces*(); *readnumber a*; *skipspaces*();
>   *iterate crp^ is an operation character*:
>   *readchar op*;
>   *skipspaces*(); *readnumber b*; *skipspaces*();
>   *.. do some calculation with a, b and op ..*
>   *enditerate*;
>   *printnumber*(*.. something ..*)

program 17.4

Operator priority

The next step in the design is to decide how to calculate the value of the formula. There is a small complication here. Conventionally 1+2×3 means 7 because it is interpreted as 1+(2×3); 3×2+1 also means 7 because it is interpreted as (3×2)+1. But type 1+2×3 on a cheap calculator and you will get the answer 9; type 3×2+1 and you will get the answer 7. Cheap calculators work from left to right without considering the relative *priority* or *precedence* of arithmetic operations. If my program is allowed to behave like a cheap calculator it can work rather like the *readsequence* procedure of chapter 10: each new operator and its succeeding numeral operates on the running total, producing a new total. Then a cheap calculator program could be as shown in program 17.5, in which I assume the definition of an *isopchar* procedure which recognises operation characters (that is, which distinguishes between '+', '-', '*', '/', '^' and the rest) together with a *calculate* procedure which can do the work of the *case* formula from program 17.1.

> *skipspaces*(); *readnumber tot*; *skipspaces*();
> *iterate isopchar*(*crp^*): *initialise op*, *x* := ?, ?
>
> > *readchar op*; *skipspaces*();
> > *readnumber x*; *skipspaces*();
> > *tot* := *calculate*(*tot*, *op*, *x*)
>
> *enditerate*;
>
> *printnumber*(*tot*)

program 17.5

This isn't a complete solution yet, by any means. It still isn't 'helpful' or 'user-friendly' when you type a wrong operation character, or leave out an operation character altogether. In some cases it doesn't calculate the value we really want, because it always works strictly from left to right. It doesn't exploit all the regularity in the problem: for example, the sequence *skipspaces*(); *readnumber* ..; *skipspaces*() appears twice, so I might make a procedure out of that sequence and clarify the program.

If I am prepared to overlook its minor deficiencies, I might use program 17.5 as the body of a *readformula* procedure, which can then be called upon to read the value of a formula from the input sequence just as the input instructions *readnumber* and *readchar* extract number and character values. Program 17.6 shows the sort of thing I mean.

-=-=-=-=-=-=-=-=-=-=-=-

Exercise 17.5
Trace the effect of program 17.6 given the input sequences from exercise 17.1.

Exercise 17.6
Abstract away from the fact that numbers are represented as sequences of digit characters and the fact that formulas may contain spaces. Imagine that the input

sequence contains alternately numbers and characters; imagine that *readelement(@x)* takes a number from the input sequence and that *readchar op* takes a character. It is then possible to prove that *readformula(@e)* moves the crp to the first character which isn't an operation character and puts the value of the formula preceding that character into *e*. Prove it. [Hint: by induction on the length of the formula; base case is length 1.]

> *def readelement(n)* =
>   *skipspaces( ); readnumber ↓n; skipspaces( )*
> *enddef*
>
> *def readformula(tot)* =
>   *readelement(↓tot);*
>   *iterate isopchar(crp^):*
>   *initialise op,x* := ?,?
>
>   *readchar op; readelement(@x);*
>   ↓*tot* := *calculate(↓tot,op,x)*
>   : *enditerate;*
> *enddef*
>
> *initialise e:=?*
> *readformula(@e); printnumber(e)*

program 17.6

Exercise 17.7
For every repetition there is a recursion and vice-versa. Find a recursive equivalent of program 17.6. [Hint: the body of the procedure isn't a *select* instruction, and the simplest solution calculates from right to left rather than from left to right.]

Exercise 17.8
What would be the effect of left-to-right calculation presented with the input '1-2-3='? What would be the effect of right-to-left calculation given the same input sequence?

-=-=-=-=-=-=-=-=-=-=-=-

17.3 FORMULAS WITH BRACKETS

If a cheap calculator won't take account of operator priorities and calculates only from left to right (or from right to left) perhaps it can be forced to give the right answer if we use brackets. How can the *readformula* procedure be adapted to handle formulas like

8+(11*3)-(14*5/36-2)

and perform the calculations in the correct order? If I can do this trick then 1+(2*3) will mean 7, even though if I type it without the brackets it will still be taken to mean 9.

A possible solution is to treat the problem as one for repetition and get lost in a forest of bracket-counting programs. A better way is to realise that the definition of a formula is recursive or self-referential, like the recurrence relations used as examples in chapter 9.

> A formula is a sequence of elements separated by operation characters.
>
> A formula element is either a numeral or it is a formula enclosed in brackets.

definition 17.1

So a formula can be made up partly of formulas which are made up partly of formulas .. Clearly a job for recursion.

The body of the *readformula* procedure from program 17.6 is still adequate, if I continue to accept that the value of a formula can be found by combining the value of its elements from left to right. Recursion comes in when calculating the value of a formula element. If the first character of the element is a digit, then the element is just a numeral; if it is a bracket, then the element is a formula enclosed in brackets. The outline of the new *readelement* procedure is shown in program 17.7. Notice that the *readnumber* instruction of program 17.6 has been replaced by a *select*; notice that the container-describing argument is passed on in the procedure call *readformula(n)*.

```
    def readelement(n) =
      skipspaces();
      select isdigchar(crp^): readnumber ↓n
        crp^='(': .. something involving readformula(n) ..
      endselect;
      skipspaces()
    enddef
```

program 17.7

Now if an element is a bracketed formula the formula doesn't include the brackets, it's enclosed by them. So before calling *readformula(n)*, the *readelement* procedure must move the crp past the opening bracket. Next, *readformula(n)* will move the crp to the end of the formula, right over the element, operation, element, .. sequence, stopping at the first non-space character which follows an element but isn't an operation character. That character should be the closing bracket if the whole formula element is properly constructed. Finally the *readelement* procedure must move the crp over that character as well, because it is part of the element. So the complete procedure is as shown in program 17.8.

Note that all the changes which have made this program able to read bracketed expressions have been made in the *readelement* procedure. It isn't necessary to make *readformula* check what comes after a formula: any attempt to do so makes

```
def readelement(n) =
  skipspaces();
  select isdigchar(crp^): readnumber ↓n
    crp^ = '(': movecrp; readformula(n); movecrp
  endselect;
  skipspaces()
enddef

def readformula(tot) =
  readelement(tot);
  iterate isopchar(crp^):
    initialise op, x := ?, ?

    readchar op; readelement(@x);
    ↓tot := calculate(↓tot, op, x)
  enditerate;
enddef
```

program 17.8

the program more complicated but no more useful.

-=-=-=-=-=-=-=-=-=-=-=-

Exercise 17.9
By drawing environment diagrams, trace the execution of *readformula(@e)* given the following inputs:

> a. (2+3)*4.
> b. (4*1)-7,
> c. 13-5*2)
> d. 42-(6+12)*5;
> e. 42-(6+12,*5:
> f. 42-(6+12a*5=

-=-=-=-=-=-=-=-=-=-=-=-

One mild drawback of program 17.8, illustrated by some of the examples in exercise 17.9, is that it is a bit too user-friendly. It doesn't matter what character you use in the closing bracket position so long as it isn't an operation character or a digit. The *readelement* procedure should be made a little more fussy, perhaps as illustrated in program 17.9.

-=-=-=-=-=-=-=-=-=-=-=-

Exercise 17.10
Repeat exercise 17.9 using the new definition of *readelement*.

Exercise 17.11
Assuming that the definition of *readformula* was modified to include the new definition of *readelement*, what would be the effect of *readformula(@e)* given the input '14-(3*(4+2x)).' (including the final position of the crp)?

```
def readelement(n) =
  skipspaces();
  select isdigchar(crp^): readnumber ↓n
       crp^='(': movecrp; readformula(n);
                 select crp^=')': movecrp
                        crp^≠')': print("closing bracket missing?")
                 endselect
  endselect;
  skipspaces()
enddef
```

program 17.9

Exercise 17.12

Making the same abstractions as in exercise 17.6 but now allowing for the presence of brackets in the input sequence, prove that if the crp is over the opening bracket of an element then *readelement(@x)* will move the crp to the position after the closing bracket. [Hint: by double induction on the 'bracketing depth' of the enclosed formula and its length. A proof like your answer to exercise 17.6 will form the base case when the enclosed formula contains no brackets.]

-=-=-=-=-=-=-=-=-=-=-=-=-=-

17.4 HOW TO HANDLE MISTAKES IN FORMULAS

There are several ways in which you might type a formula incorrectly, and accordingly different ways in which they might be spotted by the *readformula* and *readelement* procedures of programs 17.8 and 17.9. These procedures already 'notice' if there isn't a closing bracket to match each opening bracket and print a message. Suppose that a complete formula always takes up a complete line: then when the first call of *readformula* eventually terminates the crp should be over a *newline* character. If there is some other character at the crp - a comma, a full stop, even a closing bracket - then something has gone wrong. If a numeral in the formula is mistyped - say you have the SHIFT LOCK set on the keyboard so you type '%&' in place of '56' - then both condition-formulas in the *select* instruction inside *readelement* would be false and something nasty would happen.

I can think of no more user-friendly calculator than one which notices my mistake if I make one, points it out as clearly as possible and invites me to try again. To make the program notice the mistake is not difficult: it requires only minor changes to the *readelement* procedure. The clever trick is to organise things so that I can start typing again and so that the program will ignore everything in the incorrectly typed formula but nothing else.

Suppose that a mistake is noticed – a bracket missing, a numeral mistyped, the end of a formula not followed by a *newline*. Then a general description of the program's action might be as follows:

> *print a message of explanation*; *move the crp to the beginning of the next line*; *somehow start all over again*

I don't know any programming mechanism which corresponds directly to starting all over again. But starting all over again implies some form of repetition: that is, it implies that the sequence '*readformula*(@*e*); *printnumber*(*e*)' is being repeatedly executed. To start again in an indefinite repetition it is enough to terminate the current execution: then the next execution will begin and the effect is of 'starting again'. The mechanism can be illustrated by showing how the missing-bracket mistake could be more convincingly treated: see program 17.10, for example.

The normal sequence of operations in program 17.10 is *printstring, readformula, printnumber, movecrp* (the final *movecrp* consumes the *newline* character which must come at the end of the formula). If something goes wrong during the execution of *readformula* the *error* procedure is called. This procedure prints an explanatory message, invites me to try again, then carefully moves the crp to the *newline* character at the end of the line containing the dud formula, before prematurely terminating execution of the program *X*. The effect of executing *error*(..) is therefore to miss out the rest of the execution of *readformula*, to miss out the *printnumber* instruction entirely, and to resume execution at the *movecrp* so that the next *readformula* call will start with the crp at the beginning of the next line in the input sequence.

-=-=-=-=-=-=-=-=-=-=-=-

Exercise 17.13
Modify program 17.10 to cope with wrongly typed numerals. How would your program cope with the input '13*44*&'? How would it cope with the input '13*44+1&'? What explanatory message would it print, if any, in either case?

Exercise 17.14
Modify your program to cope with badly typed operation characters. How would your program cope with the inputs in exercise 17.13? How would it cope with '13*(44+1&*88'?

Exercise 17.15
Mistakes in a formula can take several guises. They can be invisible: for example, if the middle digit of a three-digit numeral is replaced by a plus sign. They can be mistakenly recognised: for example, if the last digit of a numeral is replaced by an operation character then the next character will be taken as a wrongly typed digit. If a digit is replaced by a non-digit, non-operation character then it may be taken as a badly typed operation character or a badly typed right bracket. By altering formulas so as to imitate mistakes in typing and trying out the effect of those inputs on your program, find out how reasonable its explanations of those mistakes actually are. Change your program, if necessary,

to make it print a reasonable explanation of as many mistakes in as many circumstances as possible.

```
iterate true:
  X: def error (s) = NL; printstring(s); printstring(" - try again!")
                    iterate crp^≠newline: movecrp enditerate;
                    terminate X
     enddef
     def readelement(n) =
        skipspaces ();
        select isdigchar(crp^): readnumber ↓n
               crp^='(': movecrp; readformula(n);
                         select crp^=')': movecrp
                                crp^≠')': error("closing bracket missing?")
                         endselect
        endselect;
        skipspaces ()
     enddef
     def readformula(tot) =
        readelement(tot);
        iterate isopchar(crp^):
           initialise op,x := ?,?

           readchar op; readelement(@x);
           ↓tot := calculate(↓tot, op, x)
        enditerate;
     enddef

        initialise e:=?
        printstring("formula please: ");
        readformula(@e);
        if crp^≠newline then error("What is this at the end of your formula?")
                        else printnumber(e)
        fi
  :X;
  movecrp
  enditerate
```

program 17.10

-=

APPENDIX 17.A TRY IT OUT

Exercise 17.16
The programs illustrated in this chapter show you how to build a procedure which imitates a simple calculator. Do it.

Exercise 17.17
A calculator wouldn't be complete without unary operations. Modify *readelement* so that it can handle '+element' and '-element' at least. You might like to deal with factorial in the form of '!element.'

Exercise 17.18
You may be able to give your calculator some register memories. Suppose that memories are labelled by single letters. Then you might be able to process the sequence of lines:

$$30 = a$$
$$2 = b$$
$$a*10+b$$

and print '302'. You can have the equations the other way round if you wish.

Exercise 17.19
In a cheap calculator a formula is a sequence of elements separated by *, /, +, - and ^ characters. It is possible to take account of operator priority by recognising that a formula like

$$a*b+c+d*e^f*g+h$$

would normally be evaluated as though it had been bracketed

$$(a*b)+c+(d*(e^f)*g)+h$$

The complete formula contains +, * and ^ operation symbols. Unless operator symbols are hidden by bracketing, the elements combined by addition contain * and/or ^ symbols; the elements combined by multiplication contain only ^ symbols; the elements combined by exponentiation contain no other arithmetic symbols. An 'expensive calculator' program might therefore employ three different *readelement* procedures, depending on the operation which applies to that element. Write that program.

Chapter 18
PRINTING A CALENDAR

This problem is a real old chestnut. The object is to write a program which prints the European/Roman calendar for any particular year. It's another raster printing exercise, but it's a little bit more interesting than most because the design involves some tricky formulas.

18.1 LAYOUT OF A CALENDAR

Observe that there are all sorts of different possible calendar layouts. Figure 18.1 shows the calendar for 1987, with three months arranged across the page - clearly it could be four or six or even twelve depending on the size of the paper and the size of the writing. Months could follow each other down the page rather than across. In figure 18.1 the days follow each other horizontally across the page but many calendars arrange them vertically. My weeks start with Monday; some calendars start the week with Sunday. Each of these variations makes a useful exercise problem.

18.2 PRINTING A SINGLE MONTH

Just about the only feature of the Roman calendar's layout which is absolutely fixed is the seven-day regularity of the week. In Europe Tuesday has succeeded Monday for thousands of years without a break (though not always under those names). Therefore each month in my calendar must necessarily have either seven columns or seven rows according to whether the week is printed horizontally or vertically.

Suppose that a month is printed with horizontal weeks, as a seven-by-n arrangement of numbers. How big should n be? Most people divide thirty-one by seven, giving four and a bit over, and decide that a month should be a seven-

1987

January	February	March

```
           January                        February                        March

     Mo Tu We Th Fr Sa Su        Mo Tu We Th Fr Sa Su        Mo Tu We Th Fr Sa Su
              1  2  3  4                             1                             1
      5  6  7  8  9 10 11         2  3  4  5  6  7  8         2  3  4  5  6  7  8
     12 13 14 15 16 17 18         9 10 11 12 13 14 15         9 10 11 12 13 14 15
     19 20 21 22 23 24 25        16 17 18 19 20 21 22        16 17 18 19 20 21 22
     26 27 28 29 30 31          23 24 25 26 27 28           23 24 25 26 27 28 29
                                                            30 31


            April                           May                           June

     Mo Tu We Th Fr Sa Su        Mo Tu We Th Fr Sa Su        Mo Tu We Th Fr Sa Su
              1  2  3  4  5                    1  2  3         1  2  3  4  5  6  7
      6  7  8  9 10 11 12         4  5  6  7  8  9 10         8  9 10 11 12 13 14
     13 14 15 16 17 18 19        11 12 13 14 15 16 17        15 16 17 18 19 20 21
     20 21 22 23 24 25 26        18 19 20 21 22 23 24        22 23 24 25 26 27 28
     27 28 29 30                 25 26 27 28 29 30 31        29 30


            July                          August                       September

     Mo Tu We Th Fr Sa Su        Mo Tu We Th Fr Sa Su        Mo Tu We Th Fr Sa Su
              1  2  3  4  5                    1  2            1  2  3  4  5  6
      6  7  8  9 10 11 12         3  4  5  6  7  8  9         7  8  9 10 11 12 13
     13 14 15 16 17 18 19        10 11 12 13 14 15 16        14 15 16 17 18 19 20
     20 21 22 23 24 25 26        17 18 19 20 21 22 23        21 22 23 24 25 26 27
     27 28 29 30 31              24 25 26 27 28 29 30        28 29 30
                                 31


           October                       November                      December

     Mo Tu We Th Fr Sa Su        Mo Tu We Th Fr Sa Su        Mo Tu We Th Fr Sa Su
              1  2  3  4                             1         1  2  3  4  5  6
      5  6  7  8  9 10 11         2  3  4  5  6  7  8         7  8  9 10 11 12 13
     12 13 14 15 16 17 18         9 10 11 12 13 14 15        14 15 16 17 18 19 20
     19 20 21 22 23 24 25        16 17 18 19 20 21 22        21 22 23 24 25 26 27
     26 27 28 29 30 31           23 24 25 26 27 28 29        28 29 30 31
                                 30
```

figure 18.1

by-five arrangement. Not so: look at the 1987 example, in which three of the
months need six rows because the extra days come at the end of the first week
and at the beginning of the last week in the month. Some cheap calendar-makers
print the last days of the month in the first row when this happens, so that they
can always get away with a seven-by-five arrangement, but as programmers we
abhor cheap and nasty solutions!

-=-=-=-=-=-=-=-=-=-=-=-

Exercise 18.1
Define a procedure *row* so that *row*(*i*) prints the *i*th row of a seven-by-six array of numerals

```
 1  2  3  4  5  6  7
 8  9 10 11 12 13 14
15 16 17 18 19 20 21
22 23 24 25 26 27 28
29 30 31 32 33 34 35
36 37 38 39 40 41 42
```

Use your answer in a program which prints the whole seven-by-six pattern. Careful with your layout: be sure that the numbers are aligned vertically and horizontally.

Exercise 18.2
Alter your definition of *row* so that *row*(*i*, *s*) prints the *i*th row of a seven-by-six array made up from the numbers *s*..*s*+41. For example, if *s*=−2, use it in a program which prints the pattern

```
-2 -1  0  1  2  3  4
 5  6  7  8  9 10 11
12 13 14 15 16 17 18
19 20 21 22 23 24 25
26 27 28 29 30 31 32
33 34 35 36 37 38 39
```

Exercise 18.3
Modify your *row* procedure still further so that it prints only the numbers which fall in the range 1..31, printing spaces in the other positions: for example, if *s*=−2 it might now print the pattern

```
             1  2  3  4
 5  6  7  8  9 10 11
12 13 14 15 16 17 18
19 20 21 22 23 24 25
26 27 28 29 30 31
```
(blank line)

Note that there must be a blank line at the end of this particular pattern in place of the numbers 33..39.

Exercise 18.4
Using your skill and judgement (and your knowledge of raster printing techniques) write a program which prints three patterns like that in exercise 18.3 arranged across the page:

```
             1  2  3  4                 1  2  3  4                 1  2  3  4
 5  6  7  8  9 10 11     5  6  7  8  9 10 11     5  6  7  8  9 10 11
12 13 14 15 16 17 18    12 13 14 15 16 17 18    12 13 14 15 16 17 18
19 20 21 22 23 24 25    19 20 21 22 23 24 25    19 20 21 22 23 24 25
26 27 28 29 30 31       26 27 28 29 30 31       26 27 28 29 30 31
(blank line)
```

Exercise 18.5
Modify your answer to exercise 18.4 so that each month starts on the day of the
week after the one on which the previous month finishes:

```
      1  2  3  4                      1              1  2  3  4  5
 5  6  7  8  9 10 11    2  3  4  5  6  7  8    6  7  8  9 10 11 12
12 13 14 15 16 17 18    9 10 11 12 13 14 15   13 14 15 16 17 18 19
19 20 21 22 23 24 25   16 17 18 19 20 21 22   20 21 22 23 24 25 26
26 27 28 29 30 31      23 24 25 26 27 28 29   27 28 29 30 31
                       30 31
```

Note that in this example there is no longer a need for a blank line.

Exercise 18.6
Repeat exercises 18.1-18.5, but this time based on a six-by-seven arrray of
numbers

```
1   8  15  22  29  36
2   9  16  23  30  37
3  10  17  24  31  38
4  11  18  25  32  39
5  12  19  26  33  40
6  13  20  27  34  41
7  14  21  28  35  42
```

-=-=-=-=-=-=-=-=-=-=-=-

18.3 CALCULATING A START-DAY FOR EACH MONTH

The first day of January 1987 is a Thursday. So to print the calendar of January
1987 you have to print a seven-by-six (or six-by-seven) arrangement of numbers
in such a way that the number 1 is printed in the column (or row) which stands
for Thursday: then every day which follows in that month will fall in the right
position.

Since January has four complete weeks plus three extra days, it follows that
February must always start three days later in the week than January: that is, in
1987 February must start on a Sunday. And since February starts on Sunday and
in 1987 February has four weeks exactly, it follows that March 1st 1987 must
also be a Sunday. And therefore April 1987 must start on a Wednesday, since
March has four complete weeks and three extra days. And so on for every other
month. Given the starting day of the previous month and the length of that
month you can calculate the starting day of the next month.

-=-=-=-=-=-=-=-=-=-=-=-

Exercise 18.7
Suppose that the months are numbered January=0, February=1, .. December=11.
Write a procedure which delivers the number of days in each month, ignoring the
problem of leap years.

Exercise 18.8
Suppose that the days of the week are numbered Monday=0, Tuesday=1, ..,
Sunday=6. Write a procedure which delivers the number of the day on which
month m starts, if January starts on day d. [Hint: either recursion or repetition.]

Exercise 18.9
Modify your answer to the exercises 18.7 and 18.8 to take account of the
Gregorian leap-year calculation, used in England since 1753. A year is a leap
year if its number is divisible by 4 *except* when its number is divisible by 100;
however it is a leap year if its number is divisible by 400. So 1980 was a leap
year but 1900 was not; 2000 will be a leap year.

Exercise 18.10
Write a procedure which prints any row of the seven-by-six arrangement for any
of the months of 1987, using your answers to previous exercises and the fact that
the calendar for 1987 starts on a Thursday.

Exercise 18.11
Write a program which prints a row of months from the seven-by-six style
calendar for any three successive months of 1987, in the style of figure 18.1.

Exercise 18.12
Suppose that the layout of the calendar is such that the months are arranged

Jan	May	Sept
Feb	June	Oct
Mar	July	Nov
Apr	Aug	Dec

Write a program which prints any month-row of this calendar: for example, the
second month-row contains seven-by-six arrangements for February, June and
October.

Exercise 18.13
Answer exercises 18.10-18.12 for the six-by-seven arrangement of day-numbers
within a month.

Exercise 18.14
Write a program which prints a calendar like figure 18.1 for any year, given only
the starting day of the year and its number. Put in the month-names and the
day-labels ('Mo', 'Tu', and so on).

Exercise 18.15
Answer exercise 18.14 for the six-by-seven arrangement of days.

-=-=-=-=-=-=-=-=-=-=-=-=-

A normal year has three hundred and sixty-five days, which is fifty-two complete
weeks and one extra day. A leap year has fifty-two complete weeks and two
extra days. So if year y starts on a Tuesday, year $y+1$ must start on a Wednesday,
or on a Thursday if y is a leap year.

-=-=-=-=-=-=-=-=-=-=-=-=-

Exercise 18.16
Write a procedure which calculates the day of the week in which any year in the twentieth century starts, given that 1901 started on a Tuesday.

Exercise 18.17
Write a program which prints the calendar of any year in the twentieth century.

-=-=-=-=-=-=-=-=-=-=-=-

18.4 MISTAKES IN DESIGN AND IN FORMULAS

Exercise 18.8 was careful to suggest that days should be numbered 0, 1, 2, .. Some novice programmers number their days 1, 2, 3, .. If you tried it that way you might have made some famous mistakes. Problems arise because $x \, rem \, 7$ is a number in the range 0..6, but the answer required is a number in the range 1..7. Just adding one to your answer usually isn't enough to make the calculation correct.

-=-=-=-=-=-=-=-=-=-=-=-

Exercise 18.18
Assume that the days of the week are numbered 1, 2, 3 .. rather than 0, 1, 2 .. Write a procedure which calculates the number of the starting day of year y, knowing the number of the starting day of year $y-1$. Check your answer against an official calendar; try it for various cases of leap years and different starting days.

-=-=-=-=-=-=-=-=-=-=-=-

Apparently trivial changes to a program can require great care. The exercises above produced calendars whose weeks start on a Monday. Some people prefer their calendars to start each week on a Sunday. Some eccentric might want one which starts on a Wednesday.

-=-=-=-=-=-=-=-=-=-=-=-

Exercise 18.19
Write a procedure which prints one row of the numerical arrangement for a particular month with the week starting on any particular day. A parameter to the procedure should give the starting day (Monday=0, Tuesday=1, .. Sunday=6). Be careful not to print a blank first row.

Exercise 18.20
Write a calendar-printing program which prints the calendar of any year this century, asking for the year number and on which day the week should start.

Exercise 18.21
Write a program which prints a 'cheap and nasty' calendar with only five rows of days per month by combining the first and the sixth rows. For example, the entry

for March 1987 might appear as follows:

```
30 31                1
 2  3  4  5  6  7  8
 9 10 11 12 13 14 15
16 17 18 19 20 21 22
23 24 25 26 27 28 29
```

-=

APPENDIX 18.A TRY IT OUT

This chapter's exercises ask you to write a calendar-printing program in various styles. Try several of them (but start with the exercises which print arrangements of numbers, then build up to the whole solution).

You might try to write a calendar which is accurate over several centuries. Extending forward is easy but rather pointless because nobody knows what will happen to the calendar in the future. Extending backward is more fun because the European calendar has been adjusted in various ways from an original Roman Republican model. Julius Caesar tried unsuccessfully to standardise the calculation of leap years in 45 B.C. In A.D. 8 the Emperor Augustus introduced the month names and lengths which we know today, with a leap year every four years. The Augustan (usually called Julian or old-style) calendar introduced one too many days about every one hundred and twenty-eight years because the solar year is slightly less than 365.25 days, and the calendar year slipped in comparison with the solar year.

The slip was considered unfortunate by Christians because it made the date of Easter drift slowly around the year, and in A.D. 1582 Pope Gregory XIII decreed that the calendar should be adjusted and that we should use the calculation set out in exercise 18.9. In order to bring the calendar year back into line with the sun he ordered that October 15th 1582 should follow October 4th 1582, thus eliminating ten days from that year. The adjustment didn't bring the calendar quite into line with Augustus's but instead, for doctrinal reasons, with the calendar used at the Council of Niceae in A.D. 325. The Gregorian (new-style) calendar was adopted in France that year and in most Catholic countries in 1583, but Protestants dallied.

In 1752 England and its colonies adopted the Gregorian calendar. By now the discrepancy was eleven days, because 1700 was an old-style but not a new-style leap year. September 14th 1752 followed directly after September 2nd 1752. There were riots but the change stuck. To write a calendar for Britain or the Commonwealth or the USA, then, it is necessary to cater separately for 1752, for years after 1752 and for years from 8 to 1751. The only base date you need to know is Tuesday January 1st 1901.

Before 1752 in England and its colonies New Year's Day was March 25th, the notional date of the Spring Equinox. Three hundred and sixty-five days after March 25th 1752 came April 5th 1753: April 5th is still used as the start of the taxation year in Britain. Earlier still the new year had been measured from December 25th, the notional date of the Winter Solstice. Fit that in your program if you like.

If that still isn't complicated enough for you you might extend the calendar back to 45 B.C. when the Julian calendar was introduced. Look up the details in a reference book: they are far too complicated to summarise here (and remember that there never was a year 0). Before 45 B.C. no systematic calculation is possible because the Roman priests used to cheat with the calendar for political purposes, to shorten or lengthen the period of office of particular individuals.

The Roman solar calendar isn't the only one in use by any means. You might find the rules for some other calendar and use them to print comparative calendars for particular times.

Part Four
STRUCTURES OF VALUES

You can't fit the real world inside a computer: it can't swallow a power station, or a road network, or the social security ministry, or an aeroplane flying above a city. Yet the behaviour of each of these things can be and is imitated every day by computer programs. A computer program can be a *model* which you can use to find out things about reality without having to run expensive real-world experiments. Like a constructor-set model it isn't exactly like reality but it can be sufficiently like it to give useful indications about how the real thing does behave. A computer program is a mathematical or symbolic model, unlike the mechanical models that children play with.

The parts of a good model must be systematically related in ways which are as close as possible to the ways in which the parts of the real thing are related. When a model is a computer program, some of the relationships can be described by structures of instructions, using the techniques and mechanisms introduced in this book so far. Some other relationships will be easier to capture if the program model recognises systematic relationships between values which it manipulates. Value or data structuring is an enormous subject and this book can only skim its surface.

Executions can be organised into ordered sequences, hierarchical or recursive structures, repetitive structures, choice structures, and so on, in all of the ways described in Parts One and Two of this book. There are analogous structures of values. The classical repetitive value structures are the *sequence* and the *indexed set*, introduced in chapter 19. The classical hierarchical/recursive structures are the *tree* and the *list*, introduced in chapter 21. Choice enters when hierarchical structures can be made up of alternative sorts of parts. Repetition enters when components of structures can be shared, as discussed in chapter 22.

Most mechanical codes directly represent only a few kinds of control structures and even fewer kinds of value structures. (This isn't the place to discuss why this is so: it just is so and unless you become an inventor of 'programming languages' you will have to put up with it.) You can learn to imitate the ones which you use in your program but your code doesn't provide. Nowadays you can be fairly sure that it will be easy to imitate sequences using *vectors* or *arrays.* You may be able to imitate hierarchical data structures using *reference*

403

values (pointers) in some of the ways described in chapter 21. Many other sorts of value can be imitated: for example, chapter 22 shows how sets of values can be imitated by two sorts of sequences or by procedure definitions.

The most powerful programming technique is abstraction, and it can be applied to structures of values as usefully as to instructions. When you design a program don't restrict your thinking to the structuring tools provided in a mechanical code, or even to those described in this book. Design your program as if the descriptions you want to write can be understood by the machine, then work out how to imitate your program in the mechanical code you have decided to use. This book only scratches the surface of the enormous subject of *data representation* - how to imitate the structures of values you are thinking about with the structuring tools provided in some notation.

Chapter 19
SEQUENCES AND INDEXED SETS OF VALUES

So far in this book my programs have manipulated single values: values like integers characters or procedures, which are atomic and can't be divided into parts. A number is a number is a number, a character is a character is a character. They don't have parts: what is the bottom half of a letter 'A' value? What is the first part of a number? What is the last part?

The notation used for reasoning with the input sequence, introduced in chapter 11, has so far been of theoretical interest. This chapter employs the same notation to describe practically useful values which have parts and which can be manipulated by programs. Once again the example chosen has to do with numbers and numerals, but this time the problem is examined from a different viewpoint. I show how to develop a program which can manipulate very big numbers, using sequences to represent the numbers. The message is that abstraction helps in program design: if you write a program in terms of operations on big numbers, but your programming system can't cope, don't panic! Numbers are an abstraction; abstractions can be imitated.

Computers nowadays imitate numbers with binary numerals and imitate addition, subtraction, multiplication, division and the rest of the arithmetic operations by doing algebra with numerals. Economic and technological pressures force computer designers to work with limited size numerals: for example, the machinery needed to 'add' two n-bit binary numerals is half the size of the machinery needed to do the same thing with a pair of $2n$-bit numerals, and the smaller version does its job faster than the big one. Many programming systems tamely follow the design of the machine they run on, or provide only small multiples of the numeral-width provided. A few (notably LISP systems) can imitate much larger numbers, using techniques like those described in this chapter.

Modern computers work with binary numeral-widths that are a multiple of eight. Many provide arithmetic operations on sixteen-bit numerals. There are 2^{16} different sixteen-bit numerals, giving an integer number range roughly between plus and minus thirty thousand. This is adequate for some purposes, but it is hopelessly restricted when you want to do big accurate calculations. Even thirty-two-bit numerals (BIG computer power, say the advertisements) only give a range between plus and minus two thousand million. Sounds enormous: but it's less than thirteen factorial ($13\times12\times11\times..\times2\times1$). Machine designers extend the number range by using 'floating point' representation, sacrificing accuracy in the process. That pushes the limits farther away but there are still limits. For an example in the next chapter I wanted to calculate 64! and I couldn't remember the approximation formula: even using its thirty-two-bit floating point representation my home micro couldn't tell me an approximation to the answer. In the end I did it with a calculator[†].

Computers represent numbers with sequences of binary digits. In this chapter I investigate the imitation of numbers using sequences of decimal digits.

19.1 IMITATING SEQUENCES

You must by now be aware that when computers 'perform a calculation', 'take a decision', 'send out a bill', 'make a mistake' there is always an element of pretence involved. Computers can do none of these things: what they do is to follow rules laid down by a programmer so that they imitate what a very obedient human servant might do in their place. The computer is imitating, or representing, one sort of action by another sort: appearing to make judgements while only making choices; appearing to make a calculation while only juggling with the rules of Boolean algebra, and so on.

The hardware machinery of any computer is constructed to represent certain kinds of values: typically small numbers and short bit-patterns. But a program can *represent* or *imitate* one sort of value with another, and sequences of values are extremely useful in imitation. For example: the coded messages sent around in World War II battles were sometimes long sequences of digits. Clearly each long sequence of digits wasn't supposed to represent just a number, though clearly it could do so. It was intended to represent a sentence (or a paragraph, or a letter, ..) and if the digits were grouped in the right way and you used the right code book you would discover that the enormous numeral represented a message from a commander to his troops, from a field officer to his commander, or whatever.

Computers 'actually' work with binary patterns which can represent or imitate numerals and therefore numbers. Viewed as numbers those patterns can represent other things if you simply decide on a code. The number 1 might represent the colour red, 2 the colour green, 3 the colour blue, 0 the 'colour'

[†] I don't wish to make an argument here for different, 'better' machine design with bigger numerals. A more expansive representation for numbers would be nice, but it costs money to make machines that way and whatever size you choose the representation is still limited. In the last resort a programmer has to rely on imitation to provide the mechanisms a program needs.

black: then a sequence of two-digit binary numerals can represent a garish colour television picture. Alternatively, the number 7 might represent a seven-year old female, the number −7 a seven-year old male: then a set of signed numerals can describe the age and sex of every member of a primary school class, or every person in the school, or every inhabitant in a city, or every animal in a zoo. In chapter 10 there was an explanation of how numbers can be used to represent (imitate, characterise, identify) character values, and in chapter 12 there was an explanation of how character values can do the same thing for numbers.

A large number can imitate a sequence of smaller numbers, and vice-versa. For example, the number 1024 can imitate the sequence <1,0,2,4> of numbers between 0 and 9, or the sequence <4,4,2,4> of numbers between 0 and 4 or the sequence <1,3,5,7> of numbers between 0 and 8. You can decode the sequence if you choose a number-base and then use the *digval* procedure of chapter 15 to extract a particular component of the sequence.

-=-=-=-=-=-=-=-=-=-=-=-=-=-

Exercise 19.1
If the number 1024 represents the sequence <1,0,2,4> of numbers between 0 and 9, is it possible to represent the sequence <0,1,0,2,4>? If so, what number represents it; if not, why not? How about the sequence <1,0,2,4,0>?

Exercise 19.2
Devise a way in which a sequence of small numbers each between 0 and 9, which may start and/or end with a zero, could be represented by a single positive number. What numbers would represent the sequences <1,0,2,4>, <0,1,0,2,4>, <0,0,1,0,2,4>, <1,0,2,4,0>, <1,0,2,4,0,0>, <9,9,9>, <0,0,9,0,0>, <>, <0>, <0,0>?

-=-=-=-=-=-=-=-=-=-=-=-=-=-

Exercises 19.1 and 19.2 should convince you that computers *can* manipulate values which imitate sequences. How sequences are 'actually' represented is, as usual, not so important to the programmer as the fact that it can be done. ('Actually' it is done with large binary numerals, and don't let anybody tell you otherwise!)

19.2 SEQUENCE NOTATION

If S is a sequence formula (a formula which describes a sequence) and i is a number formula, then S_i accesses the ith element of the sequence described by S. For example, if $T = <5, 3, 4, 9>$ then $T_1 = 5$, $T_2 = 3$, $T_3 = 4$, $T_4 = 9$, $T_{(T_3)} = T_4 = 9$. *Length(S)* counts the number of elements in a sequence S: $length(T) = length(<5, 3, 4, 9>) = 4$.

Sequences can be named directly: $<3, 9, 11, 41>$ is a constant formula which describes a four-element sequence. Sequence formulas may be names, constants or describe a calculation: for example, $<a, b, x, x+y>$ also describes a four-element sequence whose elements must be calculated from the values a, b, x and y. Sequence formulas like those above can be accessed immediately: for example, $<3, 9, 11, 41>_3 = 11$ and $<a, b, x, x+y>_4 = x+y$.

Sequences are values just as numbers, characters, strings and procedures are: you can use them as arguments in procedure calls, you can define names for them, you can put them into containers, you can construct arbitrarily complicated formulas which deliver them as results, and so on.

Strings, in particular, are sequences of character values. The string "hello" is nothing more nor less than the sequence $<$'h', 'e', 'l', 'l', 'o'$>$. It follows that strings can be indexed to retrieve particular elements: "hello"$_2$ is the character 'e'.

Indexing

Unless otherwise stated the first element of a sequence S is S_1 and the last is $S_{length(S)}$. For example, if $T = <9, 1, 6, 7>$ then T_0 is a meaningless formula, as is T_5. The range of numbers which index a sequence can be defined: for example, if a program includes the definition

$$let\ U = <1, 4, 9, 16>\ indexed\ 0..3$$

then U_0, U_1, U_2 and U_3 are defined. Note that although U_4 is not defined, $length(U)$ is still 4 because $length$ counts the number of elements of a sequence.

Concatenation and subsequencing

One very useful thing you can do with a sequence is lengthen or shorten it. The operation '$\oplus$' (pronounced 'cat' or 'concat') joins two sequences together. For example:

$$<\text{'h', 'e', 'l', 'l', 'o'}> \oplus <\text{' ', 't', 'h', 'e', 'r', 'e'}>$$

describes the sequence

$$<\text{'h', 'e', 'l', 'l', 'o', ' ', 't', 'h', 'e', 'r', 'e'}>$$

which is the same as the string "hello there". To lengthen a sequence you must add a new sequence on to the beginning or the end: for example, $<1, 2, 3, 4> \oplus <5> = <1, 2, 3, 4, 5>$ and $<1> \oplus <10, 20, 30> = <1, 10, 20, 30>$. The $\oplus$ operation joins two *sequences*: the formula $<x, y> \oplus 1$ is meaningless because 1 is not a sequence.

Sequences are most conveniently shortened by selecting a subsequence: "hello there"$_{4..7}$ = "lo t", the same as the sequence $<$'l', 'o', ' ', 't'$>$. Subsequences are sequences, and are indexed just like any other. In particular their first element is numbered 1: so ("hello there"$_{4..7}$)$_2$ = "lo t"$_2$ = 'o'. As in chapter 11, the shorthand $S_{i..}$ means all the elements $S'_{i..length(S)}$.

Sequence values in containers

If A names a container and S names a sequence you can reasonably write $A:=S$. Containers in my notation are infinitely stretchy: just as they can hold numbers of any size and to any accuracy they can hold sequences of any length and with any kind of elements. So you might write $A:=A\oplus<9>$ and then, if A holds the sequence $<1,3,5,7>$ before this instruction, it will hold $<1,3,5,7,9>$ after it. If A doesn't already hold a sequence the instruction is meaningless.

Again, you might write $A:=A_{1..4}$ and then, if A holds a large enough sequence it will be trimmed. For example, if A holds the sequence $<9,5,4,7,2,1,1>$ before this instruction is executed, it will hold $<9,5,4,7>$ after it. If A doesn't hold a sequence, or if it holds a sequence with less than four characters, then the instruction is meaningless.

Sometimes you might want to tinker with a sequence, to change some of its elements. If the container A contains a sequence, you might change the ith element of that sequence with the instruction $A:=A_{1..i-1}\oplus<x>\oplus A_{i+1..}$. This is such a common operation that there is a special shorthand for it: you write $A_i:=x$. Either version is meaningless if A doesn't contain a sequence or if that sequence doesn't have an ith element. Notice that the assignment instruction $A_i:=x$ builds a new sequence, just as the instruction $a:=a+1$ builds a new number[†], but the effect is just as if one element of the sequence had been changed. There's an obvious analogue using subsequences: $A_{i..j}:=B$ replaces elements i, $i+1$, .., j of the sequence stored in A.

Multiple assignments apply to sequences as well. The instruction $A_i, A_j := A_j, A_i$ exchanges the elements of a sequence. It is possible to write ambiguous multiple assignments: just as $x,x:=3,4$ has one of two possible outcomes, so does $A_i, A_i := 3, 4$. I don't give a formal treatment of multiple assignments to sequence containers in this book.

Operating on every element of a sequence

It is often very useful to be able to write programs which operate on every element of a sequence: for example, print them out one by one, add them up, double them, or whatever. Sometimes it is only necessary to put the sequence as the controlling sequence in a *for-do*. For example:

for i rt S do printnumber(i) od

will print out the components of a numerical sequence S, and

[†] Strictly, a new representation of a sequence and a new representation of a number.

$$initially\ 0$$
$$for\ i\ rt\ S\ do\ +i\ od$$

will calculate their total.

If you want to systematically alter every component of a sequence it is often convenient to use a *for-do* which runs through the indexing set. Normally $1..length(S)$ defines the indexing values of S. For example, the following program increases the value of every element of a sequence held in container V:

$$for\ i\ rt\ 1..length(V)\ do\ V_i:=V_i+1\ od$$

Hierarchies of sequences

Sequences can contain any sort of element, even other sequences, just as sequences of instructions can contain structured instructions. Hierarchical structures are then easy to devise. For example:

$$W = <<10, 15>, <-33, 94, 16>, <0, 5, 0, 6>, <>>$$

is a sequence of four sequences. Note in particular that $length(W)=4$ because W itself has four elements. It doesn't matter that each element is itself a sequence. The length of each element can be determined in this case: for example, $length(W_1)=2$ and $length(W_4)=0$.

Elements of hierarchies may be indexed hierarchically: $(W_1)_2 = <10, 15>_2 = 15$. There is a shorthand which eliminates the brackets:

$$S_{i,j} = (S_i)_j$$

definition 19.1

and which, by obvious generalisation, extends to more than two levels of structure.

19.3 INDEXED SETS

Sequences are collections of elements. Sets are collections of elements. Sequences differ from sets in that their elements are **indexed** and that therefore position within the sequence matters. The same element can occur several times in a sequence: for example, in the sequence $<a, x, b, x, c, x, d, x, e>$ there are four occurrences of x, indexed by 2, 4, 6 and 8 respectively. Normal sets don't behave like that because in a set an element either occurs or it doesn't occur: where it occurs is irrelevant. Thus $\{a, b, c, d, x\}$ describes the same set as $\{x, a, b, c, d\}$ or $\{x, a, x, b, x, c, x, d\}$ or $\{a, b, a, b, c, d, x, x, x\}$ or any of the infinite number of ways of describing this set. The element x occurs in it, and that is all you can say about *x* and this set.

Sequences are a particular form of *indexed set*, indexed by numbers. Put another way, the *indexing set* of a sequence is a particular range of numbers. In principle the indexing set can be anything you like: you can index a set by the set of colours, by the set of prime numbers less than thirty-one, by the set of filing cabinets in your bedroom, by the set of teddy-bears in your bedroom, by the set of the previous three sets in this sentence, and so on.

I use two alternative notations for indexed sets. The normal sequence notation $<a,b,c,d,e>$ describes a sequence of five elements indexed by the numbers between 1 and 5. One notation makes this explicit:

$$<a,b,c,d,e> \text{ indexed } \{1,2,3,4,5\}$$

Sometimes I write this as:

$$<a,b,c,d,e> \text{ indexed } 1..5$$

without, I hope, causing any confusion. The alternative notation for indexed sets writes each element as:

$$\text{index}ing \text{ element} = \text{index}ed \text{ element}$$

For example, the sequence above can be described as

$$\{1=a, 2=b, 3=c, 4=d, 5=e\}$$

In this last form it doesn't matter in what order the elements are introduced or how many times you say the same thing. Either of the following describes the same indexed set:

$$\{2=b, 1=a, 4=d, 3=c, 5=e\}$$
$$\{5=e, 1=a, 4=d, 2=b, 3=c\}$$

and so on through all the possible variations.

The environments of Part One are an indexed set of meanings, indexed by the set of names used in a particular part of a program.

-=-=-=-=-=-=-=-=-=-=-=-

Exercise 19.3
It is useful, in a translation program, to be able to translate names of things into foreign names of things. In translating from English to some other language you might use an indexed set D containing strings indexed by $\{mon, tue, wed, thu, fri, sat, sun\}$ and organised so that D_{mon} is the name for Monday in that other language, D_{tue} the name for Tuesday, and so on. For example, if you were translating into Martian, D_{mon} would be "Zgfrg", the Martian name for Monday. Construct the indexed set D for as many Earth-bound languages as you know, including English.

Exercise 19.4
For each of the indexed sets in your answer to exercise 19.3, what are the values

of $(D_{sun})_3$, $(D_{thu})_2$? [Don't forget that a string is a character-value sequence.]
Exercise 19.5
Continuing with the example from exercise 19.3: why is the formula $D_{(sun_2)}$ always meaningless? Why is the formula $(D_2)_{sun}$ always meaningless? How about the formula $D_{(2_{sun})}$?

-=-=-=-=-=-=-=-=-=-=-=-=-

Homogeneous and inhomogeneous indexed sets

The sequence

$$H = <0, 1, 2, 3, 5, 9, 11>$$

is *homogeneous* in the sense that all of its components are the same sort of thing - in this case they are all numbers. The sequence

$$J = <1, \text{‘a’}, \text{“hello”}, \lambda().print*>$$

is *inhomogeneous* because its elements are different sorts of things: a number, a character, a sequence of characters and a procedure.

Many programming systems make a careful distinction in their notation between homogeneous and inhomogeneous sequences. The reason is that the designer wishes to apply a particularly simple test of consistency to a program to see whether its parts fit together. We know that $x+2$ is a sensible formula provided that x names a number: we know therefore that if i belongs to the indexing set of sequence H then H_i+2 is meaningful because every one of the elements of H is a number. But we don't know whether or not J_i+2 is meaningful because the sort of thing that J_i delivers depends on the value of i. It is this sort of uncertainty which makes the designers of mechanical codes distinguish between homogeneous and inhomogeneous indexed sets and restrict the sort of things you can do with the inhomogeneous kind.

Deciding what makes a set homogeneous or inhomogeneous isn't quite as easy as it may seem. I find it natural to suppose that the sequence

<"this", "sequence", "is", "homogeneous", "surely">

is what it claims to be. Each component is a string: that is, a sequence of characters. By analogy it follows that the following sequence must also be homogeneous:

$$<<3, 5, 7>, <99, 8>, <1, 2, 3, 4, 5>, <>, <222>>$$

Many mechanical codes accept the first example as homogeneous (the most famous exception is Pascal); some accept the first and reject the second.

In general a sequence is homogeneous if you can find a way of seeing each of its components as the same sort as the others. Designers of mechanical codes have to find simple ways of imitating sequences and will invent simple rules to divide the homogeneous sheep from the inhomogeneous goats. Don't fall into the trap of believing that those rules are the only ones possible.

Sequences are a special sort of indexed set because you can do arithmetic on the index*ing* set: because 3+1=4 it is reasonable to say that S_4 is the element after S_3. But if a program environment E contains meanings for x and y there is no reason to suppose that E_x comes 'before' or 'after' E_y. Most programming sequences make a special case of structured values which can be indexed by integers. They demand that since the index*ing* value can be calculated, then the sort of value index*ed* must not depend on the calculation. In effect they demand that sequences must be homogeneous. This book isn't the place to argue whether this demand is reasonable or not. The difficulty is quite easily avoided if inhomogeneous collections are represented using sets indexed by unrelated values.

19.4 ADDING UP

You surely remember that in your childhood you had to practise arithmetic, 'doing sums' like these:

```
   742          1382
  +214          + 49
   956          1431
```

figure 19.1

You practised until you could get them right, using rules which may or may not have been justified to you. What you learnt was an *algorithm:* a procedure or program for the addition of numbers represented as multi-digit numerals[†]. You may have changed schools and had to change algorithms, because there are lots of different algorithms, all equally valid. You may have invented your own algorithm, in which case you will probably find this chapter easier to understand than other people do because you understand how your algorithm works.

It would be possible to write a computer program based on exactly the algorithm you use, but to do that you have to find out what the algorithm is. Most people learn the addition algorithm so well that it becomes part of themselves and they can no longer describe it accurately. Sometimes they can't even carry it through slowly enough for others to reconstruct it for them! The best approach is to rediscover an algorithm starting from sound principles.

[†] The very word 'algorithm' is derived from the name of the Arabic mathematician who developed the first procedures for addition, subtraction, multiplication and division in decimal notation. In Christian Europe his name was written as Al-Khoweizmi.

The normal algorithm for adding together two multi-digit numerals requires you to be able to add together two single-digit numerals. You only need to remember a few rules, like 7+2=9, 9+2=11, 1+0=1, .. - I say 'only' and 'a few', but there are fifty rules, or a hundred if you don't notice their symmetry. If I assume that a computer can add together single-digit values then I can imitate the first addition problem of figure 19.1 by program 19.1.

$$let\ A, B\ =\ <7, 4, 2>, <2, 1, 4>$$
$$initialise\ C\ :=\ <0, 0, 0>$$
$$for\ i\ rt\ 1..3\ do\ C_i := A_i + B_i\ od;$$
$$printnumseq(C)$$

program 19.1

This program is an *imitation* of the more abstract version 'print the value of 742+214'. It prints something which can be read to be the correct answer: <9,5,6>. Unfortunately it won't always work if A and B are changed: if A were <2,4,7>, for example, the program would print <4,5,11>, which doesn't look much like 461, the correct sum of 247 and 214.

Carry-over in multi-digit addition

Program 19.1 ignores carry-over - the way that one digit-addition can influence the next - and gets away with it because of the pattern of digit values in the particular numerals it works with. It also breaks one of the rules of the algorithm I learnt in childhood by working from the wrong end: because of carry-over it's harder to do multi-digit addition if you start with the hundreds digit, easier if you start with the units digit.

$$let\ A, B\ =\ <7, 4, 2>, <2, 1, 4>$$
$$initialise\ C\ :=\ <0, 0, 0>$$
$$for\ i\ rbt\ 1..3\ do\ C_i := A_i + B_i\ od;$$
$$printnumseq(C)$$

program 19.2

Program 19.2 starts at the right end by running backwards through the index values. This may not be the best way to do things: it might be better to write the numbers 'backwards', units digit first. But program design isn't entirely systematic and sometimes we must experiment, so I proceed with this design a little further.

To solve the carry-over problem requires a more fundamental change to the algorithm. If addition in one digit position produces a number too large to write as a single digit then the effect is felt in the next position to the left. For example, if $A=<2, 4, 7>$ and $B=<2, 1, 5>$ then $A_3 + B_3 = 12$, which is too large to fit. The solution is to write $C_3 = 2$, which is exactly ten smaller than the sum of

A_3 and B_3, and to add ten to the answer somehow. This is done by adding one in the next digit position to the left: this is the 'carry-over'. The new algorithm therefore adds together *three* values in each position - one digit value from each numeral and the carry-over (either one or zero) from the previous addition - and records two answers - a digit value for the current position and a carry-over for the next position. The carry-over into the rightmost digit position is always zero, because there is no previous position.

> *let A, B* = <7,4,2>, <2,1,4>
> *initialise C,D* := <0,0,0>, <0,0,0>
>
> *for i rbt* 1..3 *do*
>   *let sum* = A_i+B_i+D_i
>   *select sum*≥10: D_{i-1} := 1; C_i:=*sum*−10
>   *sum*<10: D_{i-1} :=0; C_i:=*sum*
>   *endselect*
> *od*;
> *printnumseq(C)*

program 19.3

In program 19.3 D_i is the carry into position i, the carry-over from the addition in position $i+1$. All very well, but on the last repetition, when $i=1$, it attempts to alter D_0, which doesn't exist. So the program doesn't work in its present form.

-=-=-=-=-=-=-=-=-=-=-=-

Exercise 19.6
Suppose that in program 19.3 D is a sequence indexed 0..3, so that the program doesn't contain a meaningless instruction after all: then check that the algorithm produces the right answer by pencil-and-paper execution using example sequences A and B of your own invention.

Exercise 19.7
Program 19.3 computes carry-over using a *select* instruction. The program can be made more compact if you use '+' and '*rem*' operations. Construct that program. [Hint: ten+ten=1; 9+ten=0.]

Exercise 19.8
Find an example which shows that program 19.3, even when corrected to allow access to D_0, doesn't always print the correct answer. What characterises the difference between the state of affairs it produces when the answer is correct and the one it produces when the answer is incorrect?

-=-=-=-=-=-=-=-=-=-=-=-

There are plenty of ways to solve the D_0 problem which aren't like that suggested in exercise 19.6. For example, you might use jiggery-pokery with index formulas - put D_{i+1} in place of D_i, put D_i in place of D_{i-1}, make D a four-element sequence. But all this effort is unnecessary: the sequence D isn't like the sequences A, B or C in this program. We never need to know the whole value of

D. Only two elements are ever required: the carry-over from the previous addition, used to compute the present digit-sum, and the carry-over into the next addition, which must be recorded.

$$let\ A, B\ =\ <7, 4, 2>, <2, 1, 4>$$
$$initialise\ C, D\ :=\ <0, 0, 0>, <0, 0, 0, 0>\ indexed\ 0..3$$

$\{$ *let sum* = $A_3 + B_3 + D_3$
  select sum ≥ 10: $D_2 := 1$; $C_3 := sum - 10$
       sum < 10: $D_2 := 0$; $C_3 := sum$
  endselect
$\}$;
$\{$ *let sum* = $A_2 + B_2 + D_2$
  select sum ≥ 10: $D_1 := 1$; $C_2 := sum - 10$
       sum < 10: $D_1 := 0$; $C_2 := sum$
  endselect
$\}$;
$\{$ *let sum* = $A_1 + B_1 + D_1$
  select sum ≥ 10: $D_0 := 1$; $C_1 := sum - 10$
       sum < 10: $D_0 := 0$; $C_1 := sum$
  endselect
$\}$;
printnumseq(*C*)

program 19.4

Unrolling program 19.3 to give program 19.4 shows just how *D* is used and makes it clear that the program doesn't need a sequence *D* at all. The separate environments created by the *for-do* can share a single number-container *d*, because in every assignment to *D* the particular element altered is only required for the addition which follows; vice-versa, each reference to *D* uses only the result of the immediately preceding addition.

-=-=-=-=-=-=-=-=-=-=-=-

Exercise 19.9
Construct the one-container carry-over program. Check it with the sums you used in exercises 19.6 and 19.8. [Hint: careful with the initial value of *d*.] What characterises the state left by a correct addition? An incorrect addition? [Hint: what is the final value of *d*?]

Exercise 19.10
Construct a version of program 19.3 which always produces the correct answer no matter what the values of *A* and *B*, provided that each is a sequence of digit values. [Hint: try extending *C* with the ⊕ operation.]

-=-=-=-=-=-=-=-=-=-=-=-

19.5 PRINTING NUMERALS

The numeral-printing procedures of chapters 15 and 16 use division, remaindering, exponentiation and comparisons between numbers. Program 19.3, when finally adapted to handle problems of carry-over and over-large answers, works with numbers represented by sequences of decimal digits. Working over the problem of printing numerals once more, using this new imitation, is an ideal way to illustrate how abstraction can help in the business of program design.

Recall the recursive number-printing procedure of chapter 16. Adapt it to the specific problem of printing a decimal numeral, and it becomes program 19.5. The most attractive thing about this procedure is that it has already been *proved* to solve the numeral-printing problem. It would be nicer still if it could be adapted to solve the problem when numbers have a different representation, because then I would be sure to have a solution which works.

> *def printnumber (n)* =
>   *select n<10: printdigit(n)*
>   *n≥10: printnumber (n÷10); printdigit(n rem* 10)
>   *endselect*
> *enddef*

program 19.5

The procedure definition in program 19.5 is itself an abstraction. It builds upon, but does not explain, how to divide and remainder numbers, how to compare one number with another. It builds upon mechanisms of procedure calling and of choice between alternatives. It won't execute on a computing system which hasn't been built to do all those things - *unless* you describe how the system can imitate them.

When numbers are represented by sequences of decimal digits, most ordinary programming systems can't handle program 19.5. Procedure calling and choosing between alternatives are each ok, but comparison, division and remaindering of multi-digit decimal numerals are not part of the repertoire of the average mechanical code. One way to solve the problem is to find formulas which replace all the difficult parts of the procedure definition. Procedure-calling formulas are an obvious choice - then I can write the solution as program 19.6.

> *def printnumber (S)* =
>   *select lessthan(S,* 10): *printdigit(S)*
>   ¬*lessthan(S,* 10): *printnumber (divide(S,* 10));
>   *printdigit(remainder (S,* 10))
>   *endselect*
> *enddef*

program 19.6

Program 19.6 seems to suggest that I must rewrite the *printdigit* procedure to cope with a number represented as a sequence, but that isn't so. If a number is less than ten, then its multi-digit representation will have only one significant digit. All except the units digit must be zero. I choose, because it makes calculation convenient, to represent numbers 'backwards' so that the units digit of the number is represented by S_1. Then if n is imitated by sequence S and n is less than ten, I can imitate *printdigit(n)* by *printdigit(S_1)*. Similarly, the remainder when you divide a number by ten is just the units digit of the decimal numeral representation, so *printdigit(n rem 10)* is also imitated by *printdigit(S_1)*.

Comparisons such as '*lessthan(S, 10)*' are a bit trickier, but only a little bit. One general solution to the problem of comparing two numbers is to subtract one from the other and look at the result: if $b-a$ is negative then $b<a$. Another solution, peculiar to the multi-digit representation, compares the numbers digit-by-digit.

-=-=-=-=-=-=-=-=-=-=-=-=-

Exercise 19.11
What is the multi-decimal digit representation of ten? Of one hundred? Of zero?

Exercise 19.12
Define a procedure *lessthan* so that *lessthan(A,B)* delivers true if the number represented by sequence A is less than the number represented by sequence B. Assume the sequences are the same length and are written so that A_1, B_1 are the least significant digits (units digits) of the representations. [Hint: try writing a procedure which starts its digit-by-digit comparison from one end of the sequences, then write one which starts from the other end; see which end leads to a simpler definition.]

Exercise 19.13
Modify your answer to exercise 19.12 so that A and B need not be the same length. Write a procedure call equivalent to *lessthan(S, 10)*; show the effect of this call for some interesting values of S, either by substitution or by some form of execution or environment diagram.

-=-=-=-=-=-=-=-=-=-=-=-=-

The trick with *printdigit* gives a clue about how to imitate *lessthan(S, 10)*. Ten is a special case because it is the number-base of the representation in S. If all but the units digit of a multi-digit decimal numeral are zero, then the numeral represents a number smaller than ten: so if every component of S_2 is zero then S represents a number smaller than ten. That makes *lessthan10(S)* a searching program. Answer the next exercise before looking at the answer opposite.

-=-=-=-=-=-=-=-=-=-=-=-=-

Exercise 19.14
Write the *lessthan10* procedure. What is the procedure call which corresponds to '$n<10$'?

-=-=-=-=-=-=-=-=-=-=-=-=-

The only problem left in program 19.6 is how to imitate $n \div 10$. Again, this isn't a general division problem, it is division by ten. You surely found, when you were learning to divide, that division by ten is a special case. You just throw away the last digit: for example, $3519 \div ten = 351$. Thus the numeral-printing program becomes program 19.7.

$$def\ lessthan10(S) = for\ i\ rt\ S_{2..}\ do\ select\ i \neq 0:\ deliver\ false$$
$$i = 0:\ donothing$$
$$endselect$$
$$od;$$
$$deliver\ true$$
$$enddef$$

$$def\ printnumber(S) = select\ lessthan10(S):\ printdigit(S_1)$$
$$\neg lessthan10(S):\ printnumber(S_{2..});$$
$$printdigit(S_1)$$
$$endselect$$
$$enddef$$

program 19.7

So far so good: this pair of procedure definitions could fairly easily be proved to be a faithful representation of the recursive definition from chapter 16, which itself was proved to be capable of printing decimal representations. The new program will work. But is it the best we can do?

Don't count things twice

The most untidy bit of program 19.7 is the *lessthan10* procedure. The untidiness is caused by the fact that in a procedure call *printnumber(S)* there may be a long sequence of insignificant zeros in S: that is, zeros starting the number which need not be printed. Each call of *printnumber* will call *lessthan10*, and each of those calls will investigate the first segment of S to see if it is entirely made up of zeros. Suppose that it could be guaranteed that in any call of *printnumber* there can be *no* insignificant zeros: that is, if S is indexed $1..j$ then it is guaranteed that S_j is not zero.

-=-=-=-=-=-=-=-=-=-=-=-

Exercise 19.15
What is the multi-digit representation of zero? Is it possible to write *printnumber(Z)* if Z represents zero and yet conform to the terms of the guarantee? If not, how should the guarantee be rephrased?

-=-=-=-=-=-=-=-=-=-=-=-

If a call of *printnumber* conforms to the terms of the guarantee it is possible to estimate the size of the number which S represents simply by inspecting the length of the sequence S. A number smaller than ten must necessarily have only one component. Put it another way: under the terms of the guarantee *lessthan10(S)* is bound to deliver true if $j \geq 2$, or false if $j=1$. Program 19.8 exploits this feature of the guarantee.

$def\ printnumberG(S) = select\ length(S)=1:\ printdigit(S_1)$
$\qquad\qquad length(S)>1:\ printnumberG(S_{2..});\ printdigit(S_1)$
$\qquad endselect$
$enddef$

program 19.8

-=-=-=-=-=-=-=-=-=-=-=-

Exercise 19.16
Does *printnumberG(S)* print '0' if *S* represents zero? If so, what are the terms of the guarantee? If not, modify the guarantee and/or the representation of zero and/or the procedure definition so that it does print '0'.

Exercise 19.17
Write a procedure definition *printG(S)* which contains the definition of *printnumberG* and which prints a number by calling *printnumberG(T)*, where *T* is a sequence which represents the same number as *S* and which conforms to the terms of the guarantee even though *S* itself may not.

-=-=-=-=-=-=-=-=-=-=-=-

Faster, faster!

Program 19.8 is not as computationally efficient as it might be: in particular it includes a subsequencing operation. Your experience of mechanical codes should tell you that subsequencing is usually expensive and sometimes impossible. But given a sequence *S* you can represent a subsequence of it by the whole original sequence and a description of the subsequence index values. Instead of writing *printnumberG($S_{2..}$)* I might write *printnumberG2(S, 2, length(S))* - but then I need a definition of *printnumberG2* which accepts three arguments, and I arrive at program 19.9.

$def\ printnumberG2(S,i,j) = select\ i=j:\ printdigit(S_i)$
$\qquad\qquad i<j:\ printnumberG2(S,i+1,j);\ printdigit(S_i)$
$\qquad endselect$
$enddef$

program 19.9

-=-=-=-=-=-=-=-=-=-=-=-

Exercise 19.18
Prove that an execution of *printnumberG2(S, 1, length(S))* is equivalent to an execution of *printnumberG(S)*.

Exercise 19.19
Why don't the terms of the guarantee matter in exercise 19.18?

-=-=-=-=-=-=-=-=-=-=-=-=-

One last step

The executions of *printnumberG* pass around subsequences of *S*. They might as easily use a single copy of the sequence *S* and pass around numbers describing where to find the subsequences. In practice this will often make the program more efficient because the computational effort required to make subsequences and to pass sequences as arguments is usually much greater than that involved in passing integer arguments. If the executions of *printnumberG3* share a sequence *S* then the procedure definition can be rewritten as in program 19.10.

$$def\ printnumberG3(i,j) = select\ i=j\!:\ printdigit(S_i)$$
$$i<j\!:\ printnumberG3(i+1,j);\ printdigit(S_i)$$
$$endselect$$
$$enddef$$

program 19.10

This program should remind you of the definition of the *for-do* instruction right back in chapter 6. It defines the operation of *printnumberG3*, parameterised on a sequence *i..j*, in terms of its operation on the sequence *i+1..j*. Program 19.10 doesn't look exactly like definition 6.5 only because it is running backwards through the sequence: when that is taken into account it is evident that it is equivalent to program 19.11.

$$printnumberG4(i,j) = for\ k\ rbt\ i..j\ do\ printdigit(S_k)\ od$$

program 19.11

-=-=-=-=-=-=-=-=-=-=-=-=-

Exercise 19.20
Under what circumstances is the equation *printnumberG3(I,J)* = *printnumberG4(I,J)* invalid? [Hint: consider values of *i* and *j*.]

Exercise 19.21
State the circumstances under which the equation in exercise 19.20 is valid, and prove it.

-=-=-=-=-=-=-=-=-=-=-=-=-

So what?

The development above has led in a roundabout way from an unlikely starting point to a destination which you might have expected to reach directly. The

SEQUENCES AND INDEXED SETS OF VALUES

for-do instruction is the obvious way of printing a number represented as a sequence of decimal digits; if the number is represented 'backwards' in the sequence, units digit first, then the *for-do* should obviously run backwards.

It was worth the effort of developing the obvious program from the not-so-obvious because it demonstrates a general point about program design. Abstraction allows you to write simple programs, expressed in terms of whatever mechanisms your abstract description permits. It is possible to imitate your abstract program by writing a procedure for each abstract operation and rewriting your formulas using procedure calls; but it is also possible to replace pieces of your abstract program by pieces of concrete program which don't have the same structure, provided that you justify each substitution carefully. The final imitation need not look much like the original abstraction.

19.6 SUBTRACTION, MULTIPLICATION AND DIVISION

Following the discussion in section 19.5, I give here only hints on how to write procedures which imitate subtraction, multiplication and division using sequences of decimal digits. In the case of multiplication and division the abstract version doesn't talk about sequences, but the transcription is straightforward because the abstract version uses easily imitated operations like division and remaindering by ten.

Subtraction

Subtraction is in principle very like addition, but the algorithm most people use is rather hard to understand. The difficulty is once again caused by carry-over from one digit position to the next. If you are calculating $a-b$ where a is represented by sequence A and b by sequence B, then the problem first arises when $A_i < B_i$. For example, suppose that $a=745$ and $b=183$: then in my backwards representation $A=<5, 4, 7>$, $B=<3, 8, 1>$. The answer should be $c=562$, which is imitated by the sequence $<2, 6, 5>$. In the first position $C_1=A_1-B_1=5-3=2$, which is correct. In the second position $C_2=A_2-B_2=4-8=-4$, which isn't a possible digit. The solution to the problem is to add ten in this position, writing $C_2=-4+10=6$, and to subtract ten from the whole number c by calculating $C_3=A_3-B_3-1$. This sort of carry-over is usually called *borrowing*.

-=-=-=-=-=-=-=-=-=-=-=-

Exercise 19.22
Write a program which calculates $c=b-a$, where numbers c, b and a are represented by sequences of decimal digits C, B and A.

Exercise 19.23
What will be the effect of your program if $a>b$? If $a=b$? If $a<b$?

Exercise 19.24
Alter your program so that if $a<b$ the program computes $c=b-a$. [Hint: see your answer to an earlier exercise about comparisons.]

Exercise 19.25
Define a procedure *subtract(A, B, C, s)* which accepts sequences A and B representing numbers a and b and which assigns to $\downarrow C$ and $\downarrow s$ a representation of the signed number $a-b$ as follows: $\downarrow C$ is assigned a sequence representing the magnitude of $a-b$ and $\downarrow s$ the character '+' or the character '-' according to whether $a-b$ is positive or negative.

Exercise 19.26
Write a procedure *subtract(A, sa, B, sb, C, sc)* where A and sa together represent a signed number a, B and sb together represent a signed number b and $\downarrow C$ and $\downarrow sc$ are assigned values so as to represent a signed number $a-b$.

-=-=-=-=-=-=-=-=-=-=-=-=-

Multiplication

Multiplication is repeated addition: $3\times4 = 4+4+4 = 3+3+3+3$. It is possible to base a multiplication procedure on counting repetition: see program 19.12, for example. If a and b are very large numbers, programs like 19.12 will carry out a very large number of additions. If the numbers are represented by sequences, each addition will by no means be trivial.

initially 0 *times a do +b od*

program 19.12

The multi-digit 'long multiplication' algorithm you learnt as a child is much better than program 19.12. That algorithm reduces multiplication of a pair of multi-digit numerals to a sequence of multiplications - each of a multi-digit numeral by a single-digit numeral - and a final addition. But most people know only how to use that algorithm, not how it works.

To approach a program which uses your childhood algorithm, consider the following equivalences:

$$n = (n \div y) \times y + (n \, rem \, y)$$

$$\begin{aligned}
a \times b &= ((a \div y) \times y + (a \, rem \, y)) \times b \\
&= (a \div y) \times y \times b + (a \, rem \, y) \times b \\
&= ((a \div y) \times b) \times y + (a \, rem \, y) \times b \\
&= ((a \div 10) \times b) \times 10 + (a \, rem \, 10) \times b
\end{aligned}$$

These equations are the basis of the design of a recursive multiplication program which more efficient than one which uses repeated addition because, given a

multi-digit representation of a number, division by ten and remaindering with ten
are so simple. Program 19.13 shows the algorithm. The only true multiplication
remaining in this program is that of b by $a\,rem\,10$: this can either be done by
repeated addition or by a special single- by multi-digit multiplication procedure.

$$def\,multiply(a,b) = select\ a{=}0{:}\ 0$$
$$a{\neq}0{:}\ multiply(a{\div}10,b){\times}10 + b{\times}(a\,rem\,10)$$
$$endselect$$
$$enddef$$

program 19.13

-=-=-=-=-=-=-=,=-=-=-=-=-=-

Exercise 19.27
Write the multiplication procedure so that it works with two sequences A and B.

Exercise 19.28
Division by ten is most easily imitated by subsequencing: write the version of
program 19.13 which shares sequences A and B between executions and
represents a subsequence of them with indices $a1$, $a2$, $b1$ and $b2$. [Hint: see
program 19.10.]

Exercise 19.29
Either by transforming your answer to exercise 19.28 into a repetition, or in some
other way, show that the recursive definition of multiplication given above
corresponds precisely with your childhood algorithm.

Exercise 19.30
Write a procedure *multiply* so that $multiply(A,as,B,bs,C,cs)$, where A and as
together represent a signed number a, B and bs a signed number b, assigns to $\downarrow C$
and $\downarrow cs$ a representation of the signed number $a{\times}b$.

-=-=-=-=-=-=-=-=-=-=-=-=-

Division

Since I have been discussing the representation only of integers (whole numbers)
by sequences, I shall consider only integer division. Division is repeated
subtraction: when a and b are positive, $a{\div}b$ is the number of times you can
subtract b from a without making a negative result and $a\,rem\,b$ is what's left over
when the subtraction has been carried out. Therefore, like multiplication,
division can be imitated by repetition: for example, see program 19.14, which
computes the quotient $a{\div}b$ in q and the remainder $a\,rem\,b$ in r (short for *q*uotient
and *r*emainder). This program works fine in some cases, but it breaks down if b

$$q,r:=0,a;\ iterate\ r{>}b{:}\ q,r:=q{+}1,r{-}b\ enditerate$$

program 19.14

is negative or zero, so clearly a little more care is needed. Even then it does not form the basis of a useful program because if a is very large and b is very small it will perform a lot of expensive subtractions.

Even fewer people know how 'long division' works than understand long multiplication. The algorithm is based on multiplying by ten, just as the multiplication algorithm was based on division and remaindering:

$$a \div b = ((a \div x) \times x + (a \, rem \, x)) \div b$$
$$= ((a \div (b \times y)) \times (b \times y) + (a \, rem \, (b \times y))) \div b$$
$$= (a \div (b \times y)) \times y + (a \, rem \, (b \times y)) \div b$$
$$= (a \div (b \times 10)) \times 10 + (a \, rem \, (b \times 10)) \div b$$

Here the idea is to increase b in the procedure call so as to make the number of subtractions smaller. It is essential to calculate both the quotient q and the remainder r on each procedure call, or information is lost: program 19.15 gives the abstract version. The procedure delivers a set indexed by q and r. I think the repeated subtraction which computes the final values of S_q and S_r in this program is unavoidable.

```
def divide(a, b) =
    select a<b: {q=0, r=a}
           a≥b: initialise S := divide(a, b×10)
                S_q := S_q×10;
                iterate S_r>b: S_q, S_r := S_q+1, S_r−b enditerate
                deliver S
    endselect
enddef
```

program 19.15

-=-=-=-=-=-=-=-=-=-=-=-

Exercise 19.31
Show that the recursive definition of division in program 19.15 corresponds to your own 'long division' algorithm.

Exercise 19.32
What is the repeated subtraction definition of division when either operand, or both, can be negative?

Exercise 19.33
Write the division procedure which works with signed numbers a and b to compute signed answers q and r. What is the sign of r when a is negative, b is positive?

-=-=-=-=-=-=-=-=-=-=-=-

19.7 SEQUENCES AND ARRAYS

In the notation of this book a sequence can be held in a container and therefore you can write assignment instructions like $S:=<1,2,3,4>$. You can apparently alter a part of the sequence in a container when you write $S_i:=17$, but that instruction is defined to be a shorthand for $S:=<S_1,..,S_{i-1},17,S_{i+1},..>$. Most mechanical codes don't agree. History, the properties of computing machines and the difficulties of building programming systems all press designers to imitate a sequence container with a collection of containers collectively called an *array*.

In the array imitation every element S_i is a container in its own right and each of them possesses a reference value (for example, you can write $@S_i$ in a procedure call). This messes up the substitution explanation of assignment so badly that I have avoided the difficulty in this book by insisting that a sequence is held in a single container.

19.8 IMITATING SEQUENCE OPERATIONS

The sequence operations introduced in this chapter - indexing, subsequencing, $\oplus$ and *length*(S) - are very useful in any program which manipulates sequences. Yet for various reasons few mechanical codes provide all of them or useful equivalents for the missing ones. It is possible, as always, to imitate them using other mechanisms.

Most mechanical codes provide straightforward imitations of sequence containers and of indexing. Few can directly imitate sequence expressions like $<1,2,3>$ or $<x,y>$. Many provide only fixed-size sequence containers. If S is a fixed-size container which can hold a sequence of ten items there is no point trying to put a sequence of eleven items into it. Surprisingly there is no point trying to put a sequence of *nine* items into it either: S_{10} will always exist. Procrustes has technological assistance nowadays!

Concatenation can be imitated using fixed-size containers provided that you provide enough space in each sequence container for the *longest* sequence which it will be required to hold. To represent a sequence, acquire two containers: a fixed-size container T which is large enough to hold the longest sequence you need, and an integer container t. Then together the pair T and t can represent a sequence S if $T_{1..t}=S$: that is, if t holds the length of the sequence S and T holds a sequence which starts with the elements of S (note that the values of $T_{t+1..}$ are irrelevant). The empty sequence is represented when $t=0$. Adding one component to a sequence is imitated by altering one element of T and increasing t:

$$S:=S\oplus<y> \quad = \quad t,T_{t+1}:=t+1,y$$

$$= \quad t:=t+1; T_t:=y$$
$$= \quad T_{t+1}:=y; t:=t+1$$

Subsequencing can be imitated by sequences of assignment instructions. For example, the procedure call $p(S_{6..8})$ can be represented by the sequence of instructions $U_1:=S_6$; $U_2:=S_7$; $U_3:=S_8$; $p(U,3)$. Notice that I have represented the sequence-expression argument by two arguments, one giving the components of the sequence and the other its length. Subsequencing is often most concisely imitated by *for-do* repetition. For example, the assignment $A_{1..k}:= B_{2..k+1}$ can be imitated by *for i rt* 1.*.k do* $A_i:=B_{i+1}$ *od*.

Genuine concatenation is also possible. Suppose that A is represented by TA and ta, B by TB and tb, C by TC and tc. Then the instruction $A := B \oplus C$, for example, can be imitated by three assignments:

$$TA_{1..tb}, TA_{tb+1..tb+tc}, ta :=TB_{1..tb}, TC_{1..tc}, tb+tc$$

If the code doesn't allow subsequencing then it can still be done, but with a couple of repetitions in place of the assignments to subsequences of TA.

Sequence expressions can be imitated by the use of sequence containers and assignment. For example, the procedure call $p(<a+1, b-1>)$ can be imitated by the sequence $U_1, U_2:=a+1, b-1$; $p(U, 2)$ provided that U is a new container which can hold a sequence of at least two elements.

If the sequence T and the length t are packaged together into an indexed set then they are most convincingly imitations of a variable-length sequence. For example, {*sequence*="hello", *length*=2} represents the sequence < 'h', 'e'> and {*sequence*="hello", *length*=4} represents the sequence < 'h', 'e', 'l', 'l' >

19.9 SEQUENCES AS ARGUMENTS AND RESULTS

Some mechanical codes won't allow sequence values as arguments in procedure calls. Some don't allow sequences to be delivered as the result of procedures.

Rather than delivering a result, a procedure can assign the result value to a container described by a reference argument. This sometimes makes for tedious programming, but it works. For example, program 19.15 can be rewritten as program 19.16.

If a code doesn't allow reference values, use two-stage imitation. First rewrite the program to imitate value-return with a reference argument, second use the technique introduced in chapter 10 to imitate reference arguments.

-=-=-=-=-=-=-=-=-=-=-=-=-

Exercise 19.34
Show that the local set container S in program 19.16 is unnecessary because every mention of S could be replaced by $\downarrow T$.

$def\ divide(a, b, T) =$
  $select\ a<b: \downarrow T := \{q=0, r=a\}$
    $a \geq b: initialise\ S := ?$
      $divide(a, b \times 10, @S);$
      $S_q := S_q \times 10;$
      $iterate\ S_r > b: S_q, S_r := S_q + 1, S_r - b\ enditerate$
      $\downarrow T := S$
  $endselect$
  $enddef$

program 19.16

Exercise 19.35

Rewrite program 19.16 (or your answer to exercise 19.34) to use two reference parameters q and r rather than a reference to an indexed set.

-=-=-=-=-=-=-=-=-=-=-=-

Where a code doesn't allow sequences as arguments it is possible to use subsequencing and a variation on the technique of chapter 10. Rewrite the program so that it includes one very large sequence container and store sequence arguments in it as subsequences. Then the procedure can be given the indices of its argument subsequence in place of the argument itself.

-=

APPENDIX 19.A SEQUENCES AND INDEXED SETS IN PASCAL

Pascal imitates sequences with arrays. It imitates indexed sets with records.

Arrays

Pascal arrays have to be of fixed length, they must contain homogeneous sequences and you must describe the indexing set as well as the indexed set. For example, the declaration:

```
var Q: array [1..15] of integer
```

introduces a container which can hold a sequence of fifteen integers. So also does

```
var R: array [15..29] of integer
```

but with an obviously different indexing set.

Pascal programs are written one-dimensionally, each line all on one level. Where I use a subscript to select a component of a sequence, as in 'S_i', Pascal programs use square brackets to indicate subscripting, as in 's[i]'. Indexed sets use a different dot-suffix notation, described below.

Pascal arrays are values which may be given as arguments to procedure calls and assigned to containers but unfortunately can't be printed (unless you write a program which prints each component) and can't be delivered as the result of a procedure (a Pascal `function`). The type of every argument value must be identical to the corresponding parameter description; the type of a value placed in a container must be identical to the type of the container. The easiest way to keep the system happy is to describe the type in one place

```
type a = array [1..16] of char
```

and then to describe the types of other containers by referring to that description:

```
var x,y: a;
procedure P(.. g:a ..)
    ..
x:=y; .. P(..x..)
```

Strings as sequences in Pascal

Pascal strings are sequences but they are 'packed array' rather than just 'array' values. So you write:

```
type s = packed array [1..5] of char
```

to describe the type of the Pascal string 'hello'.

You can't index strings directly: for example, you can't write the formula 'hello'[3]. Instead you must put the string into a container and index that.

Funny indexing sets in Pascal

Pascal allows you to invent 'enumerated types' and to use them as the indexing sets of array values. So, for example, you can invent

```
type direction = (north, south, east, west)
```

and then define an array type

```
type exits = array [direction] of destination
```

The elements of the indexed set must be homogeneous because although the values of the indexing set aren't ordinary numbers you can do some arithmetic (*succ/pred* style) with them. See any Pascal book or consult a helpful friend.

Indexed sets: Pascal records

Pascal allows you to construct indexed sets with non-homogeneous values. They are called *records*. For example, you can define the shape of a record containing a string, an integer and a boolean value:

```
type R = record name: packed array[1..5] of char;
                age: integer;
                female: boolean
         end;
```

This imitates an indexed set with indexing set {*name, age, female*}. Each element of the indexing set appears in the definition, labelling a description of the type of indexed value permitted. Descriptions are separated by semicolons.

Instead of subscripting, record values are indexed with a dot-suffix notation. Where I would write 'S_{name}' to describe the *name* component of the indexed set, Pascal systems use 's.name' to describe the similar component of the record. Given the definition above, a value v of type R has components v.name (a string), v.age (an integer) and v.female (true or false). Look in any reputable Pascal text for further details of the notation.

The elements of the indexing set are peculiar names because you can *only* use them meaningfully as subscripts. You can't write 'x:=name; write(Q.x)', for example. One way of explaining this might be to say that these names don't name anything but are only a sort of identifying label.

APPENDIX 19.B TRY IT OUT

Write the various calculation procedures described in this chapter. Incorporate them in a sort of super-calculator (see chapter 17). Write some more procedures, for exponentiation, factorials, or whatever you feel a good calculator needs.

Chapter 20
SEARCHING FOR SEQUENCES

A queen on a chessboard threatens to capture any other piece on the same rank (row), file (column) or diagonal as itself unless there is another piece in the way. Figure 20.1 shows an arrangement of eight queens on a chess board in which no queen threatens any other. There are ninety-two such arrangements and the famous old programming problem is to print every one of them.

figure 20.1

A solution to the eight queens problem can be seen as a sequence of eight row-positions. That makes the program which finds that solution just one amongst a family of programs which search, amongst lots of different candidate possibilities, for those which describe acceptable solutions to a problem.

20.1 SEARCHING FOR A SOLUTION

Program 20.1 shows the structure of a simple searching program which examines every possible candidate solution to a problem, applying a suitability test to each candidate in turn. Note that if none of the candidate solutions passes the test, the program is equivalent to *donothing*: otherwise it is equivalent to a sequence of executions of whatever *success* means. If the candidate solutions are difficult to compute then it may be difficult to express the program as a *for-do* but in principle every searching program must be reducible to a sequence of choices.

> *for i rt candidate solutions do*
> > *select i is ok: success*
> > > *i isn't ok: donothing*
> > *endselect*
> *od*

program 20.1

One sort of searching is to find a position in some structure which satisfies some property or other: for example, looking for the place in a haunted house where treasure is hidden. An everyday computing example of a position search is to look for occurrences of words in a text so as to make indexes, concordances and dictionaries. A text can be represented by a sequence of characters: the candidate solutions of program 20.1 are in this case the possible indices of the sequence.

-=-=-=-=-=-=-=-=-=-=-=-

Exercise 20.1
Write a procedure *aoccurs* so that *aoccurs*(P) prints the indices of the positions where the letter 'a' occurs in string P. For example, *aoccurs*("hello") should print nothing, whereas *aoccurs*("Ha Ha! said the clown") should print 2, 5 and 9.

Exercise 20.2
Write a procedure *occurs* so that *occurs*(P, c) prints the indices of the positions where character c occurs in string P. For example, *occurs*(P, 'a') is equivalent to *aoccurs*(P) and *occurs*(P, '!') tells you where there are exclamation marks in string P.

-=-=-=-=-=-=-=-=-=-=-=-

Searching programs like program 20.1 may be required to find *all* of the solutions to a problem, perhaps so that you can look at the complete set and decide which one you like best, or just *any one* solution. A program which finds one solution can easily be made by rewriting the program which finds them all. Program 20.2 shows the structure of a program which terminates as soon as one solution is

X: *for i rt candidate solutions do*
    select i is ok: success; terminate X
      i isn't ok: donothing
   endselect
od;
printstring("no solution")
:X

program 20.2

found. As before, the *for-do* is equivalent to *donothing* if no solution is found, or to a sequence '*success; terminate X; success; terminate X; ..*' if there are any acceptable candidates. And then by definition of the *terminate* instruction, the first *terminate* and everything which follows it can be deleted: so the program either prints "no solution" or executes *success* once only.

-=-=-=-=-=-=-=-=-=-=-=-

Exercise 20.3
Modify your answers to exercises 20.1 and 20.2 so that *aoccurs* and *occurs* print one index or "nothing found".

-=-=-=-=-=-=-=-=-=-=-=-

In hierarchical structures there can be searches within searches, and the structure of the searching program will reflect the structure being searched. For example, if you really want to find hidden treasure in a haunted house you must search every room: within every room you must search under every floorboard and behind every wall panel and inside every cupboard. A program which searches the house will generate a sequence of room-searches, each of which will contain a sequence of place-searches: this mirrors the way that the house is a structure of rooms, each containing a structure of hiding-places. That would make the program a search within a search, perhaps a *for-do* within a *for-do*.

Program 20.2 stops searching as soon as it finds a solution. Searches may reasonably be stopped if it becomes evident that no solution can be found. For example, when searching for treasure you may come across evidence which persuades you that the treasure is not in a particular room - say you find that the room is panelled with modern timbers and therefore wasn't built when the treasure was hidden. You can abandon your search of that room, but not of the whole house. Program 20.3 describes that kind of search.

-=-=-=-=-=-=-=-=-=-=-=-

Exercise 20.4
If you found evidence that would convince you that there is no point searching - say you found a note from Captain Kidd saying that he had found the treasure two hundred years ago - then you might abandon the entire search. Write a version of program 20.3 which prints "failed again!" if the search fails, either because it exhausts the rooms or because it finds a note from a lucky pirate.

```
X: for r rt rooms in house do
    S: for p rt places in r do
        select treasure in p: printstring("Eureka!"); terminate X
               counter–evidence in p: terminate S
               nothing in p: donothing
        endselect
    od
    :S
  od;
    printstring("failed again!")
:X
```

program 20.3

Exercise 20.5

Write a procedure *yespresent* so that *yespresent*(P, i) checks whether the word "yes" occurs at position *i* in string P. For example:

$$yespresent(\text{"but yesterday's gone"}, 5)$$

should print "hooray!", but

$$yespresent(\text{"and yet still"}, 5)$$

should print "no luck".

Exercise 20.6

Write a procedure *yesoccurs* so that *yesoccurs*(P) finds whether the string "yes" occurs anywhere in string P. For example:

$$yesoccurs(\text{"You are a yes man"})$$

should deliver true, whereas

$$yesoccurs(\text{"let a=3   printnumber(3)"})$$

should deliver false.

Exercise 20.7

Write a procedure *segoccurs* so that *segoccurs*(P, s) finds whether the string *s* occurs in string P. For example:

$$segoccurs(\text{"let a=3   printnumber(3)"}, \text{"int"})$$

should deliver true, whereas

$$segoccurs(\text{"A sailor has a wife in every"}, \text{"port"})$$

should deliver false.

-=-=-=-=-=-=-=-=-=-=-

20.2 PRINTING THE PARTITIONS OF *N*

Mathematically a *bag* or *multiset* is a set which may have repeated elements. The formula {1,2,1} describes the same multiset as the formula {2,1,1}: both have three elements, both have one element 2 and two element 1s. The formula {1,2} describes a different multiset because it has only a single occurrence of 1.

Any positive non-zero integer can be expressed as the sum of a multiset of positive non-zero integers. For example, the integer 5 can be expressed as the sum of any of the multisets {5}, {4,1}, {3,2}, {3,1,1}, {2,2,1}, {2,1,1,1}, {1,1,1,1,1}. These are the only seven multisets of positive non-zero integers which sum to 5: they are the *partitions* of 5. The problem is to write a program which finds the partitions of *n*. The technique will be based on programs 20.1 and 20.2. It will generate candidate solutions and pick the ones which have some property.

A multiset can be imitated by a sequence: for example, the sequences <1,1,2>, <1,2,1>, <1,1,2> all imitate the multiset {1,1,2} in the sense that they have the same number of elements as the multiset and the same elements. Candidate solutions to the partitions problem may therefore be represented by sequences. Those sequences[†] which sum to 5 are shown in figure 20.2. These are the candidate solutions, in the sense of program 20.1: I shall start by developing a program which prints them all and then modify it to throw away duplicates of sequences which imitate the same partition.

```
<5>
<4,1>
<3,2> <3,1,1>
<2,3> <2,2,1> <2,1,2> <2,1,1,1>
<1,4> <1,3,1> <1,2,2> <1,2,1,1> <1,1,3> <1,1,2,1> <1,1,1,2> <1,1,1,1,1>
```

figure 20.2

Generating candidate solutions

If you were asked to write a program which, given a number *n*, prints a sequence which sums to *n*, the simplest answer I can think of is given in program 20.4. That program might seem to be a bit of a cheat but program 20.5, the other obvious solution, is no more intellectually taxing.

printnumber(*n*)	*times n do printstring*("1 ") *od*
program 20.4	program 20.5

[†] Of positive non-zero integers, but I shan't write that over and over again.

-=-=-=-=-=-=-=-=-=-=-=-

Exercise 20.8
Neither program 20.4 nor 20.5 prints its output in the form illustrated in figure 20.2. Change them so that they do so.

Exercise 20.9
How many comma characters are printed by your version of program 20.5? How many '<' symbols? How many '>' symbols?

-=-=-=-=-=-=-=-=-=-=-=-

Program 20.5 invents and prints its sequence all at once. At every stage it extends the sequence with a 1. To print a different sequence it would be necessary sometimes to extend with a 2, or with a 3, or with a 4 or even with a 5: but the length of the sequence wouldn't always be the same and we certainly couldn't use *times-do* repetition to construct every example. The problem of printing *all* the sequences which sum to n can't be solved by a fixed hierarchical structure of any sort of repetitive instruction because the nesting of executions isn't the same for different length solutions. It turns out to be a job for recursion.

A hint at a possible solution is given by the grouping of sequences in figure 20.2. There is a group which all start with 1, always followed by a sequence which sums to 4; there is a group which all start with 2, always followed by a sequence which sums to 3; .. there is a group which all start with 5, followed by a sequence which sums to 0 (the empty sequence). In general each element of a group consists of k followed by a sequence which sums to $5-k$. The group which starts with 1 is the largest because it includes every subsequence which sums to 4. The sequences which sum to 4 fall into four groups: they start with 4, 3, 2 or 1 and are followed by sequences which sum to 0, 1, 2 or 3 respectively. The solution begins to look like a recursive program: to print sequences which sum to n, print a number k followed by a sequence which sums to $n-k$.

The aim is to write a program which prints *every* sequence which sums to n, each on a separate line. That means printing the number k several times, each time followed by a different sequence which sums to $n-k$. I don't know how to calculate the number of lines the program must print in general, because I don't know how many sequences sum to $n-k$ for general n and k. Suppose that instead I include k in the recursive call: that is, I call a procedure and give it both k and $n-k$, asking it to print all the sequences which sum to $n-k$ and to precede each of them with the number k. Clearly, the sequences it prints will sum to n, just because $k+(n-k)=n$.

Consider the action of the recursive call. If $n-k$ is zero, it is enough to print $<k>$ because the empty sequence $<>$ sums to zero, and $<k>\oplus<> = <k>$. Otherwise it must somehow find all the sequences which sum to $n-k$. Proceeding recursively, it might select a number j and ask for sequences to be printed which sum to $n-k-j$, each preceded both by k and by j: and then since $k+j+(n-k-j)=n$ the sequences printed will sum to n. In its turn this request may lead to a procedure call which asks for sequences which sum to $n-k-j-i$ to be printed, each preceded by k, j and i, and so on.

In general, therefore, I need a *seqpr* procedure with two parameters, one of them a sequence S which must be printed at the beginning of each line, the other a number n which is to be divided up into sequences. If *seqpr*(S, j) prints $S \oplus T$ for every sequence of positive non-zero integers T which sums to j, then *seqpr*$(<>, n)$ is an instruction which prints every sequence that sums to n. As always, I design the procedure by arguing inductively.

First, the base case could occur when $j=0$ or when $S=<>$. The second of these possibilities isn't a helpful base case because it is just exactly the problem I am trying to solve. If $j=0$, though, the only sequence of positive integers which represents it is $<>$, the empty sequence; since $S \oplus <> = S$ the procedure need only print its argument sequence S.

The inductive case is not much more difficult. If $j>0$ then each of the possible Ts must be of the form $<y> \oplus U$, where U sums to $j-y$. Therefore a procedure call *seqpr*$(S \oplus <y>, j-y)$ should do the trick, inductively. *For-do* repetition can be used to generate every possible value of y.

Try the following exercises before you look at the answer overleaf.

-=-=-=-=-=-=-=-=-=-=-=-=-

Exercise 20.10
Write the *seqpr* procedure definition: assume a basic procedure *printnumseq* which prints sequences of numbers with brackets and commas as in figure 20.2.

Exercise 20.11
Draw a complete execution diagram for *seqpr*$(<>, 3)$.

Exercise 20.12
If $j=1$ then T must be the sequence $<1>$, so printing $S \oplus <1>$ would be enough in that particular case. But why wouldn't $j=1$ be sufficient if it was the only base case in your procedure definition? [Hint: look at the final elements of the sequences in figure 20.2.]

-=-=-=-=-=-=-=-=-=-=-=-=-

Be sure you got it right

A program which can generate the sequences from figure 20.2 in the order they are given in that figure is shown in program 20.6. If I had used *runningthrough* rather than *runningbackthrough* in the *for-do* instruction the program would still generate all the sequences, but in the reverse order to that given in figure 20.2.

You may feel that the design of this program, made following a careful argument, is enough to guarantee that it is correct. As it happens the program is correct but it is always necessary to be certain. It is helpful to prove that the procedure prints all the sequences, that the sequences it prints all have the right sum and that it won't print the same sequence twice.

$def\ seqpr(S,j) =$
$\quad select\ j{=}0:\ NL;\ printnumseq(S)$
$\qquad\qquad j{>}0: for\ y\ rbt\ 1..j\ do\ seqpr(S{\oplus}{<}y{>},j{-}y)\ od$
$\quad endselect$
$enddef$
$seqpr({<}{>},5)$

program 20.6

The only tricky bit in the proofs is devising the proposition. For example: I would like to prove that $seqpr({<}{>},k)$ prints only sequences summing to k. If I rush at the problem, bull at a gate, then all seems well at first: when $k{=}0$ it prints the empty sequence, which is the only possible sequence of positive non-zero integers summing to zero. Then as strong inductive hypothesis I suppose that $seqpr({<}{>},k)$ prints sequences summing to k for every value of k between 0 and K, and show that $seqpr({<}{>},K{+}1)$ is equivalent to the instruction

$$for\ y\ rt\ 1..K{+}1\ do\ seqpr({<}y{>},K{+}1{-}y)\ od$$

which is in turn equivalent to a sequence of instructions $seqpr({<}1{>},K)$; $seqpr({<}2{>},K{-}1)$; ..; $seqpr({<}K{+}1{>},0)$. But *none* of these instructions has anything to do with the inductive hypothesis, because in every one the first argument is a *non*-empty sequence. It would have made no difference to use simple induction rather than strong induction. Bulls don't jump gates.

Try walking round the gate: if I can prove

$$P0:\ seqpr(S,k)\ \text{prints only sequences whose sum is}\ k+\sum_{i=1}^{i=length(S)}S_i$$

then I can conclude that $seqpr({<}{>},k)$ prints only sequences which sum to

$$k+\sum_{i=1}^{i=0}{<}{>}_i\ =\ k{+}0\ =\ k$$

That is, I can prove my original proposition as the consequence of something a little more general.

-=-=-=-=-=-=-=-=-=-=-=-

Exercise 20.13
Suppose that *printnumseq* isn't a basic instruction but is defined as in program 20.7 (see below). Prove that *printnumseq(S)* prints a sequence which sums to
$$\sum_{i=1}^{i=length(S)}S_i$$
[Hint: simple induction on the length of S.]

Exercise 20.14
Prove proposition P0 above. You may assume whatever helpful (and true) facts you wish about the *for-do* in the procedure definition. [Probably unnecessary hint: strong induction on k.]

> *def printnumseq(S)* =
>   *let LS=length(S)*
>   *printchar('<');*
>   *select LS>0: for i rt* 1..*LS*–1 *do printnumber(S$_i$); printchar(',') od;*
>   *printnumber(S$_{LS}$)*
>   *LS=0: donothing*
>   *endselect;*
>   *printchar('>')*
> *enddef*

program 20.7

Exercise 20.15
Prove that every sequence printed by *seqpr(S, k)* is different. [Hint: induction on *k* again; observe that *S*⊕*<y>* and *S*⊕*<y+1>* are necessarily different sequences.]

Exercise 20.16
Prove that *seqpr(<>, k)* prints every sequence of positive non-zero integers which sum to *k*. [Hint: think of a more general proposition from which you can conclude this result; then proceed very much as in exercise 20.15.]

-=-=-=-=-=-=-=-=-=-=-=-

Choosing solutions

The sequences of numbers which sum to 5 can be grouped in more than one way. Figure 20.2 groups them according to the first number in the sequence. Figure 20.3 groups them according to the multiset they represent.

<5>
<4,1> <1,4>
<3,2> <2,3>
<3,1,1> <1,3,1> <1,1,3>
<2,2,1> <2,1,2> <1,2,2>
<2,1,1,1> <1,2,1,1> <1,1,2,1> <1,1,1,2>
<1,1,1,1,1>

figure 20.3

Figure 20.3 shows that the program which prints every sequence prints all the permutations (re-arrangements) of each sequence representing a partition: that is, it prints each partition in every possible order. In each group of sequences only one of the candidates is in ascending order, only one in descending order[†]. If the

---

[†] Strictly, in *non-descending* and in *non-ascending* order. In <1,1,1,1,3>, for example, there are several adjacent equal elements so it isn't really ascending order, but because each step is either flat or ascending it is in non-descending order. The correct terms are a bit of a mouthful and I shall continue to use 'ascending' and 'descending' in their looser sense.

program only prints sequences which are in ascending order (or alternatively only those which are in descending order) then it will print each partition only once. Program 20.8 does just that.

> *def seqpr(S,j) =*
>   *select j=0: select inorder(S): NL; printnumseq(S)*
>   *¬inorder(S): donothing*
>   *endselect*
>   *j>0: for y rbt 1..j do seqpr(S⊕<y>, j–y) od*
>   *endselect*
>   *enddef*
>
> *seqpr(<>, N)*

program 20.8

-=-=-=-=-=-=-=-=-=-=-=-

Exercise 20.17
Write the *inorder* procedure. [Hint: it is a search program, looking for a position which is a counter-example to the proposition that the sequence is in order. Don't forget that a sequence with less than two elements is in both ascending *and* descending order.]

Exercise 20.18
Try out your program with some large values of *N*. Note the delays in between printing some sequences because the program is generating and then not printing lots of unsolutions.

-=-=-=-=-=-=-=-=-=-=-=-

Rejecting bad starts

Program 20.8 prints every partition by generating all the permutations, then rejecting all but a few. But suppose that you decide to print only those sequences which are in ascending order, and suppose that *N* is fairly large. Then you should realise that some procedure calls are doomed to generate no sequences at all. For example, *seqpr(<1, 2, 1>, N–4)*, will generate an enormous number of junk sequences: none of them can be accepted because every one of them will start <1,2,1,..> and therefore can't be in ascending or descending order. It is sensible to apply the *inorder* test before attempting to extend the sequence, instead of waiting until the sequence is complete before rejecting it.

-=-=-=-=-=-=-=-=-=-=-=-

Exercise 20.19
Modify program 20.8 so that the *inorder* test is applied before each extension to the sequence is used to generate a further extension. [Hint: there are at least three places in which the test could be applied, any one of which will do. Try them all before you decide which produces the nicest program.]

Exercise 20.20
Compare the execution times of your answers to exercises 20.18 and 20.19, using several different values of *N*, some large and some small. Explain the results you find.

Exercise 20.21
Modify your answers to exercises 20.18 and 20.19 to count calls to the procedures *inorder* and *seqpr* and to print out the totals when the work of the program is complete. Does the information you find back up your explanation of their different execution times in exercise 20.20? If not, try to construct a better explanation.

-=-=-=-=-=-=-=-=-=-=-=-

Avoiding bad starts entirely

The *inorder* procedure is only necessary in program 20.8 because the *for-do*, trying every possible value of *y*, sometimes generates sequences which are misordered. Suppose that you wrote the procedure in such a way that the sequence *S* was guaranteed to be ordered in every call of *seqpr(S, k)* - you may already have ensured this in the way that you placed the *inorder* test when answering the exercise above - then it would be unnecessary to check a sequence before it is printed.

The property that *seqpr* is never called with a misordered sequence *S* can be produced without any *inorder* test at all. Suppose that $S = <S_1, .., S_n>$ and is in ascending order and that $k \geq 1$: *then* $<S_1, ..S_n, 1>$ will inevitably be misordered unless $S_n = 1$. Therefore, unless *S* is empty, the *for-do* shouldn't use the sequence $1..j$ but the sequence $S_n..j$.

-=-=-=-=-=-=-=-=-=-=-=-

Exercise 20.22
Define the sequence which should be used in the *for-do* instruction in program 20.8 if partitions are to be printed only when they are in descending order.

Exercise 20.23
Write a *seqpr* procedure using a *for-do* instruction which guarantees either ascending or descending order without an *inorder* test. Run it and compare execution times again with your previous versions. This version should be the fastest so far, but only by a little. Can you explain why?

Exercise 20.24
Using your fastest definition of *seqpr*, prove that a procedure call *seqpr(<>, N)* prints all and only the distinct partitions of *N* into positive non-zero integers.

-=-=-=-=-=-=-=-=-=-=-=-

There are some further improvements you can make, but they make only a tiny difference. Consider the partitions of 5 once more: there is no ascending-order partition which starts <4,..> because the rest of the sequence would have to sum to 5-4=1 and there is no way to make a partition of 1 which starts with a number as large as 4. Similarly, there is no ascending-order partition of 5 which starts <3,..>. There are several which start <2,..> and <1,..> and never forget that there is also <5>.

The ascending-order program can be speeded up, therefore, if you ensure that in a procedure call $seqpr(S \oplus <y>, k-y)$ either $y \le k-y$ or $k=y$. You can do this by adjusting the bounds of the *for-do*, and adding an instruction for the case $y=k$.

-=-=-=-=-=-=-=-=-=-=-=-=-

Exercise 20.25
Improve the ascending-order program in the way described above, and compare its execution with the unimproved version. What activity has been eliminated from the program? Is there a large difference in execution times for large N?

Exercise 20.26
Find out how to make an improvement to the descending-order version of *seqpr*. [Hint: something to do with sequences of 1s.] Which version now runs fastest?

-=-=-=-=-=-=-=-=-=-=-=-=-

Recursive searching summarised

It is possible to generate all the partitions of N by generating all the sequences which sum to N and rejecting those which are misordered. By rejecting misordered subsequences as early as possible in their generation the program goes much faster because it does less work in recognising unsolutions. The program which is organised so that misordered sequences can't possibly be generated is fastest of all.

20.3 THE EIGHT QUEENS SEARCH

Any arrangement of eight queens on a chessboard can be described by a collection of eight coordinates, each describing the row/column (rank/file) position of a single queen. There are an enormous number of such arrangements: $64 \times 63 \times .. \times 57$ or about 2×10^{14}, which is two hundred million million. In only ninety-two cases are the queens arranged so that none of them threatens any of the others. If a computer investigated every possible arrangement and checked a thousand of them a second it would take about five hundred thousand million seconds - more than two million days or about five-and-a-half thousand years - to go through them all. Obviously that is not the way to do it.

The problem becomes more approachable when you recognise that every solution has only one queen on any particular row (rank). So you need investigate only eight positions on each row: there are 8^8 possibilities to consider which is only (only!) about sixteen million. If a computer chould check a thousand of them a second the whole set would take about four hours. That makes it a practical possibility. Most computers would be hard pressed to check a thousand board arrangements a second, so it isn't really *practical*.

The filtering technique used in section 20.2 brings the problem down into the 'easy' range, even for feeble little microcomputers. Each arrangement of the eight queens can be represented by a sequence $<S_1, S_2, .., S_8>$, where S_i gives the column position of the queen which is on row i. The sequence can be generated by some repetition or recursion which ensures that every possible arrangement is generated and investigated.

Suppose that partially-constructed unsolutions are filtered out as early as possible, just as in the partitions program. For example, a sequence might be constructed by placing a queen on row 1 and a queen on row 2. Before going any further, check if this is an unsolution in the making: if the two queens threaten each other then there is no point continuing to place queens on the other six rows, and 8^6 arrangements - about two hundred and fifty thousand - can be eliminated immediately. By rejecting unsolutions as early as possible in their development, the search for solutions will speed up noticeably.

-=-=-=-=-=-=-=-=-=-=-

Exercise 20.27
Write the eight queens program, filtering out unsolutions as early as possible. For simplicity your program can print the solutions as sequences of column positions: for example, the solution shown in figure 20.1 might be represented by the sequence <1,5,8,6,3,7,2,4>. [Hint 1: if you can't quite see the design, look at the proposition in exercise 20.30 below. Hint 2: a queen in row r, column c threatens a queen on row r', column c' if $r=r'$ (same row) or if $c=c'$ (same column) or if $r+c=r'+c'$ (same diagonal) or if $r-c=r'-c'$ (other diagonal). Hint 3: your program should print exactly ninety-two solutions. If it prints too many or too few it's wrong.]

Exercise 20.28
Your eight queens program will either be a recursive search, like the partitions program, or a nested structure with eight *for-do*s inside each other. Whichever way you did it, now do it the other way. Find out which is faster on your particular programming system.

Exercise 20.29
Modify your fastest program so that it collects some statistics about its own behaviour. Count the number of times the recursive eight queens procedure is called (or the number of times you execute a *for-do*), count the number of times it checks a board arrangement (or a partially-constructed arrangement), count the number of times it checks whether a newly placed queen threatens one already on the board. Estimate the number of calls (or *for-do*s) and checks per second which it carries out. Hence estimate how long it would take on your system to execute the program which generates and then checks every possible board position.

[Hint: to check a correct board position means checking the first queen against seven others, the next against six, the next against five, and so on: in total $8+7+6+5+4+3+2 = 35$ threat checks; assume that an incorrect board position might on average require about twenty checks before a threat is discovered.]

Exercise 20.30

The following proposition (or a different one, if your program has a design which I haven't anticipated) describes the essence of your recursive search solution:

A procedure call $eightq(S)$ will print every sequence $S \oplus T$ where the length of $S \oplus T$ is 8 and where S, T and $S \oplus T$ describe positions of queens on a chessboard such that no queen in T threatens any other in $S \oplus T$.

You can deduce from this that $eightq(<>)$ will print every solution. The proposition is not definite enough to be proved: for example, it doesn't say what 'threatens' means, or what the values in S and T should be. Clarify the proposition and then prove it.

Exercise 20.31

Modify your program so that it prints solutions as board pictures as much like figure 20.1 as possible. [Hint: leave out the black/white shading to start with.]

-=-=-=-=-=-=-=-=-=-=-=-

Faster, faster!

The eight queens problem is brought down from the ridiculous to the possible by observing that each row has only one queen on it. Similarly, each column has only one queen on it. But you can go further: any solution must be a permutation of the sequence <1,2,3,4,5,6,7,8>. There are only 8×7×6×5×4×3×2, or about forty thousand, possible permutations of this sequence. A program which generated every permutation and checked each one might be a feasible solution, just about. My home micro, running BASIC, can check about one hundred threats per second, so the brute-force permutations program would take about two hours, compared to about forty days for the brute-force sequence version.

The fastest known solutions to the eight queens problem are based on permutations and filtering out unsolutions early by checking the diagonals for threats.

-=-=-=-=-=-=-=-=-=-=-=-

Exercise 20.32

Write the eight queens program based on permutations of the sequence $<1,2,3,4,5,6,7,8>$.

Exercise 20.33

The specification for the permutations program might be based on the following proposition:

A call of *eightq*(*S, T*) will print every sequence *S*⊕*T'*, where *T'* is a permutation of *T*, and *S* and *T'* describe positions of queens on a chessboard such that no queen in *T'* threatens another in *S*⊕*T'*.

You can deduce from this that a procedure call *eightq*(<>, 1..8) will print every eight queens solution. Construct the procedure; test it out; firm up the proposition by specifying the contents of *T* and *S* and defining what 'threaten' means; prove that your procedure satisfies your firmer specification.

Exercise 20.34
Your program will print ninety-two sequences. View each sequence as an eight-digit numeral. Does your program print out the solutions in numerical order (or reverse numerical order)? If so, prove it; if not, modify your program so that it does and then prove it.

Exercise 20.35
Which is faster: your numerical-order permutations solution or your sequence solution? Find out which and explain why.

-=-=-=-=-=-=-=-=-=-=-

20.4 CONTAINER ARGUMENTS OR GLOBAL CONTAINERS

If program 20.6 were transformed to use fixed-length containers and to eliminate the use of the ⊕ operation and of sequence expressions, the result would be something like program 20.9. Observe that in every call of *seqpr*(*T, t*, ..) in this program a new container *U* is created and the values $T_{1..t}$ are copied into it, but that no assignment to *U* is made which might disturb those values. It follows that there is no need to create a new container at all. If the argument corresponding to parameter *T* describes a container which is big enough, the called and calling execution can share it. This leads to program 20.10. In this program I know that the longest sequence which can be produced has five components, so I can calculate the length of the sequence to be held in the argument container *A*.

> *def seqpr*(*T, t, j*) =
>   *select j*=0: *NL*; *printnumseq*(*T, t*)
>   *j*>0: *initialise U*:=*a container of integers, length t*+1
>
> $U_{1..t}:=T_{1..t}$;
>   *for y rbt* 1..*j do* U_{t+1}:=*y*; *seqpr*(*U, t*+1, *j*–*y*) *od*
>   *endselect*
> *enddef*
>
> *initialise A*:=*a container of integers, length* 0
>
> *seqpr*(*A*, 0, 5)

program 20.9

def seqpr (T, t, j) =
  select $j=0$: *NL*; *printnumseq*($\downarrow T, t$)
          $j>0$: *for y rbt* $1..j$ *do* $(\downarrow T)_{t+1}$:= y; *seqpr*$(T, t+1, j-y)$ *od*
  endselect
enddef

initialise A := <?, ?, ?, ?, ?>

seqpr(@$A, 0, 5$)

program 20.10

Next I observe that all the procedure executions share the same container. There is no need to share it by using an argument - it can be shared directly. Thus I arrive at program 20.11. This program is a refined version of program 20.6. In the original each procedure execution was given a sequence argument. In the refined version that argument is imitated by a number. Imitation can take surprising forms!

def seqpr (t, j) =
  select $j=0$: *NL*; *printnumseq*(A, t)
          $j>0$: *for y rbt* $1..j$ *do* A_{t+1} := y; *seqpr*$(t+1, j-y)$ *od*
  endselect
enddef

initialise A := <?, ?, ?, ?, ?>

seqpr(0, 5)

program 20.11

-=-=-=-=-=-=-=-=-=-=-=-

Exercise 20.36
Prove that the first sequence printed by program 20.11 will be <5>.

Exercise 20.37
Prove that the last sequence printed by program 20.11 will be <1, 1, 1, 1, 1>.

-=

APPENDIX 20.A TRY IT OUT

There are lots of exercises in this chapter which ask you to write programs and run them, to find out which of several possible solutions takes the least computational effort. Write and run the programs: have program races (and programming races) with your friends.

Chapter 21
RECURSIVE VALUE STRUCTURES

Chapter 2 dealt with sequential structures of executions. Chapter 3 introduced hierarchical structures. Chapter 4 showed how hierarchies could permit executions of a single procedure to be nested. Chapters 6, 7 and 8 dealt with recursive structures of executions, whose depth of nesting wasn't a single fixed value.

As it is with structures of executions, so it is with structures of values. The hierarchical value structures introduced so far are of fixed size and depth. It is time to introduce *recursive value structures*, whose levels of nesting structure within structure is not so definitely constrained.

21.1 FORMULAS AS TREES

The classic recursive value structure is the *tree*: a structure of values hierarchically interconnected in the sort of way that the execution diagrams of chapter 3 connect the executions of instructions and procedures. The classic tree-structured value is the formula. Formulas have a naturally recursive structure, as shown by the development of the calculator program 17.9 in chapter 17. That program treated a formula as a sequence of formula elements, each of which could be a numeral or a formula which was a sequence of formula elements, each of which could be a numeral or a formula, .. and so on. The depth of any particular formula structure is fixed, but just as there is no largest integer so there is no deepest formula structure.

The definition of formulas in chapter 17 is a mixture of sequential definition (a formula is a sequence of formula elements) and recursive definition (a formula may contain an element which is a formula). That definition is very practical - I used one like it when writing a compiler many years ago - but in order to discuss the properties of trees, I prefer to introduce an alternative, hierarchical definition.

Binary operations and binary trees

Consider the formula 4+5+7. Left-to-right calculation of this formula forms the sum of 4 and 5, delivering 9, then the sum of 9 and 7, delivering 16. Figure 21.1 shows a structure which reflects the structure of the calculation: sum(sum(4, 5), 7). Indeed the figure is no more than a two-dimensional picture of that one-dimensional formula, which is itself no more than a decorated version of the bracketed formula ((4+5)+7).

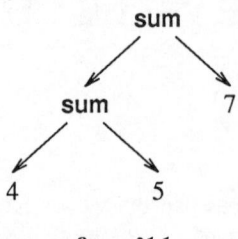

figure 21.1

The sort of picture shown in figure 21.1 is called a *tree* and is made up of *nodes* and *branches*. Branches are the lines connecting nodes; nodes are the places where branches start and finish. Each node in the tree is *labelled* or *tagged,* with a word like **sum** or a number like 5. The node at the top of the tree is called the *root* of the tree[†]. Nodes where no branches lead out are the *leaves* or *tips* of the tree: the nodes labelled 4, 5 and 7 are the leaves of the tree in figure 21.1.

Figure 21.1 describes a *binary* tree, so called because every non-leaf node contains two sub-trees. One sub-tree is identified as the left and the other as the right sub-tree. In figure 21.1 the **sum**(4, 5) node is the left sub-tree of the root. The right sub-tree is 7. Left and right ordering matter in formula structures because, for example, 1–2 is –1 and is represented by the tree formula **diff**(1, 2); 2–1 is represented by the tree formula **diff**(2, 1) and is, of course, 1. Same numbers, different order, different result.

A structure of nodes connected by lines is in general a *graph* (of which more will be said in the next chapter). The lines connecting nodes in a graph are usually called *arcs* rather than branches: trees are graphs where every node except the root has exactly one arc going in. That is, trees are hierarchical graphs.

Figures 21.2 and 21.3 show some more examples of formulas described as trees. Figure 21.2 shows the structure of 1+2×3: note that this structure describes a right-to-left calculation because the normal rules of arithmetic tell us to do multiplications before additions. Figure 21.3 shows the structure of $a+(x+y+z)\times3$. In this case the bracketing forces a mixture of right-to-left and left-to-right calculation and some of the leaves of the tree are single-character values

---

[†] Mathematical trees are always shown growing downwards, with the root of the tree at the top and the leaves at the bottom.

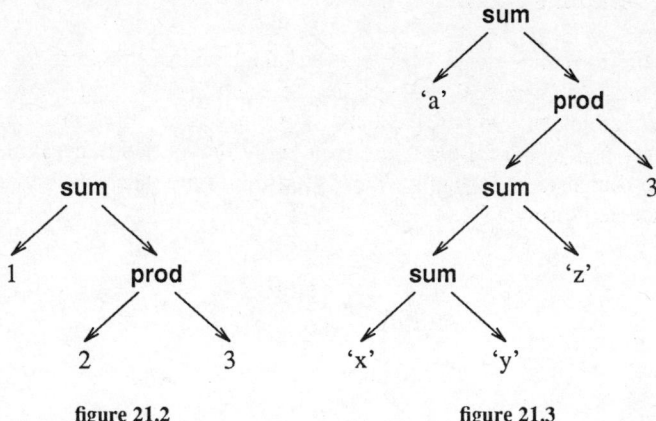

figure 21.2   figure 21.3

identifying the names in the original formula.

A sub-tree of a node is itself a tree: the tree in figure 21.4 contains a tree just like the one in figure 21.1 as its left sub-tree, and the tree in figure 21.5 appears as a part of the trees in figures 21.1 and 21.4.

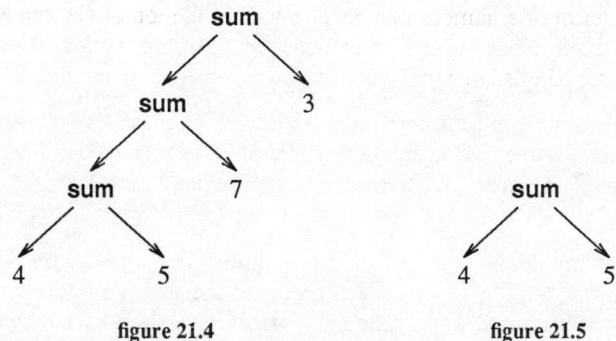

figure 21.4   figure 21.5

All these trees are perfectly reasonable as trees, but they are difficult to work with in one respect. If leaf nodes are tagged to give not only a value (like 1 or 'a') but what kind of value it is (a number or a character) it is much easier to perform calculations on the tree. Figures 21.6, 21.7 and 21.8 show the fully tagged versions of figures 21.1, 21.2 and 21.3. The fully tagged versions correspond to the following formulas:

```
sum(sum(numb(4), numb(5)), numb(7))
sum(numb(1), prod(numb(2), numb(3)))
sum(name('a'), prod(sum(sum(name('x'), name('y')),
                        name('z')),
                   numb(3)))
```

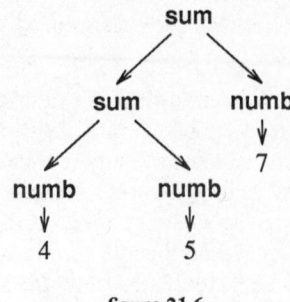

figure 21.6

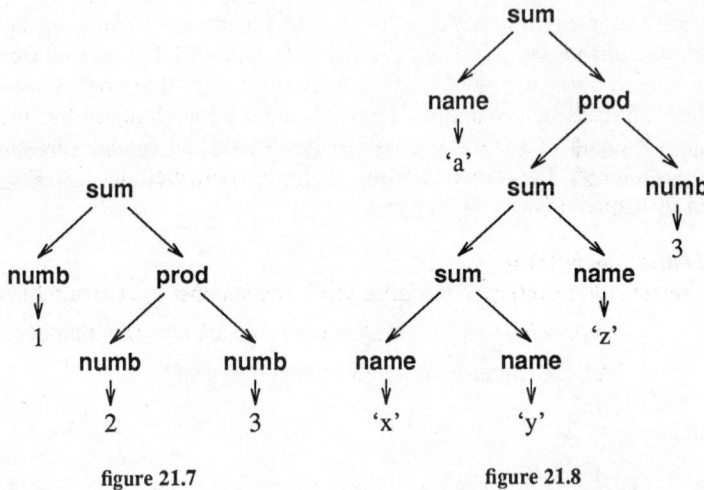

figure 21.7   figure 21.8

According to my definition, the leaves of the trees in figures 21.6, 21.7 and 21.8 are the values 4, 5, 7, .. 'x', 'y', .. According to the same definition these are not binary trees because nodes like **name**('a') aren't leaves and have only one branch leaving the node. But it makes sense to adopt a slightly different definition and to treat the nodes **name**(..) and **numb**(..), which contain only unstructured values, as leaf nodes. I shall use this alternative definition in the example programs in this chapter.

21.2 BUILDING TREES

The **sum**(..), **prod**(..), **numb**(..) and **name**(..) formulas introduced above are *constructor* formulas. If a means 6 and b means 3, the value of the formula **numb**(a+b) is the structure **numb**(9). Execution of a constructor formula is rather like a procedure call in that the values of the argument formulas are calculated but the value of the whole is the formula structure which has been built. Constructor names like **sum, prod** or **anything** are constants like 1, 'a' or $\lambda().print*$.

A constructor formula is unlike a procedure call in that there is no constraint on the number of elements between the brackets or on the kinds of values which can be used in particular positions. It may be quite reasonable to include $x(a, b)$ and $x(u, v, w)$ in the same program, for example. It may be reasonable to include $y(0, 5)$ and $y('a', \lambda().print*)$ in the same program. If it is unreasonable it will be because a particular program can only handle certain sorts of constructor if they are used in certain ways - see section 21.3 below for some example programs - and then constraints on the way that constructors are used will necessarily be part of proofs about that program.

Program 17.9 showed how the value of a formula made up of numerals, brackets and arithmetic operations could be calculated. Program 21.1 is derived from that program and shows how a formula structure which describes left-to-right calculation can itself be calculated. I haven't included anything in this program which takes account of spaces or possible mistakes in the formula presented in the input sequence, but those defects could be remedied in just the ways discussed in chapter 17.

```
def buildelement(x) =
    select isdigchar(crp^): initialise y:=? readnumber y; ↓x:=numb(y)

        isalphachar(crp^): initialise y:=? readchar y; ↓x:=name(y)

        crp^='(': movecrp; buildformula(x); movecrp
    endselect
enddef

def buildformula(f) =
    buildelement(f);
    iterate crp^='+' ∨ crp^='*':
        let op=crp^
        initialise y:=?

        movecrp; buildelement(@y);
        ↓f:=(case op of '+': sum(↓f,y) '*': prod(↓f,y) endcase)
    enditerate;
enddef
```

program 21.1

-=-=-=-=-=-=-=-=-=-=-=-=-

Exercise 21.1
Program 21.1 builds an 'f-tree', a tree which describes how to calculate the value of a formula. It treats a formula as a description of a sequence of calculations, with hierarchy imposed only by explicit bracketing. It builds a hierarchical description corresponding to left-to-right evaluation of the sequence by following the definition: 'an f-tree is either an f-element, or the sum of an f-tree and an

f-element, or the product of an f-tree and an f-element; an f-element is a number or a name or an f-tree (representing a bracketed sub-formula)'.

The following definitions lead to an alternative program, which respects the hierarchy of calculations (bracketed sub-formulas before multiplication before addition) used in normal arithmetic:

(a) An f-tree is an m-tree or the sum of an f-tree and an m-tree.

(b) An m-tree is either an f-element or the product of an m-tree and an f-element.

·   (c) An f-element is either a number or a name or an f-tree (representing a bracketed sub-formula).

Write that program. [Hint: include *buildft*, *buildmt* and *buildfe* procedures which create the different sorts of structure.]

Exercise 21.2
Add subtraction and division to your program with normal arithmetic priority (multiplication and division have equal priority, as do addition and subtraction) using constructors **diff**(*a, b*) and **quot**(*a, b*).

Exercise 21.3
Augment the definitions given in exercise 21.1 to add negation (for example, -1, -a, -3*4) to formulas and alter your program correspondingly to add **negate**(*F*) structures. [Hint: there are at least two sensible alternative ways in which the definitions can be changed.]

-=-=-=-=-=-=-=-=-=-=-=-=-

21.3 TAKING TREES APART (1)

Program 21.2 illustrates how the numerical value of a formula described by a tree structure like the ones in figures 21.6 and 21.7 can be calculated. It includes a *match* formula - an extra piece of notation which is essential when taking recursive value structures apart.

> *def valueof*(*S*) = *match S with* **numb**(*n*): *n*
>   **sum**(*a, b*): *valueof*(*a*)+*valueof*(*b*)
>   **prod**(*a, b*): *valueof*(*a*)×*valueof*(*b*)
>   *endmatch*
>   *enddef*

program 21.2

A *match* is rather like a *case* with **structure-patterns** in place of condition-formulas. The structure-patterns contain not only constructor constants like **numb** but also ordinary names like *n*. *S* matches the pattern **numb**(*n*) when it is a structure **numb**(..) with exactly one value between the brackets; in that case the name *n* identifies the value between the brackets during the evaluation of the corresponding part of the *match* formula, just as a parameter name identifies the value of the argument formula during a procedure call. For example, if *S* names the structure **numb**(48) then the *match* formula in program 21.2 will deliver 48. Similarly, *S* matches **sum**(*a, b*) when *S* is a structure **sum**(..) with exactly two values between the brackets, and in that case the names *a* and *b* take on those values during the evaluation of the corresponding arm of the *match*. For example, if *S* is the structure **sum**(**numb**(10), **numb**(44)) then *a* matches **numb**(10), *b* matches **numb**(44) and therefore *valueof*(*S*) will deliver *valueof*(**numb**(10))+*valueof*(**numb**(44)) which, after two recursive matches, it will discover to be 54.

The *match* is like a *case* in other ways: the order of the patterns doesn't matter; it is meaningless if none of the patterns match; it is potentially ambiguous; you can include an *otherwise* alternative which will be chosen only if all of the patterns fail to match.

-=-=-=-=-=-=-=-=-=-=-=-=-

Exercise 21.4
Draw an environment diagram which shows what will be delivered by program 21.2 given the structures illustrated in figures 21.6 and 21.7.

Exercise 21.5
Show, by drawing an environment diagram, that program 21.2 is meaningless given the structure illustrated in figure 21.8.

Exercise 21.6
By providing a sequence of numbers *E* indexed 1..26 (or 0..25 or 'a'..'z') which describes the meanings of single-letter names, and some means of defining those meanings, define a procedure which can be given *E* together with a tree structure like the one in figure 21.8 and which will print the appropriate numerical value.

Exercise 21.7
Modify your answer to exercise 21.6 so that *E* records not simply a value for each name but also whether that value has been intentionally associated with the name. That is, allow for the possibility that some names will have no defined value, and print out a value only if all the nodes in a tree have properly defined values.

-=-=-=-=-=-=-=-=-=-=-=-=-

Program 21.3 shows another program which takes trees apart, this time in order to print a formula. Unfortunately, the formulas it prints don't respect the rules of normal calculation: for example, given the tree of figure 21.8 it would print 'a+x+y+z*3'. Program 21.4 attempts to solve this problem by putting brackets around everything: given the tree of figure 21.8 it would print '(a+(((x+y)+z)*3))'.

-=-=-=-=-=-=-=-=-=-=-=-=-

def ptree1(S) = *match S with* **numb**(*n*): *printnumber*(*n*)
　　　　　　　　　　　　　　 name(*x*): *printchar*(*x*)
　　　　　　　　　　　　　　 sum(*a*, *b*): *ptree1*(*a*); *printchar*('+'); *ptree1*(*b*)
　　　　　　　　　　　　　　 prod(*a*, *b*): *ptree1*(*a*); *printchar*('*'); *ptree1*(*b*)
　　　　　　　　endmatch
enddef

program 21.3

def ptree2(S) =
　　match S with
　　　　numb(*n*): *printnumber*(*n*)
　　　　name(*x*): *printchar*(*x*)
　　　　sum(*a*, *b*):
　　　　　　printchar('('); *ptree2*(*a*); *printchar*('+'); *ptree2*(*b*); *printchar*(')')
　　　　prod(*a*, *b*):
　　　　　　printchar('('); *ptree2*(*a*); *printchar*('*'); *ptree2*(*b*); *printchar*(')')
　　endmatch
enddef

program 21.4

Exercise 21.8
Draw environment diagrams to show that programs 21.3 and 21.4 produce the
effects claimed for them above.

-=-=-=-=-=-=-=-=-=-=-=-

21.4 *match* INSTRUCTIONS AND *match* FORMULAS

A *match* is like a *case* or a *select* in that it contains a set of arms. Each arm
contains a structure-pattern and a program (in a *match* instruction) or a structure-
pattern and a formula (in a *match* formula).

Matching rules

A pattern which is a name (for example, *n*, *x*, *fred*, ..) matches any value and acts
as a parameter name with the matching value as its argument value. For
example, program 21.5 prints 1. Constructors can be matched by names, so
program 21.6 delivers true if and only if *x* is a structure which contains as its only

match 2 with k: printnumber(*k*−1) *endmatch*

program 21.5

$$match\ x\ with\ a(7):true\ \ otherwise:false\ endmatch$$

program 21.6

element the number 7: for example, **numb**(7), **fred**(7) or **not**(7).

A pattern which is a constant formula matches with an equivalent value: so program 21.7 prints 'yes' if $n=42$ (note the identity with *case* in this example). Constructor names are constants, so program 21.8 prints 'hello' if $n=$**numb**(3).

$$printstring(match\ n\ with\ 42:\text{``yes''}\ \ otherwise:\text{``no''}\ endmatch)$$

program 21.7

$$printstring(match\ n\ with\ \textbf{numb}(3):\text{``hello''}\ \ otherwise:\text{``no''}\ endmatch)$$

program 21.8

In general a pattern which is a structure formula $c(m_1, m_2, .., m_n)$ matches a structure $\textbf{p}(s_1, s_2, .., s_n)$ provided that c matches $\textbf{p}$ and m_1 matches s_1, m_2 matches s_2, .., m_n matches s_n. For example, program 21.9 prints 42 if $x=$**numb**(42), prints "yes" if x is a **sum** structure with two sub-trees, the left one of which is a **name** structure and the right a **numb** structure, and prints "no" in any other circumstances.

> *match x with* **numb**(*n*): *printnumber*(*n*)
>   **sum**(**name**(*a*), **numb**(*b*)): *printstring*("yes")
>   *otherwise*: *printstring*("no")
> *endmatch*

program 21.9

A structure-pattern can contain as many names as necessary, and they can be the same as the names in other patterns in the same *match*, but they must be distinct within a pattern, just as the parameter names in a procedure declaration must be distinct from each other[†].

-=-=-=-=-=-=-=-=-=-=-=-

Exercise 21.9
The only problem with program 21.3 is that it doesn't bracket **sum**s which are sub-trees of **prod**s. Design a procedure *ptree3* which doesn't have this deficiency, and show that if T is a formula which corresponds to the tree of figure 21.8, *ptree3*(T) would print 'a+(x+y+z)*3'.

-=-=-=-=-=-=-=-=-=-=-=-

[†] It would be reasonable to allow repetitions: for example, **sum**(*n*, *n*) might match a **sum** structure with two identical arms. But that would be getting a little concise for an introductory text.

Execution definition

Definition 21.1 gives the execution definition of a *match* instruction. There is an obvious equivalent definition for *match* formulas. Note that when an arm is chosen an environment is created in which the names in the pattern identify parts of the matched structure. It follows that occurrences of non-constant names in a pattern are binding occurrences.

Execution of a *match* instruction

$$match\ S\ with\ M_1{:}P_1\ M_2{:}P_2\ ..\ M_n{:}P_n\ endmatch$$
or
$$match\ S\ with\ M_1{:}P_1\ M_2{:}P_2\ ..\ M_n{:}P_n\ otherwise{:}Q\ endmatch$$

proceeds as follows:

(a) S is compared with the patterns $M_1..M_n$.

(b) If S matches with any of the patterns then one matching pattern M_i is chosen; an environment is created in which the names in the pattern M_i identify corresponding parts of S according to the match between structure and pattern; the program P_i is executed within that environment.

(c) If S doesn't match with any of the patterns and there is an arm labelled with *otherwise* then that arm is chosen and its program is executed.

(d) If S doesn't match with any of the patterns and there is no arm labelled with *otherwise* then the *match* instruction is meaningless.

definition 21.1

Substitution definition

The order of patterns in a *match* doesn't matter (definition 21.2). Arms with non-matching patterns can be deleted (definition 21.3). If all patterns are deleted, leaving only an arm labelled with *otherwise*, then that arm must be chosen

$$match\ ..\ M_i{:}P_i\ ..\ M_j{:}P_j\ ..\ endmatch\ =\ match\ ..\ M_j{:}P_j\ ..\ M_i{:}P_i\ ..\ endmatch$$

definition 21.2

If structure S does not match pattern M_i, then

$$match\ S\ with\ M_1{:}P_1\ ..\ M_{i-1}{:}P_{i-1}\ M_i{:}P_i\ M_{i+1}{:}P_{i+1}\ ..\ endmatch$$
$$=\ match\ S\ with\ M_1{:}P_1\ ..\ M_{i-1}{:}P_{i-1}\ M_{i+1}{:}P_{i+1}\ ..\ endmatch$$

definition 21.3

$$match\ S\ with\ otherwise{:}P\ endmatch\ =\ P$$

definition 21.4

If structure S matches pattern M, then

> $match\ S\ with\ M{:}P\ endmatch$
> $=\ match\ S\ with\ M{:}P\ \ otherwise{:}Q\ endmatch$
> $=\ P[n_1\backslash v_1, n_2\backslash v_2, .., n_k\backslash v_k]$

where $n_1..n_k$ are the names in pattern M, and $v_1..v_k$ are the corresponding values in structure S.

definition 21.5

If structure S matches patterns M_i and M_j and also

$$P_i[n_{i1}\backslash v_{i1}, n_{i2}\backslash v_{i2}, .., n_{ik}\backslash v_{ik}]\ =\ P_j[n_{j1}\backslash v_{j1}, n_{j2}\backslash v_{j2}, .., n_{jk}\backslash v_{jk}]$$

where $n_{i1}..n_{ik}$, $v_{i1}..v_{ik}$ are the names and values deriving from the match between S and M_i, and $n_{j1}..n_{jk}$, $v_{j1}..v_{jk}$ are the names and values deriving from the match with M_j, then

> $match\ S\ with\ ..\ M_i{:}P_i\ ..\ M_j{:}P_j\ ..\ endmatch$
> $=\ match\ S\ with\ ..\ M_i{:}P_i\ ..\ ..\ endmatch$
> $=\ match\ S\ with\ ..\ ..\ M_j{:}P_j\ ..\ endmatch$

definition 21.6

(definition 21.4). If there is a single matching pattern then it must be chosen with the bindings indicated by the pattern (definition 21.5). Arms may be combined if both of their patterns match and their programs have the same effect (definition 21.6). Ambiguous *match*es are permitted but, like ambiguous *select*s, they are not explained in substitution terms.

21.5 TAKING TREES APART (2)

Consider program 21.10, a procedure which calculates a simplified version of certain shapes of tree. It is easy to see that given a tree which represents $x{+}0$ or $0{+}x$, this program delivers the structure representing x, and that it delivers any other sort of value unchanged.

> $def\ simplify(S) = match\ S\ with\ \textbf{sum}(a, \textbf{numb}(0)){:}\ a$
> $\textbf{sum}(\textbf{numb}(0), a){:}\ a$
> $otherwise{:}\ S$
> $endmatch$

program 21.10

-=-=-=-=-=-=-=-=-=-=-=-

Exercise 21.10
What will program 21.10 do if given the structure **sum**(**numb**(0), **numb**(0))?

Exercise 21.11

What will program 21.10 do with the structure **divide**(a, b, c)?

-=-=-=-=-=-=-=-=-=-=-=-=-

It isn't hard to see that program 21.11 will deliver a structure in which there are no nodes of the form **sum**(**numb**(0), x) or **sum**(x, **numb**(0)), because it applies the technique of program 21.10 recursively to the whole tree (note the way in which the name *bin* is used to match with any binary constructor like **sum** or **prod** or **quot** or anything else). More precisely, it will do so provided that the structure it is given is like the one illustrated in figures 21.6, 21.7 and 21.8: a structure made up of binary nodes which may contain structures and leaf nodes each of which contains a non-structured value. If the tree contained a unary node **negate**(**sum**(x, **numb**(0))) then that structure wouldn't be simplified by program 21.11; if S contained a ternary node **choose**(c, **sum**(**numb**(0), x), y) then that wouldn't be simplified either.

> *def recsimp*(S) =
>   *match S with* **sum**(a, **numb**(0)): *recsimp*(a)
>   **sum**(**numb**(0), a): *recsimp*(a)
>   *otherwise: match S with*
>   *bin*(a, b): *bin*(*recsimp*(a), *recsimp*(b))
>   *otherwise: S*
>   *endmatch*
>   *endmatch*
>   *enddef*

program 21.11

-=-=-=-=-=-=-=-=-=-=-=-=-

Exercise 21.12

Programs 21.10 and 21.11 are based on the arithmetic equation $a+0=0+a=a$. Write a procedure *recsimp2* which performs over the whole tree, like program 21.11, but is based on the equation $a\times1=1\times a=a$.

Exercise 21.13

Repeat exercise 21.12, this time using the equation $a\times0=0\times a=0$.

Exercise 21.14

Combine your answers to exercises 21.12 and 21.13 with program 21.11 to make a procedure whose simplifications are based on all three equations.

Exercise 21.15

Chapter 15 introduced the notion of 'cheap' and 'expensive' calculations. Write a procedure which 'cheapens' a tree, based on the equations in program 21.11 and exercises 21.12, 21.13 and 21.14, plus the fact that $2\times a=a\times2=a+a$.

-=-=-=-=-=-=-=-=-=-=-=-=-

If the values of structures A and B are numbers a and b, then a node **sum**(A, B) might reasonably be simplified to **numb**($a+b$). Similarly **prod**(A, B) could be replaced by **numb**(*a*×*b*). A procedure which simplifies in this way, given the tree of figure 21.6, should deliver **numb**(16); given the tree of figure 21.7 it should deliver **numb**(7); given the tree of figure 21.8 it should deliver its argument unchanged.

> *def numsimp*(*S*) =
>   *match S with*
>   *bin*(*a*, *b*): *let T* = *bin*(*numsimp*(*a*), *numsimp*(*b*))
>
>   *match T with*
>   **sum**(**numb**(*a1*), **numb**(*b1*)): *deliver* **numb**(*a1+b1*)
>   **prod**(**numb**(*a1*), **numb**(*b1*)): *deliver* **numb**(*a1*×*b1*)
>   *otherwise*: *deliver T*
>   *endmatch*
>   *otherwise*: *deliver S*
>   *endmatch*
> *enddef*

program 21.12

-=-=-=-=-=-=-=-=-=-=-=-

Exercise 21.16
Combine program 21.12 with your answer to exercise 21.14. [Hint: careful of ambiguity: be sure your simplifications don't complicate. For example turn 2×1 into 2, not 1+1.]

-=-=-=-=-=-=-=-=-=-=-=-

21.6 REASONING WITH TREE STRUCTURES

Programs which manipulate recursive value structures are normally recursions or indefinite repetitions. In either case proofs will require induction. Just as simple induction depends on the fact that K is a smaller number than $K+1$, and strong induction on the fact that the members of the set $\{0, 1, 2, .., K\}$ are all numbers smaller than $K+1$, so *structural induction* depends on the fact that the sub-trees $s_1..s_n$ of a tree $c(s_1, .., s_n)$ are each smaller than the tree itself. Then if some property P can be shown to be possessed by a leaf structure $L(v_1, .., v_m)$ and inherited by a tree $c(s_1, .., s_n)$ from its sub-trees $s_1..s_n$ we have a structural induction proof.

It is possible to formalise the idea of 'smaller' and 'larger' structures by appealing to the idea of the *height* of a tree - the distance from the root to the farthest leaf - see definition 21.7. It should be clear that structural induction is equivalent to strong induction over the height of a tree, because when a node has height $K+1$ its sub-trees must, by definition 21.7, all have heights in the range $0..K$. And since you believe in strong induction (surely you do!) you can hardly

(a) The height of a leaf node (a structure which doesn't contain any sub-structures) is zero.

(b) The height of a non-leaf node is one greater than the maximum of the heights of its sub-trees.

definition 21.7

fail to believe in structural induction.

Informally, for example, program 21.2 delivers a number which is the calculated value of the formula represented by a tree structure whose leaves are of the form **numb**(N), representing the number N, and whose non-leaf nodes are of the form **sum**(A, B) or **prod**(A, B), representing (value of A)+(value of B) and (value of A)×(value of B) respectively. Evidently the procedure has the right effect given a leaf node: it just delivers N. Equally evidently, if *valueof*(A) correctly delivers the value represented by A and *valueof*(B) does the same for B, then since *valueof*(**sum**(A, B))=*valueof*(A)+*valueof*(B) the procedure delivers the correct result in this case also. Similarly for the case *valueof*(**prod**(A, B)), which completes the proof.

It is difficult to be more formal in this case because any precise definition of the value represented by a tree would necessarily be recursive and look just like the definition of program 21.2. This is often the case with very basic proofs: the proof given in chapter 7 that *times n do print* od* prints n asterisks suffers from a similar difficulty in presentation.

Consider a question which can be treated more precisely: does program 21.12 deliver a tree which represents the same value as its argument? This might be expressed formally, since we now have faith in the *valueof* procedure, by the proposition P(S):

P: *valueof*(S)=*valueof*(*numsimp*(S)) for any structure S made up of leaves **numb**(i) and non-leaf nodes **sum**(A, B) and **prod**(A, B), where i is a number and A and B are structures of the same kind as S.

The base case considers the leaf nodes. From the definition of *numsimp* and the substitution rules about *match* instructions I can calculate that

> *numsimp*(**numb**(i))
>
> = *match* **numb**(i) *with bin*(a, b): .. *otherwise: deliver* **numb**(i) *endmatch*
>
> = **numb**(i)

This tells me that *valueof*(**numb**(i)) = *valueof*(*numsimp*(**numb**(i))) and the base case is proved.

For the inductive step I need to consider two cases: one where S is a **sum** node, the other where it is a **prod**. I shall show the case of a node **sum**(A, B). The inductive hypothesis is that P applies for sub-structures of this node: that is, that *valueof*(A)=*valueof*(*numsimp*(A)) and *valueof*(B)=*valueof*(*numsimp*(B)). To make the inductive step I must show the identity of *valueof*($sum(A,B)$) and *valueof*(*numsimp*($sum(A,B)$)). First I transform the left-hand side of the equation:

> *valueof*($sum(A,B)$)

= *match* $sum(A,B)$ *with* $numb(n)$: n
>>>> $sum(a,b)$: *valueof*(a)+*valueof*(b)
>>>> $prod(x,y)$: *valueof*(x)×*valueof*(y)
>> *endmatch*

= (*valueof*(a)+*valueof*(b))[$a\backslash A, b\backslash B$]

= *valueof*(A)+*valueof*(B)

= *valueof*(*numsimp*(A))+*valueof*(*numsimp*(B))   [by inductive hypothesis]

Next I expand *numsimp*($sum(A,B)$):

> *numsimp*($sum(A,B)$)

= *match* $sum(A,B)$ *with* $bin(a,b)$: .. *otherwise*: .. *endmatch*

= (| *let* $T=bin(numsimp(a), numsimp(b))$ .. |)[$bin\backslash sum, a\backslash A, b\backslash B$]

= *let* $T=sum(numsimp(A), numsimp(B))$
> *match* T *with* .. *endmatch*

= *match* $sum(numsimp(A), numsimp(B))$ *with*
>> $sum(numb(a1), numb(b1))$: *deliver* $numb(a1+b1)$
>> $prod(numb(a1), numb(b1))$: *deliver* $numb(a1×b1)$
>> *otherwise*: *deliver* $sum(numsimp(A), numsimp(B))$
> *endmatch*

= *match* $sum(numsimp(A), numsimp(B))$ *with*
>> $sum(numb(a1), numb(b1))$: *deliver* $numb(a1+b1)$
>> *otherwise*: *deliver* $sum(numsimp(A), numsimp(B))$
> *endmatch*
>> [because the **prod** arm cannot match]

Finally I must show that *valueof*(*numsimp*($sum(A,B)$)) is *valueof*(*numsimp*(A)) + *valueof*(*numsimp*(B)). To do this it appears that I must consider two cases: one in which *numsimp*(A) and *numsimp*(B) are **numb** structures, the other in which they aren't. The latter case is in fact redundant: see exercise 21.17 below. For the former case, it is helpful to show that *valueof*(**numb**(x)) = x:

> *valueof*($numb(i)$)

= *match* $numb(i)$ *with* $numb(n)$: n
>>> $sum(a,b)$: *valueof*(a)+*valueof*(b)
>>> $prod(x,y)$: *valueof*(x)×*valueof*(y)
>> *endmatch*

= $n[n\backslash i]$ = i

Then if $numsimp(A) = $ numb(a) and $numsimp(B) = $ numb(b) we have

    $valueof(numsimp($sum$(A,B)))$

$= $ *match* sum(numb(a), numb(b)) *with*
               sum(numb$(a1)$, numb$(b1)$): *deliver* numb$(a1+b1)$
               otherwise: *deliver* sum$(numsimp(A), numsimp(B))$
    endmatch

$= valueof($numb$(a1+b1)[a1\backslash a,b1\backslash b])$

$= valueof($numb$(a+b))$

$= a+b$

$= valueof($numb$(a))+valueof($numb$(b))$

$= valueof(numsimp(A))+valueof(numsimp(B))$

The argument so far shows that given the inductive hypothesis $valueof(A)=valueof(numsimp(A))$ and $valueof(B)=valueof(numsimp(B))$, when $numsimp(A)=$numb(a) and $numsimp(B)=$numb(b) it follows that $valueof($sum$(A,B)) = valueof(numsimp(sum(A,B)))$.

-=-=-=-=-=-=-=-=-=-=-=-

Exercise 21.17
Prove that if S is a structure of the kind described in proposition P above, then $numsimp(S)$ is always a structure numb(n). Show that this completes the proof of P.

Exercise 21.18
Prove that if S is a tree consisting of leaf nodes numb(n) or name(c) and non-leaf nodes sum(A,B) or prod(A,B) where n is a number, c is a character value and A, B are structures of the same kind as S, then a procedure call $recsimp(S)$ (see program 21.11) will deliver a tree in which there are no nodes of the form sum(numb$(0),B)$ or sum$(A,$numb$(0))$.

Exercise 21.19
Using the definition of S from exercise 21.18, prove that if S contains no name nodes then $valueof(S) = valueof(recsimp(S))$.

-=-=-=-=-=-=-=-=-=-=-=-

Why use 'numb'?

The proof of proposition P would have worked just as well, given the slightly different definition of *valueof* shown in program 21.13, if I had discussed trees like the ones in figure 21.1 or figure 21.2 whose leaves are simply numbers.

Once again, the reason for introducing an extra level of structure into the tree is to make it possible to distinguish, in a single tree, between leaves which describe names - 'x', 'y' and 'z' in figure 21.3, for example - and those which describe

$def\ simpvalueof(S) = match\ S\ with$ **sum**(a,b): $simpvalueof(a)+simpvalueof(b)$
                                        prod(x,y): $simpvalueof(x)\times simpvalueof(y)$
          endmatch
  enddef

program 21.13

numbers. The *match* instruction distinguishes kinds of values in terms of the constructor which labels them, and therefore it is most convenient to provide leaf-constructors like **name** and **numb** to distinguish different sorts of leaves.

21.7 LISTS

Lists are a special sort of binary tree where the left sub-tree is always a leaf and the right sub-tree is either a list or the special leaf constructor **empty**. For example, figure 21.9 shows the list structure **cons**$(1,$ **cons**$(4,$ **cons**$(9,$ **empty**$)))$.

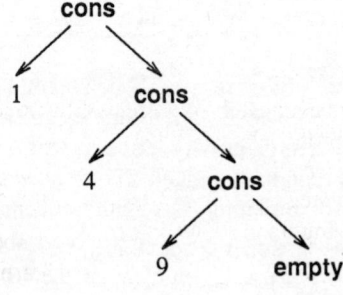

figure 21.9

Lists are very closely allied to the sequences of earlier chapters. The list of figure 21.9 can be seen as an imitation of the sequence $<1,4,9>$. The empty sequence $<>$ is represented by **empty**; if L represents a sequence S then **cons**(a,L) represents $<a>\oplus S$.

$def\ append(a,b) = match\ a\ with$ **cons**(x,y): **cons**$(x, append(y,b))$
                                  empty: b
              endmatch
      enddef

program 21.14

There are lots of famous calculations with lists which support this imitation. Program 21.14 gives a definition of *append*: if s represents sequence S and t represents sequence T then $append(s,t)$ delivers a list which represents $S\oplus T$. For example, consider the sequences $<1,2>$ and $<10,11,12>$, which are imitated by

the lists **cons**(1, **cons**(2, **empty**)) and **cons**(10, **cons**(11, **cons**(12, **empty**)))
respectively:

append(**cons**(1, **cons**(2, **empty**)), **cons**(10, **cons**(11, **cons**(12, **empty**))))
= **cons**(1, *append*(**cons**(2, **empty**), **cons**(10, **cons**(11, **cons**(12, **empty**)))))
= **cons**(1, **cons**(2, *append*(**empty**, **cons**(10, **cons**(11, **cons**(12, **empty**))))))
= **cons**(1, **cons**(2, **cons**(10, **cons**(11, **cons**(12, **empty**)))))

In this case the list calculated by *append* is a representation of the sequence
<1, 2, 10, 11, 12>, which supports my assertion.

-=-=-=-=-=-=-=-=-=-=-=-

Exercise 21.20
The length of a list is defined like the height of a tree:

(a) the length of the null list **empty** is zero.

(b) the length of a non-null list is one more than the length of its tail.

Define a procedure *length* so that *length*(L) delivers the length of list L.

Exercise 21.21
In answering exercise 21.20 you used either recursion or indefinite repetition.
Whichever way you did it, now do it the other way.

Exercise 21.22
Write a procedure *reverse* so that *reverse*(L) delivers a list whose components are
in the reverse order to those in L: for example, given the tree of figure 21.9,
reverse would deliver **cons**(9, **cons**(4, **cons**(1, **empty**))). [Hint: observe that
reverse(**empty**)=**empty**, and think inductively; *append* may be useful.]

Exercise 21.23
Define a procedure *element* so that *element*(L, i), where L represents a sequence S
and $1 \le i \le length(L)$, delivers the ith element of the list L: that is, *element*(L, i)
imitates S_i. For example, if L = **cons**(a, **cons**(b, **cons**(c, **empty**))) then
element(L, 2) = b.

Exercise 21.24
Prove that if list L imitates sequence S and list M imitates sequence T, then
append(L, S) imitates $S \oplus T$ because *element*(*append*(L, M), i) = $(S \oplus T)_i$ whenever
$1 \le i \le length(S) + length(T)$

-=-=-=-=-=-=-=-=-=-=-=-

Lists may represent sequences; sequences may represent sets if position is
disregarded. The procedure *member* is defined so that *member*(i, L) delivers true
when the number i is one of the left sub-trees in the list L, false otherwise: see
program 21.15. It should be clear that repetitions in L don't make any difference
to the behaviour of *member*.

The union of two sets $S \cup T$ is the set which contains only those elements that
occur in S or in T or both (recall the '$\vee$' operation of condition-formulas). The
intersection $S \cap T$ is the set which contains only those which occur in S and in T

$$def\ member(i, L) =$$
$$match\ L\ with\ \textbf{empty}: false$$
$$\textbf{cons}(j, M): select\ i=j:\ true$$
$$i \ne j:\ member(i, M)$$
$$endselect$$
$$endmatch$$
$$enddef$$

program 21.15

(recall the '∧' operation of condition-formulas).

-=-=-=-=-=-=-=-=-=-=-=-

Exercise 21.25
Draw execution diagrams and/or substitution derivations to calculate the result of

$$member(\ 1, \textbf{cons}(5, \textbf{cons}(1, \textbf{cons}(3, \textbf{cons}(1, \textbf{empty})))))\ )$$

and

$$member(\ 1, \textbf{cons}(2, \textbf{cons}(2, \textbf{cons}(2, \textbf{empty})))\ )$$

Exercise 21.26
What set does **empty** represent? What is delivered by $member(1, \textbf{empty})$?

Exercise 21.27
The *member* procedure of program 21.15 is recursive. Write a version based on indefinite repetition.

Exercise 21.28
If list LS imitates set S, in the sense that $member(i, LS) = i \in S$, and list LT imitates set T in the same sense, satisfy yourself that $member(i, append(LS, LT))$ imitates $i \in S \cup T$.

Exercise 21.29
Prove what you discovered in answering exercise 21.28.

Exercise 21.30
Define a procedure *union* so that if LS and LT represent sets S and T respectively and each contain no repetitions, then $union(LS, LT)$ constructs a list representing $S \cup T$ with no repetitions.

Exercise 21.31
Prove that your *union* procedure meets the specification hinted at in exercise 21.30. [Hint: see exercise 21.28.]

Exercise 21.32
Answer exercises 21.30 and 21.31 again, this time for the intersection operation $S \cap T$.

-=-=-=-=-=-=-=-=-=-=-=-

21.8 IMITATING *match* AND RECURSIVE VALUE STRUCTURES

All the mechanical codes which make any attempt to provide notation that describes recursive value structures can imitate *match* in some way or other. Usually they do so with indexed set values in place of formula structures built with constructors and *case* in place of *match*.

Matching constructors

It is sometimes useful (see, for example, programs 21.11 and 21.12) to be able to match a structure of known shape but unknown constructor. In the notation I have used in this book it is possible to distinguish between constructor-constants, such as **bin**, and names which might match with such a constant, such as *bin*. In most mechanical codes, for various reasons (some of them good ones) this distinction would be far too difficult to describe and/or far too difficult to follow mechanically. Therefore it is normally necessary to replace constructor/name matches by an enumeration of the possible alternatives.

For example, if the only binary nodes which a tree can contain are built by the **sum** and **prod** constructors, program 21.11 could be rewritten as program 21.16, expanding the inner *match* formula. Program 21.12 could be rewritten in several ways: I have chosen to do it as shown in program 21.17.

def recsimp(S) =
    match S with **sum**(*a*, **numb**(0)): *recsimp(a)*
                sum(**numb**(0), *a*): *recsimp(a)*
                otherwise: match S with
                            sum(*a, b*): **sum**(*recsimp(a), recsimp(b)*)
                            prod(*a, b*): **prod**(*recsimp(a), recsimp(b)*)
                            otherwise: S
                            endmatch
        endmatch
    enddef

program 21.16

Using indexed sets and *case*

A structure is recognised in a *match* by its constructor, the number of its components and the structure of those components. If you restrict yourself to programs in which particular constructors are always applied to the same number of components - as I have in this chapter - then it is possible to imitate structures using indexed sets.

```
def numsimp(S) =
   match S with
      sum(a, b): let T = sum(numsimp(a), numsimp(b))
                 match T with
                     sum(numb(a1), numb(b1)): deliver numb(a1+b1)
                     otherwise: deliver T
                 endmatch
      prod(a, b): let T = prod(numsimp(a), numsimp(b))
                  match T with
                     prod(numb(a1), numb(b1)): deliver numb(a1×b1)
                     otherwise: deliver T
                  endmatch
      otherwise: deliver S
   endmatch
enddef
```

program 21.17

Consider, for example, the tree of figure 21.7. In constructor terms it is
sum(numb(1), prod(numb(2), numb(3))). The leaf nodes could be written as
indexed sets containing two values - a 'tag' corresponding to the constructor and
a value. For example, I might write:

$$\{\,tag = \textbf{numb}, value = 1\,\}$$
$$\{\,tag = \textbf{numb}, value = 2\,\}$$
$$\{\,tag = \textbf{numb}, value = 3\,\}$$

The non-leaves can be written as indexed sets containing a tag and two other
values:

$$\{\,tag = \textbf{sum}, lsum = \{\,tag = \textbf{numb}, value = 1\,\},$$
$$rsum = \{\,tag = \textbf{prod}, lprod = \{\,tag = \textbf{numb}, value = 2\,\},$$
$$rprod = \{\,tag = \textbf{numb}, value = 3\,\}$$
$$\}$$
$$\}$$

It is crucial to the imitation that every structure should have an element indexed
by *tag*, because that common element is used in taking the tree apart. In this
example I have associated different *tag* component values with distinct indexing
sets: when *tag* = **numb**, the set is {*tag, value*}; when *tag* = **sum** it is
{*tag, lsum, rsum*}; when *tag* = **prod** it is {*tag, lprod, rprod*}. Distinct indexing
sets aren't necessary in my notation but they do help to emphasise the idea that
different *tag* values identify different sorts of structure, and they are usually
helpful when transcribing into a mechanical code.

Program 21.18 shows how the indexed set notation can be used in a *case*
instruction which imitates the *match* of program 21.2. The shape of the structure
IS is recognised by its *tag* component, and once recognised the other indexes can
be applied to extract the components.

$def\ valueofIS\,(IS) =$

$case\ IS_{tag}\ of\ \textsf{numb}: IS_{value}$

$\textsf{sum}: valueofIS\,(IS_{lsum}) + valueofIS\,(IS_{rsum})$

$\textsf{prod}: valueofIS\,(IS_{lprod}) \times valueofIS\,(IS_{rprod})$

$endcase$

$enddef$

program 21.18

21.9 FIXED-SIZE STRUCTURES

Few mechanical codes provide notations which allow direct description of recursive value structures. There are notable exceptions - for example, LISP and its imitators, modern 'functional programming languages' like ML[†], Hope and Miranda - but most designers have plumped for a notation which describes structures of containers holding indexed-set values.

One problem in imitating structures of values is technical. Machines are built from components which aren't infinitely stretchy and imitations of infinitely stretchy values such as trees are difficult to provide. The technical solution has always been to split descriptions of tree structures into parts, making descriptions whose components are of fixed size but unlimited number. The technique keeps information about a node in one place and information about its sub-trees elsewhere.

A description of a place where a value is remembered may reasonably stand for the value itself: then an indexed set description of the root of the tree in figure 21.7 can be separated from the description of its sub-trees. Using the same indexing set as in the previous section, it might be given as

$\{\ tag=\textsf{sum},\ lsum=..some\ place..,\ rsum=..some\ other\ place..\}$

It isn't hard to see that if the description of a storage place is of a fixed size, then the description of the root itself is of fixed size; play the same trick on every node of the tree and the job is done.

Notice carefully that this trickery introduces *three* items into the description of a structure, where previously there was only one. In place of a value there are now: (first item) a description of (second item) a storage place which holds (third item) the description of the value itself. The distinction between the description of a place, the place itself and what is found at that place should be familiar because it is used in postal addressing. For example, '327 Mile End Road' is an address which names a place, a position in a sequence of numbered places at the side of Mile End Road; the Queen Mary College main building is currently found at that place but the building isn't the place because it is possible to demolish or even to move the building and replace it with another and the place will remain.

[†] From which, I gladly acknowledge, I copied the idea of *match*.

A place is not a building. An address isn't a place because you can store an address in your pocket but you would be hard put to store a place in your pocket. A place description may reasonably stand in for a description of what is in that place, but the association is transient - like the association between a container-name and the value in the named container.

In the fixed-size imitation of structures it is the *description of the storage place* which is identified with the original structure value.

Sequences of fixed-size structures

A position in a sequence may reasonably be the 'place where a value is described'. The simplest fixed-size structure imitation of a recursive value structure uses sequences and, because positions within a sequence are numbered, it can use numbers as descriptions of places.

Consider, for example, the tree of figure 21.6. It can be described by the sequence shown in program 21.19. The first entry describes the tree as a **sum** node, whose left sub-tree is described in the second position of the sequence and whose right sub-tree is described in the fifth position. The second element of the sequence (which describes the left sub-tree of the root) describes a **sum** tree whose sub-trees are described in positions 3 and 4 of the sequence. Element 5 (which describes the right sub-tree of the root) describes the leaf node **numb**(7).

$$< \{tag=\textbf{sum}, lsum=2, rsum=5\}, \{tag=\textbf{sum}, lsum=3, rsum=4\},$$
$$\{tag=\textbf{numb}, value=4\},$$
$$\{tag=\textbf{numb}, value=5\},$$
$$\{tag=\textbf{numb}, value=7\} >$$

program 21.19

Every index of the sequence in program 21.19 identifies a tree: the value 1 identifies the whole tree; the value 2 the sub-tree **sum**(**numb**(4), **numb**(5)); the value 3 the sub-tree **numb**(4), and so on. Notice in particular how the number 4 occurs twice in the sequence, once as a place-identifying value (in $rsum=4$) and once as a number value (in $value=4$). The same applies to the number 5. This shows that it would be impossible to imitate trees like those in figures 21.1, 21.2 and 21.3 whose numeric leaf values are untagged.

Given a representation of a structure like the one in program 21.19, how can it be traversed: for example, how could the *valueof* procedure be adapted to cope with this imitation? Program 21.20 shows the answer. A tree is represented by an index i into a sequence of structure descriptions S. The description of the root of the tree will be S_i: program 21.20 is then a version of program 21.18 in which inspections of the indexed set IS are replaced by inspections of S_i.

Constructors can also be imitated. If S is a sequence of structure descriptions then $S \oplus < \{tag=\textbf{numb}, value=1\} >$ represents that set of structures augmented by

$def\ valueofS(S, i) =$

    $case\ (S_i)_{tag}$ of **numb**: $(S_i)_{value}$

        sum: $valueofS(S, (S_i)_{lsum}) + valueofS(S, (S_i)_{rsum})$

        prod: $valueofS(S, (S_i)_{lprod}) \times valueofS(S, (S_i)_{rprod})$

    $endcase$

    $enddef$

program 21.20

the structure **numb**(1). If T is a container holding a sequence of structure descriptions then the instruction $T := T \oplus <\{tag = \text{numb}, value = 1\}>$ updates that sequence, and the index of the newly constructed value is $length(T)$.

Structures of fixed-size containers

Consider the tree **sum**(**numb**(3), **name**('z')). Suppose that the three node components are to be put into three separate containers. The two leaf nodes don't refer to other structures, so I can immediately write:

$$L1 := \{tag = \text{numb}, value = 3\}; \ L2 := \{tag = \text{name}, char = \text{'z'}\}$$

These assignment instructions put descriptions of the leaves into two containers. The root description now has to include descriptions of those containers. The program

$$L1 := \{tag = \text{numb}, value = 3\}; \ L2 := \{tag = \text{name}, char = \text{'z'}\};$$
$$R := \{tag = \text{sum}, lsum = @L1, rsum = @L2\}$$

is what I require. The values in R_{lsum} and R_{rsum} identify the containers which hold descriptions of the leaves. Reference values are really no more than index values indicating particular containers within the collection of containers available to the program.

The value identifying the whole structure is $@R$ and the structure built by the whole sequence of assignments is illustrated in figure 21.10. The round blob at the top of the picture represents $@R$, and the dashed line leading from it towards the ellipse representing the container named R shows what it identifies; similarly the other container-identifying values are shown as blobs with lines leading to the ellipses representing the container they identify.

Program 21.21 shows a version of the $valueof$ procedure adapted to this new imitation. Like $valueofIS$ and $valueofS$ it accesses the parts of a structure by indexing. Its argument is a reference to a container holding a description of a structure value, and like $valueofS$ it must use the reference (the indexing value) to get at those descriptions. Program 21.21 uses the $\downarrow r$ notation in order to get hold of the container which its argument describes - the thing inside the ellipse in the diagram - just as program 21.20 used S_i.

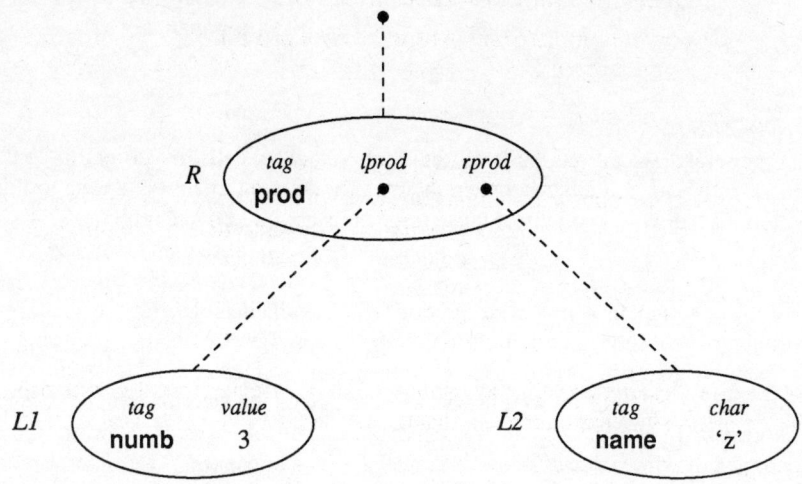

figure 21.10

$def\ valueofR\ (r) =$
$\quad case\ (\downarrow r)_{tag}\ of\ \textbf{numb:}\ (\downarrow r)_{value}$
$\qquad\qquad \textbf{sum:}\ valueofR\,((\downarrow r)_{lsum})+valueofR\,((\downarrow r)_{rsum})$
$\qquad\qquad \textbf{prod:}\ valueofR\,((\downarrow r)_{lprod})\times valueofR\,((\downarrow r)_{rprod})$
$\quad endcase$
$enddef$

program 21.21

Anonymous containers and the *ref* instruction

Structures imitating recursive value structures can be of arbitrary size. It is usually inconvenient to have to acquire named containers in order to build a structure. Many programming systems provide instructions which allow the programmer to acquire containers from a collection of anonymous containers and to access them via references.

Suppose that the formula *newcon(F)* delivers a reference to an anonymous container which is initialised to contain the value of formula F. For example, the formula

$$newcon(\{\ tag=\textbf{numb}, value=3\ \})$$

could deliver a reference to a container like the left sub-tree of figure 21.10 and then program 21.22 would deliver a reference to a structure of anonymous containers of exactly the same shape as the structure in figure 21.10. Note that the three calls to the *newcon* procedure in program 21.22 acquire three *different* containers.

-=-=-=-=-=-=-=-=-=-=-=-=-

$$newcon(\{\,tag=\textsf{sum},\,lsum=newcon(\{\,tag=\textsf{numb},\,value=3\,\}),$$
$$rsum=newcon(\{\,tag=\textsf{name},\,char=\text{'z'}\,\})\,)$$

program 21.22

Exercise 21.33
What structure would be built if the three *newcon* calls in program 21.22 acquired only one container between them? Are there alternative answers to this question? What would be built if those three calls acquired two containers?

-=-=-=-=-=-=-=-=-=-=-=-

Acquiring a container diminishes the collection available for future acquisition, ensuring that subsequent attempts don't get the same container. Acquiring a container is therefore more like executing an assignment instruction than calculating the value of a formula because it changes the state of things for later executions and calculations. In the sense of chapter 14, *newcon(F)* would be a procedure call with a side effect.

Side effects are nasty and confuse calculation. Consider, for example, programs 21.23 and 21.24. Each builds a structure of containers and delivers a reference to its root. Do they build different structures, or not? According to definition 6.3 these programs should be equivalent, but if you were able to calculate their effects using definitions like 14.8 and 14.9 it would be reasonable to conclude that program 21.23 is intended to build a structure in which there are only two containers and only one occurrence of the constructor **numb** and the number 3, whereas program 21.24 is intended to build one in which there are three containers with two occurrences of **numb** and of the number 3.

$$let\ n = newcon(\textsf{numb}(3))$$
$$deliver\ newcon(\textsf{prod}(n, n))$$

program 21.23

$$newcon(\textsf{prod}(newcon(\textsf{numb}(3)), newcon(\textsf{numb}(3))))$$

program 21.24

Since its use would violate the basic principle of substitution of equals for equals I reject the *newcon* notation, for all its shorthand advantages, and use instead a special assignment instruction to acquire anonymous containers. The *ref* instruction, written

$$ref\ x\ F$$

stores in x a reference to an anonymous container which is initialised to hold the value of formula F. I can use the instruction to build a structure like that shown in figure 21.10: program 21.25 puts in r a reference to such a structure.

In substitution terms the *ref* instruction can be treated very much in the way that *crp^* and *movecrp* treat the input sequence. I shall assume the existence of an infinite sequence H of references to new containers. Acquiring a reference to a

$$initialise\ L, R\ :=\ ?, ?$$
$$ref\ L\ \textbf{numb}(3);\ ref\ R\ \textbf{name}('z');$$
$$ref\ r\ \textbf{prod}(L, R)$$

program 21.25

new container means taking an element from H: definition 21.8 gives the formal equivalence.

$$ref\ x\ F\ =\ x := H_1; H := H_2; \downarrow x := F$$

definition 21.8

If programs 21.23 and 21.24 are rewritten to use the *ref* instruction - see programs 21.26 and 21.27 - they can then be shown to be equivalent to programs 21.28 and 21.29 respectively. These equivalences make it clear that program 21.26 acquires two containers and that program 21.27 acquires three.

$$initialise\ n := ?$$
$$ref\ n\ \textbf{numb}(3);$$
$$ref\ r\ \textbf{prod}(n, n)$$

program 21.26

$$initialise\ n1, n2 := ?, ?$$
$$ref\ n1\ \textbf{numb}(3);$$
$$ref\ n1\ \textbf{numb}(3);$$
$$ref\ r\ \textbf{prod}(n1, n2)$$

program 21.27

$$let\ n, r = H_1, H_2$$
$$H := H_3;$$
$$\downarrow n := \textbf{numb}(3);$$
$$\downarrow r := \textbf{prod}(n, n);$$

program 21.28

$$let\ n1, n2, r = H_1, H_2, H_3$$
$$H := H_4;$$
$$\downarrow n1 := \textbf{numb}(3);$$
$$\downarrow n2 := \textbf{numb}(3);$$
$$\downarrow r := \textbf{prod}(x1, x2);$$

program 21.29

-=-=-=-=-=-=-=-=-=-=-=-=-

Exercise 21.34
Prove the equivalences asserted above.

-=

APPENDIX 21.A RECURSIVE VALUE STRUCTURES IN PASCAL

If you have done your job properly, you should have a program which manipulates recursive value structures plus a proof (like the one about *numsimp* and *valueof* in section 21.6 above) or at least a proposition which you expect you could prove. You will need it when you construct your Pascal type definitions.

Step 1: Make your program Pascal-fit

Follow the steps outlined in sections 21.8 and 21.9 above: convert your program into one which uses indexed sets rather than constructors, *case* rather than *match* and structures of containers using references rather than structures of values. Your program should not use the @ operation since Pascal references (pointers) may only identify otherwise anonymous containers.

Step 2: Describe your structures

Proposition P in section 21.6 contains a description of the sort of values S which are fitting in a procedure call *valueof(S)*. They are **numb**(n) nodes, where n is a number, and **sum**(A, B) or **prod**(A, B) nodes, where A and B are structures of the same kind as S. This is a recursive specification of the sort of argument values that *valueof* will accept and it can be transcribed directly into Pascal.

Pascal represents recursive value structures with structures of containers holding indexed sets; a node in a recursive value structure will be imitated by a reference to a container holding an indexed set. In Pascal an indexed set is a `record` and reference types are indicated by the up-arrow or top-hat character '^'. Alternatives are indicated by a so-called 'variant record' defin...ion. For technical reasons you need to describe two types - one giving the list of permissible tag values, the other giving the indexing sets for each tag value. For example, the imitation of the type of value accepted by *valueof* is shown in figure 21.11. In this imitation I have chosen to use the indexing sets that I invented for the examples in sections 21.8 and 21.9 above.

Here the type `vvtag` names the set of permissible tag values (in Pascal these are constant names) and `vv` is the name of the structure type being defined. The up-arrow at the beginning of the definition indicates that it is a reference (pointer) type. The `case` inside the `record..end` brackets shows that there are alternative possible structures[†]. The name following `case` is an index name (a field name); the use of `vvtag` indicates the set of values which this particular element of the indexed set can possess. There follows a list of alternative definitions, separated

```
type vvtag = (numb,sum,prod);
     vv = ^record case tag:vvtag of
                      numb: (value:integer);
                      sum: (lsum:vv; rsum:vv);
                      prod: (lprod:vv; rprod:vv)
           end;
```

figure 21.11

[†] Notice one oddity of punctuation: a single `end` closes both the `record` definition and the `case` variant description.

by semicolons. Each alternative is labelled by one of the constant values of the type vvtag and consists of a list of index names (field names) together with a description of the type (kind, sort) of values which that particular element of an indexed set can take. The definition is recursive because, for example, the lsum element is defined to be able to hold values of the type vv which is being defined.

The definition states that every node of a vv-tree has a tag element which can take one of the values numb, sum or prod. It says that if tag has the value numb then the node has indexing set {tag, value}; that if tag has the value sum then the node has indexing set {tag, lsum, rsum}; and that if tag has the value prod then the node has indexing set {tag, lprod, rprod}.

Once a type definition has been made you can declare containers of that type, make procedures with arguments of that type, and so on. What you have done is to reveal a little of the specification of your program to the Pascal programming system.

There are some minor rules about the use of names. The constant names can be invented freely but must be distinct from any other names in the program; field names may be invented freely and need be distinct only within a particular record definition. (Notice, for example, that three of the type definition examples in this appendix include the field name tag: it would be quite ok to include all three in the same program.)

Step 3: Using structures of containers

The Pascal notation r^ means the same as my ↓r. This permits an immediate transcription of program 21.21 into Pascal: see figure 21.12. The original *match* has been converted into a Pascal case which chooses according to the possible values of the tag element of the nodes of the tree.

```
function valueof(r:vv):integer;
  begin case r^.tag of
          numb: valueof:=r^.value
          sum: valueof:=valueof(r^.lsum)+valueof(r^.rsum)
          prod: valueof:=valueof(r^.lprod)*valueof(r^.rprod)
        end
  end;
```

figure 21.12

Building structures of containers

Anonymous containers with indeterminate contents can be acquired with the instruction 'new(p)' which means the same as '*ref p* ?'. The formula p must identify a container of a pointer type like vv above. It is possible, and sensible when you are transcribing programs like the ones in this chapter, to include a tag value in the `new` instruction to help the programming system to provide a container of exactly the right size and shape: for example, if `p` is a container of type `vv` the instruction `new(p,prod)` will provide a reference to a container large enough to hold `tag`, `lprod` and `rprod` values and no more.

Once acquired with the `new` instruction, some value should be stored in the anonymous container. For example, figure 21.13 shows a program which builds a structure imitating the tree in figure 21.7. Note that the `new` instruction doesn't put any value into the container it acquires, not even a tag value. Note also the use in this program of `var` parameters in procedures `newnum`, `newsum` and `newprod` to provide an approximation to the *ref* instruction.

```
type vvtag = (numb,sum,prod);
     vv = ^record case tag:vvtag of
                    numb: (value:integer);
                    sum: (lsum:vv; rsum:vv);
                    prod: (lprod:vv; rprod:vv)
            end;
var p,L,R,R1,R2:vv;
procedure newnumb(var nv:vv; n:integer);
begin new(nv,numb); nv^.tag:=numb; nv^.value:=n end;
procedure newsum(var ns:vv; l,r:vv);
begin new(ns,sum); ns^.tag:=sum; ns^.lsum:=l; ns^.rsum:=r end;
procedure newprod(var np:vv; l,r:vv);
begin new(np,prod); np^.tag:=prod; np^.lprod:=l; np^.rprod:=r end;
begin
 .. newnumb(L,1); newnumb(R1,2); newnumb(R2,3);
    newprod(R,R1,R2); newsum(p,L,R);
 ..
end.
```

figure 21.13

Lists and the leaf constructor 'empty'

The nullary leaf constructor **empty** used in defining lists in section 21.7 is very useful when building all sorts of structures. Pascal provides a special constant reference value `nil` which doesn't correspond to **empty** but which can be used to imitate it. Pascal's `nil` is a pointer value which doesn't point to anything, a sort of empty pointer.

Figure 21.14 includes the Pascal definition of the lists of numbers discussed in section 21.7, devised in a similar way to the definition of type `vv` above. Although I don't have a formal specification of the sort of structure which can be handled by *append*, I have a very good idea about the sort of thing that I want. The indexing sets in this case are {`tag,head,tail`} when `tag=cons` and {`tag`} alone when `tag=empty`. The `append` procedure in figure 21.14 is a simple transcription of program 21.14 into Pascal, using the rules given so far in this appendix.

Figure 21.15 shows an alternative definition of the `numlist` type which takes advantage of the existence of `nil`, together with the corresponding transcription of *append*. In order to make a choice between **empty** and **cons**(a, b) the program can't look at the tag element of a referenced container because **empty** is imitated by `nil`, and `nil` doesn't point at a container. Therefore the `append` procedue must distinguish, using `if–then–else`, between **empty** and any other kind of value. That leaves only **cons**, and there is no need for a `case` to make a further discrimination. For the same reason the type definition need not describe a variant record.

Lists are unusual in that there are only **cons** nodes, left-hand leaves and right-hand **empty**, which simplifies choices between leaf and non-leaf nodes. In more general examples the `case` instruction can't be entirely eliminated from imitations of *match*. For example, figure 21.16 shows a Pascal definition imitating trees which consist of leaf nodes **empty** or **leaf**(n) and non-leaf nodes **bin**(a, b), where **empty** is imitated by `nil`. It is necessary to distinguish between **empty** and the rest using `if–then–else`, then to distinguish between **leaf** and

```
type listag = (cons,empty);
     numlist = ^record case tag:listag of
                           empty: ();
                           cons: (head:integer; tail:numlist)
               end;
procedure newcons(var nc:numlist; h:integer; t:numlist);
begin new(nc,cons); nc^.tag:=cons; nc^.head:=h; nc^.tail:=t end;
procedure append(var a:numlist; s,t:numlist);
  var r:numlist;
begin case s^.tag of
      empty: a:=t;
      cons: begin append(r,s^.tail,t);
                  newcons(a,s^.head,r)
            end
      end
end;
```

figure 21.14

```
type numlist = ^record head:integer; tail:numlist end;
procedure newcons(var nc:numlist; h:integer; t:numlist);
begin new(nc); nc^.head:=h; nc^.tail:=t end;
procedure append(var a:numlist; s,t:numlist);
  var r:numlist;
begin if s=nil then a:=t
      else begin append(r,s^.tail,t); newcons(a,s^.head,r) end
end;
```

figure 21.15

bin using case.

```
type xtag = (leaf,bin);
    xtree = ^record case tag:xtag of
                        leaf: (n:integer);
                        bin: (left,right: xtree)
            end;
procedure something(x:xtree);
begin if x=nil then .. action 1 ..
        else case x^ of leaf: .. action 2 ..
                        bin: .. action 3 ..
            end
end;
```

figure 21.16

Reference values and `var` parameters

Chapter 10, appendix 10.A, explained how to imitate reference-value arguments using `var` parameters. The `new` instruction allows a structure to be built using references to containers. Although there is no equivalent of the @ operation in Pascal, `new` allows you to get hold of reference values anyway.

If a parameter name is qualified by `var` the corresponding argument formula must be a container formula: either a container name or `r^` where `r` describes a reference value.

What to do when your program runs out of space

Programs which build structures of containers often waste space. They acquire containers and lose the references to them by storing other values into the container which holds the reference: then they acquire more containers, lose the references to those ones as well, and so on. On small machines the programming system may run out of containers and the program will crash.

The best programming systems have mechanisms called *garbage collectors*, invoked when the supply of containers is exhausted, which find and reclaim all once-used but now discarded containers. Few Pascal systems have a garbage collector. Instead they have a very dangerous instruction called `dispose` which you may feel tempted to use. If you do so it is at your own risk: it might be simpler to find a better programming system.

The instruction `dispose(p)` assumes that `p` contains a reference to a container that is now no longer required by the program and will never be referred to again. It is more or less equivalent (see definition 21.8) to $H:=<p>\oplus H$: that is, the container reference p is to be treated as if it were a reference to a new container. If a container is acquired with an instruction `new(p,..some tag..)` then for technical reasons it is essential to use the instruction `dispose(p,..exactly the same tag..)` if you should need to dispose of it.

The problem with `dispose` is that it is so easy to slip up when using it. If in fact the disposed-of container is still in use by the program (perhaps it is part of some large structure) then the chaos which can ensue is hard to describe. You will probably experience it if you ever have to use `dispose`. You have my sympathy.

Chapter 22
MODIFIABLE STRUCTURES AND GRAPHS

The trees of chapter 21 are a particular form of a structure known to mathematicians as a *graph*. Graphs are sets of places (*nodes*) joined by lines (*arcs*) which may or may not have arrows on them (be *directed*). This chapter investigates some simple graph-traversing and graph-building programs.

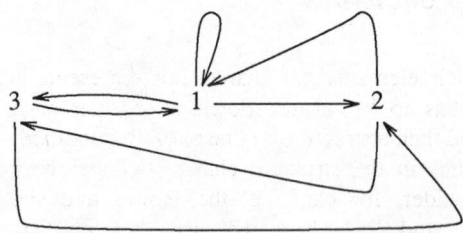

figure 22.1

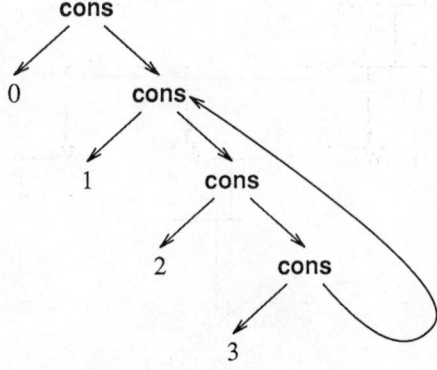

figure 22.2

Figures 22.1 and 22.2 show sample directed graphs. Figure 22.1 is a maze of three rooms connected by one-way passages starting in one of the compass directions north, south, east and west. The graph in figure 22.2 might be read as an imitation of the infinite sequence <0, 1, 2, 3, 1, 2, 3, ..>.

Graphs can in general contain *cycles* - sets of nodes which are connected by a closed path. For example, in figure 22.1 there are lots of closed paths. If you go north from node 1 you come straight back to node 1; you can go east from node 1 and then north from node 2 back to node 1; you can go west from node 1 and east from node 3 back to node 1; south from node 2 and then south from node 3 leads back to node 2; there is a path east from node 1 to node 2, south to node 3, east to node 1. In figure 22.2 there is an obvious closed path from **cons**(1, ..) to **cons**(2, ..) to **cons**(3, ..) and back to **cons**(1, ..) again.

Graphs in general allow more than one arc to enter a node: for example, in figure 22.1 there are three arcs entering node 1. As well as allowing cycles this allows the information stored in a node of a graph to be *shared* between those other nodes where the arcs originate (that is, which point to the shared node). When information is shared then it can be altered with ease.

22.1 SHARING AND UPDATING

Structures in which elements are shared can represent information concisely because nothing has to be written down more than once. If the sharing is carefully organised then a structure can be partially modified - updated - in such a way that the values in the structure change but the sharing relationships are undisturbed. Consider, for example, the family tree shown in figure 22.3. Grandparents M0 and W0 share the grandchildren G1, G2 and B1 with grandparents M1 and W1 and with parents M3 and W3. So far as English

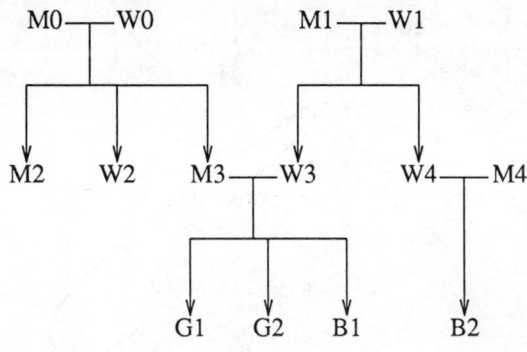

figure 22.3

relationships go, M0 and W0 have nothing to do with B2: that child is shared between parents W4 and M4, grandparents M1 and W1 and the parents of M4 (who aren't shown in this figure).

Family trees are graphs, not trees. They are rooted and acyclic (have no cycles: no paths leading from *a* back to *a* again)[†] but they allow *sharing* because some nodes have more than one arc coming in. It is a fact about this sort of graph that it can always be imitated by a forest of trees. Figure 22.4 shows the descendants (including descendants by marriage) of M0. To represent all of figure 22.3 in this way would require four trees, in each of which G1, G2 and B1 would appear twice.

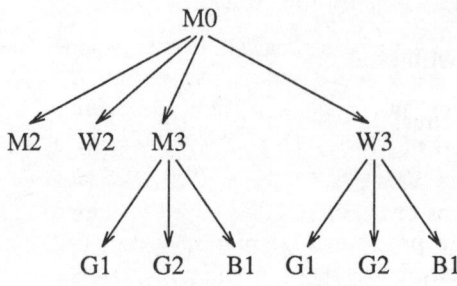

figure 22.4

Now suppose that W3 gives birth to another girl. The family tree changes to the one shown in figure 22.5 and the new child is easily seen to be a descendant of six separate individuals in the family tree. One change to the diagram updates all those descendant relationships, because the graph shares the information. The

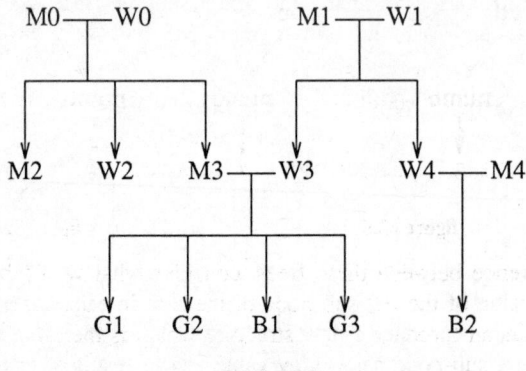

figure 22.5

[†] In most cases. Oedipus and Jocasta produced the most famous cyclic family tree: Oedipus was his own step-father and step-son, Jocasta her own daughter-in-law and mother-in-law.

forest of trees would require much more work: each of the four trees would require two changes.

When a graph uses even more sharing than my example family tree, one-place updating becomes more and more useful. Large databases of information are, in one view, large graphs of information. If *Oliver Twist* is borrowed from a library and the fact is recorded in a library computer then the list of books by Dickens, the list of books whose titles start with 'O', the list of books which deal with orphanages, the list of books on which musicals are based, .. all are in effect modified with a single stroke if information about that book is shared between them. The problems of maintaining databases of information are almost entirely to do with how to describe sharing and how to avoid replicating information[†].

Building a graph with sharing

In order to build a structure which is updatable it is important to distinguish between occurrences of values rather than values themselves. Figures 22.6 and 22.7 show structures which are similar when you consider only the tree-traversing mechanisms of chapter 21. In each structure the left and right sub-nodes of the root are **prod**(**numb**(2), **numb**(3)), and the *valueof* procedure of chapter 21 would deliver twelve given either of these structures. But they are different pictures. In figure 22.7 the left and right sub-nodes of the root are the same structure: one structure is shared. There are two occurrences of the value **prod**(**numb**(2), **numb**(3)) in figure 22.6, only one in figure 22.7.

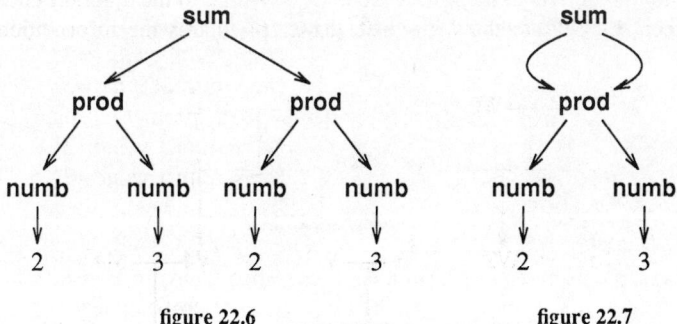

figure 22.6   figure 22.7

To see the difference between these trees, consider what would be produced if you altered the value of the left sub-node of the root in each case. By 'alter the left sub-node', I mean 'produce a new structure which is the same as the original except that the left sub-node has a new value'. The result of changing the left sub-node of figure 22.6 to **div**(**numb**(7), **numb**(3)) would certainly be the

---

[†] Database technology is well outside the scope of this book. Databases don't often use the sort of techniques which are described in this chapter, and that is all I am going to say about them.

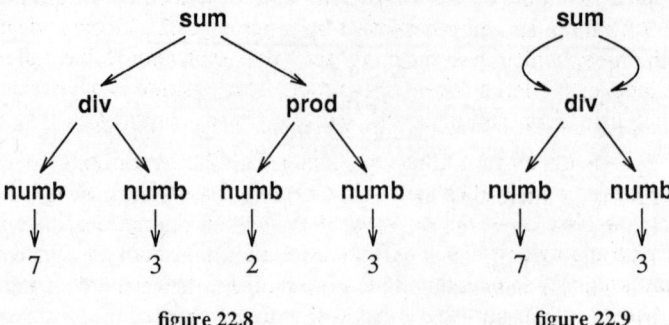

figure 22.8   figure 22.9

structure shown in figure 22.8: the result of making the same alteration to figure 22.7 might be the tree shown in figure 22.8 but it might equally reasonably be the structure shown in figure 22.9.

Chapter 21 introduced two ways of building fixed-size imitations of trees. Both techniques identify a value through a description of the place where that value is described. That is, they identify occurrences of values indirectly. When structures are described in either of those ways the effect is to enable the figure 22.9 interpretation of updating figure 22.7, because sharing relationships are described in terms of shared (commonly known) places where values are stored.

Programs 22.1 and 22.2 are formulas which describe structures like those in figures 22.6 and 22.7, using the sequence-index mechanism from chapter 21. Supposing that the corresponding structure is stored in a container t, program

$$< \{tag=\textsf{sum}, lsum=2, rsum=5\}, \{tag=\textsf{prod}, lprod=3, rprod=4\}$$
$$\{tag=\textsf{numb}, value=2\},$$
$$\{tag=\textsf{numb}, value=3\},$$
$$\{tag=\textsf{prod}, lprod=6, rprod=7\},$$
$$\{tag=\textsf{numb}, value=2\},$$
$$\{tag=\textsf{numb}, value=3\} >$$

program 22.1

$$< \{tag=\textsf{sum}, lsum=2, rsum=2\}, \{tag=\textsf{prod}, lprod=3, rprod=4\}$$
$$\{tag=\textsf{numb}, value=2\},$$
$$\{tag=\textsf{numb}, value=3\} >$$

program 22.2

$$let\ left=(t_1)_{lsum}$$
$$t_{left} := \{tag=\textsf{div}, ldiv=(t_{left})_{lsum}, rdiv=(t_{left})_{rsum}\};$$
$$(t_{left})_{ldiv} := \textsf{numb}(7); (t_{left})_{rdiv} := \textsf{numb}(3)$$

program 22.3

22.3 will produce figure 22.8 from the structure described by program 22.1 and figure 22.9 from the structure described by program 22.2. Index 1 identifies the root of the tree, which has indexing set $\{tag, lsum, rsum\}$; the value $t_{1,lsum}$ therefore indexes the left sub-tree of the root. This position is overwritten with a new value, using for sub-trees the indices already present at that position. Finally, the sub-trees of the new value are overwritten.

Program 22.4 is an interesting variation. Rather than overwriting the values in t_2, t_3 and t_4 it appends a new sub-sequence to the end of t, describing the whole new sub-tree, and alters $t_{1,lsum}$ so that it indexes the appended sub-sequence. The effect is to produce a new structure description but to leave some elements of the original structure 'isolated': that is, they do not form part of the new description. It doesn't have the same effect as program 22.3 because it doesn't preserve the sharing relationships of the original.

$t := t \oplus < \{tag=\textbf{div}, ldiv=length(t)+2, rdiv=length(t)+3\}, \{tag=\textbf{numb}, value=7\},$
$$\{tag=\textbf{numb}, value=3\} >;$$
$t_{1,lsum} := length(t)+1$

program 22.4

-=-=-=-=-=-=-=-=-=-=-=-

Exercise 22.1
Write down descriptions of the sequences produced by program 22.3 where container t holds the value of the formula from program 22.1. Hence verify that it produces a tree like that in figure 22.8. What structure does t_2 describe before the assignment, and what does it describe after it?

Exercise 22.2
Repeat exercise 22.1, this time using the formula from program 22.2.

Exercise 22.3
Repeat exercises 22.1 and 22.2, this time using program 22.4 to produce the change in t. Verify that program 22.4 transforms figure 22.7 into figure 22.8.

-=-=-=-=-=-=-=-=-=-=-=-

Programs 22.5 and 22.6 also describe structures like those in 22.6 and 22.7, this time using reference values. Execution of program 22.7 given the tree built by program 22.5 will produce the tree of figure 22.8; given the tree built by program 22.6 it will produce the tree of figure 22.9. Notice particularly that in this second case both left and right sub-trees have been altered because a container is shared.

initialise n1, n2, a, b := ?, ?, ?, ?, ?

ref a **numb**(2); *ref b* **numb**(3); *ref n1* **prod**(a, b);
ref a **numb**(2); *ref b* **numb**(3); *ref n2* **prod**(a, b);
ref r **sum**(n1, n2)

program 22.5

initialise n, a, b := ?, ?, ?

ref a **numb**(2); *ref b* **numb**(3); *ref n* **prod**(*a, b*);
ref r **sum**(*n, n*)

program 22.6

match ↓*r with*
    sum(*a, b*): *initialise x, y* := ?, ?
        ref x **numb**(7); *ref y* **numb**(3);
        ↓*a*:=**div**(*x, y*)
endmatch

program 22.7

The reference description, like the sequence-index description, separates the sharing properties of a structure from the values shared.

-=-=-=-=-=-=-=-=-=-=-=-=-=-

Exercise 22.4
Draw diagrams showing the effect of the assignment instruction in program 22.7 on the tree described by program 22.5. Show the association of names with values, of reference values with containers and of containers with the values they contain.

Exercise 22.5
Repeat exercise 22.4, this time using the tree described by program 22.6.

Exercise 22.6
Program 22.8 (see below) builds a structure in which the left sub-node of the root describes the tree **div**(**numb**(7), **numb**(3)). Is the structure delivered by this program, given each of the structures described by programs 22.5 and 22.6, the same as that built by program 22.7 or not? Justify your answer by showing the relationship between names, values and containers in the manner of exercises 22.4 and 22.5.

match ↓*r with*
    sum(*a, b*): *initialise x, y, z*:=?, ?, ?
        ref x **numb**(7); *ref y* **numb**(3); *ref z* **div**(*x, y*);
        ↓*r*:=**sum**(*z, b*)
endmatch

program 22.8

Exercise 22.7
Compare the effects of programs 22.3 and 22.7.

Exercise 22.8
Compare the effects of programs 22.4 and 22.8.

-=-=-=-=-=-=-=-=-=-=-=-=-=-

22.2 SEARCHING A MAZE

Almost every computer Adventure game that I have played includes a maze. At some stage in the game you find yourself in a room which has lots of exits, most of which lead to other rooms in the maze. If you are lucky the maze-rooms can be distinguished somehow, perhaps by slightly different descriptions of the exits from different rooms, or perhaps by some secret sign you see when you wave a magic wand or say a magic word. If you are unlucky you have to find out how to distinguish the rooms, perhaps by dropping one of your precious possessions so that you can recognise the room when you come back to it (and then sometimes it is stolen by a pirate, or a dwarf, or a dragon, or a twelve-toed sloth, or eaten by the Bugblatter Beast of Traal before you get back there!). Exits from the rooms are usually labelled with points of the compass, but just to confuse you the passages don't obey any sensible rules: if you exit north from room 1 you may get to room 2, but then going south won't usually get you back to room 1. The passages are twisty and all alike!

An n-room Adventure maze can be described by a graph. I shall use the sequence-index means of identifying elements of the graph, which makes it much easier to write down or to print in a book. A maze is then a sequence of entries, each of which describes a room. The description of each room will consist of a string which can be printed out to tell you what you 'see' in that room (some or all of the strings may be the same, just to confuse you) plus a set of exit-descriptions. Each exit-description gives the index of the room which that particular exit leads to, and the set of exit-descriptions is indexed by the direction-names you can use to move around. If a particular direction has no exit then 0 is used to imitate the **empty** sub-node.

For example: I simplify the problem by allowing only four exits from a room, indexed by N, S, E and W. I might then describe a five-room maze by the sequence:

$M = <$ { $desc$="entrance", $exits$=<1,0,2,3> indexed {N,S,E,W} },
     { $desc$="in the maze", $exits$=<3,1,0,0> indexed {N,S,E,W} },
     { $desc$="in the maze", $exits$=<4,2,1,0> indexed {N,S,E,W} },
     { $desc$="still in the maze", $exits$=<2,3,5,1> indexed {N,S,E,W} },
     { $desc$="the exit", $exits$=<1,2,0,4> indexed {N,S,E,W} } $>$

figure 22.10

In this maze room 2 lies east of room 1, because $((M_1)_{exits})_E = 2$. Room 1 is south of room 2 because $((M_2)_{exits})_S = 1$. The problem is to find your way from room 1 to room 5.

-=-=-=-=-=-=-=-=-=-=-=-=-

Exercise 22.9
Draw a picture of maze M.

Exercise 22.10
Invent a maze with a reasonable number of rooms and incorporate its description into a program so that you can wander around in the maze. Your program should print out a string description every time you 'arrive' in a room, and accept input characters n, e, s, and w to describe movement (you can have more or less directions if you like). Try it out on your friends to see if they can map it.

Exercise 22.11
Change your answer to exercise 22.10 so that you can describe the maze by typing a description to the program.

-=-=-=-=-=-=-=-=-=-=-=-=-

Adventure mazes aren't like the Hampton Court maze: you can't follow the left-hand wall and be sure of getting anywhere because passages tunnel around going under and over each other. There is a real risk of going round in circles for ever and starving to death. The problem is to design a program which can find its way around an Adventure maze without risk of starvation.

22.3 FINDING A NON-CIRCULAR PATH

Following years of heartless psychological experiments, things set running in a maze are known as mice. My program-mouse will be given a description of a maze in some form like that of figure 22.10, a starting position *a* and a finishing position *b*. It will be able to tell the difference between rooms because it knows each room by number. Its task is to print out a sequence of directions which describe a route from *a* to *b*, or say that there isn't a route between them - I might make my maze so badly that there are isolated rooms or isolated sub-mazes. Of course it must tell the truth, or it could be a very simple program indeed!

Essentially the program can follow the *seqpr* or *eightq* search technique of chapter 21. It should try each exit from room *a* in turn, and then recursively try each exit from the rooms it reaches until somehow it finds room *b*; finally it should print out its message. But it has to cope with the problem of circular paths. If the mouse always tries the northern exit first whenever it reaches a room (and why shouldn't it?) then a maze like the one in figure 22.10 would make it go round in circles immediately. If it always follows the left or the right wall then it is easy to build a maze which will trap it. Indeed, if the mouse chooses exits in any pre-planned order and doesn't otherwise attempt to avoid going round in circles then it is possible to calculate what it will do in any particular maze and it follows that there must be a maze which will trap it. The pseudo-random number sequences available in programming systems are in the end just very long sequences which eventually repeat and even a mouse which makes a pseudo-random choice could in principle and in practice be trapped by some maze or other.

If a mouse follows a path which visits the same room more than once then it has followed a cycle in the maze/graph. If the mouse abandons a path as soon as a cycle is discovered then the problem is solved. Real mice can tell when they have visited a room before, because real mice leave droppings. Even if there is a demon cleaning lady in the maze a clever mouse can *remember* which rooms it has been in before.

I suppose then that my mouse can remember the set of rooms which it has visited, and that it avoids cycles by refusing to visit the same room twice during a particular search[†]. On the *eightq* principle a recursive procedure will need to be provided with a description of the maze, the room numbers a and b, a sequence of directions followed so far (to be printed out when a solution is found) and a set of rooms already visited (and therefore not to be visited again, or a circular search would be established). My procedure might satisfy the following proposition:

> P0: If in maze M there is a sequence of moves D' leading from room i to room j which does not visit any room twice nor any of the rooms belonging to set V, then a procedure call $mouse(M, i, j, D, V)$, where i does not belong to set V, will print $D \oplus D'$ for each possible sequence D'; if no sequence D' exists the procedure call will be equivalent to *donothing*.

If a program satisfies proposition P0 you can deduce that a procedure call $mouse(M, a, b, <>, \{\})$ will print out a path from a to b if one exists, or do nothing otherwise. The qualification that i does not belong to V is needed to ensure that the search terminates, as you will see.

Given the proposition, the procedure is relatively easy to write: for example, see program 22.9. This program uses standard notation for manipulating sets: $x \in S$ should be read 'x belongs to S' or 'x is a member of S'; $x \notin S$ means 'x does not belong to S' or 'x is not a member of S'; $A \cup B$ is the union of sets A and B, the set which includes every member of A and every member of B and nothing else. If there is a path from i to j this procedure will find and print it.

The proof that program 22.9 satisfies proposition P0 goes by induction on the number of unvisited rooms: that is, the number of rooms in M minus the number of not-to-be-visited rooms in set V. If there is only one unvisited room then that room must be i: either $i=j$ - and then the procedure indeed prints $D \oplus <>$ - or the *for-do* expands to a sequence of *donothing*s, because every room which can be reached from i must either be included in V or be room i itself. If there are $K+1$ unvisited rooms then once again either $i=j$ and the procedure prints D, or the *for-do* executes a sequence made up of *donothing*s and procedure calls $mouse(M, r, j, D+<d>, V \cup \{i\})$. In each of those procedure calls the set $V \cup \{i\}$ is

---

[†] Note the qualification: it is ok to visit the same room twice, provided that it happens on different searches. For example, if a mouse is trying to find all paths from a to b, then it might go from a to c and thence to b. It might later go from a to d, and then to c again, and then again to b. But it mustn't go from a to d to c to d to c: that is, it mustn't re-visit rooms which are in the path it is trying to expand.

$def\ mouse(M, i, j, D, V) =$
$\quad select\ i=j:\ printsequence(D)$

$\qquad i \neq j:\ let\ X = (M_i)_{exits}$
$\qquad\qquad let\ V' = V \cup \{i\}$

$\qquad\qquad for\ d\ rt\ <N, S, E, W>\ do$
$\qquad\qquad\quad let\ r = X_d$
$\qquad\qquad\quad select\ r=0 \vee r \in V':\ donothing$
$\qquad\qquad\qquad\qquad\qquad r \neq 0 \wedge r \notin V':\ mouse(M, r, j, D \oplus <d>, V')$
$\qquad\qquad\quad endselect$
$\qquad\qquad od$
$\quad endselect$
$enddef$

program 22.9

one element larger than V (because $i \notin V$, which is why the qualification is needed) and in each case $r \notin V \cup \{i\}$. Therefore each procedure call is given a maze with K unvisited rooms, and by inductive hypothesis will print $D \oplus <d> \oplus D'$ or be equivalent to *donothing*.

-=-=-=-=-=-=-=-=-=-=-=-

Exercise 22.12
Make the formal proof that program 22.9 satisfies proposition P0.

Exercise 22.13
Suppose that proposition P0 had not included the requirement that i does not belong to V. What change to the procedure definition would this have caused? What changes to the proof would have been necessary?

-=-=-=-=-=-=-=-=-=-=-=-

A procedure call $mouse(M, a, b, <>, \{\})$ will print every path from a to b, and it will do nothing if there is no path. To make a program which prints only a single path, or a message if there isn't one, it is necessary to use the *terminate* instruction. Program 22.10 uses *terminate* in just this way: the program is equivalent to a labelled sequence which ends with an instruction that prints "no path" and contains a number of *printsequence* instructions each followed immediately by *terminate* instructions. If there aren't any *printsequence* instructions the procedure will terminate normally and the only thing it prints is "no path". But by the definition of the *terminate* instruction, everything following the first *printsequence* instruction can be deleted from the program, so it prints either "no path" or a single sequence of directions, as required.

T: *def mouse*$(M, i, j, D, V) =$
  select $i=j$: *printsequence*(D); *terminate* T

  $i \neq j$: *let* $X = (M_i)_{exits}$
      let $V' = V \cup \{i\}$

      for d *rt* $<N, S, E, W>$ *do*
        let $r = X_d$
        select $r=0 \vee r \in V'$: *donothing*
            $r \neq 0 \wedge r \notin V'$: *mouse*$(M, r, j, D \oplus <d>, V')$
        endselect
      od

    endselect
  enddef

  mouse$(M, a, b, <>, \{\})$; NL; *printstring*("no path")
  $:T$

program 22.10

22.4 IMITATING SETS

Suppose that you had to translate program 22.9 or program 22.10 into a mechanical code which doesn't understand set values and the operations '$\in$' and '$\cup$'. How could you imitate them in terms of values and mechanisms which the code does understand? There are several different interesting answers to that question.

Sets as value-delivering procedures

In mathematics the membership of a set can be described by its **characteristic function**: a function which delivers true if its argument is a member of the set and delivers false otherwise. For example, membership of the set E of even numbers can be described by the formula $(x \, rem \, 2) = 0$. Any number x for which this formula delivers true is an even number. In programming notation the procedure

def even$(x) = (x \, rem \, 2) = 0$ *enddef*

could be used in imitating the set of even numbers: $i \in E$ is then imitated by *even*(i).

Membership of the empty set $\{\}$ is easiest of all to imitate: it has no members, so

def empty$(x) = false$ *enddef*

will do. *Empty*(i) will deliver false for any element i.

If procedure p describes membership of set P, then membership of $P \cup \{y\}$ is described by the procedure $p1$:

$$def\,p1(x) = x{=}y \vee p(x)\ enddef$$

$P1(i)$ delivers true if $i{=}y$ or if $p(i)$ delivers true or both (which can happen if i is already in set P). A slightly different definition of the procedure makes it potentially more efficient in operation because it avoids an unnecessary procedure call when $i{=}y$:

$$def\,p1(x) = select\ x{=}y{:}true\ \ x{\neq}y{:}p(x)\ endselect\ enddef$$

You know that y is certainly in $P \cup \{y\}$; if it isn't y you're looking for then look in P and if it isn't there then it isn't in the union.

It is therefore possible represent membership of a set with a procedure, and to represent the set augmented with a new member with another procedure. This allows me to translate the *mouse* procedure into program 22.11. To make this program I have replaced $\{\}$ by $\lambda.(x).false$, $V \cup \{i\}$ by $v1$, $r \in V'$ by $v1(r)$. Does it work? Of course it does!

$T{:}\ def\,mouse(M, i, j, D, v) =$
    $select\ i{=}j{:}\ printsequence(D);\ terminate\ T$

      $i{\neq}j{:}\ let\ X{=}(M_i)_{exits}$
           $def\,v1(x) = select\ x{=}i{:}true\ \ x{\neq}i{:}\ v(x)\ endselect\ enddef$

           $for\ d\ rt\ {<}N, S, E, W{>}\ do$
              $let\ r{=}X_d$
              $select\ r{=}0 \vee v1(r){:}\ donothing$
                    $r{\neq}0 \wedge \neg v1(r){:}\ mouse(M, r, j, D{\oplus}{<}d{>}, v1)$
              $endselect$
           od
      $endselect$
     $enddef$

     $mouse(M, a, b, {<}{>}, \lambda(x).false);\ NL;\ printstring(\text{``no path''})$
  $:T$

program 22.11

-=-=-=-=-=-=-=-=-=-=-=-

Exercise 22.14
If you are lucky enough to have a programming system which allows procedure definitions within definitions, transcribe program 22.11 and try it out on a maze of your invention. [The unpacking technique of chapter 5 won't work very well with this example, but the next imitation technique provides an alternative solution.]

-=-=-=-=-=-=-=-=-=-=-=-

In the execution explanation, program 22.11 works because:

(a) every call of the procedure *mouse* creates a new environment within which the names *i*, *v* and *vl* are defined[†];

(b) the result of a call *vl*(*f*) depends not only on the argument formula *f* but also on the values of *i* and *v*;

(c) when *vl* is called it is executed within an environment which is based on *the one in which it was defined*. Although there are lots of *vl* procedures about during an execution of this program, they are all different because for each of them the values *i* and *v* are taken from their defining environment, so they all define membership of different sets.

The substitution explanation has to cope with the same problem - lots of versions of procedure *vl* - by systematically changing the identifiers used in different executions of the *mouse* procedure . This is the sort of thing that was done in chapter 5, only more exhausting this time because it happens lots of times.

-=-=-=-=-=-=-=-=-=-=-=-=-

Exercise 22.15
Program 22.11, given a maze shaped like figure 22.10 and *a*=1, *b*=5, would find the path <E,N,E>. Draw an environment diagram to verify this. [Warning: the diagram is enormous, so simplify it.]

Exercise 22.16
Show by substitution that a substantial part of the environment diagram you drew when answering exercise 22.15 is correct. [The diagram will be completely correct if you have drawn it properly, but the complete substitution is so large that I hesitate to set it as an exercise.]

-=-=-=-=-=-=-=-=-=-=-=-=-

Program 22.11 has the drawback that as the set *V'* gets larger, so the number of procedure calls required to find out whether or not *r*∈ *V'* also grows. If procedure call is an expensive operation on your programming system, program 22.11 is not a very good imitation. Nil desperandum: there are others to try.

Sets as sequences

The essential difference between a set and a sequence is that you can ask *where* in a sequence element *x* occurs, but only *whether* *x* is an element of a set. An element *x* can occur several times in a sequence, at different positions, but since you can't ask positional questions about elements of a set it is nonsense to ask

---

[†] In program 22.11 *vl* is defined within the *select*. For the purposes of the current discussion it might as well have been defined at the beginning of the *mouse* procedure.

how many times an element x occurs in a set.

Can a sequence represent a set? Answer: yes, if you only ask questions about membership and disregard any positional information. The same set can then be represented by several sequences: for example, the set $\{1,3\}$ can be represented by any of the following sequences

$$<1,3> \quad <3,1> \quad <1,1,3> \quad <3,1,3,3,3,1,1,1>$$

and an infinite number of other variations. The formula $x \in A$ can be imitated by *member*(x, AS) if AS is a sequence representing A and *member* is a procedure which searches for x in AS: see program 22.12, for example. Union of sets is obviously represented by concatenation of sequences.

> *def member* $(x, AS) = for\ i\ rt\ AS\ do\ select\ x = i:\ deliver\ true$
> $\qquad\qquad\qquad\qquad\qquad\qquad\qquad\qquad x \neq i:\ donothing$
> $\qquad\qquad\qquad\qquad\qquad\qquad endselect$
> $\qquad\qquad od;$
> $\qquad\qquad deliver\ false$
> *enddef*

program 22.12

-=-=-=-=-=-=-=-=-=-=-=-

Exercise 22.17
Why is the union of sets adequately represented by concatenation of sequences? Is it obvious? Can you prove it?

Exercise 22.18
Translate program 22.10, imitating sets with sequences. Try it out on your programming system.

-=-=-=-=-=-=-=-=-=-=-=-

On some programming systems (though by no means all) searching for an element of a sequence is cheaper than recursively calling a procedure, so the mouse which imitates sets with sequences may find a path faster than the one which imitates the characteristic function of the set. But just as it is for sets represented with characteristic functions, so it is for sets represented with sequences: the larger the set, the harder it is to find out whether or not x is an element of it. Searching new rooms far from base gets rather tedious.

Sets and subsets

Each of the previous two imitations has used a completely general representation technique. Which is to say that neither of them has taken advantage of the fact that the set V can't have just any old elements: in an n-room maze any value of V must be a subset of $\{1, 2, .., n\}$. And for representing subsets of a particular set there is a well-known trick: have a sequence S indexed $1..n$ and ensure that if element x is in the subset then $S_x = true$, but if element x isn't in the subset then $S_x = false$. That is, $S_x = x \in V$, where V is a subset of $\{1,..,n\}$. On most programming systems extracting an element of a sequence takes a constant amount of time no matter which element it is, so this is the best imitation so far because it doesn't find things harder to recall the farther it is from home.

-=-=-=-=-=-=-=-=-=-=-=-

Exercise 22.19
Translate the *mouse* procedure using the subset mechanism (without looking at the answer below).

-=-=-=-=-=-=-=-=-=-=-=-

In answering exercise 22.19 you should have produced a program equivalent to program 22.13 but there are some mistakes which it is very easy to make. If Q' is indexed $1..n$ then Q'_0 is meaningless, and the formulas '$r=0 \vee Q'_r$' and '$r\neq0 \wedge \neg Q'_r$' are each meaningless when $r=0$. One way round the problem is to make sure that Q' is indexed $0..n$ as I have done in program 22.13 and then both formulas are meaningful when $r=0$: one is true and the other false because in each case the value of Q'_0 doesn't matter. An alternative would be to change the *select* instruction into a *select* which inspects r, inside which is a *select* which inspects Q' only when $r\neq0$.

T: *def mouse*$(M, i, j, D, Q) =$
    select $i=j$: *printsequence*(D); *terminate T*

        $i\neq j$: *let* $X=(M_i)_{exits}$
            let $Q'=Q_{0..i-1} \oplus <true> \oplus Q_{i+1..}$
          for d rt $<N, S, E, W>$ *do*
              let $r=X_d$
              select $r=0 \vee Q'_r$: *donothing*
                    $r\neq0 \wedge \neg Q'_r$: *mouse*$(M, r, j, D\oplus<d>, Q')$
              endselect
          od
      endselect
      enddef
      mouse$(M, a, b, <>, <false, .., false>$ *indexed* $0..n)$;
      NL; *printstring*("no path")
  :T

program 22.13

-=-=-=-=-=-=-=-=-=-=-=-

Exercise 22.20
Transcribe program 22.13 into the code of your programming system and run this mouse in competition with either of the previous two versions.

-=-=-=-=-=-=-=-=-=-=-=-

Mouse droppings

The final imitation step is to show how to write program 22.13 so that it uses only one sequence container rather than creating a new one for each recursive call. Observe that at the beginning of the *mouse* procedure, $i \notin V$: that is, in the imitation Q_i=false. During the execution of the procedure it is necessary to examine membership of the set $V \cup \{i\}$, represented in the imitation by $Q_{0..i-1} \oplus <true> \oplus Q_{i+1..}$.

Suppose that the *mouse* procedure were to be provided with a reference QR identifying a sequence container which contains a representation of V (that is, $\downarrow QR$ contains a representation of V). Then to represent $V \cup \{i\}$ it would be enough to alter $\downarrow QR$ using the instruction $(\downarrow QR)_i := true$. And to make $\downarrow QR$ represent V again it would only be necessary to change it back, using $(\downarrow QR)_i := false$. Which suggests the sequence of instructions

$$(\downarrow QR)_i := true; \text{ for } d \text{ rt } <N, S, E, W> \text{ do } .. \text{ od}; (\downarrow QR)_i := false$$

After the first assignment the altered value held in $\downarrow QR$ represents $V \cup \{i\}$ and once the work of the procedure call is done, the original value is restored by the second assignment. It is then possible to eliminate entirely the parameter which represents V because all the executions can share the same sequence container Q. Playing a similar trick with D, and sharing M between all executions, leads to the design illustrated in program 22.14.

```
T: def mouse(i, j) =
       select i=j: printsequence(D); terminate T
             i≠j: let X=(M_i)_exits
                  Q_i := true;
                  for d rt <N, S, E, W> do
                      let r=X_d
                      select r=0 ∨ Q_r: donothing
                            r≠0 ∧ ¬Q_r:
                                    D := D ⊕ <d>; mouse(r, j); D := D_{1..length(D)-1}
                      endselect
                  od;
                  Q_i := false
       endselect
   enddef
   initialise Q, D := a sequence <false, .., false> indexed 0..n, <>
   mouse(a, b); NL; printstring("no  path")
   :T
```

program 22.14

-=-=-=-=-=-=-=-=-=-=-=-

Exercise 22.21
Transcribe program 22.14 and try it on your system (you can even do it in a recursive BASIC, now).

-=-=-=-=-=-=-=-=-=-=-=-=-

Program 22.14 is a mouse which uses sequence Q to mark its progress, but it cleans up its own droppings as it comes back. Computational hygiene pays off!

22.5 FINDING A SHORTEST PATH

The mouse of program 22.9 finds a path from room a to room b, but it doesn't necessarily find the shortest path. In a complicated maze it may be possible, by making a wrong choice early on, to go all round the maze when all that is really needed is a single move. For example, in the maze of figure 22.10 the shortest way from room 1 to room 2 is to go east, but it is also possible to go west, north, east and finally south, traversing every other room of the maze before reaching the destination.

If you have plenty of time, and the mouse has plenty of energy, it can investigate *every* path and finally print only the shortest.

-=-=-=-=-=-=-=-=-=-=-=-=-

Exercise 22.22
Modify program 22.9 - or one of your imitations of it - to print the shortest path. [Hint: keep a record of the shortest path so far; check the length of each new path against it. Another hint: what is the length of the 'shortest path so far' in an *n*-room maze *before* the mouse starts searching? Sub-hint: the best answer is not a negative number.]

Exercise 22.23
On the principle of rejecting unsolutions early, the mouse can abandon an uncompleted path which is longer than the shortest completed path found so far. Modify your program to use this technique. [Hint: consider the formulas in the *select* instruction inside the *mouse* procedure.]

-=-=-=-=-=-=-=-=-=-=-=-=-

22.6 MAPPING A GRAPH

The mouse of program 22.9 finds a path from one room to another in a maze, dragging two bits of string behind it (the set V and the sequence D) so that it can tell where it has been if it starts going round in circles and so that it can report how it got there if it ever stumbles across the destination. Each time it retreats in a search it winds up its string and forgets everything it has discovered. The task of finding a path from a to b might be simplified if you already know something about a maze.

Finding all the reachable nodes

The problem of finding all the nodes in a graph which are reachable from node a is clearly related to the problem of finding paths in a graph. It is also one of the most famous of computing solutions to a problem: so-called *garbage collector* programs search the graph of structures created by a program, mark those structures which are reachable from any roots known to the program and reclaim the space used by the unreachable ones. Just why and how garbage is created and how the programming system is designed to ensure that the garbage collector finds all and only garbage are beyond the scope of this book.

> A node y is *reachable* from a node x if and only if
>
> (a) $x=y$, or
>
> (b) x is a structure of the form $c(..y..)$, or
>
> (c) z is reachable from x and y is reachable from z.

definition 22.1

Definition 22.1 says what 'reachable' means in a graph. A node may be reachable in zero steps, in one step or recursively in more than one step via an intermediate node. When finding and recording all reachable nodes, once again the problem is to avoid going round in circles. If y is reachable from x, z is reachable from y and x is reachable from z then a careless recorder might forever march round the cycle $x–y–z–x$.

Experience with the mice of sections 22.3 and 22.4 above shows that if you are to avoid going round in circles you will need some sort of record of the nodes already encountered. Suppose that set V is used as before to mark nodes which are on a path already being investigated. Nodes in V are known to be reachable and need not be looked at again: then $reachable(G, i, V)$ might reasonably deliver $V \cup R$ where R is the set of nodes reachable from node i in graph G on a path which doesn't pass through any node in the set V. The problem of designing the procedure is simplified when you realise that it is once more based on an induction on the number of unrecorded reachable nodes.

Program 22.15 searches a graph like the ones in figures 22.6 and 22.7 in which binary nodes always contain sub-structures and unary nodes contain only unstructured values; it works on a representation of such a graph built using sequence-indexing by programs like 22.1 or 22.2. The design is based on an inductive argument. The body of the procedure examines G_i: if it is a unary node then there is nothing to do; otherwise it delivers the union of the nodes reachable through the left sub-node and those reachable through the right sub-

def reachable(G, i, V) =
  let $V' = V \cup \{i\}$
  match G_i *with leaf*(k): V'
             bin(x, y): *select* $x \in V' \wedge y \in V'$: V'
                            $x \in V' \wedge y \notin V'$: *reachable*$(G, y, V')$
                            $x \notin V' \wedge y \in V'$: *reachable*$(G, x, V')$
                            $x \notin V' \wedge y \notin V'$:
                                      reachable$(G, x, V') \cup$ *reachable*(G, y, V')
              endselect
  endmatch
  enddef

program 22.15

node, in each case basing the search on the set $V \cup \{i\}$. To be sure that the recursive call doesn't close a cycle the procedure examines x and y, the sub-nodes of G_i, to see if they are recorded in $V \cup \{i\}$ and takes action according to whether both, one, the other or neither appears there.

-=-=-=-=-=-=-=-=-=-=-=-

Exercise 22.24
Using the definition of *reachable* given in program 22.15, prove that a procedure call *reachable*(G, i, V), when presented with a graph which contains k unrecorded reachable nodes, will meet its specification. To do so you must write a specification in the form of a proposition about the procedure. [Hint: it should be important to your proof that $i \notin V$.]

Exercise 22.25
By pencil-and-paper analysis, or by writing the program and trying it out, show that *reachable*$(X, 1, \{\})$, where X is the graph of figure 22.6 built by program 22.1

  (a) finds the set $\{1, 2, 3, 4, 5, 6, 7\}$ of reachable nodes

  (b) investigates each node in the graph once only.

[Hint: if you write the program, make the *reachable* procedure print out the value of i each time it is called.]

Exercise 22.26
Repeat exercise 22.25 with the graph of figure 22.7, built by program 22.2. This time show that nodes 2, 3 and 4 are investigated more than once.

Exercise 22.27
Repeat exercise 22.25 once more with the graph built by programs 22.2 and 22.4. Show that this time node 2 is not in the set of reachable nodes.

-=-=-=-=-=-=-=-=-=-=-=-

The argument that program 22.15 terminates rests on the fact that $i \notin V$, because then you can be sure that $V \cup \{i\}$ is larger than V. But this leads to a lot of analysis of sub-structures to make sure that they aren't already part of the set V, so that the recursive procedure call can be validly applied. If that requirement is relaxed then an alternative version of the procedure can be written: see program 22.16, for example. If $i \in V$ then $reachable(G, i, V)$ should deliver V because the set R is empty. The simplification in design is worthwhile.

def reachable(G, i, V) =
  select i∈ V: V

     i∉ V: let V' = V∪{i}
       match G$_i$ with leaf(k): V'
              bin(x,y): reachable(G,x,V') ∪ reachable(G,y,V')
       endmatch
  endselect
enddef

program 22.16

-=-=-=-=-=-=-=-=-=-=-=-=-

Exercise 22.28
Construct a specification (that is, a provable proposition) which is appropriate to the definition of *reachable* given in program 22.16 and prove that program 22.16 meets it.

Exercise 22.29
Repeat exercise 22.26 using program 22.16 and show that this program also visits nodes 2, 3 and 4 more than once.

-=-=-=-=-=-=-=-=-=-=-=-=-

Program 22.17 tries to avoid visiting any node more often than necessary. V'' includes all the nodes reachable from sub-node x of i; $reachable(G, y, V'')$ will only investigate nodes reachable from sub-node y without passing through the nodes reachable from x.

def reachable(G, i, V) =
  select i∈ V: V

     i∉ V: let V' = V∪{i}
       match G$_i$ with leaf(k): V'
              bin(x,y): let V'' = reachable(G,x,V')
                     reachable(G,y,V'')
       endmatch
  endselect
enddef

program 22.17

-=-=-=-=-=-=-=-=-=-=-=-=-

Exercise 22.30
If you repeat exercise 22.26 using program 22.17 this program will also visit node 2 more than once, though it does better with nodes 3 and 4.

(a) Verify this assertion;

(b) explain why it is so;

(c) construct a graph in which programs 22.15 and 22.16 will visit nodes more than once, but program 22.17 will visit each node once only;

(d) construct a version of program 22.17 [hint: look at program 22.15] which doesn't visit node 2 twice.

Exercise 22.31
Out of the four programs 22.15, 22.16, 22.17 and the program you wrote in answering exercise 22.30, which do you prefer and why?

-=-=-=-=-=-=-=-=-=-=-=-

22.7 COPYING A GRAPH

A program which makes a copy of a tree is easy to design: to copy a leaf just make a node with the same constructor and the same contents; to copy an interior node make one with the same constructor and copied sub-structures. For example, see program 22.18, which copies a structure of values like the formula-trees discussed in chapter 21. There is an obvious structural induction which establishes that this program does its work, but it is all a bit pointless because it isn't necessary to copy a value, structured or not! The normal operation of a program copies values (for example, the instruction $x:=y$ will make a copy of the value described by y and put it in container x).

> $def\ treecopy(S) =$
> $match\ S\ with$
> $leaf(n): S$
> $bin(left, right): bin(treecopy(left), treecopy(right))$
> $endmatch$
> $enddef$

program 22.18

Structures built using the indirect description techniques of chapter 21 (structures using sequence indexing or structures of containers) aren't so easy to copy. If r is a reference to the root of a structure, then a copy of r isn't a copy of the structure. It may not be enough to get a new container and put a copy of the value held in $\downarrow r$ into it. In general it will be necessary to acquire as many containers as there are in the original structure, to put in them values built with the same constructors used in the original structure and to make the relationships between the new containers the same as those in the original structure. Program 22.19 does just that job. Its parameter r is a reference to a container holding a structure; it finds a new container and puts into it a copy (made recursively) of

$def\ refcopy(s, r) =$
　　$match \downarrow r\ with$
　　　$leaf(n):\ ref \downarrow s\ \downarrow r$
　　　$bin(left, right):\ initialise\ L, R := ?, ?$
　　　　　　　$refcopy(@L, left);\ refcopy(@R, right);$
　　　　　　　$ref \downarrow s\ bin(L, R)$
　　$endmatch$
　$enddef$
　$..\ refcopy(@x, p)\ ..$

program 22.19

the original structure. It stores a reference to the copy in $\downarrow s$. Once again, there is an obvious structural induction which shows that it gets the right number of containers and puts the right things into them.

-=-=-=-=-=-=-=-=-=-=-=-

Exercise 22.32
Make that induction. You should find that your proof depends on an assumption that the structure indicated by r is a tree.

-=-=-=-=-=-=-=-=-=-=-=-

Copying a structure with sharing

The structure built by program 22.19 doesn't have any sharing in it, as the next exercise should persuade you.

-=-=-=-=-=-=-=-=-=-=-=-

Exercise 22.33
Verify, by pencil-and-paper execution or by any other effective means, that program 22.19 will build a structure like that in figure 22.6 if given one like that in figure 22.7.

-=-=-=-=-=-=-=-=-=-=-=-

In order to take account of sharing and to build an identical copy of a structure the copying procedure must be able to convert duplicated references (references to the same occurrence of a value) in the original structure into duplicated references in the copied structure. Like searching and mapping, this means keeping some record of what you have already copied so that when you see it again you don't make a fresh copy. Suppose that X holds a list of pairs <original reference, new reference> giving a translation between nodes of the original structure and nodes in the new structure; then $sharecopy(s, r)$ might reasonably

　(a) store in $\downarrow s$ a reference to a new container holding a copy of the structure in $\downarrow r$, built wherever possible by taking account of the information in X;

(b) add to the sequence in X pairs describing any new parts of the structure it has had to build.

Program 22.20 first checks whether the container described by r has been copied already: if so, the reference to the prior copy is stored in $\downarrow s$ and X is unchanged. If r isn't recorded then it must be copied. The first arm of the *match* makes a copy of a leaf into a new container. The second arm copies the left and right arms of a binary node one after the other (note that this may update X) and copies the root node in a new container. Finally X is updated to take account of the container acquired for the leaf or the root node.

> *def sharecopy*$(s, r) =$
> B: *for* x *rt* X *do select* $x_1 = r$: $\downarrow s := x_2$; *terminate B*
> $x_1 \neq r$: *donothing*
>   *endselect*
>   *od*;
>   *match* $\downarrow r$ *with leaf*(n): *ref* $\downarrow s$ $\downarrow r$
>   *bin*(*left, right*):
>   *initialise L, R* := ?, ?
>   *sharecopy*(@L, *left*); *sharecopy*(@R, *right*);
>   *ref* $\downarrow s$ *bin*(L, R)
>   *endmatch*;
> $X := X \oplus \langle r, \downarrow s \rangle$
>   :B
> *enddef*
> .. *sharecopy*(@x, p); ..

program 22.20

-=-=-=-=-=-=-=-=-=-=-=-=-

Exercise 22.34
Prove that program 22.20

(a) builds a structure with as many distinct containers as the one it is copying;

(b) updates X to give a complete correspondence between nodes in the original structure and nodes in the copied structure.

[Hint: structural induction on the number of reachable uncopied nodes; you should need to assume that the structure has no cycles.]

Exercise 22.35
Try out program 22.20, either on paper or in a computing machine.

-=-=-=-=-=-=-=-=-=-=-=-=-

Copying with cycles

Program 22.19 is inadequate given a structure which requires sharing: program 22.20 is inadequate if a structure has cycles.

-=-=-=-=-=-=-=-=-=-=-=-=-

Exercise 22.36
Draw a picture of the structure which is built by program 22.21.

$$initialise\ s,t,u,v := ?,?,?,?$$

$$ref\ t\ ?;$$
$$ref\ u\ \mathsf{numb}(1);\ ref\ s\ \mathsf{sum}(u,t);$$
$$ref\ v\ \mathsf{numb}(2);\ \downarrow t:=\mathsf{sum}(v,s)$$

program 22.21

Exercise 22.37
If s is assigned a value by program 22.21, show that the execution of $sharecopy(@x,s)$ will not terminate.

-=-=-=-=-=-=-=-=-=-=-=-=-

The structure built by program 22.21 includes a cycle. If you tried to print it out with a program like 21.3 then you would see 1+2+1+2+1+2+.. continuing on for ever. Exercise 22.37 shows that *sharecopy* cannot cope with cycles either. The problem is that the correspondence between r and $\downarrow s$ is not recorded until after the sub-trees *left* and *right* have been copied. Yet in the tree built by program 22.21 the right sub-tree refers back to the root.

```
def cyclecopy(s,r) =
    B: for x rt X select x₁=r: ↓s:=x₂; terminate B
                       x₁≠r: donothing
              endselect
       od;
       ref ↓s ↓r; X:=X+<r,↓s>;
       match ↓r with leaf(n): donothing
                     bin(left,right):
                         initialise L,R := ?,?
                         cyclecopy(@L,left); cyclecopy(@R,right);
                         ↓(↓s):=bin(L,R)
       endmatch
    :B
enddef
.. cyclecopy(@x,p); ..
```

program 22.22

Program 22.22 is a solution to the problem of copying cyclic graphs. Once it has discovered that r has not yet been copied, it acquires a container to hold the copy which it must make and adds a pair to X. This is done first, before any copying is done, and thus r is included in the set of copied containers before the sub-trees of $\downarrow r$ are copied. Then it copies the sub-trees of $\downarrow r$. This time each is given a graph with fewer uncopied nodes, even though it may have a cyclic occurrence of r, and the induction goes through.

-=-=-=-=-=-=-=-=-=-=-=-

Exercise 22.38
Go on, push it through. (Don't bother to be ultra-formal: this is nearly the end of the book!).

-=-=-=-=-=-=-=-=-=-=-=-

22.8 BUILDING A GRAPH

There is a famous puzzle of the Farmer, the Wolf, the Goat and the Cabbage. These four are on one bank of a river. There is a boat on the river, which can carry any one or two of them. The farmer has to get all four across the river. Only the farmer can row. If the farmer leaves the wolf and the goat alone together the wolf will eat the goat; similarly, it isn't safe to leave the goat alone with the cabbage.

Finding a solution to the problem is a sort of search. The starting position has four individuals on one bank. Every move has to take the farmer from one bank to the other, with or without a passenger (that's a clue, if you don't already know the answer). Some moves lead to a disaster: for example, if the farmer first takes the wolf across the river then the goat will eat the cabbage.

$$\text{"fwgc" / ""} \quad \rightarrow \quad \text{"gc" / "fw"} \quad \text{(goat eats cabbage)}$$

Disaster positions are dead ends in the search. As usual the problem is to avoid going round in circles, but this time positions which have been visited already must be identified by their properties, not a simple sequence index or reference comparison.

A position can obviously be described by two four-element sequences. Each sequence describes one of the banks, one element of each sequence describing whether or not each of the participants is on that bank. Each element is either true or false (or if you prefer, either 0 or 1, or either -1 or +1, ..). But then since one bank is the opposite of the other, you might reasonably use only one sequence.

-=-=-=-=-=-=-=-=-=-=-=-

Exercise 22.39
Write the program which solves the Farmer, Wolf, Goat and Cabbage problem. Try it out.

Exercise 22.40
Your answer to exercise 22.39 might have found just one solution or it might
have found every one. Whichever program you wrote, now write the other one.
[Hint: there are only two solutions!]

-=-=-=-=-=-=-=-=-=-=-=-=-

Students of binary arithmetic should have noticed that if a position in the
problem can be described by a four-element sequence of binary values, no more
than $2^4 = 16$ distinct positions can arise during an investigation of the Wolf, Goat
and Cabbage problem. Despite dead ends, every one of the sixteen positions can
be reached by valid moves in the problem. To show that this is so, it is sufficient
to build a copy of the graph of positions. This is almost identical to the problem
of finding reachable positions in an existing graph.

-=-=-=-=-=-=-=-=-=-=-=-=-

Exercise 22.41
Draw the complete graph of the Wolf, Goat and Cabbage problem. Hence verify
that there are sixteen valid positions (including all those where the goat and/or
the cabbage come to a sticky end).

Exercise 22.42
Write a program which builds a representation of the graph. [Hint: because there
are so few positions, it is simplest to build a sequence-indexing representation.]
Your program should print out the locations of the participants in each node of
the graph, and indicate the positions directly reachable from each of them.

-=-=-=-=-=-=-=-=-=-=-=-=-

22.9 IMITATING STRUCTURES OF INDEXED SETS

Maze M of figure 22.10 is a hierarchical structure. It is a homogeneous sequence
in the sense that every element is of the same kind. It isn't homogeneous in the
very strong sense that every element of every element is of the same kind.

Almost all programming systems can imitate sequences of sequences (of
sequences ..) but if they don't provide an imitation of indexed sets then a
sequence like M can't be immediately transcribed. The simplest way around the
problem is to split up the sequence of indexed sets into a collection of sequences,
each with a different name. For example, M could be split into:

$Mdesc$ = <"entrance", "in the maze", "in the maze", "still in the maze",
            "the exit">

$Mexits$ = < <1, 0, 2, 3>, <3, 1, 0, 0>, <4, 2, 1, 0>, <2, 3, 5, 1>, <1, 2, 0, 4> >

At the expense of replacing M_{desc} by $Mdesc$, M_{exits} by $Mexits$ and replacing every argument *M* by two arguments *Mdesc* and *Mexits*, programs which use the original structure can be transcribed into codes which don't permit sequences of indexed sets.

-=

APPENDIX 22.A TRY IT OUT

Surely no programmer can resist the challenge of writing programs which build mazes, search mazes, get other people lost in mazes, ..

Chapter 23
A FINAL FLOURISH

This chapter is my final word in this book about searching. It starts by introducing an alternative means of searching. It ends with one of the most intricate and intractable searching problems, the problem of finding a knight's tour of a chessboard.

23.1 BREADTH-FIRST SEARCHES

Suppose that you have to build a mouse to search an infinite maze but the puzzler (he/she who sets the puzzles) guarantees that there is a finite path between rooms a and b. Anything based on program 22.9 would be almost useless in those circumstances. If the program started off in the wrong direction, down a path which didn't lead to the destination, it would necessarily keep going and it would disappear over the infinite horizon and never come back. That program works only if it can explore every path through the maze, and in an infinite maze there may be an infinite number of infinitely long paths which lead from a and don't pass through b after a finite number of steps.

Program 22.9 is not entirely useless in an infinite maze. You might think that to find one path out of an infinite number gives it zero chance. Not quite: suppose that the shortest path has length p, and that in every room the mouse can go four ways (north, south, east or west). Then after p consecutive moves the mouse will have generated a path length p and the chance is at least 1 in 4^p that it's picked the right one. Even if it hasn't chosen the right path all is not lost: it might chance on one of the slightly longer ones - a path length $p+1$ or $p+2$ or even $500p$. Provided it hasn't taken entirely the wrong path there will be a glimmer of hope even if there is only one needle in the infinite haystack. All we know is that program 22.9 would *probably* fail - which is bad enough, after all.

Suppose that the puzzler put the mouse in an infinite maze and told it the value of p, the length of the shortest path from a to b. Now a mouse which was cleverer than program 22.9 could find that path by investigating every path in turn and giving up on each one as soon as its length exceeds p. In effect the mouse is searching a finite area of the infinite maze and eventually, no matter how unlucky it is in its choice of directions, it must find room b.

An even cleverer mouse could find room b even if the puzzler kept the value of p a secret. When program 23.1 terminates $xp=p$ and the path is found.

$xp:=0$; *iterate path not found*: $xp:=xp+1$;
                                    investigate all paths length xp
       enditerate

program 23.1

A very systematic and very clever mouse could do better still. All journeys start with a single step: the paths of length 2 start with paths of length 1 and paths of length $y+1$ are just the paths of length y with a single move tacked on the end of them. Now suppose that the mouse is extending a path length y to find a path length $y+1$ and it reaches a room which is on the end of a path length $y-z$. That particular $y+1$ path is useless and the mouse can forget about it.

-=-=-=-=-=-=-=-=-=-=-

Exercise 23.1
Satisfy yourself that in a maze of two-way passages, if the mouse always forgets useless paths then whenever it discovers a new useless one, $z=0$ or $z=1$.

Exercise 23.2
Describe a procedure which is given a description of all the paths leading from room a which are of length y and delivers a description of all the paths which are of length $y+1$.

-=-=-=-=-=-=-=-=-=-=-

This latest search technique is called a **breadth-first** search, whereas program 22.9 describes a **depth-first** search. The difference is in the way that the two programs explore the graph of nodes reachable from room a. The breadth/depth terminology comes from a view of the search as expanding a tree of possibilities.

Depth-first searches go as far as possible along a single path until they either succeed or fail; when they fail they backtrack to a previous position and push on as deeply as possible down a new path from that position. Breadth-first searches operate as if there was an army of mice, all moving in step and all carrying out a search together. In breadth-first searching no particular searching mouse is allowed to get ahead of the others and mice which fail just drop out of the search. In either kind of search, failure occurs when a mouse finds a room in the maze with no unexplored rooms reachable from it.

Now imagine a breadth-first search in a very large finite maze. The program can proceed just as if the maze was infinite. If the maze is very large, so that the average length of a path from a to b is much larger than the shortest path between them, this program might expect on average to perform better than one based on program 22.9 (for example, better than your answer to exercise 22.18). But how to build it? One way is to record what each mouse in the breadth-first search remembers: the rooms at the end of the paths. Record for each room in the maze whether a path has been found which leads to it; if a path has been found record that path. Expand all paths one step at a time and all in step, in the manner of the systematic and ultra-clever mouse: if the expansion leads to an unexplored room then the path just found must be one of the shortest ways from *a* to that room (that is, there isn't a shorter one).

-=-=-=-=-=-=-=-=-=-=-=-=-

Exercise 23.3
Write the breadth-first program. Try it on some mazes of your own invention. [Hint: the solution may be either recursive or repetitive; think hard about both kinds of solution before you develop either of them.]

-=-=-=-=-=-=-=-=-=-=-=-=-

23.2 SEARCHES WITHOUT WALLS

Figure 23.1 shows a *trackword*, a type of problem invented by Clive Doig[†]. The problem is to find all the words of three letters or more which can be traced out by starting at one letter and moving one place left, right, up, down or diagonally without visiting any position more than once. For example, if you start at the letter T in the top left the sequence down, down, down-and-right, right traces out the word TRUE. Each of Mr Doig's trackwords is a single convoluted nine-letter word. Figure 23.1 hides the word PETROLEUM, but I had to use a computer to find that out!

TOP
REL
MUE

figure 23.1

The programming problem is to trace out all the three-, four-, five-, six-, seven-, eight- and nine-letter sequences which can be generated from the diagram using the rules. As always, the problem is to avoid going round in circles.

-=-=-=-=-=-=-=-=-=-=-=-=-

Exercise 23.4
Go on, write the program. There are over fifty English words hidden in figure 23.1.

[†] This example appeared in the *Radio Times*, May 1986, and is reproduced by permission of Clive Doig. There are lots more examples in *Clive Doig's Radio Times Puzzle Book*, Penguin, 1984.

Exercise 23.5
Try your program with some different trackwords.

-=-=-=-=-=-=-=-=-=-=-=-

23.3 THE KNIGHT'S TOUR: A MAZE WITHOUT WALLS

There are sixty-four squares on a chessboard. A chess knight can move two squares up, down, left or right followed by one square at right angles to that move. It is possible to make a *knight's tour* of the board, starting at any square and visiting every other square once, finishing back at the square you started from. It is possible to write a program which finds a knight's tour - indeed it could find every one of the possible knight's tours if you let it run long enough. There are millions of knight's tours, so I suppose you wouldn't want to wait that long.

This problem is superficially similar to the trackword problem but it is much larger. It is larger even than that of the eight queens. Brute force won't work at all: every solution can be thought of as a way of numbering the squares 1 to 64, but there are something like 10^{90} such numberings, and only a very small fraction of them are knight's tours.

Filtering out unsolutions is the only way. The problem is a sort of maze search in which the early moves of the tour build the walls for the later moves. Filtering has to be carried very carefully because the number of possible unsolutions is so astronomically enormous. Figure 23.2 shows some of the ways in which a badly designed program can go wrong.

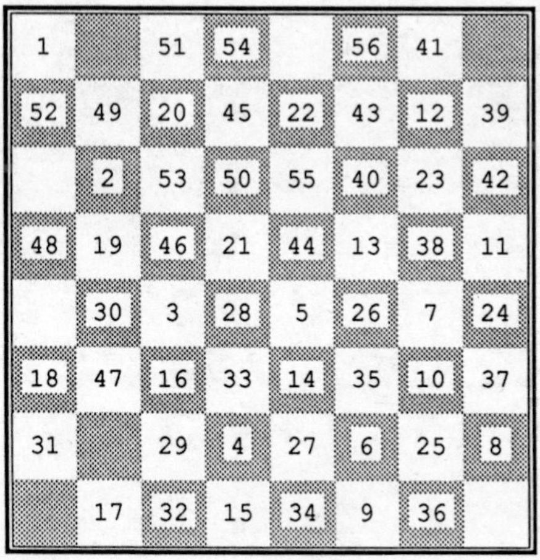

figure 23.2

This search has reached the fifty-sixth step on the top row but it is hopeless to go on for several reasons:

(a) the move 6-7 left a dead end (a square reachable from only one other square) in the bottom right-hand corner and then move 9-10 isolated it entirely;

(b) move 19-20 left the original square (number 1) unreachable, so the tour can't finish properly;

(c) move 23-24 left a dead end in the top right-hand corner;

(d) move 29-30 did the same for the bottom left-hand corner;

(e) there are two pairs of squares in the left-hand half of the board each of which is reachable only from the other.

The techniques of searching and filtering unsolutions used in this book can indeed lead to a program which finds knight's tours. The filtering techniques I know depend on counting the set $D(s)$ of the descendants of s: that is, unvisited squares reachable from a square s.

Consider the partial tour shown in figure 23.3, which shows the position after the first five moves of figure 23.2. The unvisited squares reachable from the knight's position are marked a, b, c, d and e. From each of a, b, c and d several unvisited squares are reachable, but from the corner-square e only one. If the next move is to a, b, c or d then a dead end has been created at e and you have an unsolution. One rule, therefore, is that if one of the descendants of the current square has only one descendant of its own, pick that one and ignore all the others. A subsidiary rule is that if there are two or more one-way descendants then whichever way you go you will create a dead end, so give up that particular

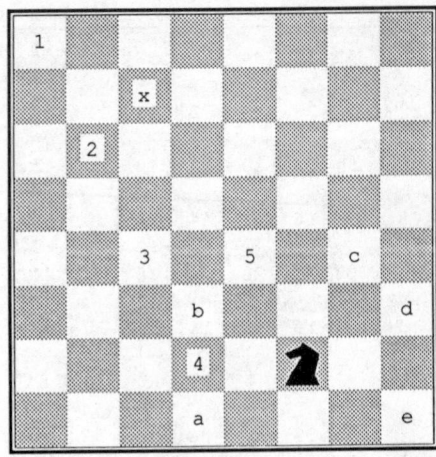

figure 23.3

position immediately.

The descendant rules have to be applied carefully. Consider the square marked x in figure 23.3. It is the only unvisited square reachable from position 1 and if the tour is to end properly the last-but-one move must be to this square. Even though eventually x might be reachable from only one unvisited square it can't be a dead end. This problem can be resolved in various ways: I usually count square 1 as a reachable descendant.

Application of the one-way rules will ensure that no dead ends are created. If the program doesn't isolate square 1 until the very last moment then it will find all the tours.

-=-=-=-=-=-=-=-=-=-=-=-=-

Exercise 23.6
Write the knight's tour program and try it out. [Hint: you will find it rather sensitive to starting position. It will probably find tours more easily when it starts from the middle of the board. Another hint: you may like to practise on a smaller board, but a knight's tour isn't possible on a board with an odd number of rows and columns.]

-=-=-=-=-=-=-=-=-=-=-=-=-

Suppose that a tour has reached square *s* and that all the unvisited squares reachable from s have more than one descendant. Is there any reason to prefer any move over any other? Answer: yes, in practice there is. Suppose that *r* is reachable from *s*, and that from *r* you can reach two unvisited squares. If the next move isn't *s* →*r* then a new corner-square has been created, a little sequence of three squares which must be traversed in the right order. Create too many of them and you may make an unsolution by creating a closed loop. Figure 23.4,

1						33	24
16					25		
	2	17			34	23	32
	15					26	
		3	18	5	20	31	22
14		12		10	29	8	27
			4	19	6	21	30
	13		11		9	28	7

figure 23.4

which was generated by a program using just the one-way rule and the don't-isolate-1 rule has one such nasty configuration in the bottom left-hand corner. It is an unsolution, but it takes the program a long time to realise it.

Suppose that you find a descendant r with two descendants of its own and you prefer the move $s \rightarrow r$ over all the others: the other moves must still be searched eventually, but it turns out that your program finds its first solutions more quickly. This *twin-descendant* rule is a great help in knight's tour racing, where generally the problem is to find the first thousand solutions faster than anyone else. For example, my own program, when it included the twin-descendant rule as well as the others, generated figure 23.5 with only one false step in the search.

1	50	9	40	63	38	19	34
8	41	64	37	48	35	62	21
51	2	49	10	39	20	33	18
42	7	52	55	36	47	22	61
53	56	3	46	11	60	17	32
6	43	54	27	30	25	14	23
57	28	45	4	59	12	31	16
44	5	58	29	26	15	24	13

figure 23.5

Positively the last flourish

For reasons which I have never seen satisfactorily explained, this is not quite the end of the story. If at each stage of the search you sort the descendants of the current square into order depending on their own number of descendants, and then visit them in ascending order of number of descendants (notice that this technique supersedes the twin-descendant rule) the program becomes fastest of all. I repeat, I don't properly understand why this is so.

-=-=-=-=-=-=-=-=-=-=-=-

Exercise 23.7
Write the improved knight's tour program. Try it out.

Exercise 23.8
Find some more unsolution filtering rules if you can. [Good luck!]

Part Five
TRANSCRIBING INTO OTHER CODES

The main advantage of using an abstract notation for programs is clarity of expression. An abstract program is shorter than a mechanical transcription and can use notation designed to fit a particular programming purpose. A mechanical code must be designed for universal implementation or international standardisation and programs written in it must be crammed into its straitjacket. One important consequence of the difference is that an abstract program is much easier to reason about and much easier to change into a similar but different program.

The appendices in earlier chapters have given rules for the transcription of programs into Pascal, although Pascal is certainly not the only suitable 'target' for transcription. Of all mechanical codes it is perhaps the most widely used for the teaching of novices and near-novices and I have given transcription rules for Pascal for that reasons. In addition, because there is an ISO Standard for Pascal, I can write transcription rules knowing that they will be applicable throughout the world.

But what to do if you want to experiment with working programs and you can't get hold of a Pascal programming system? The answer is to use what you've got: make up transcription rules for the code or codes you can use. If you are a complete novice you may find this a bit of a tall order: you should find a helpful friend or colleague or teacher who can help you (and, as stated in the preface, I should be glad to help other teachers to prepare and distribute transcription rules for other codes).

This part is really for use when you have become fairly confident in your programming skills and would like to be able to experiment with different programming systems. It gives hints about how to make transcriptions and advice about how to get around the difficulties you can expect to meet.

Chapter 24
INVENTING TRANSCRIPTION RULES

This book divides the description of programming notation into various parts: basic instructions, sequences, procedures, structured instructions. I have followed the same framework in this chapter.

If you are faced with the problem of transcribing into an unfamiliar code you should proceed as follows. First, read the definition of the code (the 'manual') looking at each instruction, formula and program structure and asking yourself what programming purpose it serves. That is, don't necessarily try at first to understand the details of all the components of the code; you should build up instead an idea of the sort of instructions, formulas and structures which you might be able to transcribe fairly directly into it.

It isn't necessary to find direct equivalents for the program structures you have used in your program, because there are rules, set out in earlier chapters and in sections 24.3 and 24.4 below, which tell you how to translate between structures. Second, therefore, find out what program structures can be transcribed directly into the code and then look in this book for hints on how to translate your procedure definitions and structured instructions into ones which fit the mechanical code's straitjacket.

Third, try to find direct equivalences in the code for the basic instructions and formula operations which you require. You will find hints on how to do this in sections 24.1 and 24.5 below.

The fourth stage you already know. Many codes don't provide full sets of operations on sequences. Most provide no operations on sets. Many provide no operations on structured values. Part Four has already given hints and rules for translating programs which do use structured values into programs which use the restricted collection of operations which you can expect to find in a mechanical code.

I cannot pretend that to move from the abstract version to the concrete mechanical implementation is always such a simple matter that it requires no ingenuity. Sometimes 'transcription' is really translation and a programmer must be almost as creative in translating as in devising a program. But in general transcription is straightforward and it gets more automatic the more experienced you become.

And that's it! So now you really can program in Ada™, FORTRAN, BASIC, COBOL, ..

Caveat

This chapter doesn't give hints about transcription into *every* possible code. At present there are at least three different programming paradigms which are competing for our allegiance:

(a) *Sequential* or *imperative* programming, which is the sort taught in this book. It is the oldest of the three paradigms and the basis of most mechanical codes in the late 1980s.

(b) *Functional* programming, which is based on the lambda calculus and the work of Landin and is more or less like the notation in this book but without sequences of executions, input, output, assignment or unlimited repetition (and usually without counting repetition or premature termination). Functional programming got started in the late 1950s with LISP but it is still not the choice of the majority.

(c) *Relational* or *logic* programming, for which Prolog is the main mechanical code. Logic programming has recently taken off in Britain in a big way.

The hints in this chapter cover only sequential codes[†].

24.1 BASIC INSTRUCTIONS

The basic instructions, so far as this book is concerned, are those which don't contain other instructions: output instructions, input instructions, assignment instructions, premature termination instructions. Procedure calls are dealt with in section 24.3 below.

[†] I have chosen to base this book on sequential programming for several reasons, the most compelling of which is that it will equip you to cope with most of the programming systems which you are likely to come across in the near future. Also, by concentrating so much of my treatment on reasoning about programs, I aim to equip you for the changes which are taking place in the practice of programming.

Output instructions

The treatment in this book starts with the basic instructions *print**, *printspace* and *NL*. If you want to transcribe your answers to exercises from this book then you should start by finding a direct equivalent for these basic output instructions. Most codes have them.

You could be unlucky. Some *very* old codes (for example, FORTRAN and COBOL) output line-by-line rather than character-by-character: that is, the smallest output instruction outputs a sequence of characters on the current line and moves the cpp down to the next line. Don't despair! - a little ingenuity can solve the problem. If *print** and *printspace* assemble a sequence of characters, and then *NL* outputs the assembled sequence, the problem is solved.

Specifically, invent an 'output sequence' O in which you accumulate a line of output. Invent the basic procedure *printline* which is given a sequence of characters and prints it as a line of text (it won't be hard to find an equivalent instruction in your code). At the beginning of your program write

$$initialise\ O:=<>$$

Transcribe *printchar*(c) into $O:=O+<c>$, and similarly transcribe *print** and *printspace*. Transcribe *NL* into *printline*(O). At the end of your program write

$$if\ O=<>\ then\ donothing\ else\ printline(O)\ fi$$

Input instructions

Most codes have equivalents of *readchar* and *readnumber* at least. It may be necessary to imitate *crp^*/*movecrp* using *readchar*, as described in chapter 11, section 11.6.

If your code won't input character-by-character then you can use a trick very similar to the *printline* one. I suppose that you can find an imitation of the instruction

$$readline\ X$$

which reads a sequence of characters representing an entire line of input and puts it into container $X^{\dagger}$. At the beginning of your program, put

$$initialise\ I:=<>$$

Then *crp^* can be imitated by the formula

$$(\!|\ if\ I=<>\ then\ readline\ I\ else\ donothing\ fi;\ deliver\ I_1\ |\!)$$

and *movecrp* can be imitated by

---

† You may need to ensure that *readline* puts a *newline* code at the end of each line it reads.

$$if\ I = <> \ then\ readline\ I\ else\ donothing\ fi;\ I:=I_2..$$

Definition 11.1 tells you how to imitate *readchar* in terms of *crp^* and *movecrp*.

Assignment instructions

If your code allows any use of memory at all, it will have an assignment instruction. The only difficulty you might encounter is that you may not be allowed to store certain sorts of values - for example, procedure values - in containers. See below under 'Second-class values' for hints about how to proceed in those circumstances.

Terminate and *deliver*

Terminate and *deliver* can be imitated with *goto*, as described in chapter 14.

Some modern codes (for example, Modula-2) have no *goto* and no general equivalent of *terminate* or *deliver*. The only way out is to be ingenious and rewrite your program without the offending structures. It isn't usually very difficult: for example, termination of an infinite repetition like the one in program 24.1 can be imitated by use of an assignment instruction and a changed condition-formula, as in program 24.2. There are tricky terminations which can't easily be imitated without using *goto*, but I haven't described any of them in this book.

$$B: iterate\ true: select\ C_1: terminate\ B$$
$$..$$
$$endselect$$
$$enditerate$$
$$:B$$

program 24.1

$$initialise\ b:=true$$
$$iterate\ b: select\ C_1: b:=false$$
$$..$$
$$endselect$$
$$enditerate$$

program 24.2

Invent your own basic instructions

The basic instructions described in this book were chosen in order to support the treatment of calculations with programs and proofs about programs. If you are writing a program which does something other than print asterisks on a screen then you should expect to invent new instructions appropriate to your task. For example, in chapter 22 I found it convenient to write the *mouse* program (program 22.10) using the set operations union ($\cup$) and member ($\in$). Once the program was designed and proved to meet its specification I could consider how to implement set operations in terms of those more likely to be provided in a mechanical code.

This is really nothing more than an argument for 'as if' programming. Write your programs as if the notation you need were defined; be sure to define exactly what your new notation means, perhaps giving rules for transcription into some already defined notation like the one in this book; transcribe your final program according to your explanation of its meaning.

24.2 SEQUENCE

So far as the programs discussed in this book are concerned you can't do without sequences of execution. If your code doesn't support sequences of executions then it must support a kind of functional programming or relational/logic programming. In which case learn about that sort of programming.

24.3 PROCEDURES

Following Landin, my notation follows the rules of the lambda-calculus. Procedures may be activated recursively; they may contain free names which are bound as parameters of enclosing procedures; they will accept parameters of any kind and may deliver results of any kind.

Recursion

This is the most difficult of the transcription tasks and the most unnecessary. When FORTRAN, the first of the modern mechanical codes, was invented in the mid 1950s the usefulness of recursion wasn't widely understood, nor was it known how to make a programming system which could imitate the execution of recursive programs. Now, more than thirty years later, that original invention still casts a shadow. Recursion is often regarded as 'difficult' and 'advanced': for example, it is often treated in the last chapter of books about programming.

With the development of LISP in the late 1950s, and later the development of Algol 60, recursion became more widely understood and the imitation problem was solved. Recursion is now so widely accepted as a programming mechanism that even the next standard version of FORTRAN will almost certainly provide it. Nevertheless you may be stuck with an old-fashioned version of an old-fashioned code.

Some forms of recursion are very easily imitated. A **tail-recursive** procedure definition is one like program 24.3: that is, one whose body is a *select* instruction in which the only references to the procedure *f*, even indirectly, come at the *end* of some of the arms of the *select*. For example, procedure *A* from chapter 9 (program 9.1) is tail-recursive: in that procedure *x* is the pair $<n,p>$; *i* and *j* are both 1; C_1 is $n=0$; P_1 is *donothing*; C_2 is $n>0$; Q_1 is $p()$ and *g* is $<n-1,p>$.

$$def f(x) = select\ C_1{:}P_1\quad C_2{:}P_2\ ..\ C_i{:}P_i$$
$$\qquad\qquad C_{i+1}{:}Q_1;f(g_1)\quad C_{i+2}{:}Q_2;f(g_2)\ ..\ C_{i+j}{:}Q_j;f(g_j)$$
$$\qquad endselect$$
$$enddef$$

program 24.3

Tail-recursive programs can always be transcribed directly into repetitive programs. In general, provided that there is no ambiguity in choosing between condition-formulas $C_1..C_i$ on the one hand and $C_{i+1}..C_{i+j}$ on the other, program 24.3 transcribes into program 24.4, and in particular program 9.1 transcribes into program 24.5.

$$def f(y) = initialise\ x{:=}y$$
$$\qquad iterate$$
$$\qquad\quad C_{i+1}{:}Q_1;x{:=}g_1\quad C_{i+2}{:}Q_2;x{:=}g_2\ ..\ C_{i+j}{:}Q_j;x{:=}g_j$$
$$\qquad enditerate;$$
$$\qquad select\ C_1{:}P_1\quad C_2{:}P_2\ ..\ C_i{:}P_i\ endselect$$
$$enddef$$

program 24.4

$$def\ A2(m,p) = initialise\ n{:=}m$$
$$\qquad\qquad iterate\ n>0{:}\ p();\ n{:=}n-1\ enditerate$$
$$\qquad enddef$$

program 24.5

-=-=-=-=-=-=-=-=-=-=-=-

Exercise 24.1
Prove both the general and the particular equivalence asserted above.

-=-=-=-=-=-=-=-=-=-=-=-

In general a recursive program can always be imitated by a repetitive program which uses a sequence ('stack') of values representing environments. That is how the environment diagram model of execution works and it is the way that almost every programming system works. But if I were to describe that imitation

I would have to explain how to imitate an entire programming system and this book isn't the place for that.

My best advice is to find a programming system which *does* permit recursion. My second-best advice is to be ingenious in searching for repetitive solutions. For example the Fibonacci series, computed recursively in chapter 9 (program 9.11) is normally computed repetitively as in program 24.6. This is by no means the most efficient way to do it: there is a version which is based on multiplication of matrices, but *that* isn't what this book is about, either.

$$def\ Fib(n) = initialise\ x, y := 1, 1$$
$$for\ i\ rt\ 3..n\ do\ x, y := x+y, x\ od$$
$$enddef$$

program 24.6

Nested definitions

Chapter 5, definition 5.4, gives a rule for converting nested definitions into un-nested ones. The conversion is useful in various circumstances. You may be using a mechanical code (for example, FORTRAN) which doesn't allow nested definitions or one (for example, LISP or BCPL) which doesn't allow names free in a procedure definition to be bound by a binding occurrence in an enclosing definition.

A third possibility is that you may be using a programming system (for example, most LISP systems and some BASIC systems) which uses so-called 'dynamic binding': an execution mechanism in which the environment created on procedure call is based on the *calling* environment, rather than the 'static binding' described in this book where the environment is based on the one in which the procedure was *defined*. If you can't see the difference between these mechanisms, consider program 24.7, which will print either 'dynamic' or 'static' depending on which interpretation of environment creation you take.

$$let\ s = \text{``static''}$$
$$def\ p() = printstring(s)\ enddef$$
$$def\ q() = let\ s = \text{``dynamic''}$$
$$p()$$
$$enddef$$
$$q()$$

program 24.7

If you treat every procedure definition according to definition 5.4 then none of them will have free names, except for procedure names[†] defined in the outermost

---

[†]   And perhaps their result containers: see 'Result restrictions' below.

program environment. If you further ensure that none of those procedure names are re-bound anywhere else in the program then every procedure name will be given a meaning only in that global environment and it won't matter whether your programming system uses dynamic or static binding. For example, program 24.8 will print 'static' whatever kind of programming system you use.

$$let\ s=\text{"static"}$$
$$def\ p(s) = printstring(s)\ enddef$$
$$def\ q(t) = let\ s=\text{"dynamic"}$$
$$p(t)$$
$$enddef$$
$$q(s)$$

program 24.8

Argument restrictions

Some programming systems won't let you use certain kinds of values as arguments: for example, some primitive Pascal systems don't allow procedure-valued arguments. Some programming systems (for example, many BASICs) won't let you use *any* kind of value as an argument. When either of these difficulties occurs there are usually ways to avoid them (plus the universal alternative: find a better programming system!).

If a certain sort of value is not permitted to be an argument but a reference to a container holding that sort of value is permitted[†] then you can convert the definition

$$def\ p(a) = Q\ enddef$$

into

$$def\ p(r) = Q[a\backslash\downarrow r]\ enddef$$

and every procedure call $p(b)$ into $p(@b)$, if b is a container formula, or $x:=b; p(@x)$ otherwise.

If reference values won't solve the problem, assignment will. Since you are always allowed to assign a value to a container[‡] even thought you cannot pass it as an argument, you can use the global variable technique outlined in chapter 10, section 10.12. In the simplest case you might convert program 24.9 into program 24.10. But in general p will be a recursively activated procedure and you will have to convert $p(b)$ into program 24.11, which remembers the present argument value in a new container y during the recursive call, or into one of the programs

---

[†] Yes, it happens. For example, in BCPL and some elderly Cs.

[‡] Or imitate its assignment - see 'Second class values' below.

$$def\ p(a) = Q\ enddef$$
$$p(b)$$

initialise $a:=?$
$$def\ p() = Q\ enddef$$
$$a:=b; p()$$

program 24.9   **program 24.10**

$(\ initialise\ y:=a$
$\quad a:=b; p(); a:=y$
$)$

program 24.11

$$S:= <a>\oplus S;\ a:=b; p();\ a, S:=S_1, S_2.$$

program 24.12

$$S:=S\oplus <a>;\ a:=b; p();\ a, S:=S_{length(S)}, S_{1..length(S)-1}$$

program 24.13

24.12 or 24.13, which use a sequence S to 'stack' the present argument value during the call.

Result restrictions

Sometimes certain values can't be delivered as the result of a procedure call. Once again assignment can solve the problem. In place of *deliver F* write an assignment instruction which stores the value of F in some container, followed if necessary by a *terminate* instruction to end the execution of the procedure. There are at least two ways in which the result container can be described.

In some notations (for example, Pascal) procedures may not deliver a value of certain kinds, but they can be given a reference to a container as an argument. Then it is possible to convert the instruction $x:=p(b)$ into the procedure-calling instruction $p(b, @x)$, to convert the procedure definition

$$def\ p(a) = Q\ enddef$$

into

$$def\ p(a, r) = B:Q:B\ enddef$$

and to replace *deliver F* within Q by the sequence

$$\downarrow r:=F;\ terminate\ B$$

For example, program 24.14 may be imitated by program 24.15.

Notice that in program 24.15 the formula $x\times power(x, n-1)$ has been 'linearised': that is, converted from a hierarchical calculation to a sequence of operations. In this program the value of x^{n-1} is assigned to t, then that value is used to compute the result $x\times t$.

$$def\ power(x, n) = select\ n=0: 1$$
$$n>0: x\times power(x, n-1)$$
$$endselect$$
$$enddef$$
$$.. z:=(power(2, 64)); ..$$

program 24.14

$$def\ power(x, n, r) = select\ n=0: \downarrow r:=1$$
$$n>0: initialise\ t:=?$$
$$power(x, n-1, @t); \downarrow r:=x\times t$$
$$endselect$$
$$enddef$$
$$.. power(2, 64, @z); ..$$

program 24.15

It may sometimes be necessary to linearise the calculation of formulas before the technique is applied: for example the instruction

$$printnumber(p(x)+p(y))$$

could become the sequence

$$res1:=p(x); res2:=p(y); printnumber(res1+res2)$$

which is then in a form suitable for treatment.

If you can't use reference values then a 'result container' can be associated with every procedure: rp with procedure p, rq with procedure q, $rfred$ with procedure $fred$, and so on. Each instruction *deliver F* in the body of a procedure p can then be imitated by the sequence

$$rp:=F; terminate\ <body\ of\ p>$$

For example, an alternative imitation of program 24.14 is shown in program 24.16.

$$initialise\ rpower:=?$$
$$def\ power(x, n) = select\ n=0: rpower:=1$$
$$n>0: power(x, n-1); rpower:=x\times rpower$$
$$endselect$$
$$enddef$$
$$.. power(2, 64); z:=rpower; ..$$

program 24.16

Care is required when one procedure call can affect the value of another procedure's result container: for example the program

$$f(0); g(1); printnumber(rf+rg)$$

may not always be a valid imitation of the instruction

$$printnumber(f(0)+g(1))$$

-=-=-=-=-=-=-=-=-=-=-=-=-=-

Exercise 24.2
Why not? Can you construct definitions of f and g which justify the assertion
above?

-=-=-=-=-=-=-=-=-=-=-=-=-=-

24.4 STRUCTURED INSTRUCTIONS

Computers are hardware imitations of simple programming systems. Most
computers work entirely using assignment, reference values, *if–then* and *goto*. It
follows that everything you can do with structured instructions you can imitate
using just that simple repertoire. It *does not* follow that this is a pleasant or
amusing thing to do. Quite the contrary: it is tedious and frustrating and you
would be justified if you resented the necessity to do it, when that necessity
arises.

Choice

Select instructions can be imitated by *if-then-else,* up to a point (see chapter 8,
section 8.11). *If-then-else* can be imitated by *if-then* and *goto*, as described in
chapter 14, section 14.6: for example *if a then B else C fi* can be imitated by the
sequence

> *if a then goto L1*;
> *B*; *goto L2*;
> *<label L1> A*;
> *<label L2>*

Case instructions can be transcribed into *selects*, then transcribed as above.
Transcriptions of *match* instructions were described in chapter 21.

Repetition

For-do can be imitated by *iterate*. For example, *for N rt S do P od* can be
imitated by

$$\textit{initialise } i := 1$$

$$\textit{iterate } i \leq length(S) \text{: } let \, N = S_i$$

$$P; i := i+1$$

$$\textit{enditerate}$$

provided that i isn't free in P. If the successive elements of the sequence S are easy to calculate then a simpler imitation is possible. For example, the instruction *for N rt a..b do P od* can be imitated by the program

$$\textit{initialise } N := a$$

$$\textit{iterate } N \leq b \text{: } P; N := N+1 \textit{ enditerate}$$

Single-armed *iterate* instructions can be imitated by *if-then* and *goto*. The instruction *iterate c:P enditerate* is imitated by the program

$$\textit{<label L1> if} \neg c \textit{ then goto L2;}$$

$$P; \textit{goto L1;}$$

$$\textit{<label L2>}$$

Multi-armed *iterate*s can be converted into single-armed instructions using one or other of the definitions 12.4 or 12.5.

24.5 SECOND-CLASS VALUES

In most mechanical codes you can read numbers, print numbers, pass numbers as arguments to procedure calls, deliver numbers as the results of procedure calls and store numbers in containers. Numbers are *first-class values*. Usually the same is true of character values. But other values are *second-class* because there are some of these things which you can't do with them. For example, in most mechanical codes you can't read or print a sequence value (though you can write a procedure which provides that operation). In Pascal you can't deliver a sequence value as the result of a procedure call. In most of those BASICs which allow procedure arguments you can't provide a sequence-valued argument[†].

The general solution to the problem is to alter your program so that it refers to the second-class value *indirectly* via a first-class value which identifies it. For example, I suppose that numbers are always first-class values. Suppose that sequence-valued arguments aren't allowed in your mechanical code but that you want to transcribe program 24.17 into it. Strings are sequences, so you certainly have a problem[‡]. The solution is to replace each sequence-valued argument by a number and to provide an imitation of any instruction or formula which uses the true argument value. Then program 24.17 could be transcribed as program

---

[†] I don't wish to single out Pascal and BASIC: most codes have some second-class values.

[‡] The mechanical equivalent of *printstring* is naturally exempt from the restriction.

def twice(s) = *NL*; *printstring(s)*; *printstring(s) enddef*
twice("hello"); *twice*("goodbye")

program 24.17

def twice(s) = *NL*; *printstringarg(s)*; *printstringarg(s) enddef*
def printstringarg(i) = *case i of* 1: *printstring*("hello")
                                   2: *printstring*("goodbye")
                          endcase
enddef
twice(1); *twice*(2)

program 24.18

24.18.

One particularly galling omission from many codes is procedure-valued arguments. In such codes you can't write a direct equivalent of a simple example like program 4.3. You can get around the problem just as before: number the procedure values, or identify them with strings or characters or whatever else happens to be a useful first-class value. Then, for example, you might transcribe program 4.3 as program 24.19.

def r3(p) = *apply(p)*; *apply(p)*; *apply(p) enddef*
def one() = *print* enddef*
def two() = *NL enddef*
def three() = *NL*; *print**; *print**; *print* enddef*

def apply(i) = *case i of* 1: *one()* 2: *two()* 3: *three() endcase enddef*
r3(1); *r3*(2); *r3*(3)

program 24.19

Note that you might often have to unpack the procedure definitions, in the manner of section 24.3 above, so that *apply* can validly call upon any procedure; notice also that you will need several versions of *apply* if you pass as arguments some parameterless procedures, some procedures which take one argument, some procedures which take two, and so on.

SUBJECT INDEX

INDEX OF DEFINITIONS

INDEX OF FIGURES

INDEX OF PROGRAMS